Convicts

Clare Anderson provides a radical new reading of histories of empire and nation, showing that the history of punishment is not connected solely to the emergence of prisons and penitentiaries, but also to histories of governance, occupation, and global connections across the world. Exploring punitive mobility to islands, colonies, and remote inland and border regions over a period of five centuries, she proposes a close and enduring connection between punishment, governance, repression, and nation and empire building, and reveals how states, imperial powers, and trading companies used convicts to satisfy various geopolitical and social ambitions. Punitive mobility became intertwined with other forms of labour bondage, including enslavement, with convicts a key source of unfree labour that could be used to occupy territories. Far from passive subjects, however, convicts manifested their agency in various forms, including the extension of political ideology and cultural transfer, and vital contributions to contemporary knowledge production.

Clare Anderson is Professor of History at the University of Leicester.

Convicts
A Global History

Clare Anderson

CAMBRIDGE
UNIVERSITY PRESS

University Printing House, Cambridge CB2 8BS, United Kingdom

One Liberty Plaza, 20th Floor, New York, NY 10006, USA

477 Williamstown Road, Port Melbourne, VIC 3207, Australia

314–321, 3rd Floor, Plot 3, Splendor Forum, Jasola District Centre, New Delhi – 110025, India

103 Penang Road, #05–06/07, Visioncrest Commercial, Singapore 238467

Cambridge University Press is part of the University of Cambridge.

It furthers the University's mission by disseminating knowledge in the pursuit of education, learning, and research at the highest international levels of excellence.

www.cambridge.org
Information on this title: www.cambridge.org/9781108840729
DOI: 10.1017/9781108887496

© Clare Anderson 2022

This publication is in copyright. Subject to statutory exception and to the provisions of relevant collective licensing agreements, no reproduction of any part may take place without the written permission of Cambridge University Press.

First published 2022

A catalogue record for this publication is available from the British Library.

Library of Congress Cataloging-in-Publication Data
Names: Anderson, Clare, 1969– author.
Title: Convicts : a global history / Clare Anderson.
Description: Cambridge, United Kingdom ; New York, NY : Cambridge University Press, 2021. | Includes bibliographical references and index.
Identifiers: LCCN 2021026925 (print) | LCCN 2021026926 (ebook) | ISBN 9781108840729 (hardback) | ISBN 9781108814942 (paperback) | ISBN 9781108887496 (ebook)
Subjects: LCSH: Convict labor – History. | Convict labor – Cross-cultural studies. | Imperialism – Cross-cultural studies. | BISAC: HISTORY / World
Classification: LCC HV8888 .A53 2021 (print) | LCC HV8888 (ebook) | DDC 365/.65–dc23
LC record available at https://lccn.loc.gov/2021026925
LC ebook record available at https://lccn.loc.gov/2021026926

ISBN 978-1-108-84072-9 Hardback
ISBN 978-1-108-81494-2 Paperback

Cambridge University Press has no responsibility for the persistence or accuracy of URLs for external or third-party internet websites referred to in this publication and does not guarantee that any content on such websites is, or will remain, accurate or appropriate.

For Hugh Rowell Duffield
and
James Samuel Duffield

Contents

	List of Figures	*page* viii
	List of Maps	x
	List of Tables	xi
	Acknowledgements	xii
1	Introduction	1
	Part I	35
2	Empires and Colonies	37
3	Nations, Borders, and Islands	73
4	Enslavement, Banishment, and Penal Transportation	100
5	Imperial Governance	133
6	Insurgency, Politics, and Religion	172
	Part II	217
7	Punishment and Penal Systems	219
8	Encounters, Exploration, and Knowledge	249
9	Medicine, Criminality, and Race	287
10	The Human Sciences	319
11	Escape and Extradition	360
12	Conclusion	390
	Appendix: Principal and Selected Imperial and Latin American Sites of Punitive Relocation	406
	Bibliography	413
	Archives	458
	Index	466

Figures

1.1 Marçal de Corria, by G. Ramage, 1887	*page* 2
1.2 Expedition [left to right] Mar[ç]al [de Corria], [George A.] Ramage, H.N. R[idley], T.[S.] Lea, Da Silva [Sylvano de Barro?]	3
1.3 Convict village	4
1.4 The square, Fernando [de] Noronha. My horse, Marcal, in background	5
2.1 The naval base on Ireland Island in the Bermudas, by Captain Henry Rolfe RN, 1839	58
2.2 Sick convicts going to hospital!!! Bermuda	59
3.1 Kuniyoshi Utagawa, Sashū ryūkei Kakuta nami daimoku (Banishment to Sado Island: On the Waves at Kakuta), woodblock print, c. 1835	80
3.2 Miniature *geta* (sandals) and *shamisen* (musical instrument)	88
3.3 Rosary, made from plum seeds	88
4.1 Sketches of a flag taken from the insurgent slaves at Barbados, 1816	113
4.2 A view in Belize, 1829	116
4.3 View of Sierra Leone, 1838	121
5.1 HM Penal Settlement on the Mazaruni, c. 1842–3	149
6.1 The Central Jail at Port Blair – 663 cells	193
6.2 Convict uprising at Castle Hill 1804	197
7.1 Convictos en la Nueva Olanda [Convicts in New Holland], by Felipe Bauza, c. 1790	224
7.2 The International Prison Congress in the Middle Temple Hall [London]	226
7.3 *Pénitencier dépôt des condamnés aux travaux forces.* Photographer: E. Robin, c. 1870	233
8.1 Leafy sea dragon, by William Buelow Gould, c. 1832	272
9.1 Anthropometry Studio, Saint-Laurent-du-Maroni, French Guiana	296

9.2 An Arab type of convict. A combination of ideality and
     homicidal mania   299
9.3 Berezowski, the Polish Anarchist who attempted to murder
     Napoleon III, and Tsar Alexander II, in the Champs Elysées.
     One of the Lowest Types of Criminal Faces. An illustration of
     the ease with which it is possible to disguise the chin, typical
     of moral weakness, and the wild-beast mouth, which nearly
     all Criminals have, by means of moustache and beard   300
10.1 Devil's Island, painted by convict   325
11.1 Five escaped French convicts in British Guiana, 1902   387

Maps

1.1 Key global destinations of convict flows, 1800–1900	page 18
1.2 Convict flows in the French Empire, 1541–1953	23
1.3 Penal transportation in the British Empire, 1618–1874	25
1.4 Penal transportation in British Asia, 1787–1939	27
2.1 Convict mobility in the Portuguese Empire since 1415	39
2.2 Punitive mobility in the Spanish Empire, c. 1760–1950	48
2.3 Convict flows in the Netherlands Empire, seventeenth to twentieth centuries	54
2.4 Convict hulk sites in Bermuda, 1824–63	60
3.1 Xinjiang, China	76
3.2 Hokkaido's *shūchikan*, showing road building and *tondenhei* villages	86
3.3 Convict mobility in post-independence Latin America	94

Tables

1.1 Global convict flows, 1415–1976   *page* 12
1.2 Global labour mobility, 1415–1976   15

Acknowledgements

The research for this book was conducted over a period of more than twenty-five years. It began with my PhD, which was a study of the Indian penal settlement in Mauritius during the first half of the nineteenth century. My interest in Indian convict flows continued with a larger history of the Indian Ocean and South and Southeast Asia, and I then moved on to work on penal transportation from British colonies to New South Wales and Van Diemen's Land. I am grateful to several funders for their generous support. The Arts Research Board and Carnegie Trust for the Universities of Scotland funded my PhD, and the British Academy, National Maritime Museum, and Economic and Social Research Council (award no. R000271268) supported later work. During this period, archivists and staff were unfailingly supportive as I worked for long periods in a range of archives. They include the National Archives at Kew, the British Library (especially the India Office), National Library of Scotland, National Archives of Mauritius, Archives Office of Tasmania, National Archives of India, and Tamil Nadu State Archives. I thank also Madhumita Mazumdar and Vishvajit Pandya, who I had the pleasure of working with on the Economic and Social Research Council funded collaboration 'Integrated Histories of the Andaman Islands' (award no. RES-000-22-3484). We appreciated the generosity of many islanders at this time, including Zubair Ahmed, Sheikh Farooq Alam, Mukeshwar Lal, Francis Xavier Neelam, Rashida Iqbal, and John Lobo and his family.

In 2013, the European Research Council, under the European Union's Seventh Framework Programme, awarded me funding for the 5-year project 'The Carceral Archipelago: transnational circulations in global context, 1415–1960' (award no. 312542). This was transformational in that it enabled me to undertake a sustained period of research on penal colonies and settlements in other global locations, in dialogue with numerous other researchers. I thank the wonderful team who worked with me on this project during the period 2013–18: Anne Ablett, Adam J. Barker, Rachel Dawes, Carrie Crockett, Christian G. De Vito, Eureka Henrich, Aaron Jaffer, Sarah Longair, Emma Battell Lowman, Anna McKay, Takashi Miyamoto, Kellie

Moss, Mikhail Nakonechny, Lorraine M. Paterson, Maureen Rail, Katy Roscoe, Manuela Sánchez Noriega, Minako Sakata, and Emily Whewell. Thanks also to Katherine Foxhall and Zoe Knox, who co-supervised the project PhD students, and the project's Advisory Board: Tim Coates, Simon Dixon, Judith Pallot, Miranda Spieler, Hamish Maxwell-Stewart, Ann Laura Stoler, and Kerry Ward. I am grateful also to the participants in our international conference at the University of Leicester in 2015, especially our inspirational keynote speakers, Hilary Carey and Mary Gibson.

It would have been impossible to research this book without the generous and enthusiastic support of a wide range of institutions. For work on the French Empire, I am grateful to the Archives Nationales d'Outre Mer, the archives of French Guiana (Guyane) including in Cayenne and at the Camp de la Transportation in Saint-Laurent-du-Maroni, and the archives of Guadeloupe, Martinique, Réunion Island, and New Caledonia. My interest in the British Empire again took me to the British Library, National Archives at Kew, and National Library of Scotland, and also to the Bermuda Archives, Archives of the Royal Botanic Gardens Kew, Jamaica Archives and Records Department, National Archives of Trinidad and Tobago, National Library of Australia, Rare Books and Special Collections of Princeton University Library, Salvation Army International Heritage Centre London, Walter Rodney Archives Guyana, and the Western Cape Archives and Records Service. I greatly appreciate the generosity of Minako Sakata, who took me to visit penal colony sites in Hokkaido; Deborah Atwood, who showed me around the Royal Naval Dockyard, Bermuda; and Louis-José Barbançon, Emmanuelle Eriale, and Yves Mermoud who taught me so much when I visited New Caledonia.

The Carceral Archipelago team convened panels at two conferences of the European Network of Universal and Global History: Paris (2014) and Budapest (2017). These were key to the development of the overarching project, and the conceptualization and then realization of two publications: the (open access) edited volume *A Global History of Convicts of Penal Colonies* (2018) and a special issue of the *International Review of Social History* (2018), the latter in collaboration with the 'labour camps' project at the International Institute for Social History, Amsterdam. I had the chance to share drafts of chapters of this book in Paris, Budapest, and Amsterdam, and at many other conferences and seminars. These include at the Australian National University, Canberra; Harvard University; École des hautes études en sciences sociales, Paris; Institute of Historical Research, London; Menzies Centre for Australian Studies (King's College London); New York University, Abu Dhabi; University of Bern; University of the Free State Bloemfontein; University of Guyana; University of Hull; University of Pittsburgh; University of Tasmania;

University of Warwick; University of the West Indies (Mona); University of the Western Cape; University of Wollongong; and the University of Zurich. I thank the organizers of these events, and all those who responded to my work with provocations, comments, and suggestions.

I count some terrific scholars as colleagues and friends. They include the authors of the chapters of the 2018 volume: Tim Coates, Christian G. De Vito, Johan Heinsen, Jean-Lucien Sanchez, Matthias van Rossum, Hamish Maxwell-Stewart, Ryan Edwards, Sarah Badcock, Judith Pallot, Minako Sakata, Mary Gibson, Ilaria Poerio, and Ann Laura Stoler. The scholarship of Louis-José Barbançon, Ian Duffield, Isabelle Merle, Lorraine M. Paterson, Anoma Pieris, Ronit Ricci, Joanna Waley-Cohen, and Kerry Ward also stands out as inspirational. Otherwise, huge gratitude for the terrific work and scholarly company of Robert Aldrich, Richard B. Allen, Sunil Amrith, Dave Anderson, David Arnold, Rochana Bajpai, Alison Bashford, Crispin Bates, Alain Blum, Ulbe Bosma, Huw Bowen, James Bradley, Dan Branch, Trevor Burnard, Antoinette Burton, Gwyn Campbell, Jane Carey, Marina Carter, Indrani Chatterjee, Clive Dewey, Felix Driver, Saul Dubow, Margot Finn, Durba Ghosh, Anna Greenwood, Joanna de Groot, Catherine Hall, Gad Heuman, Isabel Hofmeyr, Christina Hughes, Tricia Jeffery, Preben Kaarsholm, Isaac Land, Alan Lester, John McAleer, Andrea Major, Margaret Makepeace, Hilary Marland, Kirsten McKenzie, Claire Mercer, Clare Midgley, Jim Mills, Paul Nugent, Di Paton, Doug Peers, Satyendra Peerthum, Marcus Rediker, Kirsty Reid, Anita Rupprecht, Sujit Sivasundaram, Kate Smith, Debs Sutton, Vijaya Teelock, Kristy Warren, Angela Woollacott, and Anand Yang. Tamsin O'Connor, and Hamish Maxwell-Stewart and Clare Smith were exceptionally generous hosts in Brisbane and Hobart when I was finalizing sections of the book in 2018, and later Hamish generously read chapter drafts. It has been a privilege to find new friends in Guyana as I researched Mazaruni. Mellissa Ifill, Estherine Adams, Shammane Joseph-Jackson, and Queenela Cameron: I salute you! We all remember with great fondness four terrific scholars who passed away as I worked on this manuscript: Tina Picton-Phillipps (1946–2016), Satadru Sen (1969–2018), Pieter Spierenburg (1948–2018), and Ian Duffield (1937–2019).

Finally, I am thankful to co-workers and friends at the University of Leicester, especially in the David Wilson Library, Leicester Institute for Advanced Studies, and School of History, Politics and International Relations. For their collegiality and friendship I am especially grateful to Richard P. Anderson (now at the University of Aberdeen), Tammy Ayres, Kate Boehme (now at the University of Nottingham), Svenja Bethke, John Coffey, Lucy Evans, Corinne Fowler, Iain Gillespie (now at the

University of Dundee), Zoë Groves, Martin Halliwell, Sally Horrocks, Dylan Kerrigan, Prashant Kidambi, Steve King (now at Nottingham Trent University), Zoe Knox, Di Levine, Paul Moore, Henrietta O'Connor, Maeve Ryan (now at Kings College London), Kevin Schürer, Deb Toner, and Charlotte Walsh. Michael Watson, Lucy Rhymer, Emily Sharp, Melissa Ward, and the Cambridge University Press team supported this project from its inception. Thanks also to Raghavi Govindane and my terrific copy editor Vicki Harley. Kate McIntosh compiled the index and Lorraine M. Paterson organized the Bibliography, doing a brilliant job of sorting out some of the footnotes along the way. Laura Vann-Leeds drew the maps. My talented friend of more than twenty-five years Mark Summers checked the *rōmaji* (Japanese) text. Thank you all. I also hope that the book is richer for changes made in response to the close and insightful reading of the two anonymous reviewers of the manuscript; all errors and omissions are, of course, my own.

Samuel Duffield has been a wonderful partner and companion for more than twenty years. Sam, you are always full of surprises! Our sons Hugh and James grew up with 'mum's project', and as they become young adults it gives me pleasure to dedicate this book to them. It remains a source of great sadness to us all that Sam's father, the remarkable historian of convicts and penal colonies (and so much more) Ian Duffield, died before this work was finished. Ian was ever loyal and supportive of those of us fortunate enough to become his friend. I present these chapters in tribute to him, and in the hope that they will do justice to his pioneering scholarship in writing global, and connected, history from below.

1 Introduction

A British Expedition to the Brazilian Penal Colony of Fernando de Noronha in 1887

On 9 July 1887, the botanists and collectors Henry Ridley, T. S. Lea, and George A. Ramage left the English port of Southampton on an expedition to Brazil's island penal colony of Fernando de Noronha. They were on a mission to collect animal, mineral, and plant specimens for London's British Museum. The men travelled first to the city of Pernambuco (Recife), on Brazil's mainland, and from there to Villa los Remédios, the island's main settlement. On arrival, they went to see the governor, Captain Dom Joaquim Agripino Furtado de Mondouça, and he gave them rooms and allocated them two *sentenciados* (convicts) as assistants: Sylvano de Barro and Marçal de Corria. (Figures 1.1 and 1.2).[1] Five decades earlier, during his round-the-world voyage on *The Beagle*, Charles Darwin had spent a few hours on the island, and in 1871 the survey ship *HMS Bristol* had anchored there. American naturalist John

---

[1] RBG Archives HNR/5/4 Henry Ridley Book of Travels 1887–1912: Of the island of Fernando Noronha and the expedition thereto by T. S. Lea, George Ramage, and Henry N. Ridley to which is added an historical account of the island; Alexander Rattray, 'A Visit to Fernando Noronha', *Journal of the Royal Geographical Society of London*, 42 (1872), 431–8. See also Peter M. Beattie, *Punishment in Paradise: Race, slavery, human rights, and a nineteenth-century penal colony* (Durham, NC: Duke University Press, 2015); Peter M. Beattie, '"Born under the Cruel Rigor of Captivity, the Supplicant Left It Unexpectedly by Committing a Crime": Categorizing and Punishing Slave Convicts in Brazil, 1830–1897', *The Americas*, 66, 1 (2009), 11–55. On Fernando de Noronha in relation to other contemporary Latin American penal colonies, see Ryan C. Edwards, 'Post-Colonial Latin America, since 1800', in Clare Anderson, ed., *A Global History of Convicts and Penal Colonies* (London: Bloomsbury, 2018), 245–70; Ricardo D. Salvatore and Carlos Aguirre, 'Colonies of Settlement or Places of Banishment and Torment? Penal Colonies and Convict Labour in Latin America, c. 1800–1940', in Christian G. De Vito and Alex Lichtenstein, eds., *Global Convict Labour* (Leiden: Brill, 2015), 291–6 (273–309). The Portuguese had colonized Fernando in 1741, to impede contraband trade. Following independence in 1822, Brazil claimed it.

2 Introduction

Figure 1.1 Marçal de Corria, by G. Ramage, 1887
Source: Archives of the Royal Botanic Gardens, Kew: HNR/5/4 Henry Ridley Book of Travels.

C. Branner had also visited in 1876.[2] Darwin had noted Fernando de Noronha's thick and dense forests, as had a Royal Naval ship that had touched the coast in 1884. However, excepting coconut groves, by 1887 there were few trees on the island, for they had been cut down to open land for cultivation and to prevent convicts from using the wood to make boats in which to escape (Figures 1.3 and 1.4).[3]

---

[2] John C. Branner, 'Notes on the Fauna of the Islands of Fernando de Noronha', *The American Naturalist*, 22, 262 (1888), 863–4 (861–71); John C. Branner 'The Convict-Island of Brazil – Fernando de Noronha', *The Popular Science Monthly*, 25 (1889), 35 (quote), 38–9 (33–40). Darwin was mainly concerned with the island's geology. See the diary entry dated 20 February 1832, at John van Wyhe, ed., *The Complete Works of Charles Darwin Online* http://darwin-online.org.uk/content/frameset?viewtype=side&itemID=CUL-DAR32.39-40&pageseq=1 (accessed 4 October 2018).

[3] Argentina's penal colony of Ushuaia (1902–47) was also deforested, as a photograph in the collections of the British-based Howard League for Penal Reform attests. See MRC MSS 16A/723/3: 'Ushuaia, Penal Colony of Argentina in Tierra del Fuego. Remains of forests cut down by convict labour, because they facilitated escapes. Photograph sent by Commander Keevil RN who visited it in 1933? 34?' Just five years after the 1887 visit,

Introduction 3

Figure 1.2 Expedition [left to right] Mar[ç]al [de Corria], [George A.] Ramage, H.N. R[idley], T.[S.] Lea, Da Silva [Sylvano de Barro?]
Source: Archives of the Royal Botanic Gardens, Kew: HNR/1/2/7 Photographs of Fernando de Noronha, 1887.

Convict Marçal de Corria, who spoke English, acted as Ridley, Lea, and Ramage's guide. He told them that he had been transported to the island for murder and though he had once made his escape to the mainland, at the end of the previous year he had won a probationary ticket for helping the governor put down a military mutiny.[4] With de Corria's help, the party collected dozens of specimens: rocks and minerals, plants, and animals, including earthworms, spiders, scorpions, cockroaches, earwigs,

---

contemporaries were connecting the island's barren appearance, and the near-total absence of woodland, to a sharp decrease in rainfall and a sharp increase in the risk of severe drought. See 'A Brazilian Convict Island', *Chambers Journal*, 25 Feb. 1893, 117 (116–19), and Beattie, *Punishment in Paradise*, 21. For an environmental history of Ushuaia, including the relationship between forestry and penology, see Ryan Edwards, 'From the Depths of Patagonia: The Ushuaia Penal Colony and the Nature of "The End of the World"', *Hispanic American Historical Review*, 94, 2 (2014), 271–302; Ryan C. Edwards, 'Convicts and Conservation: Inmate labor, fires and forestry in southernmost Argentina', *Journal of Historical Geography*, 56, 2 (2017), 1–13.

[4] This is certainly the enslaved man 'Marçal', who Beattie notes conspired to escape with five non-enslaved inmates. See Beattie, '"Born Under the Cruel Rigor of Captivity"', 28–9 (n. 38).

Figure 1.3 Convict village
Source: Archives of the Royal Botanic Gardens, Kew: HNR/1/2/7 Photographs of Fernando de Noronha, 1887.

grasshoppers, locusts, crickets, dragonflies, fish, geckos and birds. The men spent their days in the field, and their evenings drying and pressing plants, skinning birds, labelling rocks, writing up notes, repairing equipment, and sketching. Convict de Corria took them everywhere. He showed them where best to collect, he carried their loads, and he told them the local names of the resources that they gathered. Ridley later wrote:

We all grew very fond of him, for, besides his extensive local knowledge, he was full of quaint fun. He seemed to know everyone on the island, and was expert in fishing, showing us how the small fry in the rock-pools of the shore might be poisoned with a species of vetch, a device which, though perhaps unsportsmanlike, filled up our collecting bottles with but little trouble. He was always ready to help us to carry home specimens, even of considerable weight, and the contents of his basket were always an important item when we overhauled the day's takings in the evening.

Before leaving Brazil, Ridley, Lea, and Ramage sent home a range of specimens, and de Corria promised that he would send on further samples. This he did, collecting Burra (weeping grass) seeds, and giving them

Introduction

Figure 1.4 The square, Fernando [de] Noronha. My horse, Marçal, in background.
Source: Archives of the Royal Botanic Gardens, Kew: HNR/1/2/7 Photographs of Fernando de Noronha, 1887.

to the governor for shipment. Ultimately, the materials gathered by the botanists and collectors and their Brazilian convict assistant ended up in the natural history section of the British Museum.[5]

At the time of Ridley, Lea, and Ramage's visit in 1887, there were 1,400 convicts on Fernando de Noronha. Peter M. Beattie writes that the

---

[5] RBG archives HNR/5/4: Of the island of Fernando Noronha; letter from Marçal de Corria to Henry Ridley, 26 December 1887; 'The Island of Fernando do Noronha in 1887' by Rev. T.S. Lea – read at the evening meeting of the Royal Geographical Society 23 April 1888 (printed in *Proceedings of the Royal Geographical Society*, 10 [1888], 431 [424–34]). John Branner criticized T. S. Lea's article, for its view of the 'excellence' of the convict system. He stated that if Lea had been able to speak Portuguese, he would have got 'a clear insight' into the true nature of the penal colony, which included an illegal flogging of such violence that Branner himself had been unable to watch. Branner, 'The Convict-Island of Brazil', 36–7 (footnote). Of course, their difference in views might also be explained with respect to the introduction of the new 3-stage penal regime in 1879, and Fernando's transfer from the authority of the military to the judicial wing of government, in the years between Branner and Lea's visits in 1876 and 1887. See also Beattie, *Punishment in Paradise*, 83–4, 89, 116–7, 191–2.

island was 'a large, if exceptionally isolated, plantation where convicts provided most of the labour'.[6] On average, around nine tenths of the convicts were men. Some were soldiers and slaves, and others were Indigenous or free.[7] Whilst most were ordinary criminal offenders, government also used the island to confine a few political prisoners. During the first half of the nineteenth century, they included the leaders of the Cabanos Revolt (1832–5) and the Cabanagem and Praieira rebellions (1835–40, 1850).[8] The convicts were organized into military-style sections or companies and moved through the stages of a three-class penal system. In 1885, the government had passed by-laws which directed that the penal colony would become part of a new graduated penal system in Brazil, based on the globally influential model developed by Sir Walter Crofton in Ireland. Under Crofton's Irish system, prisoners served a relatively short period of initial solitary cellular imprisonment in Dublin, on basic rations. They were then sent to Spike Island, where they were separated at night and worked in association by day. Next, they were transferred to an 'intermediate' prison on probation, in Lusk, where they wore their own clothes and worked on farms. Depending on their conduct, prisoners could be remanded back to the previous stages, and have to work their way back up again. Finally, came conditional liberation. The Brazilian government decreed that Fernando would receive convicts during the 'intermediate' stage of their incarceration, under terms of probation. However, in the final instance it never actually implemented the by-laws, and Fernando's convict system instead incorporated all three elements of the scale. The Justice Ministry had introduced this following an inspection by penal experts Conselheiro Fleury and Bandeira Filho in 1879. Prior to their visit to the island, both men had visited prisons in Europe.[9]

The convicts on the island worked hard, for labour was central to the regime. The first-class convicts made a living by making and selling shell

---

[6] Beattie, *Punishment in Paradise*, 4.
[7] RBG archives HNR/5/4: Life on the Islands, n.d. See also Beattie, *Punishment in Paradise*, 4–5; Salvatore and Aguirre, 'Colonies of Settlement', 291. For a roughly contemporary description of Fernando: E. C. Wines, *The State of Prisons and of Child-Saving Institutions in the Civilized World* (Cambridge, MA: University Press, John Wilson and Son, 1880), 553–6. Brazil abolished slavery in 1888.
[8] Beattie, *Punishment in Paradise*, 90, 130–3.
[9] Beattie, *Punishment in Paradise*, 50–9, 116–7, 191–2. On Crofton, see Lawrence Goldman, 'Crofton, Sir Walter Frederick (1815–1897)', *Oxford Dictionary of National Biography* (Oxford University Press, 2004); online edition, 23 September 2004, https://doi.org/10.1093/ref:odnb/65325 (accessed 7 May 2020). Following the US national prison congress in Cincinnati in 1870, American reformers sent Spanish translations of documents on the Crofton system to Latin American states. See Wines, *The State of Prisons and of Child-Saving Institutions*, 548.

boxes, hats, and boots, or preparing crabs and lobsters. Those in the second class worked as farmers, or in handicrafts, fishing, quarrying, or stonecutting. The island was self-sustaining in terms of maize production, and exported manioc, castor seeds, and cotton. Convicts received a share of profits. Third-class convicts repaired roads, walls, and paths. Those in the lower classes could move up a penal stage according to satisfactory work and conduct, but those who did not submit to the labour and penal regime were downgraded, flogged, fettered, and confined. The ultimate sanction was banishment to neighbouring Ilha Rata (Rat Island), where convicts had to sustain themselves through fishing and foraging. All the convicts had to go to evening mass, where a convict band played. As a reward for good behaviour, and in the belief that family units fostered social stability, government permitted convict men and women to marry. First-class convict men could call for their wives. Though born free, government compelled convicts' children to attend school until they turned 14, when the girls were sent to a mainland convent, and the boys made to enlist in the army. In these ways, as Beattie argues, Fernando de Noronha served multiple purposes: 'as a site for punishment, exile, rehabilitation, colonization and production'.[10] The penal colony endured until the proclamation of the Brazilian republic in 1889. Public opinion then turned against the island, and the new government wound down and eventually abandoned it in 1897.[11]

The shipment of convicts and political prisoners to Fernando de Noronha is part of the history of punishment and governance in Brazil. It is also part of a much larger national, regional, and global history of punitive mobility. The existence and operation of an island penal colony such as Fernando de Noronha into the late 1890s disrupts the dominant narrative of carceral history: that in the nineteenth century the closed walls of the cellular penitentiary largely replaced other modes of punishment or architectures of confinement. Rather, Fernando de Noronha was one among many carceral sites that reveal the persistence of alternative forms of punishment, for a much longer period of time than historians and penologists have previously assumed.[12] Convicts were sent long distances and offshore, to work on and in plantations, farms, households, quarries, mines, forests and jungles, to build penal infrastructure, and to labour on public works such as road, bridge, canal, and dockyard construction. The long life of such penal mobility, to islands and colonies as

---

[10] Beattie, *Punishment in Paradise*, 7 (quote), 24, 28, 78, 108, 110–16, 118–21.
[11] Beattie, *Punishment in Paradise*, 86–90, 140–2; Salvatore and Aguirre, 'Colonies of Settlement', 292–3.
[12] For an expansive discussion of a large literature, see Mary Gibson, 'Global Perspectives on the Birth of the Prison', *American Historical Review*, 116, 4 (2011), 1040–63.

also to remote inland or border regions, can be accounted for in the close and enduring connection between punishment and nation and empire building. States, imperial powers, and, sometimes, even trading companies used convicts to satisfy geopolitical and social ambitions. Convicts constituted a supply of unfree labour that could be used to occupy territories for economic and commercial reasons. In turn, those territories became places to which socially and politically 'undesirable' people could be removed. As is evident in the case of Fernando de Noronha, penal colonies were bound up with colonization, resource extraction, and productivity. The penological influences brought to bear on the island also show that the operation of places of punitive relocation, and the management of convicts and political prisoners, became intertwined with global circulations of ideologies of punishment and rehabilitation, including of enslaved, Indigenous, and military populations. Thus, punitive mobility is connected to the history of governance and repression, and to the creation of new modalities of work and organization including racialized labour regimes. It also produced new kinds of classifications and social structures in which governments encouraged and nurtured family formation as a route to both convict reform and permanent settlement.[13]

Marçal de Corria's work with British botanists and collectors in 1887 also suggests that convict expertise made a vital contribution to the local practices and global circulations that together shaped contemporary knowledge production and straddled nations and empires. It is well established that science as a global practice emerged out of local encounters and exchanges, rather than centrifugal European transfers of knowledge, in which multiple global nodes were connected in chains of scientific production. Local mediators played a key role in these circuits, which were facilitated by new technologies of preservation and transportation.[14] If the very existence of Fernando de Noronha disrupts accepted views on the history of punishment and provides a new lens through which to consider the coercive basis of nation-making and governance, the employment of a formerly enslaved convict in a European-led scientific expedition injects the social and geographical global margins

---

[13] Clare Anderson, 'Introduction', in Anderson, ed., *A Global History of Convicts and Penal Colonies*, 1–35. These themes are also discussed in regard to prison labour in De Vito and Lichtenstein, eds., *Global Convict Labour*.

[14] Anne Coote, Alison Haynes, Jude Philp, and Simon Ville, 'When Commerce, Science, and Leisure Collaborated: The Nineteenth-Century Global Trade Boom in Natural History Collections', *Journal of Global History*, 12, 3 (2017), 319–39; Lissa Roberts, 'Situating Science in Global History: Local Exchanges and Networks of Circulation', *Itinerario*, 33, 1 (2009), 9–30; Sujit Sivasundarum, 'Sciences and the Global: On Methods, Questions, and Theory', *Isis*, 101, 1 (2010), 147–8 (146–58).

Introduction 9

into intellectual histories of scientific mediation in an important new way.[15] Convicts and penal colonies, it would seem, played a role in the making of the modern world, with respect not just to the history of punishment, but of governance, labour, nation and empire, and global knowledge exchange.

Convicts and Punitive Relocation: Definitions, Themes, and Concepts

This book uses Ridley, Lea, and Ramage's expedition to the penal colony of Fernando de Noronha in 1887 as the starting point for a global approach to the history of convicts since 1415. This represents the time when Portugal first used convicts (*degredados*) for imperial expansion in the North African *presidio* (fort) of Ceuta. After this date, the European empires, Russia, China, Japan, and numerous independent Latin American nations transported, banished, and deported men and women to *presidios*, penal colonies, and other punitive destinations all over the world. This practice endured into the 1970s in the case of Spain, and later still in parts of Latin America and Russia. Convicts, exiles, and deportees were rendered mobile through a variety of legal avenues, from judicial conviction and military court martial, to administrative removal and banishment. Though it does not perfectly capture such differences, the book uses the nomenclature 'convicts' to describe generally people subjected to various forms of punitive mobility. Where specific groups are the focus of discussion – including transportation convicts but also nationalist agitators who during the period since the nineteenth century were held in separate penal facilities without expectation of labour – they are referred to more precisely. Otherwise, the book terms the mobility of convicts, deportees, and exiles at large 'punitive mobility' or 'punitive relocation', and where appropriate uses more precise descriptors such as 'penal transportation', 'convict indenture', 'deportation', or 'penal

---

[15] For the long eighteenth century, see Simon Schaffer, Lissa Roberts, Kapil Raj, and James Delbourgo, eds., *The Brokered World: Go-betweens and global intelligence, 1770–1820* (Sagamore Beach, MA: Watson Publishing International, 2009); David Arnold, *The Tropics and the Traveling Gaze: India, landscape, and science, 1800–1856* (Seattle: University of Washington Press, 2006); Kapil Raj, *Relocating Modern Science: Circulation and the construction of knowledge in South Asia and Europe* (Basingstoke: Palgrave, 2006); James Delbourgo and Nicholas Dew, eds., *Science and Empire in the Atlantic World* (London: Routledge, 2008); Ricardo Roque and Kim A. Wagner, 'Introduction: Engaging Colonial Knowledge', in Ricardo Roque and Kim A. Wagner, eds., *Engaging Colonial Knowledge: Reading European archives in world history* (Basingstoke: Palgrave, 2012), 1–32.

impressment'.[16] '*Presidios*' describes the Iberian forts in which convicts were kept alongside soldiers, the enslaved, and other workers; and 'penal colonies' designates places in which systems made efforts to separate convicts from neighbouring populations, whether they were Indigenous, enslaved, free, or migrant. The book identifies other, mixed locations as 'penal settlements' or 'sites of punitive relocation'. All were distinct from prisons and penitentiaries, which incarcerated and immobilized inmates. As we will see, though sites of punitive relocation sometimes blended features of mobility and immobilization, it is important to appreciate different carceral forms in understanding continuities and shifts in the history of punishment, and the perhaps surprising endurance of punitive movement into the modern age.

Underpinning the argument is the contention that convicts were agents of occupation, colonization, and frontier expansion, and were labour pioneers. Convicts were highly mobile, moving geographically across, around and within nation states and land and sea-borne empires. The chapters that follow examine the multivalent relationships that existed between convicts and punitive relocation and governance, and nation building and imperial expansion. They explore histories of punishment and state repression, the occupation and settlement of borderlands and colonies, the forging of new global connections, the development of scientific and medical knowledge, and the spread of political or anti-colonial ideologies.[17] In this regard, the book's objective is to write a new global history from below. In doing so, it focuses on the lives of convicts and pays attention to the ways in which they found agency in and resisted their punitive relocation. This included by mutiny and rebellion, sometimes with political intent, and through the establishment of economic, social, cultural, and intimate relationships, forged at least partly outside the purview or surveillance of states and empires. Escape is a key theme. The book also foregrounds the place of convicts and punitive mobility in the global circulation and exchange of knowledge, practices, and people, highlighting flows in penal thinking, systems of classification and connections, and relationships and encounters between convicts and Indigenous men and women, free settlers, and indentured and enslaved workers. Through this approach, the book draws out comparisons and distinctions between

[16] Christian G. De Vito, Clare Anderson, and Ulbe Bosma, 'Penal Transportation, Deportation and Exile: Perspectives from the Colonies in the Nineteenth and Twentieth Centuries', *International Review of Social History*, 63, S26 (2018), 6 (1–24).
[17] See also Uma Kothari, 'Contesting Colonial Rule: Politics of exile in the Indian Ocean', *Geoforum*, 43 (2012), 697–706.

the various polities under discussion, and between convicts, colonized peoples, and subaltern experiences.[18]

During a more than six-century-long period, there were hundreds of thousands of punitive relocations; millions when imperial Russia and the Soviet Union are included (see Table 1.1).[19] Convicts, exiles, and deportees moved multi-directionally, crossing land, rivers, seas, and oceans. They went outwards from national and imperial centres, across borders and frontiers, and between overseas possessions. They travelled on foot, by carts, wagons, boats, and ships, and, later, on steamers and trains. Penal journeys were often lengthy and multi-staged, and even after convicts arrived in *presidios*, penal colonies, and other punitive destinations, they remained highly mobile. Some made multiple attempts at escape, or successfully fled. Others could be made subject to further movement according to geopolitical and labour needs, or alternatively put under some form of penal restraint such as incarceration or solitary confinement. Therefore, in common with parallel flows of free, enslaved, and coerced migrants, there is often no easy definition of the start and end points of convict journeys. A networked approach that is appreciative of what Nick Gill and others have recently termed 'carceral circuitry' is vital to understanding their character.[20]

Hamish Maxwell-Stewart argues that convict mobility and expendability were so significant and extensive for the European empires that convicts were 'the shock troops of colonialism'. 'In the absence of transportation and associated systems of unfree labor migration', he writes, 'it is difficult to envisage how early-modern European states could have attracted migrants to their New World possessions.' The importance of convicts during the early years of colonization was connected to labour shortages and associated high wage rates. For that

---

[18] Related interventions are Clare Anderson, *Subaltern Lives: Biographies of colonialism in the Indian Ocean world, 1790–1920* (Cambridge University Press, 2012); Tony Ballantyne and Antoinette Burton, eds., *World Histories From Below* (London: Bloomsbury, 2016).

[19] Sarah Badcock and Judith Pallot, 'Russia and the Soviet Union from the Nineteenth to the Twenty-First Century', in Anderson, ed., *A Global History of Convicts and Penal Colonies*, 289 (271–305).

[20] Nick Gill, Deirdre Conlon, Dominique Moran, and Andrew Burridge, 'Carceral circuitry: New directions in carceral geography', *Progress in Human Geography*, 42, 2 (2018), 183–204. See also Clare Anderson, Carrie M. Crockett, Christian G. De Vito, *et al.*, 'Locating Penal Transportation: Punishment, Space, and Place c. 1750 to 1900', in Karen M. Morin and Dominique Moran, eds., *Historical Geographies of Prisons: Unlocking the usable carceral past* (London: Routledge, 2015), 147–67; Tony Ballantyne, 'Mobility, Empire, Colonisation', *History Australia*, 11, 2 (2016), 7–37; Prabhu Mohapatra, 'Eurocentrism, Forced Labour, and Global Migration: A Critical Assessment,' *International Review of Social History*, 52, 1 (2007), 110–15; Kerry Ward, *Networks of Empire: Forced migration in the Dutch East India Company* (Cambridge University Press, 2009).

Table 1.1 *Global convict flows, 1415–1976*

Polity	Dates of operation[a]	Estimated no. of punitive relocations
Portuguese Empire	1415–1961	120,000[b]
Spanish Empire	1494–1976	110,000
Habsburg Empire	1526–1918	? 3,000+[c]
French Empire	1541–1953	100,000
Imperial Russia	1590–1917	1,900,000
British Empire	1618–1945	376,000
Netherlands Empire	1619–1942	202,000
Scandinavian Empires	1640–1765	2,000
China	1644–1912	134,000
Japan	1881–1908	14,000
Italian Empire	1886–1943	? 5,500[d]
USSR	1928–1953	25,000,000[e]

Source: Clare Anderson, 'Introduction: A Global History of Convicts and Penal Colonies', in Clare Anderson, ed., *A Global History of Convicts and Penal Colonies* (London: Bloomsbury, 2018), 2 (1–35).

[a] The 'Dates of operation' column has been altered as research has progressed.

[b] Since the first publication of these figures, estimates for the Portuguese Empire have been revised from 100,000 to 120,000, using Timothy J. Coates, 'The Long View of Convict Labour in the Portuguese Empire, 1415-1932', in Christian G. De Vito and Alex Lichtenstein, eds., *Global Convict Labour* (Leiden: Brill, 2015), 146, 156 (144–67).

[c] The figure for the Habsburg empire is for 1744–68 only. See Stephan Steiner, '"An Austrian Cayenne": Convict Labour and Deportation in the Habsburg Empire of the Early Modern Period', in De Vito and Lichtenstein, eds., *Global Convict Labour*, 132–8 (126–43).

[d] For the Italian Empire, Francesca Di Pasquale, 'The "Other" at Home: Deportation and Transportation of Libyans to Italy During the Colonial Era (1911-1943)', *International Review of Social History*, 63, S26 (2018), 211–13.

[e] Figures for the USSR have also been revised upwards. See Carrie Crockett, 'Russia: Convict Labour and Transportation, 1696–1960', http://convictvoyages.org/expert-essays/russia-1696-1960 (accessed 17 October 2018).

The figures do not include deported vagrants or sex workers, or penal impressments. Estimates suggest that these were extensive. The Spanish transported more than 60,000 vagrants during the period 1730–69 alone, and the French impressed at least 600,000 into imperial military service. See De Vito, 'The Spanish Empire, 1500–1898', 71, and Dominique Kalifa, *Biribi: Les Bagnes coloniaux de l'Armée Française* (Paris: Perrin, 2009).

Neither do they include the following punitive relocations, for which figures are currently unavailable: Ottoman Empire (1453– ?), Argentina (1810–), Chile (1821–1975), Mexico (1821–), Ecuador (1837–1958), Brazil (1857–1950), Panama (1873–2004) and the Belgian Congo (1908–60).

reason, it is important to note that they did not necessarily provide an alternative to more desirable free labour; often they were the preferred choice. However, and because of the infrastructural development and other work completed by convicts, gradually many places became more

Introduction 13

attractive to free migrants. Convict labour then began to undercut free wages and so settlers sought to end transportation. It was often where particular locations remained unattractive to free settlers, often due to high death rates, that penal transportation persisted.[21]

Maxwell-Stewart's insights on European empires suggest that punitive mobility did not exist in isolation, and to understand its significance for the expansion of national and imperial power, it is necessary to appreciate the importance of associated labour systems. The book proposes that penal transportation and its punitive corollaries were part of a continuum of labour practices that also incorporated the expropriation of Indigenous labour, enslavement, indenture, and other forms of bonded work.[22] Punitive mobility co-existed with what Pieter Spierenburg described as 'penal bondage', which was undertaken in workhouses, galleys, and dockyards across Western Europe.[23] So different were their development in the sixteenth and seventeenth centuries that Johan Heinsen calls for the reconceptualization of early-modern extramural labour as a practice of assemblage.[24] Convict work was also connected to the imperial workforce, which was itself extraordinarily diverse. Spain, for example, was able to access labour via tribute, contract, enslavement, and servitude, both in Europe and the colonies. According to Evelyn P. Jennings, a close relationship developed between the economic, political, and labour needs of empire, and it was this that underpinned Spain's 'resilience and longevity' as an imperial power.[25] Other such links emerge in the imperial melting pot of the turn-of-the-nineteenth-century Caribbean. Enslaved persons sentenced to transportation generated compensation for their former owners and profits for the merchants who purchased, shipped, and sold them on between empires. Upon resale,

---

[21] Hamish Maxwell-Stewart, 'Transportation', 639–40, 647 (quotes). See also Clare Anderson and Hamish Maxwell-Stewart, 'Convict Labour and the Western Empires, 1415–1954', in Robert Aldrich and Kirsten McKenzie, eds., *The Routledge History of Western Empires* (London: Routledge, 2014), 102–17.

[22] Clare Anderson, 'After Emancipation: Empires and Imperial Formations', in Catherine Hall, Nicholas Draper, and Keith McClelland, eds., *Emancipation and the Remaking of the British Imperial World* (Manchester University Press, 2014), 113–27; Seymour Drescher, 'Capitalism and Slavery after Fifty Years', *Slavery and Abolition*, 18, 3 (1997), 220–1 (212–27).

[23] Pieter Spierenburg, 'Prison and Convict Labour in Early Modern Europe', in De Vito and Lichtenstein, eds., *Global Convict Labour*, 108–25.

[24] See also Johan Heinsen, 'Historicizing Extramural Convict Labour: Trajectories and Transitions in Early Modern Europe', *International Review of Social History*, 66, 1 (2021), 111–33.

[25] Evelyn P. Jennings, 'The Sinews of Spain's American Empire: Forced Labor in Cuba from the Sixteenth to the Nineteenth Centuries', in John Donoghue and Evelyn P. Jennings, eds., *Building the Atlantic Empires: Unfree labor and imperial states in the political economy of capitalism, ca. 1500–1914* (Leiden: Brill, 2015), 26 (25–53).

they were effectively re-enslaved. Penal conscription and penal enslavement are also relevant to this discussion. During the early-modern period, European debtors and West African 'criminals' were sold into armies and enslavement. Russia, Portugal, Spain, France, and Britain all produced penal units for service in colonial outposts, including in continental Africa, India, and the Americas.[26]

Table 1.2 details the absolute number of punitive relocations against those of other labour flows. Imperial Russia and the USSR dominate; otherwise convict movement was more limited than the vast mobilities associated with slave trading, Asian indentured labour, and the modern penal labour camps of Italy, Spain, and Nazi Germany – notwithstanding free migration within Asia and from Europe to the New World. However, in appreciating the importance of punitive mobility within a larger framework of migration and labour history, three things are especially noteworthy in framing general themes. First, penal transportation extended over a very long period, preceding, coexisting with and outlasting other forms of exploitative mobility, including enslavement and indenture. Second, even relatively small numbers of convicts could form either a substantial proportion or the majority of settler populations. Both points are important because they suggest that not only did convicts play a key role in occupation and expropriation, but they also prepared land and infrastructure for permanent settlement, for themselves and their descendants, and for other non-convict migrants.[27] Third, from the earliest times, states and empires used transportation, exile, and deportation as tools of governance and repression. The 'political prisoner' did not, as scholars sometimes represent, develop exclusively or even primarily in the modern age.[28]

Some attention to historicity and the changing character of punitive relocation during the long period under consideration in the book is necessary here. With the exception of the Soviet Union's archipelago of *gulag*, established in the twentieth century and in which forced mobility and relocation was a key component of almost all political repression and judicial punishment, from the period after 1800 elsewhere penal transportation, penal servitude, and administrative deportation were usually reserved as penalties for specific offences or acts.[29] This was sometimes

---

[26] Maxwell-Stewart, 'Transportation', 637–8, 639.   [27] Anderson, 'Introduction', 5–8.
[28] Padraic Kenney, '"I felt a kind of pleasure in seeing them treat us brutally." The Emergence of the Political Prisoner, 1865–1910', *Comparative Studies in Society and History*, 54, 4 (2012), 863–89.
[29] Laura Piacentini and Judith Pallot, '"In Exile Imprisonment" in Russia', *The British Journal of Criminology*, 54, 1 (2014), 20–37; Judith Pallot, 'Russia's Penal Peripheries: Space, Place and Penality in Soviet and Post-Soviet Russia', *Transactions of the British Institute of Geographers*, New Series, 30, 1 (2005), 98–112. The reference to the '*gulag*

Introduction 15

Table 1.2 *Global labour mobility, 1415–1976*

Polity	Dates	Estimated nos
Indian Ocean slave trading, by Europeans	1500–1850	ᵃ489,000
Asian indenture in the Caribbean and Indian Ocean	1834–1916	1,451,000
Punitive mobility, European empires, China, and Japan	1415–1976	1,066,500ᵇ
Migration: India, China, Japan, and Africa to the Americas	1846–1940	2,500,000
Migration: Africa, Europe, Northeast Asia and Middle East to Southeast Asia, Indian Ocean rim, South Pacific	1846–1940	4,000,000
European penal labour camps	1750–1950	5,000,000
Punitive mobility, Russia and USSR	1590–1953	11,900,000–26,900,000
Foreign forced labour, Nazi Germany	1939–45	13,500,000
Atlantic slave trade	1500–1866	12,521,000
Migration: Northeast Asia and Russia to Manchuria, Siberia, central Asia, Japan	1846–1940	48,500,000ᶜ
Migration: India and Southern China to Southeast Asia, Indian Ocean rim, South Pacific	1846–1940	50,000,000ᵈ
Migration: Europe to the Americas	1846–1940	^ 56,500,000

Source: Anderson, 'Introduction', 7.
ᵃ Richard B. Allen's estimate is between 431,000 and 547,000. See Richard B. Allen, 'Satisfying the "Want for Labouring People": European Slave Trading in the Indian Ocean, 1500–1850', *Journal of World History*, 21, 1 (2010), 64 (45–73).
ᵇ Does not include penal impressment, or the mobility of vagrants and other social 'undesirables'.
ᶜ, ᵈ, ᵉ Adam McKeown's estimates are: ᶜ46–51 million, ᵈ48–52 million, and ᵉ55–58 million. See Adam McKeown, 'Global Migration, 1846-1940', *Journal of World History*, 15, 2 (2004), 155–89.
These figures do not include the overland migrations of North America, regional migration in the Caribbean and Southeast Asia, immigration into Africa, or internal migration in Europe, Russia, India, or China. Note also that many free labour flows were seasonal and/ or circulatory and are thus difficult to capture statistically.

the case in the earlier period, where convicts were shipped outwards from Europe, including by trading companies or private merchants, convicts having been sold into contracts of indenture or military service. These early-modern flows sometimes included political exiles, as noted above. They often also incorporated other socially 'undesirable' or marginal populations such as vagrants, sex-workers, and orphans, who were effectively criminalized, as well as enslaved people, semi-coerced or impressed

archipelago' comes from former convict Aleksandr Solzhenitsyn's famous *The Gulag Archipelago: An experiment in literary investigation* (New York: Harper and Row, 1974).

soldiers and sailors, indentured workers, and people subject to administrative deportation on the orders of a governor or local official. The lines between these groups were often blurred, to the extent that Beattie refers to the lack of distinction between them as 'category drift'.[30]

It is challenging to make generalizations across this long period and wide terrain. The Italian Empire is an important exception in regard to the deportation of insurgents (or potential insurgents) from North African colonies to Italy, rather than intra-colonially for labour purposes, as was the more usual pattern. This manoeuvre was primarily repressive and often collective, with the choice of destination at least in part due to the existence of 'internal' penal colonies (*colonie coatti*) in Sicily, Sardinia, and on offshore islands.[31] However, otherwise and repeatedly over time and place convicts were used to colonize, occupy, or expand territory, and even where labour projects were inefficient or failed, they were put to work. Many though by no means all convict flows were overwhelmingly male, and men and women were often treated differently. What certainly shifted over time was that, from the end of the eighteenth century, commonly efforts were made to separate convicts from other populations, both during their penal journey and following their arrival. This was related to changing ideas about punishment, deterrence, and rehabilitation, and the corresponding desire for discrete punitive sites. Work remained important to this endeavour, and connections between convicts and other populations through associated and wider labour markets remained. However, the goal was not necessarily the permanent settlement of convicts, but labour extraction tied to punishment and sometimes though not always reform, including through religious reflection. Further, in practice, during the later period penal transportation and in some cases administrative deportation were reserved for crimes that were serious but not viewed as meriting judicial execution, or for repeat or habitual offenders and capital reprieves. These varied considerably according to context. As Timothy J. Coates argues, in relation to the labour needs of the early-modern Portuguese Empire, convicts were too valuable to kill.[32]

A global perspective on punitive mobility also reveals the important finding that during the nineteenth century transportation, deportation,

---

[30] Beattie, *Punishment and Paradise*, 6. See also Pieter Spierenburg, ed., *The Emergence of Carceral Institutions, 1550–1900* (Rotterdam: Erasmus University Press, 1984).

[31] Francesca Di Pasquale, 'The "Other" at Home: Deportation and Transportation of Libyans to Italy During the Colonial Era (1911–1943)', *International Review of Social History*, 63, S26 (2018), 211–31.

[32] Timothy J. Coates, 'The Portuguese Empire, 1100–1932', in Anderson, ed., *A Global History of Convicts and Penal Colonies*, 38–9 (37–64).

and exile were more globally expansive than at any point in world history (Appendix 1, Map 1.1). This suggests that the period since the mid-seventeenth century was not an era in which Enlightenment rationality underpinned a 'great confinement', as has been argued following Michel Foucault's seminal work on the era of the birth of the prison. Rather, the logic of nation and empire building demanded the global relocation of convicts on a massive scale.[33] Not only did punitive mobility coexist with incarceration, but during this period penal settlements and colonies became spaces of international discussion and experimentation.[34] At this time, the European empires and East Asian powers, imperial Russia, and much of Latin America remained strongly attached to remote sites of punishment: inland, offshore, or overseas. The ready accessibility of convicts as research assistants or subjects also suggests that penal colonies acquired further functions in relation to wider histories of exploration, collecting, medicine, and ethnographic research. In taking a global history perspective on their histories, the book offers a fundamental revision of penological narratives. It compels us to establish a new narrative of punishment that is connected not just to the emergence of prisons and penitentiaries, but to histories of nation and empire over a period of more than 500 years.

By the nineteenth century, the similarities in the exercise and experience of different forms of punitive relocation are suggested by common descriptions of convict destinations as 'colonies'.[35] For example, in lamenting the failure of cellular prisons to reform repeat offenders, British Inspector of Prisons Arthur Griffiths urged the introduction of a new type of punishment. He wrote: 'If convict labor is worth anything, it is worth keeping at home, to be used for the benefit, direct or indirect, of the taxpayer who bears the charges. ... *The penal colony of the future is to be established in our midst and in full view of all.*' He further wrote: 'the word "colony" is used in a restricted sense – that of its original meaning as a place worked by husbandmen, planted out, but at no great distance, nor beyond sea.' Griffiths' proposal was underpinned by his knowledge of contemporary

---

[33] The arguments most closely associated with the work of Michel Foucault in *Madness and Civilization: A History of Insanity in the Age of Reason* (London: Tavistock, 1967) and *Discipline and Punish: The birth of the prison* (New York: Vintage, 1975). See also Gibson, 'A Global History of the Prison'; David Garland, *Punishment and Modern Society: A study in social theory* (Oxford: Clarendon, 1991); Norval Morris and David Rothman, eds., *The Oxford History of the Prison: The practice of punishment in western society* (Oxford University Press, 1998).

[34] Anderson, 'Introduction', 9–10.

[35] For a broader analysis of the word 'colony' as a political concept, see Ann Laura Stoler, 'Colony', *Political Concepts: A critical lexicon*, 1 (2011). Stoler usefully points to the 'tangled projects and investments' that spanned a range of different kinds of colonies – settler, penal, entrepôt.

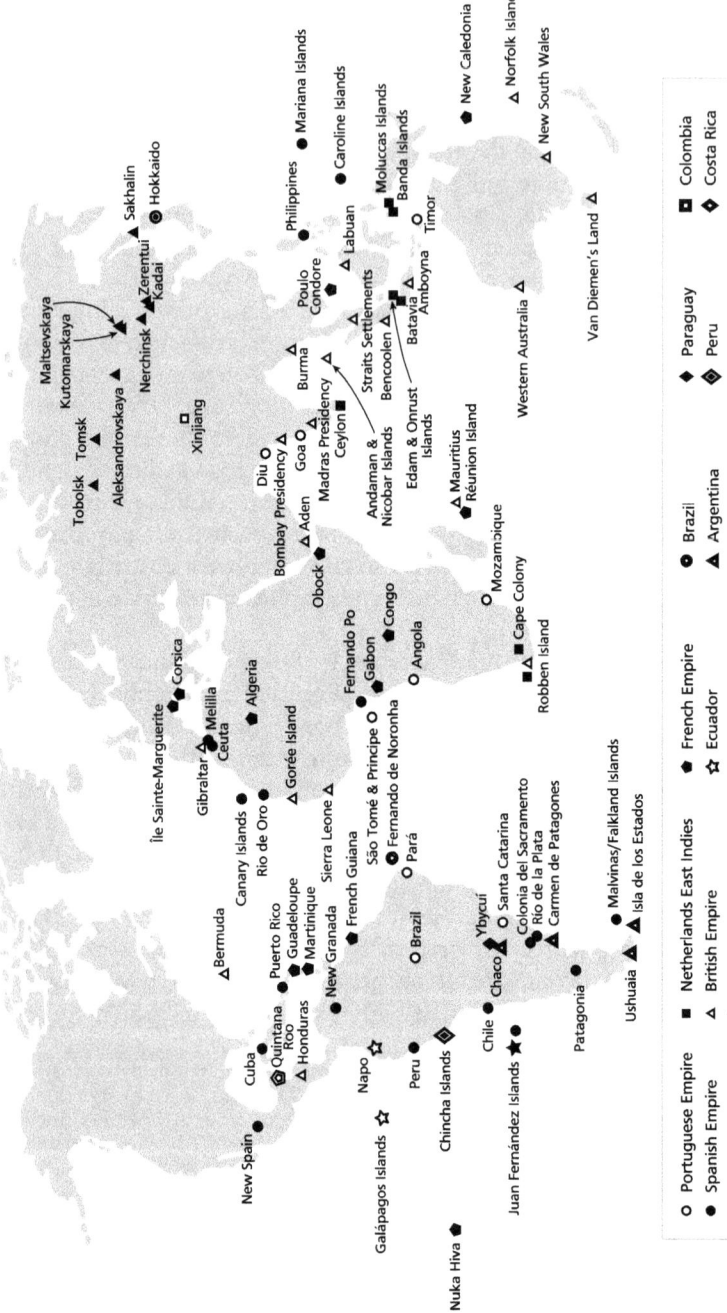

Map 1.1 Key global destinations of convict flows, 1800–1900

Italian agricultural colonies, as well as the Dutch pauper colonies of Frederiksoord and Willemsoord, and the French juvenile reformatory at Mettray.[36] Later chapters draw out the importance of such penal knowledge. Here, note that Mettray (est. 1839) in particular was much visited and admired. It was organized along village lines, with the children placed in 'families', under the care of trained officers. At least during its early years, the settlement enjoyed extraordinary success, measured by the tiny handful of offences committed by its former inmates after release.[37] In the 1850s, Matthew Davenport Hill, the famous English recorder (judge) of Birmingham, remarked: 'No Mahomedan believes more devoutly in the efficiency of a pilgrimage to Mecca than I do in one to Mettray.'[38]

---

[36] Arthur Griffiths, 'Penal Colonies – Agricultural and Industrial', *North American Review*, 163, 482 (1896), 682 (quotes, my emphasis), 683–6 (676–87). See also Bill Forsythe, 'Griffiths, Arthur George Frederick (1838–1908)', *Oxford Dictionary of National Biography* (Oxford University Press, 2004); online edition, September 2004, https://doi.org/10.1093/ref:odnb/33581. George Dubois (member of the board of directors of the general society of prisons, France) expressed a near-identical sentiment when he described one penitentiary in Sicily as 'a kind of transportation'. See George Dubois, *Report on Incorrigibility*, in E. C. Wines, *The Actual State of Prison Reform Throughout the Civilized World: A discourse pronounced at the opening of the international prison congress of Stockholm, August 10, 1878* (Stockholm: Centra-Tryckeriet, 1878), 130.

[37] Société Paternelle, *Fondation d'une colonie agricole de jeunes détenus à Mettray* (Paris: Benjamin Duprat, 1839); James McClelland, *On Reformatories for the Destitute and Fallen (being the substance of a paper read at the statistical section of the British Association)*, to which is appended, Report on Agricultural Colonies, by M. Demetz, Honorary Counsellor of the Imperial Court of Paris (Glasgow: James Maclehose, 1856). See also Ceri Crossley, 'Using and Transforming the French Countryside: The "Colonies Agricoles" (1820–1850)', *French Studies* 44, 1 (1991), 36–54; Felix Driver, 'Discipline without Frontiers? Representations of the Mettray Reformatory Colony in Britain, 1840–1880', *Journal of Historical Sociology*, 3, 3 (1990), 272–93; Luc Forlivesi, Georges-François Pottier, and Sophie Chassat, *Éduquer et punir. La colonie agricole et pénitentiaire de Mettray (1839–1937)* (Presses Universitaires de Rennes, 2005); Mary Gibson and Ilaria Poerio, 'Modern Europe, 1750–1950', in Anderson, ed., *A Global History of Convicts and Penal Colonies*, 334–6 (337–70). On agricultural colonies more broadly, see Jeroen J. H. Dekker, 'Punir, sauver et éduquer: la colonie agricole "Nederlandsch Mettray" et la rééducation résidentielle aux Pays-Bas, en France, en Allemagne et en Angleterre entre 1814 et 1914', *Le Mouvement Social*, 153 (1990), 6–90; Jeroen J. H. Dekker, *The Will to Change the Child: Re-education homes for children at risk in nineteenth century Western Europe* (Frankfurt am Main: Peter Lang, 2001); Albert Schauwers, 'The "Benevolent" colonies of Johannes van den Bosch: Continuities in *the Administration of Poverty in the Netherlands and Indonesia*', *Comparative Studies in Society and History*, 43, 2 (2001), 298–328; Ann Laura Stoler, *Duress: Imperial durabilities in our times* (Durham, NC: Duke University Press, 2016), chapter 3.

[38] Matthew Davenport Hill, *Mettray: A letter from the Recorder of Birmingham to Charles Bowyer Adderley, Esq., M.P.* (London: Cash, 1858), 8. Mettray was globally famous. For instance, Major G. Hutchinson referred to Hill's praise in *Reformatory Measures Connected with the Treatment of Criminals in India* (Lahore: Punjab Printing Company's Press, 1866), 131. See also Driver, 'Discipline Without Frontiers?', 272–3.

From the Ancient to the Modern World: a Brief Overview of Convict Mobility

This book straddles a range of themes and concepts, across global contexts. Though it takes the early fifteenth century as a starting point, there is a long history of punitive mobility stretching back to the Ancient World. This can be usefully presented here. From around the third century BC to the end of the Western Empire in AD 476, the Romans deployed convict labour in Europe, coastal North Africa, the Balkans, and parts of Western Asia and the Middle East. They used convicts in large numbers, with enslaved, formerly enslaved and free workers: skilled and unskilled, local and migrant. Punishment was status dependent, and the Romans primarily reserved penal labour for the enslaved, non-elites, and non-citizens, the latter being people living in provinces such as Sicily and Sardinia and subject to Roman rule. Convicts laboured on public works (*opus publicum*), and in mines and quarries (*opus metalli*). The Romans considered transportation to distant locations as an additional punishment, but they did not use it on a large scale. It was mainly restricted to *opus metalli* convicts. On the other hand, they did not put privileged citizens to hard labour, but sent them into banishment, including on Mediterranean islands.[39] In Britain during the early Middle Ages, banishment was a punishment for serious crime, though it seems to have gone into demise by the sixteenth century.[40] In this period, abjurers faced exile. They had either escaped criminal conviction but had been so defamed that they had to leave their communities, or had gone overseas following a felony, confessed, and avoided a trial if they promised not to return. Between 1180 and c. 1350, more than 75,000 such exiles went to France.[41] Far distant from Europe in East Asia, from at least the second century BC, the first Chinese dynasty, the Qin, banished offenders to state borders and remote frontiers.[42] Japan used offshore islands for the same purpose, and

---

[39] Miriam J. Groen-Vallinga and Laurens E. Tacoma, 'Contextualizing Condemnation to Hard Labour in the Roman Empire', in De Vito and Lichtenstein, eds., *Global Convict Labour*, 52–4, 65–6, 68, 71–3, 77–8 (49–78). A fascinating interpretation of one of these mines, Phaeno in Palestine, is David Mattingly, Paul Newson, Oliver Creighton, *et al.*, 'A landscape of imperial power: Roman and Byzantine *Phaino*', in Graham Barker, David Gilbertson, and David Mattingly, eds., *Archaeology and Desertification: The Wadi Faynan landscape survey, South Jordan* (Oxford: Council for British Research in the Levant, 2007), 333–4 (305–48).
[40] Sarah Tarlow and Emma Battell Lowman, *Harnessing the Power of the Criminal Corpse* (Basingstoke: Palgrave, 2018), 47–8.
[41] William Chester Jordan, *From England to France: Felony and exile in the High Middle Ages* (Princeton University Press, 2015), 6.
[42] Joanna Waley-Cohen, *Exile in Mid-Qing China: Banishment to Xinjiang, 1758–1820* (New Haven, CT: Yale University Press, 1991), 36–7.

for the exile of elites, in the centuries before the Meiji restoration of 1868.[43]

The scope, scale, and chronology of convict mobility in the age of European empires might be briefly summarized as follows (see also Table 1.1 and Appendix 1). From 1415, Portugal sent European, African, and Asian convicts multi-directionally around its empire, alongside other social 'undesirables' including vagrants, sex workers and orphans, and soldiers and the enslaved. Convicts went to colonies including Goa, Timor, Ceylon (now, Sri Lanka), and Malacca (Melaka) in the East Indies, to pre-independence Brazil, to the sugar islands of Sao Tome and Principe, and to penitentiary colonies in the African colonies of Angola and Mozambique. Some convicts were impressed into military service. Transportation to some of these destinations continued until 1974.[44] Following Portugal, from the sixteenth century onwards, the Spanish shipped convicts to and between overseas *presidios* in North Africa and the Americas. These included Ceuta, which had been ceded from Portugal in 1668, Oran, Melilla, Louisiana, Chile, Colonia del Sacramento, and New Spain. Remarkably, by the late 1500s, convicts constituted almost eighty per cent of the workforce of Spain's Caribbean galleys.[45] As in the Portuguese Empire, Spanish convicts often travelled alongside soldiers and the enslaved, or people from the social underclasses. By the mid-seventeenth century, Spanish convicts were either sentenced to hard labour or military service and were known as *presidiarios* or *desterrados* respectively. Some were sent by administrative order, rather than following criminal trial. Spain also sent convicts from Europe and the colonies to the Philippines, including the Mariana Islands and the Caroline Islands, and to Puerto Rico and Cuba, before the independence of the latter in 1898. Until 1950

---

[43] Minako Sakata, 'Japan in the eighteenth and nineteenth centuries', in Anderson, ed., *A Global History of Convicts and Penal Colonies*, 308, 317 (307–35).

[44] Timothy J. Coates, 'Preliminary Considerations on European Forced Labor in Angola, 1880–1930: Individual Redemption and the "Effective Occupation" of the Colony', *Portuguese Literary & Cultural Studies 15/16 Remembering Angola* (2010), 79–106; Timothy J. Coates, *Convicts and Orphans: Forced and state-sponsored colonizers in the Portuguese empire, 1550–1755* (Stanford University Press, 2001); Timothy J. Coates, *Convict Labor in the Portuguese Empire, 1740–1932: Redefining the empire with forced labor and new imperialism* (Leiden: Brill, 2014); Coates, 'The Portuguese Empire, 1100–1932', 37–64; Timothy J. Coates, 'The Depósito de Degredados in Luanda, Angola: Binding and Building the Portuguese Empire with Convict Labour, 1880s to 1932', *International Review of Social History*, 63, S26 (2018), 115–67; Zachary Kagan-Guthrie, 'Repression and Migration: Forced Labour Exile of Mozambicans to São Tomé, 1948–1955', *Journal of Southern African Studies*, 37, 3 (2011), 449–62.

[45] Jennings, 'The Sinews of Spain's American Empire', 45.

and 1976 respectively, convicts also went to the Canary Islands and Fernando Po (now, Bioko), and Rio de Oro.[46]

During the early-modern period, and in parallel with Portuguese and Spanish practices, the French transported convicts (*bagnards* or *forçats*) to Corsica, and deported 'undesirable' children to the island of La Désirade, off Guadeloupe in the French Antilles. In 1541, convicts were part of the colonizing force sent to Quebec. For the brief period, 1717–20, France also rounded up on the streets of French cities ex-prisoners, exiles, vagrants, orphans, and sex workers, and sent them to its new colony of Louisiana. A few noble families also had their rebellious kin exiled. In Sharon Lee Dawdy's words: 'It was colonization by abduction.' In France, it was a private company, the *Compagnie d'Occident* (Company of the West, or Company of the Indies after 1719), that managed convict shipments.[47] Later, in the revolutionary 1790s, government sent political prisoners (*déportés*) to French Guiana and the Seychelles. From the middle of the nineteenth century, France began shipping convicts and political prisoners to and around its colonies in North Africa, Indochina, India, the Indian Ocean, and the Caribbean. Concurrent with transportation flows to Algeria and Île Sainte-Marguerite, the main nineteenth and twentieth-century destinations were French Guiana and New Caledonia, though smaller numbers of *forçats* (or *transportées*) and *déportés* also went to Martinique, Réunion Island, Corsica, Poulo Condore (Côn Son Island), Obock (Djibouti), and Gabon (Map 1.2). Disastrous mortality rates among Europeans in French Guiana led to the suspension of their transportation to the colony in 1867, though the French resumed it when shipments to Nouméa (New Caledonia) ended in 1896. In the meantime, after 1887, the French shipped the first repeat offenders (*relégués*) alongside convicts. Whilst the penal

---

[46] Christian G. De Vito, 'The Spanish Empire, 1500–1898', in Anderson, ed., *A Global History of Convicts and Penal Colonies*, 65–95; Stephanie Mawson, 'Unruly Plebeians and the *Forzado* System: Convict Transportation between New Spain and the Philippines during the Seventeenth Century', *Revista de Indias*, 73, 259 (2013), 693–730; Stephanie Mawson, 'Convicts or *conquistadores*? Spanish soldiers in the Seventeenth-Century Pacific', *Past and Present*, 232, 1 (2016), 87–125; Eva Mehl, *Forced Migration in the Spanish Pacific World: From Mexico to the Philippines, 1765–1811* (Cambridge University Press, 2016); Ruth Pike, *Penal Servitude in Early-Modern Spain* (Madison: University of Wisconsin Press, 1993), chapters 3, 7, and 8.

[47] Bernard Allaire, *La rumeur dorée: Roberval et l'Amérique* (Montreal: Les Éditions La Presse, 2013), 69–71; Shannon Lee Dawdy, *Building the Devil's Empire: French colonial New Orleans* (University of Chicago Press, 2009), 143, 150 (quote), 150–2; James D. Hardy, Jr., 'The Transportation of Convicts to Colonial Louisiana', *Louisiana History: The Journal of the Louisiana Historical Association*, 7, 3 (1966), 207–20; Jean-Lucien Sanchez, 'The French Empire, 1542–1976', in Anderson, ed., *A Global History of Convicts and Penal Colonies*, 124–5, 127 (123–55); Miranda Frances Spieler, Empire and Underworld: *Captivity in French Guiana* (Cambridge, MA: Harvard University Press, 2012), 18–20, 38–41, 65–73.

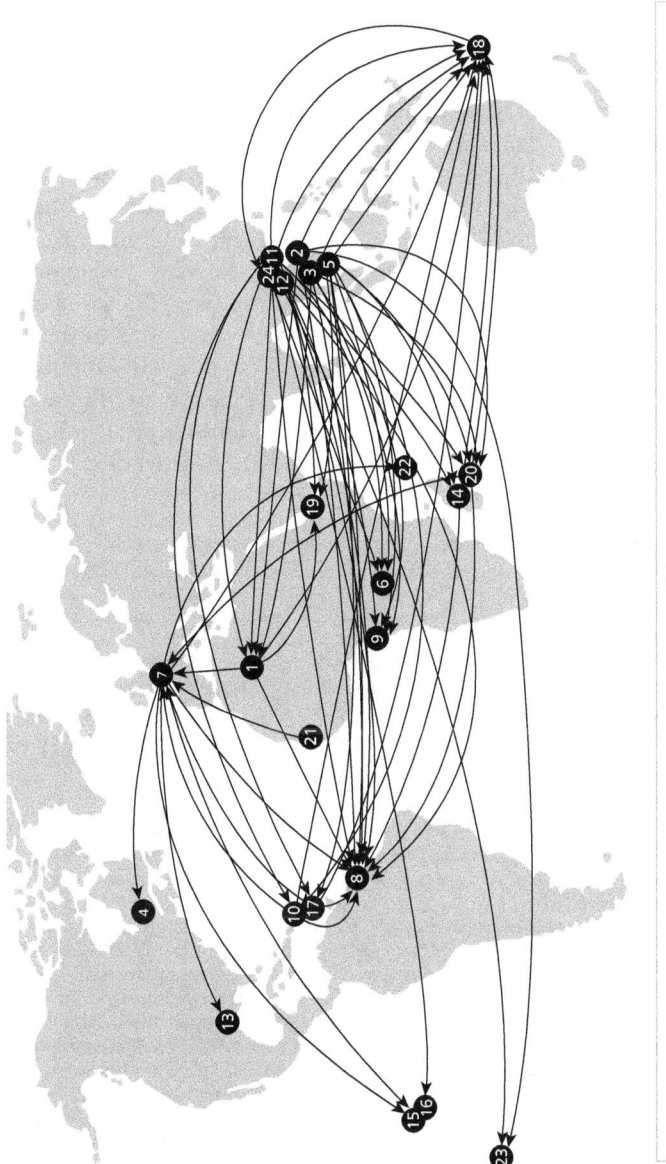

1. Algeria	6. Congo	11. Kouang Tchéou Wan	16. Marquesas (Hiva Oa)	21. Senegal
2. Annam	7. France	12. Laos	17. Martinique	22. Seychelles
3. Cambodia	8. French Guiana	13. Louisiana	18. New Caledonia	23. Tahiti
4. Canada (Québec)	9. Gabon	14. Madagascar	19. Obock	24. Tonkin
5. Cochinchina	10. Guadeloupe	15. Marquesas (Nuku Hiva)	20. Réunion Island	

Map 1.2 Convict flows in the French Empire, 1541–1953
Note: The lines of connection in this and subsequent maps do not represent actual convict routes.

colony of New Caledonia closed in 1921, that of French Guiana remained open until 1953.[48]

In the seventeenth century, Britain sold British and Irish convicts into contracts of indenture, a process which, as in the French Empire, private merchants managed. Convicts went to the Americas, mainly Barbados, Virginia, Maryland, and the Chesapeake, and to the overseas possession of Tangier (1661–84). The Transportation Act of 1717 and Declaration of Independence in 1776 opened and then closed the American colonies off to convicts. Subsequently, government transported a few convicts to the African coast, and then after 1787 more substantial numbers, including political (or 'gentleman') convicts, to the Australian colonies, including New South Wales, Van Diemen's Land, Norfolk Island, Port Phillip, and Western Australia. Though the bulk of convicts were from Britain and Ireland, some of these colonies also received convicts from the wider empire, including Caribbean colonies like Jamaica, the Cape Colony (part of modern South Africa), and Mauritius. Western Australia was the only remaining Antipodean penal colony when transportation ended in 1868 (Map 1.3).[49]

---

[48] Louis-José Barbançon, *L'archipel des forçats. Histoire du bagne de Nouvelle-Calédonie (1863–1931)* (Lille: Presses universitaires du Septentrion, 2003); Alice Bullard, *Exile to Paradise: Savagery and civilization in Paris and the South Pacific* (Stanford University Press, 2000); Danielle Donet-Vincent, *De soleil et de silences. Histoire des bagnes de Guyane* (Paris: La boutique de l'histoire, 2003); Odile Krakovitch, *Les femmes bagnardes* (Paris: Perrin, 1998); Isabelle Merle, *Expériences Coloniales: La Nouvelle-Calédonie, 1853–1920* (Paris: Belin, 1995); Lorraine M. Paterson, 'Prisoners from Indochina in the Nineteenth-Century French Colonial World', in Ronit Ricci, ed., *Exile in Colonial Asia: Kings, convicts, commemoration* (Honolulu: University of Hawai'i Press, 2016), 220–47; Michel Pierre, *Bagnards: La terre de la grande punition, Cayenne, 1852–1953* (Paris: Éditions Autrement, 2000); Peter Redfield, *Space in the Tropics: From convicts to rockets in French Guiana* (Oakland: University of California Press, 2000); Sanchez, 'The French Empire, 1542–1976', 126–8; Spieler, *Empire and Underworld*; Stephen A. Toth, *Beyond Papillon: The French overseas penal colonies, 1854–1952* (Lincoln: University of Nebraska Press, 2006). Military impressment continued until 1972. See Dominique Kalifa, *Biribi: Les Bagnes coloniaux de l'Armée Française* (Paris: Perrin, 2009).

[49] Emma Christopher and Hamish Maxwell-Stewart, 'Convict transportation in global context, c. 1700–88', in Alison Bashford and Stuart Macintyre, eds., *The Cambridge History of Australia, Volume 1: Indigenous and colonial Australia* (Cambridge University Press, 2013), 68–90; A. Roger Ekirch, *Bound for America: The transportation of British convicts to the colonies, 1718–1775* (Oxford: Clarendon Press, 1987); Farley Grubb, 'The Transatlantic Market for British Convict Labor', *The Journal of Economic History*, 60, 1 (2000), 94–122; Hamish Maxwell-Stewart, 'Transportation from Britain and Ireland, 1615–1875', in Anderson, ed., *A Global History of Convicts and Penal Colonies*, 183–210; Gwenda Morgan and Peter Rushton, *Eighteenth-Century Criminal Transportation: The formation of the criminal Atlantic* (Basingstoke: Palgrave, 2004); Gwenda Morgan and Peter Rushton, *Banishment in the Early Atlantic World: Convicts, rebels and slaves* (London: Bloomsbury, 2013); Wilfrid Oldham, *Britain's Convicts to the Colonies* (Sydney, NSW: Library of Australian History, 1990); A.G.L. Shaw, *Convicts and the Colonies: A study of penal transportation from Great Britain and Ireland to Australia and other parts of the British Empire* (Melbourne University Press, 1966).

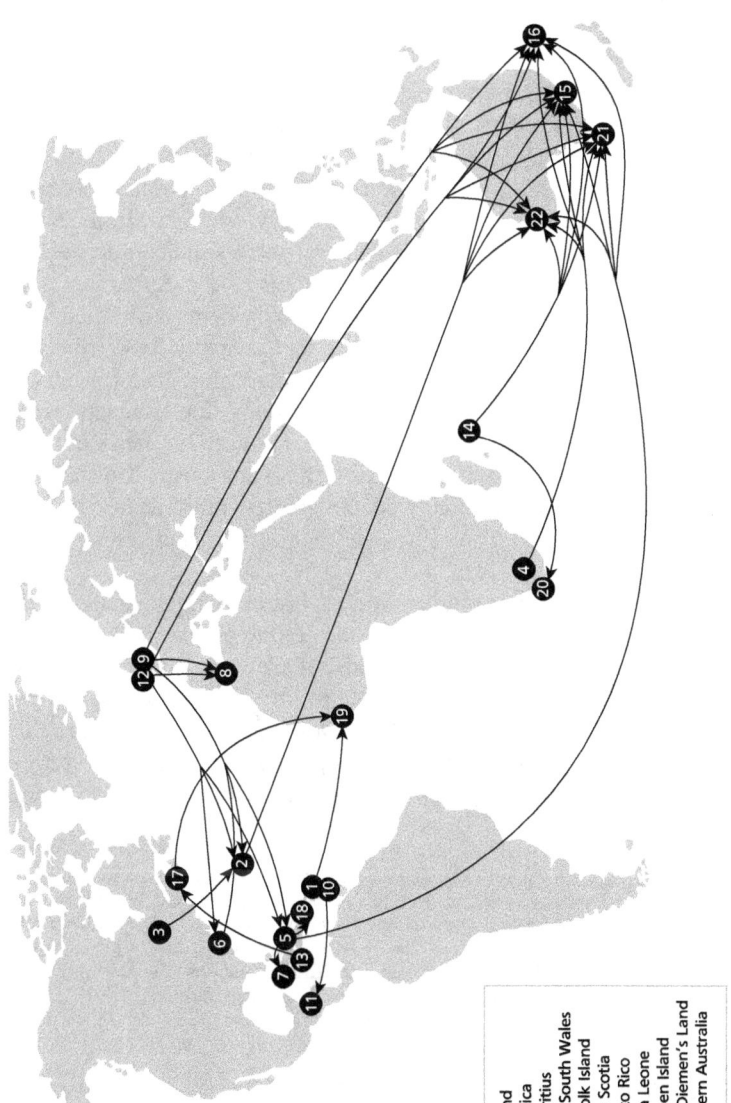

Map 1.3 Penal transportation in the British Empire, 1618–1874

1. Barbados
2. Bermuda
3. Canada
4. Cape Colony
5. Caribbean
6. Chesapeake
7. Cuba
8. Gibraltar
9. Great Britain
10. Grenada
11. Honduras
12. Ireland
13. Jamaica
14. Mauritius
15. New South Wales
16. Norfolk Island
17. Nova Scotia
18. Puerto Rico
19. Sierra Leone
20. Robben Island
21. Van Diemen's Land
22. Western Australia

However, after this date, Britain clung on to other imperial sites of punitive relocation. It shipped convicts from Britain and Ireland to the hulks of Bermuda and Gibraltar until 1863 and 1874, respectively, and maintained a penal colony for Indian and Burmese convicts in the Andaman Islands right up to the Japanese occupation of the Second World War. In the latter case, sent alongside ordinary criminal convicts were smaller numbers of nationalists, or freedom fighters.[50] Transportation to the Andamans was a continuation of earlier multi-directional convict shipments around the Bay of Bengal and to Mauritius, which the East India Company (EIC) directed from the 1780s. The EIC was a trading company that had powers of governance in South Asia. The first destinations for convicts were Bencoolen and Penang (Prince of Wales Island), followed by sites including Singapore, Malacca, Aden, and Arakan and the Tenasserim Provinces in Burma. Overall, the Andamans received the greatest number of convicts, not just in British Asia, but of any single destination or penal colony in the whole British Empire (Map 1.4).[51]

In the seventeenth and eighteenth centuries, but on a much smaller scale and only ever outwards from Scandinavia, the empire of Denmark–Norway sent convicts to New Sweden on America's Delaware River, and to St Thomas in the Caribbean.[52] Finally, amongst the European powers, the Dutch East India Company (Vereenigde Oost-Indische Compagnie, or VOC) shipped convicts within and around its possessions. Especially during its peak years of global influence, c. 1640–1750, this included to and from the

---

[50] Maxwell-Stewart, 'Transportation from Britain and Ireland'; Hamish Maxwell-Stewart, 'Transportation', in Paul Knepper and Anja Johansen, eds., *The Oxford Handbook of the History of Crime and Criminal Justice* (Oxford University Press, 2016), 635–54. On Bermuda, see C. F. E. Hollis Hallett, *Forty Years of Convict Labour: Bermuda 1823–1863* (Pembroke, Bermuda: Juniperhill Press, 1999). On Gibraltar, see Arthur Griffiths, *Secrets of the Prison-House or Gaol Studies and Sketches, Volume I* (London: Chapman and Hall, 1894), part 2: chapter 1, and Lawrence A. Sawchuk, Lianne Tripp, and Michelle M. Mohan, '"Voluntariness of Exposure": Life in a Convict Station', *Prison Journal*, 90, 2 (2010), 203–19.

[51] Clare Anderson, 'Transnational Histories of Penal Transportation: punishment, labour and governance in the British Imperial World, 1788–1939', *Australian Historical Studies*, 47, 3 (2016), 381–97. On transportation in British India, see Clare Anderson, 'The British Indian Empire, 1789–1939', in Anderson, ed., *A Global History of Convicts and Penal Colonies*, 211–43; Clare Anderson, Madhumita Mazumdar, and Vishvajit Pandya, *New Histories of the Andaman Islands: Landscape, place and identity in the Bay of Bengal, 1790–2012* (Cambridge University Press, 2016), chapters 1, 3, and 5; Anoma Pieris, *Hidden Hands and Divided Landscapes: A penal history of Singapore's plural society* (Honolulu: University of Hawai'i Press, 2009); Satadru Sen, *Disciplining Punishment: colonialism and convict society in the Andaman Islands* (New Delhi: Oxford University Press, 2000).

[52] Johan Heinsen, *Mutiny in the Danish Atlantic World: Convicts, sailors and a dissonant empire* (London: Bloomsbury, 2017); Johan Heinsen, 'The Scandinavian Empires in the Seventeenth and Eighteenth Centuries', in Anderson, ed., *A Global History of Convicts and Penal Colonies*, 97–121.

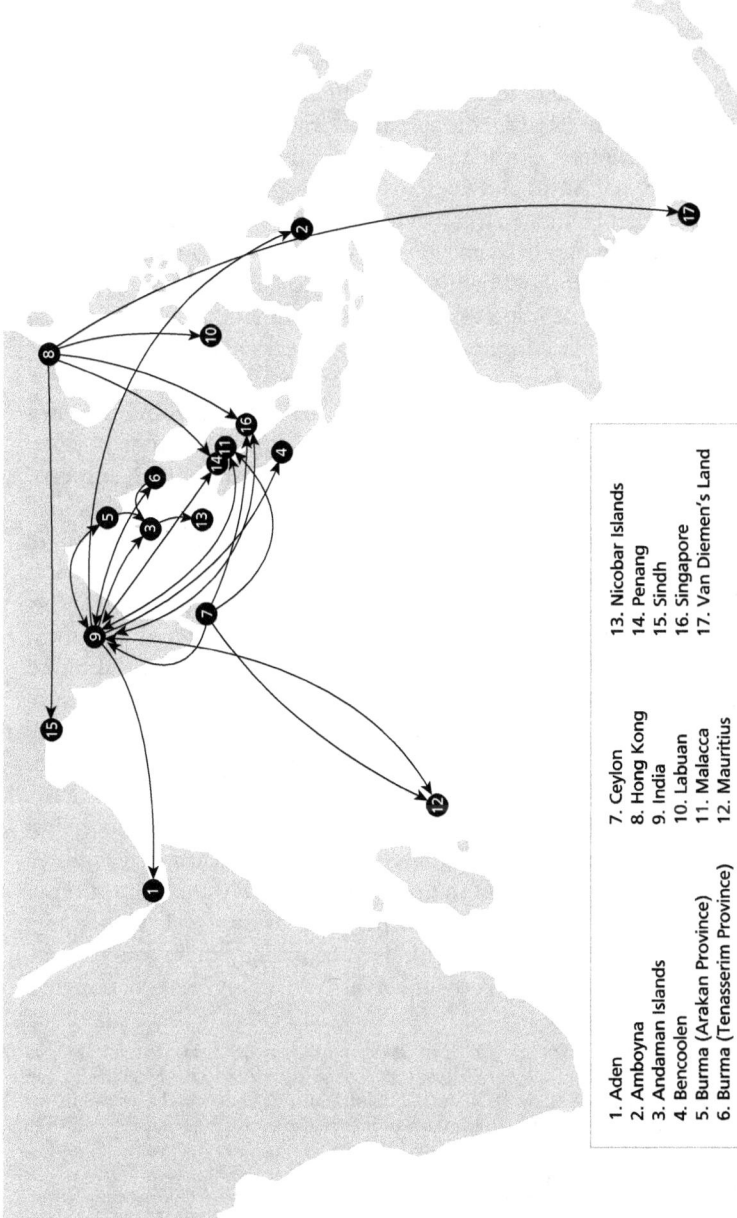

Map 1.4 Penal transportation in British Asia, 1787–1939

centre of its Asian empire, Batavia, the Banda Islands (especially Rosingain), the islands of Onrust and Edam, Ceylon, the Coromandel Coast of India, and the Cape Colony. Unlike its European counterparts, it never transported convicts from the Netherlands to the colonies.[53] Even Germany, which never established penal colonies, considered setting them up. In 1911, following its occupation of parts of Africa and the Pacific, the government sent the police criminologist Robert Heindl on a global tour, and he visited New Caledonia, the Andaman Islands, and Ceuta. Heindl was firmly anti-transportation, citing as critiques its expense, high mortality rates, and failure to produce effective agricultural settlers and workers. 'It is a contradiction to try to make farmers and pioneers of culture out of the shipwrecks of society, out of the products of a large city – out of vagabonds', he wrote.[54]

As Table 1.1 shows, in terms of numbers, the convict mobilities associated with imperial Russia greatly overshadow those of other polities. After 1590, through the centuries until the revolution of 1917, imperial Russia transported, resettled, and exiled deportees to numerous *katorga* (penal hard labour) sites. The Baltic had a few *katorga*, but most were in Western and Eastern Siberia, including on Sakhalin Island. Convicts travelled to the Russian Far East overland and by sea, initially as workers and from the 1730s also as colonists. Convicts considered the most dangerous were supposed to be sent the furthest distances. They laboured at public works, in agriculture, or in mines. Convicts fell into one of numerous categories. Only sometimes were those convicted of criminal offences sentenced to hard labour, but government stripped them of their civil identity (as in the empires of Denmark–Norway and France). On the other hand, when local communes ordered punitive relocation, convicts could return after serving their sentence. An unusual feature of punitive relocation in Russia was that women formed a substantial proportion of convict settlers, perhaps as high as 30 per cent of the total. If they met certain conditions, free women could also accompany their convict husbands (and husbands, their convict wives). In many places, convicts

---

[53] Matthias van Rossum, 'The Dutch East India Company in Asia, 1595–1811', in Anderson, ed., *A Global History of Convicts and Penal Colonies*, 157–81; Matthias van Rossum, 'The Carceral Colony – Colonial Exploitation, Coercion and Control in the Netherlands East-Indies, 1810s–1940s', *International Review of Social History*, 63, S26 (2018), 65–88; Ronit Ricci, *Banishment and Belonging: Exile and diaspora in Sarandib, Lanka and Ceylon* (Cambridge University Press, 2019); Ward, *Networks of Empire*.

[54] Robert Heindl (translated by Bertha R. Wolf), 'Penal Settlement and Colonization', *Journal of the American Institute of Criminal Law and Criminology*, 13, 1 (1922), 59 (56–60). See also Robert Heindl, *Meine Reise nach den Strafkolonien, mit vielen originalaufnahmen* (Berlin-Wien: Ullstein und Co., 1913); Matthew Fitzpatrick, 'New South Wales in Africa? The Convict Colonialism Debate in Imperial Germany', *Itinerario*, 37, 1 (2013), 59–72; Warren Rosenblum, *Beyond the Prison Gates: Punishment and welfare in Germany, 1850–1933* (Chapel Hill: University of North Carolina Press, 2008), 77–87, 91–8.

flooded the labour market, and, unable to find work, ex-convicts prohibited from returning home slipped into poverty and destitution.[55]

As noted above, Chinese dynasties exiled convicts, including to Manchuria in the northeast. They also set up *tun* (military agricultural colonies) for the confinement of Indigenous peoples who had resisted the migration of Han Chinese and associated land incursions in the southwestern province of Sichuan and the island of Taiwan. After 1759, when it annexed Xinjiang, right up to 1911, the Qing sent tens of thousands of disgraced officials, criminal offenders and political exiles to the place previously known as *Xiyu* (Western Regions). They were kept in *tun* or in separate penal colonies (*fantun* or *qiantun*). This kind of exile was known as banishment to the frontier (*fapei* or *waiqian*). It was the most severe punishment short of death, often used following commutation of sentence, and co-existed with life exile (*liu*) and military life exile (*jun* or *chongjun*) to more proximate locations.[56] Also in East Asia, the modernizing post-1868 Meiji regime in Japan passed a new penal code in 1880, which systematized the pre-restoration practices of island *tokei* (servitude) and *rukei* (exile), mainly to offshore islands in the south and west. Subsequently, following the extensive translation and discussion of European penological texts, and an official visit to the British Indian convict settlement in Singapore, Japan sent convicts to five places in the northern island of Hokkaido: Abashiri, Kabato, Kushiro, Sorachi, and Tokachi (1881–1908). They worked on road building and in mines, and the consequences of both were profound changes to the island's landscape and the forced relocation of the Indigenous Ainu. Ultimately, their presence enabled the incorporation of the island as a new 'homeland territory' of the nation state of Japan.[57]

---

[55] Sarah Badcock, *A Prison Without Walls? Eastern Siberian Exile in the Last Years of Tsarism* (Oxford University Press, 2016); Badcock and Pallot, 'Russia and the Soviet Union'; Daniel Beer, *The House of the Dead: Siberian exile under the Tsars* (London: Allen Lane, 2016); Andrew A. Gentes, '*Katorga*: Penal Labor and Tsarist Siberia', in Eva-Maria Stolberg, ed., *The Siberian Saga: A history of Russia's Wild East* (Frankfurt: Peter Lang, 2005), 73–85; Andrew A. Gentes, *Exile to Siberia, 1590–1822* (Basingstoke: Palgrave, 2008), 14; Andrew A. Gentes, *Exile, Murder and Madness in Siberia, 1823–61* (Basingstoke: Palgrave, 2010); Zhanna Popova, 'Exile as Imperial Practice: Western Siberia and the Russian Empire, 1879–1900', *International Review of Social History*, 63, S26 (2018), 131–50.

[56] Waley-Cohen, *Exile in Mid-Qing China;* Joanna Waley-Cohen, 'Banishment to Xinjiang in Mid-Qing China, 1758–1820', *Late Imperial China*, 10, 2 (1989), 44–71.

[57] Hideki Hatakeyama, 'Convict labor at the Sumitomo Besshi copper mine in Japan', *International Journal of Social Economics*, 25, 2/3/4 (1998), 365–9; Takashi Miyamoto, 'Towards an Evolutionary History of Penological Information in Modern Japan', http://staffblogs.le.ac.uk/carchipelago/2014/04/16/towards-an-evolutionary-history-of-penological-information-in-modern-japan/ (accessed 17 July 2017); Takashi Miyamoto,

After winning independence from the Iberian powers in the early nineteenth century, several independent Latin American states took over the carceral remnants of the Portuguese and Spanish Empires, or set up new penal colonies, often on islands. They included not only Brazil's Fernando de Noronha (1822–89), but Chile's Juan Fernández archipelago (1821–1930) and the Galapagos Islands of Ecuador (1837–1958). Later, from the end of the nineteenth century, Mexico, Colombia, and Argentina established new sites of penal relocation in remote or island spaces, including Islas Marías (est. 1908), Isla de los Estados (1884–99), and Ushuaia (1902–47).[58] Here, there was a *de facto* if not *de jure* blurring of the use and experience of imprisonment, penal servitude, administrative deportation, and penal transportation. The distinctions and convergences were often a question of degree: of distance travelled, relative isolation, island or inland character, and the nature of penal work.

Twentieth-century European dictatorships subjected a very large number of convicts to punitive mobility and hard labour, but these histories as also those of the USSR and modern China lie beyond the scope of this book. This is because the purpose of such penal relocation was (and in some cases still is) to repress entire populations, and in this regard penal labour or re-education camps cannot always be easily distinguished from concentration or death camps. Nonetheless, a brief survey of the field is useful for comparative purposes. In 1926, the Italian Fascist government introduced a law on internal exile (*confino*), which underpinned later political and social repression. It repurposed pre-existing penal colonies, and set up new ones, including in Italian-occupied Yugoslavia.[59] Similarly, and connected to the Civil War, between 1936 and 1947, General Francisco Franco's military dictatorship in Spain established almost 200 concentration camps for political and social repression. Confined in them were dissidents and other enemies of the state, and their moral redemption was tied to their performance of forced labour.[60] Following its seizure of power in 1933, the Nazi government also set up

---

'Convict Labor and Its Commemoration: the Mitsui Miike Coal Mine Experience', *The Asia-Pacific Journal: Japan Focus*, 15, 1 (2017), 3 (1–15); Minako Sakata, 'Japan in the eighteenth and nineteenth centuries'; Minako Sakata, 'The Transformation of Hokkaido from Penal Colony to Homeland Territory', *International Review of Social History*, 63, S26 (2018), 109–30.

[58] Edwards, 'Post-Colonial Latin America, since 1800'; Salvatore and Aguirre, 'Colonies of settlement'; Jane M. Rausch, 'Using Convicts to Settle the Frontier: A Comparison of Agricultural Penal Colonies as Tropical Frontier Institutions in Twentieth-Century Colombia', *SECOLAS Annals*, 34 (2002): 26–48.

[59] Gibson and Poerio, 'Modern Europe', 352–5.

[60] Gibson and Poerio, 'Modern Europe', 356–7.

'preventative detention camps' to imprison political opponents. It then established concentration camps for 'racial' or 'antisocial' enemies. Compulsory labour was always a feature of these sites of confinement, and the German Reich used inmates to develop camps and workshops. However, later in the 1930s and into the Second World War, the goal of the camps shifted: from the correction of people considered 'anti-social', to forced labour production and the extermination of so-called enemies, both for the benefit of the state. For instance, the Nazis introduced a system of forced labour recruitment for Polish workers, and mainly sent them to work on German farms. After the outbreak of the Second World War, French, British, Soviet, and other prisoners-of-war also worked both in agriculture and construction. Meantime, there was an expansion in the number of labour camps, and this was intertwined with the development of what Marc Buggeln calls 'industrial projects', mainly factories and notably the manufacture of armaments. Here, businesses paid a daily, not hourly, fee for the hire of inmates, and so working days were long. When Jews and others including antifascists, communists, sex workers, and Roma arrived in concentration camps such as Auschwitz-Birkenau, they were divided into groups according to their fitness to work. The unfit were murdered right away, and the fit starved and worked to death. From 1941, the Nazis opened the first of a string of separate camps entirely purposed for the murder of deported Jews. Meantime, in what Buggeln describes as 'radical destructiveness', the Nazi regime accepted that most of the inmates in its labour camps would die. This was possible because they constituted a small minority, perhaps three per cent, of the overall labour force. It was the larger number of forced foreign labourers, who made up almost one third of the workforce, free or unfree, that was vital to the war effort. As Buggeln puts it: 'National Socialism was a dictatorship based on mobilization, characterized by movement, not rigidity.' This flexibility was in evidence not just in the highly responsive and ever-changing nature of its labour system, but in the way that it moved, incorporated, and exploited workers from all over Europe. The extent of this was such that by the end of the Second World War, Germans made up less than a quarter of the population of the labour camps.[61] During the Nazi era, prisons were also used as instruments of what Nikolaus Wachsmann describes as 'legal terror'. As Wachsmann

---

[61] Marc Buggeln, 'Forced Labour in Nazi Concentration Camps', in De Vito and Lichtenstein, eds., *Global Convict Labour*, 333–60 (quote, 341); Gibson and Poerio, 'Modern Europe', 359–61. See also Jane Caplan and Nikolaus Wachsmann, eds., *Concentration Camps in Nazi Germany: The new histories* (London: Routledge, 2010); Nikolaus Wachsmann, *Hitler's Prisons: Legal terror in Nazi Germany* (New Haven, CT: Yale University Press, 2004).

explains, it is not altogether easy to ascertain whether their larger purpose was productivity or extermination: 'no simple answer can do justice to the complex realities'. The authorities certainly used labour to exterminate prisoners, for racial or political reasons, and accepted that death would be a consequence of it. However, unlike concentration camp inmates, the majority of prisoners survived the violence and poor conditions.[62]

In the twentieth century, the government of the USSR set up a vast network of prisons, work camps, and corrective settlements known collectively as the *gulag*. These built on and often overlaid geographically the earlier imperial *katorga*. However, the Soviet sites were distinct from these in that they were underpinned more by a desire to repress and exploit entire populations than to remove, punish, or extract labour from convicted offenders. Indeed, the twentieth-century sites included *spetsposelenia* (later called *trudposelenia*), which were 'special' (later, 'work') settlements, established in the north of European Russia, the Urals, and Western Siberia. They confined 'undesirable' populations, including notoriously whole ethnic groups such as the Kulak. Initially used as colonizers, government later put convicts to forced labour in the realization of Stalin's Five-Year Plans.[63] Following the establishment of the People's Republic in 1949, and influenced by the USSR, from the 1950s the communist party of China also set up the *laogai* (concentration camp) system. Its objective was to 'remould' and 're-educate' through labour. These huge camps accommodated men and women sent either by administrative order or following judicial process. They still exist today, containing unknown thousands of convicts, political prisoners, and so-called 'undesirables' including minority ethnic and religious groups.[64]

*

This book straddles global contexts to address a common set of themes. Integrating an extensive historiography with a wide range of primary

---

[62] Wachsmann, *Hitler's Prisons*, 227–8 (quote, 227).

[63] Anne Applebaum, *Gulag: A history of the Soviet camps* (London: Penguin, 2003); Badcock and Pallot, 'Russia and the Soviet Union'; Jehanne M. Gheith et al., *Gulag Voices: Oral histories of Soviet detention and exile* (Basingstoke: Palgrave, 2010); Judith Pallot, 'Russia's Penal Peripheries', 98–112; Lynn Viola, 'Historicising the Gulag', in De Vito and Lichtenstein, eds., *Global Convict Labour*, 361–79; Lynne Viola, *The Unknown Gulag: The lost world of Stalin's special settlements* (Oxford University Press, 2007); Lynne Viola, 'The Aesthetic of Stalinist Planning and the World of the Special Villages', *Kritika: Explorations in Russian and Eurasian History*, 4, 1 (2003), 101–28.

[64] Philip F. Williams and Yenna Wu, *The Great Wall of Confinement: The Chinese prison camp through contemporary fiction and reportage* (Oakland: University of California Press, 2004), 2–3, 45–9. See also Harry Wu Hongda, *Laogai: the Chinese gulag* (Boulder, CO: Westview Press, 2004).

research, it is split into two parts, linked by a commitment to writing a global history of punishment, governance, knowledge formation, agency, and resistance. The chapters take a comparative approach to understanding the purpose and nature of punitive mobility, and convict experiences of it, drawing out commonalities and distinctions across various case studies to foreground themes of connection and circulation. They highlight those sites of punitive relocation that are least known, historically, though in balancing the material the chapters include discussion of all destinations. Otherwise, the geographical scope of the book has been determined by blending new research on the British and French Empires, Meiji-era Japan, and Fernando de Noronha, with the available secondary literature. Thus, the Caribbean, Indian Ocean, Australia, Pacific, and South Asia, for which there exists a rich convict historiography, receive more attention than China and parts of Africa, where research is more limited. Readers seeking more detailed area studies knowledge are encouraged to consult the footnotes, which include a wealth of sources that are largely focused on single polities and systems.

Part I examines when, why, and how empires and nations used punitive mobility, from the fifteenth to the twentieth centuries. Drawing on a range of examples including the European empires, independent Latin American nations, Russia, China, and Japan, it links convict relocation to governance, political economy, and enslavement. The chapters focus on the relationship between convict work and the history of unfree migration and coerced labour, the role of punitive mobility in population management and social control, and the relationships between convicts and the enslaved. The chapters reveal significant parallels across contexts, as well as the interconnectedness of imperial geopolitics. Convict agency is a central theme; woven into the discussion of empires and nations, it is a key means of establishing how convicts as political agents experienced punitive mobility, how they created new religious and social formations, and how convict flows became vectors of insurgency.

Part II shifts to an examination of the place of punitive mobility in the history of punishment, and of the role of convicts in the formation of knowledge systems and classifications. The chapters open with a close study of the global interchange of ideas about and practices of punishment, including through international meetings and penal tours. They move on to consider the relationships between convicts and Indigenous and other peoples in sites of punitive relocation, and their role in scientific 'discovery' and the collection of specimens. Here, the book focuses particularly on the British and French Empires to show how scientists also studied convicts in investigations into the relationship between crime and physiognomy, and in experiments into tropical disease. This is connected to ethnographic studies and a census of convicts in imperial Russia, to argue that convicts were important in the development of both medical research and the human sciences, which in their interest in issues such as convict sexuality and descent were themselves often linked. The final chapter of the section returns to the theme of convict agency and insurgency, and the global chains of carceral circuitry, to consider the nature and impact of convict escape. Often transnational in form, as we will see evasion not only challenged effective governance, it was also a means of spreading anti-imperial ideologies. Ultimately, however, such resistant mobility led to the development of new forms of repression through enhanced international cooperation and the passing of new laws to curtail illicit movement, and had further, unintended, political consequences.

Part I

2 Empires and Colonies

This chapter establishes the reach of punitive relocation across a range of imperial contexts, from the late Middle Ages into the twentieth century. It employs a series of case studies to stress its dual importance as a source of the unfree labour necessary for the expansion of empires and as a means of governing colonized populations. The first part of the chapter covers the American, African, and Asian empires of Portugal, Spain, Scandinavia, and the Netherlands, from the fifteenth century onwards. In these locations, punitive mobility supplied labour for public works, land clearance, mines, plantations, and the army, and it was a means of controlling labourers. The chapter will show that across the territories of the Iberian empires, Denmark–Norway and Sweden, and in the Netherlands East India Company (Vereenigde Oost-Indische Compagnie, or VOC), sometimes convicts and their descendants became settlers, and when they did not, they laid the ground for free migration or satisfied wider imperial ambitions by clearing land and building basic infrastructure. In the meantime, convicts were able to work for their own profit, including through opening businesses, farming, or manufacturing goods and crafts.

The second part of the chapter centres on the colonial hulks of Bermuda and Gibraltar, where British and Irish convicts worked on the construction of naval infrastructure in the nineteenth century. Following the loss of the American colonies at the end of the revolutionary war in 1783, the British needed Atlantic-facing naval stations, and both colonies served a vital strategic purpose. Two distinctive features of the convict hulks, in contrast to the larger and better-known penal colonies in Australia, were that all the convicts were men, and that they were prohibited from staying in Bermuda or Gibraltar after completion of sentence. The absence of convict women and the ban on settlement are important because they reveal that, in comparison to other transportation sites, Britain's intention was not to use convicts for colonization, but to harness the energies of a temporary, mobile labour force to bolster its naval power. Even to contemporaries this presented a striking contrast with their

Australian equivalents, where it was routine to assign convicts to work for free settlers, and few returned home.[1]

Convicts shipped to and around these global sites resisted their fate in numerous ways, and as in the national contexts explored in Chapter 3, this is an important theme. Convict responses to the modalities of penal labour were active and passive, collective and individual, non-violent and violent. They went on strike or assaulted their overseers, feigned sickness or worked slowly and ineffectively, absented themselves from work or escaped altogether, and refused to answer questions or told lies. It is important to note that because of their employment at hard labour, on farms and in mines, many convicts had access to tools such as pickaxes and hammers that they could use with murderous intent. Moreover, because they were employed outdoors, often in working parties accommodated in temporary camps, they had opportunities to make plans to revolt or to abscond. Convict resistance could be a powerful means of tempering or effecting changes to penal labour. However, imperial administrations responded to it with brutal retribution and spectacular levels of violence, and this meant that though everyday forms of resistance impacted on working practices and productivity, rebellions, mutinies, and escapes usually failed.

The European Empires since 1415

There is an exceptionally long history of convict labour in the Portuguese Empire. This can be rooted in the history of labour relocation and exploitation, or exile (*degredo*), within Portugal during the medieval period, through to the 1950s in the Portuguese empire (Map 2.1).[2] During all periods, the Portuguese subjected convicts (*degredados*) to multi-directional mobility, sending them outwards from Portugal to imperial possessions, between overseas colonies, and during the early-modern period from the colonies to the Iberian peninsula. They worked at various occupations, under differing degrees of supervision and control. In terms of punitive mobility to Iberia, according to the seventeenth-century account of French doctor Gabriel Dellon, convicted in Goa (India) during the Inquisition and sentenced to galley labour in Lisbon, convicts worked in the shipyard where they were employed in unloading ships, portering, rope making, and collecting stones

---

[1] TNA CO37/113/8 3 March 1846 no. 8 folios 100–115: Governor William Reid, Bermuda, to William Ewart Gladstone, secretary of state for war and the colonies, 3 March 1846.

[2] Timothy J. Coates, 'The Portuguese Empire, 1100–1932', in Clare Anderson, ed., *A Global History of Convicts and Penal Colonies* (London: Bloomsbury, 2018), 46–7 (37–64); Timothy J. Coates, *Convicts and Orphans: Forced and state-sponsored colonizers in the Portuguese Empire, 1550–1755* (Stanford University Press, 2001); Timothy J. Coates, *Convict Labor in the Portuguese Empire, 1740–1932: Redefining the empire with forced labor and new imperialism* (Leiden: Brill, 2015), 14.

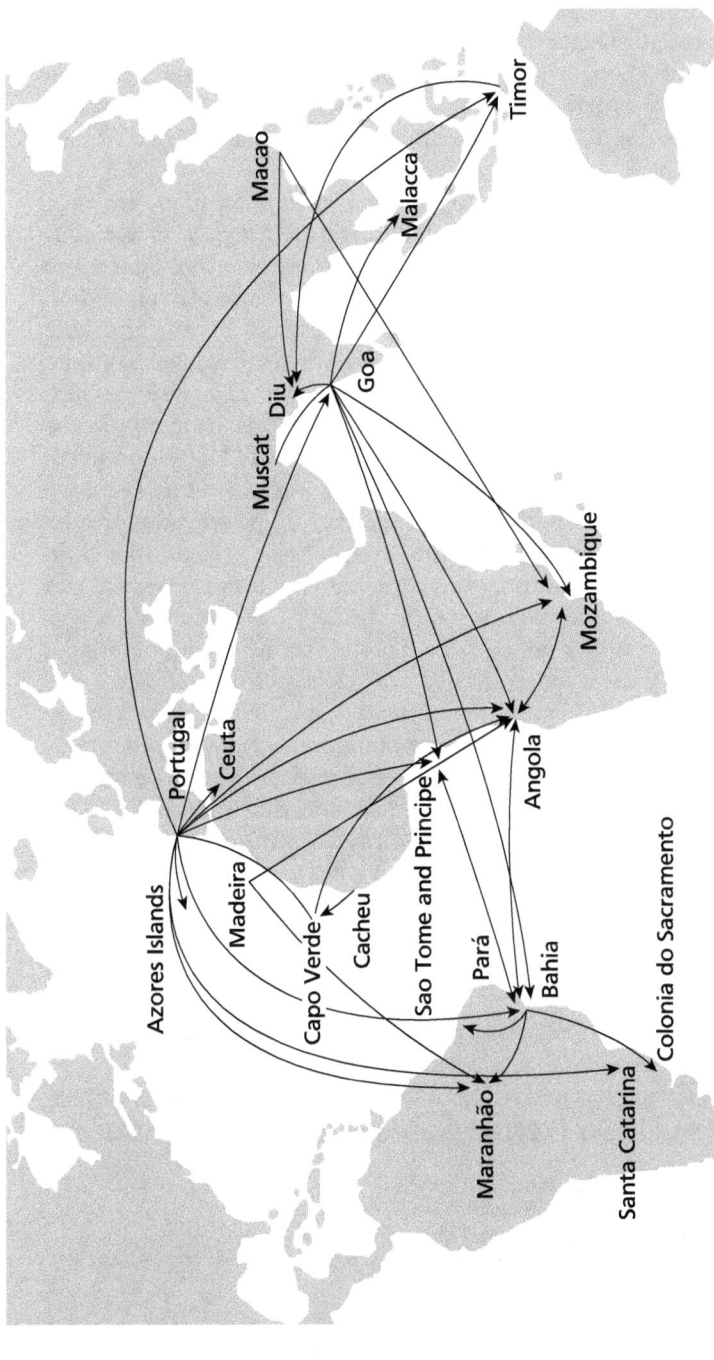

Map 2.1 Convict mobility in the Portuguese Empire since 1415

and sand for ballast. Dellon's unique account reported that fugitive slaves were also present among the convicts.[3] Another key site of internal exile in the 1600s was Castro Marim, a small frontier town that enjoyed an important strategic position near the border of southeastern Portugal. Convicts worked on the saltpans there.[4]

From the fifteenth century, Portugal had a small population, but large imperial ambitions. Besides their value in Portugal itself, *degredados* were thus potential colonizers. Increasingly at this time convicts were conscripted into the army, which lessened the empire's reliance on enslaved labour and on foreign troops. Convict soldiers were vital to the great era of Portuguese overseas expansion during the fifteenth century, when following the capture of Ceuta in North Africa (1415), Portugal took other *presidios* (forts), including Tangiers, along the coast of what is now Morocco. Dating from the arrival of the famous navigator Diogo Cão in Angola in 1484, the bulk of the Portuguese population in the rest of Africa was also composed of *degredados*.[5] Of especial significance were the needs of the Portuguese army during wars with the Dutch Republic (1598–1663) and Spain (1640–1668). In a continuation of fifteenth-century practice, convicts became soldiers and fought in military campaigns in some of Portugal's overseas possessions. These included conflicts in Sao Tome and its neighbouring island, Principe, and in India, Ceylon, Malacca, Angola, and Brazil. There was a strong association between the seriousness of a convict's crime and the distance travelled, with the furthest destinations reserved for the most serious offenders. Convicts during this period possessed useful work skills, and those who were not themselves conscripted worked alongside soldiers. On occasion, they became engaged in procuring enslaved Africans for trade, or in selling European goods. In the case of Sao Tome, they supervised enslaved labour on sugar plantations. This was also the case in Brazil, where convicts worked as farmers and sharecroppers, reared cattle, or went down the mines. Some convicts even became priests. The small number of women *degredadas* were almost without exception sent to Brazil. The voyage was relatively short, the climate healthy, and there was a particularly skewed gender ratio among the Portuguese population that government wished to redress.[6]

Timothy J. Coates has pieced together the history of Portuguese transportation, from a highly fragmented archive, to show that convicts and

---

[3] Anant Kakba Priolkar, *The Goa Inquisition* (Bombay University Press, 1961), Part II, 75–77, cited in Coates, 'The Portuguese Empire', 45–6.
[4] Coates, 'The Portuguese Empire, 1100–1932', 46–7.
[5] Gerald J. Bender, *Angola under the Portuguese: The myth and the reality* (London: Heinemann, 1978), 60.
[6] Coates, 'The Portuguese Empire', 39–40, 79; Timothy J. Coates, 'The Long View of Convict Labour in the Portuguese Empire, 1415–1932', in Christian G. De Vito and Alex Lichtenstein, eds., *Global Convict Labour* (Leiden: Brill, 2015), 147–8 (144–67).

their families possessed some degree of agency. He reveals that, in some cases, *degredados* successfully petitioned to change their destination, in exchange for a lengthier term. In others, they had their families accompany them, or chose their occupations, restricted only by a prohibition from leaving their punitive destination. In 1800, for instance, the free woman Maria Fernandes petitioned for permission to accompany her convict husband to Maranhão (Brazil). In 1818 and 1820, *degredados* João Monteiro and Antonio Dias Perdigão petitioned to take their wives and families to the same location. Those convicts who were still alive upon completion of their term received a certificate and were free to go.[7]

Following independence in 1822, Brazil was no longer a destination for convicts. India was also closed to convicts following penal reform in 1869. However, from the middle of the nineteenth century, and in the context of Portugal's 1867 abolition of both the death penalty and punishment by labouring at public works, convicts enabled the nation to consolidate control over its imperial possessions in Africa.[8] These included Sao Tome and Principe, but then extended to the Cape Verde islands and most significantly Angola and Mozambique. In the middle of the nineteenth century, the Portuguese were still enlisting convicts in the army. This was remarked upon by the famous Scottish explorer David Livingstone and the British commissioner in Luanda, Edmund Gabriel. They claimed that penal enlistment produced a remarkable change in the men, which they put down to the impossibility of escape and fear of being sent to São José do Encoje, a remote inland district which as a site of additional punishment they compared to Australia's Norfolk Island.[9] At this time, the Portuguese took the view that the best way to develop the African economy was through the settlement of white farmers, and from the second half of the nineteenth century they tried to encourage free migration by offering paid passage, land, livestock, and subsidies. This was part of a package of policies, practices, and goals associated with lusotropicalism, the belief that the absence of racism among the Portuguese population would underpin egalitarian imperial relationships.[10] However, with few exceptions, settlement schemes were what Gerald J. Bender describes as 'disastrous failures', both socially and

---

[7] Coates, *Convict Labor in the Portuguese Empire*, 23–4; Coates, 'The Long View of Convict Labour', 150. See also Bender, *Angola under the Portuguese*, 74.

[8] Coates, *Convict Labor in the Portuguese Empire*, 28. Note that Portugal recognized Brazilian independence only in 1825. In practice Portugal previously only used the death penalty for treason and had abolished public works in 1838.

[9] David Livingstone and Edmund Gabriel, 'Explorations into the Interior of Africa', *Journal of the Royal Geographical Society of London*, 25 (1855), 233–4 (218–37).

[10] Bender, *Angola under the Portuguese*, xxvii, 3, 23–4. As Bender points out: 'lusotropicalism is a romantic myth (at best) or an invidious lie (at worst) used to obscure the realities of Portuguese colonialism' (3).

economically.[11] Thus, from the middle of the nineteenth century, the character of punitive mobility changed. The Portuguese no longer considered convicts the sole means of colonization and settlement, but as a workforce that could build the infrastructure to encourage free migration on a larger scale. During the earlier period, there had been a close association between convicts and colonization. In possessions such as Goa and Brazil, few convicts had returned home upon completion of sentence. In contrast, during the later period, about half of the *degredados* who survived their term left the colony after serving their time.[12]

In the later period, in common with the other global powers, Portugal was concerned with the modernization of its penal code and reforms to punishment. However, an important factor in the stimulation of penal transportation to the African colonies was Portugal's abolition of the slave trade (1836) and enslavement (1869), and its consequent search for an alternative supply of unfree labour.[13] As the overseas minister put it in the nineteenth century, whereas once the colonies had been 'a nest of slaves', they had since become 'nests of convicts'.[14] The use of transportation was also connected to the desire to populate Angola and Mozambique. As Coates argues, in the nineteenth century, the central concern of the Portuguese state was the ongoing failure of these colonies to become economically profitable.[15] For instance, several members of the influential Lisbon Geographical Society (est. 1875), including most notably Francisco Xavier da Silva Telles, studied convict labour as a means of colonization.[16] However, with women constituting less than five per cent of the convict population, even by the 1890s, this was never likely to succeed.[17]

In the 1880s, Portugal set up agricultural penal settlements in Angola, first inland at Malanje and second in a place it called Esperança (Hope). Poor planning, inferior land, and an inadequate supply of convicts doomed them to failure. A shift in strategy, towards the employment of

---

[11] Bender, *Angola under the Portuguese*, 58.
[12] Coates, 'The Portuguese Empire', 40; Coates, *Convict Labor in the Portuguese Empire*, 111–12.
[13] Enslaved persons remained *libertos* (bound to their former owners) until 1878. Independent Brazil did not abolish slavery until 1888. On enslavement, immigration, and the Brazilian economy see Bender, *Angola under the Portuguese*, 24.
[14] Coates, *Convict Labor in the Portuguese Empire*, 79.
[15] Coates, *Convict Labor in the Portuguese Empire*, 40.
[16] Coates, *Convict Labor in the Portuguese Empire*, xxvi, 5, 7 31–3; Coates, 'The Long View of Convict Labour', 153; Bender, *Angola under the Portuguese*, 86n80. Bender notes that Telles' study of convicts in Angola during the period 1883–9 revealed that though they were on average in their late 20s on arrival, their post-arrival life expectancy was just 13.6 years. See Bender, *Angola under the Portuguese*, 86–8. The original text is Francisco Xavier da Silva Telles, *A Transportação Penal e a Colonização* (Lisbon: Sociedade de Geografia de Lisboa, 1903).
[17] Coates, *Convict Labor in the Portuguese Empire*, 69–70, 73–4.

convicts in a military agrarian penal settlement called Mochico was no more successful. Sandy soil, ill health, lack of knowledge of agriculture, and interruptions to the supply of clothes and rations were factors, but so was the high rate of convict desertion. One commander opined in 1896: 'The degredados cannot be counted on. When they work, twelve do the work of two; when they eat ... two consume the amount of twelve, and they are always ready to flee when they fear punishment.'[18] Meantime, in part because of the association between convicts and colonies, Portuguese efforts to encourage free migration remained so unsuccessful that, even by the 1880s, free migrants constituted just one third of the white population of Angola. Renewed efforts to establish agricultural penal settlements at Capelongo and Pedras Negras during 1919–20 also failed.[19]

What was perhaps unique about Portuguese practice compared to that of other empires was the creation of what Coates describes as two 'urban penal colonies' in Angola and on Mozambique Island. By far the largest was the *Depósito de Degredados* (Convict Depot), located in Luanda's Fortress of São Miguel. 'It is no exaggeration', Coates writes, 'to say that Angola from the 1880s until 1932 was built on the labor of convicts'.[20] The smaller institution, the *Depósito Geral dos Sentenciados* (General Depot for Sentenced Persons) was in São Sebastião on Mozambique Island. Though both penal colonies received Europeans, the depots were otherwise racialized. Luanda also received convicts from the Portuguese Atlantic (Cape Verde, Guinea, and Sao Tome and Principe), and Mozambique Island those from Portuguese Asia (India, Macau, and Timor).[21] Like the punitive destinations of other empires and nations ranging from France to Japan, and consistent with Crofton's famous Irish system, these depots co-existed with Portuguese jails. A period of overseas *degredo* sometimes followed a stretch of domestic imprisonment, with *degredados* moving through a punitive repertoire made possible by empire. This was the case, for instance, with sentences for first-degree murder. Such convicts included Francisca Rosa, sentenced for infanticide in 1910 by the court of Bragança to six years in prison and ten years of transportation with labour, or twenty without.

---

[18] Bender, *Angola under the Portuguese*, 80–6 (quote, 83); Coates, *Convict Labor in the Portuguese Empire*, 48–9.
[19] Bender, *Angola under the Portuguese*, 86–7, 91–3.
[20] Coates, *Convict Labor in the Portuguese Empire*, 91.
[21] Coates, 'The Portuguese Empire', 54 (quote); Coates, 'The Long View of Convict Labour', 152–65; Coates, *Convict Labor in the Portuguese Empire*, 50–67. As Coates notes, little is known about the contemporary Asian *depósitos* of Diu (India) and Timor, established in the 1910s and operational until at least the 1950s. See Coates, *Convict Labor in the Portuguese Empire*, 54–5.

After serving her first term, she went to Angola. The courts also awarded *degredo* alongside a pecuniary fine.[22]

As well as *degredados*, the *depósitos* received other categories of convicts: recidivists (*addidos*), vagrants (*vadios*), and military deportees. Vagrants were not guilty of a specific crime but were classified as criminals. They had refused to work, and their deportation was viewed as a means of correcting idleness through labour or conscription into the army. During the nineteenth century, and into the twentieth, the state sent them from Portugal and the colonies to Angola, Mozambique, and Angola. For instance, in 1907 the governor of Cape Verde recommended that a group of vagrants, including men named Adolpho Maria Rodrigues (described as 'disorderly') and Luiz Filippe ('bad behaviour and refused to work'), be transferred to Angola. That vagrants and military deportees are altogether missing from convict statistics has both obfuscated the fact of their existence across the Portugal's African empire and masked the complex and varied legal regime that underpinned its history of convicts and penal colonies.[23]

The convicts of Luanda and Mozambique Island were highly mobile, to such an extent that Coates describes the *depósitos* as 'hubs' in a larger labour system. The organization of convict work was inextricably linked to changing ideas of reformative work, which will be explored in more detail in Chapter 7. As in the Fernando de Noronha case that opened Chapter 1, there was a system of penal stages, through which convicts could move, and which was dependent on time spent in the colony and on behaviour. Government put those at its lowest end to hard labour in or outside the depot, under military superintendence. It put those in the middle to outdoor labour during the day and confined them in the depot at night. It leased out those at the top of the scale to private employers, under bond, and they were employed all over the colony. However, the Portuguese also organized the *depósitos* along military principles, and placed convicts in separate companies according to their crime, sentence, and whether they were from Portugal or the colonies. These further racial hierarchies were complemented by divisions of gender and law, for the depots put men and women in separate companies and kept vagrants apart from convicts. As Coates stresses for Luanda: 'The types of convict labour and the objectives of their work in Africa were *to extract whatever possible useful labour from these individuals* to build the infrastructure in the colony.'[24]

---

[22] Coates, *Convict Labor in the Portuguese Empire*, 108–10.
[23] Coates, *Convict Labor in the Portuguese Empire*, 75, 77–80 (quotes, 77).
[24] Coates, 'The Long View of Convict Labour', 156. Emphasis in original. See also Coates, *Convict Labor in the Portuguese Empire*, 50–67, 92–101.

Convicts worked in one of four ways: for an individual under bond, for the military, in town, or in prison workshops. Thus, they laboured on the streets and in the docks, and as bookbinders, carpenters, metalworkers, locksmiths, tailors, and cobblers. The small number of women worked mainly as laundresses. It is difficult to calculate the value of convict labour, or the profit and loss of the colony, though convicts were present throughout Angola and especially in Luanda. *Degredados* who expressed a desire to settle in one of the colonies, and who had experience of agriculture, could be leased land before completing their sentences. Ownership transferred to them after ten years of successful cultivation. Given the urban profile of the bulk of *degredados*, the number of convicts accepting this offer was probably low. During the nineteenth century, convicts made up somewhere between one tenth and one third of the white population of Luanda. Perhaps surprisingly, but because of their mobility, some were able to establish taverns. Others entered commerce and became involved in slave trading, forming networks that stretched inland from the coast. This continued after release, when ex-convicts were especially engaged in setting up drinking houses in Luanda. Coates argues that this produced 'a brotherhood of the spirits, a nexus of convicts and former convicts centred on taverns and alcohol'. Such establishments reached across communities of convicts and ex-convicts. They were places of information that aided convicts in planning escapes and obtaining forged papers, and in finding employment after release. Moreover, they were one means through which convicts became intermediaries between the free Portuguese and African populations.[25] However, it is important not to overstate the apparent freedoms of punitive relocation. During the period of their confinement, convicts faced the severe penalties that characterized the punishment of disciplinary infractions during this era: chaining to the walls of a tiny underground cell (*cova de onça*) or confinement in a dark cage-like structure (*segredo*). The horrors of such punishments were detailed in two books written by the political prisoner João Pinheiro Chagas, who was confined in Luanda between 1892 and 1893.[26] But for those who survived and worked out their sentence in the colony, there was the prospect of government-issued free land. In 1880s Angola, about half of the *degredados* stayed in the colony after serving their time. A few got married; to each other or to Angolans. As noted above, Portugal's ultimate goal was to use convicts to

---

[25] Coates, *Convict Labor in the Portuguese Empire*, 84 (quote), 91, 93, 104–5. Coates notes that there was no one account of income and expenditure, and that the prison and military budgets were often blended (105).
[26] Coates, 'The Portuguese Empire', 57–8; Coates, 'The Long View of Convict Labour', 157–8, 161; Coates, *Convict Labor in the Portuguese Empire*, 46–7, 62–4, 72.

prepare for free settlement, and thus it paid the costs of repatriation where ex-convicts wished to return to their place of conviction.[27]

When António de Oliveira Salazar became Prime Minister of Portugal in 1932, the New State (*Estado Novo*) instituted a series of tight fiscal policies. That same year, Portugal closed the Luanda and Mozambique *depósitos* to new arrivals, and later transferred the remaining inmates to other prisons. It promulgated a decree that suggested *degredado* labour should be mobilized 'for the benefit of the Metropole's economy'. Nonetheless, the Portuguese continued to transport convicts sentenced in Angola, Sao Tome, Cape Verde, and Guinea to a new site at Roçados, inland near the Namibian border. It closed in 1936, when the state transferred the convicts to a new agricultural penal settlement in Damba (est. 1935) and to other public works projects. The Portuguese abolished the entire system in 1954.[28]

Portugal's punitive practices were mirrored in the Spanish empire from a slightly later period. Convicts (*forzados*) made up a significant proportion of the galley rowers who defended Spanish interests in the Caribbean, Pacific, and Peru during the sixteenth to eighteenth centuries. This included in the capital of Spain's first New World colony of Santo Domingo (Haiti) and in Cuba, where convict rowers in Havana outnumbered enslaved African crew. As well as working on the galleys, government put *forzados* to other occupations, including domestic servitude, fishing, shoemaking, carpentry, caulking, and salvage.[29] At this time, the Spanish also sent convicts from Europe and the colonies to their *presidios* in North Africa and the Americas, and employed them alongside the enslaved. They were an especially important source of labour in ports, building fortifications and arsenals and working as hauliers.[30] As in the Portuguese empire, there was also a close link between penal conviction and military enlistment. Stephanie J. Mawson describes the 'half-starved, under-clothed and unpaid' convicts who made up at least one quarter of

---

[27] Coates, 'The Portuguese Empire', 40; Coates, *Convict Labor in the Portuguese Empire*, 111–12, 114–5.

[28] Bender, *Angola under the Portuguese*, 91–3 (quote, 92); Coates, *Convict Labor in the Portuguese Empire*, 117.

[29] David Wheat, 'Mediterranean Slavery, New World Transformations: Galley Slaves in the Spanish Caribbean, 1578–1635', *Slavery and Abolition*, 31, 3 (2010), 329–30, 334–5 (327–44).

[30] Wheat, 'Mediterranean Slavery, New World Transformations', 335. In the mid-eighteenth century, the Spanish took captive a group of shipwrecked British travellers, and they were kept alongside Spanish convicts. See the description in *The Narrative of the Honourable John Byron (Commodore in a Late Expedition round the World) Containing an Account of the Great Distresses Suffered by Himself and His Companions on the Coast of Patagonia, From the Year 1740, till their Arrival in England, 1746. With a description of St. Jago de Chili, and the manners and customs of the inhabitants. Written by himself* (London: S. Baker and G. Leigh, 1768), 212.

the companies of soldiers stationed across the Spanish Pacific, including the Philippines, in the seventeenth century. Many originated in the viceroyalty of New Spain, in the Americas, and especially its capital, Mexico City.[31]

The Spanish in the Americas compelled Indigenous people to work, and they laboured alongside convicts, soldiers, and the enslaved. For example, in the 1500s, the Spanish Crown awarded *encomiendas* (labour tribute) to loyal settlers, and Indigenous *encomendados* (tributary labourers) were especially important in establishing mines on the American mainland and in Cuba. However, as Evelyn P. Jennings reminds us, there was a staggering decline in Indigenous populations. Of Cuba, she notes: 'Overwork and disruption killed thousands; despair compelled thousands more to choose suicide over subjugation.' Consequently, Spain found a new source of forced labour for its West Indian possessions in the enslavement of Indigenous peoples in the circum-Caribbean. However, in 1542 and 1543, it abolished both *encomiendas* and Indigenous enslavement. The consequence of this was a new reliance on enslaved Africans and convicts.[32] The number of *forzados* particularly increased after 1748, when Spain abolished the Mediterranean galleys (Map 2.2). Contemporaries viewed the recruitment of convicts as a cheaper alternative to the purchase of enslaved Africans, and by 1770 convicts outnumbered them in Cuba by two to one. In what was, in part, an exercise in social discipline in the face of drought and famine, the large majority of *forzados* were from Mexico. By the 1820s, with the independence of Spain's continental possessions, including Mexico, this supply of convicts was cut off. It was replaced by convicts from Spain and Cuba, which remained a Spanish colony until 1898. Vagrants and military deserters augmented their numbers, but most significant all was contract and indentured labour, from places as diverse as the Canary Islands, the USA, Yucatán (Mexico), and most of all China.[33]

---

[31] Stephanie Mawson, 'Convicts or *conquistadores?* Spanish soldiers in the Seventeenth-Century Pacific', *Past and Present*, 232, 1 (2016), 95, 100 (87–125). See also Stephanie Mawson, 'Unruly Plebeians and the *Forzado* System: Convict Transportation between New Spain and the Philippines during the Seventeenth Century', *Revista de Indias*, 73, 259 (2013), 693–730; Eva Mehl, *Forced Migration in the Spanish Pacific World: From Mexico to the Philippines, 1765–1811* (Cambridge University Press, 2016); Ruth Pike, *Penal Servitude in Early-Modern Spain* (Madison: University of Wisconsin Press, 1993).

[32] Evelyn P. Jennings, 'The Sinews of Spain's American Empire: Forced Labor in Cuba from the Sixteenth to the Nineteenth Centuries', in John Donoghue and Evelyn P. Jennings, eds., *Building the Atlantic Empires: Unfree labor and imperial states in the political economy of capitalism, ca. 1500–1914* (Leiden: Brill, 2015), 35–7, 40–1 (25–53) (quote, 36). See also Pike, *Penal Servitude in Early-Modern Spain*, 136–7.

[33] Jennings, 'The Sinews of Spain's American Empire', 45–50. See also John Tutino, *From Insurrection to Revolution in Mexico: Social bases of agrarian violence, 1750–1940* (Princeton University Press, 1986), chapter 2.

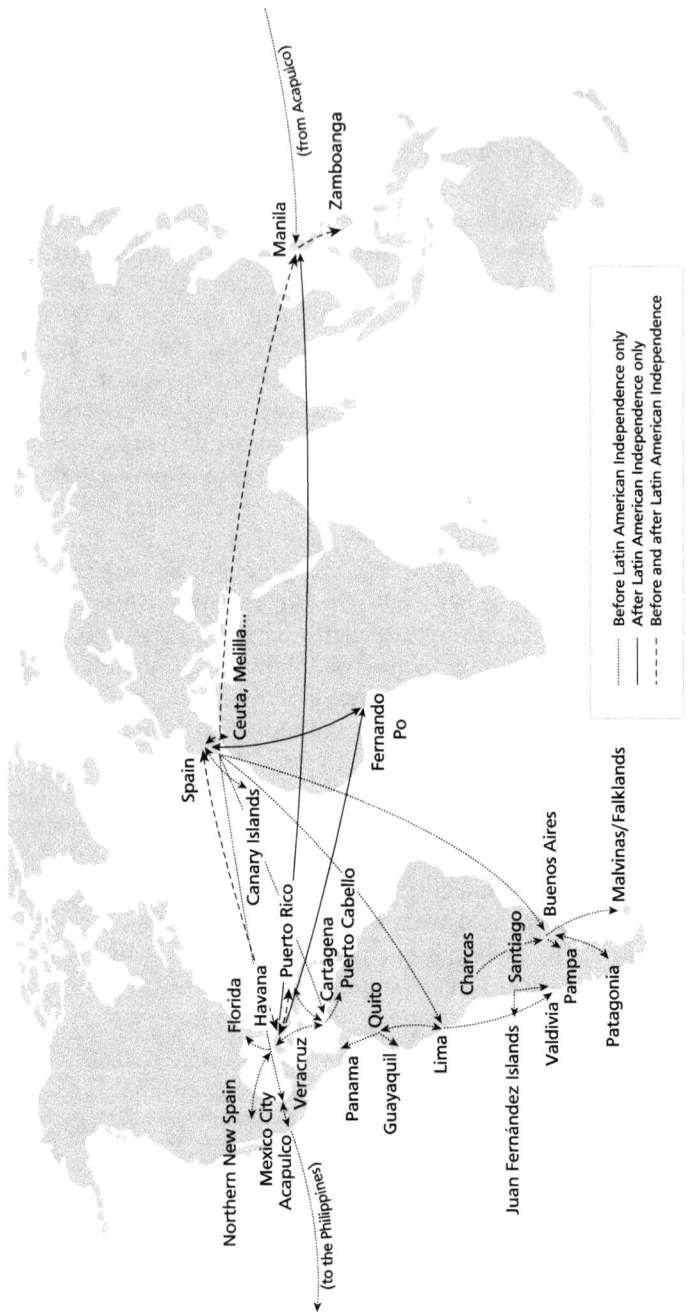

Map 2.2 Punitive mobility in the Spanish Empire, c. 1760–1950
Note: I am grateful to Christian De Vito, who conceptualized this map.

Across the Spanish Empire, large-scale convict revolts were rare, but escapes were frequent, effected after breaking chains and scaling walls, or altering records to indicate that it was time for their release. Convicts were also active petitioners, writing numerous and repeated pleas for improved conditions or direct favours.[34] On occasion, they did resist the penal regime in dramatic fashion. In one case in 1583, a group of nine convicts of the galliot *Santiago* broke out in open mutiny off the coast of Santo Domingo. Led by a Spaniard called Alonso de Reyna, they attacked the officers and then killed Captain Ruy Díaz de Mendoza, his convict servant, and a soldier and gunner, shouting 'Freedom! Freedom!' With the captain's death, the convicts had apparently plotted to cut the ropes holding the galliot's weapons to the sides of the deck. This they did, following which they elected a Spanish convict, Pedro de Vargas, as their leader. They called de Vargas 'general', and designated others as master, master-at-arms, and corporal. In scenes reminiscent of the Indian convict mutinies explored later in Chapter 6, throwing overboard their convict dress, they clothed themselves in garments belonging to the captain and dined at his table. Excepting the pilots, the mutineers left the rest of the crew, as well as a few sick convicts, on shore at La Isabela. They retained control of the *Santiago* for a full seven weeks, until two convicts murdered de Vargas, having proclaimed that they did not need a general, 'since on board the ships every one of them would share in the command'.[35] Ultimately, with the breakdown in solidarity, this mutiny failed, but in the years that followed, as in other punitive sites, Spanish convicts continued to engage in more subtle forms of labour resistance, including through feigning sickness.[36]

During the first part of the nineteenth century, Spain extended practices of penal transportation to support the shipment to and employment of convicts in overseas mines and textile factories (*obrajes*). As in Portugal's African colonies, in some of the Spanish possessions there was a gradual disaggregation of convicts from other labourers, especially soldiers, and as in the Portuguese world this was connected to changing ideas about punishment and convict reform. In the earlier period, like their Portuguese contemporaries, many different groups had laboured in

---

[34] Christian G. De Vito, 'The Spanish Empire, 1500–1898', in Anderson, ed., *A Global History of Convicts and Penal Colonies*, 67–8 (65–95).

[35] Richard Boulind, 'Shipwreck and Mutiny in Spain's Galleys on the Santo Domingo Station, 1583', *The Mariner's Mirror*, 58, 3 (1972), 297–330 (quote, 311). This article includes a full English translation of the key source on the mutiny, 'A Contemporary Narrative of the Loss of the Galleys of Spain's Santo Domingo Squadron under the Command of Ruy Díaz de Mendoza, Off La Isabela, Hispaniola, 1583, Compiled by the Galleys' Accountant [Emasavel]', 302–12. Note: a galliot is a single-masted galley, or flag galley.

[36] Pike, *Penal Servitude in Early-Modern Spain*, 140–1.

concert.[37] Cuba, on the other hand, which remained a Spanish colony until 1898, experienced a succession of different forced labour regimes. Until the middle of the sixteenth century, this was grounded in Indigenous tribute labour. For the next two centuries, it was based on enslavement. During the 1700s, the enslaved were joined by convicts, and in the 1800s convicts were joined by indentured labourers.[38] Paralleling Portuguese practices of punitive labour, of especial significance in regard to Spain's efforts at penal modernization was its creation of separate penal colonies in the Philippines, and its development of the North African *presidio* of Ceuta. Initially colonized by the Portuguese, in 1415, in 1668 Ceuta passed to Spanish control, and it received convicts right up to 1912.[39] In common with the other Spanish *presidios* in North Africa – Oran, Melilla, and to a lesser extent Peñón de Vélez and Peñón de Alhucemas – Ceuta was not considered an 'overseas' colony, but an extension of domestic legal space.[40] Ceuta's significance increased following a royal decree of 1834, which divided the Spanish prisons into three classes. These were provincial houses of correction for petty offenders, mainland *presidios* for prisoners sentenced for up to eight years, and the overseas settlements for those under punishment for more than eight years.[41]

Christian G. De Vito has shown that, during the nineteenth century, the Spanish combined the use of judicial sentences of penal transportation with both administrative deportation, ordered by high-ranking colonial officials, and army-managed military relocation. This created what he describes as 'a broad toolkit to maintain colonial order, discipline subaltern labour, and prevent or curb anti-colonial insurgencies.'[42] In regards to labour discipline, in Cuba from the 1830s to 1860s, for instance, the threat of penal transportation was a means to manage enslaved labour on sugar plantations. Following the abolition of slavery in Cuba in 1880 was a six-year period of apprenticeship (*patronato*), and the Spanish passed

---

[37] De Vito, 'The Spanish Empire', 84–5. See also Mehl, *Forced Migration in the Spanish Pacific World*, 80–119; Jennings, 'The Sinews of Spain's American Empire', 32–3.

[38] Jennings, 'The Sinews of Spain's American Empire', 27.

[39] De Vito, 'The Spanish Empire', 68; Mehl, *Forced Migration in the Spanish Pacific World*, 227–66; Pike, *Penal Servitude in Early-Modern Spain*, chapters 3, 7, and 8.

[40] Christian G. De Vito, 'Punitive Entanglements: Connected Histories of Penal Transportation, Deportation, and Incarceration in the Spanish Empire (1830s–1898)', *International Review of Social History*, 63, S26 (2018), 176 (169–89). See also Lauren Benton, *A Search for Sovereignty. Law and geography in European empires, 1400–1900* (Cambridge University Press, 2010), chapter 4.

[41] Rafael Salillas, *La vida penal en España* (Madrid: Imprenta de la Revista de la Legislación, 1888), cited in Arthur Griffiths, *Secrets of the Prison-House or Gaol Studies and Sketches, Volume I* (London: Chapman and Hall, 1894), 347–8.

[42] De Vito, 'Punitive Entanglements' 171.

aggressive anti-vagrancy laws designed to tie formerly enslaved people to the plantations. During this era, again transportation was used as a means of labour discipline, punishing those who had deserted their former workplaces and refused to engage in new employment. Convict destinations included the Isla de Pinos (Isle of Pines), off the Cuban coast.[43] One of the goals of punitive mobility in another Spanish possession, the Philippines, was also labour management. Here, the Spanish used convicts to colonize the southern islands of Mindanao and Jolo, and to create what De Vito describes as 'one of the most significant institutional innovations in the field of punishment in the nineteenth-century Spanish Empire: military penitentiary colonies'. These colonies were markedly distinct from convicts' earlier destinations, where formerly they had worked side by side with other labourers: enslaved, coerced, conscripted, and free.[44]

These Philippine institutions remained somewhat exceptional in the Spanish empire, however, and during the nineteenth and twentieth centuries most usually convicts continued to labour with other kinds of workers. For example, in Puerto Rico in the second half of the nineteenth century, transported convicts and locally convicted prisoners – alongside enslaved, indentured, and military labour from Africa, China, and Spain – built the north–south road that connected the island. In Cuba, convicts constructed railways, worked in quarries, and built and repaired the basic infrastructure of Havana. This included through work on the roads, sewers, and aqueducts. As we will see below, as in the French Empire during the same period, the Spanish also leased out convicts for plantation labour.[45] Perhaps the main distinction between the penal practices of Spain and Portugal was Spain's abolition of outward transportation, from Europe to the colonies, in 1836. Subsequently, and unlike Portugal's penal institutions in Luanda and Mozambique Island, Spain's military penitentiary colonies and other sites of penal transportation in the Philippines, Cuba, and Puerto Rico no longer received convicts from Europe. The North African *presidios* were, however, considered part of Spain, and thus Spain continued to send convicts to sites like Ceuta and Melilla. The only exceptions were related to convict conscription into the army during the campaign to retake Santo Domingo (1861–5), and in the Cuban war of independence and Spanish-American war (1895–8). Otherwise, and importantly, though Spain abolished penal transportation to overseas colonies in 1836, subsequently the scale and reach of administrative deportation and military relocation expanded dramatically.[46] Note also that in contrast to Portugal from the eighteenth

---

[43] De Vito, 'Punitive Entanglements', 172–3. The Isla de Pinos has been known as Isla de la Juventud (Isle of Youth) since 1978.
[44] De Vito, 'Punitive Entanglements', 173.   [45] De Vito, 'Punitive Entanglements', 174.
[46] De Vito, 'Punitive Entanglements', 176.

century, the Spanish did not allow released *forzados* to return home, and at least some were resettled in Puerto Rico.[47]

Convict transportation in the Scandinavian empires operated on a much smaller scale than in the Iberian empires and differed in significant ways. Sweden and Denmark–Norway moved convicts from Europe to their Atlantic possessions of New Sweden on America's Delaware River (1638–55) and St Thomas in the Caribbean but did not send convicts between colonies. However, as in the empires of Portugal and Spain, punitive mobility and labour needs were linked. The convicts of New Sweden, for instance, worked for the New Sweden Company, a trading company closely related to the Crown, either in building fortifications or on tobacco plantations. Johan Heinsen shows that there was just one enslaved man in New Sweden at this time, and convicts made up the vast bulk of the colonial labour force. Also present were indentured labourers, and though their legal status was distinct from that of convicts, they shared experiences. Indeed, the Company routinely referred to both groups as 'slaves'.[48]

Coerced labour also played a central role in the making of Denmark's Atlantic Empire. The state had exploited convict labour since the medieval period, when it sentenced felons to enslavement in the King's Yard. What was new in the seventeenth century was Danish imperial ambition.[49] The Danish West India and Guinea Company occupied St Thomas (now part of the US Virgin Islands) in 1672. Before this, it moved hard labour convicts from all over Denmark, including Norway and Iceland, around the realm, and across land and sea. Destinations included Trunken, the naval dockyard prison, and other military or naval fortresses, including in Copenhagen. Denmark's Caribbean settlers always envisaged St Thomas as a plantation colony, for the cultivation of sugar, tobacco, and sugar, but they had no ready access to West African slave markets. However, the Crown had granted the Company access to hard labour convicts through the terms of its charter. The practice of sending convicts to St Thomas was, therefore, as Heinsen puts it, an Atlantic world extension of existing centripetal flows. Convicts performed a wide variety of work tasks, including land clearance, construction, cultivation, and fishing. Enslaved Africans always performed plantation labour, however, which shows that the Danes instituted racialized work practices to keep them apart from convicts.[50]

---

[47] Pike, *Penal Servitude in Early-Modern Spain*, 141–2.
[48] Johan Heinsen, 'The Scandinavian Empires in the Seventeenth and Eighteenth Centuries', in Anderson, ed., *A Global History of Convicts and Penal Colonies*, 97, 101–2 (97–121).
[49] Johan Heinsen, *Mutiny in the Danish Atlantic World: Convicts, sailors and a dissonant empire* (London: Bloomsbury, 2017), 6, 127.
[50] Heinsen, 'The Scandinavian Empires', 104–9; Heinsen, *Mutiny in the Danish Atlantic World*, 34–5.

Underpinning the convict labour regime of St Thomas were extraordinary levels of violence. In one case, Governor Jørgen Iversen beat several convicts and indentured labourers to death. He claimed in his defence that they had died of dropsy following the assault, dropsy being the 'idleness disease'. Iversen's discipline was in part rooted in the solidarity and refusal of other convicts and servants to beat or shackle their recalcitrant compatriots. Plots to escape were omnipresent, and the authorities lamented the convicts' constant insubordination.[51] They complained that they would not work, ran away, or mimicked the enslaved in throwing themselves to the ground to avoid punishment. In 1681, for example, Norwegian convict Anders Pedersen bolted into the woods, in the company of another convict. They stole meat and beer from the Company stores. Pederson's companion was caught and returned to labour, but Pederson was later shot and died.[52] By this time, convict transportation had slowed considerably, though the country transported what Heinsen describes as a 'slow trickle' of convicts in the decades before 1750, including to the Finnmark in northern Norway. As in Britain during this period, some of them were sold into indenture. The purchase of St Croix in 1733 had enhanced further Denmark's labour needs. However, unlike Portugal and Spain, following the dramatic *Havmanden* mutiny of 1683 (see Chapter 6), contemporaries expressed the view that convicts would corrupt the colonies and ruin the Company, degrading the Danish in the eyes of enslaved Africans. Moreover, convicts were more expensive than the enslaved, because they were costlier to feed and maintain. As Chapter 5 will show, identical arguments re-emerged a century later, following British proposals to transport white convicts to the Caribbean.[53]

The final case study explored here is the Netherlands VOC, which made extensive use of convict labour (Map 2.3). Especially during its peak years of global influence, c. 1640–1750, it shipped convicts within and around its possessions, notably the centre of its Asian Empire, Batavia, as well as the Banda Islands (especially Rosingain), the islands of Onrust and Edam, Ceylon, the Coromandel Coast of India, and the Cape. Convict destinations in part depended on conviction, and the most serious offences were punished in the most far-flung locations. Sentences – either banishment from a locality or punishment in chains (*kettingstraffen*) – always included hard labour. The VOC sent convicts to work on its settlements' *gemeene werken* (public works), including the construction of roads, canals and forts, and often alongside enslaved and *corvée* (obligated) labour. It employed convicts

---

[51] Heinsen, 'The Scandinavian Empires', 109–10.
[52] Heinsen, *Mutiny in the Danish Atlantic World*, 27. Dropsy refers to a build-up of fluid and swelling (oedema).
[53] Heinsen, *Mutiny in the Danish Atlantic World*, 171–2.

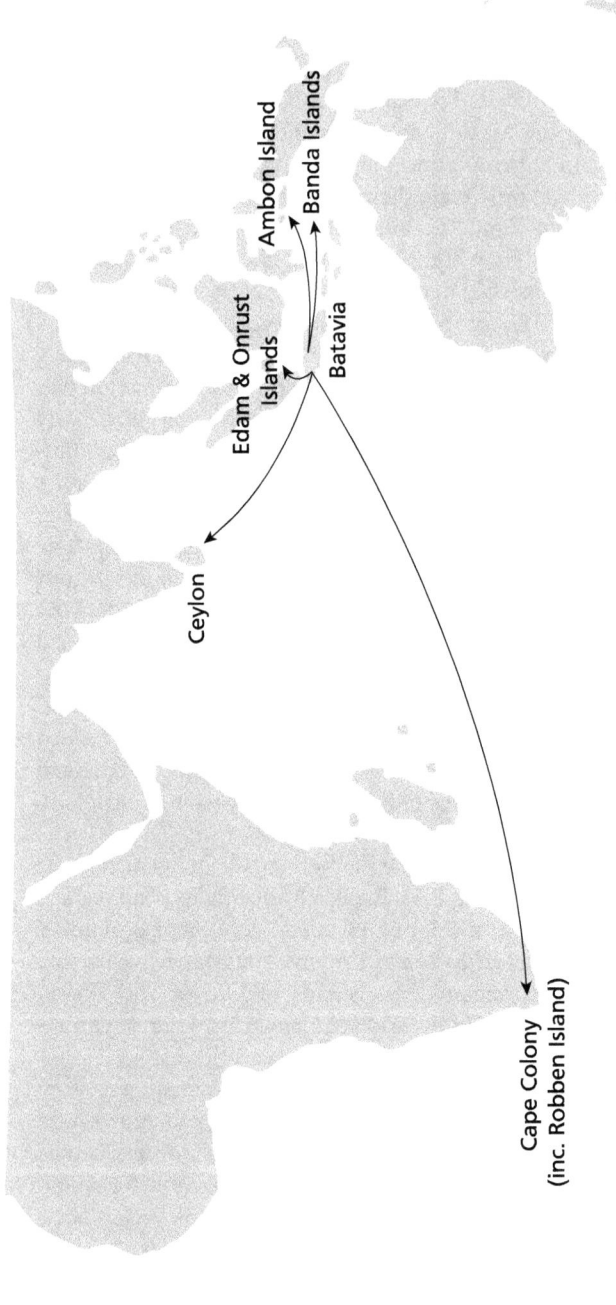

Map 2.3 Convict flows in the Netherlands Empire, seventeenth to twentieth centuries

also in arsenals (*batterije*), warehouses (*materiaalhuis*), forges (*smederij*), and the gold and silver mines of Java and Sumatra. Occupations on VOC islands included caulking ships on the wharves, making limestone (from shells), land clearance, logging, and carpentry – and in Edam, in the Bay of Batavia, the most important island destination for convicts – making rope.[54] At the end of the eighteenth century, and into the nineteenth, in the turmoil of the Anglo-Dutch wars (1780–4), Batavian revolution (1795), and Napoleonic Wars (1803–15), the VOC lost its possessions in the East Indies, South Asia, and southern Africa. However, the Anglo-Dutch Treaty of 1814 restored Java to the Netherlands. Convict labour then became even more important to the colonial work force in the Dutch East Indies, as convict occupations diversified to include labour on spice plantations of Banda, mining in Banka and Padang (western Sumatra), and military construction.[55]

As noted above, the Portuguese and Spanish transported only small numbers of convict women, and those who were shipped to or around the *presidios* and viceroyalties were not separated from men, though they were kept to 'domestic' forms of labour such as cleaning and needlework. This was also the case for most women in Dutch Asia. However, the VOC sent Christian women from across the empire to a special institution in Batavia: the *tuchthuis* (house of discipline), which was run by nuns. The numbers were tiny, and at the start of the eighteenth century there were perhaps just five or six women in the 'house' at any one time. However, just as in the Iberian imperial context they worked at domestic tasks such as sewing, under the direction of its 'mother'.[56]

With this important exception in regard to convict women, in the Netherlands empire convict mobility was always multi-directional and attached to specific labour requirements. However, the Netherlands was unusual amongst the European powers during this period in one key respect: it never transported convicts outwards from Europe, but only shipped convicts between, its imperial possessions. Thus, Matthias van Rossum, in common with De Vito's arguments on the Spanish empire, suggests that penal transportation in the Dutch Asian context was not solely a means of supplying labour, but of managing and disciplining workers in the colonies. They included contract labourers from Europe, Ceylon, Java, and China, as well as enslaved men and women, and locally raised *corvée*. The

---

[54] Matthias van Rossum, 'The Dutch East India Company in Asia, 1595–1811', in Anderson, ed., *A Global History of Convicts and Penal Colonies*, 158–9 (157–81).

[55] van Rossum, 'The Dutch East India Company in Asia', 175. On this later period, see Matthias van Rossum, 'The Carceral Colony – Colonial exploitation, coercion and control in the Netherlands East-Indies, 1810s–1940s', *International Review of Social History*, 63, S26 (2018), 65–88.

[56] van Rossum, 'The Dutch East India Company in Asia', 168.

consequence of this was the concentration of unfree labour, with the *kettinggangerskwartier* (chain-gang quarter) of Batavia, for instance, holding some 1,000 men.[57] There were continuities in the interrelationship between convict, slave, *corvée*, and contract labour, and the use of the penal system as a means of labour control, during the later period. However, as in other imperial locations, unfree labourers resisted the work regime. There were convict revolts on the island of Edam in 1772, 1779, and 1782, and this preceded wider resistance by sailors and the enslaved.[58] As I have argued previously: '[I]t was the relative openness of transportation journeys, *presidios*, and penal settlements and colonies that opened up spaces for such manifestations of convict agency.'[59]

With the conclusion of the Napoleonic Wars, and after the abolition of the VOC, the Netherlands government took direct control of the East Indies, and convict transportation around imperial sites continued as late as 1943. The Dutch employed convicts in various capacities, including as soldiers in military expeditions, labourers on public works, miners of tin and coal, manufacturers of uniforms and furniture, and producers of rubber.[60] This brings us, full circle, back to the Portuguese empire which, as Zachary Kagan-Guthrie explains, in the twentieth century used punitive relocation to discipline Indigenous and migrant labour in the colony of Mozambique and to provide labour for the sugar island of Sao Tome. Some of the convicts sent to Sao Tome were *indesejáveis* (undesirables), deported for terms of years, including for insubordination or 'disrespectful' behaviour. Others were Jehovah's Witnesses, members of one of the Zionist churches, or had been involved in strikes and political activity. A substantial proportion were deported on the orders of provincial administrators, rather than through judicial sentence. Still more were 'out-of-place' migrant workers, such as Mozambicans expelled from Southern Rhodesia (now, Zimbabwe) for participating in political activity, including widespread strikes in 1948. Such deportations continued until 1956, ceasing at the request of the Portuguese authorities in Sao Tome, though the punishment of 'internal exile' continued for some years after that.[61]

---

[57] van Rossum, 'The Dutch East India Company in Asia', 164, 167.
[58] van Rossum, 'The Dutch East India Company in Asia', 157–8, 173–4.
[59] Clare Anderson, 'Introduction: A Global History of Convicts and Penal Colonies', in Anderson, ed., *A Global History of Convicts and Penal Colonies*, 22 (1–35).
[60] Klaas Stutje, 'From across the Water: Nusakambangan and the Making of a Notorious Prison Island', *International Review of Social History*, 64, 3 (2019), 493–513; van Rossum, 'The Carceral Colony'.
[61] Zachary Kagan-Guthrie, 'Repression and Migration: Forced Labour Exile of Mozambicans to São Tomé, 1948–1955', *Journal of Southern African Studies*, 37, 3 (2011), 452–3, 455–6, 458 (quote), 459, 461–2 (449–62). American missionaries first introduced Zionist Christian practices in southern Africa at the start of the twentieth century.

Convict Hulks in Nineteenth-century Bermuda and Gibraltar

Britain first sent British and Irish convicts to the imperial outpost of Bermuda in 1824, to work on the construction of the naval dockyard (Figures 2.1 and 2.2). This was over thirty years after the First Fleet sailed to Botany Bay, creating the nucleus of the first, and better known, Australian penal colony. Over 9,000 convicts served their sentence in Bermuda, held in seven hulks (decommissioned naval vessels), moored off Ireland Island and the town of St George's on the island of the same name (Map 2.4).[62] Convict numbers peaked in 1848, during the Great Irish Famine (1845–52), when unprecedented shipments of convicts arrived. Most had been convicted of theft and were serving the relatively short term of seven years. The convict establishment closed in 1864, once the dockyard was complete.[63] The labour was formidable, and the convicts were mainly engaged in the quarrying of hard, marine limestone and the construction of an extensive breakwater. This massive building project required a range of skills, and convicts also worked as sawyers, carpenters, and blacksmiths. They loaded and unloaded stores and coal; undertook caulking, copper and ironwork on naval ships; heated boilers and cleaned barracks; built and fitted out storehouses and workman's cottages; made general repairs to government buildings; and stitched convicts' clothes and shoes. The convicts built a water tank, wash houses, storehouses, landing jetties, a lime kiln, and houses for the chaplain and deputy superintendent. Convicts also built Grey Bridge, which opened in 1849 to connect the dockyard site at Ireland Island to Boaz Island, where convict barracks had started to replace some hulk accommodation. Under the promise of pay and enhanced rations, a small number of the Grey Bridge convicts undertook the challenging and dangerous task of working underwater in a diving bell to lay its foundations. Overall, contemporaries calculated, Grey Bridge cost one third of what the same structure would have cost to build in England. Otherwise, no convict labour went to waste, and those unfit for labour were

---

[62] The hulks were the *Antelope* (arrived 1824), *Dromedary* (1826), *Coromandel* (1827), *Weymouth* (1829), *Tenedos* (1843), *Thames* (1844), and *Medway* (1848). The hulks moored off St George's were *Thames* and *Antelope*, but only for a brief period during the 1840s and 1850s, while convicts completed work for the Ordnance Department.

[63] TNA CO37/116/2 6 January 1847 no. 2 folios 7–16: Henry Grey (3rd Earl Grey), secretary of state for war and the colonies, to Governor Charles Elliot, Bermuda, 2 March 1847. I reached the figure of 9,000 by collating figures from C. F. E. Hollis Hallett, *Forty Years of Convict Labour: Bermuda 1823–1863* (Pembroke, Bermuda: Juniperhill Press, 1999); *Annual Reports on the Convict Establishments at Bermuda and Gibraltar* (London: George E. Eyre and William Spottiswoode, 1859–63); and the TNA CO37 series, especially the Report of Dr Charles Edwards, 1863, at CO37/186.

Figure 2.1 The naval base on Ireland Island in the Bermudas, by Captain Henry Rolfe RN, 1839
Source: National Museum of Bermuda.

Empires and Colonies

Figure 2.2 Sick convicts going to hospital!!! Bermuda
Source: State Library of New South Wales, PXA280: Sketches of convicts, 1860 (artist unknown).

designated light tasks such as making mats, ropes, brushes, and baskets.[64] There was no alternative labour supply, particularly following the abolition of slavery in 1833. In Bermuda, this was immediate and unfollowed

---

[64] For a detailed summary of the nature and organization of convict labour in Bermuda, see Clara F. E. Hollis Hallet, 'Bermuda's Convict Hulks', *Bermuda Journal of Archaeology and Maritime History*, 2 (1990), 90–5 (87–104); Hollis Hallett, *Forty Years of Convict Labour*.

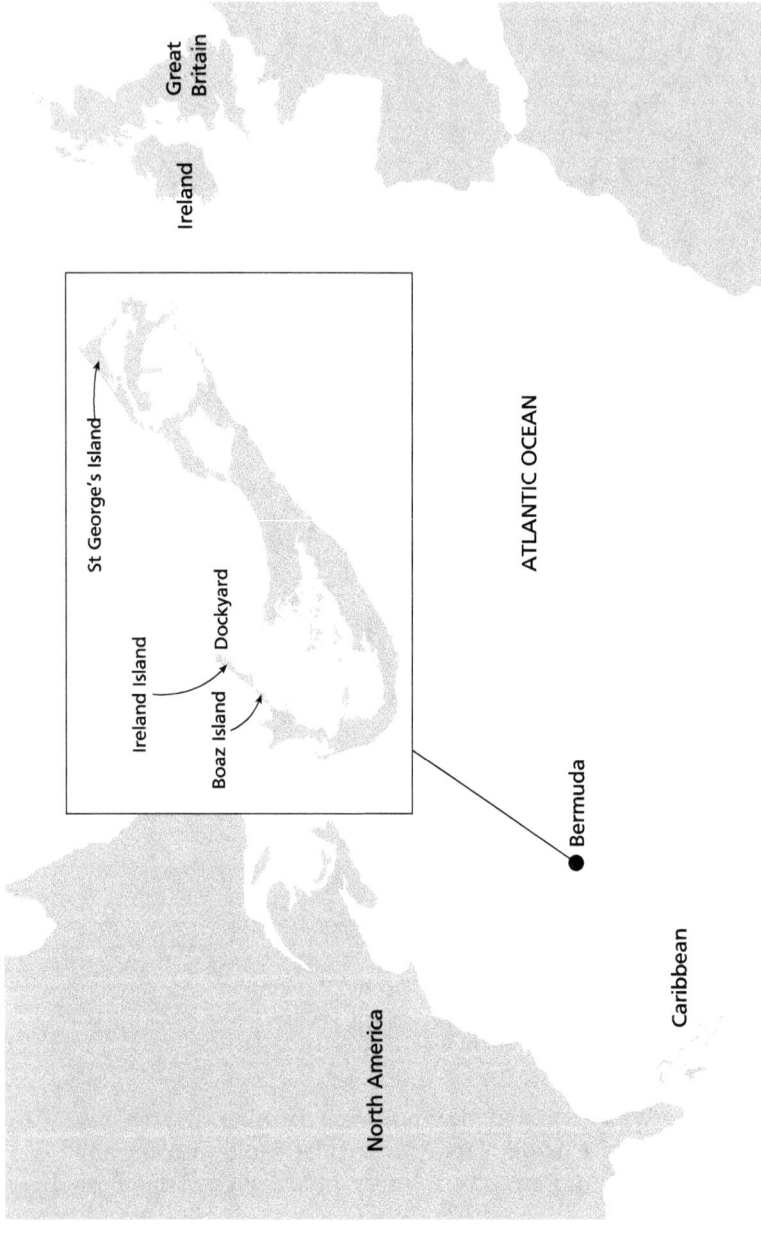

Map 2.4 Convict hulk sites in Bermuda, 1824–63

by the period of apprenticeship that tied formerly enslaved people to their previous owners, as implemented in other British colonies.[65]

In the nineteenth century, and despite the praise of the cost-effectiveness of constructing Grey Bridge, there was some dispute about whether convict labour in Bermuda was efficient or not. Whilst the annual reports of the convict establishment printed in British parliamentary papers painted a largely positive view, one governor, William Reid, claimed that these masked what he termed the 'abuses' of penal transportation. He wrote: 'the small amount of labour accomplished by the Convicts in the Dock yard, is a subject of perpetual complaint.' Reid calculated the value of a day's convict work in Bermuda at about two thirds of that of a hired labourer (2s 6d), because convicts loitered, unless made to perform task work. He lamented the absence of rewards and underscored the importance of religious instruction. 'I look on the system at Bermuda, as one of coercion without hope', he informed Secretary of State for War and the Colonies William Ewart Gladstone, 'which it is very desirable should be altered.'[66]

In Reid's view, one means of offering such hope to convicts was to grant them permission to make and sell small items made out of limestone. Though prohibited, according to Reid the manufacture and sale of such objects was already common practice, and if properly regulated would not interfere with the discipline and good order of the establishment.[67] Certainly, the production of fancy goods (and art) was entirely in keeping with the flair and creativity displayed by convicts working as taxidermists, artists, and craftsmen in Britain's Australian colonies and Japanese Hokkaido (Chapter 7). Moreover, it enabled convicts to pass time, engage in leisure activities, and enter local and international markets. In Bermuda, convicts made dice, dominoes, chess pieces, beads, rings, buttons, charms, and pipes, at least some of which they kept or sold to other convicts. They worked with bone as well as stone.[68] In 1862, the deputy comptroller general remarked on the

---

[65] For example: TNA CO37/100/45 2 May 1839 no. 21 folios 195–200: Governor Sir William Reid, Bermuda, to Constantine Phipps (1st Marquis of Normanby), secretary of state for war and the colonies, 2 May 1839. Antigua was the only other British colony which did not introduce a period of apprenticeship for the formerly enslaved preceding final emancipation.

[66] TNA CO37/113/8 3 March 1846 no. 8 folios 100–115: Reid to William Ewart Gladstone, secretary of state for war and the colonies, 3 March 1846.

[67] TNA CO37/113/8 3 March 1846 no. 8 folios 100–115: Reid to Gladstone, 3 March 1846.

[68] Some of these artefacts are now on display at the National Museum of Bermuda, which is located at the key site of convict labour, The Dockyard. See also the following resource, which is an account of the remarkable excavation of the *Dromedary* hulk: http://www.bermudahulks.com/ (accessed 31 July 2018). Later, an overseer later noted the work of one convict in stuffing and selling birds outside the convict establishment. TNA CO37/

extent of their clandestine work, writing that over the past year there had been a considerable demand for such goods, not only from the navy but from Bermudians. Convicts could always, he concluded, command high prices.[69] A convict overseer, W. J. Henry, noted at this time that sailors and convicts worked together, and were often seen selling and buying these goods, or planning sales and purchases. According to Henry, this was an element of broader solidarities which existed between different labourers.[70]

The Gibraltar convict establishment opened almost twenty years after that of Bermuda, and the first convicts arrived in 1842.[71] It remained open until 1875, receiving over 4,500 male convicts during its more than thirty-year history. The bulk were from England and Ireland, but the hulks also held a few courts martialled British soldiers and Spaniards, the latter convicted in the colony.[72] The first convicts worked on the construction of a breakwater, and their appeal lay in Governor Robert Wilson's calculations on the value of their labour. Free workers were paid more than convicts ($1 compared to 2d per day), but the former were in short supply and Wilson claimed that convicts did more work.[73] The commander of the Royal Engineers, Colonel George Harding, later added that the establishment could put convicts to the kind of hard labour that free workers refused to do. This included excavations, heavy digging, unloading trucks, and carrying and laying large stones – sometimes standing in water up to waist height – and as in Bermuda work in diving bells.[74]

However, as in Bermuda, there were disputes about the value of convicts, and not all contemporaries agreed with Wilson and Harding's positive view. Captain Henry Wray of the Royal Engineers, for example, who worked four

---

177 20 February 1861 no. 18: Overseer Joseph Kemp, *Medway* hulk, to Governor Freeman Murray, Bermuda, 27 September 1860.

[69] TNA CO37/182 15 May 1862 no. 60: Governor Sir Harry St George Ord, Bermuda, to Henry Pelham-Clinton (5th Duke of Newcastle), secretary of state for the colonies, 15 May 1862, enc. Henry Trotter, deputy comptroller in charge to St George Ord, 13 May 1862.

[70] TNA CO37/182 15 May 1862 no. 60: Trotter to St George Ord, enc. Examination of the Overseer, W.J. Henry, 12 May 1862.

[71] TNA CO91/160 3 November 1842 no. 147: Governor Sir Robert Wilson, Gibraltar, to Edward Smith-Stanley (14th Earl of Derby), secretary of state for war and the colonies, 3 November 1842, enc. George Harding, commanding Royal Engineer, to Wilson, 2 November 1842. See also TNA CO91/160 17 November 1842: Wilson to Smith-Stanley, 17 November 1842.

[72] Gibraltar figures from *Annual Reports on the Convict Establishments at Bermuda and Gibraltar* (London: George E. Eyre and William Spottiswoode, 1859–63); *Reports of the Directors of Convict Prisons on the Discipline and Management of … the Convict Establishments at Gibraltar …* (London: George E. Eyre and William Spottiswoode, 1864–1875); TNA CO91 series, 1842–65.

[73] TNA CO91/168 27 May 1844 no. 125: Wilson to Smith-Stanley, 27 May 1844; TNA CO91/172 8 February 1845 no. 24: Wilson to Smith-Stanley, 8 February 1845.

[74] TNA CO91/192 2 January 1849 no. 4: Wilson to Grey, 2 January 1849.

years in Gibraltar and seven in the penal colony of Western Australia, argued that only piece or task work produced the desired results; in his view this was the case for all forms of forced labour.[75] Nonetheless, the range of convict employment was impressive. As in Bermuda, most convicts in Gibraltar were employed on public works, under the charge of the departments of the Royal Engineers and the Admiralty. They worked in blasting and cutting stone, repairing the parade ground, making new roads, building boundary walls, constructing drains, making and improving gardens, building new defences, and extending one of the settlement's breakwaters. Those working for the Admiralty laboured on the New Mole breakwater, to accommodate large ships, and at Europa Quarry and in dockyard workshops. They also painted and repaired naval buildings.[76] The overall objective was to prepare shore and land for the building and refitting of ships.[77] In 1868 alone, Admiralty convicts quarried 25,300 tons of stone, whilst five convict divers worked underwater to build the foundation for a further breakwater expansion.[78] Otherwise, convict tailors and shoemakers were employed in making and repairing shoes and clothes. Carpenters, painters, shipwrights, sawyers, plumbers, blacksmiths, and tinmen worked on the barracks, hulks, and boats, and made and repaired buckets and mess kits, lamps and chains, brushes, ropes, hammocks, and nets. Other convicts worked as clerks and teachers, officers' servants and cooks, inspectors of weights and measures, boatmen and boatswain's mates, and hospital washer men.[79]

As in the case of Brazil and the Portuguese Empire, the strategic imperatives of convict employment in Bermuda and Gibraltar coincided with the development of ideas about the reformative value of labour in the nineteenth century. Convicts could receive mitigation of sentence for good behaviour and hard work.[80] On the other hand, misconduct or

---

[75] Cited in C. P. Measor [Deputy Governor of Chatham Convict Prison], *The Convict Service: A Letter to Sir George Cornewall Lewis* [home secretary] *on the administration, results and expense of the present convict system; with suggestions* (London: Robert Hardwicke, 1861), 38.

[76] PP 1859 Session 2 (2523) Annual reports on the convict establishments at Bermuda and Gibraltar; preceded by instructions on the form to be observed in such reports: Gibraltar, report of the chief of the establishment, 1 January 1859, 33.

[77] TNA CO91/196 3 April 1850: Unattributed report, Gibraltar, 7 May 1850.

[78] PP 1870 (C.204) Report of the directors of convict prisons on the discipline and management of Pentonville, Millbank, and Parkhurst prisons, and of Portland, Portsmouth, Dartmoor, Chatham, Brixton, and Woking prisons for male convicts, with Woking and Fulham prisons for female convicts; also the convict establishments at Gibraltar, Western Australia, and Tasmania, for the year 1869: Gibraltar, comptroller's report (Captain Arthur Griffiths, acting comptroller), 1 January 1869, 430–1.

[79] TNA CO91/193 27 March 1849 no. 16: Nature of principal employment of convicts on the establishment, n.d.

[80] TNA CO91/176 14 February 1846 no. 20: Report of John Allen, Foreman of works, Wellington's Front, n.d.

labour shirking would have negative consequences. Some contemporaries claimed that this meant that convicts were more compliant and easier to control.[81] Whatever the case, convict labour supply was what Acting Comptroller Arthur Griffiths described in the 1860s as 'naturally more elastic', it being easy to reduce or increase numbers at a day's notice.[82] It was not so much that government desired convicts where free workers were unavailable, but that as a highly malleable and mobile workforce, which could be subjected to physical discipline, convicts were its first choice. If this was true for Britain's naval interests, it was also the case in numerous other contexts, including the East India Company settlements in the Indian Ocean, during the same period.[83]

Until the 1850s, all convicts sent to Bermuda and Gibraltar had been sentenced to transportation. However, in 1853 government passed the Penal Servitude Act, which specified that sentences of hard labour should be served either in Britain or in one of the colonies. From then on, Bermuda and Gibraltar received such men, the first batch in 1856.[84] This caused considerable difficulties, because unlike transportation convicts penal servitude men could not earn remission of sentence by good conduct. The annual report for Gibraltar of 1856 described the prisoners' subsequent 'gloomy and unsatisfactory appearance'.[85] In Bermuda, there was what Assistant Superintendent John Kirkham described as an unprecedented number of assaults on overseers, which he attributed to convict disaffection over these changed legal categories.[86] In mid-1858, the convicts on the *Medway* threatened an all-out mutiny. Vice-Admiral Houston Stewart wrote that they considered themselves unjustly treated and refused to work or speak to their officers. Governor Freeman Murray visited the hulk, spoke to some of the men, flogged the organizers of the resistance, and then forced the convicts to march out. When they went slow, he inflicted lashes on the prisoners at the front, after which the convicts fell into line. Murray next went on to the hulk *Tenedos*, and flogged a few other

---

[81] TNA CO91/176 14 February 1846 no. 20: Report of Lieutenant B.H. Martindale, Royal Engineers, n.d.

[82] PP 1870 (C.204) Report of the directors of convict prisons: Gibraltar, comptroller's report (Arthur Griffiths, acting comptroller), 1 January 1869, 432.

[83] Clare Anderson, 'Transnational Histories of Penal Transportation: punishment, labour and governance in the British Imperial World, 1788–1939', *Australian Historical Studies*, 47, 3 (2016), 389 (381–97).

[84] TNA CO91/227 4 July 1856 no. 130: Major General Governor and Commander-in-Chief Sir James Fergusson, Gibraltar, to Henry Labouchere, secretary of state for the colonies, 14 July 1856.

[85] TNA CO91/232 21 January 1857 no. 22: Report of the overseer, chaplain, and surgeon for 1856.

[86] TNA CO37/169/14 26 March 1859 no. 34 folios 102–3: Annual Report of Assistant Superintendent John Kirkham to Murray, 21 January 1859.

prisoners described as 'the worst and most prominent characters'.[87] Following such discontent, the British government decided that those convicted by the 1853 Act could volunteer for transportation to Western Australia, with a ticket-of-leave (i.e. on probation), after serving part of their sentence with good conduct.[88] The same pattern was repeated in Bermuda. Nonetheless, in 1860 Comptroller General Harry Blair noted the 'insolence, disrespect, and want of obedience' of the penal servitude men. He further explained: 'a spirit of discontent and disinclination to labour seemed to creep over them. The stimulus to exertion was gone, and with it, the amount of labour considerably decreased.'[89] Ultimately, government realized its error and strongly influenced by further convict unrest in 1860 revised the Act, so that penal servitude prisoners received longer initial sentences but could earn remission of them for good conduct. In effect, this put both groups of men in the same legal position.[90]

This kind of organized resistance had a long history in Britain's convict establishments. In common with convicts transported to other imperial locations, the men of Bermuda and Gibraltar resisted penal labour in various ways: by attempting to escape, feigning illness, working slow, or refusing to submit to corporal punishment. Few if any escape attempts succeeded, however. For instance, the absconding of four men in 1845 ended when a ship found them 600 miles north of Bermuda. The men had been employed in building the colony's lighthouse and had got away in a pilot boat after stealing provisions and water.[91] Another Bermuda escapee had previously served time in the British penal colony of New South Wales, and fled the *Coromandel* hulk in 1847 in the company of another man. Following their recapture, Governor Charles Elliot refused to put the two men (Thomas Thompson and William Jackson) on trial, because the punishment for escape was transportation, and he believed that this would further encourage absconding. The colonial secretary agreed and ordered that Bermudian convicts who committed transportation offences should in lieu of removal from the colony be sentenced to local imprisonment for the same period.[92]

---

[87] TNA CO37/167 (Admiralty): Houston Stewart, vice-admiral and commander-in-chief, to the secretary to the Admiralty, 8 June 1858.

[88] TNA CO91/236 12 May 1858 no. 92: Fergusson to Stanley, 12 May 1858.

[89] TNA CO91/251 27 January 1861 no. 10: Report on the Discipline and management of HM's convict prison Gibraltar for the year 1860, Harry Blair, 1 January 1861. This report is reproduced in PP 1861 (2785) Annual reports and despatches on the convict establishments at Bermuda and Gibraltar for 1860.

[90] TNA CO91/246 6 January 1860 no. 4: Newcastle to Horatio Waddington, permanent under-secretary of state of the Home Office, 30 March 1860.

[91] TNA CO37/112/1 11 October 1845 no. 40 folios 7–9: Reid to Stanley, 11 October 1845; TNA CO37/114/15 18 August 1846 no. 47 folios 141–3: Reid to Grey, 18 August 1846.

[92] TNA CO37/116/8 19 January 1847 no. 8 folios 83–90: Elliot to Grey, 19 January 1847; Grey to Elliot, 3 March 1847. The men were Thomas

Meantime, Thompson and Jackson faced brutal punishment, based on the norms of naval discipline. One of the men, who had previously attempted to abscond, got 96 lashes, the other 72. Both were put in irons, day and night and lost their right to a pardon. Their uniforms were given 'marks of degradation', their hair cut close, and their beards shaved.[93]

Across the British Empire, including in the Australian colonies and British Asia, overseers always inflicted floggings in full view of other convicts. As Raymond Evans and William Thorpe have shown, this created intensely violent, humiliating, and emasculating experiences and spectacles of punishment and deterrence.[94] In an 1847 case, for example, Bermuda convict William Allison refused to leave his hammock and come on deck when called, threatening one of the guards with what overseer William Harriott later described as 'very abusive language'. Harriott ordered that Allison receive 48 lashes, during which he yelled threats at the overseers: 'You may blow my brains out but I'll drive a knife into your b_y heart the first time I catch any of you.'[95] Governor Elliot ordered that if there was any further disorder, there would be no pardons on the ship for a whole year, unless other convicts informed on the organizers. In this, he made the convicts collectively responsible for reporting on plots or unrest.[96]

Less dramatic but sometimes more effective were convict labour negotiations. Indeed, convicts were occasionally able to turn to advantage Britain's desire for unfree workers in negotiating better conditions for themselves. In 1847, for example, four men working in Bermuda's Grey Bridge diving bell refused to continue their work unless a ration of spirits (liquor), recently withdrawn, was restored. The governor supported them, writing to Colonial Secretary Grey that although it was 'impossible to permit work of any kind to go into operation under consent to stipulations proposed by the Prisoners', they had previously worked well and he had every reason to believe that they would continue to do so. He did not mention the difficulty of finding convicts willing to undertake this

---

Thompson and William Jackson, but it is not clear which of them had previously served time in New South Wales.

[93] TNA CO37/116/13 6 February 1847 no. 11 folios 123–55: Elliot to Grey, 6 February 1847. This number of floggings far exceeded what was permitted under convict regulations in the Australian colonies. I thank Hamish Maxwell-Stewart for this insight.

[94] Raymond Evans and William Thorpe, 'Power, Punishment and Penal Labour: *Convict Workers* and Moreton Bay', *Australian Historical Studies*, 25, 98 (1992), 90–111. See also Clare Anderson, 'The Execution of Rughobursing: The Political Economy of Convict Transportation and Penal Labour in Early Colonial Mauritius', *Studies in History*, 19, 2 (2003), 185–97.

[95] TNA CO37/117/4 2 May 1847 no. 41 folios 22–55: Elliot to Grey, 2 May 1847, enc. Overseer William Harriott, *Thames* hulk, to Elliot, 23 April 1847.

[96] TNA CO37/117/4 2 May 1847 no. 41 folios 22–55: Elliot to Grey, 2 May 1847; NAB Convict Hulk Establishment, 1847–9: 23 April 1847.

unpleasant and dangerous work, though presumably this was an important consideration. Even Grey described the diving bell as 'laborious work'.[97] However, convict strikes were not always successful. In another case, in Gibraltar in 1860, following a reduction in the bread ration (from 27 to 20 ounces per day), convicts refused to work. Six of the men were flogged with up to 48 lashes. The convicts continued in their strike, and so were put on half rations, after which they eventually capitulated.[98] In what seems to have been a related act of resistance, that same year, four convicts attacked Assistant Surgeon Gross. Wilson had grabbed him during a medical examination, crying out to the others: 'Now you Buggers on to the Slaughter – "Bread Ho", "Bread Ho".' The five men were tried in the Supreme Court and sentenced to life imprisonment and hard labour in the colony.[99]

In Gibraltar, British and Irish convicts worked alongside Spanish convicts. The Spanish had committed offences in the colony and were transferred to the convict chain gang if sentenced to transportation. The colony passed an ordinance in 1846, banning the practice, but it continued for some years afterwards.[100] The Spaniards were few compared to another group of workers employed alongside convicts in both Bermuda and Gibraltar: soldiers. The relationship between penal and military discipline is well known, particularly as we have seen in the early-modern Iberian empires, and in penal settlements and colonies where the army and navy provided convict guards and overseers. Because convicts and soldiers worked side by side, invariably they compared the conditions under which they toiled, and on occasion soldiers complained that convicts enjoyed better treatment.[101] Governor William Reid of Bermuda even claimed that convicts goaded soldiers and sailors with evidence of their working

---

[97] TNA CO37/11/6 12 January 1847 no. 6 folios 51–73: Elliot to Grey, 12 January 1847, Grey to Elliot, 30 March 1847.
[98] TNA CO91/246 10 August 1860 no. 87: Governor Sir William Codrington, Gibraltar, to Newcastle, 10 August 1860, enc. B. S. Stehelin and F. Warden, visitors of the prison, to Codrington, 3 August 1860. The strike, but not the violent measures taken against the strikers, is mentioned in PP 1861 (2785) Annual reports and despatches on the convict establishments at Bermuda and Gibraltar for 1860: Report of Harry Blair, the comptroller general of convicts, 1 January 1861.
[99] TNA CO91/246 13 August 1860 no. 88, Codrington to Newcastle, 13 August 1860, enc. Blair to Codrington, 10 August 1860; TNA CO91/246 19 September 1860 no. 101: Codrington to Newcastle, 19 September 1860.
[100] TNA CO91/170 31 October 1844 no. 251: Wilson to Stanley, 31 October 1844. See also TNA CO91/185 27 February 1847 no. 35: Wilson to Grey, 27 February 1847; TNA CO91/227 15 January 1856 no. 9: Report of Chief Justice James Cochrane, Gibraltar, 4 January 1856.
[101] TNA CO37/88/23 15 November 1828 no. 19 folios 66–7: Governor Sir Hilgrove Turner, Bermuda, to Sir George Murray, secretary of state for war and the colonies, 15 November 1828.

conditions.[102] Though they started and finished work at the same time, soldiers were not issued with the alcohol, biscuits, and tobacco that convicts enjoyed during their half-hour rest, and due to guard duty spent just one night in three in a bed. Moreover, as Governor Sir Robert Gardiner explained in 1852, by good behaviour convicts in Gibraltar could halve the term of their sentence. Because soldiers had to serve a stipulated period of service, if they deserted, and were sentenced to transportation, with good service they could secure their release before their original term of military service had been due to expire.[103] Governor Sir William Codrington underscored this in 1863 when he wrote: 'The question of long and irksome loss of liberty is not uppermost in a soldier's mind when he makes this comparison; but the amount of labour, of physical comfort, and or immunity from night work is before his eyes daily.' Codrington was concerned that soldiers' awareness of the penal labour regime tempted them to commit crimes that would ameliorate the conditions of their working lives, for they knew that a sentence of penal servitude was what he called an '"ipso facto" discharge'.[104]

The desire to use convicts as a labour force was not always fully compatible with changing ideas about the nature of effective punishment, or ideas about convict reformation. This was the source of numerous disputes between the Admiralty and Royal Engineers, which directed convict work, the comptrollers general of convicts, and colonial governors, who had ultimate responsibility for the Bermuda and Gibraltar establishments. Of especial interest here are the relationships between establishment personnel such as overseers, doctors, and chaplains. One event of 1846 reveals some of the underlying conflicts about punishment and health. Surgeon-superintendent Henry Goldney reported on 300 convicts, recently arrived in Bermuda from Millbank Prison:

At the period of embarkation the prisoners had not a healthy appearance. A pallid dejected aspect prevailed throughout the whole. Many had long been subject to prison discipline, carried out under the silent system, and being obliged suddenly to discontinue it on embarkation, they became extremely sensible to noise, so as to interrupt all sleep for several nights, producing an irritable state of mind amounting evidently to a strong predisposition to Cerebral derangement. Many became subject to fits of an epileptic character, paroxysms of a short duration, requiring only temporary treatment, but the cases were both numerous and troublesome.[105]

---

[102] TNA CO37/113/8 3 March 1846 no. 8 folios 100–115: Reid to Gladstone, 3 March 1846.
[103] TNA CO91/205 3 June 1852 no. 59: General Sir Robert Gardiner, Governor of Gibraltar, to Sir John Pakington, secretary of state for war and the colonies, 3 June 1852.
[104] TNA CO91/262: 20 June 1863 no. 47: Codrington to Newcastle, 20 June 1863.
[105] TNA CO37/114/23 14 September 1846 no. 55 folios 217–26: Reid to Grey, 14 September 1846, enc. Surgeon-Superintendent Harry Goldney to Reid, 15 September 1846.

After the ship set sail, their fitness gradually improved. Goldney reported specifically on one man, William Baker, who had attempted suicide four times, thrice in Millbank and once in Pentonville: '[A]fter being on board a few weeks [he] came to me and said, "Sir do you recollect me? I have been one of the most happy men aboard the ship; it was the prison and silence that made me wretched and tired of life."'[106]

Another example of the gap between expectations of punishment and healthfulness, in the eyes of medical officers, dates from 1860. Herbert Beck, acting chief medical officer in Bermuda, then critiqued the employment of invalids at stone breaking. Like convicts in the punishment gang, invalids lost their gratuity and liquor ration. This was hardly fair, Beck complained, for they had no control over their poor health.[107] The same year, the chief medical officer of Gibraltar complained that climate, monotony, homesickness, and anxiety caused convicts to age prematurely. He added that treatment regimens were often ineffective for those who had been confined for long periods of time and recommended that convicts be moved to other sites of punishment after five years in the colony. It seems that a year earlier, the acting chief medical officer of Bermuda had made precisely the same point.[108]

There were more intense conflicts over convict labour and religion, for from the 1830s onwards an important feature of penal transportation in the British imperial context was the promotion of Christianity as a means of convict reform, rehabilitation, and ultimately salvation. In Bermuda and Gibraltar, hulk chaplains were Church of England ministers, and charged with religious instruction and education. Yet chapel service and bible study took convicts away from public works. As Hilary Carey has recently suggested: 'A series of religious issues plagued the secular management of convicts in Bermuda.' This was particularly the case following the

---

[106] TNA CO37/114/23 14 September 1846 no. 55 folios 217–26: Reid to Grey, 14 September 1846, enc. Goldney to Reid, 15 September 1846. For comparable material on the mental health impacts of separate confinement on convicts shipped to the Australian colonies during 1848–9, see Katherine Foxhall, *Health, Medicine, and the Sea: Australian voyages, c. 1815–1860* (Manchester University Press, 2012), 38–9. Foxhall draws on the reports of Surgeon-Superintendent Colin Arrott Browning. Evidence of Browning's religious zeal among transportation convicts can be found in his earlier book, *The Convict Ship, and England's Exiles* (London: Hamilton, Adams and Co., 1847). See also Charles Bateson, 'Browning, Colin Arrott (1791–1856)', Australian Dictionary of Biography, National Centre of Biography, Australian National University, http://adb.anu.edu.au/biography/browning-colin-arrott-1838/text2121, published first in hardcopy 1966 (accessed 7 May 2020).

[107] PP 1860 (2662) Annual reports on the convict establishments at Bermuda and Gibraltar for 1859: Report of Herbert Beck, acting chief medical officer, Bermuda, 20 January 1860.

[108] PP 1860 (2662) Annual reports on the convict establishments at Bermuda and Gibraltar for 1859: Report of Julius Williams, chief medical officer, Gibraltar, 5 January 1860.

appointment of Reverend John Guilding in 1856, for he was a firm believer in the possibility of convicts' moral reformation through the effective use of the separate system.[109] Indeed, in 1858 Guilding declared his mission as 'bringing ignorant and depraved men to a sense of sin and repentance, and the practical knowledge of pure and Evangelical Religion'. Though convict transportation to Bermuda might have had its origins in the colonial desire for convict labour, as Carey has shown, it was Guilding's religious critique, and his representation of the Bermuda hulks as 'dens of infamy and pollution' and 'hells of abomination' in which convicts sought sexual pleasure, that ultimately underpinned the decision to abolish them in 1863.[110]

Disputes over convict labour and education greatly occupied Guilding and the new Deputy Superintendent of Convicts, Captain Montagu Pasco, who had taken up his post two years before Guilding arrived.[111] One of Guilding's first acts had been to reorganize the establishment library. 'I have been criticized that the books are of too high an order for the class for whom they are intended', he wrote. 'But ... [t]he Convict Class it must be remembered is a very mixed one. No society perhaps is comprised of so many elements. There are collected, besides the sweepings of our towns and the ignorant laboring man, many who are intelligent by nature and education, the mechanic, the clerk, nay even men who have occupied the position of gentlemen.'[112] Guilding also established a busy schedule of religious services, prayers, communion, evening lectures, and schooling in writing, reading, arithmetic and general knowledge. These took up a good deal of time, and consequently Pasco frequently suspended his classes, and ordered the convicts back to work. Governor Murray wrote: 'I was not a little astonished when I discovered ... that he considered the instruction of the Prisoners and their moral reformation to be of far less importance than their labor.' Indeed, Pasco had previously reported to Murray: 'The moral culture of the men at school ... and the successful progress of the works are incompatible.'[113] Governor Murray ruled in favour of the chaplain, and ultimately the colonial secretary approved Pasco's dismissal, claiming that he had discovered that he

---

[109] Hilary Carey, *Empire of Hell: Religion and the campaign to end convict transportation in the British Empire, 1788–1875* (Cambridge University Press, 2019), 276–80.

[110] Carey, *Empire of Hell*, 277–8. In 1859, Guilding visited prisons in Pennsylvania and New York during a trip to the USA, thus viewing the differing regimes of the Eastern State Penitentiary and Auburn prison. See TNA CO37/174 28 January 1860 no. 14: Report of Chaplain John Guilding, 1 January 1860.

[111] Carey, *Empire of Hell*, 278–9. On Pasco's appointment, see TNA CO37/146/71 26 June 1854 no. 66 folios 307–20: Acting Governor Montgomery Williams, Bermuda, to Newcastle, 26 June 1854.

[112] TNA CO37/160 26 May 1857 no. 60 folio 403ff: Guilding to Murray, 18 May 1857.

[113] TNA CO37/165 27 February 1858 no. 22: Murray to Henry Herbert (4th Earl of Carnarvon), under-secretary of state for the colonies, 26 February 1858, enc. Pasco to Murray, 10 January 1858.

had flogged a mutinous convict without first seeking his approval.[114] However, at the same time, Murray represented Guilding's claims about the prevalence of so-called 'unnatural crime' as unproven and 'greatly exaggerated'. The convicts lived in such close association, the governor wrote, that sexual relationships could not possibly be kept secret.[115] Nonetheless, at this time, due to the diminished number of penal servitude prisoners available for work in the three remaining establishments of Bermuda, Gibraltar, and Western Australia, the Colonial Office was debating which one to close. It settled on Bermuda.[116] Gibraltar lasted a few more years, ultimately shutting down in 1874.

None of the convicts were allowed to settle in these colonies. Indeed, the Bermuda House of Assembly passed an Act to this effect as early as 1830, and resisted any further efforts at change, including an 1841 proposal by Governor Reid to allow the best-behaved men to stay in the colony. It stressed the 'considerable uneasiness' of the population at the prospect of convict settlement, noting that because so many men were mariners, women and children were left alone for much of the time, including those widowed or orphaned by the deaths of husbands and fathers at sea. It petitioned the governor: 'To let loose ... among such persons ... a set of sanguinary men, originally expelled from their own country for their crimes, and since hardened in an association of congregated villains, would be intolerable.'[117] It seems that a few convicts returned to Britain and Ireland, and others were allowed to leave on ships short of crew and offering convicts a free passage, if they were willing to work. However, after 1850, following objections to ex-convict arrivals in the ports of New York and Baltimore, the USA was closed as a destination.[118]

*

This chapter has argued that a key element of punitive relocation, cutting across empires, was the desire to extract work from convicts and to

---

[114] TNA CO37/165/74 19 June 1858 folios 477–85: Murray to Herbert, 19 June 1858.
[115] TNA CO37/177 19 April 1865 no. 47: Murray to Newcastle, 29 March 1865.
[116] TNA CO37/177 19 April 1865 no. 47: Newcastle to Murray, 12 July 1865.
[117] TNA CO37/113/9 14 March 1846 no. 9 folios 116–34: Reid to Gladstone, 14 March 1846, enc. Address from the House of Assembly of Bermuda to the Governor, 12 April 1830.
[118] For Honduras, see TNA CO37/122/28 21 August 1848 no. 71 folios 157–66: Elliot to Grey, 21 August 1848, Grey to Elliot, 14 November 1848. For the USA, see TNA CO37/133/40 14 December 1850 no. 137 folios 334-41: Elliot to Grey, 14 December 1850; TNA CO37/133/10 18 September 1850 no. 107 folios 52–67: Elliot to Grey, 18 September 1850; TNA CO37/134 (Foreign Office) 11 November 1850: Edward John Stanley (2nd Baron Stanley of Alderley), under-secretary of state for foreign affairs and HM's Minister at Washington, to Herman Merivale, permanent under-secretary of state for the colonies, 11 November 1850.

manage colonial workers. The imperial powers moved convicts multi-directionally and employed them in an extraordinarily diverse range of occupations. Their mobility and labour were connected to the wider goals of imperial expansion, punishment, and deterrence. During the early-modern period, in the empires of Portugal, Spain, France, the Netherlands, and Denmark–Norway convicts routinely travelled and worked alongside people of the social underclasses, and Indigenous, military, and indentured labour, as well as the enslaved. In some cases, there existed racialized labour regimes. Women always made up a minority of convicts, and the small numbers sent into transportation were put to household or other kinds of gendered labour, including in the Dutch East Indies. Often, convicts were conscripted into the army, or hired out to free settlers, and in some colonies, both practices endured well into the twentieth century. In places like Portuguese Africa administrators hoped that convicts would become colonizer-settlers. Further, as the early-modern cases show, numerous empires and polities used the threat of punitive relocation as a means of managing populations, including people from numerous legal categories.

The British hulk establishments of Bermuda and Gibraltar present a contrasting example, for in these colonies convicts constituted a mobile, male-only labour force that was deployed to complete work and then leave. However, alongside critique of the punitive merits of convict labour, and its impacts on health and well-being, contemporaries disputed its value, particularly in comparison to the productivity of free workers. Moreover, as the nineteenth century progressed, there were fundamental incompatibilities between the character of punishment and the demands of labour, and this could lead to disputes, including between convict overseers, chaplains, and doctors. This was in part related to the endemic nature of labour resistance, for convicts everywhere showed remarkably similar tactics in confronting or refusing penal work. Administrators used extreme violence in response to violent outbreaks and escape attempts, but convicts had some success in garnering changes to work patterns when they used more subtle means. Moreover, within the context of relatively open penal sites, convicts demonstrated creativity when they engaged in trade, opened businesses, or made and sold small objects. We will return to the theme of convict resistance in Chapter 6, which is an exploration of punitive mobility, religion, and political ideology. In the meantime, the Chapter 3 turns to the use of convicts by expansionist nation states, and their role in occupying and developing internal frontiers and offshore islands.

3 Nations, Borders, and Islands

Common and intertwined goals underpinned punitive relocation across numerous national and imperial contexts. If Chapter 2 explored the case of European empires, this one appreciates the scope, scale, and experience of convict mobility in the expansionist regimes of mid-Qing China, post-Meiji restoration Japan, continental Europe, and in the independent nation states of Colombia, Ecuador, Bolivia, Chile, Argentina, Mexico, and Peru. Spanning the period from the eighteenth to twentieth centuries, it shows that government sent convicts over long distances, including to borders and offshore islands, for a combination of reasons. As in European empires, these included the management of troublesome or insurgent populations, the occupation and development of geopolitical frontiers, the encouragement of free migration, and the appropriation of convict labour. Engaged in global conversations about punishment, governments also used punitive mobility to inflict severe punishment, provide a strong deterrent against crime, and in some cases to rehabilitate offenders.

Chapter 5 will return to the relationship between punitive mobility and population management, whilst Chapter 7 will examine contemporary debates about convicts. Here, as in previous pages, the chapter focuses on the labour dimensions of punitive mobility, noting that its various objectives were not always compatible, and that convict agency sometimes challenged or compromised its success. In the Chinese case, for instance, serious offenders were supposed to travel the furthest distances and yet simultaneously to those regions in greatest need of labour. Punitive mobility in China also had little to do with rehabilitation. Likewise, the harsh conditions that convicts faced during road-building programmes in Japan overrode the convict reform agenda. The desire to implement graduated systems of punishment in Argentina's penal colony of Ushuaia took much longer than anticipated, because they were incompatible with the demand for timber. This meant that for at least the first two decades of its existence, convicts were kept to logging work. The experiences of convicts sent to El Frontón in Peru also had everything to do with severe punishment and labour profit, and nothing to do with rehabilitation. Meantime, convict movement into the interiors of Colombia, Ecuador, and Bolivia was intimately connected to free labour migration. For these reasons, it is useful to conceptualize convict mobility as a system operated by a range of stakeholders who did not always have identical desires and goals regarding governance, punishment, work, and geopolitical expansion. The various places under discussion here are extraordinarily distinct, and there are important political, economic, social, and cultural differences between them. However, the overall argument is that in each case the desire to use convict labour to consolidate and to expand territory powered their mobility, including across internal frontiers, and sometimes in the face of political threat. As we will see, convicts resisted and subverted this intention in diverse ways.

Yi ju liang de, or Achieving Multiple Ends by a Single Means

In 1768, the Qing government banished the eminent scholar Ji Yun for a 'serious breach of confidentiality', after he warned a distant relative named Lu Jianzeng of his imminent arrest. Ji Yun's punitive journey took him away from his wife and children across the length of the Chinese Empire: from the capital city of Beijing to the far western Central Asian province of Xinjiang, which the Qing had annexed in 1759. He remained there for one year, an unusually short period of time, but wrote and compiled materials that enable insights into the lives and experiences of both elite and ordinary convicts. As for other exiled scholars and officials, there were few restrictions on his mobility. He first lived in the compound of Lieutenant-Governor Wenfu, who oversaw Xinjian's capital, Ürümqi, and later moved in with a friend from home, Tian Baiyan. Yun was put to work drafting official papers and documents and was allowed to send personal letters. After his release and return to Beijing in 1771, he took on various senior government roles, and became joint chief editor of the Imperial Manuscript Library.[1] Later, he published poems and stories, since used as historical sources by scholars of nineteenth-century Xinjiang.[2]

---

[1] Joanna Waley-Cohen, *Exile in Mid-Qing China: Banishment to Xinjiang, 1758–1820* (Yale University Press, 1991), 5–6, 148, 150n55, 152–3. The Hanlin Academy was an elite scholarly institution that served the Chinese court. Note that Lu Jianzeng's grandson was married to Ji Yun's eldest daughter. Tian Baiyan had taught poetry to Lu Jianzeng.

[2] Waley-Cohen, *Exile in Mid-Qing China*, 155–6.

At the time of Yun's punitive journey, the Qing commonly moved troublemakers (*weifei*) to its frontier regions, especially to Xinjiang, which lies across the Gobi Desert on the old Silk Road between the northern reaches of Mongolia and Tibet (Map 3.1). This policy was underpinned by the principle of *yi ju liang de*, or achieving multiple ends by a single means: the infliction of severe punishment on offenders, their rehabilitation through work, and colonization. Punishment in far-distant locations was especially harsh in China because it disrupted the practice of ancestor worship in a convict's home place. But the immediate background to punitive mobility in mid-Qing China was an intense period of demographic growth, which had led to overcrowding and unrest and, as migrants moved out from the inner provinces, competition for arable land. The Qing wanted to exploit Xinjiang's natural resources, subjugate its peoples, and establish a Han Chinese presence to counterbalance the local population. This would create what Joanna Waley-Cohen describes as a 'buffer zone' against Russian and Kazakh expansion from the west. Thus, convicts went either to *tun* (military agricultural colonies) or to separate penal colonies (*fantun* or *qiantun*). Most convicts were ordinary criminal offenders, but political offenders, including religious sectarians, were also sent alongside disgraced officials. Some faced punitive mobility on the principle of 'collective responsibility', following the execution of their relatives. Those found guilty of the most serious crimes alongside the majority of political exiles were enslaved: in northern Xinjiang, to the army, and in the south, either to local officials or the local administration. Though government sent at least 134,000 convicts to Xinjian, they made up no more than five per cent of the settler population of the region. However, unless they were government officials, after serving their sentence the Qing compelled them to stay in the region. This meant that by the start of the twentieth century, and the fall of the dynasty in 1912, they constituted one of the area's largest groups of Han Chinese.[3]

The punishment of *fapei* (banishment to the frontier) was distinct from other forms of punitive mobility under the Qing because it held out the possibility of self-renewal (*zixin*). This was to be achieved through labour. As Waley-Cohen writes, 'work formed an integral part of the government colonization project and [convicts'] performance affected their prospects for formal emancipation.'[4] For this reason frontier convicts were not subjected to violent punishments, which would have impacted on their fitness for labour. Before 1759, the Qing had sent them to Manchuria, enslaving the most

---

[3] Waley-Cohen, *Exile in Mid-Qing China*, 1–2, 6–7, 9–11, 12–15, 17, 19, 23, 25 (quote), 26–7, 31, 33–4. 36, 53, 56, 166–7. The China statistic is drawn from Clare Anderson, 'Introduction: A Global History of Convicts and Penal Colonies', in Clare Anderson, ed., *A Global History of Convicts and Penal Colonies* (London: Bloomsbury, 2018), 2 (1–35).
[4] Waley-Cohen, *Exile in Mid-Qing China*, 56.

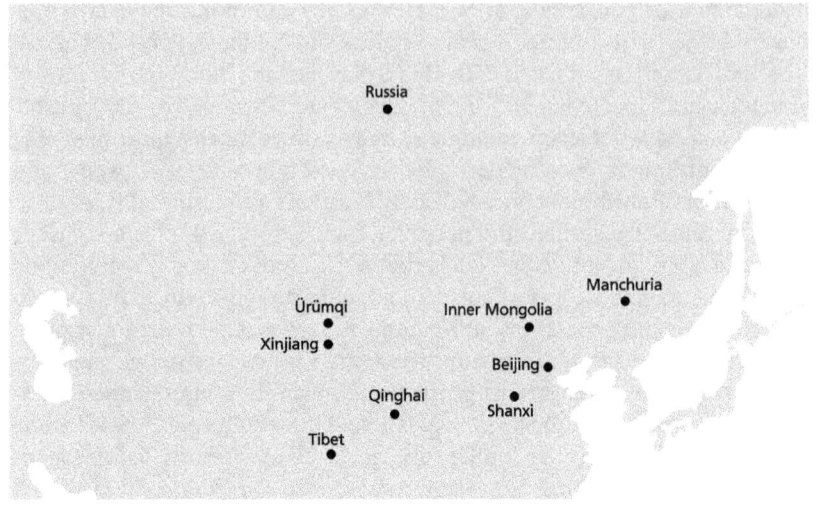

Map 3.1 Xinjiang, China

serious offenders, and working the remainder in military agricultural colonies, on river patrols, or in dockyards. Some were engaged in agriculture, crafts, and trade. However, it was in Xinjiang that government explicitly connected convict labour to the project of colonization, dispatching convicts where they were most required. Employment in the northern regions included land clearance and farming, and mining for lead and iron. In a few cases, convicts undertook military service. Government found it difficult to balance labour demands with the desire to exile the worst offenders over the longest distances. Nonetheless, its colonizing intentions are clear when we consider that, except for a brief period in the early 1760s, until 1799 government bore the expense of sending wives and children with their convict husbands and fathers, as long as the women were under 60 and in good health.[5] The Qing desired the transformation of convict families into productive settlers. In contrast and unlike ordinary convicts, disgraced officials such as Yun were only ever meant to be temporary residents of the frontier, and they were put to rather different kinds of work. Some were sent to hard labour (*kuchai*), but most were employed in government service (*dangchai*), which greatly reduced the expense of administration in the new settlements and encouraged the wider goal of self-sufficiency.[6]

---

[5] Waley-Cohen, *Exile in Mid-Qing China*, 56–8, 64–5, 66–8, 71–2, 167, 169–75. Note that the children of convicts were born free: Waley-Cohen, *Exile in Mid-Qing China*, 167–8.

[6] Waley-Cohen, *Exile in Mid-Qing China*, 139–46.

The scholar Yun made several observations on the lives of ordinary convicts, noting, for instance, that that those engaged in agriculture lived on the land but waited out the harsh winters in Ürümqi, and that because of highly imbalanced gender ratios the state employed women to make marriage matches. He also wrote of the presence of skilled artisans among the convicts, of their skills as storytellers, singers, and actors, and of their New Year celebrations.[7] Not included in his writings is the evidence of numerous incidents of escape otherwise detailed in official reports. Prior to the dispatch of convicts, government compiled registers, which included details of each individual's crime, place of origin, age, and any distinguishing marks, as well as descriptions of the shape of their fingerprints. In order to distinguish convicts from free men and women, excepting some political offenders and those of high rank who would one day return home, convicts were tattooed on the forehead. Descriptive rolls and tattoo marks were an important means of marking status and identifying convicts in the event of their desertion.[8] Nonetheless, convicts were able to bribe tattooists to make only slight marks or to efface them altogether by burning the skin or using ointments. This was necessary because escaped convicts faced summary execution.[9] In the eighteenth century, it took between six and nine months to reach Xinjiang, presenting many opportunities for desertion. Ordinary convicts travelled on carts and banished officials in sedan chairs, spending the nights lodged in prisons or inns. In extreme cases, convicts committed suicide. In terms of resistance more generally, as Waley-Cohen shows, Qing officials were especially nervous that Muslims would stoke up unrest in the communities that they passed through. Given that some convicts were under punishment for rebellion, and others under the principle of collective responsibility, this was not entirely irrational. As for escape, when one man, Li Erman, was recaptured close to his home he described how since he had gone on the run he had been forced to beg for food and sleep in temples. He added that he had been reunited with his son, and that they had supported themselves by selling

---

[7] Waley-Cohen, *Exile in Mid-Qing China*, 179–81.
[8] Waley-Cohen, *Exile in Mid-Qing China*, 112–17. Following the introduction of transportation in 1789, the East India Company compiled similar registers in the Bengal, Madras, and Bombay presidencies. Bengal and Madras convicts were tattooed on the forehead by a process called *godna* and showed similar dexterity in blurring or removing the marks. The British did not abolish this practice until 1849. See Clare Anderson, *Legible Bodies: Race, criminality and colonialism in South Asia* (Oxford: Berg, 2004), 15–25, 30–36, 39–41.
[9] Waley-Cohen, *Exile in Mid-Qing China*, 118. The arguments about the disruption of ancestral rites reveal interesting parallels here with arguments about penal transportation as a culturally appropriate and severe punishment in nineteenth-century British India and Hong Kong. See Clare Anderson, 'A Global History of Exile in Asia', in Ronit Ricci, ed., *Exile in Colonial Asia: Kings, convicts, commemoration* (Honolulu: University of Hawai'i Press, 2016), 23–4 (37–79).

wheat cakes.[10] In 1768, there was an uprising among over 200 convicts at the Changji agricultural colony, west of Ürümqi, the only such event in eighteenth-century China. Around half of the convicts were killed during the rebellion, and in its aftermath, government cut to death its leaders, executed the remainder, placing the corpses on public display.[11]

The Hokkaido *shūchikan* of Meiji Restoration Japan

In April 1879, Kiyoshi Tsukigata and seven other officials from Japan's Home Ministry travelled from Tokyo to Hokkaido. The Meiji restoration government (1868–1912) had charged them with choosing a site for the establishment of a new *shūchikan* (penitentiary) on the island formerly known as Ezochi.[12] By this time, not only was there already a small jail attached to a match factory in the port of Hakodate, the administrative centre of Hokkaido, but there existed an experimental agricultural station eleven miles north in a place called Nanae. An Indigenous Ainu man called Rekonte, from a village called Oyafuru near the port of Ishikari, guided Tsukigata and his companions in their investigations. Their work included the observation and analysis of topography, timber, and soil, and Tsukigata proposed the land around a place that the Ainu called Subetsu as the ideal site for the prison. After its establishment, he became the first governor of what was known as Kabato *shūchikan*, and the town that grew up around it today bears Tsukigata's name.[13]

Since the first half of the eighteenth century, during the latter part of the Tokugawa Shogunate era (1603–1868), Japanese merchants had established trading relationships with the Ainu of Ezochi and managed some of the island's fisheries. However, they were only present in part of the island, and it was not until the Japanese government was faced with the threat of Russian colonization from its existing possessions in neighbouring Sakhalin Island and the Kurils that it sought to occupy the whole island.[14] The idea of using convicts to colonize and develop those areas

---

[10] Waley-Cohen, *Exile in Mid-Qing China*, 121, 131, 134–7.
[11] Waley-Cohen, *Exile in Mid-Qing China*, 183–5.
[12] In reference to its Indigenous hunter-gatherer inhabitants, the Ainu, Ezochi is literally translated as 'land of barbarians'.
[13] For a full discussion of the period before c. 1855, see Minako Sakata, 'Japan in the Eighteenth and Nineteenth Centuries', in Anderson, ed., *A Global History of Convicts and Penal Colonies*, 310–12 (307–35). At this time, the agricultural station grew Japanese, Chinese, and other varieties of crops such as rice, wheat, soya, and adzuki beans alongside non-indigenous trees. It was the site of a water mill and wheat and rice cleaners and grinders. See also Kiyoshi Tsukigata, 'Hokkaidō kairanki, 1880', in Tsukigatamurashi hensan iinkai, ed., *Tsukigatamurashi* (Tsukigata: Tsukigatamura Yakuba, 1942), 142–4, 149–50 (142–56).
[14] In the nineteenth century, Japan occupied part of Sakhalin, which it called Karafuto. In 1875, with the signing of the Treaty of St Petersburg, it gave up its claim to Sakhalin in

of Ezochi that were not under Japanese control or influence stretched back to the turn of the nineteenth century, when intellectual Rimei Honda first advocated it. The Japanese did not take steps towards formal annexation at this time. However, during the later period the outward-looking and modernizing Meiji government became increasingly aware of the penal practices of other global powers. It noted the abolition of the death penalty in some nations, and the use of transportation convicts to open up what earlier observers had referred to as 'barren land', or *terra nullius* (nobody's land), such as in the Australian penal colonies and Siberia.[15] Its interest in global debates was such that it received and distributed copies of the proceedings of the first International Penitentiary Congress, which was held in London in 1872, and which we will explore in depth in Chapter 7.[16]

Dating from the seventh century, there existed in Japan a long history of removing social 'undesirables' to remote islands (*entō*), either as exiles or convicts under sentences of hard labour. They included the Izu, Oki, Iki, Goto, Amami, and Amakusa islands in western Japan, and the southern Okinawa archipelago in the East China Sea.[17] Exiles were not put to work but left to fend for themselves under the watch of village headmen. Convicts were required to work, though they were not used to clear or develop land. One famous case is the exile of the Buddhist monk Nichiren. He was a devotee of the Lotus Sudra sect, and believed that enlightenment could be achieved on Earth. For this belief, he came into conflict with Japanese rulers, and they exiled him to Sado Island, off the northern coast in the Sea of Japan, during the years 1271 to 1274 (Figure 3.1). In a practice akin to that of early-modern Europe, from the eighteenth century onwards, the Tokugawa Shogunate also sent vagrants, petty offenders, and gamblers to Sado, criminalizing them and putting them to work in the island's silver and gold mines. Vagrants worked specifically as *mizugae-ninsoku* (water-bailers). According to Yoshirō Hiramatsu, this had the effect of stigmatizing the work and lowering wages, thus creating an ongoing and 'chronic need' for

---

exchange for some of the Kuril Islands. At their closest meeting points, Sakhalin and Hokkaido are just 25 miles apart.

[15] Sakata, 'Japan in the Eighteenth and Nineteenth Centuries', 313, 315. A copy of Honda's 1791 manuscript, copied in 1854, is in Hokkaido University Library: *Ezo tochi kaihatsu guzon no taigai*. On Japan's engagement with European and North American forms of punishment earlier in the nineteenth century, see Daniel V. Botsman, *Punishment and Power in the Making of Modern Japan* (Princeton University Press, 2005), 117–29.

[16] Neil Pedlar, *The Imported Pioneers: Westerners who helped build modern Japan* (Sandgate: Japan Library Ltd, 1990), 187–8. Germany and Prussia were also influential in three areas of Japanese reform: the creation of international law, the writing of the constitution, and the establishment of a police force. See Pedlar, *The Imported Pioneers*, 188–9; Yoshirō Hiramatsu, 'History of Penal Institutions: Japan', *Law in Japan: An Annual*, 6 (1973), 30, 32–3 (1–48).

[17] Sakata, 'Japan in the Eighteenth and Nineteenth Centuries', 317.

Figure 3.1 Kuniyoshi Utagawa, Sashū ryūkei Kakuta nami daimoku (Banishment to Sado Island: On the Waves at Kakuta), woodblock print, c. 1835
Source: The British Museum, 1913,0415,0.10.

prisoners.[18] During the whole Tokugawa period, punitive relocation, with or without labour, varied in regards to length of sentence and choice of destination, depending not just on the nature of the crime but on the social rank of the offender. In total, the numbers sent from the mainland were small; perhaps amounting to just twenty people per year. However, in many cases they were not allowed to return to the mainland, enhancing demographic impact in this island location and giving the punishment a remarkably deterrent character.[19]

---

[18] On the exile of commoners and *samurai* (warrior class) before the Meiji restoration, see Hiramatsu, 'History of Penal Institutions', 7–8, 12–19 (quote, 8). On Sado island, see Botsman, *Punishment and Power*, 99–100. For an English-language contemporary source, note Shigejiro Ogawa and Kosuke Tomeoka, 'Prisons and Prisoners', in Marcus B. Huish, ed., *Fifty Years of New Japan, Volume I, compiled by Shigenobu Okuma* (London: Smith, Elder and Co., 1910), 296–9 (296–319). This argument has also been made for the indenture of British and Irish convicts in the eighteenth-century Americas. See Emma Christopher and Hamish Maxwell-Stewart, 'Convict Transportation in Global Context, c. 1700–88', in Alison Bashford and Stuart Mcintyre, eds., *The Cambridge History of Australia, Volume 1: Indigenous and colonial Australia* (Cambridge University Press, 2013), 73 (68–90). I am grateful to Hamish Maxwell-Stewart for pointing out the comparison here.

[19] Carl Steenstrup, *A History of Law in Japan until 1868* (Leiden: Brill, 1996), 61, 153–4; Hiramatsu, 'History of Penal Institutions', 7–8, 12–19; Yoshirō Hiramatsu, 'Tokugawa Law', *Law in Japan: An Annual*, 14 (1981), 20, 21, 24, 41, 47 (1–48).

When the Meiji government seized power in 1868, the prison administration was placed under the Ministry of Justice (*Shihōshō*), which passed orders to the effect that all such offenders would be sent to Hokkaido. However, it suspended the use of the sentence until new prison facilities had been constructed. It then passed the 1870 *Shinritsu Kōryō* (New Criminal Law), ordering under-sentence convicts to the same locations as other offenders, but with more rigorous labour.[20] At this time, the Meiji government was making active efforts to reform law and punishment, in part because the 'unequal' treaties with foreign powers, signed between 1858 and 1869, introduced the principle of extraterritoriality via consular courts. This exempted foreign nationals from Japanese law, because the foreign powers did not view the justice system as adequately modern.[21] Shortly before Tsukigata's survey mission to Hokkaido, in 1872 the Ministry of Justice had sent a group of officials to France, where they researched the French penal system, and appointed legal scholar Gustave Emile Boissonade as a professional advisor in the creation of a new western-style penal code. This was the 1873 *Kaitei Ritsurei* (*Revised Criminal Law*), which replaced flogging, exile, and transportation with penal servitude, i.e. imprisonment with labour.[22] Efforts at reform were brought into sharp focus by the changing geopolitics of the region. Japan had lost Sakhalin to Russia in 1875, and as a consequence Hokkaido became its northern-most border. Government attempts to encourage migration – chiefly by vagrants, *samurai* who had lost the Boshin War of 1868–9 that had marked the end of the Tokugawa Shogunate, and farmer-soldiers (*tondenhei*) – had not been successful. However, in order to stave off the threat of Russian invasion, there was an urgent need to populate the island.[23] As Minako Sakata has shown, at this time the Meiji government envisaged Hokkaido as a colony, only later and with its incorporation into the Japanese nation state viewing it as what she terms a 'homeland territory'.[24]

---

[20] Hiramatsu, 'History of Penal Institutions', 22–4, 27; Sakata, 'Japan in the Eighteenth and Nineteenth Centuries', 317–20.
[21] Takashi Miyamoto, 'Convict Labor and Its Commemoration: the Mitsui Miike Coal Mine Experience', *The Asia-Pacific Journal: Japan Focus*, 15, 1, 3 (2017), 3 (1–15). On European representations of sanguinary Japanese punishments, that justified extraterritoriality, see Botsman, *Punishment and Power*, 139–40.
[22] Hiramatsu, 'History of Penal Institutions', 22–4, 27; Sakata, 'Japan in the Eighteenth and Nineteenth Centuries', 317–20.
[23] Sakata, 'Japan in the Eighteenth and Nineteenth Centuries', 322.
[24] Minako Sakata, 'The Transformation of Hokkaido from Penal Colony to Homeland Territory', *International Review of Social History*, 63, S26 (2018), 109–30.

The immediate catalyst to the establishment of the *shūchikan* in Hokkaido, however, was neither the modernizing thrust of the Meiji regime nor the desire to secure borders against Russian interests, but the eruption of a series of anti-government revolts, notably the Satsuma Rebellion (or Seinan War) of 1877.[25] This created a penal crisis, for there was a shortage of accommodation for the incarceration of political prisoners. Thus, a new 1880 penal code (*Kyūkeihō*), written by Boissonade under the full influence of European law, dismantled much of the Tokugawa penal system.[26] It specified that sentences of imprisonment with labour (*tokei*) and exile (*rukei*) would be imposed on Honshū, Japan's main island. Although Hokkaido was unmentioned, sentences of imprisonment without labour would be served 'on other islands'. The code also stipulated that women sentenced to penal servitude would be kept in mainland prisons. Those sentenced to imprisonment without labour could be made subject to transportation.[27]

It was following the passing of this French-influenced code that government built eight new *shūchikan*: in Miyagi and Tokyo (Honshū); at Miike on the island of Kyūshū; and in Hokkaido at Kabato (1881), Sorachi (1882), Kushiro (1885), Abashiri (1891) and Tokachi (1895). In Hokkaido, earlier migrant settlements were largely clustered around Sapporo, which was by then the capital. Thus, government established all the Hokkaido prisons in sparsely populated areas in the interior. Simultaneously, with the opening of the first Hokkaido *shūchikan* in 1882, Deputy Director of the Prisons Department Shigeya Ohara went on a tour of prisons in Belgium, France, and Prussia, and then further revised the prison rules. As in Europe and European empires, and later in Latin America, these created penal stages. First, convicts would be kept in holding prisons (*kariyūkan*) in Honshū or Kyūshū. They would then be sent north, where they were sent out to work daily from their penitentiary base. Without exception, the convicts transported to Hokkaido were male; all were sentenced for at least 12 years; and 90 per cent of them were aged between 20 and 50 years. Despite their importance in catalysing the penal colonization of Hokkaido, political offenders who were not subject to hard labour overall made up less than 0.2 per cent of all

---

[25] Hiramatsu notes that 43,000 persons were sentenced in the wake of the Satsuma Rebellion. See 'History of Penal Institutions', 31.
[26] Botsman, *Punishment and Power*, 141, 143; Karl-Friedrich Lenz, 'Penal Law', in Wilhelm Röhl, ed., *History of Law in Japan since 1868* (Leiden: Brill, 2005), 608–10 (607–26); Ogawa and Tomeoka, 'Prisons and Prisoners', 307–9.
[27] Lenz, 'Penal Law', 608–10; Hiramatsu, 'History of Penal Institutions', 10–16, 19–21; Sakata, 'Japan in the Eighteenth and Nineteenth Centuries', 319–20; Sakata, 'The Transformation of Hokkaido', 13–14.

transportations.[28] They included a man called Kenshi Okunomiya, who later wrote of his experiences of Kabato. He appreciated its openness, which meant that he was able to talk, read, and study. Meantime, the prison administration exploited his education, putting him to work in conducting a survey of the prisoners.[29] With the exception of the small number of political offenders, the gender, age, and sentencing profile of the ordinary Hokkaido convicts suggests that there was no place in the *shūchikan* for those who were deemed unsuitable or unable, or who were not required, to undertake labour.

When Tsukigata was first appointed to the Kabato *shūchikan* of Hokkaido, he was instructed to use convicts to develop agriculture. Finding that neither they nor their warders possessed experience of farming, five years into his governorship he proposed that instead convicts should be employed in cutting down the forests and building a road connecting the inland areas to the island's ports. Writing of the potential for Hokkaido to become a 'northern paradise', he argued that this would benefit the free settlers who through the sale or grant of cleared land and better communications would be encouraged to migrate.[30] Sakata has argued that Tsukigata's change in perspective instigated a fundamental shift in Japanese policy: from earlier ideas about the potential value of convicts as settlers, which were modelled on British, French, and Russian

---

[28] Hiramatsu, 'History of Penal Institutions', 33–6; Lorenz Ködderitzsch, 'The Courts of Law, Appendix: Execution of Penalty', in Wilhelm Röhl, ed., *History of Law in Japan since 1868* (Leiden: Brill, 2005), 760 (711–69); Sakata, 'Japan in the Eighteenth and Nineteenth Centuries', 321–2. Convict transportation statistics (which exist for the period 1886–1903 only) are located at: Kabato shūchikan, ed., 'Kabato shūchikan enkaku ryakki', in Asahikawashi henshū kaigi, ed., *Shin Asahikawashishi* 6 (c. 1892) (Asahikawa: Asahikawashi, 1993), 526–7; *Hokkaidō shūchikan tōkeisho* (3 vols) (Tokyo: Hokkaidō shūchikan, 1892–94); *Hokkaidō shūchikan nenpō* (Tokyo: Hokkaidō shūchikan, 1896–1900), 5–9. I thank Minako Sakata for these and subsequent Japanese-language references. The reference to 12-year minimum sentences is from William W. Curtis, *Applied Christianity in Hokkaido: An attempt at prison reform in Japan* (Boston, MA: American Board of Commissioners for Foreign Missions, n.d. [c. 1894]), 2. Note also that high-ranking police officer Motohiro Onoda's study of European prison design influenced the architecture of the *shūchikan*.

[29] Kenshi Okunomiya, 'Gokuri no Ware', in Kenshi Okunomiya, ed., *Okunomiya Kenshi Zenshū* (Tokyo: Kōryūsha, 1988), 157, 159–60 (141–70). Okunomiya was a civil rights activist, sentenced to penal servitude for life in 1887. He was in Kabato *shūchikan* during the period 1889–97, when he was released in the amnesty that followed the Empress Dowager Eishō's death. His memoir 'Gokuri no Ware' was published serially in the *Tōkyō Shimbun* [newspaper] in 1897. However, he was arrested again in 1910, sentenced to death, and executed in 1911. Minako Sakata kindly supplied this reference and information.

[30] Sakata, 'Japan in the Eighteenth and Nineteenth Centuries', 233. See also National Diet Library, Tokyo: Kiyoshi Tsukigata, 'Hokkaidō kaitaku shigi', c. 1885; Tsukigata Kabato Museum Archives: Kiyoshi Tsukigata, 'Hokkaidō shūchikan no yakushūjigyō nitsuki jōshin', c. 1885.

history and policy, to a focus on the use of convicts to anticipate later free migration from the Japanese mainland. This was made stark in the question submitted by Japan to the St Petersburg International Penitentiary Congress in 1890, the first to which it sent a delegation. It asked whether convicts should undergo a period of severe incarceration on the mainland, before they were sent into transportation 'to occupy uncultivated land for colonization'.[31] Japan's changing views can be seen in its subsequent alteration of its policy on ex-convicts. Government initially envisaged their release in Hokkaido, as settlers. In 1896, it decided that instead they would be sent back to Tokyo.[32]

In common with its European contemporaries, by the end of the nineteenth century the Meiji government viewed penal work, accompanied by 'moral education', as a means of convict reform. In 1888, the Prison Society of Japan was established, and though participation remained voluntary, it encouraged religious instruction in jails. Initially, Buddhist, Shinto, and Confucian priests were present among prisoners, and after 1878 they were joined by Christian chaplains.[33] This was influenced by the Christian warden of Kushiro, Terusaki Oinoue, who later became general superintendent of all the Hokkaido *shūchikan*. Around the year 1894, Oinoue welcomed the famous American missionary William W. Curtis on a tour of Hokkaido, and he noted that Christian chaplaincy in the *shūchikan* had been pioneered by one of the first converts in Japan, Taneaki Hara. Earlier, Hara had been a seller of woodblock prints in Tokyo but was sentenced to three months' imprisonment in 1883 for commissioning an anti-government print. Shocked by his experiences, after his release he devoted himself to prison work. Curtis claimed that the writings of contemporary reformers such as E. C. Wines had greatly influenced Hara, and that he had even entered into

---

[31] C. D. Randall, *The Fourth International Prison Congress St. Petersburg, Russia* (Washington DC: Government Printing Office, 1891), 85. The delegates were: Nishi Tokujiro (chairman and envoy extraordinary), Katchi Masuo (secretary to the envoy), and Omae Taizo (assistant diplomat). See excerpt from 'Government Gazette', *Dainippon Kangoku Kyōkai Zasshi*, 23 (vol. 3, issue 3, 1890). I am grateful to Takashi Miyamoto for kindly supplying translations from the *Bulletin of the Association for Japanese Penitentiaries*, here and below. Note that Japan also sent a delegation to the Paris congress in 1895. *Report of the Delegates of the United States to the Fifth International Prison Congress held at Paris, France, in July, 1895* (Washington DC: Government Printing Office, 1896), 20.

[32] W. W. Curtis, 'Prison Reform in Japan', *Missionary Herald* (June 1896), 237 (235–7); W. W. Curtis, 'Prison Reform in Japan', *The Missionary Review of the World*, 22 (1899), 656–7 (649–58). In the intervening period, a few locally convicted juveniles from Hakodate prison were discharged into the care of a prison chaplain, Wada Yoshihide. He rented a piece of government land, and the ex-prisoners reclaimed it for agriculture. See Mankichi Sugimoto, 'Reformatory Projects in Hokkaido', *Dainippon Kangoku Kyōkai Zasshi*, 29 (vol. 3, issue 9, 1890), 46.

[33] Ködderitzsch, 'The Courts of Law, Appendix', 764–5.

correspondence with the New York Prison Society (see also Chapter 7). In 1884, Hara became chaplain of Kobe prison, from where he went to Hokkaido with a group of convicts being transferred to Kushiro. He visited the sulphur mine at Atosanupuri, where conditions were dreadful and afterwards called upon Oinoue to end the use of convict labour there. Oinoue was so impressed that he appointed him chaplain of Kobe prison. Oinoue converted to Christianity, and the two men granted prisoners books, including religious texts like *Seisho no Tomo* (*Bible Friend*). Buddhist and Confucian teaching remained important too. Curtis wrote of religious quotations hung in each cell: 'These aphorisms, selected by the warden or the instructor, look the men in the face as they enter their cells day by day until they are thoroughly familiar, then are replaced by new ones.' Curtis described how each prison had a chapel or hall, and on Sundays prisoners received a compulsory 'moral address'. Optional Sunday schools combined Bible study and classes in Shintoism, Buddhist scripture, and classic Confucian texts. In 1895, Oinoue appointed Reverend Kosuke Tomeoka to Sorachi. He went to the USA to study prison reform and visited seventy penal institutions. While Tomeoka was away, control of the prisons was transferred from the Hokkaido Department to the central government. In the climate of jingoism during the Sino-Japanese War (1894–5), the government accused Oinoue of disloyalty. It appointed a new general superintendent of all five prisons and withdrew the Christian chaplains. Tomeoka subsequently found work in Tokyo's Sugamo prison. There, he established an aid organization for some of the 16,000 prisoners (including from Hokkaido) who were released under amnesty when the Empress Dowager Eishō died in 1897.[34]

In terms of labour, each of the five *shūchikan* was associated with a different form of outdoor work (Map 3.2). Kabato and Tokachi prisons were largely agricultural, and Abashiri supplied road labour. Sorachi was the base for the Horonai mine, and Kuchero for the Atosanupuri sulphur mine. Rates of mortality and morbidity were so high in the latter that it only lasted for two years, after which production was switched to road building, land clearance, and the construction of housing for *tondenhei* (solder-settlers). A key feature of the system in Hokkaido during its first ten years was that convicts could be hired out to settlers. However, this

---

[34] Curtis, *Applied Christianity in Hokkaido*, 2–12 (quotes, 4); 'Prison Reform in Japan'; W. W. Curtis, 'Japan Mission: Prison Work in the Hokkaido', *Missionary Herald* (November 1896), 486–7. See also Botsman, *Punishment and Power*, 191–3; Hiramatsu, 'History of Penal Institutions', 53–4. Prisoner Kenshi Okunomiya also described the chaplains in his memoir 'Gokuri no Ware', 162–9.

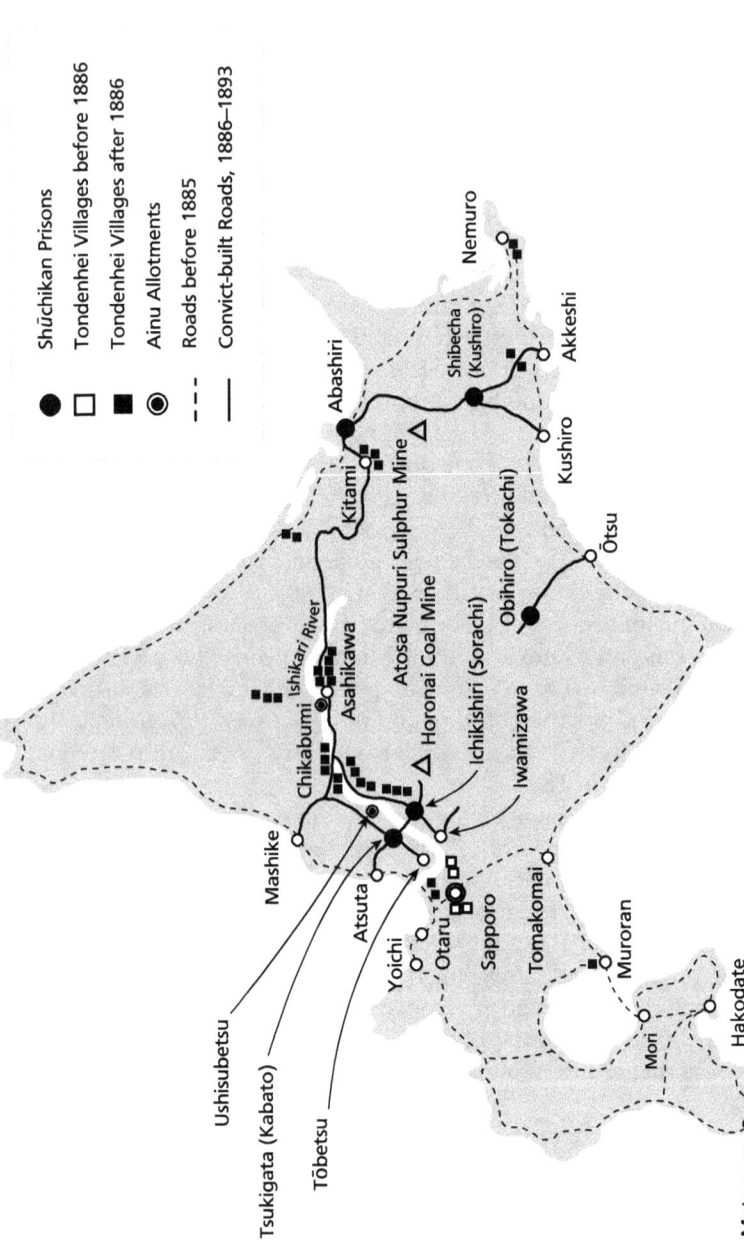

Map 3.2 Hokkaido's *shūchikan*, showing road building and *tondenhei* villages
Note: Thanks go to Minako Sakata, whose research underpinned this map.

went into decline because it was seen as contrary to good discipline.[35] It is important to appreciate in particular the nature and scale of convict road building. Governor Takeshiro Nagayama had observed convicts working on the Trans-Siberian railway in Russia and supported the employment of convicts on the roads in Hokkaido. This history is deadly: in 1891 almost half of the convicts labouring on the Chuo-Doro road, which connected Abashari to central Hokkaido, died.[36] Also, note that as in European empires, convict and military labour were strongly related. During the period 1891–96, the Japanese government established eighteen *tondenhei* villages in Hokkaido. These soldier-settlers were used not for military purposes, but in parallel with the transportation convicts as a labour force.[37]

The history of Japanese convict labour is remarkable. Convicts cleared forests to create agricultural settlements and used the logs for building purposes. They built roads, bridges, canals, schools, and lodging houses. Each *shūchikan* also incorporated workshops engaging convicts in carpentry, ironwork, coopering, tailoring, and the manufacture of shoes, harnesses, saddles, and tools. Prisons also had machinery for rice cleaning and produced the dietary staples of *miso* (soya bean paste) and soya sauce. The missionary Curtis claimed that in order to prevent competition with the free market, such products were not sold outside the prisons.[38] However, there existed shops which sold convict-made goods, and similarly to purchases made from the Bermuda hulks settlers bought storage chests, Buddhist altars (*butsudan*), iron braziers, and kettles.[39] Examples of these manufactures were even exhibited at the 1891 St Petersburg International Prison Congress, alongside those of other nations.[40] They may have included objects such as toothpicks and rosaries, or miniature representations of *geta* (sandals) and bottles, which convicts made out of materials such as wood, seeds, and gourds (Figures 3.2 and 3.3).

---

[35] Hiramatsu, 'History of Penal Institutions', 37.
[36] This is revealed in the dramatic fall in the number of convicts in Abashiri: 1,200 in 1891 (the year the prison opened), 769 in 1892, and following the arrival of a replacement supply of convicts, 1,288 in 1893. Sakata, 'Japan in the Eighteenth and Nineteenth Centuries', 321. See also *The Largest and Oldest Prison Museum in Japan* (Abashiri: Abashiri Prison Museum, 2015), 4.
[37] Hiramatsu, 'History of Penal Institutions', 33–6. See also Sakata, 'Japan in the Eighteenth and Nineteenth centuries', 322.
[38] Curtis, *Applied Christianity in Hokkaido*, 3.
[39] Chiaki Oguchi, *Nihonjin no sōtaiteki kankyōkan: 'konomarenai kūkan' no rekishichirigaku* (Tokyo: Kokon shoin, 2002), 45–6 (25–55).
[40] Randall, *The Fourth International Prison Congress*, 103; Curtis, *Applied Christianity in Hokkaido*, 2; Exhibitions at the International Prison Congress', *Dainippon Kangoku Kyōkai Zasshi*, 23 (vol. 3, issue 3, 1890).

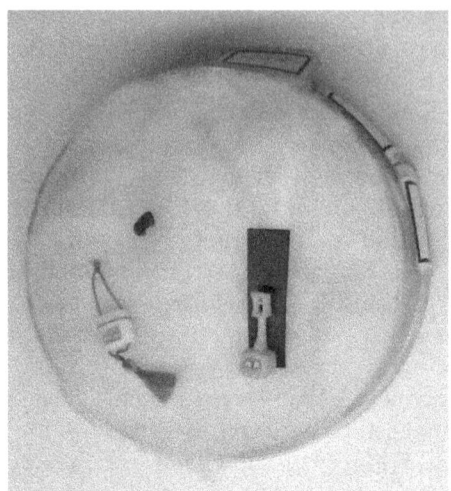

Figure 3.2 Miniature *geta* (sandals) and *shamisen* (musical instrument)
Source: Kabato Museum, Tsukigata. Photograph by the author, 2014.

Figure 3.3 Rosary, made from plum seeds
Source: Kabato Museum, Tsukigata. Photograph by the author, 2014.

A late nineteenth-century study of the Horonai convict mine by professor of criminal law Asatarō Okada provides important insights into convict experiences of labour. Okada found sanitation and ventilation inadequate, discipline ineffective, and illness and injury commonplace. Indeed, he reported that between 1884 and 1885 between a quarter and one third of the convicts suffered work injuries. A feature of the mine was that convicts worked alongside free labourers, and Okada criticized the ease with which convicts were able to obtain luxuries like tobacco. Compared to prisoners, he noted, they were subject to little supervision and therefore were able to distil liquor, leading to gambling and what Okada described as indecency. It is perhaps no coincidence that Sorachi prison closed in the same year that Okada published his critique.[41]

By encouraging free settlement through land clearance and infrastructural development, the *shūchikan* were successful in their promotion of dramatic population growth. Between 1883 and 1897, the population in Abashiri doubled; and in Tokachi, it rose 21-fold.[42] Meantime, as the number of free settlers grew, complaints about convicts mounted. Anti-transportationists in government started to critique road gang labour, and settlers wished to distance themselves from convicts, blaming them for crime. Government began to argue that the presence of convicts deterred what it considered as more desirable free migration. However, the abolition of convict transportation came gradually. It was instigated with the 1897 amnesty, after the death of the Empress Dowager. Sorachi and Kushiro *shūchikan* closed in 1901, and in 1907 the penal code was revised and the transportation system was altogether abolished.[43] The demise of penal transportation to Hokkaido is thus explained not by any increase in humanitarian concern, but by the emergence of an alternative labour force of settlers willing to work for very low wages. This was particularly important because though the Japanese state oversaw road gangs and other kinds of infrastructural labour, it chartered private companies to undertake engineering works and mining, and those companies hired convicts at a rate of ten per cent of a free worker's wage. This meant that once there was a surplus of workers, and wages fell, free labour could compete economically with convict transportation, even though paid workers remained subject to a harsh regime. Thus, not only did the employment of convicts by contractors in turn-of-the-century Hokkaido

---

[41] Ködderitzsch, 'The Courts of Law, Appendix', 766.
[42] Sakata, 'Japan in the Eighteenth and Nineteenth centuries', 322.
[43] Hiramatsu, 'History of Penal Institutions', 42. Both villages ultimately combined to form present-day Urausu. The new penal code came into force in 1908. See Ködderitzsch, 'The Courts of Law, Appendix', 769; Hiramatsu, 'History of Penal Institutions', 47–8.

facilitate capital accumulation, the convict system underpinned ongoing exploitation in the labour market.[44]

The appeal of mobile convict labour, however, proved remarkably enduring. Twenty-five years later, following Japan's military occupation of Chinese Manchuria in 1933, government again used Japanese prisoners to work on railway and road construction intended to bolster national security. When the Sino-Japanese war broke out in 1937, to support the Pacific War effort convicts were put to work on naval installations in eastern Hokkaido and airbases on the South Sea Islands. Following the occupation of the Hainan Islands in 1939, the Japanese shipped convicts from its new colonies in Korea and Taiwan to work in the mines and construct a naval railway. Though the Japanese expressed the view that such labour would be a route to the citizenship of Koreans and Taiwanese, it is clear that they were sent to the most dangerous sites and were exposed to much greater levels of violence than their mainland counterparts. Many died. As Sakata argues: 'Hokkaido was the point of departure of the wartime convict labour regime, which, in turn, was a legacy of nineteenth-century convict labour practice.'[45]

'Internal' Penal and Agricultural Colonies

Beyond Japan, other polities enforced sentences of imprisonment or penal servitude through the movement of prisoners to remote inland spots or offshore islands. Between the fifteenth and seventeenth centuries, through a practice known as *sürgün*, the Ottomans shipped thousands of convicts including from Anatolia to Cyprus and the Balkans, around the Balkans, and from the Balkans to Constantinople (Istanbul) and Anatolia. Many of them worked in construction, playing an especially important role following the conquest of Constantinople in 1453. Stephan Steiner argues that the system provided considerable incentives and prospects for both the destination states and the *sürgün*s. This distinguished it from later deportations of the Habsburgs (1526–1918), which was more concerned with getting rid of unwanted elements of the population than using convicts as pioneer settlers.[46] Nonetheless, the latter provides an interesting example of punitive

---

[44] Osamu Tanaka, 'Shihonshugi kakuritsuki Hokkaidō ni okeru rōdō keitai: Shūjin rōdō o chūshin toshite', *Keizaironshū* (March 1955), 67–112. In an interesting parallel, in 1873 prisoners in Miike jail were put to work in the coal mine of the same name. In 1889, the Japanese government handed the mine over to the private company Mitsui, which leased prison labour until 1931, following the signing of the International Labor Organization's convention on forced labour. See Miyamoto, 'Convict Labor and Its Commemoration', 3–5.

[45] Sakata, 'The Transformation of Hokkaido', 129.

[46] Stephan Steiner, '"An Austrian Cayenne": Convict Labour and Deportation in the Habsburg Empire of the Early Modern Period', in Christian G. De Vito and Alex Lichtenstein, eds., *Global Convict Labour* (Leiden: Brill, 2015), 139–42 (126–43).

mobility during this period, because it targeted women in particular and, though ultimately it proved economically unprofitable, it established gendered divisions of penal labour. Between 1744 and 1768, the Habsburgs passed over 3,000 sentences of *temesvarer wasserschub* (deportation by water). A *keuschheitskommission* (committee of chastity) rounded up sex workers and so-called *liederliche weiber* (women of ill repute), alongside vagrants, petty offenders, religious dissenters (including Protestants), and political insurgents. They came not just from Vienna, but from all over the Holy Roman Empire, and they were relocated in Transylvania or the Banat of Timişoara, the same Balkan sites previously used by the Ottomans. There were four types of penal labour. Women were employed in workhouses at spinning and knitting. Men worked on the streets of Timişoara, cleaning the streets and sewers, digging trenches, and maintaining fortifications. Minor offenders, including both men and women, were sent out to the countryside, working with local farmers, artisans, and merchants. Steiner describes the continuous deportations along the Danube river as 'the most extended forced migration activity *ever* on an institutionalised basis in Central Europe.'[47]

As noted in Chapter 1, by the sixteenth century the 'penal bondage' associated with workhouses, galleys, and public works had become an important form of punishment in the Netherlands, Britain, and France.[48] From the eighteenth century, France, Italy, and Spain sent convicts to dockyard prisons (known in French as *bagnes*), and central and northern European states set up public works in the interior. As Mary Gibson and Ilaria Poerio explain: 'reformers recast the value of outdoor work from that of repression through painful heavy labour to reform through healthy occupations in the countryside'. These new penal locations were often in rural areas that were separated from towns and cities by land or water, and they confined people under both criminal sentence and preventative detention. This included convicts from North African colonies such as Libya.[49] So far, the book has demonstrated that there was a pattern whereby convicts and other criminalized populations across a wide range of contexts experienced punitive mobility in very similar ways. In the nineteenth century, this began to change with the emergence of isolated penal settlements that blended features of incarceration and

---

[47] Steiner, "An Austrian Cayenne", 132–8 (quote, 132). Emphasis in the original.
[48] Pieter Spierenburg, 'Prison and Convict Labour in Early Modern Europe', in De Vito and Lichtenstein, eds., *Global Convict Labour*, 108–25.
[49] Mary Gibson and Ilaria Poerio, 'Modern Europe, 1750–1950', in Anderson, ed., *A Global History of Convicts and Penal Colonies*, 338 (337–70). See also Mary Gibson, *Italian Prisons in the Age of Positivism, 1861–1914* (London: Bloomsbury, 2019), 133–5, 204–7, and Francesca Di Pasquale, 'The "Other" at Home: Deportation and Transportation of Libyans to Italy During the Colonial Era (1911–1943)', *International Review of Social History*, 63, S26 (2018), 211–31.

removal over land or sea. Subsequently, internal penal colonies began to replace the more diffuse carceral approach of the earlier period.

Following unification (*risorgimento*) in 1871, for example, the Italian government established eight islands of police exile (*domicilio coatto*). These islands received ordinary and political convicts, sentenced through a separate non-judicial system, and including vagrants, beggars, anarchists, and socialists. There was not enough work on the islands for all of them, and for this reason Gibson and Poerio describe the *domicilio coatto* as 'a strange hybrid system' of confinement without labour or rehabilitation.[50] Nonetheless, by the start of the twentieth century Italy had set up further penal colonies, mainly on islands, including the previously deserted Pianosa, as well as Gorgona and parts of Sicily and Sardinia. Convicts were used to prepare land and infrastructure for much-desired free settler farmers, and worked in reclaiming land, cultivation, animal husbandry, and building houses.[51] This change is apparent in various imperial locations too, including in the British Empire. In 1843, for instance, the colony of British Guiana inaugurated Her Majesty's Penal Settlement Mazaruni in an isolated upriver location. A decade later, neighbouring Trinidad set up an identical establishment in the Irois Forest. Both engaged convicts in resource extraction, including of granite and timber.[52] Most famous of all, perhaps, was Robben Island, which from the seventeenth century was used by the Netherlands VOC and then by the British, in the latter case as a destination for locally convicted offenders and as a holding place for convicts awaiting transportation to the Australian colonies.[53] Further, Britain extended techniques of penal confinement to new

---

[50] Gibson and Poerio, 'Modern Europe', 343.
[51] Gibson and Poerio, 'Modern Europe', 347; Francesca Di Pasquale, 'On the Edge of Penal Colonies: Castiadas (Sardinia) and the "Redemption" of the Land', *International Review of Social History*, 64, 3 (2019), 427–44. Similarly, by the third quarter of the nineteenth century, Greece's sole penitentiary was on the island of Corfu. See E. C. Wines, ed., *Transactions of the Third National Prison Reform Congress, held at Saint Louis, Missouri, May 13–16, 1874: Being the third annual report of the National Prison Association of the United States* (New York: Office of the Association, 1874), 483.
[52] TNA CO111/177: Governor Henry Light, British Guiana, to Lord Stanley, secretary of state for war and the colonies, 15 March 1841, enc. Court of Policy, 4 March 1841; TNA CO111/203: Light to Stanley, 16 October 1843; TNA CO295/197: Governor Robert Keate, Trinidad, to Henry Labouchere, secretary of state for the colonies, 21 December 1857.
[53] Harriet Deacon, ed., *The Island: A history of Robben Island 1488–1990* (Cape Town: David Philip, 1997). On Britain's use of the island as a local prison and transportation holding depot in the nineteenth century, see Clare Anderson, 'Convicts, Carcerality and Cape Colony Connections in the 19th Century', *Journal of Southern African Studies*, 42, 3 (2016), 429– 42. Following independence from Britain in 1961, the new Republic of South Africa reinvigorated the island as a site for the incarceration of political prisoners.

kinds of governance and management across empire, including of Indigenous peoples, famine and plague victims, so-called hereditary criminals, and migrant workers in breach of labour laws.[54] In another imperial context, Congo Free State, the Belgians developed *colonies agricoles pour relégués dangereux* (*CARD*, or agricultural colonies for dangerous repeat offenders). Famous among them was a remote jungle site called Ekafera, for *relégués* (repeat offenders), including religious rebels. This was a place of relocation as well as containment, for sentencing implied removal over long distances. Ekafera and other *CARD* sites existed in parallel with forced labour, incarceration, and fertility clinics set up to control family life. As Nancy Rose Hunt has shown, Congolese people observed their 'semi-captivity' and the 'camp-like' character of their lives.[55]

From the start of the nineteenth century, the newly independent nations of Chile, Argentina, Brazil, and Mexico also began to relocate and exploit convict labour in order to effect the economic development of offshore islands (Map 3.3). Jane Rausch has connected this to contemporary continental European institutions. She suggests that Latin American representatives first learned about agricultural penal colonies in Italy at the American National Congress of Penitentiary and Reformatory Discipline, held in Cincinnati in 1870.[56] Ricardo D. Salvatore and Carlos Aguirre have shown that there were important continuities between pre- and post-independence punitive practices in Latin America, notably regarding convict mobility. However, in the later period, penal relocation was repurposed to produce regimes in which states used punishment to control social protest and discipline the working poor, to extend national frontiers, and develop export industries. Moreover, national governments established penal colonies at different times, and for different reasons, and their efforts did not always meet with success.[57] During the colonial period, the Spanish

---

[54] Aidan Forth, *Barbed-Wire Imperialism: Britain's empire of camps, 1876–1903* (Oakland: University of California Press, 2017); Cole Harris, *Making Native Space: Colonialism, resistance and reserves in British Columbia* (Vancouver: University of British Columbia Press, 2002); Vijayalakshmi Teelock, ed., *The Vagrant Depot of Grand River, its Surroundings and Vagrancy in British Mauritius* (Port Louis: University of Mauritius Press, 2004).

[55] Nancy Rose Hunt, *A Nervous State: Violence, remedies, and reverie in colonial Congo* (Durham, NC: Duke University Press, 2016), 167–77, 185–8, 195–7.

[56] Jane M. Rausch, 'Using Convicts to Settle the Frontier: A Comparison of Agricultural Penal Colonies as Tropical Frontier Institutions in Twentieth-Century Colombia', *SECOLAS Annals*, 34 (2002), 27. For the proceedings of the Congress, see *Transactions of the National Congress of Penitentiary and Reformatory Discipline, held at Cincinnati, Ohio, October 12–18 1870, edited by E. C. Wines, Chairman of the Publishing Committee* (Albany, OH: The Argus Company, 1871).

[57] Richard D. Salvatore and Carlos Aguirre, 'Colonies of Settlement or Places of Banishment and Torment? Penal Colonies and Convict Labour in Latin America,

Map 3.3 Convict mobility in post-independence Latin America. I am grateful for Christian De Vito's assistance in the production of this map.

Crown had sent convicts (*destierro*) from the Viceroyalty of Peru and the Captaincy General of Chile to the Juan Fernández islands. It released the

<blockquote>
c. 1800–1940', in De Vito and Lichtenstein, eds., *Global Convict Labour*, 275, 306 (273–309). See also Ryan C. Edwards, 'Post-Colonial Latin America, since 1800', in Anderson, ed., *A Global History of Convicts and Penal Colonies*, 249–56 (245–70).
</blockquote>

convicts upon arrival, with basic provisions, and they had to find their own livelihood. Following independence (1810–18), Chile continued to send convicts to Juan Fernández, including political prisoners. A succession of mutinies rocked the islands, from the 1820s to early 1850s, and conditions were so poor that convicts often acted in concert with their soldier guards. During the first half of the nineteenth century, government tried and failed to attract free settlers or set up private industries. It was the economic failure of the islands, together with the impact of ongoing and violent convict revolts and escapes, that led to their closure in 1852. Chile did not transport convicts to the islands for another fifty years, when it established a penal colony at Más Afuera. This remained open until 1930.[58]

Quite different was Argentina's penal colony in Tierra del Fuego, the Ushuaia penitentiary (*Penal de Ushuaia*). Ryan Edwards has described it as 'a combination of internal settler colony and town of forced migration'.[59] Established in 1895, Ushuaia remained open until 1947. President Julio A. Roca noted its model was Britain's Australian penal colonies. Argentina's ultimate objective was to secure sovereignty in the region, and the idea was that following sentences of hard labour, convicts would become settlers. In the meantime, there was what Edwards calls 'a co-constitutive relationship between penology and forestry' in the development of the frontier. Work in the forests followed by chopping wood were the most common convict occupations, the latter keeping the settlement's stoves and furnaces burning in the face of the bitter cold.[60] Convicts were also employed in the construction of a radial penitentiary, using local materials. This opened in 1902, though initially attempts to implement a system of penal stages failed. This was because the demand for timber in the prison and the neighbouring town was so high than in practice convicts often went out to work in the forests with little supervision. By the 1920s, however, such a regime was in place, founded on the principles of positivist thinking, and the idea that work was rehabilitative. Convicts were separated according to their crime, attended school, and put to work. Inside the penitentiary, in common with other global sites of

---

[58] Salvatore and Aguirre, 'Colonies of Settlement or Places of Banishment and Torment?', 275–82. The Juan Fernández islands are otherwise famous as the place where Alexander Selkirk was shipwrecked. This is said to have been the origin of Daniel Defoe's *Robinson Crusoe* (1719). Salvatore and Aguirre draw on the important nineteenth-century history by Benjamin Vicuña Mackenna: *Juan Fernández, Historia verdadera de la isla de Robinson Crusoe* (Santiago de Chile: Rafael Gover, 1883).

[59] Ryan Edwards, 'From the Depths of Patagonia: The Ushuaia Penal Colony and the Nature of "The End of the World"', *Hispanic American Historical Review*, 94, 2 (2014), 276 (271–302).

[60] Ryan C. Edwards, 'Convicts and conservation: inmate labor, fires and forestry in southernmost Argentina', *Journal of Historical Geography*, 56 (2017), 1, 6–9 (1–13).

transportation at the turn of the twentieth century, convicts worked. Not only did they continue to supply firewood for the *Penal* and town, they worked at occupations including carpentry, ironwork, and shoemaking. They also made bricks, furniture, uniforms, and paper. Some convicts were sent out to public works labour, and constructed streets, pavements, sewage systems, and the harbour, as well as houses for free settlers. Though the convicts were engaged in productive labour, Argentina only partially satisfied its objective of penal colonization. The isolation of Tierra del Fuego meant that few ex-convicts wanted to settle, even though government offered land grants and their labour was in high demand. Government never realized plans to encourage marriage between convicts and Indigenous women. On the other hand, Ushuaia relied on convict labour for public works, free settlers relied on the penitentiary for employment, and businesses made profits from supplying the penitentiary with various goods. Salvatore and Aguirre write: 'the town of Ushuaia grew in time to become a city ... thanks to the systematic and disciplined work of convicts'. Though perhaps it was senior prison personnel and local businessmen who most benefitted from land grants, the importance of the penal colony was such that by the time the penitentiary closed in 1948, Tierra del Fuego was fully incorporated into Argentinian territory.[61]

In regard to international influence and the operation and limitations of punishment, labour, and rehabilitation, there are some parallels between Ushuaia and Brazil's Fernando de Noronha, as described in Chapter 1. Both also shared features with Mexico's penal colony of Islas Marías, which opened in 1908. In this case, the Mexican government was relatively unconcerned with using convicts as colonizers. Many were petty thieves (*rateros*), their deportation ordered administratively rather than by a criminal court.[62] They worked in a range of occupations, including in quarries and construction, cutting firewood, and as farmers and pearl divers, as well as in prison workshops. Bad behaviour was punishable with assignment to severe labour, working in the salt quarries, which convicts called *infierno blanco* (white hell). Some convicts could be hired out to free enterprise, including in the timber industry. Finally, as in Ushuaia, a large settlement grew up around the penal colony. Unlike the Argentinian case, and despite Mexico's initial disinterest in penal colonization, numerous ex-convicts settled in Islas Marías, either bringing their families from the

---

[61] Salvatore and Aguirre, 'Colonies of Settlement or Places of Banishment and Torment?', 283–90 (quote, 289). See also Edwards, 'Post-Colonial Latin America', 255–6; Edwards, 'From the Depths of Patagonia, 288.
[62] Edwards, 'Post-Colonial Latin America', 253.

mainland or marrying locally. The islands were not far from the mainland, and this made them far more attractive to settlers than the wilds of Patagonia.[63]

The penal colony of El Frontón, just off the coast of Callao in Peru, was different again. It was one of three main penal institutions, alongside the Lima penitentiary and Guadalupe jail, each of which contained inmates of different legal status. Opened in the late 1910s, El Frontón received *rematados* (prisoners sentenced to different terms), *penitenciados* (sentenced to serve in a penitentiary), political prisoners (including strikers), and vagrants. The convicts worked in the island's quarries (*canteras*), and they cut stone used for construction purposes in rapidly developing Lima. If there was a convict population of at least 250, El Frontón turned a profit. This economic imperative underpinned both the transfer of prisoners from Guadalupe, when numbers dipped, and from 1925 to 1928 the mass deportations of vagrants, when Peru's vagrancy laws were at their height. Despite the productive value of convict labour, political detainees and visitors to El Frontón reported on such horrific conditions that Aguirre has argued that it was akin to 'a quasi-slave plantation'. Indeed, he notes 'torments and tortures ... to an extent difficult to find in the other prisons'. Convicts were starving and shoeless. Buildings were in poor condition, overcrowded, and infested with vermin. Guards put recalcitrant convicts in the *lobera*, a natural cave which exposed them to the ocean, or *la parade*, a vertical hole carved out of stone. Director of El Frontón 1921–5, Hermilio Hergueras, apparently wrote that convicts 'have to work themselves to death while they are at the Island'.[64]

During this period, convict relocation in Latin America coexisted with other forms of migration, including from China. This is especially relevant to understanding the motivation for the creation of inland penal agricultural colonies in nations such as Colombia, Ecuador, and Bolivia. Governments used convicts – and vagrants – alongside free migrants to push state frontiers into the interior, at the same time claiming them to be sites of penal reform through labour. In the first decades of the twentieth century, for example, Colombia set up agricultural penal colonies to develop the eastern tropical plains of Los Llanos (Acacías in Meta, 1922–present) and following war with Peru it did the same on the Amazonian frontier (Araracuara in Caquetá, 1937–71). In Acacías, convicts were put to work in development, cultivation, and processing of

---

[63] Salvatore and Aguirre, 'Colonies of Settlement or Places of Banishment and Torment?', 298, 303–4.

[64] Carlos Aguirre, *The Criminals of Lima and Their Worlds: The prison experience, 1850–1935* (Durham, DC: Duke University Press, 2005), 104–7, 111–12 (quotes, 106, 107).

sugar. They were supposed to receive free land grants upon completion of their sentences, but they did not, and so most returned home. However, the presence of the penal colony did encourage later free migration. The case of Araracuara was somewhat different, because it was in a remote and isolated location. Free migration did not follow, but the settlement both encouraged the return of Indigenous peoples previously pushed out of the area through rubber extraction and firmly established the Colombian presence in the region.[65]

*

This chapter has argued that a key element of punitive relocation across new and expansionist nations was the exploitation of convict labour for the occupation and development of frontier territories, including inland and offshore on islands. Nation states employed convicts in an extraordinarily wide range of occupations, often alongside other marginal populations who were themselves criminalized. This work was in some cases connected to, and in others overrode, other goals of punishment, deterrence, and reform. In contexts as diverse as Japan and Colombia, governments used convicts as colonizers, hoping that they would prepare the land and infrastructure necessary to encourage free migration. However, the rhythm of punitive relocation varied considerably, for it was dependent on the balance between the governance of populations and economic goals. This is revealed in the case of China, as also in Italy, Japan, and Peru's El Frontón, and more generally in the relationship between punitive relocation, the larger economy and population structures.

As in the imperial contexts noted in Chapter 2, some governments viewed convicts as an expendable workforce, and this was reflected in the choice of working environments, the violence of punitive sites, and high convict death rates in some locations. By the 1800s, however, other contemporaries started to view work as a key element of rehabilitation, and there was considerable global interchange in ideas and practices of convict management. Over time, there developed a tendency to separate convicts from other workers, creating distinct working patterns and institutions. As in the later European colonies, administrations sometimes introduced penal classes based on sentence served and good behaviour. In some places, including Hokkaido as described in the present chapter and Bermuda (see Chapter 2), religious education became important. Opening Part II of the book, Chapter 7 takes further the theme of

---

[65] Edwards, 'Post-Colonial Latin America', 254. See also: Rausch, 'Using Convicts to Settle the Frontier', 26–48.

governance, in its analysis of the global nature of discussions and innovations in convict management. In the meantime, Chapter 4 picks up some of the earlier discussion on convicts and other labour regimes, centring on the relationship between punitive mobility and one related and very specific category of labour: enslavement.

4 Enslavement, Banishment, and Penal Transportation

During the eighteenth and early nineteenth centuries, Britain's West Indian sugar colonies routinely subjected enslaved populations to banishment and penal transportation, sending them to far away littorals and islands. As Chapter 2 suggested, this was part of a pattern of relationality between punitive mobility and the management of colonial labour globally. In the Caribbean, British magistrates sentenced and resold enslaved runaways, rebels, and lawbreakers to Spanish colonies like Puerto Rico and Cuba, and to the Danish colony of St Thomas. They also instigated mass banishments and transportations, following so-called conspiracies and plots, and revolts, including to British settlements and colonies in Honduras, Sierra Leone, and Australia. Commonly, the British sentenced the leaders of uprisings to death, deporting those who turned informer, or who the courts (or courts martial) deemed less culpable. From the eighteenth century, this was routine in numerous places, including Antigua (1729, 1736), Tobago (1774, 1801), Jamaica (1760, 1776, 1796, 1806), Saint Vincent (1796), and Grenada (1797).[1]

This chapter opens with an examination of the history of banishment and penal transportation in the British Caribbean. It highlights their use in the management of enslaved people and reveals the mechanisms through which enslaved convicts moved around the region, including to territories occupied by French, Spanish, and Danish settlers. It will show that the question of how to punish free and enslaved people sentenced to transportation became a key element of the larger question of legal reform in the British Caribbean, following the abolition of the slave trade in 1807 and the reform of the 'Bloody Code' in England in the 1820s. The place of transportation within a framework of the amelioration of enslavement (c. 1823–38) was important to these legal discussions.[2] The second part of the chapter moves on to construct a detailed narrative of the penal

---

[1] Michael Craton, *Testing the Chains: Resistance to Slavery in the British West Indies* (Ithaca, NY: Cornell University Press, 1982), *passim* and chapters 21 and 22.

[2] PP 1826–27 (559) *Criminal and civil justice in the West Indies. (Second series.) First report of the commissioners of enquiry into the administration of criminal and civil justice in the West Indies. Jamaica: Abstract of Statute Law of Jamaica*; PP 1828 (577) *Criminal and civil justice in the West*

transportation of a group of over one hundred enslaved rebels in the aftermath of the Barbados Rebellion of 1816. This includes the refusal of the superintendent of Honduras to land them, their near shipwreck in the Bahamas, and their arrival and fate at their final destination: Sierra Leone. The chapter presents the conviction and journey of the 1816 rebels as an allegory for a slave voyage in reverse. It uses it as an entry point into an examination of the connections between, and the multi-directional circulations associated, with enslavement, imperial governmentality, penal transportation, and other forms of colonial bondage and repression. It positions the enslaved rebels at the heart of this story of entanglement.[3] Also significant is the role of the British superintendent and commander of the settlement of Honduras, George Arthur who, like other colonial officials, fostered a wide range of transnational carceral links and mobilities. Such administrators moved around the repressive spaces of empire, stationed in the African and Creole slave colonies of the Caribbean, the largely European and Irish convict colonies of Australia, and the Asian penal settlements scattered across the littorals and islands of the Bay of Bengal and the Indian Ocean. In consequence, they created common languages and practices for the discipline and management of both enslaved and convict labour, and Indigenous peoples. The Barbadian rebels, meantime, maintained and created their own lines and networks of filiation and association, expressing cultural and spatial creativity and agency in seemingly unpromising circumstances.

Enslavement, law, and punishment

By the start of the nineteenth century, there were established systems for the penal transportation of enslaved persons in many parts of the British

---

Indies and South America. (Second series.) Second report of the Commissioners of Enquiry into the Administration of Criminal and Civil Justice in the West Indies and South American Colonies. United colony of Demerara and Essequebo, and colony of Berbice; PP 1829 (334) *Criminal and civil justice in the West Indies and South America. Second series. Third report of the commissioners of inquiry into the administration of criminal and civil justice in the West Indies and South American colonies. Honduras and the Bahama islands;* PP 1826–7 (36) *Third report of the commissioner of inquiry into the administration of civil and criminal justice in the West Indies. Antigua, Montserrat, Nevis, St. Christopher, and the Virgin Islands. General conclusions;* PP 1826–27 (551) *Trinidad. Report of His Majesty's commissioners of legal enquiry on the colony of Trinidad.* An excellent summary of the reports is: *Substance of the Three Reports of the Commissioner of Inquiry, into the Administration of Civil and Criminal Justice in the West Indies, extracted from the parliamentary paper, with the general conclusions, and the commissioner's scheme of improvement, complete and in full* (London: Joseph Butterworth and Son, 1827).

[3] There are parallels with the mobility of the Jamaican maroons here, which Fortin describes as having a 'ripple effect' across the Atlantic World. See Jeffrey A. Fortin, '"Blackened Beyond Our Native Hue": Removal, Identity and the Trelawney Maroons on the Margins of the Atlantic World, 1796–1800', *Citizenship Studies*, 10, 1 (2006), 7 (5–34).

Caribbean. At the forefront of the desire to ship rebels or lawbreakers out of the colonies, as well as the legislation for other penal measures which even colonial administrators recognized 'sound harshly to the English ear', was the influence of revolution in Saint-Domingue (now, Haiti) and, to a lesser degree, the winning of independence in Spanish America (1808–26). The prospect of enslaved people overthrowing colonial regimes was terrifying to Caribbean plantation owners, who used law and punishment to deter insurgency. As is evident from a focus on the largest British Caribbean colony, Jamaica, in regard to the sentence of penal transportation, the system was neither extra-judicial nor ad hoc. The 1696 Slave Code specified transportation as a punishment for a wide range of felonies. Slave courts in each parish tried enslaved persons. Three justices of the peace, assisted by a jury of twelve, heard transportation offences, and for conviction the jury's verdict had to be unanimous. If sentenced to transportation, juries valued each enslaved person, with the maximum set at £100 or £50 in the case of runaways.[4] This played a useful role in plantation economies because it compensated masters for loss of property in a way that other punishments did not, with the key exception of the death sentence. Almost certainly, government set the lower rate for runaways to discourage slave owners from using the courts to get rid of enslaved men and women who routinely absconded from work. However, the use of banishment and transportation to punish absconding was part of an empire-wide pattern of labour management. Indeed, transportation convicts in the Australian colonies also faced sentence extensions in ways that those punished for other crimes did not. This was especially the case for women.[5] In the Caribbean, Diana Paton's meticulous research suggests that between 1802 and 1825 alone, parish slave courts in Jamaica sentenced almost 700 enslaved men and women to transportation.[6]

---

[4] PP 1826–27 (559) *First report of the commissioners of enquiry ... Jamaica*, 34, 41–2, 80, Appendix D: Answers of the Judge of the Vice Admiralty Court (William Roden Rennals), 238. The inclusion of the punishment of transportation in the slave code is noted in Jonathan Dalby, *Crime and Punishment in Jamaica, 1756–1856* (Mona, Jamaica: University of the West Indies Press, 2000), 78. In British Guiana, the maximum valuation for all enslaved persons sentenced to transportation was 1,000 guilders, or approximately £70. See PP 1828 (577) *Second report of the Commissioners of Enquiry ... United colony of Demerara and Essequebo, and colony of Berbice*, iv.

[5] Hamish Maxwell-Stewart and Michael Quinlan, 'Female Convict Labour and Absconding Rates in Colonial Australia', *Tasmanian Historical Studies*, 22 (2017), 19–36; Hamish Maxwell-Stewart and Michael Quinlan, 'Voting with Their Feet: Absconding and Labor Exploitation in Convict Australia', in Marcus Rediker, Titas Chakraborty, and Matthias van Rossum, eds., *A Global History of Runaways: Workers, Mobility, and Capitalism, 1600–1850* (Oakland: University of California Press, 2019), 156–77. Thanks to Hamish Maxwell-Stewart for this insight.

[6] Diana Paton, 'An "Injurious" Population: Caribbean-Australian Penal Transportation and Imperial Racial Politics', *Cultural and Social History*, 5, 4 (2008), 458n14 (449–64).

Following conviction, the governor of the colony reviewed the indictment (formal accusation), evidence, and sentence, and either reprieved, pardoned, or commuted the sentence, or issued a transportation warrant. The provost marshal sold the enslaved person, and used the proceeds, minus any costs, to pay their former owner the value of their human property. If the sale did not cover their full value, the receiver general paid the slave owner the difference.[7] It is important to note that judicial transportation did not emancipate enslaved persons. In law, a compensatory payment to a slave owner was 'a purchase at the public expense', which transferred enslaved persons to the property of the king. This legal position was clarified during the Colonial Office's consideration of the 1833 case of two enslaved men, George Hackett and Joseph Denny, who were sentenced to execution in Barbados and subsequently pardoned because of 'technical objections'. Permanent Counsel James Stephen proposed that government sell them, so that on 1 August 1834, when the Slavery Abolition Act came into force, they would become apprentices to their purchasers.[8] In the meantime, a system of bonds ensured that transportations took place. The purchaser of the enslaved person delivered to the provost marshal the very large sum of £500, showing the profits that could be made from the conviction of enslaved persons, and gave an oath that he would transport them within thirty days. Into the early nineteenth century, purchasers usually took transportation slaves to the Spanish colonies, including what was described as 'the Spanish main', likely the neighbouring coast of the Spanish Viceroyalty of New Granada, or else the islands of Puerto Rico and Cuba. Their new owners employed them in what one contemporary described as 'severe' hard labour, including in the mineral and metal mines in these locations.[9]

If an enslaved person was still in Jamaica thirty days after their supposed shipment, the bond would be forfeited, and the enslaved person would appear before a justice of the peace who would direct their resale for transportation. There were also measures to prevent enslaved persons' return. Anybody who knowingly brought a transportation slave back to Jamaica, or organized, aided, or assisted their return would be fined the

---

[7] TNA CO23/91/9 18 January 1834: James Stephen, assistant under-secretary of state for the colonies, 'Disposal of Colonial Convicts', n.d. Famously, James Stephen was the architect of the 1833 Slavery Abolition Act.
[8] TNA CO28/112 (Law Officers): legal opinion, James Stephen, permanent counsel Colonial Office, 18 September 1833.
[9] TNA CO23/91/9 18 January 1834: 'Disposal of Colonial Convicts'. New Granada incorporated the territories of present-day Colombia, Ecuador, Panama, and Venezuela, as well as parts of Brazil, Guyana, and Peru. Today, the sum of £500 would be worth over £30,000.

sum of £300 and be sent to prison for between three and twelve months.[10] After Britain's abolition of the slave trade in 1807, the ships on which such transportation slaves travelled needed copies of the appropriate paperwork, for otherwise the enslaved persons could be seized as illegally trafficked. Indeed, in 1826, vice-admiralty court judge William Roden Rennals recalled the condemnation of a ship carrying sixteen enslaved persons into transportation in Cuba, two years after the abolition of the slave trade in 1807. The ship had proof that they were transportation convicts, but they did not have certified copies of the judgements, which the law required to prove they were not being illegally trafficked.[11] The court thus condemned the ship, and it is likely that the men on board were impressed into labour apprenticeship in Jamaica or another colony, in the same way as those men, women, and children who were taken from illegal slave trading vessels at this time and known as Liberated Africans.[12]

There are glimpses in the archives of who the enslaved men and women sold into transportation in Jamaica were. One case followed the discovery of a plot in St George's parish in 1806. One enslaved man, Marcus, had told others about the revolution in Saint-Domingue, allegedly urged on by a French planter who told them that they would be free under French rule. The British executed him, together with another enslaved man, Tom. They condemned five others, Romulus, Perigrine, Captain, Anthony Gutzmir, and Adam Williamson, to transportation. As in several other cases, it is unclear whether their sentences were carried out.[13] Slave

---

[10] PP 1826–27 (559) *First report of the commissioners of enquiry . . . Jamaica*, 34, 41–2, 80, 238. £300 is equivalent to around £18,000 today.

[11] PP 1826–27 (559) *First report of the commissioners of enquiry . . . Jamaica*, 34, 41–2, 80, 238.

[12] Richard Anderson and Henry B. Lovejoy, eds., *Liberated Africans and the Abolition of the Slave Trade, 1807–1896* (New York: University of Rochester Press, 2020); Richard Anderson, 'The Diaspora of Sierra Leone's Liberated Africans: Enlistment, Forced Migration, and "Liberation" at Freetown, 1808–1863', *African Economic History*, 41 (2013), 103–40; Marina Carter, V. Govinden, and S. Peerthum, *The Last Slaves: Liberated Africans in 19th-Century Mauritius* (Port Louis, Mauritius: Centre for Research on Indian Ocean Societies, 2003); Bronwen Everill, *Abolition and Empire in Sierra Leone and Liberia* (Basingstoke: Palgrave, 2012); Anita Rupprecht, '"When he gets among his Countrymen, they tell him that he is free": Slave Trade Abolition, Indentured Africans and a Royal Commission', *Slavery and Abolition*, 33, 3 (2012), 435–55; Anita Rupprecht, 'From slavery to indenture: scripts for slavery's endings', in Catherine Hall, Nicholas Draper, and Keith McClelland, eds., *Emancipation and the Remaking of the British Imperial World* (Manchester University Press, 2014), 77–97; Padraic X. Scanlan, 'The Colonial Rebirth of British Anti-Slavery: The Liberated African Villages of Sierra Leone, 1815–1824', *American Historical Review*, 121, 4 (2016), 1084–113; Padraic X. Scanlan, *Freedom's Debtors: British Antislavery in Sierra Leone in the Age of Revolution* (New Haven, CT: Yale University Press, 2017).

[13] TNA CO137/118/24: Governor Eyre Coote, Jamaica, to William Windham, secretary of state for war and the colonies, 20 February 1807, enc. Minutes of the Privy Council, 19 February 1807; Coote to Windham, 10 March 1807, enc. Minutes of the Privy Council, 9 March 1807.

Court records for the parishes of Hanover and Middlesex survive for the period 1819–23 and 1825 respectively and, though it is not clear whether these records are complete, it is possible to glean sentencing patterns. They show that the Hanover court sentenced a total of twenty-five men and two women to transportation for a range of felonies, including burglary, theft, and assault. It tried most of them (twenty) as 'frequent', 'incorrigible', 'notorious', or 'persistent' runaways. Though we know nothing about their experiences when on the run, evidently the colonial administration employed transportation as a deterrent against the unauthorized mobility of enslaved persons, and as a punishment for escape. In one Hanover case, a man called Tom had been absent for three whole years when he was tried and convicted. In another, a woman called Bell and a man called Cupid had frequently run away together. Robert, owned by a man called William Grant, broke into Grant's house, stealing shoes and a ham.[14] The men sentenced by the Middlesex court included two runaways referred to as Leicester and Liverpool, as well as a third man called George, sentenced for obeah, and Brown, for theft. The jury valued each of them at £50.[15] There are also three cases in 1823–4, where enslaved men received sentences of life transportation for escaping from Kingston workhouse. They were Tommy and York, described as 'very bad characters', and George. As in the cases above, the Slave Courts did not specify the destination – though they did sometimes note that if the enslaved persons returned to Jamaica, they would face the death penalty.[16]

Other islands in the Caribbean used the same transportation system as Jamaica. Montserrat and Saint Vincent, for example, also sold convicts to unspecified destinations. For instance, in 1821, three enslaved persons in Montserrat were found guilty of stealing money from the custom house and sentenced to transportation 'to any of the islands'. Saint Vincent sent convicts 'to some other part of the world', according to the judges'

---

[14] NAJ IA/2/1/1: Hanover Slave Court, Parish of Hanover.
[15] PP 1826–27 (559) *First report of the commissioners of enquiry ... Jamaica*, Appendix Q: Statement of Committals in the County Gaol of Middlesex, Jamaica, from 4 November 1825 to 21 February 1826, 342. Tom's case was heard on 10 July 1821, Bell and Cupid's on 9 July 1822, and Robert's on 26 September 1821. See NAJ IA/2/1/1 Hanover Slave Court. Obeah is a form of spiritual healing that was criminalized and subject to prosecution by the British. See Diana Paton, *The Cultural Politics of Obeah: Religion, Colonialism and Modernity in the Caribbean World* (Cambridge University Press, 2015). On court records in Jamaica generally, see Agnes Butterfield, 'Notes on the records of the supreme court, the chancery, and the vice-admiralty courts of Jamaica', *Bulletin of the Institute for Historical Research*, 15 (1938), 88–99.
[16] NAJ IB2/19: Port Royal, summary slave trials, 1819–34.

discretion.[17] Other islands specified the locations to which convicts should be sent. In one 1821 case, Grenada sentenced an enslaved convict called John Charles to Trinidad, for the crime of 'burning a negro house' at the Mount Rose estate. The main witness against him was another slave, Joseph. During the trial, John Charles complained that Joseph was having a relationship with his wife, and it seems that after John Charles had been transported, Joseph moved in with her. He subsequently argued with her family, and it was alleged at the time that he threatened to have her brother transported as well.[18] The Bahamas Slave Court sentenced enslaved convicts to be sold into transportation, specifically to Cuba.[19] On the other hand, Nevis and Honduras did not use transportation at all, and Saint Christopher (now, Saint Kitts) applied it only for capital respites (i.e. convicts sentenced to death but transported following commutation of sentence). Cases included that of an enslaved man, described as 'a black boy', who was sentenced to death for burglary but then pardoned by the governor. Thirteen further capital pardons during the period 1815–22 specified that offenders agree either to join the convict work gang or be subject to transportation.[20]

During this period, other colonies preferred sentences of banishment to transportation. Though they may have been legally distinct, in practice there was little difference between the enslaved's experiences of them. It seems that the first British settlers of Dominica, which the French transferred to Britain by the 1763 Treaty of Paris following the end of the Seven Years War, took with them enslaved people under sentences of banishment from other islands. According to the chief justice of Dominica, Thomas Atwood, they put them to work in clearing forest land. These enslaved persons had little shelter from the wet climate, and

---

[17] PP 1826–7 (36) *Third report of the commissioner of inquiry . . . Antigua, Montserrat, Nevis, St. Christopher, and the Virgin Islands. General conclusions*, 37, Appendix I, Examinations, 137; PP 1830–31 (334) *Gaols, West Indies. Copies of Correspondence relative to the State of the Gaols in the West Indies and the British Colonies in South America; and also, of any instructions which have been sent out from the Colonial Office relative to such Prisons, 30 March 1831*, 5, 14.

[18] PP 1826–7 (36) *Third report of the commissioner of inquiry . . . Antigua, Montserrat, Nevis, St. Christopher, and the Virgin Islands*, Appendix II, Documents Grenada, Guardians of St Patrick's to Major Sweeney, 30 September 1821, 274.

[19] PP 1829 (334) *Third report of the commissioners of inquiry . . . Honduras and the Bahama islands*, 32, 43, 70, Appendix A, Examinations, 121. Note that the maximum value of the transported slave was fixed at £60.

[20] PP 1826–7 (36) *Third report of the commissioner of inquiry . . . Antigua, Montserrat, Nevis, St. Christopher, and the Virgin Islands*, Appendix I, Examinations, 137; Appendix II, Documents Saint Christopher, Return of the Number of Slaves Convicted, Sentenced and Acquitted; from 1815 (when the Act passed giving them the benefit of Trial by Jury,) to 1822, 235; PP 1829 (334) *Third report of the commissioners of inquiry . . . Honduras and the Bahama islands*; Appendix A, Examinations, 89.

no previous experience of this kind of work. Many died, and others fled into the forests where they also perished.[21] In Antigua, the courts could order 'persons considered dangerous to the public peace' to leave the island for a destination of their own choosing.[22] Trinidad, which had been a Spanish colony until 1797, used Spanish law, which did not allow transportation. The island's courts instead used the penalty of banishment to an unspecified destination, selling convicts on the condition that purchasers remove them.[23] In the united colony of Demerara-Essequibo, created by the British after they had been ceded by the Netherlands, the British did not use transportation either. They followed Dutch-Roman law, considering all offences committed by enslaved persons as *crimen qualificatum*, or aggravated.[24] Demerara-Essequibo used banishment, in preference to transportation, for the punishment of enslaved people, sometimes in combination with other punishments like flogging, fines, or imprisonment. In keeping with British practice elsewhere, however, government compensated slave owners for their losses. British judges sent enslaved convicts over Little Abary Creek, the river which at the time separated Demerara-Essequibo from Berbice. Interesting details emerge from one recorded case of 1806. An enslaved man called Frederick, convicted of housebreaking, was on his way into banishment when he carried out a robbery on board the ship. The courts sentenced him to flogging, branding, and 50 years' work in chains. In 1825, he appears in the list of enslaved persons confined in the Demerara workhouse, together with another man, Adonis, also sentenced to flogging, branding, and banishment, for theft and receiving stolen goods. It seems that government had not banished Adonis, because 'no fit station could be found'.[25] The Commission of Legal Enquiry in the West Indies, which

---

[21] Thomas Atwood, *The History of the Island of Dominica: Containing a description of its situation, extent, climate, mountains, rivers, natural productions, &c. &c. Together with an account of the civil government, trade, laws, customs, and manners, of the different inhabitants of that island. Its conquest by the French, and restoration to the British dominions* (London: J. Johnson, 1791), 224–5.

[22] PP 1826–7 (36) *Third report of the commissioner of inquiry ... Antigua, Montserrat, Nevis, St. Christopher, and the Virgin Islands*, Appendix I, Examinations, 137.

[23] PP 1826–27 (551) *Trinidad. Report of His Majesty's commissioners of legal enquiry on the colony of Trinidad*, Appendix A, 11, 54–5. The island was formally ceded to the British by the Treaty of Amiens (1802). Note that the governor of Trinidad forbade the use of punishments permitted under Spanish but not under English law.

[24] This meant that enslaved and free people were treated entirely differently in the courts. This included the use of interrogations to elicit confessions, and a presumption of guilt should the accused take flight, practices which dated from the 16th century. See J. Henry, *Report on the Criminal Law at Demerara, and in the Ceded Dutch Colonies: drawn up by the desire of the Right Hon. The Earl Bathurst* (London: Henry Butterworth, 1821), 66, 100–1.

[25] PP 1828 (577) *Second report of the Commissioners of Enquiry ... United colony of Demerara and Essequebo, and colony of Berbice*, Appendix A: Examinations of the Public

carried out wide-ranging investigations during the period 1826–9, reported the Demerara fiscal's view that banishments were 'a mere mockery' of punishment.[26] In practice, as the chief justice of Trinidad also testified during the enquiry, it enabled colonies to reciprocally exchange convicts with each other and did not seem to deter against or reduce crime.[27]

All these cases relate to the punishment of individuals, or small groups of individuals, who appeared before Slave Courts. What of those men and women who the British tried and convicted for acts of collective rebellion or treason? From as early as the 1730s, the British banished enslaved 'conspirators' in Antigua to Saint Kitts and Danish Saint Croix.[28] Here, let us explore the mass deportations that followed Fédon's Rebellion in British Grenada in 1795–6, for they offer especially detailed insights into the debates and controversies that surrounded the implementation of the punishment at the end of the eighteenth century. The 1763 Treaty of Paris had ceded Grenada to Britain, alongside Dominica, but many free inhabitants remained loyal to the French. Inspired by the revolutions in France and Saint-Domingue, and led by the 'free coloured' planter Julien Fédon, in 1795 men and women from all communities including the enslaved broke out in open revolt in support of the new French republic. It took the British a year to regain control of the island. With 6,000 enslaved and 1,000 free people dead, as Kit Candlin has shown, it was 'the deadliest slave revolt in the history of the British Caribbean'.[29]

Under commission from King George III, in 1796, Lieutenant-Governor Alexander Houston set up a special court, known as the Court of Oyer and

---

Functionaries of Demerara and Berbice, 138, 144; Appendix T: Return from the Colony Workhouse, Demerara, List of slaves confined in the Colony Workhouse of Demerara, 12 February 1825, 270–1. Prior to his conviction for housebreaking, Frederick had a previous conviction, for highway robbery, for which he had been flogged and branded. Note that in 1831, Demerara, Essequibo, and Berbice merged to form the colony of British Guiana.

[26] PP 1828 (577) *Second report of the Commissioners of Enquiry ... United colony of Demerara and Essequebo, and colony of Berbice*, Abstract of the Examinations of the several Public Functionaries connected with the Administration of Justice in the United Colony of Demerara and *Essequibo*, and the Colony of *Berbice:*- With Observations thereon, 14. The fiscal of Demerara was the public prosecutor.

[27] TNA CO318/69: Commissioners of Legal Enquiry in the West Indies, Volume 13, Report on Trinidad, 18 June 1827.

[28] Craton, *Testing the Chains*, 119–20.

[29] Kit Candlin, *The Last Caribbean Frontier, 1795–1815* (Basingstoke: Palgrave, 2012), chapter 1; Kit Candlin, 'The role of the enslaved in the "Fedon Rebellion" of 1795', *Slavery and Abolition*, 39, 4 (2018), 685–707. See also Edward L. Cox, 'Fedon's Rebellion 1795–96: Causes and Consequences', *The Journal of Negro History*, 67, 1 (1982), 7–19; Craton, *Testing the Chains*, 207–10.

Terminer, to try the rebels for treason.[30] But the court exercised far more than the judicial powers invested in it, leading Home Secretary the Duke of Portland to criticize its 'extraordinary and unparalleled proceedings'. He wrote: 'I should never have thought it possible that the Spirit of Revenge could have possessed itself of British Minds, and I should have been more apprehensive of the Lenity than of the Severity of my Countrymen.'[31] Indeed, despite ordering the execution of 14 rebels, it continued to pass capital sentences, and refused condemned men the right of appeal. Portland accused it of attacking the rights of the king's representative (the governor) and confusing the office of judge and executioner. 'I am really at a loss for terms to express my indignation and astonishment', he wrote.[32] Shortly afterwards, the court was dissolved, because of what Houston's successor Charles Green described as 'some informality of proceedings'. He commissioned a second court.[33] In the meantime, Portland had directed Houston to deport the rebels, ideally by sending them to France or any part of Europe then under French control.[34] However, before these instructions arrived, Houston had asked Admiral Henry Harvey, commander-in-chief of the naval station in the Leeward Islands, to take the rebel slaves into naval service. He had refused and so Houston had put them to work on the roads and fortifications.[35]

Lieutenant-Governor Green issued a commission for the establishment of a third Court of Oyer and Terminer, and this began hearing cases in June 1797.[36] This court found 3 white and 59 'free coloured' people guilty of high treason, but Green respited the capital sentences on the condition that they banish themselves for life from all British territories.[37] By this time, another 100 enslaved persons had been sentenced to death by the first two courts, but they were reprieved on condition of transportation. Government paid John and James McBurnie the vast sum of £2,000 to take all of them away, ordering the men not to land them anywhere to the east of Cuba, in any British colony, 'or in any other than a civilized country.' It requested reports of the date and location of

[30] TNA CO101/34/48 4 July 1796: Lieutenant-Governor Alexander Houston, Grenada, to John King, under-secretary of state Home Office, 4 July 1796. Courts of Oyer and Terminer also heard felony cases (violent offences).
[31] TNA CO101/34/49 n.d. August 1796: William Cavendish-Bentinck (3rd Duke of Portland), home secretary, to Houston, n.d. August 1796.
[32] TNA CO101/34/49 n.d. August 1796: Portland to Houston, n.d. August 1796.
[33] TNA CO101/35: Governor Charles Green, Grenada, to Portland, 27 May 1797.
[34] TNA CO101/34/49 n.d. August 1796: Portland to Houston, n.d. August 1796.
[35] TNA CO101/34/54 16 September 1796: Houston to Portland, 16 September 1796.
[36] TNA CO101/35: Green to Portland, 27 May 1797.
[37] TNA CO101/35/19 24 June 1797: Green to Portland, 24 June 1797; TNA CO101/35/20 12 July 1797: Green to Portland, 12 July 1797, enc. The Petition of the Prisoners now confined in Gaol and under sentence of Death, n.d.

everyone's disembarkation.[38] Other than the Fédon banishments and transportations, the most famous case of mass deportation followed the conclusion of the Second Maroon War in Jamaica in 1796. After the passing of an Act of Deportation, the British sent around 1,500 maroons to Nova Scotia. Four years later, it transferred them to Sierra Leone, where it employed some of them in colonial policing. Indeed, across empire the British routinely employed particular kinds of convicts as policemen or overseers, including men who had previously served in the military in British India and the Australian colonies. In Sierra Leone, by 1841 most of the maroons had left the colony and returned to Jamaica.[39]

It is difficult to track the fate of individuals who were sentenced to banishment, sold into transportation, or deported. However, in some cases it is evident that they did not become compliant in the hands of their new owners. Some of the enslaved people sent overseas for rebellion carried political desires, as well as social and cultural practices, with them. The theme of punitive mobility as a vector for politics and religion is taken forward in Chapter 6. Here, note that two of the Antiguans sent to Danish Saint Croix in 1737, Sam Hector (alias Quaw) and George Foot, were among the leaders of the slave revolt in the island in 1759.[40] 'Coromantees', enslaved Akan people originating from the Gold Coast (now, Ghana) and who were shipped to Honduras after Tacky's revolt in Jamaica (1760), rebelled in its British enclave later that decade.[41] In other cases, banishment and transportation appears to have constituted a collective experience, which fostered cultural cohesion. Following the Second Carib War of 1795–6, in Saint Vincent, for instance, the British banished a staggering 5,000 'Coromantees' and 'Black Caribs', or Garifuna, descended from Indigenous Amerindians and Africans, to the offshore island of Balliceaux, among other localities. From there, it transferred some of them to the island of Roatán, a Spanish possession off the

---

[38] TNA CO101/35/20 12 July 1797: Green to Portland, 12 July 1797, enc. Grenada: agreement for shipping, 5 July 1797; TNA CO101/35/24 13 September 1797: Portland to Green, 13 September 1797.

[39] Mavis C. Campbell, *Back to Africa. George Ross and the Maroons: From Nova Scotia to Sierra Leone* (Trenton, NJ: Africa World Press, 1993); Ruma Chopra, *Almost Home: Maroons between Slavery and Freedom in Jamaica, Nova Scotia, and Sierra Leone* (New Haven, CT: Yale University Press, 2018); Craton, *Testing the Chains*, chapter 17; Fortin, "'Blackened Beyond Our Native Hue'"; John N. Grant, *The Maroons in Nova Scotia* (Halifax, NS: Formac Publishing Company Ltd, 2002); James W. St. G. Walker, *The Black Loyalists. The search for a promised land in Nova Scotia and Sierra Leone, 1783–1870* (New York: Africana Publishing and Dalhousie University Press, 1976).

[40] Craton, *Testing the Chains*, 124. Note that in the seventeenth and eighteenth centuries, the Danish also sent convicts to Saint Croix. See Johan Heinsen, *Mutiny in the Danish Atlantic World: Convicts, Sailors and a Dissonant Empire* (London: Bloomsbury, 2017).

[41] Craton, *Testing the Chains*, 140.

Honduras coast. From Roatán, the banished men and women moved themselves onto the mainland, first to the port of Truxillo (now, Trujillo), and then by 1802 southwards along the Mosquito (Miskito) coast, then part of the viceroyalty of New Spain. They carried various Saint Vincent customs with them, including the celebration of festivities at Christmas and food ways. According to the census of 1861, the 'Black Caribs' numbered 1,825. Subsequently, they flourished, and today constitute what Michael Craton has described as 'the nearest approximation to a truly Afro-American *nation* in the Caribbean region'. The population is around 40,000 strong, spread mainly across Honduras, Belize, and Guatemala, with smaller numbers elsewhere in Central America.[42]

From Barbados to Sierra Leone, via Honduras

On the evening of Easter Sunday, 14 April 1816, the British Caribbean island of Barbados erupted in a well-planned slave uprising, which has since become known as Bussa's Revolt. It began in St Philip and quickly spread to other parishes. Enslaved men and women including the ranger (head slave) Bussa (Busso) and carpenter King Wiltshire on Bayleys plantation, and a driver and a domestic at Simmons estate, Jackey and Nanny Grig, led 400 men and women into rebellion, setting ablaze one fifth of the sugar cane in the island, destroying other property, and forcing plantation owners and their families to take flight. Three free black men – Cain Davis, Roach, and Richard Sergeant – mobilized support and assisted them. Barbados was the most established of Britain's sugar colonies, and in a context where enslaved men and women outnumbered the white population by almost five to one, the British responded swiftly and with severity. They enacted murderous reprisals and placed the island under martial law, quashing the rebellion within just three days. Around 200 people died in fighting with British troops, and in the aftermath of the revolt the British executed 144 more – mainly enslaved people but also a handful of free black men. It hanged about half of them in the fields. As the Barbados House of Assembly's official enquiry put it, the rebellion was 'a rude shock' to the colony and resulted in British losses calculated at a massive £170,000.[43]

---

[42] Craton, *Testing the Chains*, 138, 204–7 (quote, 207). See also Nigel O. Bolland, *The Formation of a Colonial Society: Belize, from conquest to Crown colony* (Baltimore, MD: Johns Hopkins University Press: 1977), 3. Mid-nineteenth-century descriptions of the 'Black Caribs' can be found in John Young, *Narrative of a Residence on the Mosquito Shore, with an account of Truxillo, and the adjacent islands of Bonacca and Roatan; and a vocabulary of the Mosquitian language* (London: Smith, Elder and Co., 1847), 130–5.

[43] TNA CO28/85 30 April 1816: Governor James Leith, Barbados, to Henry Bathurst (1st Earl Bathurst), secretary of state for war and the colonies, 30 April 1816; Edward Codd, military commander Barbados, to Leith, 25 April 1816; TNA CO28/85

The motivations of the rebels were undoubtedly mixed and were and remain contested. This was because the official enquiry took a pro-slavery position, and because British troops killed many of the leaders during the revolt who otherwise would have given testimony. According to the military commander of the island, Colonel Edward Codd, enslaved people believed that following abolitionist William Wilberforce's introduction of the Slave Registry Bill in 1815, demanding for the first time their registration, the British parliament desired their emancipation, but the island's planters were withholding it. There is evidence for this in the proceedings of the courts martial, which interrogated slaves about their motivations, and in clergymen's discussions with the condemned men who they attended at the scaffold. But it is also clear from the House of Assembly's enquiry that the success of the 1791–1804 revolution in French Saint-Domingue – the only slave uprising in history to overthrow a colonial government – was an influence. The witnessing of enslaved people in this regard reveals the Barbados revolt as part of a much larger struggle for black emancipation in the Caribbean.[44] Indeed, Colonel Codd informed the governor that the rebels had told him: 'the Island belonged to them, and not to white men'. He added that they had flown a flag on which they had drawn a picture of a black man marrying a white woman (Figure 4.1). This 'served to inflame the passions', for it was a visual statement of an imperial world turned upside down.[45]

---

21 September 1816: Leith to Bathurst, 21 September 1816; *The Report From A Select Committee of the House of Assembly, appointed to inquire into the origin, causes, and progress, of the late insurrection* (Barbados: W. Walker, Mercury and Gazette Office/London: T. Cadell and W. Davies, 1818), 3–4. £170,000 equates to at least £6 million today. See also Hilary McD. Beckles, *Bussa: The 1816 Revolution in Barbados* (Cave Hill and St Ann's Garrison, Barbados: University of the West Indies and Barbados Museum and Historical Society: 1998); Hilary McD. Beckles, 'The Slave-Drivers War: Bussa and the 1816 Barbados Slave Rebellion', *Boletín de Estudios Latinoamericanos y del Caribe*, 39 (1985), 85–110; Michael Craton, *Testing the Chains*, chapter 20.

[44] *The Report From A Select Committee of the House of Assembly*, 5–6, 10–12, 34–7, 56–7. On the process of courts martial during the revolt, see Jerome S. Handler and Ronald Hughes, 'The 1816 Slave Revolt in Barbados and the Petition of Samuel Hall Lord', *Journal of the Barbados Museum and Historical Society*, 47 (2001), 267–86. On differing accounts of the rebellion, see David Lambert, 'Producing/ Contesting whiteness: rebellion, anti-slavery and enslavement in Barbados, 1816', *Geoforum*, 36 (2005), 35–40 (29–43). Note that following the revolution, Saint-Domingue was renamed Haiti.

[45] TNA CO28/85 30 April 1816: Codd to Leith, 25 April 1816. Leith's aide-de-camp reported in October that there remained 'considerable alarm' among white women in the island. See TNA CO28/85 21 October 1816: Thomas Moody, late aide-de-camp to Leith (now deceased), to Bathurst, 20 October 1816; TNA MFQ1/112; TNA ADM1/337 (enc. in despatch from Admiral John Harvey, 30 April 1816). Three years later in 1819, the 1st Viscount Combermere (Stapleton Cotton), governor of Barbados, informed Bathurst of the discovery of a flag dating from the time of the insurrection, by a doctor visiting a sick female slave. Its motto was 'Royal Sufferers', and was taken to commemorate those executed after the 1816 rebellion. Combermere wrote: 'Three bloody hands, three keys, and three lions rampant, disposed in some thing like heraldic

Enslavement, Banishment, and Penal Transportation

Figure 4.1 Sketches of a flag taken from the insurgent slaves at Barbados, 1816
Source: The National Archives, Kew: MFQ1/112.
Note: The text reads, anti-clockwise from the top: 'happiness Remains forever with endavourance', 'G[eorge]R[eins] Royal endavourance for: E Ver', 'endavourance for ever', 'happiness for ever remain with endavourance', 'Bretanier are happy it lead any such Sons as endavourance', 'GOD Allways saves endavourance'. The images are: an African drum (on which is inscribed 'GR'), a slave ship flying the English and royal navy flags, an African man (wearing the clothes of an English gentleman), an African couple (in a marriage ceremony?), a British admiral, holding a flag ('G[eorge]R[eins] Royal endavourance for: E Ver'), Britannia seated upon a lion, three crowns, two hatchets or battle axes, and two crossed flint locks (guns). I thank Hamish Maxwell-Stewart for assistance in identifying the weaponry illustrated here.

order, were interpreted to mean Revenge, Secrecy and Courage. The supporters were Justice, with her scales unequally poised, and blind folded on one side, and a negress dressed as a Huntress on the other.' See TNA CO28/88/1 15 January 1819: Combermere to Bathurst, 15 January 1819. Note that bloody hands can also represent tyranny, and keys freedom or liberation. The figure of the huntress is one of power.

By the autumn of 1816, around 100 men remained under sentence of death, but having restored British authority in the island, Governor James Leith was unwilling to carry out further hangings. His desire, as he put it in a letter to the Secretary of State for War and the Colonies the Earl Bathurst, was to 'blend moderation with severity', in order to guarantee 'safety and tranquillity'.[46] Leith referred the matter to the Legislative Council of Barbados, and it recommended the penal transportation of all those capitally convicted.[47] This left Leith with the problem of where they should go. He thought Vieques (Crab) Island, off Puerto Rico, was an idea site, for there was plentiful work available in felling timber. However, Britain had not occupied the island, and both Denmark and Spain had claims on it. He discounted both Sierra Leone and the island of Bulama, off the coast of what is now Guinea-Bissau, as too far away and expensive. Leith despaired that any other British or European colony would agree to accept the rebels, and so he asked the colonial secretary for directions. Bathurst ordered the men's transportation to Honduras. The appeal of this location lay in the fact that at this time no European power had formally claimed it, though from the late seventeenth century the British had granted themselves rights to fell timber and had begun importing enslaved workers to the detriment of the Indigenous Maya.[48] And so, on 25 January 1817, the British embarked 106 Barbados rebels and 18 other 'dangerous persons' on the ship *Francis May*, setting the sails for the coast of Central America. Though courts martial had sentenced

---

[46] TNA CO28/85 30 April 1816: Leith to Bathurst, 30 April 1816.
[47] TNA CO28/85 21 September 1816: Leith to Bathurst, 21 September 1816.
[48] TNA CO28/85 30 December 1816: Leith to Bathurst, 21 September 1816; Acting Governor John Spooner, Barbados, to Bathurst, 30 December 1816 (Governor Leith died in October 1816). The 1783 Treaty of Versailles gave the British rights to cut logwood in some areas of Honduras, and the 1786 Convention of London expanded these. A superintendent ran the British settlement of Honduras through tri-annual public meetings with the minority free population, after 1765 using regulations known as 'Burnaby's Code'. On Honduras, see Bolland, *The Formation of a Colonial Society*, 3, 6, 28–30. Note that the Spanish founded Vieques as a colony in 1843, and Puerto Rico annexed it in 1854. The uninhabited island of Bulama (now, Bolama) had been subject to a failed British attempt at colonization, in 1792–4. As in Sierra Leone, enslavement was illegal, and colonists envisaged it as a potential model for African freedom. Interestingly, the president of the colonization society, the Bulama association, was the mayor of London Paul Le Mesurier. He was pro-transportation, and may have been interested in the island following the closure of the American colonies to British and Irish convicts in 1775, and the subsequent failure of British transportation schemes to West Africa. See Deirdre Coleman, 'Bulama and Sierra Leone: Utopian islands and visionary interiors', in Rod Edmond and Vanessa Smith, eds., *Islands in History and Representation* (London: Routledge, 2003), 73 (63–80); Billy G. Smith, *Ship of Death: A voyage that changed the Atlantic world* (New Haven, CT: Yale University Press, 2013).

the 106 rebels, the remaining 18 had not been subject to judicial process. However, having been implicated in the rebellion, their owners had refused to take them back, fearing that their presence would ferment discontent on the plantations. The governor with the support of the Legislative Council decided to sentence them to banishment.[49] The legal status of this group, who had never stood trial, is somewhat murky. Equally opaque is whether their owners were paid compensation for their loss of property, which was usual practice.[50] The case of the Barbadians was unusual in other ways too, for the British did not resell them into slavery, as for other contemporary transportations in the Caribbean. President of the Council of Barbados, acting governor John Spooner, described them as 'slave convicts'.[51]

Spooner later reported that when the 124 Barbadian rebels were embarked on board the *Francis May* for transportation in January 1817, 'the greatest attention was paid to the comfort of these unhappy persons'. This included the supply of provisions, medicines and 'other necessaries' for the 21-day voyage.[52] The ship anchored in Honduras three weeks after it left the port of Bridgetown, on 17 February 1817, one man having died on the way (Figure 4.2).[53] Its arrival caused uproar. The Colonial Office had not given notice to the British superintendent and commander of the settlement, George Arthur. The magistrates (who represented the British settlers) thus boarded the *Frances May*, inspected the convicts, called a public meeting, and asked Arthur not to land them.[54] Arthur told the magistrates that he was duty bound to follow the orders of government, at the same time complaining to Bathurst that he had no secure place to confine the Barbadians and feared insurrection and loss of life.

---

[49] TNA CO28/86/2 4 February 1817: Spooner to Bathurst, 4 February 1817. All convicts were sent into transportation with paperwork that included details of their name, age, and conviction.

[50] For Jamaica, see PP 1826–27 (559) *Criminal and civil justice in the West Indies ... Jamaica*, 41. For British Guiana, see PP 1828 (577) *Criminal and civil justice in the West Indies and South America. (Second series.) ... United colony of Demerara and Essequebo, and colony of Berbice*, 272: 'Demerara Ordinance relating to slaves condemned by Sentence of Criminal Courts' (Appendix V), iv. There are no surviving records of the compensation paid to the owners of the enslaved Barbados rebels.

[51] TNA CO28/85/15 30 December 1816: Spooner to Bathurst, 30 December 1816.

[52] TNA CO28/86/2 4 February 1817: Spooner to Bathurst, 4 February 1817; CO123/26 26 February 1817: Instructions for the master of the ship Francis Mary, relative to the treatment of the convicts which he is to convey to the Bay of Honduras, n.d. Provisions consisted of ship bread, yams, cornmeal, salted fish, salt, rice, molasses, and ginger.

[53] TNA CO28/86/9 3 June 1817: Superintendent and Commander George Arthur, Honduras, to Bathurst, 3 June 1817.

[54] TNA CO28/86/9 3 June 1817: Spooner to Bathurst, 3 June 1817, enc. Arthur to Spooner, 17 March 1817; John Alder Burdon, *Archives of British Honduras, Volume II, From 1801 to 1840* (London: Sifton Praed and Co., 1934): Magistrates' Meetings, 17, 18, 20, 24 and 25 February 1817 (189–94).

Figure 4.2 A view in Belize, 1829
Source: Cambridge University Library, Royal Belize Almanack, 1829, Royal Commonwealth Society Case.d.391. Reproduced by kind permission of the Syndics of Cambridge University Library.

He wrote: '[T]he whole settlement has been thrown into a most alarming state of violence and convulsion.'[55] Shortly afterwards Arthur repeated this sentiment to acting governor Spooner in Barbados.[56] In the meantime, the Honduras magistrates sent their own letter of protest to Bathurst, in which they represented him as 'the author of this heavy Calamity and direful disgrace'. They feared that the convicts would join with Indigenous Amerindians and communities of maroon (escaped) slaves and overwhelm them.[57] The context for their fears was not just

---

[55] Burdon, *Archives of British Honduras, Volume II:* Magistrates' Meeting, 24 February 1817 (191–3); TNA CO123/26 26 February 1817: Arthur to Bathurst, 26 February 1817. On George Arthur in Honduras: see Alan Lester and Fae Dussart, *Colonization and the Origins of Humanitarian Governance: Protecting Aborigines across the nineteenth-century British empire* (Cambridge University Press, 2014), chapter 2.

[56] TNA CO28/86/9 2 June 1817: Arthur to Spooner, 17 March 1817. For a summary of events, see also A. G. L. Shaw, *Sir George Arthur, Bart, 1784–1854: Superintendent of British Honduras, Lieutenant-Governor of Van Diemen's Land and of Upper Canada, Governor of the Bombay Presidency* (Melbourne University Press, 1980), 27–8.

[57] Burdon, *Archives of British Honduras, Volume II:* Chairman, Public Meeting of Magistrates, to Bathurst, 26 February 1817 (194–8 [quote, 194]). See also TNA CO123/26

the role that the convicts had played in the Barbados rebellion, but the fact that at this time there were just 149 white settlers in Honduras, compared to 933 free 'people of colour' and 2742 enslaved persons. '[H]ow is all intercourse between them and the negroe population to be guarded against or avoided? & how can an intercourse subsist without Contamination?', the magistrates asked.[58]

Despite the uproar, in directing the transportation, Bathurst believed that he was following established practice.[59] The settlement's British residents were adamant that he was mistaken. To support their outrage, they directed the keeper of records in the settlement to look out evidence of their previous refusal to allow such shipments to land and represented their 'determined opposition ever to allow this Settlement to become a receptical [sic] for Convicts, and other dangerous Characters'.[60] Meantime, Arthur gave Bathurst two reasons for denying entry to the convicts. First, that the settlement had no code of laws or judicature, and so the British had no legal authority over its inhabitants. Second, in the past settlers had taken 'energetic measures' to prevent the introduction of convicts, passing regulations to this effect and requiring the masters of incoming vessels to take affidavits that they were not carrying them on board. These were dated 1792, 1793, 1802, 1809, and 1814, and had forbidden the landing of any person concerned in rebellion, or sent from a jail or workhouse, under pain of a fine of £500.[61]

---

26 February 1817: Marshall Bennett, Chairman of the Public, Honduras, to Bathurst, 26 February 1817, enc. Minutes from the public records of Honduras extracted and arranged by the magistrates, pointing out the measures which have from time to time been adopted by this community, to resist the introduction of convicts and others of a dangerous character into this settlement, drawn up at the request of the committee nominated by the public to address the Right Honorable Earl Bathurst upon the state of the country.

[58] Burdon, *Archives of British Honduras, Volume II:* Census, 1 December 1816 (188); Burdon, *Archives of British Honduras, Volume II:* Magistrates' Meeting, 25 February 1817 (193–4); Chairman, Public Meeting of Magistrates, to Bathurst, 26 February 1817 (197).

[59] Indeed, previously, Edward Long had noted flows of convicts from Jamaica to Honduras. See *The History of Jamaica or, General Survey of the Antient and Modern State of that Island, with Reflections on its Situation, Settlements, Inhabitants, Climate, Products, Commerce, Laws, and Government, Volume 2* (London: T. Lowndes, 1774), 462 (note). Long owned enslaved persons, and believed in polygenesis (the descent of humankind from different ancestors). His derogatory views on Africans were extreme even by the standards of the late eighteenth century.

[60] Burdon, *Archives of British Honduras, Volume II:* Magistrates' Meeting, 25 February 1817 (193–4); Chairman, Public Meeting of Magistrates, to Bathurst, 26 February 1817, 195.

[61] TNA CO123/26 26 February 1817: Arthur to Bathurst, 26 February 1817; TNA CO123/26 11 March 1817: Bathurst to Leith, 7 November 1816, Bennett to Bathurst, 26 February 1817; Burdon, *Archives of British Honduras, Volume II:* Magistrates' Meeting, 25 February 1817 (193–4).

Arthur's claims about the absence of a legal code, and the settlers' previous rejection of white convicts were not wholly true. In regard to the legal code, in 1765, the commanding officer of Jamaica William Burnaby had drawn up the civil law of the settlement. This included the establishment of courts of justice, with cases heard by five magistrates and a jury of 13, and agreement on the levying and collection of taxing and logging. Burnaby's Code, as it was called, was printed in 1809, growing to incorporate additional regulations and alterations as necessary. Though these regulations were not law, as a parliamentary commission of enquiry reported in 1829, it was 'by common consent of the inhabitants, considered as binding upon them, and as such are strictly acted upon and enforced'.[62]

The aftermath of the American revolutionary war (1775–83) provides important context for Arthur's second claim: that previously the settlement had refused to land shipments of white convicts. As noted earlier, following Independence, the American colonies refused to accept transportation convicts from Britain and Ireland. However, the courts continued to pass such sentences. By the second half of the 1780s, England's hulks were becoming increasingly overcrowded, and government was desperately looking for new transportation destinations. During that decade, it drafted prisoners into military service, and put them to work in slave forts on Africa's Gold Coast, including Cape Coast Castle. This was disastrous, and only a tiny handful of the few hundred men so transported survived. The British made plans to establish a further destination in the southwest of the continent (in present-day Namibia), at Das Voltas, though these were never realized. It was the failure of this African experiment in the context of the larger search for alternative transportation destinations which culminated, famously, in the sailing of the 'First Fleet' of convicts round the Cape and across the southern Indian Ocean to Botany Bay in 1787. This marked the founding of the first Australian penal colony, New South Wales.[63]

In the meantime, in 1784, after the newly independent American colonies had refused to accept them, 86 British convicts were diverted

---

[62] PP 1829 (334) *Third report of the commissioners of inquiry ... Honduras and the Bahama islands*, 3–6.
[63] Emma Christopher, *A Merciless Place: The lost story of Britain's convict disaster in Africa* (Oxford University Press, 2011); Emma Christopher and Hamish Maxwell-Stewart, 'Convict Transportation in Global Context, c. 1700–88', in Alison Bashford and Stuart McIntyre, eds., *The Cambridge History of Australia, Volume 1: Indigenous and colonial Australia* (Cambridge University Press, 2013), 68–90; Wilfrid Oldham, *Britain's Convicts to the Colonies* (Sydney, NSW: Library of Australian History, 1990), chapters 4 and 6.

from North America to Honduras on a ship called the *Mercury*.[64] The convicts threatened to overwhelm the free white population of Honduras, which at this time numbered fewer than twenty men. At first, the settlers would not allow the ship to anchor, and resolved to fine anybody who hired a convict £100 per man. Despite the initial furore, however, and in the context of the labour needs in the logging industry, the settlers eventually agreed to allow the convicts on shore. They put them to work in gangs: clearing land, building huts, and cutting wood. After further disputes about their fate, ultimately the settlers sold the convicts – presumably into contracts of indenture, as had been routine for British and Irish convicts sent to the Americas in the eighteenth century.[65] In a second case of 1785, the London-based merchant George Moore, who had a contract with government for convict transportation, sent another thirty convicts to Honduras on the *Fair American*. He planned to employ them in the settlement cutting logwood for his own profit. Home Secretary Lord Sydney warned the settlers not to land the convicts, though in fact they stayed for a month. It is not entirely clear what happened next. At the time, it was suggested that either they were removed from Honduras and left on the Spanish island of Cay Chapel, sold to a Jamaican and taken away, or distributed among the British settlers.[66] In a third case in 1791, settlers refused to land 217 insurgents sent by the French from Saint-Domingue to English Cay on *La Manuel*. They chartered two ships to take them back via Jamaica.[67] Finally, in 1802, Jamaica tried to send enslaved men imprisoned in Kingston jail to Honduras, suggesting that they could work as 'pioneers', the term then

---

[64] Mollie Gillen discusses the case of the *Mercury*, and the later cases discussed below, in 'The Botany Bay Decision, 1786: Convicts, Not Empire', *The English Historical Review*, 97, 385 (1982), 747–8 (740–66).

[65] John Burdon, *Archives of British Honduras: Volume I, From the earliest date to A.D. 1800* (London: Sifton Praed and Co., 1931): 'Private Records', Meeting of Inhabitants at a private house, 9 August 1784 (146).

[66] Burdon, *Archives of British Honduras: Volume I:* Evan Napean, under-secretary of state Home Office, to Superintendent Despard (150–1), Board of Council, Mosquito Shore, 13 February 1786 (152), Narrative of Daniel Hill, 4 July 1788 (169–70).

[67] TNA CO123/26 26 February 1817: Arthur to Bathurst, 26 February 1817; TNA CO123/26 11 March 1817: Bathurst to Leith, 7 November 1816, Bennett to Bathurst, 26 February 1817, enc. Minutes from the public records of Honduras; Burdon, *Archives of British Honduras, Volume II:* Magistrates' Meeting, 25 February 1817 (193–4). Historian Ashli White has described the flow of exiled slaves, free people of colour, and white planters (former slave owners) to France, Cuba, the USA, and the British colony of Trinidad as the region's first refugee crisis: 'The Saint-Dominguan Refugees and American Distinctiveness in the Early Years of the Haitian Revolution', in David Patrick Geggus and Norman Fiering, eds., *The World of the Haitian Revolution* (Bloomington: Indiana University Press, 2009), 255 (248–60). See also Darrell Meadows, 'Engineering Exile', *French Historical Studies*, 21, 1 (2000), 67–102.

used for soldiers employed on public works. This came to nothing, following protestations from the settlement magistrates.[68]

So, to at least some extent, there was precedent for the shipment of the 1816 Barbados rebels to Honduras. Nonetheless, Superintendent Arthur remained firm in his resolve to leave them on board the *Frances May*. Conditions must have been dreadful, and as they began to sicken with dysentery, he ordered them off the ship, and onto the vessel *Indian*.[69] Once the *Frances May* had been cleaned, Arthur sent them back on board and over to the offshore island of Triangle Cays, and later on to Moho Rey, where they were put to work clearing land in a bid to 'restore health'. By this time, including the man who had perished after leaving Bridgetown, 25 of the convicts were dead. For months, Arthur awaited directions from the Colonial Office, and in the meantime, he made a series of increasingly desperate pleas to the secretary of state. A whole year later, Bathurst ordered that the men be shipped on to the West African colony of Sierra Leone. Arthur kept back eight 'good men', as he described them, for employment in the settlement. He put the rest to sea, including ten men whose conduct he described as exemplary.[70]

---

[68] Burdon, *Archives of British Honduras, Volume II:* Magistrates' Meeting, 2 January 1812 (149).

[69] TNA CO123/26 11 March 1817: Arthur to Bathurst, 11 March 1817.

[70] The eight men retained in Honduras had been employed as carpenters, coopers, and seamen, and were especially useful because there were no military artificers in the settlement. Arthur named them as Jack, Paulett, Foley (for employment on the government schooner), Winnabar (Royal Artillery), John, King, Ned, and Payne (Fort George commissariat). See TNA CO123/26 22 September 1818: Arthur to Bathurst, 22 September 1818, enc. Garrison Orders, 17 September 1818. The 'List of convicts recommended for their good conduct' is as follows:

Men's names	Owners' names in Barbadoes
Prince	H. Hunt esq.
Tom Mingo	H. ?Novend
Nat	J. Sim[m]ons esq.
Jack Sprat	J. Probert esq.
Oronoque	Thos ?Estiel esq.
Cuffie Ned	Genl. Biaffet
Page	Col. Callender
Daniel	John Croskendale esq.
Sampson	Mrs Doughty
Castello Clark	Saml Clarke esq.

This list was enclosed in TNA CO267/49 16 January 1819. Note that Cuffie (Cuffee) Ned was one of the small number of enslaved men who testified before the Select Committee: *The Report from a Select Committee of the House of Assembly*, Appendix C (27–8). However, he was never sentenced to transportation for his role in the 1816

Figure 4.3 View of Sierra Leone, 1838
Source: *Church Missionary Paper*, no. 89 (1838), via http://www
.liberatedafricans.org/image_gallery/01_sierra_leone/prints/1838_
cmpaper_viewofsierraleone.jpg (accessed 27 April 2018).

Their journey continued as badly as it had begun. The *Francis May* was forced to make an unscheduled stop in the Bahamas, where it was declared unseaworthy, and the convicts were transferred onto another vessel, the *Speculator*. The group finally arrived in the Sierra Leone's capital, Freetown, a full two years into their penal transportation, and almost three years after the Barbados rebellion (Figure 4.3). By this time, the original party of 124 numbered just 88.[71]

Sierra Leone was not at this time a penal colony, but it was imbricated in networks of coercive imperial governance that connected the Caribbean to the American colonies, to the colony of Nova Scotia, and to Great Britain. The British philanthropic association the Committee for the Relief of the Black Poor (chaired by abolitionist Granville Sharp) had established Freetown, Sierra Leone in 1787, as a site for the settlement of

---

rebellion. Rather, he was one of a few enslaved men shipped out of the colony as 'dangerous characters'. See Handler and Hughes, 'The 1816 Slave Revolt in Barbados', 271.

[71] TNA CO267/49 16 January 1819: Council President and Commander in Chief William Vesey Mannings, Bahamas, to Lieutenant Colonel Governor Charles MacCarthy, Sierra Leone, 21 November 1818, enc. Certificate of Lieut. Col. George Arthur of the arrival and treatment of the Insurgents on their landing at Honduras (n.d.).

destitute Africans living in London.[72] They included formerly enslaved loyalists who had fought with the British during the American War of Independence and had since become refugees. Enslaved Americans who had escaped to freedom in Nova Scotia following the War of Independence went to the settlement in 1792. Over 500 Jamaican maroons followed in 1799. The maroons were from quasi-independent communities of escaped slaves, dating from the British occupation of Jamaica in the mid-seventeenth century. In 1796, the British had deported one large group of them from Trelawny to Halifax, Nova Scotia, following the end of the Second Maroon War (1795–6). They petitioned to leave and were sent on to Freetown.[73] When the Barbadians arrived in 1819, Sierra Leone was also the place where illegally trafficked slaves seized after the abolition of the slave trade in 1806 were settled, 'liberated' into government service in the colony. Their numbers soon swamped those of the earlier settlers and their descendants.[74] Britain's intention in regards to all these groups was to encourage them to engage in settled cultivation and domestic servitude, and to learn trades, both in preparation for their eventual freedom, and in order to spread 'civilization' into west Africa.

Though Bathurst did not record his rationale for his decision to transport the 1816 rebels to West Africa, it was surely determined by his understanding that if not a penal colony Sierra Leone was a place of forced resettlement, if not solely punitive relocation, for persons of African origin. Moreover, the skills of plantation slaves were a perfect match for the productive needs of the colony, and Barbadians could be easily dispersed among the largely African-descended population. In this regard, this slave voyage in reverse lays open to view the close links

---

[72] Stephen Braidwood, *Black Poor and White Philanthropists: London's Blacks and the foundation of the Sierra Leone Settlement 1786–1791* (Liverpool University Press, 1994); Cassandra Pybus 'Washington's Revolution (Harry that is, not George)', *Atlantic Studies: Global Currents*, 3, 2 (2006), 183–99.
[73] Fortin, '"Blackened Beyond Our Native Hue"'.
[74] Richard Peter Anderson, *Abolition in Sierra Leone: Re-building lives and identities in nineteenth-century West Africa* (Cambridge University Press, 2020); Everill, *Abolition and Empire*; Christopher Fyfe, *A History of Sierra Leone* (Oxford University Press, 1962), 136; David Northrup, 'Becoming African: Identity Formation among Liberated Slaves in Nineteenth-Century Sierra Leone', *Slavery and Abolition*, 27, 1 (2006), 1–21; Suzanne Schwarz, 'Reconstructing the Life Histories of Liberated Africans: Sierra Leone in the Early Nineteenth Century', *History in Africa*, 39 (2012), 175–207. The Nova Scotians claimed that the Sierra Leone Company reneged on its promise to grant them land free of all expenses. Whatever the Company's intention had been, this sowed the seeds of discontent for decades afterwards, because the Nova Scotians lacked security of tenure and so refused to either pay rent and cultivate their land, or give it up: TNA CO267/98 27 May 1829: Lieutenant Governor H. J. Ricketts, Sierra Leone, to Sir George Murray, secretary of state for war and the colonies, 27 May 1829.

between enslavement, transportation, and other forms of colonial bondage and repression. For the first couple of years after their arrival, the British put the Barbadians to work, but also treated them according to the norms of punishment across the British Empire, which at the time included incentives to good behaviour. 'I shall explain to them', Governor Charles MacCarthy wrote to Bathurst in 1819, 'that their future emancipation from all manner of restraint, will depend upon the Instructions I shall receive from your Lordship, and their good conduct.'[75] Bathurst subsequently directed MacCarthy to either remit their sentences or grant other indulgences, if their behaviour warranted it.[76] Meantime, the Barbadians mainly chose to live in and around the colony's capital, Freetown. This disappointed those officials who had held out hopes that these colonially born people (for they were all Barbados-born Creoles) might teach the skills of plantation agriculture to the recently enslaved and then 'liberated' Africans then growing in number in Sierra Leone.[77]

During this period, colonial administrators treated the Barbadians in the same way as the Liberated Africans. It divided them into small parties, and either employed them on public works labour in Freetown or sent them out to the newly established villages to search for work. Some took up trades, and others worked for merchants or settlers, and even took Liberated Africans into service.[78] In 1826, a British parliamentary Commission of Inquiry visited Sierra Leone, and as part of its larger investigations it interviewed one of the Barbadians, a man called Samuel Lane. This reveals a great deal about the rebels' fate in transportation.[79] Of the 87 arrivals, Lane knew 34 to be alive. Otherwise, he supposed 26 were dead, and did not know the whereabouts of 25 others. The Commission described the men as 'industrious and useful', and in its report reproduced Lane's account of every known Barbadian still in the colony, which included details of their occupation, place of residence, and marital status. Samuel Lane told the commissioners that he was married and had found employment as a wheelwright,

---

[75] TNA CO267/49 16 January 1819: MacCarthy to Bathurst, 16 January 1819.
[76] TNA CO267/49 25 June 1819: MacCarthy to Bathurst, 25 June 1819.
[77] TNA CO267/82 22 April 1827: Governor Sir Neil Campbell, Sierra Leone, to Bathurst, 22 April 1827.
[78] TNA CO267/49 24 January 1819: MacCarthy to Bathurst, 23 January 1819; TNA CO267/49 25 June 1819: MacCarthy to Bathurst, 25 June 1819.
[79] TNA CO267/91 Commission of Inquiry Sierra Leone, 1825–8, Appendix B: Statement of Saml Lane, taken March 6th 1826. Lane's testimony is reproduced in full as an appendix to Evelyn O'Callaghan's work of historical fiction: *The Earliest Patriots; being the true adventures of certain survivors of 'Bussa's Rebellion' (1816), in the island of Barbados and abroad* (London: Karia Press, 1986), 55–8.

employed by an American settler. The other Barbadians, he reported, worked either at trades, on farms or as servants. They included the 'free coloureds' Cain David and Richard Sergeant, who allegedly played a key role in the 1816 rebellion; Jackey [or Jacky], who in 1816 had been the head driver at Simmons estate in Barbados; and Prince William, the driver at Grove plantation. David and Sergeant were both married and working as tailors. David had a 'shingle house', a sign of wealth, in Maroon Town (a district of Freetown), and Sergeant a lot and house in Freetown. Jackey was unmarried, owned a lot and a more ordinary 'grass house', and worked as a superintendent on a farm belonging to one Mr Burbers. Prince William was working as a groom and was married, though his two children had died. Samuel Lane stated: 'Lot and Grass House at Grass field lives with Mr Maccawly gains a great deal of money – better off than any one of the Barbadians.'[80] 'Mr Maccawly' must have been Kenneth Macaulay, the second cousin of the famous abolitionist, and former governor of Sierra Leone, Zachary. Indeed, during this period, Kenneth worked for the firm Babington and Macaulay, which made immense profits from processing captives and other cargo seized from illegal ('prize') slave trade vessels in the colony.[81]

The commission noted with satisfaction that by this time at least some of the Barbadians were teaching the Liberated Africans tropical cultivation. It added, of Samuel Lane:

He is of opinion that those Barbadians who are present in the Colony would prefer remaining here as Freemen to returning to Barbadoes to be in slavery.

Those who had Masters that were cruel and whipped them, are better off here – but those who kind owners were better off in Barbadoes as slaves.

Samuel Lane was in happier circumstances there than here. He is of opinion there are more bad Masters than good ones.[82]

This led the commissioners to the extraordinary conclusion that although the Barbadians 'seemed generally to be contented with their condition ... there was by no means that *decided* expression of satisfaction which

---

[80] TNA CO267/91 Commission of Inquiry Sierra Leone, 1825–8, Appendix B: Statement of Saml Lane, taken March 6th 1826; *The Report From A Select Committee of the House of Assembly*: 'The Confession of Robert, a Slave belonging to the Plantation called "Simons"', 30–1 (29–31). See also Beckles, 'The Slave-Drivers War'. Note that 'shingle houses' were roofed in flat pieces of hard wood which looked like slates, but over time turned up at the edges. In contrast, grass houses were thatched in the broad leaves of the local elephant grass.

[81] Catherine Hall, *Macaulay and Son: architects of imperial Britain* (New Haven, CT: Yale University Press, 2012), 70–2. Scanlan, *Freedom's Debtors*, 105.

[82] TNA CO267/91 Commission of Inquiry Sierra Leone, 1825–8, Appendix B: Statement of Saml Lane, taken March 6th 1826.

perhaps many would have expected from the change in their circumstances'.[83]

Buried in the detail of Samuel Lane's interview with the commissioners is a passing reference to the departure of three of the Barbadians for the Gambia, and the return of two.[84] One of them was almost certainly a man called Will Lord. His former owner was John Thomas Lord, whose son Samuel Hall Lord (?1788–1844), was one of the most famous slave owners in Barbados. The family enslaved several hundred people on several estates, including in Long Bay. One opulent mansion, built in the years following the 1816 revolt, was known as 'Sam Lord's Castle'.[85] At the start of 1817, Samuel Lord had petitioned the Colonial Office about Will Lord. He claimed that the evidence against him and another of his enslaved property, Kitt, had been fabricated by others who had since been executed for revolt, and that both men had saved the lives of his sisters Elizabeth and Sarah. He requested their vindication and liberation.[86] Bathurst rejected the petition as unfounded, writing that Samuel Lord was mistaken. In 1824, Samuel Lord petitioned again, this time asking for a royal pardon so that Will Lord could return to his family in Barbados. These petitions detail how Will Lord had exchanged several letters with his family, that his brother had accompanied Samuel Lord's sisters (themselves owners of enslaved property) to England, and that Will Lord had asked his family to send him the £10 cost of the passage to London. Samuel Lord reported that Will Lord's family had told him that they had sent him the money, and so they were anticipating

---

[83] PP 1826–27 (312) *Sierra Leone. Report of the commissioners of inquiry into the state of the colony of Sierra Leone. First part; viz. I. Extent and boundaries of the colony. II. Number and condition of the population, by classes. III. Liberated African, and engineer departments. IV. Provision for religious instruction and the education of youth. V. Agriculture. VI. Trade. VII. Revenue and expenditure. VIII. Judicial and civil establishments. IX. Observations on the climate of Sierra Leone, and its dependencies on the River Gambia, and on the Gold Coast*, 8–15; TNA CO267/91 Commission of Inquiry Sierra Leone, 1825-8, Appendix B: Statement of Saml Lane, taken March 6th 1826.

[84] TNA CO267/91 Commission of Inquiry Sierra Leone, 1825-8, Appendix B: Statement of Saml Lane, taken March 6th 1826. The presence of 'apprentice settlers' from Sierra Leone in the Gambia is noted in PP 1826–27 (552) *Sierra Leone. Report of the commissioners of inquiry into the state of the colony of Sierra Leone. Second part; viz. I. Dependencies in the Gambia. II. [Ditto] on the Gold Coast*, 29 June 1827, 8.

[85] A. H. Wightwick Haywood, 'Sam Lord and his Castle', *Journal of the Barbados Museum and Historical Society*, 30 (1963), 114–26. For details of the compensation paid to Lord following emancipation in 1833, see Legacies of British Slave-ownership database: Samuel Hall Lord, https://www.ucl.ac.uk/lbs/person/view/6720 (accessed 2 February 2018).

[86] The 1818 petition (in TNA CO28/87) is reproduced and analysed in Handler and Hughes, 'The 1816 Slave Revolt in Barbados', 267–86. Handler and Hughes point out that TNA CO papers include the only known record of a court martial held in the aftermath of the 1816 revolt.

his arrival at any time.[87] In 1825, the Colonial Office again rejected Samuel Lord's petition, claiming the court martial had been 'as fair a trial as any of the others'.[88]

Will Lord appears in Samuel Lane's 1826 list of Barbadians in Sierra Leone. He seems to have done well in the colony. His entry is near-identical to that of Prince William, noted above: 'Groom (Married) has a lot and a Grass House in grass fields – lives with Mr Maccauley, gains a great deal of money is better off than any one of the Barbadians.'[89] There is no record of Will Lord's voyage to England. However, the first census of England, recorded in 1841, tantalizes us with details of a man of the same name (the only man so named in the country) living at no. 2 Cumberland Terrace, near Regents Park, not far from Sarah Lord, where he was working as a carpenter. The head of the household was recorded as Sir Archibald Edmonstone. He lived at the property with his wife Lady Emma, a baby daughter (also Emma), and seven servants. The census notes that 'Will Lord' was aged 55 and had not been born in the parish in which he was living.[90] If this was Will Lord, the Barbadian rebel, his residence in London marks a further stage in a quite extraordinary journey of enslavement, conviction, and freedom.

After a short period of time, the British treated the Barbadian rebels in Sierra Leone in the same way as the Liberated Africans. From the records of

---

[87] TNA CO28/94: Samuel Hall Lord to Bathurst, n.d. (1824), Lord to Bathurst, 1 December 1824. Note that Samuel Lord's sister Elizabeth Sarsfield Lord lived in Barbados until her death in 1851. See https://www.ucl.ac.uk/lbs/person/view/4496 (accessed 27 February 2019). Nothing is known of the life of his other sister, Sarah, though in 1841 somebody of that name, aged 40, was living with a 20-year old Richard Lord, and of independent means, in a smart address in London's West End. See HO107/686/13: England Census 1841 St Pancras, Middlesex, enumeration district 13, folio 10, page 15 (available via paid subscription to ancestry.com). Also: https://www.ucl.ac.uk/lbs/person/view/6619 (accessed 27 February 2019). There are numerous works on the English census. Perhaps the best-known is E. A. Wrigley and R. S. Schofield, *The Population History of England 1541–1871: A reconstruction* (Cambridge University Press, 1981).

[88] TNA CO28/95/31 5 May 1825: Governor Sir Henry Warde, Barbados, to Bathurst, 5 May 1825, enc. Captain Delhoste, private secretary to the governor, to Warde, 27 April 1825.

[89] TNA CO267/91 Commission of Inquiry Sierra Leone, 1825–8, Appendix B: Statement of Saml Lane, taken March 6th 1826.

[90] TNA HO107/684/17: England Census 1841 St Pancras, Middlesex, enumeration district 19, folio 4, page 3 (available via paid subscription to ancestry.com). On Archibald Edmonstone, see G. C. Boase, revised by Elizabeth Baigent, 'Edmonstone, Sir Archibald, third baronet (1795–1871)', *Oxford Dictionary of National Biography* (Oxford University Press, 2004); online edition, 23 September 2004, https://doi.org/10.1093/ref:odnb/8496 (accessed 7 May 2020). 'Will Lord' does not appear in any subsequent census, though a 'William Lord' died in the St Marylebone workhouse in 1849. See LMA: *Board of Guardian Records, 1834–1906/ Church of England Parish Registers, 1813–1906, p89/mry1/352* (available via paid subscription to ancestry.com).

Samuel Lane's interview with the commissioners, it is evident that their success was evaluated based on their employment, ownership of land and houses, marital status, and wealth. In many ways, the encouragement of settlement, work, and cultivation anticipated the later apprenticeship system, instituted in Britain's sugar colonies (excepting Antigua and Bermuda) after the Emancipation Act came into effect on 1 August 1834. Excepting children under the age of six years, apprenticeship did not free enslaved persons, but forced them to work for their former owners, as previously, for three quarters of their time, and to find other paid employment. Government claimed this as necessary preparation for eventual freedom and self-sufficiency. Though the Act was supposed to remain in force for up to eight years, it came under sustained attack from abolitionists until the colonies emancipated apprentices in full on 1 August 1838. If we consider apprenticeship as part of a continuum of labour exploitation, the attempted use of the Jamaican Nova Scotians and maroons, Liberated Africans, and Barbadian slave convicts to effect colonization, this shows the fluidity of the boundaries between apparently distinct labour regimes as well as the depth of trans-imperial practices of coerced mobility. Moreover, as Chapters 2 and 3 demonstrated, this was anticipated in the common experiences of other categories of labour during the earlier period, including vagrants, orphans, sex-workers, and soldiers. The kinds of work that the 'black loyalists', maroons, Barbadian rebels, and Liberated Africans in Sierra Leone did – whether as servants, agriculturalists, or on public works – were common features of many coerced labour regimes, including enslavement, indenture, and penal transportation, as also in workhouses, galleys, and armies. Moreover, Samuel Lane's testimony, Will Lord's mobility, and the history of the transportation of the Barbados rebels more generally, provide insights not just into subaltern experience, but into what I would like to call a subaltern politics of comparison.[91] The Barbados 'slave-convicts' both imagined and moved through networks that paralleled those of colonial officials, and most significantly in so doing themselves created new lines of connection and stimulated new forms of imperial punitive practice in and between the islands and coast of the Caribbean and Central America, and the littorals, ports, and cities of West Africa and southern England.[92]

---

[91] Ann Laura Stoler and Carole McGranahan, 'Refiguring Imperial Terrains', *Ab Imperio*, 2 (2006), 17–56.

[92] Alan Lester has drawn attention to the need for focus on the relationship between imperial networks and subaltern agency and called for their theorization in relation to the shape and function of these connections. Of concern to him are 'the changes in social discourse and practice wrought by the mobile individuals themselves'. See Alan Lester : 'Personifying Colonial Governance: George Arthur and the Transition from Humanitarian to Development Discourse', *Annals of the Association of American Geographers*, 102, 6 (2012), 1469, 1470 (quote) (1468–88). On imperial networks, see

A focus on George Arthur, the superintendent and commander-in-chief of Honduras, who managed the on-shipment of the Barbados rebels to Sierra Leone in 1817, is relevant here. Like other colonial officials, he carried specific and tangible practices of governance around British spheres of influence. As Alan Lester and A. G. L. Shaw have identified, his long, unbroken service makes him an especially compelling figure.[93] Arthur was experienced in governing and repressing various imperial populations, including Indigenous, enslaved, and convict people, and he married the daughter of a Jamaican slave owner.[94] A pronounced anti-slavery campaigner and evangelical humanitarian, in Honduras Arthur introduced codes of amelioration, collected information on violence against slaves, and freed Indigenous (Amerindian) people enslaved on the Mosquito Coast. This made him very unpopular with the settlers, even before he was caught in the middle of the conflicting desires of the Colonial Office and the Honduras settlers, when the Barbados rebels arrived in 1816. In 1824, following what appears to have been a breakdown in health, and directly from Honduras, Arthur accepted the post of Lieutenant-Governor of the newly separate colony of Van Diemen's Land. There, he established the reformatory system of punishment that, taking convicts through penal stages to ultimate liberation on good behaviour, he claimed was the best in the world (see Chapter 7).[95] He also put into operation the famous 'black line' of 1830–1, the violent means of driving Indigenous peoples from their homelands through what Lyndall Ryan has conceptualized as 'an important instrument of British imperial power'.[96] At the same time, he embodied the contradictions of

---

also Catherine Hall, *Civilising Subjects: Metropole and Colony in the English Imagination, 1830–1867* (Cambridge University Press, 2002); Zoë Laidlaw, *Colonial Connections, 1815–45: Patronage, the Information Revolution and Colonial Government* (Manchester University Press, 2005); Desley Deacon, Penny Russell, and Angela Woollacott, eds., *Transnational lives: Biographies of Global Modernity, 1700–present* (Basingstoke: Palgrave Macmillan, 2010).

[93] I draw here on David Lambert and Alan Lester's now classic collection of essays: *Colonial Lives across the British Empire: Imperial Careering in the Long Nineteenth Century* (Cambridge University Press, 2006). On George Arthur, see Shaw, *Sir George Arthur, Bart*; Alan Lester, 'Personifying Colonial Governance'; and A. G. L. Shaw, 'Arthur, Sir George, first baronet (1784–1854)', *Oxford Dictionary of National Biography* (Oxford University Press, 2004); online edition, May 2013, http://www.oxforddnb.com/view/article/707 (accessed 9 July 2014).

[94] His wife was Elizabeth Sigismund Smith, daughter of Jamaican slave owner Colonel Sir John Frederick Sigismund Smith. See Shaw, 'Arthur, Sir George'; and Legacies of British slave ownership database: John Frederick Sigismund Smith, https://www.ucl.ac.uk/lbs/person/view/15990 (accessed 12 May 2018).

[95] Lester, 'Personifying Colonial Governance', 1479.

[96] Lyndall Ryan, 'The Black Line in Van Diemen's Land: success or failure?', *Journal of Australian Studies*, 37, 1 (2013), 3 (3–18). Ryan's argument is that there was not one but three 'black lines', during the fifteen-month long period of Arthur's military campaign.

empire, for after shifting from the Caribbean to the Antipodes he was able to 'recode', in Lester's words, slave 'amelioration' as Indigenous 'protection' – and, I would like to suggest, also as convict 'rehabilitation'.[97] From Van Diemen's Land, the Colonial Office appointed Arthur to the post of Lieutenant-Governor of Upper Canada. He arrived in the aftermath of the 1837–8 rebellion and, having ordered the execution of two of the leaders, he enforced the transportation of 102 rebels to Van Diemen's Land. By then, of course, Arthur was in possession of direct experience of repressive mass transportation (from Barbados), and of the penal regime in the Australian colonies. Shortly after Canadian Confederation, in 1842, Arthur took up the governorship of the Bombay Presidency, where he remained until he retired in 1844. Lester argues that, here, Arthur in his interest in the Indian peasantry transformed his earlier discourse and practice of humanitarian *protection* to one of humanitarian *development*.[98] Indeed, among other experiments in cultivation, he became interested in cotton production, fearing that American competition would impact on the Indian market in China He established and then abandoned a government farm, complaining of Indians' 'ancient customs and prejudices'.[99] In Bombay, he also became involved in the routine administration of convict transportation to India's penal settlements in the Straits Settlements, which did not cease until 1868. This included transportation after the Kolhapur rebellion in 1844. Given Arthur's prior knowledge of the management of convict voyages, it should not surprise us that on one occasion, after two violent convict ship mutinies on the part of rebels, he ordered the fitting of heavy irons before future embarkations from the Bombay presidency's Tannah jail.[100]

We come back to the story of Bussa's rebels in the larger context of abolition, emancipation, and apprenticeship in the 1830s. In the late 1830s and 1840s, agents from Jamaica and British Guiana (and French Guiana) began to recruit workers from Sierra Leone as plantation labour. During the same period, they also began to import indentured labour from India and China, and other workers from places such as Barbados,

---

On the black war, see also James Boyce, *Van Diemen's Land* (Melbourne, VIC: Black Inc., 2008).

[97] Lester, 'Personifying Colonial Governance', 1481.
[98] Lester, 'Personifying Colonial Governance', 1482. (Emphasis in original).
[99] Shaw, *Sir George Arthur, Bart, 1784–1854*, 255–6 (quote 256).
[100] IOR P/403/56 (Bombay judicial consultations, 11 March 1846): Minute of Governor George Arthur, 26 February 1846. On Arthur's repression of the Kolapur rebellion, see Shaw, *Sir George Arthur, Bart, 1784–1854*, 263–5. Shaw notes that Arthur remained interested in convict transportation, before his death in 1854, and often corresponded with new colonial secretary Charles Grant (1st Baron Glenelg). He defended convict assignment, and was critical of the probation system and Grey's 'exile' transportations. See Shaw, *Sir George Arthur, Bart, 1784–1854*, 282.

Germany, Madeira, and Malta.[101] The colonial government in Sierra Leone signalled that it would take any person who refused to migrate off its stores, and make them responsible for their own subsistence. At this time, some of the maroons decided to go back to Jamaica, arriving in September 1841.[102] Almost certainly buoyed on by the colony's desire to resettle Liberated Africans and others in the Caribbean, and by the departure of the maroons, in July 1841 the surviving Barbados convicts petitioned the Queen, seeking permission to return home. Their formulaic 'humble' petition reveals little, apart from this firm desire.[103] Dr Richard R. Madden was one of the special magistrates sent to Jamaica in 1833 to oversee the implementation of the Emancipation Act.[104] A decade later, government appointed him commissioner in Sierra Leone, where he met the Barbadians. He strongly supported their request, noting that a man he described only as their 'spokesperson' owned land and was 'of very superior manners and address'. Generally, he added, they were a 'well-ordered set of people'.[105] The spokesman was almost certainly Jacob Thomas, a veterinarian who had made money as a publican, married and had a child, owned property, and sent his daughter to school in England.[106] The three other signatories included John Morgan, who was a carpenter. He was also married and owned property.[107]

---

[101] Selections from a large literature are: Marina Carter, *Servants, Sirdars and Settlers: Indians in Mauritius, 1834–1874* (New Delhi: Oxford University Press, 1995); David Dabydeen and Brinsley Samaroo, eds., *India in the Caribbean* (London: Hansib, 1987); Kay Saunders, ed., *Indentured Labour in the British Empire 1834–1920* (London: Croom Helm, 1984); Verene A. Shepherd, *Maharani's Misery: narratives of a passage from India to the Caribbean* (Mona, Jamaica: University of the West Indies Press, 2002); Hugh Tinker, *A New System of Slavery: the export of Indian labour overseas 1830–1920* (Oxford University Press, 1974).

[102] Campbell, *Back to Africa*; Chopra, *Almost Home*, 183–4; Craton, *Testing the Chains*, chapter 17; Fortin, '"Blackened Beyond Our Native Hue"'; Walker, *The Black Loyalists*.

[103] TNA CO267/164 Acting Governor John Carr, Sierra Leone, to Lord John Russell, secretary of state for war and the colonies, 5 July 1841 enc. The Humble Memorial of Your Majesty's Most dutiful Barbadian Subjects, being Inhabitants of the Colony of Sierra Leone, n.d. – John Proverbs, John Morgan, Robert Chapman, J. Thomas ('acting for and on behalf of the other Barbadian subjects'); draft reply, Russell to Carr 30 September 1841. This petition is reproduced as an Appendix to O'Callaghan, *The Earliest Patriots*.

[104] Rupprecht, 'From slavery to indenture', 77.

[105] PP 1842 (551) (551-II) *Report from the Select Committee on the West Coast of Africa; together with the minutes of evidence, appendix, and index. Part II.* Appendix and Index, Appendix 15: 'Report of Commissioner of Inquiry on the Western Coast of Africa, Sierra Leone' 247.

[106] Beckles, *Bussa*, 43 (citing Fyfe, *A History of Sierra Leone*).

[107] TNA CO267/91 Commission of Inquiry Sierra Leone, 1825–8, Appendix B: Statement of Saml Lane, taken March 6th 1826. Samuel Lane gave no details of the other two signatories, John Proverbs and Robert Chapman.

The Colonial Office raised no objections to the petition, and moreover in a marginal note on the papers, a person unknown expressed bafflement about who the Barbadians were, and why they were in Sierra Leone.[108] Memories were short, it seems, and with abolition and emancipation, the political context of the Caribbean had changed greatly over the previous 25 years. The secretary of state granted the Barbadians permission to return, though there are no records to suggest that they ever did.[109] Some of them may have gone back to Barbados in ways that escaped the attention of the Colonial Office, or perhaps they chose to travel to the region with one of the Caribbean emigration agents then active in Sierra Leone, and then to find their own way back to Barbados. A decade later, on several occasions settlers even complained to the governor that recruiters had kidnapped or duped their relatives into enslavement in French Guiana. In one case of 1859, the Foreign Office appears to have made efforts to locate these people and have them sent back. The French then claimed that they had in fact signed labour contracts, and that they were only returning them because those contracts had expired.[110] This suggests that in common with other forms of mobile labour, the desire to increase economic and social capital was certainly a stimulus. Such was not entirely incompatible with semi-coerced labour recruitment, as seen for example during the first years of Indian indentured recruitment in the 1830s and 1840s, when allegations of kidnapping were rife. Indeed, interestingly, later in 1859 at least one group of prisoners in Sierra Leone volunteered for emigration to Cayenne in exchange for free pardons.[111]

*

The multiple points of intersection between punitive mobility and enslavement are apparent from the analysis presented here. The chapter has shown that in the eighteenth and nineteenth-century British Empire, banishment and transportation were tools for the control of enslaved

---

[108] TNA CO267/164: Carr to Russell, 5 July 1841. [109] Beckles, *Bussa*, 45–6.
[110] TNA CO267/264: Acting Governor Alexander Fitzjames, Sierra Leone, to the Duke of Newcastle (Henry Pelham-Clinton, 5th Duke), secretary of state for the colonies, 22 August 1859; TNA CO267/270: Governor Stephen J. Hill, Sierra Leone, to Newcastle, 5 February 1861; J. H. Isnard, vice consul of France, Sierra Leone, to Hill, 4 February 1861.
[111] TNA CO267/264: Fitzjames to Newcastle, 22 August 1859, enc. The Information and Complaint of Sarah Johnson of Circular Road of the City of Freetown in the Colony of Sierra Leone married woman, 18 July 1859; Names of prisoners who are willing to emigrate to the French West India colonies and have received pardon from his Excellency the Governor in Chief as per Warrant dated opposite each name, taken from the record of the gaol on this 20th day of July 1859; draft reply, Newcastle to Fitzjames, 18 November 1859.

populations. They were applied to individuals convicted of petty crime and running away, as well as collective acts of resistance or rebellion, in colonies using English, Spanish, and Dutch-Roman law. Routinely, the Crown purchased enslaved convicts from their owners, and resold them in other colonial locations. The chapter has also suggested that after the abolition of the slave trade, discussions about the punishment of enslaved persons in the Caribbean became part of larger debates on amelioration, and, after abolition, they were relevant to the institution of standardized penal practice. Here, the decision to send the 1816 Barbados rebels to Sierra Leone is significant, for it reveals some of the connections between punitive mobility and other kinds of coerced displacement and resettlement. By the time that that the Barbadian convicts arrived in Freetown, the colony was a place in which the British had resettled London's black poor, America's black loyalists, Jamaica's deported maroons, and illegally trafficked African captives.

Sierra Leone enables us to see connections between governmentality, enslavement, penal transportation, and other forms of colonial bondage and repression. These are evident not only in the life histories and testimonies of the enslaved persons discussed in this chapter, including notably Samuel Lane and Will Lord, but in the circulation of colonial personnel. Here, it has been suggested that the life and work of George Arthur in South America, the Caribbean, the Australian colonies, and India was especially important. And yet, despite their subjection to punitive mobility, as the chapter has shown, enslaved persons who were banished or transported found agency in repressive colonial regimes, from Jamaica and Honduras to the Mosquito Coast and Freetown. In Chapter 6, the discussion focuses again on punitive mobility as a conduit for insurgent politics and religious practice. Chapter 5 now develops the British story into the later part of the nineteenth century. It reveals its links to punitive mobility amongst the European powers in the wider Caribbean, and in stressing the regional dimension also restates the importance of transnational cooperation for colonial population management in the aftermath of the abolition of enslavement.

5 Imperial Governance

If Chapter 4 established the British Caribbean as part of larger imperial networks of enslavement and penal transportation that stretched across the Atlantic and Indian oceans, this chapter takes an even wider geographical perspective, taking the narrative of colonial governance in the colonies from the 1820s into the 1870s. First, it develops earlier insights on the relationships been enslavement, punishment, and convict mobility in the French, Spanish, and British empires, from the late eighteenth century onwards. This argues for an interconnected approach to punitive European geopolitics. The spectre of revolution like that experienced in French Saint-Domingue (Haiti) between 1791 and 1804 encouraged hopes of emancipation by enslaved people and stirred up fears of rebellion among slave owners, in and beyond the Caribbean. Indeed, the dissolution of much of the Spanish Empire through the independence of Latin American nations in the decades that followed also impacted on British punitive strategies. All the European powers banished and transported enslaved men and women, revealing the extent and complexity of political, legal, and geographical networks and connections. In contrast to several of the case studies explored in Chapter 2 and Chapter 3, such punitive mobility was not always driven by the labour requirements of colonization or settlement, but in geographically distant places like Martinique and Réunion Island, by the common need to manage and discipline colonial labour. There are strong parallels here between the practices of the French and Spanish empires, and the Netherlands Vereenigde Oost-Indische Compagnie (VOC).

In the early nineteenth century, the independence of various territories in the Spanish Empire closed off a range of punitive destinations to convicts from other polities. British judicial process thus shifted from the resale of formerly enslaved convicts in proximate colonies to their penal transportation to more distant locations. The first part of the chapter will show how they travelled first to England or Bermuda, and then on to New South Wales and Van Diemen's Land. Such voyages were undertaken by individuals convicted of various criminal offences, as well as rebels of Jamaica's Baptist War (1831–2).[1] At this time, British imperial policy became saturated with concerns about the need for consistency between English law and colonial law, and the need for appropriate kinds of punishment with respect to a person's civil status, as well as their race and gender.[2] As Chapter 4 noted, after the abolition of enslavement, in most colonies formerly enslaved persons remained bonded to their former owners during the period to 1838 when the British granted final emancipation. Known as 'apprentices', like free men and women such bonded labour could also be sentenced to penal transportation by colonial courts.[3]

Part two of the chapter shows that during the 1830s, there developed in Britain and the Australian colonies growing anti-transportation sentiments, and this impacted on the wider empire in ways that to date are only partially appreciated. In 1837, as the abolitionist Molesworth Committee was sitting, the Home Office prohibited any further shipments of Caribbean convicts to the Antipodes. Given the closure of other European colonies to convicts, and ongoing difficulties in finding ships to carry them to London pending departure for Sydney or Hobart, Britain's West Indian colonies had for some years been interested in the

---

[1] Michael Craton, *Testing the Chains: Resistance to Slavery in the British West Indies* (Ithaca, NY: Cornell University Press, 1982), *passim* and chapters 21 and 22.

[2] Note that Scotland had its own justice system. From the sixteenth century Wales used English law, although until the nineteenth century in all but one county (Monmouthshire) it was administered in slightly different ways. I thank Angela Muir for this detail.

[3] Clare Anderson, *Subaltern Lives: Biographies of colonialism in the Indian Ocean world, 1790–1920* (Cambridge University Press), chapter 5; James Bradley and Cassandra Pybus, 'From Slavery to Servitude: The Australian Exile of Elizabeth and Constance', *Journal of Australian Colonial History*, 9 (2007), 29–50; Lesley C. Duly, '"Hottentots to Hobart and Sydney": The Cape Supreme Court's Use of Transportation, 1828–38', *Australian Journal of Politics and History*, 25 (1979), 39–50; James Hugh Donohoe, *The Forgotten Australians: The non-Anglo or Celtic convicts and exiles* (Sydney, NSW: published by the author, 1991); Ian Duffield, 'From Slave Colonies to Penal Colonies: The West Indians Transported to Australia', *Slavery and Abolition*, 7, 1 (1986), 25–45; Ian Duffield, 'The Life and Death of "Black" John Goff: Aspects of the Black Convict Contribution to Resistance Patterns During the Transportation Era in Eastern Australia', *Australian Journal of Politics and History*, 33, 1 (1987), 30–44; Ian Duffield, '"Stated This Offence": High-Density Convict Micro-Narratives', in Lucy Frost and Hamish Maxwell-Stewart, eds., *Chain Letters: Narrating convict lives* (Melbourne University Press, 2001), 119–35; Ian Duffield, 'A Storm in a Teapot? Five Stories About the Trials of Priscilla's Life and their Household Remedy, Arsenic Trioxide', in *To the Islands: Australia and the Caribbean*, special edition of *Australian Cultural History*, 21 (2002), 19–31; V. C. Malherbe, 'Khoikhoi and the Question of Convict Transportation from the Cape Colony, 1820-1842', *South African Historical Journal*, 17 (1985), 19–39; Diana Paton, 'An "Injurious" Population: Caribbean-Australian Penal Transportation and Imperial Racial Politics', *Cultural and Social History*, 5, 4 (2008), 449–64; Cassandra Pybus, *Black Founders: The unknown story of Australia's first black settlers* (Sydney: University of New South Wales Press, 1996).

establishment of a penal colony in the Caribbean region. From the 1830s, and as the numbers awaiting transportation grew, they reignited debates on the desirability or otherwise of establishing a regional site. This never happened, though British Guiana and Trinidad each established penal settlements for locally convicted felons, which the Colonial Office compared to their Australian counterparts. It is interesting to note that in discussions about the abolition of the slave trade at the turn of the nineteenth century, pro-slavery campaigners had justified it through the comparison of judicial enslavement and penal transportation. This provides important background for understanding the use of the language of enslavement more generally as a rhetorical device in broader debates about the abolition of transportation and its aftermath in the Caribbean.

French, Spanish, and British Connections in the Eighteenth and Nineteenth Centuries

In the eighteenth and nineteenth centuries, the French and Spanish in the Atlantic world banished and transported enslaved men and women. This was connected to British imperial practice and reveals something of the nature and extent of political, legal, and geographical networks in the region. For instance, in 1787, the French administration in the island of Saint-Domingue sold 33 'unruly' enslaved persons in Tobago.[4] The management of enslaved persons' resistance and criminal offending accelerated during the Haitian revolution. Indeed, in a well-known case of 1791 the French sentenced around 200 enslaved persons, part of a group of around 2,000 known as the Swiss Confederates, to transportation. The free black population had recruited them to threaten French planters with rebellion if they did not meet their demands for political rights. Once the French conceded, and in a context where the free population likely promised them freedom in exchange for their support, they betrayed their enslaved comrades and, in the face of a great deal of popular outrage, the government deported them. In dubious circumstances, the captain of the ship *Emmanuel* took them to Goff's Cay in Honduras, where he sent a member of his crew, Peter McCulloch, on shore to sell them. McCulloch told their potential buyers, who were British, that the men had nothing to do with the rebellion. They did not believe him and refused the vessel permission to land. The captain sailed on to the small island of English Cay and dumped the enslaved men on shore with just three days' rations and no water. Three British settlers

---

[4] David Patrick Geggus, *Haitian Revolutionary Studies* (Bloomington: Indiana University Press, 2001), 111.

rowed out to the island and told the men that if they did not return to shore, they were going to take them to Jamaica and then on to Saint-Domingue. Consequently, the enslaved convicts readily agreed to go, and they were put to work as mahogany cutters. Their residence only lasted for about six weeks, however, because other British settlers were unhappy about their presence and voted to send them to Jamaica. Their arrival caused such alarm that the Jamaican authorities immediately ordered them on to Saint-Domingue. After their ship landed, government put them to chain gang labour in the northwestern port of Môle Saint Nicolas, ostensibly to work on its fortifications. It is unclear what happened next. Contemporary accounts claimed that the French killed some of them and kept others on a hulk moored offshore.[5]

In the French colony of Martinique, the courts also sold off enslaved people who committed criminal offences. Indeed, contemporaries blamed one such group of men, working on canal construction, for starting the famous Carbet insurrection of 1822. The acting British governor of neighbouring Saint Lucia wrote at the time: 'The undertaker of the canal instead of hiring negroes to make a job of it bought all the bad subjects he could get cheap several he bought at auction when they were fined off by the Proprietors after being disgraced for some weeks in the chain gang.' The rebellion itself broke out when a group of enslaved people living near St Pierre killed their master and declared their intention to massacre the island's population. As Lorelle Semley explains, this followed the issue of a subversive pamphlet by wealthy planter Cyrille-Charles-Auguste Bissette, which supported the rights of free people of colour. However, the French quickly defeated the rebels.[6] The carceral loop continued with the removal of around forty rebels to the colony of Senegal. The terms of their administrative deportation prohibited them from returning to Martinique. However, they managed to reach other Antillean islands, France, and even the USA, before the French decreed their right to return in 1831.[7]

---

[5] Geggus, *Haitian Revolutionary Studies*, chapter 7, esp. 108–15. Nigel O. Bolland notes that since a slave uprising of 1773, settlers remained fearful of rebellion and were 'panic struck' when the Saint-Domingue convicts arrived. See *The Formation of a Colonial Society: Belize, from conquest to Crown colony* (Baltimore, MD: Johns Hopkins University Press: 1977), 74–5.

[6] TNA CO28/91/46 7 November 1822 (private): Acting Governor General J. M. Mainwaring, Saint Lucia, to Governor Henry Warde, Barbados, 23 October 1822, enc. letter from unknown member of Privy Council, 20 October 1822.

[7] François-André Isambert, *Affaire des déportés de la Martinique, 1823–1824: mémoires, consultations, pieces justificatives, etc.* (Paris: Constantin, 1825). See also Lorelle Semley, *To Be Free and French: Citizenship in France's Atlantic empire* (Cambridge University Press, 2017), 115–6.

Later, Martinique established a Provostial Court. This court of summary justice bypassed the usual procedures of the Royal Court and sentenced dozens of rebels to execution and other punishments. In the face of mounting critique, in 1827 the French authorities abolished it, but as part of a larger package of administrative reforms they gave the Privy Council the right to transport enslaved persons believed to be guilty of the two most feared crimes in the colony: poisoning and arson. Consequently, until the 1840s, the Privy Council routinely sent enslaved men and women into penal transportation. Their destinations included Senegal, French Guiana, and the Spanish colony of Puerto Rico. It is important to note that in sharp contrast to the British practices described in Chapter 4, these transportations were extra-legal in character. Paradoxically, as John Savage has noted, what was in effect an administrative measure necessitated an appreciation of enslaved people as legal and ultimately political subjects. Indeed, on some occasions the Privy Council ordered the payment of compensation to slave owners. On the other hand, as in the British case, metropolitan administrators criticized the selling of enslaved persons to third parties for transportation. Concerned that it was inadequately punitive, they cited cases of transported slaves who had encouraged others to commit offences to enjoy a better quality of life. This included the notorious case of one man who had apparently (and famously) become an assistant to the governor of Puerto Rico. And so, with the July Monarchy's passing of the 1845 Mackau Law, which gave enslaved people the right to be heard in court and own property, thus paving the way for the abolition of slavery in 1848, the extra-legal transportation of enslaved persons started to fall out of use.[8]

As in Martinique, the Privy Council of French Guiana sent enslaved convicts into transportation. In 1845, for example, it ordered the 'exceptional exclusion' of the *galérien* (galley slave) Maxime. He had twice escaped from jail, and the governor described him as a subject of terror in the colony.[9] However, across the Atlantic in the western Indian Ocean colony of Réunion Island, practices differed, and the enslaved were subject to judicial trial and conviction by one of the island's three Courts of Assizes, which were located in Saint-Paul, Saint-Denis, and

---

[8] John Savage, 'Unwanted Slaves: The Punishment of Transportation and the Making of Legal Subjects in Early Nineteenth-Century Martinique', *Citizenship Studies*, 10, 1 (2006), 35–7, 42–6, 51n.33, 51n.40 (35–53). See also Bernard Moitt, *Women and Slavery in the French Antilles, 1635–1848* (Bloomington: Indiana University Press, 2001), 120–1. I thank Lorraine M. Paterson for these references.

[9] ANOM H21/B: Governor Marie-Jean François Layrle, French Guiana, to Ange René Armand (Baron de Mackau), minister of the navy and the colonies, 25 June 1844, 12 August 1844 and 13 February 1845.

Saint-Pierre. In a few cases, these courts condemned enslaved men to hard labour, and shipped them to France for onward transfer to French Guiana. In 1837, for example, the Saint-Paul court sentenced a 39-year old enslaved Malagasy (Madagascan) named Carlin to life, for the crime of rape.[10] In 1842, and despite his plea of innocence, the Saint-Denis assizes sentenced the 29-year old Creole Marville for life, for the murder of the enslaved woman Marie Louise. He had been *marron* (maroon, or escaped) for about six weeks at the time.[11] In 1842, the Saint-Paul court also convicted the enslaved Creole Paul for a violent robbery that he had committed on the run.[12] In 1844 the Saint-Denis court convicted Pierre Jean of setting fire to the hut of an enslaved woman called Pauline. He was also in a state of *marronage*, and following the arson attacked Pauline and a man called Agénor, presumably her paramour.[13] In 1844, the Saint-Denis Court of Assizes found enslaved man Casimir guilty of murdering Ferdinand, an enslaved *commandeur* (driver), and robbing his house.[14] In another 1845 case, the Saint-Paul assizes sentenced to life the 32-year old enslaved Malagasy Edouard, for the attempted murder of a man called Eusèbe.[15]

It could take years to find vessels willing to carry enslaved convicts out of the French colonies. In a few cases, shipments took so long that by the time enslaved convicts reached France, enslavement had been abolished. This was true for Marville, Carlin, Casimir, and Edouard, who sailed from Réunion to the Breton port of Lorient on the steamship *Cassini*. It was also the experience of another three men: Pierre Jean, Joseph, and Noël. Pierre Jean had been convicted in 1839, Joseph in 1842, and Noël in 1846, but they were not sent out of Réunion until 1850, when they sailed for France on the *Reine-Blanche*. From there, they went on to French Guiana.[16] The court had tried Noël together with an enslaved

---

[10] ADLR 122W651: Extract from the register of the Court of Assizes, Saint-Paul, 22 March 1837; List of convicts embarked on the government steamer *Cassini* for Lorient, 16 March 1850.

[11] ADLR 2U72: Trial of Marville, Indictment of Saint-Denis Court of Assizes, 31 August 1840, Interrogation of Marville, 24 July 1840; ADLR 122W651: List of convicts embarked on the government steamer *Cassini* for Lorient, 16 March 1850.

[12] ADLR 122W651: Extract from the register of the Court of Assizes of Saint-Paul, 22 December 1842.

[13] ADLR 122W651: Extract from the register of the Court of Assizes of Saint-Denis, 12 October 1844.

[14] ANOM H280 Casimir no. 3116: Extract from the register of the Court of Assizes of Saint-Denis, 7 August 1844, Extract from the register of civil status, Saint Georges (French Guiana); ADLR 122W651: List of convicts embarked on the government steamer *Cassini* for Lorient, 16 March 1850.

[15] ADLR 122W651: Extract from the register of the Court of Assizes Saint-Paul, 25 June 1845.

[16] ADLR 122W651: Governor Marie-Bon-Ézéchiel Barolet de Puligny, Réunion Island, to Governor Eugène Maissin, French Guiana, 1 May 1850, enc. List of five convicts

woman called Souria, for the murder of Noël's wife, Alida.[17] It is not known how many enslaved convicts survived the long and protracted voyage to French Guiana. However, records show that at least one of the men noted above, Casimir, arrived in Cayenne in 1852. He died three years later in Saint-Georges.[18]

At the height of Spain's power in the seventeenth century, its empire extended across much of central and north America, and the Caribbean, including Cuba, Puerto Rico, Santo-Domingo, and Trinidad. The capital of the viceroyalty was New Mexico. During this period, up to the outbreak of the Mexican war of independence in 1810, Spain conscripted convicts from this region into military companies in the Philippines. This was known as the *forzado* (forced) system. Stephanie Mawson has argued that its introduction was a 'response to the emergence of an unruly and disobedient plebeian underclass in the cities and along the highways'. It emerged in parallel with other forced labour schemes, including work in mines and *obrajes* (textile workshops), and was perfectly in keeping with utilitarian Spanish jurisprudence, and the philosophy of 'social cleansing'. Indeed, the Spanish authorities put *plebe* (plebeian) convicts to work rather than subjecting them to imprisonment or execution.[19] In some cases, as Christian De Vito, has shown, the Spanish sent enslaved men to the mines of Almadén, in mainland Spain. In others, notably Havana (Cuba) and San Juan (Puerto Rico), enslaved men worked alongside convicts.[20] The imbrication of punishment in Spanish imperial labour relations was such that De Vito introduces the concept of 'punitive pluralism' to describe their co-existence. This endured much later than was the case in the British and French empires, for in Cuba enslavement was not abolished until 1880, and apprenticeship (*patronato*) ended only in 1886.[21]

---

embarked for France on *La Reine-Blanche*, 11 May 1850. Pierre Jean, Joseph, and Noël were accompanied by the formerly enslaved men Elie Lionel and Sévère Pithye, who were convicted after abolition in 1849.

[17] ADLR 2U81: Trial of Noël and Souria, Indictment of Saint-Denis Court of Assizes, 17 September 1846.

[18] ANOM H280 Casimir no. 3116: Extract from the register of the Court of Assizes of Saint-Denis, 7 August 1844; Extract from the register of civil status Saint Georges (French Guiana); ADLR 122W651: List of convicts embarked on the government steamer *Cassini* for Lorient, 16 March 1850.

[19] Stephanie Mawson, 'Unruly Plebeians and the *Forzado* System: Convict Transportation between New Spain and the Philippines during the Seventeenth Century', *Revista de Indias*, 73, 259 (2013), 694–5 (quote, 694) (693–730) 694–5.

[20] Christian G. De Vito, 'The Spanish Empire, 1500–1898', in Clare Anderson, ed., *A Global History of Convicts and Penal Colonies* (London: Bloomsbury, 2018), 67, 72 (65–95).

[21] Christian G. De Vito, 'Connected Singularities. Convict Labour in Late Colonial Spanish America (1760s–1800)', in Christian G. De Vito and Anne Gerritsen, eds.,

Chapter 4 presented an account of the relationship between enslavement and punitive mobility in the British Empire in the eighteenth and early nineteenth centuries. Taking the story forward beyond the 1820s, the history of penal transportation in the British Empire was intertwined with the history of Spanish imperialism. This is because between 1808 and 1826, all the Spanish colonies excepting Puerto Rico and Cuba won their independence. Of relevance to transportation practices in the Anglophone Caribbean were two events: first, the transformation of the neighbouring Spanish Viceroyalty of New Granada, on mainland Latin America, into the United Provinces of New Granada, during 1810–16; and second, following a brief period of Spanish occupation, in 1819 the declaration of Gran Colombia. A few years after the passing of the 1821 manumission law, Gran Colombia began to free enslaved persons. There, and in other parts of independent Latin America, liberal governments also passed 'free womb' laws (*libertad de vientres*), which decreed that the children of enslaved women would be born free.[22] It seems that in the context of this very gradual emancipation, the former Spanish colonies refused to admit transportation slaves into their provinces. Though Puerto Rico and Cuba remained under Spanish rule until 1898, following a royal decree of 1836 they followed suit.[23] The only convicts sent to the Spanish Empire's two remaining islands during the nineteenth century were transported much later: convicts impressed into the army during the Cuban war of independence (1895–8) and the Spanish American war (1898).[24] Meanwhile, the gradual closure of the former Spanish colonies to convicts also left the British Caribbean with the problem of where to send its convicts.

As a consequence of the closure of the Spanish colonies, in 1822, Britain's Colonial Office directed the colonies to ship transportation felons, whether formerly enslaved or free, to England, where their

---

Micro-Spatial Histories of Global Labour (London: Palgrave, 2018), 171–202; Evelyn P. Jennings, 'The Sinews of Spain's American Empire: Forced Labor in Cuba from the Sixteenth to the Nineteenth Centuries', in John Donoghue and Evelyn P. Jennings, eds., *Building the Atlantic Empires: Unfree labor and imperial states in the political economy of capitalism, ca. 1500–1914* (Leiden: Brill, 2015), 25–53.

[22] On the 1821 manumission and 'free womb' laws, see Aline Helg, *Liberty and Equality in Caribbean Colombia, 1770–1835* (Chapel Hill: University of North Carolina Press, 2004), 8, 140, 163, 169–70, 217, 245.

[23] PP 1826–27 (559) *Criminal and civil justice in the West Indies. (Second series.) First report of the commissioners of enquiry into the administration of criminal and civil justice in the West Indies. Jamaica: Abstract of Statute Law of Jamaica*, 80; TNA CO23/91/9 18 January 1834: James Stephen, assistant under-secretary of state for the colonies, 'Disposal of Colonial Convicts', n.d.

[24] The Spanish also sent a group of prisoners of war from Santo Domingo to Cuba, but Cuba deemed it 'inconvenient' and sent the men on to Spain.

transhipment to one of the Australian penal colonies would be arranged.[25] Ultimately, this direction was incorporated into the 1824 Transportation Act, and included both convicts sentenced to transportation and capital respites.[26] Following the arrival of the first convict hulk in 1824, some of the Caribbean colonies also sent convicts to Bermuda, to await their onwards transportation. Finding a vessel to take convicts to England or Bermuda was not easy, because colonial administrations sought free passage. As in the French Empire, this led to the build-up of a backlog of transportation convicts.[27] One of the shortcomings of the transportation archive is that it is not always clear whether convicts actually went overseas.[28] Nonetheless, there were dozens of cases in which convicts were kept in jail for months or even years.[29] Long waiting times were compounded by the fact that at the same time a larger imperial conversation was taking place in which the Colonial Office called for the alignment of laws on capital crime. By 1837, in England, only murder, attempted murder, and treason still carried the death penalty. Before the abolition of enslavement, the implication of these changes in the Caribbean was to put enslaved and free persons on the same legal footing in regards to the right to give evidence in court and to claim benefit of clergy, the latter of which was a request for a reduction of sentence upon

---

[25] TNA CO28/91/55 8 December 1822: Governor Sir Henry Warde, Barbados, to Henry Bathurst (1st Earl Bathurst), secretary of state for war and the colonies, 8 December 1822.

[26] TNA CO137/178/43 1 May 1831: Chief Justice W. A. Scarlett, Jamaica, to Governor Somerset Lowry-Corry (Earl of Belmore), Jamaica, 15 April 1831.

[27] TNA CO28/103/2 15 January 1829: Provost Marshall J. Walrond, Bermuda, to Governor J. B. Skeete, Bermuda, 15 January 1829; TNA CO28/103/37 21 July 1829: Governor James Lyon to George Murray, secretary of state for war and the colonies, 21 July 1829.

[28] For examples of actual transportations, from Barbados, see TNA CO28/102/29 5 April 1828: Skeete to William Huskisson, secretary of state for war and the colonies, enc. Court of Grand Sessions of Oyer and Terminer, 11 December 1827; TNA CO28/103/17 30 March 1829: Lyon to Murray, 30 March 1829; TNA CO28/110 2 October 1832: George Lamb, under-secretary of state Home Office, to Henry Grey (3rd Earl Grey), under-secretary of state for war and the colonies, 2 October 1832, enc. R. Skinner, superintendent of Bermuda convict hulk *Coromandel*, to J. H. Capper, superintendent of convicts, 15 August 1832; TNA CO28/111: Skeete to F. J. Robinson (1st Viscount Goderich), secretary of state for war and the colonies, 3 February 1833; TNA CO28/109/93 1 December 1832: Lyon to Goderich, 1 December 1832.

[29] For example, TNA CO28/111/101 31 December 1833: Sir Lionel Smith, governor of Barbados and governor-in-chief of the Windward Islands, to Edward Smith-Stanley (14th Earl of Derby), secretary of state for war and the colonies, 31 December 1833, enc. List of men under sentence of transportation from Barbados (to Bermuda), December 1833. See also Melanie J. Newton, 'The King v. Robert James, a Slave, for Rape: Inequality, Gender, and British Slave Amelioration, 1823–1834', *Comparative Studies in Society and History*, 47, 3 (2005), 583–610.

a first conviction.[30] At the start of 1830, Home Secretary Sir Robert Peel raised 'serious objections' to the transportation of Caribbean convicts to Bermuda. He stated that convict labour on dockyard construction was only temporary, and black convicts were 'ill suited' to it. This was the period of amelioration, in the run up to emancipation. Though he did not elaborate, Peel may have been concerned that if enslaved people worked alongside white convict chain gangs, it would upset the racial order of the colony. Indeed, he was unconcerned about their shipment to the majority white colonies of New South Wales and Van Diemen's Land. Thus, he instructed Colonial Secretary Sir George Murray to use his discretion to arrange the necessary passages.[31]

During the period 1831–7, at least 170 convicts were sent to London, of whom 140 were sent on to the Antipodes.[32] However, despite the Australian option and in contravention of colonial law, some Caribbean colonies continued to sell enslaved convicts. Tortola (now, the British Virgin Islands), for example, sentenced nine enslaved persons to be sold and banished during the period 1825–30. Four of them were ended up in Spanish Puerto Rico, and one in St Thomas in the Danish Antilles.[33] Governor Charles Maxwell's legal counsel complained that this type of transportation had 'grown out of a principle of convenience rather than of law', rooted in the inability of the Treasury to pay slave-owners compensation equivalent to the value of the enslaved person.[34] Colonial Secretary Viscount Goderich viewed the practice as dangerously close to slave

---

[30] TNA CO28/93/85 30 December 1824: Warde to Bathurst, 2 December 1824. The court sentenced Richard Streams to death, but the jury recommended him for mercy. Judge Lucas described him as 'turbulent and evil disposed'. See TNA CO28/93/48 30 June 1824: Warde to Bathurst, 30 June 1824. Richard Newton ('an incorrigible offender') had stolen a cow. See TNA CO28/102/29 5 April 1828: Skeete to Huskisson, 5 April 1828, enc. Court of Grand Sessions of Oyer and Terminer, 11 December 1827.

[31] TNA CO23/91/9 18 January 1834: 'Disposal of Colonial Convicts'.

[32] Paton, 'An "Injurious" Population', 453. For detailed information on these transportations, read Paton's appendices alongside those of Duffield, in 'From Slave Colonies to Penal Colonies'.

[33] TNA CO239/29 30 April 1832: Governor William Nicolay, Saint Christopher, to Goderich, 30 April 1832, enc. Return of slaves sentenced to banishment from the British Virgin Islands between the years 1825 and 1832. Note that according to this return, the colony only banished enslaved persons between 1825 and 1830, and that in 1831 the governor pardoned 4 other enslaved persons sentenced to banishment: John Swallow, William Martin, Lancaster, and Shelley.

[34] PP 1831–32 (733) *Papers presented to Parliament, by His Majesty's command, in explanation of the measures adopted by His Majesty's government for the melioration of the condition of the slave population in His Majesty's possessions in the West Indies, on the continent of South America, and at the Mauritius. [In further continuation of the papers presented in July 1832, no. 649]*: Governor Charles Maxwell to Goderich, Tortola, 19 November 1831, enc. H. J. Woodcock (King's counsel) to Maxwell, 10 August 1831, 91–4.

trading, abolished in 1807, because each convict was transported as 'an article of merchandize, rather than as a criminal who is to undergo the sentence of the law'. As it gave slave-owners a financial interest in criminal conviction, he argued, 'such an abuse... cannot be tolerated'.[35] In law, as he noted, only the governor could select transportation destinations, and other convict shipments were unauthorized and illegal.[36] Other Colonial Office discussions at this time drew attention to the illegality and 'questionable propriety' of such sales.[37]

The exchange between Governor Maxwell and the Colonial Office came precisely at the time of an 11-day revolt in Jamaica, since known as the Christmas Uprising or Baptist War. Disappointed that emancipation had not been forthcoming, in a massive assault on imperial authority tens of thousands of enslaved people joined forces to break out in open rebellion. The British repressed the uprising with the same force that they had employed during the 1816 rebellion in Barbados – and went on to display during a revolt that involved several thousand enslaved persons in Demerara in 1823. Indeed, following the Demerara uprisings, the British conducted a series of elaborate and gruesome public hangings, which included the public display of executed bodies at visible locations on the affected plantations. Though the courts returned most other rebels to their owners, they reprieved and banished to Saint Lucia one of the surviving leaders, Jack Gladstone, together with a man called Cato. The judges had spared Gladstone from a death sentence because he had both turned informer and testified about the negative influences of missionaries in Demerara. The latter helpfully supported the British view of them as an undesirable presence in the colony.[38]

Almost a decade after the Demerara revolt, the British executed almost 350 enslaved rebels from Jamaica's Baptist War, following conviction by what Michael Craton describes as 'drumhead courts-martial'.[39] Indeed,

---

[35] PP 1831–32 (733) *Papers presented to Parliament, by His Majesty's command, in explanation of the measures adopted by His Majesty's government for the melioration of the condition of the slave population in His Majesty's possessions in the West Indies*, Goderich to Maxwell, 2 January 1832, 95–6 (quote, 96). See also TNA CO239/29 30 April 1832: Goderich to Maxwell, 4 July 1832.

[36] PP 1831–32 (733) *Papers presented to Parliament, by His Majesty's command, in explanation of the measures adopted by His Majesty's government for the melioration of the condition of the slave population in His Majesty's possessions in the West Indies*, Goderich to Maxwell, 2 January 1832, 96.

[37] TNA CO23/91/9 18 January 1834: 'Disposal of Colonial Convicts'.

[38] Craton, *Testing the Chains*, 285. Jack Gladstone's father was Quamina, who led the rebellion. The British executed him and hung his body in chains outside the *Success* plantation, where both men had lived. See Emilia Viotti da Costa, *Crowns of Glory, Tears of Blood: the Demerara slave rebellion of 1823* (Oxford University Press, 1994), 244.

[39] Craton, *Testing the Chains*, chapter 22 (quote, 314).

at the time Governor Belmore reported the magistrates had ignored his demand that he make the decision on all capital cases, and conducted executions immediately after trials.[40] For its part, the Colonial Office was anxious that further hangings would fan the flames of further unrest.[41] Consequently, Belmore commuted over a dozen capital sentences to penal transportation. As during the earlier period, however, Jamaica found it difficult to find ships willing to take its convicts to England, and therefore many of these enslaved rebels remained in jail on the island.[42] By 1835, with the addition of several men sentenced for arson, murder, or attempted murder, there were 20 of them. They included apprentices, convicted of various offences in the aftermath of emancipation in 1834.[43]

Given the distances and societies that they crossed, the carceral journeys of enslaved or formerly enslaved people were always remarkable. They were dangerous too, and an unknown number died during transportation voyages. For example, one enslaved man from Barbados, Benjamin Walrond, had been sentenced to death in December 1830 for assault with intent to kill. He had struck his owner, Andrew Trevor, who later died. The governor commuted the sentence to penal transportation for life, but whilst awaiting shipment there was a hurricane and Walrond escaped from jail. He remained at large for four years, when he was recaptured and sent to London.[44] There, he was kept on the *Justitia* hulk, where he died in 1838.[45] Enslaved Jamaican Horatio Sandys escaped from transportation twice. In 1828, with five other defendants, he had been sentenced to death for 'malicious cutting'. However, the Supreme Court had commuted his capital sentence on condition that he transport himself from Jamaica. If he returned, it ordered, he would face execution. It seems that Sandys chose to go to Cuba, and not long afterwards in 1829 he returned home. However, the governor did not carry out the sentence of death, ordering only that he go back. Sandys, he stated, had been guilty only of 'obeying that natural feeling which is

---

[40] TNA CO137/182/4 9 April 1832: Lowry-Corry to Goderich, 9 April 1832.
[41] TNA CO137/182/32 28 May 1832: Goderich to Lowry-Corry, 31 July 1832.
[42] TNA CO137/183/35 9 June 1832: Governor the Earl of Mulgrave, Jamaica to Goderich, 3 November 1832.
[43] TNA CO137/198/13 6 March 1835: Governor Howe Peter Browne (Marquess of Sligo), Jamaica, to Robert Hamilton-Gordon (4th Earl of Aberdeen), secretary of state for war and the colonies, 6 March 1835; TNA CO137/197/24 29 January 1835: Browne to Hamilton-Gordon, 29 January 1835.
[44] TNA HO17/18/23 Petitions: Benjamin Walrond or Benjamin Waldon or Benjamin Waldron; TNA CO28/116/32 9 December 1835: Smith to Charles Grant (1st Baron Glenelg), secretary of state for war and the colonies, 9 December 1835.
[45] TNA HO94/4 Convict prison hulks: registers and letter books: 1572 Ben Walrond, age 40, died 17 April 1838 (available via paid subscription to ancestry.com).

common to every man of desiring to return to the Land of his Birth'.[46] In 1831, Sandys returned to Jamaica again.[47] The authorities then embarked him for England, with several other transportation offenders. They included the enslaved transportation convict Alexander Simpson who had been sentenced following the Christmas Uprising.[48] Simpson made it to Van Diemen's Land, but Sandys died a month after shipment from the English hulks.[49]

Jamaica was not the only colony that was somewhat tardy in taking up the Australian transportation option. Indeed, it was only after the start of the period of emancipation and apprenticeship that the Caribbean colonies generally accelerated their use of it. Barbados only transported convicts to New South Wales to any significant degree between 1834 and 1836. Governor Sir Lionel Smith explained this as the consequence of the need for 'strong though just Laws, for the proper control of People coming out of Slavery, that they would not abuse Liberty'.[50] In one case in British Guiana, one man was executed and four sent to the London hulks for transportation, following riots which broke out in Essequibo when the terms of apprenticeship were explained. The secretary of state was highly critical of the confused explanation that he claimed had provoked the rioting, and noted the men's 'docile, industrious, and decorous' conduct since their arrival.[51] During this period, Grenadian slave owner (and former council president administering the government of Grenada), John Henry Earle Berkeley, wrote in a letter to the colonial secretary that Chief Justice Sanderson had shown undue severity in sentencing apprentices to terms of transportation. This included for first offences of petty theft. Berkeley had already petitioned the governor for the pardon of his apprentice, Robert, who had stolen money from him,

---

[46] TNA CO137/178/43 1 May 1831: Lowry-Corry to Goderich, 1 May 1831.
[47] TNA CO137/179/26 30 September 1831: Lowry-Corry to Goderich, 30 September 1831.
[48] TNA CO137/181/37 16 March 1832: Lowry-Corry to Goderich, 16 March 1832; TNA CO137/181/42 22 March 1832: Lowry-Corry to Goderich, 22 March 1832. Simpson is discussed by Ian Duffield, in '"Stated This Offence": High-Density Convict Micro-Narratives', in Lucy Frost and Hamish Maxwell-Stewart, eds., *Chain Letters: Narrating convict lives* (Melbourne University Press, 2001), 119–35.
[49] TNA ADM101/25/8/1 Folios 2–3, 6: Journal of His Majesty's Hired Convict Ship *Emperor Alexander*, William Donnelly Surgeon, between the 13th March and 16th August 1833, during which time the said ship has been employed in conveying convicts from England to Van Diemen's Land (Sandys was taken ill on 15 April and died on 20 May).
[50] TNA CO28/117/66 27 July 1836: Smith to Glenelg, 27 July 1836.
[51] TNA CO111/138 22 June 1835: Governor Sir James Carmichael-Smyth, British Guiana, to Thomas Spring Rice, secretary of state for war and the colonies, 11 October 1834, draft reply, Glenelg to Carmichael-Smyth, n.d. It is not clear whether the men returned to British Guiana.

and even visited him twice on the *Justitia* hulk in Woolwich. He argued that formerly enslaved people had seen their masters' money as their own. To warn new apprentices against the 'vicious habit' of taking it, it would be better to put them to work on the public roads, in full public view. The solicitor and attorney general told the Colonial Office that Robert's sentence was illegal, but he died before he could be released. These law officers also decided that the other six sentences were legal but 'unduly severe'. The Colonial Office advised the Home Office to release some of the offenders, though their fate is unknown.[52]

Though there was no provision for women in the hulks or England, a small number of Caribbean women did reach London for onwards shipment. In the 1820s and 1830s, they included Maria, from Honduras, and Priscilla, Ann Powell, and Cecelia Williams (also known as Celia Marshal), from Jamaica.[53] In 1830, Priscilla had been found guilty of the attempted murder by poisoning of her owner William Samuells, his enslaved housekeeper Jane Jones, and her young daughter. Jane was likely Samuells' mistress, and the child his daughter. Priscilla travelled on to Sydney on the *Elizabeth* in 1836, though we know nothing of her fate in New South Wales.[54] Ann Powell was given a free pardon in London, and was not sent.[55] Embarked from the hospital hulk *Unite* for Sydney, Cecelia Williams never made it, dying at sea in April 1837. According to the ship's surgeon, she was of 'nervous habit of body' and had been 'in delicate health before embarkation'. He wrote in his report of her death that she had been subject to strong 'hysterical paroxysms', which the night before she died had been especially 'severe'.[56]

---

[52] TNA CO101/84/39 11 April 1837: John Henry Earle Berkeley, former temporary administrator of Grenada, to Glenelg, 11 April 1837, draft reply, Glenelg to Berkeley, 5 May 1837; TNA CO101/84/40 23 May 1837: Berkeley to Glenelg, 23 May 1837, draft reply, Glenelg to Berkeley, 2 June 1837. With his uncle, Thomas Berkeley, John Henry Earle Berkeley owned five plantations in Grenada, and one in St Christopher. By the time of emancipation, the former was mortgaged, and compensation for 538 slaves was awarded to the mortgagee, Archibald Paull. The men received £2,022 14s 9d for the 119 enslaved on the Hutchinson Estate in St Christopher. See https://www.ucl.ac.uk/lbs/person/view/1460485689 (accessed 15 May 2018).

[53] TNA CO123/38 1 November 1827: Major General Edward Codd, Superintendent and Commander-in-Chief, at Belize, Honduras, to Goderich, 1 November 1827; TNA CO137/209/95 25 February 1836: Browne to Glenelg, 25 February 1836, Glenelg to Browne 9 April 1836; TNA CO137/212/55 6 August 1836: Browne to Glenelg, 6 August 1836. The women are listed as having been transferred to the Woolwich hulks, in TNA HO9/9 Convict prison hulks: registers and letter books (nos. 6693, 6694, 6695).

[54] Duffield, 'A Storm in a Teapot?'. Duffield notes that Jane Jones' child remains unnamed in the CO archives.

[55] Paton, 'An "Injurious" Population', 463 (Appendix 1).

[56] TNA ADM 101/66/7/3 Folios 14–18: Medical and Surgical journal of the female convict ship *Sarah and Elizabeth* for 15 December 1836 to 3 May 1837 by John Rankine,

Penal Settlements and Convict Depots in the British Caribbean

As noted in previous chapters, the imperial powers used punitive mobility as a means of managing colonial labour. In the British Empire, the colonies sent convicts into penal transportation and put local prisoners to work on infrastructural and development schemes. The 1830s were an exceptionally active period in terms of British parliamentary interest in colonial imprisonment and transportation. There was a parliamentary enquiry specific to the Caribbean, a more globally expansive committee that reported on all British colonies, and the Molesworth report, which recommended the abolition of transportation to New South Wales and the establishment of a new penal colony for the British Empire. Finally, in 1837, the Colonial Office banned the transportation of non-white convicts from the Caribbean and Cape to the Australian colonies. All took place against a backdrop of growing anti-transportation sentiment, which reverberated beyond the Australian colonies during the period 1849–50.

The global ramifications of these discussions are apparent in Governor Henry Light's 1839 proposal for the establishment of a new site of transportation in the interior of British Guiana, which has previously escaped the notice of historians. Though he did not mention the Molesworth report, his proposition was surely a response to it. Indeed, Light compared Guiana to New South Wales, and suggested that the forests around the Mazaruni River could satisfy all the timber needs of the Royal Navy. Convicts could be set to work in logging and digging the canals necessary to facilitate the movement of resources and commodities around the colony. Indigenous people would make excellent guards and, as in the era of enslavement (and in the Australian colonies), government could pay them to return runaways. Convict labour, he added, would more than repay the cost of any financial investment.[57] The Colonial Secretary, the 1st Marquess of Normanby, was dismissive of Light's plan, but in reasoning why wrote only of numerous, but unarticulated, objections.[58] Probably they included not just the challenges that the climate posed, but opposition to the introduction of white convicts into a former slave colony, as in Bermuda earlier on. Indeed, as discussed

---

Surgeon, during which time the said ship was employed in her passage from England to Port Jackson, New South Wales.

[57] TNA CO111/164 29 July 1839 no. 121: Governor Henry Light, British Guiana, to Constantine Phipps (1st Marquess of Normanby), secretary of state for war and the colonies, 29 July 1839.

[58] TNA CO111/164 29 July 1839 no. 121: Note of Robert Vernon (1st Baron Lyveden), under-secretary of state for war and the colonies, 25 September 1839, Normanby's draft response.

below, at this time Trinidad and Jamaica refused to receive white convicts claiming they would degrade empire in the eyes of only recently emancipated men, women, and children.

Governor Light did not lose sight of his idea, however, and four years later in 1841 made a new proposal that blended features of incarceration with transportation. This time, he suggested that locally convicted prisoners sentenced to more than a few months in prison go to an isolated penal settlement. His intention was to put the prisoners to work, in felling timber and in mining granite, the latter then imported from England at huge expense. This hard labour would be reformative and benefit the colony economically. 'By convict labour', Light wrote to Lord John Russell, the new secretary of state for war and the colonies, 'the materials may be obtained at a trifling expense'. Georgetown would then have 'such facilities of improvement as to authorise the prospect of its being unequalled in South America'. Light won the support of the colony's legislative body, the Court of Policy, and following an exploratory mission into the interior by keeper of Georgetown Jail Patrick Horan, and 'practical quarrier' J. P. Sparman, they selected what appeared to be the healthiest most productive spot for the penal settlement. Horan described it as 'an old Indian post' near the confluence of the Mazaruni, Cayuni, and Essequibo rivers.[59]

The combined economic and penal impulses driving the establishment of the settlement is clear in Horan's financial projections of the likely value of the timber and granite at the site, and his rejection of numerous other places that he inspected.[60] Light himself laid the first stone of what became Her Majesty's Penal Settlement (HMPS) Mazaruni, and he directed that free labourers should clear the land and build accommodation for the soon-to-arrive convicts. He appointed Horan as first superintendent. On 6 June 1842, the first batch of fifty-five locally convicted prisoners arrived, and according to Horan's plan they were put to work quarrying granite, which would give 'the quickest and probably most lucrative return' (Figure 5.1).[61]

---

[59] TNA CO111/177 15 March 1841 no. 28: Light to Lord John Russell, secretary of state for war and the colonies, 15 March 1841 (quote); TNA CO111/181 2 November 1841 no. 147: Light to Smith-Stanley, 2 November 1841; WRNAG AB1/73 Court of Policy: Report of Patrick Horan, keeper of H.M. colonial prison of Georgetown, Demerara, appointed to explore the lower Essequebo and its tributary rivers, the Mazaroonie and Cyoni, up to the first falls, for the purpose of selecting an eligible site for the establishment of a penal settlement, 19 May 1841 (quote).

[60] WRNAG AB1/73 Court of Policy: Report of Patrick Horan, 19 May 1841; WRNAG AB1/73 Court of Policy: Report of Patrick Horan, keeper of H.M. colonial prison of Georgetown, appointed ... to examine and report as to the eligibility of the site of the Indian post called 'Sela', and its vicinity, on the Demerary River, for a penal settlement, 29 April 1841.

[61] WRNAG AB1/78 Court of Policy: Report of Patrick Horan, superintendent of HM penal settlement in the river Massaroonie in the county of Essequibo, British Guiana, 17 May 1842; TNA CO111/191: 10 June 1842 no. 100: Ordinance 1 1842, An ordinance

Figure 5.1 HM Penal Settlement on the Mazaruni, c. 1842–3
Source: British Library Additional MS. 16,936.37 & 38: From a collection of views of scenery, buildings, etc., in Guiana; drawn by E. A. Goodall, who accompanied Sir Robert Schomburgk on an expedition 1842 and 1843, to settle the boundaries. Presented by the Secretary of State for the Colonial Department. HM's Penal Settlement on the Mazaruni; two views.[62]

Light clearly envisaged the penal settlement as an exercise in unfree labour extraction, productivity, and reform. In this regard, Mazaruni was entirely in keeping with penal settlements and colonies in other global locations. At this time, contemporaries believed that hard labour would not only be of economic value but rehabilitate convicts and act as a deterrent against crime. However, Mazaruni differed from other sites of punitive relocation during this period in two interrelated respects, for it opened within a decade of emancipation. The role of the penal settlement in managing labour relations was widely recognized during this period, and not just by colonial officials. For example, the famous German botanist Richard Schomburgk, commissioned by the Royal Geographical Society to explore the interior of British

---

to empower the Governor to remove convicted offenders sentenced to imprisonment and hard labor from the different gaols of British Guiana to the penal settlement; Light to Smith-Stanley, 10 June 1842.

[62] On Goodall's paintings of British Guiana, in particular his ethnographic images of Indigenous people, see Michael St John-McAlister, 'Edward Angelo Goodall (1819–1908): An Artist's Travels in British Guiana and the Crimea', *British Library e-Journal*, article 5 (2007).

Guiana,⁶³ expressed the view that Britain established Mazaruni to terrorize the colony's black population.⁶⁴ As Governor Philip Edmond Wodehouse put it later in 1855: '[The prisoner] must pass a life of regular industry – he must, in short, be brought into that condition into which, since the first Emancipation illusions were dispelled, their best friends [i.e. colonists] have anxiously but unsuccessfully endeavoured to bring the whole [black] population of our West Indian Colonies.'⁶⁵ In other words, one of HMPS Mazaruni's key functions was social discipline, and the training of formerly enslaved people and their descendants in productive and remunerative work. In this regard, from its very inception, it was a heavily racialized penal site.

Alongside its extractive potential for the mining of granite, and the relationship between resource exploitation, work, prisoner reform, and social discipline, the perceived benefits of the penal settlement were also connected to the desire to better incorporate Guiana's Indigenous population into the colonial economy, by integrating them into the colonizing goals of the administration. On the banks of the river almost opposite the settlement lay the Church Missionary Society station of Bartica (est. 1829). The Indigenous people living there, known as Amerindians, were at the time being schooled and encouraged to settle down and cultivate land. This was typical of missionary activity, and in Light's view they were becoming 'moral and industrious'. However, Bartica's isolation from Georgetown impeded the station's further expansion or development. Light conceptualized the building of the penal settlement not simply as a means of putting prisoners to productive labour, and thus reforming them, but also as an exercise in Indigenous moralization. He noted that the penal settlement was a means of opening up

---

⁶³ Pauline Payne, *The Diplomatic Gardener: Richard Schomburgk: Explorer and botanic garden director* (North Adelaide, SA: Jeffcott Press, 2007), 6. Payne notes that Joseph Hooker (see Chapter 8) was an admirer of Schomburgk's work.

⁶⁴ *Richard Schomburgk's Travels in British Guiana 1840–1844. Translated and Edited, with Geographical and General Indices, and Route Maps, by Walter E. Roth* [Stipendiary Magistrate of the Demerara River District], Volume I (Georgetown: "Daily Chronicle" Office, 1922), 201–2. The original German text was Richard Schomburgk, *Reisen in Britisch-Guiana in den Jahren 1840–44* (Leipzig: Verlagsbuchhandlung von J. J. Weber, 1847). See also TNA CO111/150 30 August 1837 no: 375: Carmichael-Smith to Glenelg, 30 August 1837, enc. report by Mr Schomburgk, n.d. Schomburgk was particularly admiring of the Pennsylvania system of separate and silent confinement, instituted in the Eastern State Penitentiary, believing it well suited for British Guiana. The alternative was a regime where prisoners were separated at night, but allowed to associate with each other during the day, though sometimes in silence. This was often known as the Auburn system, following its introduction in a prison of the same name in New York in the 1820s. See David J. Rothman, 'Perfecting the Prison: United States, 1789–1865', in Norval Morris and David Rothman, eds., *The Oxford History of the Prison: The practice of punishment in western society* (Oxford University Press, 1998), 105–7 (100–16).

⁶⁵ TNA CO111/305 19 July 1855 no. 102: Governor Philip Edmond Wodehouse, British Guiana, to Russell, 19 July 1855.

communication between the entire region and Georgetown, and thus encouraging the incorporation of Indigenous men and women into the colonial economy.[66] His hope was that the constant flow of convicts and commodities up and down the river would bring the entire area out of isolation, and following Indigenous incorporation would ultimately encourage free settlement.[67] Meantime, he envisaged the use of Indigenous people in penal governance; and as in most other contemporary sites of punitive relocation, those living around the penal settlement were paid to return prisoner runaways.[68]

In both respects, Mazaruni had a close relationship to the mission station. Indeed, beyond economic integration and the employment of Indigenous people to capture convict runaways, its first chaplain was recruited from Bartica. Later in the 1860s and 1870s, the Reverend Canon Farrar, who was chaplain of the penal settlement, set up three new Indigenous missions: St Edwards, The Holy Name, and St Mary's.[69] The settlement also became connected to the site of a new lazaretto. Between 1843 and 1844, the Mazaruni convicts cleared land and then constructed buildings for lepers on the island of Kaow, five miles distant along the Essequibo river.[70] The penal settlement, mission station, and lazaretto formed part of a carceral junction, at the point where the Mazaruni, Cayuni, and Essequibo rivers meet. In an upriver location far distant from Georgetown, prisoners, Amerindians, and lepers became linked to each other, not solely through colonial practices of confinement, but in their encounters, religious practices, and labour. Supplies were shifted from HMPS Mazaruni to Kaow Island, both of which contained signalling stations. Doctors worked between the prison hospital and the lazaretto. Priests ministered to Indigenous converts and prisoners.[71]

---

[66] TNA CO111/191: 10 June 1842 no. 100: Light to Smith-Stanley, 10 June 1842.
[67] TNA CO111/191: 10 June 1842 no. 100: Light to Smith-Stanley, 10 June 1842.
[68] TNA CO111/241: 27 February 1847 no. 40: Light to Grey, 27 February 1847. Previously under-secretary, Henry Grey became secretary of state for war and the colonies in 1846.
[69] TNA CO111/191 10 June 1842 no. 100: Light to Smith-Stanley, 10 June 1842; F. P. L. Josa, *The Apostle of the Indians of Guiana: A memoir of the life and labours of the Rev. W.H. Brett, B.D., for forty years a missionary in British Guiana* (London: Wells, Gardner, Darton and Co., 1887), chapter 13.
[70] TNA CO111/209 14 March 1844 no. 54: Blue Book, 14 March 1844; TNA CO111/215 2 December 1844 no. 250: Light to Smith-Stanley, 2 Dec 1844. On the history of leprosy in British Guiana, see Ramesh Gampat, *Guyana: From Slavery to the Present: Volume 2. Major Diseases* (Bloomington, IN: Xlibris, 2015), chapter 14.
[71] TNA CO111/215 2 December 1844 no. 250: Light to Smith-Stanley, 2 December 1844, enc. Minute by the penal settlement commission, 30 November 1844; TNA CO111/260 18 December 1848 no. 160: Light to Grey, 18 December 1848, enc. Acting governor William Walker, British Guiana, to the commissioners of enquiry, 16 October 1848; TNA CO111/191 10 June 1842 no. 100: Light to Smith-Stanley, 10 June 1842.

Six months after HMPS Mazaruni opened, in 1843, Governor Light reported on the settlement's progress. He claimed that it had become a place of reformation, as well as punishment, and was already turning a profit. The 'wilderness' had been tastefully landscaped, and through the judicious cutting down or otherwise of trees, the penal settlement he claimed constituted a 'picturesque scene' (Figure 5.1). There were workshops and guards' buildings, and a house for the superintendent; the hospital and chapel were under construction. All the work had been carried out by gangs of prisoners. Light explained that they were unfettered and unflogged, and subject to 'moral influence alone'. He also claimed that the penal settlement was so dreaded that in the last report from the inspector general of police, there had been a fifty per cent reduction in crime in the rural districts, and a thirty per cent decrease in the towns.[72] By 1844, Light was claiming that Mazaruni was 'perhaps... the most perfect example for convicts of any part of the colonial empire of Great Britain'. Once the initial infrastructure had been completed, convicts began to clear more land, and continued work in quarrying, planting, and logging.[73] Mazaruni quickly became linked to free enterprise outside the settlement: by 1848 convicts in the sawmill were employed in cutting logs into lumber for private businesses.[74] Moreover, by the 1850s, after serving their sentence in the settlement (or jail), prisoners were obliged to sign a one-year contract of indenture on one of the colony's sugar estates, whilst on probationary tickets-of-leave.[75]

Close to British Guiana in the Caribbean Sea was the colony of Trinidad, which from the 1850s also employed locally convicted prisoners on the Mazaruni model. Stationed at Carrera Island, prisoners cut

[72] TNA CO111/199 11 January 1843 no. 3: Light to Smith-Stanley, 11 January 1843. On the 'picturesque' nature of the penal settlement, see also TNA CO111/246 19 December 1847 no. 220: 'Observations in regard to the penal settlement and prisons generally in British Guiana' (Henry Light), 9 July 1847. Light's full quote is: '[T]he work of Horan would have done honor to the Landscape taste of some of our professors – his grouping of trees, and adjusting this grouping to the different points of the three great rivers and the numerous islands made it then the most picturesque scene that could be imagined.' Light repeated this sentiment in his evidence to an 1849 parliamentary committee, describing Mazaruni also as productive of 'a wholesome terror in those disposed to commit offences'. PP 1849 (297): *Report from the Select Committee on Ceylon and British Guiana, Minutes of Evidence*, 14.
[73] TNA CO111/215 2 December 1844 no. 250: Light to Smith-Stanley, 2 December 1844.
[74] University of Pennsylvania, Rare Book and Manuscript Library, John Nicholson diary, 1848–50, 3rd WI Reg, Eve Leary Barracks, Demerara, 'An expedition from Demerara to the penal settlement up the Massaruni River', 28 March 1848. Nicholson did not elaborate on the terms of this arrangement. However, the fact that it is unmentioned in the CO archives suggests that the arrangement was both unofficial and lucrative for at least some of the personnel and convicts involved.
[75] TNA CO111/321 4 November 1858 no. 126: Wodehouse to Edward Bulwer-Lytton (1st Baron Lytton), secretary of state for the colonies, 4 November 1858.

a canal between the mainland and a place called Point Gourde. Almost half a mile long, fifteen feet wide, and four feet deep, the canal eased the passage of fishermen who previously had to navigate strong currents in the area. Named Hart's Canal after Lovelace Hart, the island's superintendent of prisons, it took two years to complete.[76] The colonial government established the first convict depot proper in Chaguanas forest, just south of the capital, Port of Spain. In 1871, the British parliament instituted an enquiry into prison discipline in the colonies, and by this time Inspector of Prisons Lionel Fraser described Chaguanas as a place of hard labour: much dreaded by convicts and a source of profit to the colony. The convicts were employed in laying a tramway leading from the forest to the bay, cutting and hauling heavy timber, and loading it onto the tramway trucks.[77] The second Trinidad depot was established in the Irois Forest, in the southwest of the island, in 1858. Like Chaguanas, it was dedicated to timber extraction, and as we will see in Chapter 8 also became a place of experimental agriculture. The founding regulations called for the training of convicts in tasks such as squaring wood, splitting sleepers, and making shingles, in preference to free labour. Government departments could apply for this timber, through the Department of Public Works.[78] As the demand for timber decreased, at the start of 1864 government broke up the depot.[79] However, the remaining prisons in Trinidad quickly became full, and the governor reinstituted it a few months later. The convicts continued to work in felling timber and cutting firewood, and a few were sent out to clear and repair Hart's Canal.[80] Subsequently, convicts worked in agricultural cultivation, but at the end of 1872 Irois closed for good, and a third convict depot opened on Carrera Island.[81] The Carrera Island depot became permanent in 1877, with convicts used not only to construct their jail accommodation, but to quarry and break stone for the purpose of road building. At this time, the inspector of prisons reported that the value of their work covered

---

[76] Anthony de Verteuil, *Western Isles of Trinidad* (Port of Spain: The Litho Press, 2002), 44–5.
[77] *Papers Relating to the Improvement of Prison Discipline in the Colonies* (London: H.M.'s Stationery Office, 1875): Report of the inspector of prisons in Trinidad, Lionel M. Fraser, for year ending 31 December 1873, 30.
[78] TNA CO295/199 2 April 1858 no. 53: Governor Robert William Keate, Trinidad, to Lord Edward Stanley, secretary of state for the colonies, 2 April 1858, enc. regulations for the government of the Convict Establishment at the Irois Forest.
[79] TNA CO295/226 20 February 1864 no. 24: Keate to Henry Pelham-Clinton (5th Duke of Newcastle), secretary of state for the colonies, 20 February 1864.
[80] TNA CO295/228 5 October 1864 no. 127: Governor Manners Sutton, Trinidad, to Edward Cardwell (1st Viscount Cardwell), secretary of state for the colonies, 5 October 1864.
[81] *Papers Relating to the Improvement of Prison Discipline in the Colonies*, 31.

the cost of their incarceration.[82] Though the large majority were put to work in the quarries and forests, some prisoners in Trinidad displayed remarkable creativity in their work. The Chaguanas prisoners manufactured polished tables and made mats and blinds from palm leaves. Just as Japan's convict manufactures were displayed at the International Penitentiary Congress in 1891 (Chapter 3), Trinidadian convicts' wooden tools and implements including axe handles, felloes, and spokes were displayed in the 1886 Colonial and Indian Exhibition, held in London's South Kensington.[83]

There are significant connections to be made between emancipation, indentured migration, and the establishment of these three convict depots. In effect, Trinidad was following the precedent set in neighbouring British Guiana. Carrera, Irois, and Chaguanas played a similar role to Mazaruni in managing colonial labour, including the formerly enslaved and indentured workers who began to arrive in 1845. Their parallel function in this respect can be seen in the 1873 transfer of Trinidad's superintendent of prisons, Thomas Sealy, to Mazaruni.[84] In Carrera, convict occupations grew to include collecting sand and burning wood, and the depot even extended to neighbouring Cronstadt Island. Those long-sentenced inmates who desired it were taught a trade, including carpentry, painting, masonry, metalwork, boat-building, cooking, and baking. Others were employed at washing and mending clothes, coir picking, or metal breaking. Despite this apparently wide array of occupations, Superintendent of Prisons G. T. White lamented in 1894: 'Many of the committals were of a class that it is very difficult to know what to do with: laziness is almost a disease with them; work is the only thing that they are afraid of, and it is almost impossible to get them to do any.' Here, he was referring to Indian indentured labourers. They constituted around half of all inmates and were mainly imprisoned for travelling without the required pass or other breaches of immigration ordinances.[85] As a consequence, and up until ten years before the abolition of indenture in 1917, they were treated differently to ordinary prisoners. They did not undertake an initial

---

[82] de Verteuil, *Western Isles of Trinidad*, 44–9.
[83] J. H. Collens, *A Guide to Trinidad: A handbook for the use of tourists and visitors* (London: Elliot Stock, 1888), 123–4. Felloes are the outer rims of wheels. The 1886 exhibition included a clay figure of a convict postman in the British Andaman Islands penal colony, as well as a model of a carpet loom and examples of jail uniforms from Indian prisons. See *Colonial and Indian Exhibition, 1886: Empire of India, special catalogue of exhibits by the Government of India and private exhibitors* (London: William Clowes and Sons: 1886), 37, 42.
[84] *Papers Relating to the Improvement of Prison Discipline in the Colonies*, 26.
[85] NATT Council Paper 42, 1898: Report of the Inspector of Prisons for the year 1897.

penal stage, and worked in garden gangs, either at Government House or in the Botanic Gardens.[86]

The problem for the colonial authorities was how to render conditions in prisons more severe than conditions on the sugar estates, for all kinds of workers. Lionel Fraser, inspector of prisons, wrote of the principle of less eligibility in 1875, when he asked:

> If a man commits a crime and is sent to gaol ... can it be contended that physically he is worse off than when working on the estate? In the gaol he is well lodged, and fed ... with food identical with [sic] that which he consumes when at liberty ... The labour to which he is put is not more severe than that to which he has been accustomed on the estates ... What then does such a prisoner really suffer by imprisonment?[87]

The fact remained that inmates were under restraint, and as in other contexts, the Trinidad prisoners attempted to find agency in their fate. Fraser himself called for the separation of female inmates at night, to prevent 'depravity' between them.[88] Other medical officers claimed that Carrera Island prisoners deliberately made themselves too sick to work. They ate their own faeces or blinded themselves by rubbing limestone or crushed-up crab into their eyes. One indentured labourer sent to prison apparently told the superintendent of prisons that he was hoping for repatriation.[89] White's 1894 report noted that the inmates' sole desire was 'to get into the infirmary and remain there at any cost'.[90] They drank seawater to such an extent that by 1898 convicts were no longer allowed to go to the beach to bathe.[91] The inspector of prisons reported that the closure of Chaguanas in 1894 was a consequence of the open nature of the depot, from which prisoners constantly escaped. Though most were recaptured, this caused 'much trouble and inconvenience'. The prisoners were transferred to Carrera Island, along with their barracks. These had been dismantled and were rebuilt on this alternative site.[92]

---

[86] NATT Council Paper 148, 1907: Report of the Inspector of Prisons for the year 1906-7.
[87] *Papers Relating to the Improvement of Prison Discipline in the Colonies*, 29.
[88] *Papers Relating to the Improvement of Prison Discipline in the Colonies*, 30.
[89] de Verteuil, *Western Isles of Trinidad*, 50.
[90] NATT Council Paper 40, 1895: Report of the Inspector of Prisons for the year 1894.
[91] NATT Council Paper 22, 1899: Report of the Inspector of Prisons for the year 1898.
[92] NATT Council Paper 40, 1895: Report of the Inspector of Prisons for the year 1894.

Anti-transportation and the Idea of a West Indian Penal Colony

As mentioned above, in the early nineteenth century there emerged growing criticism of the Australian penal colonies in Britain. Critics argued that convicts wrote home with positive accounts of life in the colonies, and so ordinary working people believed that transportation offered them otherwise unavailable economic and social prospects. Others attacked the cost of transportation, argued that it had a detrimental effect on free settlement in the colonies, or concluded that it was no longer a deterrent. Therefore, in 1819 government set up a commission of enquiry, chaired by John Bigge, previously chief justice of Trinidad.[93] In three reports of 1822 and 1823 it presented a highly critical account of New South Wales (which then incorporated Van Diemen's Land). The commission attacked Governor Lachlan Macquarie's liberal treatment of convicts and his favourable policies towards ex-convicts, who were known as emancipists. One of its findings was that transportation lacked certainty as a punishment, because convict experiences varied widely according to the treatment that they received from their masters. Subsequently, there was a shift in policy as reformers sought to transform penal transportation into 'an object of real terror'. In New South Wales, this meant that convicts were leased out to landholders and a proper scale of punishment was established. The Bigge reports also prompted the setting up of a limited constitutional government through a legislative council, the establishment of Van Diemen's Land as a separate colony, and extensive legal reforms.[94] It is noteworthy that the report also circulated widely, for example influencing transportation policy in the East India Company's (EIC) penal settlements in the Straits

---

[93] J. M. Bennett, 'Bigge, John Thomas (1780–1843)', Australian Dictionary of Biography, National Centre of Biography, Australian National University, http://adb.anu.edu.au/biography/bigge-john-thomas-1779/text1999, published first in hardcopy 1966 (accessed 7 May 2020).

[94] The two reports dealing with convicts are PP 1822 (448) *New South Wales. Report of the commissioner of inquiry into the state of the colony of New South Wales*, 19 June 1822; PP 1823 (33) *New South Wales. Report of the commissioner of inquiry, on the judicial establishments of New South Wales, and Van Diemen's Land*, 21 February 1823. See also Bennett, 'Bigge, John Thomas (1780–1843)'; Raymond Evans, '19 June 1822: Creating "An Object of Real Terror": the tabling of the first Bigge Report', in Martin Crotty and David Andrew Roberts, eds., *Turning Points in Australian History* (Sydney: University of New South Wales Press, 2009), 48–61; John Ritchie, *Punishment and Profit: The reports of Commissioner John Bigge on the Colonies of New South Wales and Van Diemen's Land, 1822–1823: Their origins, nature and significance* (Melbourne, VIC: Heinemann, 1970); *The Evidence to the Bigge Reports: New South Wales under Governor Macquarie, Volume 2: the written evidence*, selected and edited by John Ritchie (Melbourne, VIC: Heinemann, 1971).

Settlements.[95] Meanwhile, the British Home Secretary, Sir Robert Peel, expressed the view that the disciplinary regime of Bermuda was much more effective than that of New South Wales. Indeed, it was Peel who in 1822 had introduced the bill authorizing convicts to be employed at hard labour in any colony designated by the king. The Convict Labour Act passed into law in 1823, the year before the first convict hulks arrived in the island's dockyard.[96]

In the aftermath of the Bigge reports, attacks on transportation continued, and in 1831 parliament set up a second select committee, on secondary (i.e. non-capital) punishments. Its purpose was 'to ascertain means by which transportation would be rendered more severe and more dreaded'. One line of enquiry for the committee was the calling of a number of witnesses to explore whether 'crimes of a deeper dye' might be punished through especially severe transportation: from Britain to the Caribbean colonies.[97] As discussed in Chapter 4, there was precedent in transportation (and self-banishment in order to avoid a criminal trial) to islands such as Barbados, St Christopher's, and Jamaica in the seventeenth and eighteenth centuries, before the closure of the American colonies to British and Irish convicts following independence in 1782.[98] The 1831 select committee considered the historic destination of Jamaica as well as the newly acquired island of Trinidad. It interviewed Major-General Sir Lewis Grant, governor of Trinidad; Joseph Marryat MP, who had previously visited Trinidad; and William Burge MP, former attorney general of Jamaica. Marryat and Burge

---

[95] IOR P/136/31 (Bengal judicial consultations, 26 August 1824): W. E. Phillips, superintendent of convicts, Penang, minute on the treatment of convicts, 15 April 1824. Phillips noted: 'A perusal of several publications which have lately appeared, concerning New South Wales, has rendered me desirous of bringing under consideration of the board and of the Supreme Government, the condition and treatment of transported convicts here ... To amend the existing system and devise a plan of government and regulation for the future management of the convicts cannot be very difficult to anyone, who will refer to the various acts for the better regulation of places of confinement, and for treating and employing convicts, and the publication of various pieces on the regulation of New South Wales.'

[96] Brenda Gean Mortimer, Rethinking Penal Reform and the Royal Prerogative of Mercy During Robert Peel's Stewardship of the Home Office 1822–7, 1828–30, PhD thesis, University of Leicester, 2017, 49–50.

[97] PP 1831 (276) *Report from the Select Committee on Secondary Punishments: together with the minutes of evidence, an appendix of papers, and an index*, 27 September 1831: minutes of evidence, 105–22 (quotes 106, 122).

[98] Trevor Burnard, 'European Migration to Jamaica, 1655–1780', *William and Mary Quarterly*, 53, 4 (1996), 769–96; Gwenda Morgan and Peter Rushton, *Banishment in the Early Atlantic World: Convicts, rebels and slaves* (London: Bloomsbury, 2013).

owned enslaved people, and during this period were pro-slavery, actively lobbying parliament against emancipation.[99]

Governor Lewis Grant's long military service in the West Indian colonies had begun in Tobago in 1802. He had lived in Trinidad for some fifteen years, and with emancipation looming, and coinciding with the evidence gathering of the 1831 select committee, he approached Colonial Secretary Goderich privately, with a plan to transport English convicts to the island. His interest was in the 1831 Swing rioters, who he represented as agriculturalists unaccustomed to crime, and with the potential to form what he called a 'nucleus' of a free, white population, especially if their families travelled with them. The colonial secretary wrote to Home Secretary Lord Melbourne recommending the plan, not just because it would have the effect of separating political offenders from other transportation convicts who he described as morally depraved, but because it would be cheaper than sending them to New South Wales, and could form the basis of the population described by Grant.[100] Grant later testified before the parliamentary select committee on the benefits of white convicts. Before sending for their families and establishing themselves, such convicts could work on the fortifications or as mechanics (the contemporary description for skilled labourers).[101] Slave owner Burge, on the other hand, strongly opposed convict transportation to the Caribbean, fearing enslaved persons would see 'the degraded state of convicts' and this would impact on the hierarchies of race that underpinned labour relations. He concluded: 'I think it is extremely dangerous as a political measure.'[102] Marryat, also a slave owner, remarked similarly: 'If [convicts] are to be kept in irons, the moral effect would be very bad. If the slave population see a white man working as a slave, the whole frame of society would be disorganized, and very great danger would

---

[99] Legacies of British slave-ownership database: William Burge https://www.ucl.ac.uk/lbs/person/view/13564; Joseph Marryat https://www.ucl.ac.uk/lbs/person/view/11416 (accessed 15 April 2018).

[100] TNA CO295/89 12 January 1831: Governor Major-General Sir Lewis Grant, Trinidad, to Goderich, 12 January 1831, draft reply, 14 January 1831; TNA CO295/89 17 February 1831 (private): Grant to Goderich, 17 February 1831; CO295/89 23 March 1831: Grant to Grey, 23 March 1831. Acting governor Colonel Sir Charles Smith, commanding engineer in the West Indies, was also in favour of the plan. See TNA CO295/89 19 April 1831: Smith to Grey, 19 April 1831; TNA CO295/89 15 June 1831: Smith to Grey, 15 June 1831; TNA CO295/89 3 July 1831: Smith to Grey, 3 July 1831.

[101] PP 1831 (276) *Report from the Select Committee on Secondary Punishments*... minutes of evidence, 105–22, and Appendix 8: papers relative to the locating [of] convicts in Trinidad, letter from Sir Major-General Sir Lewis Grant to Grey, 29 May 1831, 149–53.

[102] PP 1831 (276) *Report from the Select Committee on Secondary Punishments*... minutes of evidence, 118.

arise.'[103] Despite his initial enthusiasm, Goderich developed other objections when it emerged that Trinidad's plan was to treat the convicts 'as indulgently as circumstances would permit'. This meant that there would be no labour benefit to offset against the cost of the system.[104] Ultimately, the select committee did not propose any change to secondary punishment, and asked for the resumption of the enquiry the following year.[105] This did not happen, the discussion on Trinidad ended, and there were no further investigations until 1837, when the government set up a third select committee, chaired by Sir William Molesworth.

The Molesworth Committee was concerned with whether transportation was feared and was thus a deterrent punishment, and whether it was an effective means of reforming convicts. It also reported on the impact of transportation on 'morality' in the penal colonies, and on issues of economy and cost. Finally, it considered whether it was possible to reform the system, and if not, what should replace it. The committee concluded that penal transportation was founded in violence, produced immorality and 'unnatural vice', and in other respects New South Wales and Van Diemen's Land were comparable to slave colonies. In the context of the 1831 committee's concerns about the moral effect of convicts and enslaved people working in close proximity to each other in the Caribbean, Molesworth's interest in property rights in convicts in particular is interesting. Earlier in 1832, Archbishop of Dublin Richard Whately, who supported the building of penitentiaries at home over transportation overseas, had described convict transportation as 'domestic slavery'. He called the New South Wales government a 'large slave merchant' which on the arrival of each transportation ship gave away to free settlers 'several hundred slaves'.[106] This view was also expressed by famous penal reformer Alexander Maconochie (see Chapter 7).[107] Maconochie cited at length what he described as an 'anonymous' account of a visit to New South Wales:

---

[103] PP 1831 (276) *Report from the Select Committee on Secondary Punishments* ... minutes of evidence, 121.

[104] See TNA CO295/89 19 April 1831: Grey to Smith (draft reply), 25 May 1831.

[105] PP 1831 (276) *Report from the Select Committee on Secondary Punishment*, 3.

[106] Richard Whately, *Thoughts on Secondary Punishments, in a letter to Earl Grey, to which are appended, two articles on transportation to New South Wales, and on secondary punishments; and some observations on colonization* (London: B. Fellowes, 1832), 116 (emphasis in original). Following critique of this text, Richard Whately published *Remarks on Transportation, and on a recent defence of the system; in a second letter to Earl Grey* (London: B. Fellowes, 1834).

[107] Alexander Maconochie, *Australiana: Some thoughts on convict management, and other subjects connected with the Australian penal colonies* (Hobart Town, Van Diemen's Land: J. C. MacDougall, 1839), 6.

[T]he prisoner servants were treated as badly as I can conceive any slaves to be out of the West Indies ... The system of assignment is on the face of it only a disguised system of slavery. The assignee's master is bound to feed, clothe, and lodge his servant, as an owner does his slave. This is the wages of both; and if indolent or insolent, both receive the slave's stimulus – the lash. In the present enlightened age slavery is almost universally admitted to have a degrading and debasing effect on the slave. If it was so in the West Indies, why should it be otherwise in Van Diemen's Land.[108]

In these ways, whilst slave owning lobbyists like MPs Burge and Marryat feared the consequences of mixing indiscriminately white convicts and enslaved Africans and Creoles, anti-transportation rhetoric drew strength from critiques of enslavement.[109]

As is well known, ultimately, Molesworth passed resolutions to the effect that transportation to New South Wales and the settled districts of Van Diemen's Land should be discontinued and substituted with imprisonment and hard labour, at home or 'overseas'. If the latter, penal colonies should be located in places where there were no free settlers, and convicts should be compelled to leave following completion of their sentence. Only long-sentenced offenders should go to the colonies.[110] Following the Molesworth report, in 1840, transportation to New South Wales ceased. In response to its critique of the arbitrary nature of convict assignment (to private masters), the system in Van Diemen's Land was reformed, with transportation divided into penal

---

[108] Maconochie, *Australiana*, 37.

[109] J. B. Hirst, *Convict Society and Its Enemies: A history of early New South Wales* (Sydney, NSW: Allen and Unwin, 1983), 26–7; Kirsten McKenzie, *Scandal in the Colonies: Sydney and Cape Town 1820–50* (Melbourne University Press, 2004); Kirsten McKenzie, 'Discourses of Scandal: Bourgeois Respectability and the End of Slavery and Transportation at the Cape and New South Wales, 1830–1850', *Journal of Colonialism and Colonial History*, 4, 3 (2003). doi:10.1353/cch.2004.0011. An important gendered analysis of transportation, slavery, sexuality, and abolition is Kirsty Reid, *Gender, Crime and Empire: Convicts, settlers and the state in early colonial Australia* (Manchester University Press, 2007), esp. chapters 4 and 6.

[110] PP 1837 (518) *Report from the Select Committee on Transportation; together with the minutes of evidence, appendix, and index*, 14 July 1837; PP 1837–38 (669) *Report from the Select Committee on Transportation; together with the minutes of evidence, appendix, and index*, 3 August 1838, xli–xliii, xlvi–xlvii. Note: the report is printed in paper no. 669 only. See also John Ritchie, 'Towards Ending an Unclean Thing: The Molesworth Committee and the Abolition of Transportation to New South Wales, 1837–40', *Australian Historical Studies*, 17, 67 (1976), 144–64; Norma Townsend, '"The Clamour of ... Inconsistent Persons": Attitudes to Transportation within New South Wales in the 1830s', *Australian Journal of Politics and History*, 25, 3 (1979), 345–57. The most recent literature is: Isobelle Barrett Meyering, 'Abolitionism, Settler Violence and the Case against Flogging: A Reassessment of Sir William Molesworth's Contribution to the Transportation Debate', *History Australia*, 7, 1 (2010), 6.1–6.18, and David Andrew Roberts, 'Beyond "the Stain": Rethinking the Nature and Impact of the Anti-transportation Movement', *Journal of Australian Colonial History*, 14 (2012), 205–79.

stages through which convicts could move on the basis of time served and conduct.¹¹¹ At the same time, as part of broader knowledge circulations (Chapter 7), global critics of penal colonies repeatedly made reference to the Molesworth Committee's discussions about the prevalence of so-called sexual immorality by and between men. France alluded to the Molesworth report in its 1851 Mackau Commission, on the desirability or otherwise of penal colonies, for example. It referred to 'monstrous abuses and disorders' in the Australian colonies, and the need for a balanced gender ratio.¹¹² They used numerous other documents, including the Bigge reports, in other debates.¹¹³

During the same period, criticisms of transportation in the Caribbean colonies were also emerging. Especially during the period of apprenticeship, colonial administrators questioned the value of penal transportation as a means of punishment and deterrence. In 1836, Secretary of State for War and the Colonies Lord Glenelg complained that not only did the Caribbean population have no knowledge of their likely fate in the Australian colonies, but the demand for labour in the British West Indies was so great that it was preferable to put them to work on the public roads. He called for the adoption of 'some general scheme of secondary punishment producing a more wholesome terror, subjecting

---

[111] *The Convict Probation System: Van Diemen's Land 1839–1854: A study of the probation system of convict discipline; together with C. J. La Trobe's 1847 report on its operation, and the 1845 report of James Boyd on the probation station at Darlington, Maria Island*, commentary and notes by Ian Brand (Hobart, TAS: Blubber Head Press, 1990).

[112] ANOM COL/H3: Commission de déportation: rapport (1851). The Mackau Commission proposed New Caledonia as the perfect location for a penal colony. See Jacqueline Dutton, 'Imperial Eyes on the Pacific Prize: French Visions of a Perfect Penal Colony in the South Seas', in John West-Sooby, ed., *Discovery and Empire: The French in the South Seas* (University of Adelaide Press, 2013), 271 (245–82). See also Whately, *Remarks on Transportation*, Appendix No. 5: Extracts from the Remarks of the French Commissioners on the American System of Secondary Punishments. Note that information flowed towards Molesworth too. For example, we know from a digitized example that he owned a copy of the East India Company's 1838 *Report of the Committee on Prison Discipline*: http://books.google.co.uk/books/reader?id=4BQPAQAAMAAJ&printsec=frontcover&output=reader&pg=GBS.PP1 (accessed 1 July 2014).

[113] A famous French critique of penal transportation that drew on the Bigge reports is Jules de la Pilorgerie, *Histoire de Botany Bay, etat present des colonies pénales de l'Angleterre, dans l'Australie, ou examen des effets de la deportation, considéreée comme peine et comme moyen de colonisation* (Paris: Paulin, 1836). See also ANOM COL/H2/1: *Mémoire sur la Déportation des Forçats, présenté en 1828, par M. Martemarie* (Havre: Imprimerie de Stanislas Faure, 1840) [presented to AM. Hyde de Neuville, minister of the navy and the colonies]. Translations of many Australian colonial documents are located in the papers of de Michaux, who was under-secretary to the ministry of the navy and the colonies. See ANOM COL/H59: Dossiers de Michaux, *Documents sur la transportation Anglaise en Australie*, Paris, September 1864: *Resumé* and *Appréciations en ce qui touch le guyane française*. See also Colin Forster, *France and Botany Bay: The Lure of a Penal Colony* (Melbourne University Press, 1996), 128–42.

their Revenues to smaller charges, and relieving the Australian colonies from an inconvenience to which they ought not to be subjected'.[114] In the same year, the Governor of Barbados, Sir Lionel Smith, informed Colonial Secretary Glenelg that the legislative council had given him the power to commute transportation sentences to hard labour on the grounds that transportation was expensive and took workers out of the colony. Glenelg approved this change in policy, though clearly concerned to avoid claims of re-enslavement, he directed that prisoners' chains should neither be 'more galling' than those used in England nor worn by women.[115]

In 1837, against the background of Glenelg's earlier critique, the appointment of the Molesworth Committee, and anti-transportation comparisons between convictism and enslavement, the Colonial Office prohibited further shipments of convicts from the Caribbean to the Australian colonies. It declared black convicts as 'injurious', in what according to Diana Paton was a deliberate attempt to racially differentiate the colonies.[116] The constant delays and expense of transportation, via England, was certainly an important consideration. Later correspondence suggests that mortality and morbidity among black transportation convicts was an additional factor. Clearly, the Colonial Office also associated some colonies like New South Wales with European settlement and others including in the Caribbean with the 'native' production of tropical commodities like sugar, coffee, and tobacco. Indeed, Glenelg argued: 'as applied to the negro race, this mode of punishment fails to possess most of the essential qualities of an efficient secondary punishment'.[117] Moreover, not only were military convicts sentenced by courts martial excluded from the measure, the Colonial Office paid their costs.[118] At this time, around fifty black convicts per year were so

---

[114] TNA CO101/82/7 17 September 1836: Glenelg to Governor John Beckles, Grenada, 17 September 1836.

[115] TNA CO28/117/66 27 July 1836 no. 53: Governor Sir Lionel Smith, Barbados, to Glenelg, 27 July 1836, Glenelg to Governor Murray MacGregor, Barbados, 28 November 1836, 354–5; CO28/119 24 February no. 43: Extracts of message from the House of Assembly to Murray MacGregor, 21 February 1837. Murray MacGregor replaced Smith as governor of Barbados in 1836.

[116] On penal transportation to the Australian colonies, debates around its abolition, and Glenelg's 1837 prohibition, see Paton's important article, 'An "Injurious" Population', esp. 452–5. Also: TNA CO23/91/9 18 January 1834: 'Disposal of Colonial Convicts'; TNA CO318/128 (Home Office): Glenelg to Phillipps, 31 May 1837.

[117] PP 1837 (521) Abolition of slavery: Glenelg's circular despatch to the governors of the West India colonies, &c., 25 May 1837; TNA CO28/164 20 April 1846 no. 22: William Ewart Gladstone, secretary of state for war and the colonies, 20 April 1846; Gladstone to Governor Sir Charles Edward Grey, Barbados, 15 June 1846.

[118] TNA CO28/122/20 22 February 1838 no. 30: Murray MacGregor to Glenelg, 22 February 1838 (Colonial Office circular, 30 December 1837).

sentenced in the West Indian colonies, though in practice most were not transported, but put to hard labour in prisons or workhouses.[119] It is interesting to note that the prohibition never applied to the western Indian Ocean sugar colony of Mauritius. This was perhaps because it escaped attention from its practice of shipping convicts directly to New South Wales and Van Diemen's Land, rather than via England.[120] Somewhat anomalously, the Cape Colony in Southern Africa was, however, included.[121]

The 1837 prohibition had two related impacts. First, some colonies continued to sentence convicts to transportation, and if they were not sent away after a period of time according to law, they had to be released. Thus Glenelg advised them to substitute imprisonment or hard labour for transportation, but they saw them as unsatisfactory punishments lacking in deterrence.[122] Consequently, and following the 1824 Transportation Act (which empowered the Crown to appoint places for the transportation of British subjects),[123] as well as Molesworth's recommendation on the establishment of 'overseas' penal colonies, the colonial secretary and the Caribbean colonies then reinvigorated earlier discussions on a regional penal colony. They had raised the desirability of such a site previously, in the larger context of British reforms to criminal law in the 1830s, and the abolition of capital punishment for crimes other than murder. This had meant that as the most important secondary punishment, transportation sentences increased. As noted above, as early as 1831, Colonial Secretary Goderich had proposed the setting up of a Caribbean penal colony, but nothing further happened.[124] In 1835, Governor Blayney Townley-Balfour suggested the Bahamas as an ideal location, for convicts could be employed in salt raking or on the roads.

---

[119] Paton, 'An "Injurious" Population', esp. 452–5; TNA CO23/91/9 18 January 1834: 'Disposal of Colonial Convicts'.

[120] Clare Anderson, *Subaltern Lives: biographies of colonialism in the Indian Ocean world, 1790–1920* (Cambridge University Press, 2012), chapter 3.

[121] Clare Anderson, 'Convicts, Carcerality and Cape Colony Connections in the 19th Century', *Journal of Southern African Studies*, 42, 3 (2016), 436 (429–42).

[122] TNA CO318/128 (Home Office): Glenelg to Phillipps, 31 May 1837. An example response is PP 1837–38 (596) Report of Captain J.W. Pringle, on prisons in the West Indies. Jamaica. Printed, 17 July 1838, 5.

[123] 1824 Transportation Act (5 Geo. IV cap. 84). Note that after 1837 in the Leeward Islands the courts in St Christopher, Nevis, and Montserrat always substituted imprisonment and hard labour for terms of years; whilst Antigua, Dominica, and Tortola repealed transportation statutes. See TNA CO7/106 25 June 1856 no. 10: Governor Ker Baillie Hamilton, Antigua, to Henry Labouchere, secretary of state for the colonies, 25 June 1856.

[124] TNA CO137/178/57 26 May 1831 no. 5 folios 278–81: Lowry-Corry to Goderich, 24 May 1831.

Again, no action followed.[125] Two years later, the governor of Barbados addressed the House of Assembly. 'The population can hardly be supposed to possess any definite notions respecting the place to which criminals are sent, or the penalties awaiting them there', he said, and reiterated Glenelg's earlier plea for a punishment that might induce 'wholesome terror'.[126] Following the 1837 prohibition on sending convicts to the Australian colonies, Jamaica raised the issue again in 1839.[127] Eventually, an 1840 order in council enabled colonial governors to appoint transportation destinations, though directed that convicts could not be sent to places that refused to receive them. This was a significant constraint, and, as a result, some locations such as Saint Lucia chose to keep its prisoners rather than send them away. They were employed in what the lieutenant-governor called 'useful labour', under 'a system of reformatory discipline'. The men's work included draining marshes, repairing the roads, and extending the wharves. The women made prison clothes. All attended religious services, which the governor of Barbados considered 'a material part of any efficient system of prison discipline'.[128]

In Governor Light's first proposal for a penal settlement for British Guiana, he suggested that it might be open to convicts from the other West Indian colonies. Just a few months after it opened in 1843, the Governor of Jamaica, James Bruce (8th Earl of Elgin), sent Inspector of Prisons John Daughtrey to the colony, with a view to discussing the matter.[129] Daughtrey had recently returned from a tour of prisons in the USA. Like Governor Light, he admired the separate and silent Pennsylvania system, and the building of Jamaica's first penitentiary was underway.[130] Almost simultaneously, the Governor-in-Chief of the

[125] TNA CO23/93/45 3 April 1835 no. 20 folios 172–5: Governor Blayney Townley-Balfour, Bahamas, to Aberdeen, 3 April 1835. On such proposals, see also Paton, 'An "Injurious" Population', 452–3.
[126] TNA CO28/129/16 no. 124 folios 83–92: Message from Murray MacGregor to the Speaker and House of Assembly, 24 January 1837.
[127] TNA CO37/240 5 December 1839 no. 28: Governor Charles Metcalfe, Jamaica, to Russell, 5 December 1839; draft reply, 16 January 1840.
[128] TNA CO28/173 11 September 1850 no. 7: Colebrooke to Grey, 11 September 1850, enc. Lieutenant-Governor C.H. Darling, Saint Lucia, to Colebrooke, 19 and 22 March 1849 (quotes). After 1833, Saint Lucia was part of the Windward Islands (with Grenada, Saint Vincent, and the Grenadines), which were administered from Barbados.
[129] TNA CO137/274 19 August 1843 no. 145: Governor James Bruce (8th Earl of Elgin), Jamaica, to Smith-Stanley, 19 August 1843, Elgin to Light, 7 August 1843, Light to Elgin, 26 September 1843; TNA CO137/375 1 November 1843 no. 170: Elgin to Smith-Stanley, 1 November 1843, Light to Elgin, 4 October 1843 (quote). Daughtrey was inspector of prisons between 1841 and 1861. On his career, see Diana Paton, *No Bond but the Law: Punishment, Race and Gender in Jamaican State Formation, 1780–1870* (Durham, NC: Duke University Press, 2004), 127–9.
[130] Paton, *No Bond but the Law*, 128–34.

Windward Islands Charles Edward Grey, and the Governor-in-Chief of the Leeward Islands, Charles Fitzroy, asked British Guiana to receive their convicts. Light put the issue to the Court of Policy, the colony's legislative council, which rejected it because as he explained: 'The Colonists took fire at the idea of British Guiana becoming the Botany Bay of the West Indies, and were unwilling to risk the good name at the outset of their great scheme of influx of emigrants.'[131] Light later wrote privately to Governor Elgin, expressing his regret at the legislature's decision. 'I still hope my views will be effected', he noted, 'but at the moment the feeling is too strong to overcome.'[132] The Court of Policy remained steadfast in its rejection of Mazaruni as a regional penal colony, despite the financial benefits it would have brought in the form of the colonies' contribution to its overall cost.[133] It also turned down an approach from the East India Company, which wanted to send to Mazaruni white convicts sentenced to transportation in India.[134] There was perhaps some truth in the Court's claim that in the aftermath of abolition the existence of a penal settlement in the colony would deter indentured or other forms of labour that had some degree of choice over their destination. Indeed, in 1843, Light was claiming that emigration agents in West Africa and working for Jamaica and Trinidad, were telling the potential Liberated African migrants of Sierra Leone that Guiana was 'Felon Colony' (see also Chapter 4).[135] Mazaruni, in the meantime, continued to receive prisoners from all over British Guiana. Though the majority were born in the colony, reflecting the demography of migration flows to the colony during this period, the settlement also received Barbadian, European, Portuguese, African, and Asian prisoners.[136]

The opening of Mazaruni and British Guiana's refusal to accept convicts from the wider Caribbean coincided with a Colonial Office circular to the colonies, again igniting discussions about a penal colony for the West Indies. The Colonial Office had neither the power nor the authority to order the colonies to finance it, though, and for this and other reasons,

---

[131] TNA CO111/203 16 October 1843 no. 163: Light to Stanley, 16 October 1843 (quote), enc. Extract from the minutes of the proceedings of the Honorable the Court of Policy, of the Colony of British Guiana, 19 September 1843; TNA CO28/157/21 October 1842 no. 32 folios 259–60A: Governor-in-Chief Charles Edward Grey, Windward Islands (Barbados), to Smith-Stanley, 21 October 1843, Light to Grey, 3 October 1843; TNA CO111/203 16 October 1843 no. 163: Governor-in-Chief Charles Fitzroy, Leeward Islands (Antigua), to Light, 14 September 1843.
[132] TNA CO111/203 16 October 1843 no. 163: Light to Elgin, 4 October 1843 (private).
[133] TNA CO111/305 19 July 1855 no. 102: Wodehouse to Russell, 19 July 1855.
[134] TNA CO111/257 13 September 1848 no 93: Walker to Grey, 13 September 1848.
[135] TNA CO111/203 16 October 1843 no 163: Light to Smith-Stanley, 16 October 1843.
[136] PP 1849 (297) *Select Committee on Ceylon and British Guiana*, Appendix 14, 310–11.

the proposals that emerged from time to time never came to anything.[137] The lieutenant-governor of Saint Vincent, for example, stated that its offshore islands (the Grenadines) had no water supply, and in any case the legislature would never sanction it. The lieutenant-governor of Grenada noted that most of the small islands were privately owned.[138] In 1844, the governor of Barbados proposed Saint Lucia. He lamented the total lack of discipline on the public works, as the convicts were 'daily seen and spoken to on the highway and thoroughfares by their acquaintances and seem to become hardened and stubborn'. He added that they loathed the work, and resisted 'as far as they dare', but their constant return to prison proved that the punishment was not deterrent. He believed that once the colonies had paid the cost of convict shipment, Saint Lucia could become self-sufficient. It also had the advantage of being 'a natural prison' meaning that there would be no need to construct costly buildings or employ a large number of guards. The convicts could be employed in building roads and clearing land for plantations, and if the settlement were established in the mountains, the climate would be suitable for Europeans too. However, this plan was not realized, the sticking point being the inability of the Crown to grant a tract of land.[139] At this time, and reluctantly, Colonial Secretary Earl Grey agreed that Barbados could send its convicts to other locations, but as other colonies had to agree to receive them, it is unlikely that such transportations ever took place.[140]

In 1844, Colonial Secretary Lord Edward Smith-Stanley wrote to Governor of Jamaica Elgin to request that he host a conference on the establishment of a regional penal colony, with the governors-in-chief of the Windward Islands (based in Barbados), Leeward Islands (Antigua) and Trinidad.[141] There was considerable private interest in the matter, including from planters keen to secure a new source of unfree labour following emancipation.[142] The conference took place in February 1845,

---

[137] TNA CO111/305 19 July 1855 no. 102: Russell to Wodehouse, n.d.; TNA CO123/78 (Foreign Office): marginal note [author illegible], 21 April 1849.

[138] TNA CO28/159/35 20 April 1844 no. 14 folios 212–30: Lieutenant-Governor R. Doherty, Saint Vincent, to Smith-Stanley, 17 April 1843; Lieutenant-Governor A. Doyle to Smith-Stanley, 3 May 1843.

[139] TNA CO28/159/35 20 April 1844 no. 14 folios 212–30: Grey to Smith-Stanley, 20 April 1844.

[140] This was later reported in: TNA CO123/78 (Foreign Office): Consul-General W. D. Christie, Mosquito Coast, to Henry John Temple (3rd Viscount Palmerston), foreign secretary, 8 March 1849.

[141] TNA CO318/161: colonial circular, 16 August 1844.

[142] TNA CO318/164: J.H. Milner, Barbados, to Smith-Stanley, 21 January 1845, enc. 'On the establishment of a Penal Settlement for the West India Colonies', n.d. Milner described himself as 'a Jamaica planter and a resident for some time in that island'. According to the Legacies of British Slave-ownership database, he had not previously owned enslaved persons: https://www.ucl.ac.uk/lbs/ (accessed 10 May 2018).

but came to no firm decision.[143] The colonial secretary continued to hope that the Guiana Court of Policy would eventually capitulate and agree to receive Caribbean convicts. However, it remained firm in its resolve.[144] Other proposals continued to trickle into the Colonial Office. In 1846, the governor of Barbados asked for the reinvigoration of transportation to Van Diemen's Land, but the colonial secretary refused, on the grounds of cost and health.[145] In 1849, following a suggestion from the council president of the island E. B. Baynes, Governor James Macaulay Higginson of Antigua suggested Montserrat as a penal colony. Baynes had described it as 'the Montpellier of the West Indies', writing: 'There is scarcely to be found in any part of the globe a purer or more salubrious air than that breathed on the more elevated portions of this delightful island.' What Higginson described as a 'proper system of prison discipline' could be enforced on the island and offer the hope of rehabilitation and reform. Higginson claimed that there had been a recent increase in crime and blamed this on the absence of the penal option of transportation.[146] As on previous occasions, the issue stalled.[147] Another proposal came during the same year from the British consul-general in Honduras. The Colonial Office turned it down, noting that the British parliament could not be asked to fund it, and there was no hope that the colonies would co-operate.[148] The chief justice of Barbados despaired that nothing would happen unless a parliamentary act defined the principle of the establishment, laid down details, and regulated the amount that each colony should provide. If it were left to each colony to join or not, there was little hope that any such plan could succeed. According to him, the law on deportation, noted above, was not a good substitute for transportation.[149]

In 1850, the governor of Barbados requested British, Irish, or Caribbean convicts to build a new harbour of refuge in Bridgetown, comparing the nature of the works to those being constructed by convicts

---

[143] TNA CO318/161: colonial circular, 16 August 1844; TNA CO7/81 25 January 1845 no. 1: Fitzroy to Smith-Stanley, 25 January 1845; TNA CO7/81: 24 March 1845 no. 2: Fitzroy to Smith-Stanley, 24 March 1845.
[144] TNA CO28/187 10 June 1857 no. 29: Governor Sir Francis Hincks, Barbados, to Labouchere, 10 June 1857; Hincks to Wodehouse, 12 September 1856; Wodehouse to Hincks, 2 May 1857.
[145] TNA CO28/164 20 April 1846 no. 22: Grey to Gladstone, 20 April 1846; Gladstone to Grey, 15 June 1846.
[146] TNA CO7/93 26 December 1849 no. 47: Governor James Macaulay Higginson, Antigua, to Grey, 26 December 1849, enc. Council President E. D. Baynes, Montserrat, to Higginson, 4 December 1849.
[147] TNA CO7/93 26 December 1849 no. 47: draft reply to Higginson, 31 January 1850.
[148] TNA CO123/78 (Foreign Office): Christie to Palmerston, 8 March 1849; Grey's note, 21 April 1849; draft reply 5 May 1849.
[149] TNA CO28/172 29 August 1850 no. 54: Chief Justice R. Bowcher Clarke to Governor William MacBean George Colebrooke, Barbados, 27 August 1850.

in Bermuda. However, former Governor of Bermuda, and Governor-In-Chief of the Windward Islands, William Reid, reported that the proposal was 'a work of magnitude beyond the means of Barbados, even if aided by a penal settlement', and the Colonial Office took the suggestion no further.[150] Later calls for the reintroduction of transportation to Bermuda in 1853 solicited an unsympathetic response from the colonial secretary, who lamented their 'local jealousies' and lack of 'public spirit'.[151]

Across the Atlantic world to India, in 1857 the British faced what was one of the greatest threats to empire in the nineteenth century. Mutineers and rebels broke out in rebellion against the ruling East India Company across large parts of north India, and the British only regained control after some months. The mutineers and rebels destroyed or broke open dozens of prisons and released thousands of prisoners. This left the Company with an unprecedented penal crisis; for it had little secure prison accommodation for newly convicted mutineers and rebels, let alone recaptured prisoners. There existed in 1857 Indian penal settlements in Penang, Malacca, and Singapore (Straits Settlements) and in Burma, but they refused to take transportation rebels on the grounds that they might spread discontent and unrest among their convict populations.[152] The revolt impacted on Britain's far-distant Caribbean colonies in two interrelated ways: first, it interrupted the supply of indentured labour; second, it appeared to offer plantation owners, in the form of people convicted of mutiny and rebellion, an additional if short-term labour supply. Indeed, Governor Robert William Keate reported from Trinidad: 'the present disturbed state of India has caused doubts to arise of a full supply of labor being obtained from thence during the present season, and has consequently fixed the attention of Planters more decidedly on such other sources as they consider to be within their reach'.[153]

Consequently, following the resumption of British control, there were discussions between the Board of Commissioners for the Affairs of India (otherwise known as the Board of Control) and the Colonial Office about

---

[150] TNA CO28/173 11 September 1850 no. 7: Colebrooke to Grey, 11 September 1850; TNA CO28/173 (Ordnance Office) 20 November 1850: Report of Lieutenant-Colonel William Reid, Commanding Royal Engineers, Barbados, 11 November 1850.

[151] TNA 28/174 23 March 1853 no. 3: Colebrooke to Newcastle, 23 March 1853; Newcastle's note, n.d.

[152] On the destruction of prisons during the rebellion, and discussions on new transportation destinations, see also Clare Anderson, *The Indian Uprising of 1857–8: prisons, prisoners and rebellion* (London: Anthem Press, 2007), chapter 4; Jill C. Bender, *The 1857 Uprising and the British Empire* (Cambridge University Press, 2016), 43–9.

[153] TNA CO28/188 27 January 1857 no. 6: Keate to Hincks, 23 December 1857.

the shipment of mutineers and rebels to British colonies. Some officials argued that whilst mutineers who had killed British soldiers should be executed, those from mutinous regiments should be transported, and those who had simply deserted their regiments and then returned home should be sent out of India as emigrants.[154] Indeed, there was a fine line between overseas emigration and penal transportation, and in the nineteenth century potential migrants drew lines of association between them.[155] The Board of Control at first proposed the passing of legislation to enable the East India Company to transport convicts to territories beyond its control. The government did not support this, however, and instead directed that colonies interested in receiving such convicts should approach directly the secretary of state.[156] Colonial interests, driven by the desire for new sources of labour, were extremely proactive in doing so. The West Indies Committee, a powerful lobby of absentee planters based in London, requested the shipment of 1857 rebels to the Caribbean. At this time, British Guiana's Court of Policy adopted three resolutions calling for up to 30,000 sepoys (soldiers), including a limited number of what it described as 'grave' offenders.[157] Other potential destinations included Grenada[158] and Western Australia.[159] However, by the time these requests reached London, the East India Company had taken the

[154] Charles Raikes, *Notes on the Revolt in the North-Western Provinces of India* (London: Longman, Brown, Green, Longmans and Roberts, 1858), 153–5. Charles Raikes served as acting judge of Agra, 1853–7, and then civil commissioner of Farrukhabad.

[155] See Clare Anderson, 'Convicts and coolies: rethinking indentured labour in the nineteenth century', *Slavery and Abolition*, 30, 1 (2009), 93–109.

[156] TNA CO318/218 (India Board): Wodehouse to Labouchere, 11 January 1858, draft reply 5 February 1858.

[157] TNA CO111/317 9 December 1857 no. 59: Acting Governor Lieutenant-Governor William Walker, British Guiana, to Labouchere, 9 December 1857, enc. Extracts from the Minutes of the Court of Policy, 26 November 1857; TNA CO111/320 8 June 1858 no. 71: Governor Sir Philip Edmond Wodehurst to Lord Edward Stanley, secretary of state for the colonies, 8 June 1858. See also George K. Alapatt, 'The Sepoy Mutiny of 1857: Indian Indentured Labour and Plantation Politics in British Guiana', *Journal of Indian History*, 59, 1–3 (1981), 303–8 (295–314).

[158] TNA CO318/218 (India Board): William Leach, Board of Commissioners for the Affairs of India [Board of Control], to Herman Merivale, under-secretary of state for the colonies, 1 February 1858; Thomson Hankey to Labouchere, 8 February 1858, enc. Memorial of the Agricultural and Horticultural Society of Grenada on behalf of the colony generally. Before emancipation, Thomson Hankey had enslaved property on Grenada, and had substantial economic interests in the colony. He was a former governor of the Bank of England and at this time the Liberal MP for Peterborough. See Legacies of British Slave-ownership database: Thomson Hankey, https://www.ucl.ac.uk/lbs/person/view/45726 (accessed 10 May 2018). Hankey informed Labouchere that the president of the agricultural and horticultural society had asked him to forward the petition.

[159] IOR L/PJ/296: Bengal judicial despatch to the Court of Directors, no. 8, 10 March 1858; *The Times*, 19 November 1857. Western Australia was still a penal colony, for British and Irish convicts, during this period.

decision to send the 1857 convicts to the newly re-colonized Andaman Islands, with the first batch of mutineer-rebels arriving in March 1858.[160]

In the Caribbean, the 1857 discussions had the impact of informing the wider Caribbean of the existence of the Irois penal settlement in Trinidad. But like British Guiana, Trinidad also refused to accept other West Indian convicts, the Legislative Council worrying that it would impact negatively on free immigration.[161] A decade later, the British government partly solved the issue with the passing of the Colonial Prisoners Removal Act 1869, which authorized 'the removal of prisoners from one Colony to another for the purposes of Punishment'. As Robert Aldrich has shown, though the host colonies had to agree to receive any convicts transported under the Act, the wording was otherwise vague. Moreover, British colonies only ever agreed to receive royal exiles and not ordinary offenders.[162] British Guiana, for example, never took prisoners, even those under sentences of imprisonment and penal servitude.[163] Perhaps for that reason, the British government extended the Act in 1884 to include provisions on the transfer of some prisoners to the United Kingdom. It remains in force today in Britain's Overseas Territories in the Caribbean and elsewhere.[164]

*

In the history of governance and convict mobility in imperial contexts, there are connections within and between Britain's imperial world and

---

[160] For a detailed history of the first eighteen months of the penal colony, see Anderson, *The Indian Uprising of 1857–8*, chapter 5.

[161] TNA CO295/197 21 December 1857 no. 134: Keate to Labouchere, 21 December 1857; TNA CO28/188 27 January 1858 no. 6: Keate to Hincks, 23 December 1857; TNA CO295/199 2 April 1858 no. 53: Keate to Stanley, enc. regulations for the government of the Convict Establishment at the Irois Forest.

[162] Robert Aldrich, *Banished Potentates: Dethroning and exiling indigenous monarchs under British and French colonial rule, 1815–1955* (Manchester University Press, 2018), 12–13.

[163] Colonial Prisoners Removal Act 1869 (32 & 33 Vict. cap. 10), http://www.legislation.gov.uk/ukpga/Vict/32-33/10/introduction (accessed 15 May 2018). For an example of Caribbean correspondence on the Act (with Barbados), see TNA CO28/209 3 November 1869: Granville Leveson-Gower (2nd Earl Granville), secretary of state for the colonies, to Governor Sir Rawson William Rawson, Windward Islands (Barbados), 22 December 1869; Governor Sir John Scott, British Guiana, to Rawson, 12 October 1869.

[164] TNA CO321/17/27 1 May 1877 no. 23 folios 268–91: Lieutenant-Governor George Cumine Strahan, Windward Islands [Barbados] to Henry Herbert (4th Earl of Carnarvon), secretary of state for the colonies, 1 May 1877. Strahan was later governor of Tasmania. See also Colonial Prisoners Removal Act 1884 (47 & 48 Vict. cap. 31), http://www.legislation.gov.uk/cy/ukpga/Vict/47-48/31 (accessed 15 May 2018). British Overseas Territories never became independent, and since decolonization they have remained under the sovereignty and jurisdiction of the United Kingdom. In the Caribbean, they are: Anguilla, British Virgin Islands, Cayman Islands, Montserrat, and the Turks and Caicos Islands. Bermuda is another such territory in the region.

the geopolitics of punitive relocation in the French, Spanish, and Danish empires. From the turn of the nineteenth century, the Saint-Domingue revolution and independence in Spanish America had an important influence on the agency of enslaved peoples, and on British policy and practice. Both the French and the Spanish were engaged in penal transportation, including through the shipment or sale of convicts to and in other colonies. The French read closely British parliamentary discussions on transportation during their own debates on penal colonies. Moreover, similarly to the British Empire, French colonies such as Guadeloupe, Martinique, and Réunion Island used penal transportation as a means of managing enslaved labour on sugar plantations. Following the independence of many Spanish colonies, the British shipped convicts to London for onward transportation to the Australian colonies. However, in 1837, concerned to limit such transportation to white convicts, the Colonial Office ended this practice, leading to a backlog in jails. Consequently, debates arose about the possibility of establishing a regional penal colony. Despite the creation of penal settlements for locally convicted offenders in British Guiana and Trinidad, disagreements over finance and location meant that such an institution was never built. Following the report of the anti-transportation Molesworth Committee, there were suggestions that the Caribbean could be the site of a new penal colony for Britain and Ireland. Contemporaries claimed that the presence of white convicts would impact negatively on a racial hierarchy that included recently emancipated slaves, and this also came to nothing.

From the nineteenth century, convict transportation from Britain and Ireland to the Australian colonies was increasingly subject to critique, in part through rhetorical appeals to the idea that penal transportation itself was a form of enslavement. This manoeuvre was grounded in the recognition that punitive mobility was a means of governing and managing colonial populations, as demonstrated here and in Chapter 4. If punitive mobility was a response to resistance, it could also have unintended consequences. Chapter 6 resumes themes first explored in Chapter 4, to demonstrate how penal transportation and administrative deportation facilitated the spread of anti-colonial practices and discourses. This was the case in European empires and across post-colonial Latin America, where convicts and exiles broke out in open mutiny or carried and adapted aspects of culture and religion. It is clear that the history of punitive relocation is at once a history of rebellion and resistance, played out not just on continents, but on islands, oceans, and seas.

6 Insurgency, Politics, and Religion

This chapter explores the ways in which convicts used their trans-local or global mobility as an opportunity to extend the ambit and reach of their political beliefs. These were sometimes those same deeply held ideologies which the authorities had criminalized and punished through banishment, exile, or penal transportation. The chapter opens with a series of examples drawn from the convict histories of the Dutch and English East India companies, and the Danish–Norwegian Empire, from the seventeenth century onwards. These trace the spread of resistance to imperial governance in the early-modern period by people subjected to punitive mobility, including through religious practice. It goes on to focus on the history of penal transportation and servitude in Ireland, revealing its global dimensions, and foregrounding its relationship to convict unrest in Britain's hulks and penal colonies. Finally, it suggests that there were important continuities between insurgency, politics, and religion in the Spanish Empire and its successor nation states, including in Chile, Ecuador, Argentina, Peru, and Mexico.

This history of insurgency, politics, and religion also enables us to envisage punitive spaces as sites of cosmopolitanism and cultural transformation. If convicts carried political ideologies to their punitive destinations, their mobility also facilitated cultural and religious dissemination, adaptation, and transformation. Chapter 4 considered the example of the Garifuna of Latin America, deported en masse from Saint Vincent in the late eighteenth century. Here, the discussion is taken forward to include convicts and Islam in the Cape Colony, the character of shipboard mutiny in the Atlantic and Indian Ocean worlds, caste practices in the British colony of Mauritius, Irish unrest on the Bermuda hulks and in the Australian colonies, and the history of African–Cuban 'secret societies' in the Spain's *presidio* of Ceuta. Overall, the chapter frames punitive mobility as a vector for community formation, nationalism, and resistance to the changing geopolitical formations created by empires. It suggests that this was evident from the early-modern period into the twentieth century, and shows that the history of the prison as a vehicle for politics and political education has its origins not solely in modern states and organized movements, but at least partly in practices of punitive mobility rooted in early-modern global penal practices, and convict responses to them.[1]

Religion and Resistance in Early-Modern European Empires

During the period of the British occupation of the Cape Colony from 1815, during the five decades after the Union of South Africa became a self-governing British dominion in 1910, and following independence in 1961, Robben Island has been geographically and imaginatively represented as an offshore prison near Cape Town. Perhaps the most famous prisoner of modern times, at least in the post-imperial British world, is Nelson Mandela. Mandela was an African National Congress leader who was incarcerated on Robben Island between 1964 and 1982 for his political campaigns against apartheid, and was later South Africa's first democratically elected and black president.[2] Mandela and other political detainees in Robben Island continued to organize resistance from their prison cells, including through programmes of political education that encompassed reading, writing, and training. Along with several other revolutionaries, Mandela later penned a detailed account of his imprisonment.[3]

The focus on the modern history of Robben Island has, to at least some extent, obscured its earlier importance as a site of punitive relocation that, from the fifteenth to early nineteenth centuries, served the empire of the Dutch United East India Company (Verenigde Oost-Indische

---

[1] Padraic Kenney, '"I felt a kind of pleasure in seeing them treat us brutally." The Emergence of the Political Prisoner, 1865–1910', *Comparative Studies in Society and History*, 54, 4 (2012), 863–89.

[2] Fran Lisa Buntman, 'Resistance on Robben Island 1963–1976', in Harriet Deacon, ed., *The Island: a history of Robben Island 1488–1990* (Cape Town: David Philip, 1997), 93–136; Fran Lisa Buntman, 'How Best to Resist? Robben Island after 1976', in Deacon, ed., *The Island*, 137–67; Fran Lisa Buntman, *Robben Island and Prisoner Resistance to Apartheid* (Cambridge University Press, 2003).

[3] Nelson Mandela, *Long Walk to Freedom: the autobiography of Nelson Mandela* (London: Little, Brown, 1994). On prison writings in South Africa, see Elleke Boehmer, 'Robben Island', *Journal of Postcolonial Writing*, 41, 2 (2005), 223–31; C. J. Driver, 'The View From Makana Island: Some Recent Prison Books from South Africa', *Journal of Southern African Studies*, 2, 1 (1975), 102–19; Paul Gready, 'Autobiography and the "Power of Writing": Political Prison Writing in the Apartheid Era', *Journal of Southern African Studies*, 19, 3 (1993), 489–523; David Schakwyck, 'Writing from Prison', in Sarah Nuttall and Cheryl-Ann Michael, eds., *Senses of Culture: South African Culture Studies* (New York: Oxford University Press, 2000), 279–97.

Compagnie, or VOC), and its indigenous allies. During this period, Robben Island was part of the VOC's empire, though far distant from its other spheres of influence including in India, Ceylon (now, Sri Lanka), Sumatra, Batavia (in Java), Sulawesi, and the Moluccas (Maluku Islands). The VOC used the island for the transportation of convicts sentenced under criminal law, as well as for the banishment and exile of native rulers, Muslim scholars (*ulema*), and political prisoners. It made almost all of them subject to forced labour, which blurred different judicial sentences. They worked in gathering shells (used to make lime for construction purposes), stone-cutting, the extraction of oil from seal blubber, and the collection of firewood. In this way, and in common with convicts and exiles in numerous global polities (Chapters 2 and 3), they became part of the VOC's larger system of forced migration and coerced labour extraction, including from enslaved persons and *corvée* (obligated) workers.[4] By the middle of the eighteenth century, there were at least forty convicts and exiles on Robben Island, sent from all over the Company's empire in South and Southeast Asia. They included Europeans and Asians, the latter known collectively and inaccurately as *Indiaanen*.[5] To a significant extent, *Indiaanen* convicts and exiles carried the history and practice of rebellion and insurgency with them. As is well known, they spread Islam to the Cape and in so doing became vectors for the circulation of religious knowledge that was antithetical to the beliefs of the Dutch.[6]

In 1751 Radja Boekit [Raja Boukit], the former Regent of Padang and a political prisoner on Robben Island, led a plot of rebellion against the Dutch soldiers and European convicts also held there.[7] Boekit had been transported from Batavia to the Cape in 1749, for joining a rebellion against the VOC in West Sumatra. His co-conspirator was a man known

---

[4] Nigel Penn, 'Robben Island 1488–1805', in Deacon, *The Island*, 9–32; Paul Truter, 'The Robben Island Rebellion of 1751: A Study of Convict Experience at the Cape of Good Hope', *Kronos*, 31 (2005), 36–8 (34–49). More globally expansive histories of convict banishment and transportation in the Netherlands VOC are Matthias van Rossum, 'The Dutch East India Company in Asia, 1595–1811', in Clare Anderson, ed., *A Global History of Convicts and Penal Colonies* (London: Bloomsbury, 2018), 157–81; Ronit Ricci, 'From Java to Jaffna: exile in Dutch Asia in the eighteenth century', in Ronit Ricci, ed., *Exile in Colonial Asia: Kings, convicts, commemoration* (Honolulu: University of Hawai'i Press, 2016), 94–116; Kerry Ward, *Networks of Empire: Forced migration in the Dutch East India Company* (Cambridge University Press, 2009). Ronit Ricci's *Banishment and Belonging: Exile and diaspora in Sarandib, Lanka and Ceylon* (Cambridge University Press, 2019) appeared as this book was being finalized.

[5] Kerry Ward, *Networks of Empire*, 271.

[6] Ward, *Networks of Empire*, 20 (also 191, 231–7); Michael Laffan, 'Looking Back on the Bay of Bengal: An African Isolate Reoriented', in Michael Laffan, ed., *Belonging across the Bay of Bengal: Religious rites, colonial migrations, national rights* (London: Bloomsbury, 2017), 207–22.

[7] I draw this account of the rebellion from Truter, 'The Robben Island Rebellion of 1751', and Ward, *Networks of Empire*, 270–80.

to us as Robbo of Buton. Convicted of ordinary criminal offences, he had been subjected to punitive mobility twice: first from the island of Buton in Southeast Sulawesi to the Cape Colony, and second from the Cape to Robben Island. It seems that events proceeded as follows. Boekit and Robbo called a meeting among the Sulawesi convicts, during which they agreed to break out in revolt on 26 June, the arrival date of a ship due to embark a cargo of shells. The men resolved that they would kill the Dutch postholder sergeant, his two corporals, and the remaining Europeans on the island, storm the ship, throw the crew overboard, load it with provisions, and set the sails for the East Indies. However, the Dutch foiled the plot before the ship arrived. A European corporal complained that he had been robbed of money, and two European convicts Lodewijk Rets and Marten van der Klugt reported the theft and discovery of knives. The Dutch accused an Asian convict named September Van Ternate, and under threat of a brutal flogging he implicated a second man, Djan Marrowang. Marrowang claimed that both of them had been responsible, and so the Dutch chained them together and flogged them. They tried to escape, but failed, and upon recapture they were again beaten. It was during this second flogging that Van Ternate revealed Boekit's plot, and named the convicts involved. Afterwards, he claimed that he had lied in order to put a stop to the beating, but the Dutch believed his initial story, and sent Boekit, Buton, and 13 other convicts to Cape Town to stand trial. They were all found guilty and sentenced to public execution. Boekit and Buton were tied to wooden crosses, their limbs broken, and left to die in agony. Seven other *Indiaanen* were tied up and their limbs broken, and then killed with a blow to the chest. The remaining six were hanged. The Dutch put the bodies of all 15 men on public display on a hill near Table Mountain, the Lion's Rump, in close proximity to the corpses of two recently executed slave runaways.

Public executions and corporeal display were common features of the governance and punishment of convicts and enslaved persons during this and later periods, and by numerous polities, including in the Caribbean, as discussed in the previous two chapters. At stake in the repression of the 1751 plot specifically was a more than century long history of political exile to the Cape, accompanied by constant fears of insurgency. For example, in 1681 the VOC had shipped more than a dozen men from Makassar in South Sulawesi, including three princes with their families and entourages. Fearful of their influence and potential power, the VOC transferred some of them to Robben Island, and others to isolated inland posts. At the time, keen to secure the lucrative spice trading routes to the islands further east of Sulawesi, including the Moluccas, the Company had signed a number of treaties with indigenous polities. Both the

Company and the native powers used banishment as a means of getting rid of their opponents. The VOC in Batavia, for instance, exiled prisoners of high rank from polities openly hostile to it, whilst the Javanese princes in other parts of the island including northern Cirebon used the Company's extant networks of forced migration for the same purpose. As Kerry Ward explains, Company law recognized indigenous legal authority, which meant that there were few practical distinctions between differential conviction, penal transportation, banishment, and political exile.[8] As we will see, the VOC later transferred some of the East Indies exiles in the Cape to Robben Island. The island became part of a carceral scale of punishment by distance. As the most far-flung punitive destination from the East Indies, it was reserved for the most 'dangerous' or serious criminals and exiles, as well as men of power, influence, and rank. Otherwise, the VOC used Onrust and Edam islands in the Bay of Batavia, Banda, and Rosingain (Rozengain) in the Banda archipelago as sites of punishment and as holding stations for those sentenced to more distant locations. Other than Robben Island, this included Ceylon and Allelande, an island off Tuticorin (Thoothukudi) on the southeast Coromandel Coast of India.[9]

One of the consequences of transportation and exile across the VOC's empire was the spread of Islam to the Cape, despite Dutch efforts at keeping those exiles defined more as 'Muslims' than 'royals' away from urban areas.[10] Perhaps the most famous religious exile of all was Shaykh Yusuf of Makassar, who scholars have represented as the man responsible for Islamization in southern Africa. Yusuf had been the leader of the Bantenese rebellion against the Dutch and was exiled alongside a second man, Hajji Mataram, following his capture in 1683. His death in isolated Faure (near Stellenbosch) in 1699 sparked a fierce debate over the repatriation of his body. Ultimately, he had two gravesites, one in Gowa near Makassar in Indonesia, and the other in the Cape. Other notable individuals in the spread of religious belief across the Indian Ocean included Sayyid 'Alawi, a Yemeni priest who was banished from Java in 1744, following the Chinese War of 1741–3. Tuan Guru (Abdullah bin Abd al-Salam), a noble exiled from the northern island of Tidore in the Moluccas in 1780, played a key role in the establishment of Malay-language schools. The Dutch exiled a fourth man, the Muslim scholar Noriman, also known as Tuan or Oupa Skapie, from Cirebon in 1773. The VOC viewed him as so important that it permitted his children to travel with him. These and many other political exiles, priests, and religious leaders spent time on Robben Island. That is not to suggest that

---

[8] Ward, *Networks of Empire*, 194–9, 259, 260–1 (paraphrased reference, 261).
[9] Ward, *Networks of Empire*, 269–70.   [10] Ward, *Networks of Empire*, 231–7.

there existed necessarily a unity of politics among them. For instance, 'Alawi was present in Robben Island at the time of the 1751 plot but appears nowhere in the VOC's records of the investigation, suggesting that he was unconnected with the planned uprising. Michael Laffan argues that it was only when the VOC evacuated Robben Island at the onset of the Fourth Anglo-Dutch War (1780–4), and put the exiles in Cape Town's slave lodge, that they started to develop a sense of community cohesion.[11] Indeed, it was this politically inspired move to the mainland which provided such exiles with a wider opportunity to interact with other Muslims, including from Indonesia and the eastern islands. Though the VOC prohibited the practice of Islam in the forts and cities under its control, the *Indiaanen* exiles were able to celebrate in private what were in essence Sufi or mystical forms of Islam. This included praying, reading from the Qur'an, *dhikr* (communal recollection), and feasts in honour of the birthday of the Prophet.[12] As Ward has shown, it is possible to recognize common features straddling Southeast Asian and Cape Islam, including the authoritarian relationship between *guru* (teacher) and *murid* (student), the transmission of religious power through miraculous feats, and the veneration of Saints.[13]

Though evidence of religious practice during this period is sparse and fragmentary, extraordinary details of the nature of Islamic practice in the Cape emerged during the criminal trial of 'Mahomedan priest' Noriman in 1786. Noriman stood accused of supplying a group of enslaved runaways, including one Jonas van Batavia, with an amulet and black powders, which were believed to have protective powers. Noriman escaped punishment, but the Dutch were so nervous about the prospect of a general conspiracy against them, that they returned him and Imam Abdullah (Tuan Guru) to Robben Island, where they were kept until 1791 and 1793 respectively.[14] Shortly afterwards, in 1795, the British

---

[11] Laffan, 'Looking Back on the Bay of Bengal', 209; Michael Laffan, 'From Javanese Court to African Grave: How Noriman Became Tuan Skapie, 1717–1806', *Journal of Indian Ocean World Studies*, 1, 1 (2017), 38–59 (quote, 41); Michael Laffan, 'The Sayyid in the Slippers: An Indian Ocean Itinerary and Visions of Arab Sainthood, 1737–1929', *Archipel*, 86 (2013), 191–227. For an account that is especially attentive to the transoceanic cultural 'afterlives' of Shaykh Yusuf, see Saarah Jappie, '"Many Makassars": Tracing an African-Southeast Asian Narrative of Shaykh Yusuf of Makassar', in Scarlett Cornelissen and Yoichi Mine, eds., *Migration and Agency in a Globalizing World* (Basingstoke: Palgrave, 2018), 47–66 (quote, 49).

[12] Laffan, 'From Javanese Court to African Grave', 46–7; Laffan, 'The Sayyid in the Slippers', 216–7.

[13] Ward, *Networks of Empire*, 236.

[14] Laffan, 'From Javanese Court to African Grave', 48–54. See also Titas Chakraborty, 'Slave trading and slave resistance in the Indian Ocean world: the case of early eighteenth-century Bengal', *Slavery and Abolition*, 40, 4 (2019), 723–4 (706–26).

occupied the Cape, staying until 1803 when the Dutch regained control.[15] During this period, Imam Abdullah led demands for rights to spaces for prayer, free residence, and burial grounds (in the Cape, grave complexes, or *mazaars*, are known as *kramats*). In 1799, under British rule, the first mosque was built. Upon the return of the Dutch, in 1804, Muslims were granted religious freedom, and in 1805, they were gifted rights to a burial ground on Signal Hill close to the grave of Sayyid 'Alawi.[16] If the punitive relocation associated with empire and diplomacy in the Indonesian archipelago of the Netherlands VOC resulted in collective acts of resistance, it also underpinned the spread of Islamic scholarship and religious practices. This created bonds not just between political exiles, but with those transported for ordinary criminal offences – and as the Dutch greatly feared ultimately between convicts and the enslaved.

Mutiny and Revolt

The role of punitive relocation in creating solidarities between convicts, and sometimes between convicts and other coerced workers, is well documented. Here, the chapter draws on the work of Johan Heinsen on Denmark–Norway and its empire in the seventeenth and eighteenth centuries. Denmark–Norway's imperial history began in 1620, when it established a post in Tranquebar (now, Tharangambadi) on India's Coromandel Coast. Convicts of noble birth and political offenders were occasionally banished there, at the king's behest, until it was replaced as a punitive destination by the new colony of St Thomas in the Lesser Antilles, which was established in 1672. Like the Dutch Cape, Denmark–Norway's Caribbean colony also received priests, thus providing an outlet for people Heinsen describes as 'religious troublemakers'.[17] Heinsen writes that there existed a 'culture of flight' among prisoners and convicts, both in Denmark–Norway's imperial centre in Copenhagen and in St Thomas. Those undergoing sentences of hard labour in Denmark planned escapes in the *Trunken* prison, which was located in the naval dockyard on Bremerholm. Not infrequently, men were incarcerated together and later ran together. Convicts also planned their escapes on board ships, enacting resistance grounded in 'fictive kinship'. Their close relationships with each other could be a source of solidarity, just as they

---

[15] The British seized the Cape from the Dutch again in 1806.
[16] Laffan, 'From Javanese Court to African Grave', 55; Ward, *Networks of Empire*, 233.
[17] Johan Heinsen, 'The Scandinavian Empires in the Seventeenth and Eighteenth Centuries', in Anderson, ed., *A Global History of Convicts and Penal Colonies*, 104 (97–121).

were during the middle passage of enslaved men and women travelling to the plantations of the Atlantic world, and for British and Irish convicts transported to the Australian colonies over a century later. Indeed, the Australian convicts called each other 'messmates'.[18]

Convicts often also developed strong bonds with other coerced labourers, as was the case during a dramatic mutiny on board the *Havmanden* in 1683. The Danish West India and Guinea Company was in charge of this ship, which was on its way to the Caribbean carrying around two hundred passengers, about half of whom were convicts. Led by a convict, convicts and sailors, including men previously imprisoned together in the *Trunken*, seized the vessel. However, the mutiny failed after the group split. The convict captain dumped some of the convicts in the Azores, and the ship was wrecked off the coast of Sweden. Nine of the mutineers were tried and hanged. Other groups of convicts who disembarked in St Thomas in the years that followed continued to plan and effect their escape, wanting to go to St Croix, St John, or Puerto Rico. The latter Spanish colony was not only a place of banishment for enslaved men and women during this period (see Chapter 5), but already a destination for maroon (escaped) slaves. Nonetheless, as Heinsen shows, the violent and dramatic event on the *Havmanden* catalysed the collapse of the Danish West India and Guinea Company.[19]

The Danish West India and Guinea Company was not the only trader to experience mutiny on a convict vessel. In fact, in the years between 1827 and 1859 there were over a dozen attempted or successful mutinies on board ships chartered by the English East India Company (EIC) to transport convicts from the presidencies of Bengal and Bombay, and from Hong Kong, to penal settlements in the Straits Settlements (Penang, Malacca, and Singapore), Burma, Mauritius, and Aden; and on convict vessels travelling in the other direction, from the Straits Settlements and Burma to the Indian presidencies.[20] Up to twenty transportation ships

---

[18] Marcus Rediker, Cassandra Pybus, and Emma Christopher, 'Introduction', in Marcus Rediker, Cassandra Pybus, and Emma Christopher, eds., *Many Middle Passages: Forced migration and the making of the modern world* (Berkeley: University of California Press, 2007), 4 (1–19). The authors here cite the seminal work of Richard Price and Sidney W. Mintz, *The Birth of African-American Culture: An anthropological perspective* (Boston, MA: Beacon, 1992). Note also Hamish Maxwell-Stewart, '"Those Lads Contrived a Plan": Attempts at Mutiny on Australia-Bound Convict Vessels', *International Review of Social History*, 58, S21 (2013), 188 (177–96).

[19] Johan Heinsen, *Mutiny in the Danish Atlantic World: Convicts, sailors and a dissonant empire* (London: Bloomsbury, 2017), 71–5, 131–44, 145–54; Heinsen, 'The Scandinavian Empires'.

[20] Detailed accounts of convict ship mutinies can be found in Clare Anderson, '"The Ferringees are Flying – the ship is ours!": the convict middle passage in colonial South and Southeast Asia, 1790–1860', *Indian Economic and Social History Review*, 41, 3 (2005),

sailed out of India each year, carrying a total of around 25,000 convicts into transportation. Most had been convicted of serious but non-capital offences such as armed or gang robbery, and for the tiny number of women who were transported infanticide.[21] Some EIC administrators believed that penal transportation was a particularly harsh punishment for Hindus, for sea voyages (across the *kala pani*, or black water) fatally compromised their caste. This was because convicts of all classes and religions were chained together, and shared crockery, latrines, and water pumps. Thus, for convicts of high caste, the journey itself was an important element of the punishment. This was also, Company officials believed, the case for Muslims of high status, who they claimed also suffered religious infringements.[22] There was also a belief prevalent amongst Company administrators in the Southeast Asian trading factories (commercial settlements) that Buddhist Malays and Chinese convicts especially feared transportation. This was because it severed family ties, and so after death they would not be granted the burial rites necessary for a successful transition to the afterlife.[23]

Though the EIC had established its first penal settlement in 1789, in Penang, there were just two mutinous incidents before the Company lost its trading monopoly in 1834. During this early period, although there were no ships specially fitted out for convicts, the EIC commonly transported them alongside other passengers, notably *sipahis* (soldiers), and cargos of trading goods. The sudden change in the frequency of mutiny appears to have come in the context of a slight increase in the number of annual transportations. Most important, however, was a fundamental shift in practice, in which with the loss of its monopoly in 1834 the Company no longer used its own vessels to transport convicts but put out tenders for private hire. There appears to have been an immediate and perhaps inevitable downgrading of security on board these chartered

---

143–86; Clare Anderson, 'Convict Passages in the Indian Ocean, c. 1790–1860', in Rediker, Pybus, and Christopher, eds., *Many Middle Passages*, 129–49; Clare Anderson, 'The Age of Revolution in the Indian Ocean, Bay of Bengal and South China Sea: A Maritime Perspective', *International Review of Social History*, 58, S21 (2013), 229–51. Unless indicated otherwise, the material on Indian convict mutinies that follows here is drawn from these publications.

[21] Clare Anderson, 'The British Indian Empire, 1789–1945', in Anderson, ed., *A Global History of Convicts and Penal Colonies*, 211–43.

[22] Clare Anderson, 'The Politics of Convict Space: Indian Penal Settlements and the Andamans', in Alison Bashford and Carolyn Strange, eds., *Isolation: Places and practices of exclusion* (London: Routledge, 2003), 41–5 (40–55); Clare Anderson, 'Convicts and coolies: rethinking indentured labour in the nineteenth century', *Slavery and Abolition*, 30, 1 (2009), 101–3 (93–109).

[23] IOR P/142/38 (Bengal judicial consultations, 1 October 1845): J. Davis, secretary to government Hong Kong, to Edward Smith-Stanley (14th Earl of Derby), secretary of state for war and the colonies, 29 January 1845.

vessels, not least because arrangements became somewhat piecemeal and irregular, and unlike EIC ships they did not routinely carry soldiers. There were often inadequate numbers of armed guards on board and, keen to keep the cost of the passage down, captains routinely exploited convicts in the performance of shipboard tasks. This meant that convicts had unprecedented freedom of mobility, and thus opportunities, compared to the earlier period, to take control of ships and attempt to sail to freedom. Indeed, it is notable that there were no such mutinies on board ships embarking from the Madras presidency (from Chingleput (Chengalpattu)), which through fear of convict uprisings from the early 1840s onwards only ever used troop ships for transportation purposes.

Convicts were ingenious in their escape plans. They were commonly locked together at night, on a single chain padlocked at one end. If one man feigned sickness or for other reasons was released, the other convicts could slip out. In other cases, they used silk thread to gradually cut through their chains, using wax and dye to plug the holes so that they remained unseen. It is important to note that, in common with transportation convicts across a range of global contexts, Indian convicts often experienced both long periods of confinement, and lengthy journeys from their homes, places of trial, and conviction to their final destination. They travelled in chain gangs called *challan*, which seem to have underpinned the formation of new relationships. If Australian convicts called each other 'messmates', Indians called each other *bhai*, a Hindustani word which signals a brother or a friend. Those Indians transported to the French Kreol-speaking British colony of Mauritius talked of each other as *compatriots* (countrymen) or *camarades* (fellow soldiers). This suggests that they thought of each other in military terms, a language of association that was so powerful that convicts on the island were commonly referred to as *sipahis*. As Chapter 3 showed, the broader social and economic factors at work in these descriptions was that frequently convicts and soldiers were employed in the same kind of infrastructural labour. The work of Indian convicts also resembled that of ordinary labourers, and the blurring between labour categories was such that across the other side of the Indian Ocean in the Bay of Bengal's Straits Settlements, convicts called themselves *kumpanee ke nauker*, or servants of the EIC.[24]

The long and close confinement and journeying associated with the punishment of transportation, and the concurrent development of close bonds between Indian convicts, enabled mutiny plots. Sometimes convicts prepared them while awaiting embarkation, for instance by sewing

---

[24] IOR P/136/31 (Bengal judicial consultations, 26 August 1824): W. E. Phillips, superintendent of convicts, Penang, minute on the treatment of convicts., 15 April 1824.

nails and metal files into their bedding. However, they always broke out either in response to violent and arbitrary treatment on the part of the captain and crew, or poor conditions such as the issue of short rations, water shortages, or overcrowding – and sometimes a combination of both. Inadequate guarding and access to unsecured weapons were important factors in the success of mutinies, as was the presence of convict women, who enjoyed more freedom of movement on board ship and could supply vital intelligence that assisted planning. Most significant of all for the successful seizure of vessels was the presence of convicts who had previously been to sea.

For example, two of the thirty-four *Virginia* convicts, who mutinied just south of Goa on their way to Singapore in 1839, were seafarers. They murdered the captain, Charles Whiffin, landed on the coast, and made for home. The EIC went after the convict party, arresting them all, and paying little heed to their protestations of poor treatment. In 1841, it re-embarked two of them on the convict ship *Freak*, and incredibly they again mutinied. This time, after murdering the captain and chief mate, they sailed to the Mentawai Islands off the coast of western Sumatra, in the mistaken belief that they were in the Nicobars. They next steered the ship up the coast, landing at the northern province of Aceh, where they claimed that they were traders with opium, cotton, dates, and other goods for sale. Some of the convicts later testified that a man they called a 'rajah' ('king') had heard rumours about the mutiny and had been to inspect and buy some of their wares. The convicts presented him with the captain's watch, sword and gun, and a chronometer (mechanical timepiece). The 'rajah' then enlisted fourteen of the mutineers as *sipahis* in his service, including one of the convicts who had killed Captain Whiffen of the *Virginia*.[25] Meanwhile, upon receiving intelligence from Aceh, seemingly from the 'rajah' himself, the EIC despatched a boat from Penang, and a party of soldiers found and arrested the mutineers. It sent them to Penang for trial on charges of piracy, following which eight were hanged, three transported for life to Moulmein (now, Mawlamyine) in Burma, and the remainder sent into transportation to serve their original sentences.

Such convict mutinies possessed a political character, for they constituted dynamic and violent responses to the practices and degradations of Company occupation and rule. The larger background at work here was the EIC's occasional use of transportation sentences to repress war, revolt, and rebellion. Indeed, some of the very first transportations were

---

[25] This man may have been the acting sultan of Aceh, Alauddin Ibrahim Mansur Syah, or one of the many 'pepper rajahs' living along the coast during this period.

of Polygars from the former Tirunelveli kingdom of south India. The Company tried and sentenced them in the wake of the wars of 1799–1805, and shipped them around the coast to Bengal as well as to Penang.[26] Other contemporary transportations followed the Maratha Wars (1803–5, 1816–19), endemic and ongoing peasant and tribal (*Adivasi*) revolt against the intrusions of Company administration and jurisdiction in areas of the Bengal Presidency, the Anglo-Sikh Wars (1845–6, 1848–9), the Santal *hul* (rebellion), and, as noted in Chapter 5, the 1857 revolt. There were sometimes direct links between subaltern resistance on land and convict mutiny at sea. Three examples follow here. Two of the convict leaders of the mutinous *Catherine*, sailing from Bombay to Singapore in 1838, were Bhils: Kondajee Bapoo and Ram Chunder Valalloo. They had been sentenced to transportation for their resistance against British territorial aggression in the forests of western India during the 1830s. The Bhils were one of several *Adivasi* groups, including also the Kols of the Bengal presidency and the Konds of the Madras Presidency, who from the 1810s had broken out in rebellion against EIC land incursions and increasing revenue demands.[27] The Bhils on the *Catherine* planned to run the ship aground and flee to a place that they described as 'Chitripoore Ram Rajah's country', probably the Hindu Saraswat Brahmin community (in what is now Kannada), where they believed they could live in safety. In a similar case, 12 of the of 79 convicts on the *Recovery*, sailing from Bombay to Singapore in 1846, were Marathas, convicted and transported for insurrection, rebellion, and treason. They planned a mutiny whilst awaiting embarkation, after which they broke out of the holds, overpowered the sentries and guards, and got up on deck – though the crew managed to force them into retreat, killing one man and wounding five. Third, following victory in the Anglo-Sikh Wars, the EIC was able to extend its control in the northwest of the Indian subcontinent by annexing the Punjab, and sentencing hundreds of soldiers to imprisonment or transportation. In 1850, a *challan* of Punjabi convicts mutinied on the river steamer *Kaleegunga*, which was taking

---

[26] IOR P/408/8 (Bombay law proceedings, 1799): John Spencer and John Smee, Malabar commissioners, to secretary to government of Bombay, 16 December 1798 and 14 February 1800; IOR P/321/95 (Madras judicial consultations, 1803): R. Rickards, principal collector Malabar, to George Buchan, chief secretary to government Fort St George, 2 October 1803, Buchan to Rickards, 22 October 1803; TNSA Madras judicial consultations volume 98, 1814: F. H. Baber, magistrate North Malabar, to the officer commanding the Mysore Division, 11 July 1814.

[27] Clare Anderson, *Convicts in the Indian Ocean: Transportation from South Asia to Mauritius* (Basingstoke: Macmillan, 2000), 28–32. On the EIC's military campaign against the Konds, see Felix Padel, *The Sacrifice of Human Being: British rule and the Konds of Orissa* (New Delhi: Oxford University Press, 1995), chapter 2.

them from Allahabad to Calcutta for onward shipment to Burma. The men had risen after their guards let two men off the common chain to relieve themselves, and the rest of the convicts took the chance to escape. They reached for eighteen loaded guns, stored next to their sleeping quarters, and with military experience in their favour they killed three guards, jumped off the boat, and swam to shore. The British secretary to the government of Bengal later described their leader, Narain Singh, as a 'notorious Sikh general', who the Company had tried and convicted for the crime of treason. He had acted in concert with two of his military subordinates.

Punjabis also instigated the most dramatic convict mutiny ever seen in the British imperial world, which took place on the *Clarissa* during a voyage from the Bengal presidency to Burma in 1854. It was an uprising of unprecedented scale, sparked off by poor conditions – overcrowding, short rations, and an inadequate supply of drinking water – against the background of the Company's recent annexation of the Punjab. Most of the 133 convicts on board the *Clarissa* were from the province, and they were led by a man describing himself as a Sikh from Lahore: Soor Singh. The convicts murdered the captain, chief mate, and second mate, and a total of 31 crew members including their guards. After taking control of the ship, they destroyed the convict register and logbook, ran the ship aground, armed themselves, and waded to the shore near the small town of Ye, situated between Moulmein and Tavoy (now, Dawei) on the Burmese coast. Assuming military command, leader Soor Singh dressed himself in the captain's coat and boots, and put on the gold necklace, sword, and sash that had belonged to the *subadar* (head) of the guard. He armed six other convicts, gave them what a boatswain later described as 'caps and accoutrements', and called them 'his sepoys'. Soor Singh then assembled all the convicts on the beach. Convict Beejah Sing later testified that he had announced to them: '[Y]ou shall be taken to the Burma Raja's and there be all free men.' Soor Singh and six other men set out to find him, planning to offer their services in the belief that they were in territory outside of the Company's control. However, Soor Singh's party was mistaken, and though they found the 'rajah', a gunfight broke out, and Soor Singh and six of his men were shot dead. The EIC ultimately recaptured the rest of the men, and the court sentenced 4 of the 129 surviving convicts to death for the piratical seizure of the vessel. It directed that remainder of the convicts continue their transportation journey but specified that they were to be kept at hard labour for the entirety of their term.

Not long after the *Clarissa* mutiny came the 1857 revolt. Soldiers, peasants, and urban dwellers across North India rose up against the

Company, in the largest anti-British rebellion of the nineteenth century.[28] The Company retaliated swiftly and brutally, using execution and transportation as means of quelling and punishing mutineers and rebels. Given the presence of *sipahi* convicts, skilled in handling weapons, on transportation ships, it is unsurprising that there were at least two outbreaks on vessels taking 1857 convicts to the penal settlements. This included forty-four convicts bound for Singapore on the *Julia*. They managed to grab the ship carpenter's tools and use them to kill the chief guard and sentry. The ship's officers only contained them by opening fire and shooting two convicts dead. They ordered the remainder up on deck, chained them to the bower cable (the strong chain connected to the anchor), and left them in the shadow of the loaded forecastle gun. When the ship arrived in Singapore the authorities promptly ordered it on to the Andaman Islands, which a monthly previously in March 1858 the Company had established as a penal colony. At the end of 1858, another ship was transporting thirty-seven 1857 rebels from Multan to Karachi on the *Frere*, ready for shipment to the Andamans. They managed to slip off their fetters and rush the deck. Before the ship's command were able to properly regain control, seven convicts had escaped.

As mentioned above, the Netherlands VOC and Denmark–Norway used exile and transportation to get rid of religious rebels. For the Dutch, this had unintended consequences in that it enabled the Islamization of the Cape. Here, note that in the world of the EIC there was sometimes a politico-religious dimension to mutiny at sea. This reflected that of subaltern rebellion during this period more generally, in which religion sometimes played an important role.[29] The enquiry following the mutiny on the Bombay Presidency ship *Recovery* revealed that the convicts had sworn on the Qur'an to rebellion, before the ship had even set sail. Rumours reached the authorities that some 'Arabic' vessels would be waiting in the harbour to aid their escape. This was not the case, but the convicts nonetheless rose, upon the signal '*din*', the Qur'anic cry of devotion and duty. A convict on board the mutinous

---

[28] C. A. Bayly, *The New Cambridge History of India II.i: Indian society and the making of the British Empire* (Cambridge University Press, 1988), chapter 6; Crispin Bates et al., eds., *Mutiny at the Margins: New perspectives on the Indian uprising of 1857* [6 vols] (London: Sage, 2013–2014); Rudrangshu Mukherjee, *Awadh in Revolt 1857–1858: A study of popular resistance* (New Delhi: Oxford University Press, 1984); Rudrangshu Mukherjee, '"Satan Let Loose Upon Earth": The Kanpur Massacres in India in the Revolt of 1857', *Past and Present*, 128, 1 (1990), 92–116; E. T. Stokes, *The Peasant and the Raj: Studies in agrarian society and peasant rebellion in colonial India* (Cambridge University Press, 1978); E. T. Stokes (ed. C. A. Bayly), *The Peasant Armed: the Indian Revolt of 1857* (Oxford: Clarendon Press, 1986).

[29] Ranajit Guha, *Elementary Aspects of Peasant Insurgency in Colonial India* (New Delhi: Oxford University Press, 1983), 1–2, 38–9.

vessel *Freak* testified that one of the mutineers had described the bleeding of the fatally wounded captain as the letting of liquor or 'poison'. The same men had called shoes found and tossed overboard as 'infidels' things'. It seems that the *Freak* convicts had wanted to go to the holy city of Mecca, but because they thought they were unlikely to reach it, they decided to head for Aceh. A convict named Michael Antony, who turned informer, stated their belief that 'all are Musselmen there and they would be safe'. He reported that the convict's leader, Hadjee Hussain, had asked the second mate where Aceh was, and the second mate had replied that it was 'a Mohamedan country' where any English vessel was plundered and its crew killed.[30]

Furthermore, convicts sometimes mutinied as a consequence of crews' failure to respect specific cultural practices relating to the preparation and eating of food. High-caste Hindus routinely refused cooked food on board vessels, and the Company regarded this as an indication of their laziness or unwillingness to submit to discipline. One of the *Virginia* mutineers, Saduck Ali, who later mutinied on the *Freak*, apparently claimed on his arrest that the Hindu convicts on board had resolved to die rather than to eat cooked rice. Convicts' refusal to eat cooked food appears generally to have been related to the shortage of water. An Indian medical attendant working on the ship *Boanerges*, which was carrying convicts from Karachi to the Andaman Islands in the aftermath of the 1857 revolt, later reported that Hindus would not eat their rations because they had been unable to wash themselves first.[31]

It is also evident that convicts transported for acts of resistance against the EIC instigated rebellion and revolt following their punitive relocation. In the 1840s, the Company transported a few dozen convicts to the Yemeni port of Aden (then part of the Bombay Presidency). Some of them had been convicted of 'insurrection and bearing arms' during the EIC's efforts to incorporate the princely (independent) state of Kolhapur into its territories. In 1845, they led a bloody escape attempt.[32] On a much larger scale was the resistance that followed the transportation of convicts to the Andamans in 1858. Following the arrival of the first

---

[30] IOR P/403/6 (Bombay judicial consultations, 2 March 1842): deposition of convict Michael Anthony, 7 June 1841.

[31] IOR P/146/21 (Bengal judicial proceedings, 27 October 1859): Superintendent J. P. Walker, Port Blair, to Rivers Thompson, junior secretary to government Bengal, 10 September 1859, enc. judicial enquiry regarding the treatment of the convicts on board the ship *Boanerges* from Calcutta to Port Blair, 5–8 September 1859.

[32] IOR P/403/47 (Bombay judicial consultations, 13 August 1845): political agent Aden to W. Escombe, secretary to government Bombay, 27 June 1845; governor's minute, n.d. On the history of Kolhapur in the nineteenth century, see *Imperial Gazetteer of India, Volume XV: Karachi to Kotayam* (Oxford: Clarendon Press, 1908), 383.

transportation ships, convicts made constant attempts at escape, spurred on by their belief either that a sympathetic 'rajah' lived somewhere in the islands' jungles, or that there was a road connecting the Andamans to mainland Southeast Asia. After a ten-day march, some convicts thought, they would find service with a man they called the king of Burma. They would then return to destroy the penal colony.[33]

In other cases, resistance had complex precedents. An example from Mauritius enables insights here. In 1817, sixteen Bengal Presidency convicts faced trial in the Tribunal de Première Instance (Court of First Instance), at the time the principal criminal court of the island. They were accused of deserting the Bel Ombre sugar estate, where they were employed as plantation labourers, and of armed resistance to their arrest. The sixteen men were drawn from the first batches of Indian convicts sent to the island in 1815 after it had been ceded to the British after the Napoleonic Wars.[34] Some of these convicts hailed from the *Adivasi* areas of Midnapur, a district of Bengal that had been in open revolt against the EIC, during both the Chuar Rebellion (1797–1800) and the Naek Revolt (1806–1816). The Company had convicted some of them of 'political' crimes, and others for ordinary offences like banditry or armed extortion. However, there is no question that a proportion of these men were peasant rebels. The EIC had suspended transportation between 1811 and 1813, due to concerns over its cost and penal effectiveness, and so some of them had been in prison for several years before they embarked for Mauritius.[35]

By May 1817, seventy-five of these Indian convicts had been hired out to the Bel Ombre estate, where they were put to work side-by-side with the plantation's enslaved, in the cultivation of various crops.[36] In

---

[33] IOR P/188/53 (India judicial proceedings, 7 May 1858): J. P. Walker to C. Beadon, secretary to government of India, 23 April 1858; Beadon to Walker, 7 May 1858; IOR P/206/61 (India judicial proceedings, 29 July 1859): Dr Browne's report on sanitary state of the Andamans, n.d.; Statement of convict no. 276 Doodnath Tewarry, 26 May 1859. See also M. V. Portman, *A History of our Relations with the Andamanese, Volume I* (Calcutta: Office of the Superintendent of Government Printing, 1899), 279–86.

[34] The discussion of the trial is largely based on material from the NAM JB127: Trial of the Bel Ombre Convicts – Bessharut Kan, Jhunkoo, Jowaher, Ruttunah, Kéhurée, Kunnye, Maumray, Mooteeah, Sadut Khan, Mewashee, Bessarat, Kinaour, Kallouah, Myseraly, Maddow, and Karam Khan.

[35] Anderson, *Convicts in the Indian Ocean*, 31–2.

[36] TNA CO167/40: Return shewing the number of convicts employed with individuals during the months of February, March, April, May, June, and July 1817. The owners of Bel Ombre were Charles Telfair, British governor Robert T. Farquhar's private secretary, and Louis Blancard, the civil commissioner of the district (Savanne). Farquhar himself was former lieutenant-governor of Penang, which at the time was also a penal settlement for Indian convicts. He not only ignored the ongoing importation of slaves to Mauritius after the abolition of the trade in 1807, as did Telfair, but from his Penang posting he

July 1817, forty-seven of the convicts made their way back to the public works department barracks at Grand River, the headquarters of the penal settlement. They complained of short rations. Later reports suggested that not only had their overseers diverted their food to the plantation household, but the convicts were made to eat out of the same pots as enslaved workers. This, it was alleged, forfeited their caste. The convicts also complained of brutal treatment at the hands of their overseer, a British soldier called William Holmes. Dr Robert Erskine, the chief medical officer of the colony, oversaw an investigation. His report on one convict, Saprar Jackel, noted 'many marks of severe violence on the back and buttocks, and also deep and extensive ulceration'.[37] Nevertheless, the outcome of the investigation was the flogging of thirty-two of the convicts, and their return to Bel Ombre.[38]

When the convicts arrived back at the estate, overseer Holmes threatened them with further beatings, and so eighteen of them immediately ran off.[39] Two weeks later, an enslaved watchman called Pyrame came to Bel Ombre to report that the convicts had attacked him and stolen his gun. Four days later, one of the convict deserters, Myseraly, returned. He claimed that the convicts had joined with a band of armed maroons (enslaved deserters). They were planning to set fire to Bel Ombre, kill Louis Blancard, cut overseer Holmes into 'small pieces', and escape to Madagascar. Blancard set out with Holmes, nine soldiers, and two slaves called Sofala and Figaro. Myseraly led the way. He took them to what was by then an abandoned camp. The party followed a trail into the hills where they found the convicts.[40] A violent confrontation followed. The convicts, armed with their *rattans* (canes), charged. Sofala fired at them but missed. The convicts then ran at Blancard, who also shot at them, this time killing two convicts and seriously injuring two, who he took into

---

knew the value of Indian convicts as replacements for slaves. See Anthony Barker, *Slavery and Anti-Slavery in Mauritius, 1810–33: The conflict between economic expansion and humanitarian reform under British rule* (Basingstoke: Palgrave, 1996); Anthony Webster, 'British Expansion in South-East Asia and the Role of Robert Farquhar, Lieutenant-Governor of Penang, 1804-5', *Journal of Imperial and Commonwealth History*, 23, 1 (1995), 1–25.

[37] TNA CO167/40: Robert Erskine, chief medical officer, to Lieutenant Jenkins, acting superintendent of convicts, 24 July 1817.

[38] TNA CO167/40: Interview of William Clover, chief overseer of convicts, by Francis Rossi, superintendent of convicts, 21 September 1818.

[39] NAM JB127: Trial of the Bel Ombre convicts; TNA CO167/40: Acting Governor G. J. Hall to J. Pépin, acting procureur-général [attorney general], 13 September 1818.

[40] Pépin claimed in September 1818 that Blancard, Myseraly, the soldiers, Holmes, Sofala, and Figaro found the convicts at the same time (TNA CO167/40: Pépin to Hall, 16 September 1818). I have chosen to give the version presented at the trial (NAM JB127: Trial of the Bel Ombre Convicts).

custody.[41] The other convicts escaped back into the woods, but a few days later they showed up once again at the Grand River convict barracks.[42] The outcome of the trial was that although the court found the convicts guilty of desertion, because they were already under sentence, it had no further powers of punishment. It returned them to Grand River, where Superintendent of Convicts Francis Rossi subsequently ordered their transfer to public works in the faraway port of Mahebourg.[43]

Of interest in this discussion of transportation, insurgency, resistance, and religion are not solely the poor treatment and apparent caste violations that underpinned the rebellion, but the background of the thirteen Bel Ombre convicts. All of them had been convicted in India between 1812 and 1815, and four of the men had been awaiting their transportation for three or four years. By the time that these thirteen men were assigned to Bel Ombre in May 1817, the majority of them had been in Mauritius for a year, and all had arrived at least four months previously. Two of them had been co-offenders, and seven had been involved in riots that had broken out in the Bengal Presidency's transportation holding jail at Alipur during 1815–16. In a twist of coincidence, Francis Rossi had been there at the time, and later wrote of the seriousness of unrest that had involved 200 prisoners. Finally, two groups of two convicts and one of three had been transported on the same ships (*Helen*, *Lady Elliot*, and *Lord Minto*). Just two of the men had no known links to the others.[44] The convicts' antecedents are such that, speculatively, the long journey into transportation of these convicts, including for some several years of incarceration including during jail riots, nurtured ties of fraternity that enabled the later outbreak.

It would be a mistake, however, to suggest that all convicts developed collective identities and shared solidarities. Some of the mutinies

---

[41] NAM JB127: Trial of the Bel Ombre convicts, enc. report of Jean Louis Desnoyeur, medical officer Savanne district, 9 August 1817.

[42] NAM JB127: Trial of the Bel Ombre convicts, enc. Governor Robert T. Farquhar to J. M. M. Virieux, procureur-général, 11 August 1817.

[43] A full and detailed account of the trial can be found in Clare Anderson, 'The Bel Ombre Rebellion: Indian convicts in Mauritius, 1815–53', in Gwyn Campbell, ed., *Abolition and its Aftermath in Indian Ocean Africa and Asia* (London: Routledge, 2005), 50–65. Francis Rossi was later superintendent of police in the penal colony of New South Wales, where he was assigned an enslaved woman from Mauritius called Thérésia, transported for the attempted murder of her master's daughter, likely in retaliation for sexual assault. See Clare Anderson, *Subaltern Lives: biographies of colonialism in the Indian Ocean word, 1790–1920* (Cambridge University Press, 2012), 77–8; Neville Potter, Francis Nicolas Rossi: The ambivalent position of a French nobleman in 19th-century New South Wales, PhD Thesis, Australian National University, 2017.

[44] Anderson, 'The Bel Ombre Rebellion', 57–9.

described above, and the Bel Ombre rebellion itself, involved only limited numbers of convicts. Other mutinies and rebellions were fractured by the differing motivations and ambitions of their perpetrators. Notably, the Bengali convicts on the ship *Clarissa* disassociated themselves from events, claiming that the Punjabis had impressed them into service against their will. Moreover, convicts did not necessarily carry preexisting forms or expressions of political consciousness into transportation. In 1855, for instance, the Santals, the third largest tribal group in India, rose in rebellion (*hul*), in the Bengal Presidency. They were aggrieved by the deforestation of their land associated with logging for sleepers for the EIC's expanding network of railways, and the bonded labour and low wages that characterized the Company's favouring of landlords (*zamindars*) and moneylenders (*mahajans*) in its economic and social policies.[45] During and after the *hul*, the Company sentenced hundreds of Santals to imprisonment or transportation, for criminal offences like treason, rebellion, plunder, and robbery. They shipped those sentenced to transportation to the Burmese port of Akyab (now, Sittwe) in Arakan and placed those sentenced to imprisonment in Alipur jail. Alipur's prisoner population swelled in the aftermath of the later and more widespread 1857 revolt, and so the EIC transferred all the Santali prisoners to Arakan. The convicts in the settlement experienced unprecedentedly high death rates, which peaked at 80 per cent in the first year.[46] This was the result of the transfer of prisoners in a state of exhaustion following the uprising, and their employment at hard labour. A number of convicts protested against their transportation by going on hunger strike. However, the Santals did not. EIC administrators in Burma ridiculed the demands of the striking convicts and contrasted their actions to the willingness of the Santals to eat a wide range of food stuffs, including those obtained by foraging. Compared to caste Hindus, civil assistant surgeon J. W. Mountjoy reported, Santals possessed 'the wisdom of the barbarian'.[47] Despite the Santals' transportation for rebellion, their pliability meant that ultimately they became so popular with the

---

[45] The now-classic account of the *hul* is Ranajit Guha, *Elementary Aspects of Peasant Insurgency in Colonial India* (New Delhi: Oxford University Press, 1983).

[46] Fred. J. Mouat, *Report on the Jails of the Lower Provinces of the Bengal Presidency for 1858–9* (Calcutta: John Gray General Printing Department, 1859), 28.

[47] Mouat, *Report on the Jails of the Lower Provinces of the Bengal Presidency for 1858–9*, Appendix I: J. W. Mountjoy, civil assistant surgeon, Akyab, to R. Shepherd, second principal assistant commissioner, Arakan, 11 September 1857, enc. annual report Akyab jail hospital. The imprisonment and transportation of the 1855 Santal rebels is discussed in detail in Clare Anderson, '"The Wisdom of the Barbarian": rebellion, incarceration, and the Santal body politic', *South Asia: Journal of South Asian Studies*, 31, 2 (2008), 223–40.

administration that a substantial proportion of them became overseers (*tindals*) over their fellow convicts. The use of convicts as overseers was a routine element of Indian convict management that provided an escape from hard labour and opportunities for personal gain through contraband trafficking and extortion. This meant that convicts coveted overseer positions. It seems to have derived from military practice and organization, including not just in the army but also at sea where *tindals* were petty officers who oversaw lascars (South Asian seamen). Nonetheless, at the time, the use of convicts as overseers diverged from the norm of global practices where guards or soldiers were most usually employed.[48]

Adivasis and peasants transported overseas from South Asia before the 1857 revolt are rarely regarded as political offenders. Historically, those appellations were most usually reserved for banished elites, especially disposed royals.[49] They included several dozen Kandyan nobles exiled by the British from Ceylon after the great rebellion of 1817–18. The British sent them to jails across South India and to the island of Mauritius, where they were kept separately from the Indian convicts at a site called Powder Mills.[50] Following the 1857 revolt, after killing two of his sons, the British also exiled the deposed Mughal Emperor, Bahadur Shah Zafar, to Rangoon (now, Yangon). His wife Zeenat Mahal and other family members accompanied him.[51] There were two further exiles in British India. The Burmese rulers, King Thibaw and Queen Supayalat,

[48] Fred. J. Mouat, *Report on the Jails of the Lower Provinces of the Bengal Presidency for 1859–60* (Calcutta: Savielle and Cranenburgh Printers, Bengal Printing Co. Ltd, 1860), Appendix I, 115. The use of convicts as overseers was made famous through J. F. A. McNair, *Prisoners Their Own Warders; A record of the convict prison at Singapore in the Straits Settlements established 1825, discontinued 1873, together with a cursory history of the convict establishments at Bencoolen, Penang and Malacca from the Year 1797* (Westminster: Archibald Constable and Co., 1899).

[49] They are the focus of Robert Aldrich, *Banished Potentates: Dethroning and exiling indigenous monarchs under British and French colonial rule, 1815–1955* (Manchester University Press, 2018).

[50] NAM RA54: Governor Robert Brownrigg, Ceylon, to Acting Governor Major-General Gage John Hall, 18 May 1818; TNA CO54/73: Brownrigg to Henry Bathurst (1st Earl Bathurst), secretary of state for war and the colonies, 8 January 1819; IOR F/4/421: Transportation of persons banished from Ceylon to certain parts of the Company's dominions [1813]; IOR F/4/1594: Proceedings relating to the Kandyan prisoners [1836]. Note that the EIC never administered Ceylon. It became a British Crown colony following ceding of Dutch territories by the Treaty of Amiens, during the Napoleonic Wars (1802). British victory in the Second Kandyan War extended control in 1815. For a discussion of petitions written by the Kandyans in Mauritius, see Clare Anderson, 'A Global History of Exile in Asia, c. 1700–1900', in Ricci, ed., *Exile in Colonial Asia*, 29–30 (37–79). On Kandyan exile more broadly, see also Aldrich, *Banished Potentates*, chapter 2; Robert Aldrich, 'Out of Ceylon: The Exile of the Last King of Kandy', in Ricci, ed., *Exile in Colonial Asia*, 48–70.

[51] Aldrich, *Banished Potentates*, 84–7; William Dalrymple, *The Last Mughal: the fall of a dynasty, Delhi, 1857* (London: Bloomsbury, 2006).

were banished to South India at the end of the third Anglo-Burmese war (1885), and six members of the Manipur royal family were sent to the Andaman Islands penal colony, following defeat in the Anglo-Manipur war in 1891. One of them died shortly after their arrival, but as for the Kandyans in Mauritius the others lived entirely separately from the convicts, at the top of Mount Harriet, the summer retreat of the penal colony's British administration. Unlike ordinary transportees, they were allowed to receive goods and money from their relatives.[52]

Ireland, British India, and the Australian Colonies

In the early twentieth century, the British incarcerated Indian nationalists in the notorious Andaman cellular jail (est. 1906), forever associating the islands with political repression (Figure 6.1). The British referred to these nationalists as 'terrorists'; Indians called them 'revolutionaries' or 'freedom fighters'.[53] At least some of them associated their activities with the 1857 revolt. Notable was one of the intellectual founders of Hindu nationalism, V. D. Savarkar, who argued that wars of independence were synonymous with revolutions. The British later arrested Savarkar, in England, where he was a member of the revolutionary, underground organization Abhinav Bharat Society (Young India Society). They charged him with offences including procuring and distributing arms, sedition, and waging war. Sent to Bombay for trial, in 1911 he was

---

[52] Aldrich, *Banished Potentates*, 97–105. Full background to the Manipur exiles can be found in Caroline Keen, *An Imperial Crisis in British India: The Manipur uprising of 1891* (London: I.B. Tauris, 2015). See also NAI Home (Port Blair 'B' proceedings), June 1892, 76–80: Petitions from Manipuri prisoners requesting relatives and friends may send them goods, Chief Commissioner Norman McLeod Horsford to the secretary to the government of India, 9 May 1892.

[53] Barendra Kumar Ghose, *The Tale of My Exile* (Pondicherry: Arya Office, 1922); Bhai Parmanand, *The Story of My Life* (New Delhi: S. Chand and Co., 1982); V. D. Savarkar, *The Story of My Transportation for Life (A biography of black days of Andamans)* (Bombay: Sadbhakti Publications, 1950); Bejoy Kumar Sinha, *In Andamans, the Indian Bastille* (Kanpur: Profulla, C. Mitra, 1939). See also David Arnold, 'The Self and the Cell: Indian Prison Narratives as Life Histories', in David Arnold and Stuart Blackburn, eds., *Telling Lives in India: Biography, autobiography, and life history* (Indiana University Press, 2004), 29–53; J. Daniel Elam, 'Commonplace Anti-Colonialism: Bhagat Singh's Jail Notebook and the Politics of Reading', *South Asia: Journal of South Asian Studies*, 39, 3 (2016), 592–607; J. Daniel Elam and Chris Moffat, eds., 'Writing Revolution: Practice, History, Politics in Modern South Asia', *South Asia: Journal of South Asian Studies*, 39, 3 (2016); Durba Ghosh, *Gentlemanly Terrorists: Political violence and the colonial state in India, 1919–1947* (Cambridge University Press, 2017); Kama Maclean and J. Daniel Elam, eds., *Revolutionary Lives in South Asia: Acts and afterlives of anticolonial political action* (London: Routledge, 2014); Taylor Sherman, *State Violence and Punishment in India, 1919–1956* (London: Routledge, 2009).

Figure 6.1 The Central Jail at Port Blair – 663 cells
Source: Archives and Special Collections, SOAS Library, SOAS MS380828: 'Islands of No Return' by Charles J. Bonington, with accompanying photographs, 1937–86.

sentenced to two life terms in the Andamans.[54] A few 1857 convicts were still alive at the start of the twentieth century. Savarkar claimed in his later memoir, *The Story of My Transportation for Life*, that one rebel had congratulated him: 'for my incarceration in this prison for an attempt to overthrow the Raj similar to the one they had planned in their day'.[55]

One of the many striking elements in *The Story of My Transportation for Life* is Savarkar's description of the cellular jail as a place of education and political consciousness. He described clandestine meetings among political prisoners, lessons in Indian and European history, politics, and economics, and discussions of religion, literature, and science. Forbidden from possessing pencils or paper, prisoners used nails or thorns to write on the whitewashed walls of their cells. They moved cells once a month, and left poems, essays, and other writings for the next occupant, sometimes in tiny vernacular script that was illegible to jail officers. Savarkar claimed that using their own possessions, and bundles sent to them from mainland India, they built up a library of a thousand books, in English, Hindi, Bengali, Sanskrit, and Marathi. The Andaman administration kept political prisoners in the cellular jail for the entirety of their sentence, but all ordinary prisoners had to pass an initially harsh penal stage there before going out to work gangs in the districts. Savarkar claimed that he and his compatriots took the chance to communicate with them, telling them about the nationalist *swadeshi* movement, which encouraged domestic production and the boycott of foreign imports. Their idea was that ordinary convicts would then carry their knowledge into the islands' convict villages, where the British employed literate men as clerks and overseers.[56]

Transportation and incarceration were spaces for learning, education, and politicization in several other contexts. As Robert Aldrich has argued, they presented opportunities for gaining geopolitical experience, making new contacts, developing ideologies, and strategizing.[57] As noted above, this included South Africa's Robben Island during the apartheid era.[58]

---

[54] Vinayak Chaturvedi, 'A Revolutionary's Biography: The Case of V. D. Savarkar', *Postcolonial Studies*, 16, 2 (2013), 128, 130, 131 (124–39); Kama Maclean, *A Revolutionary History of Interwar India: Violence, image, voice and text* (London: Hurst and Co., 2015); Ujjwal Kumar Singh, *Political Prisoners in India* (New Delhi: Oxford University Press, 1998).
[55] Savarkar, *The Story of My Transportation for Life*, 73.
[56] Savarkar, *The Story of My Transportation*, 151–4, 265–72. See also Arnold, 'The Self and the Cell', 41–2.
[57] Aldrich, *Banished Potentates*, 6.
[58] Crain Soudien, 'Nelson Mandela, Robben Island and the Imagination of a New South Africa', *Journal of Southern African Studies*, 41, 2 (2015), 353–66; Paul Gready, *Writing as Resistance: Life Stories of imprisonment, exile, and homecoming from apartheid South Africa* (Lanham, MD: Lexington Books, 2003).

Education was also a feature of the detainee camps for Mau Mau rebels in Kenya (1952–64) and in Zimbabwe during the political upheavals following the unilateral declaration of independence from Britain in 1965. In British colonial Africa, as in the Andaman Islands, prisoners used the time they had for study and discussion. They worked through political ideas of the decolonized nation, reflecting on race, masculinity, class, and religion. Incarceration in jail was an experiential metaphor for colonization, and thus prisons became places for the production of ideas about the nation and the self. As Jocelyn Alexander writes: 'African prison writings can tell us about political visions and social relationships, about the shaping of identity and the assertion of agency.'[59]

Another pertinent theme of Savarkar's memoir of the Andamans was the contemporary political situation in Ireland. His book reproduced what he claims was a conversation with the man in charge of the cellular jail, Irishman David Barrie, when he first arrived. According to Savarkar, Barrie attempted to connect the histories of Ireland and India, telling him that though he had fought for Irish freedom, violence would never achieve success. On a later occasion, Barrie apparently lamented to the political prisoners in his charge: 'Why do you consider me as your enemy? If you suffer, it is the government to blame and not I. I am innocent.'[60] Despite his attempts to garner sympathy, according to Savarkar, Barrie's Irishness also became a point of conflict. Savarkar claimed that the political prisoners ridiculed him for his inability to speak in his mother tongue and viewed him as a slave to the English. He wrote:

We Indians are prepared to fight for freedom with our lives. But you serve those who throw a few crumbs of office at you. You bark like dogs for the master who feeds them. You regard as your own the British Empire that has enslaved your people as much as they have enslaved us, and are proud to be the watch-dogs of that Empire.[61]

Though Savarkar did not make the connection, he could also have compared his fate to the recent history of several thousands of Irish transported by the British, first as indentured servants to the Americas, and then as convicts, over a 200 year period from the middle of the

---

[59] Jocelyn Alexander, 'Prisoners' Memoirs in Zimbabwe: Narratives of Self and Nation', *Cultural and Social History*, 5, 4 (2008), 396 (395–409); Arnold, 'The Self and the Cell'. See also Marshall S. Clough, *Mau Mau Memoirs: History, memory and politics* (Boulder, CO: Lynne Rienner Publishers, 1998); Luise White, 'Separating the Men from the Boys: Constructions of Gender, Sexuality and Terrorism in Central Kenya, 1939–1959', *International Journal of African Historical Studies*, 23, 1 (1990), 1–25.
[60] Savarkar, *The Story of My Transportation for Life*, 230.
[61] Savarkar, *The Story of My Transportation for Life*, 235. On Savarkar's portrayal of Barrie, see also Arnold, 'The Self and the Cell', 41.

seventeenth century. These repressive transportations began with England's Cromwellian invasion of Ireland during the period 1649–53, which completed occupation. At this time, the English sent some convicts to the plantations of Barbados. Irish men and women later constituted a proportion of the convicts indentured in the American colonies, mainly Maryland and Virginia, between 1718 and 1776. From 1788, the Irish also formed part of the more general convict population of the Australian colonies, and then Bermuda and Gibraltar.[62] Of significance for the argument here is that transportation proved a vector for the spread of the revolutionary politics and ideology of the United Irishmen. They were Protestants who wanted autonomous rule in Ireland and the removal of Anglican landowners' privileges in politics and public life. The French revolution inspired them in their secular-republican and revolutionary politics, and with a membership of over half a million they instigated rebellions in 1798 and 1803–4. The Britain punished these uprisings through transportations to New South Wales. According to Ian Duffield, the Irish proved 'dangerous ship's cargo'. They threatened two mutinies in 1793, later declaring that their intention had been murder and escape. In 1801, mutiny broke out on board an Irish convict vessel, with thirteen Irishmen killed in its suppression.[63]

Upon the arrival of United Irishmen in New South Wales, there followed more disturbances and anti-government plots. In 1800, the British foiled a plan to seize a ship and sail to the shores of North America.[64] In 1804, after a series of attempted risings in Sydney, several hundred Irish mounted the largest convict rebellion in the history of the colony, at Castle Hill (Figure 6.2). A whaling ship had recently arrived, bearing news of the outbreak of a second rebellion in Ireland in 1803. The convicts' strategy and tactics were remarkably close to those of the Irish rebellion of 1798, and their goal was to return home as revolutionary republicans. Governor Philip King declared martial law, defeated them in battle, and sentenced some of the survivors to execution and hanging in chains, and others to the chain gang. He ordered another group to travel north to establish a new settlement in Newcastle.[65] Meantime, some of the Castle Hill fugitives

---

[62] Maxwell-Stewart, 'Transportation from Britain and Ireland', *passim*. Irish convicts are among those discussed by George Rudé, *Protest and Punishment: The Story of the social and political protesters transported to Australia 1788–1868* (Oxford: Clarendon Press, 1978).
[63] Ian Duffield, 'Cutting Out and Taking Liberties: Australia's Convict Pirates, 1790-1829', *International Review of Social History*, 58, S21 (2013), 201–3 (quote, 201) (197–227).
[64] Duffield, 'Cutting Out and Taking Liberties', 201–3.
[65] J. E. Gallagher, 'The Revolutionary Irish', *Push from the Bush*, 19 (1985), 2–33; Anne-Maree Whittaker, *Unfinished Revolution: United Irishmen in New South Wales, 1800–1810* (Darlinghurst, NSW: Crossing Press, 2010); Anne-Maree Whittaker, 'Swords to Ploughshares? The 1798 Rebels in New South Wales', *Saothar*, 23 (1998), 13–22.

Insurgency, Politics, and Religion 197

Figure 6.2 Convict uprising at Castle Hill 1804
Source: National Library of Australia: Rex Nan Kivell Collection, NK10162.

were captured on the Hawkesbury river, north of Sydney, where they were planning to seize the first boat they came across and go to sea.[66]

Though the large majority of the approximately 167,000 convicts transported to the Australian colonies were ordinary criminal offenders, there were some further political transportations. Fifteen naval mutineers protesting against poor pay and conditions in England's Spithead and the Nore were transported in 1797, for example.[67] In the 1830s, as noted in Chapter 5, a small number of enslaved rebels were transported out of Jamaica following the Baptist War of 1831–2. They included Jamaican Alexander Simpson who when asked by a clerk about the nature of his offence stated: 'mutiny and exciting the slaves to rebellion. I was a slave

---

[66] Duffield, 'Cutting Out and Taking Liberties', 203.
[67] Ann Veronica Coats and Philip MacDougall, eds., *The Naval Mutinies of 1797: Unity and perseverance* (Woodbridge: Boydell and Brewer, 2011). Stressing the 'common political ideology' that emerged out of Atlantic mutinies of the 1790s is Niklas Frykman, 'Connections between Mutinies in European Navies', *International Review of Social History*, 58, S21 (2013), 88 (87–107).

myself.'[68] Duffield shows how black convicts, including another man called John Goff, carried community-of-origin forms of resistance with them to the Australian colonies. These included bushranging, which Duffield argues mirrored maroon communities in slave colonies, and attempts to form alliances with Aboriginal peoples.[69] The most famous of the 'political' convicts sent to the Australian colonies were the machine breakers known as Swing rioters, who were transported in the 1830s. They were agricultural workers who had undertaken a widespread uprising against mechanization in southern and eastern England.[70] A third group comprised just under 100 Americans, transported to Van Diemen's Land in 1840. Members of the patriot army, or republican activists, in 1838 they had conducted border raids into the colony of Upper Canada, to liberate their northern neighbours from British oppression. Though several of them wrote memoirs, they did not engage in explicitly political activity, and eventually most of them returned home[71]

Following the Castle Hill uprising, the next series of political transportations from Ireland specifically came after the formation of the Young Ireland confederation, which split from other nationalists during the devastating period of the Great Famine of 1845–9. At this time, Ireland lost up to 30 per cent of its population through starvation, disease, and

[68] Ian Duffield, '"Stated This Offence": High-Density Convict Micro-Narratives', in Lucy Frost and Hamish Maxwell-Stewart, eds., *Chain Letters: narrating convict lives* (Melbourne University Press, 2001), 120 (119–35). See also James Bradley and Cassandra Pybus, 'From Slavery to Servitude: The Australian Exile of Elizabeth and Constance', *Journal of Australian Colonial History*, 9 (2007), 29–50; Ian Duffield, 'A Storm in a Teapot? Five Stories About the Trials of Priscilla's Life and their Household Remedy, Arsenic Trioxide', in *To the Islands: Australia and the Caribbean*, special edition of *Australian Cultural History*, 21 (2002), 19–31; Diana Paton, 'An "Injurious" Population: Caribbean-Australian Penal Transportation and Imperial Racial Politics', *Cultural and Social History*, 5, 4 (2008), 449–64.

[69] Ian Duffield, 'The Life and Death of "Black" John Goff: Aspects of the Black Convict Contribution to Resistance Patterns During the Transportation Era in Eastern Australia', *Australian Journal of Politics and History*, 33, 1 (1987), 37–9 (30–44).

[70] TNA CO48/297 17 July 1849 no. 116: Henry Grey (3rd Earl Grey), secretary of state for war and the colonies, to Governor H.G. Smith, Cape Colony, 30 November 1849. This letter appears out of sequence and appears to have been misfiled in the records. The classic account of the Swing riots is Eric Hobsbawm and George Rudé, *Captain Swing: A Social History of the great English agricultural uprising of 1830* (New York: W. W. Norton and Company, 1973). On the Australian transportations, see Bruce W. Brown, The Machine Breaker Convicts from the Proteus and the Eliza, MA thesis, University of Tasmania, 2004; David Kent and Norma Townsend, *The Convicts of the Eleanor: Protest in Rural England, New Lives in Australia* (London: Pluto Press and Merlin, 2002); David Kent and Norma Townsend, eds., *Joseph Mason: Assigned convict 1831–1837* (Melbourne University Press: 2013).

[71] Hamish Maxwell-Stewart and Cassandra Pybus, *American Citizens, British Slaves: Yankee political prisoners in a British penal colony 1839–1850* (East Lansing: University of Michigan Press, 2002).

emigration. Mirroring the wider political context for the rebellion of the United Irishmen in 1798, the 1848 revolution in France inspired the Young Irelanders. A key figure in the movement was John Mitchel (1815–75), who set up the newspaper *United Irishmen*, using the 1798 motto: 'Our independence must be had at all hazards.' The British arrested Mitchel, charging him with sedition, but then dropping the case. They then tried and convicted him under the newly passed Treason Felony Act of 1848. Sentenced to fourteen years' transportation, Mitchel went to the Bermuda hulks.[72] He joined 704 recently arrived Irishmen, mostly, it was said at the time, convicted for stealing food or other agrarian offences. Sixty-eight of them were under the age of nineteen, and of those twelve were under sixteen and one was just thirteen years old. Governor Charles Elliot remarked that they appeared shorter and younger than their actual age. Elliot placed Mitchel on the *Dromedary*, having first removed all the Irish who had recently arrived and were in a discontented state. Still, the hulk held 1500 convicts, including 800 from Ireland. They were in what Elliot described as 'a state of great excitement on which [Mitchel] had acted a conspicuous part'.[73] That the Irish were not in good health is unsurprising. To the depredations of the famine years were added the hardships of incarceration and the voyage across the Atlantic Ocean. More than half of new arrivals from Ireland had scurvy, and some of them died.[74]

It was not long before the governor reported finding what he described as an 'inflammatory newspaper' in the cabin of the Catholic chaplain, the Reverend MacLeod, who lost no time in asking for permission to visit Mitchel. Elliot refused, stating that he wanted the convicts to be kept free of 'political excitement'.[75] Describing Mitchel as a very dangerous man, for this reason he decided not to send him out to public works.[76] By this time, Mitchel had been gifted a gold-edged Bible, by a woman living in New York who claimed to be 'a daughter of one of the Patriots of 1798'.[77]

---

[72] Seán McConville, *Irish Political Prisoners, 1848–1922: Theatres of War* (London: Routledge, 2003), chapter 2 (quote, 21n34). The Act was 11 & 12 Vict. cap. 12.

[73] TNA CO37/122/8 22 June 1848 no. 47 folios 51–4: Governor Charles Elliot, Bermuda, to Grey, 22 June 1848. Between 1848 and 1851, almost as many convicts were transported to Bermuda from Ireland (759) as from England (810): TNA CO37/139 18 March 1852 no. 18: Elliot to Grey, 18 March 1852, enc. Return of convicts sent to Bermuda, n.d.

[74] C. F. E. Hollis Hallett, *Forty Years of Convict Labour: Bermuda, 1823–1863* (Pembroke, Bermuda: Juniperhill Press, 1999), 41–2, 59.

[75] TNA CO37/122/14 5 July 1848 (private): Elliot to Grey, 5 July 1848.

[76] TNA CO37/122/40 21 September 1848 no. 82 folios 250–60: Elliot to Grey, 21 September 1848.

[77] TNA CO37/122/37 5 September 1848 (private): Elliot to Grey, 5 September 1848, enc.: Reverend R. Baird to Elliot, 10 August 1848.

Meantime, suffering from asthma, he was moved to the hospital ship *Tenedos*, and then shifted back to the *Dromedary* after news arrived that stoked fears that his escape was being planned in the USA. Governor Elliot claimed that an emissary from what he described as 'the Irish associations in the US' had gone to Bermuda on the pretext of being a debt collector and made it as far as the convict public works at Ireland Island before he was detected and sent away.[78]

Against this background, Secretary of State for War and the Colonies Henry Grey took the decision to send Mitchel and some of the other Irish convicts to the Cape Colony. The larger context for this was previous discussion about the Cape as a transportation destination. Governor Charles Somerset had first mooted the idea of sending British convicts as road labourers in 1825, and in 1841 the EIC proposed that it receive white soldiers convicted in India.[79] In 1842, the Colonial Office raised the prospect of the transportation of juvenile convicts, with conditional pardons, from England's Parkhurst prison.[80] In both cases, colonists raised strong objections.[81] Natal was incorporated into the Cape Colony in 1843, and new Colonial Secretary, William Ewart Gladstone, with the support of penal reformer Alexander Maconochie, proposed the transportation of convicts to work as labourers on harbour improvements. However, this plan, and further proposals in 1846 and 1848, also came to nothing.[82] Mitchel and other nationalists were not at this time viewed

---

[78] TNA CO37/122/40 21 September 1848 no. 82 folios 250–60: Elliot to Grey, 21 September 1848.

[79] TNA CO48/68 8 June 1825 no. 174: Governor Charles Somerset, Cape Colony, to Bathurst, 8 June 1825; TNA CO48/81 7 July 1826: Somerset to R. W. Hay, 7 July 1826; IOR P/141/62: J. Moore Craig, acting secretary to government Cape Colony, to G. A. Bushby, secretary to government of India, 6 November 1841; Governor George Napier, Cape Colony, to Lord John Russell, secretary of state for war and the colonies, 23 October 1841. Copies of this correspondence are also in TNA CO48/213 and PP 1849 (217) *Transportation. Convicts. Transportation (Cape of Good Hope). Copies of correspondence with the governors of the Cape of Good Hope and Ceylon, respecting the transportation of convicts to those colonies; and correspondence with the Governor of Bermuda, on the removal of convicts from that station to the Cape*, 4 April 1849. Other relevant sources are: IOR P/403/6 Minute of George William Anderson, officiating governor of Bombay, 23 February 1842; PP 1849 (217) *Transportation. Convicts. Transportation (Cape of Good Hope):* Note of Commandant Richard Wolfe, Robben Island, 25 September 1841, Napier to Russell, 23 October 1841, Napier to Smith-Stanley, 2 July 1842. See also Clare Anderson, 'Convicts, Carcerality and Cape Colony Connections in the 19th Century', *Journal of Southern African Studies*, 42, 3 (2016), 437–9 (429–42).

[80] TNA CO48/220 2 July and 15 August 1842 nos. 127 and 154: Napier to Smith-Stanley, 2 July 1842, 15 August 1842; TNA CO48/221 Napier to Smith-Stanley, 7 September 1842.

[81] TNA CO48/220 27 August 1842 no. 158: Napier to Smith-Stanley, enc. memorial ('by certain ministers of the gospel'), n.d.

[82] On proposals to introduce convicts during this period, see A. F. Hattersley, *Convict Crisis and the Growth of Unity: Resistance to transportation in South Africa and Australia* (Pietermaritzburg: University of Natal Press, 1965).

as entirely culpable for their original transportation. Indeed, Reverend James Kennedy in Bermuda noted the extraordinary circumstances in which many of them had been transported, for either famine-related thefts or 'political offences committed under fear and at times of excitement'.[83] Nonetheless, Governor Elliot maintained that Mitchel should be kept apart from other convicts. The party left Bermuda for the Cape in April 1849, on the ship *Neptune*, after a speech in which the governor told them that if they behaved well during the voyage, they would be given a ticket-of-leave immediately upon arrival.[84]

Following a lengthy sea passage during which the ship was first presumed lost, and then detained at Pernambuco in Brazil, the *Neptune* finally reached the Cape in September 1849. Grey had sent ahead orders that the colony disembark the convicts, drawing attention to Colonial Secretary John Montagu's prior experience of transportation in Van Diemen's Land. Appointed to the Cape in 1843, Montagu had almost twenty years' service in the Australian colony, as private secretary to the governor.[85] However, Governor Harry Smith refused the ship permission to land, and it remained anchored in Simon's Bay during considerable anti-transportation agitation. Following a five-month long period of meetings, protests, and petitions, eventually Grey ordered the ship on to Van Diemen's Land. It arrived in April 1850, after almost a year at sea. Mitchel was immediately granted a ticket-of-leave.[86] Already in Van Diemen's Land were other Irish republican convicts, including

---

[83] TNA CO37/126/14 8 February 1849 no. 13 folios 120–6: Elliot to Grey, 8 February 1849, enc. Reverend James Kennedy, 3 February 1849.

[84] TNA CO37/126/47 22 April 1849 no. 42 folios 350–79: Elliot to Grey, 23 April 1849, enc. Elliot's visit to the ship, n.d.

[85] PP 1849 (217) *Transportation. Convicts. Transportation (Cape of Good Hope):* Grey to Smith, 19 March 1849; TNA CO37/126/48 23 April 1849 no. 43 folios 380–93: Elliot to Grey, 23 April 1849. For extensive anti-transportation correspondence and petitions, see also TNA CO48/296 and TNA CO48/297. On Montagu, see E. I. Carlyle (revised by Lynn Milne), 'Montagu, John (1797–1853)', *Oxford Dictionary of National Biography* (Oxford University Press, 2004); online edition September 2004, https://doi.org/10.1093/ref:odnb/19028. During Montagu's Van Diemonian posting, transportation discipline had changed significantly, with the introduction of a probation system. Convicts progressed through their sentence in penal stages, beginning in chain gangs and ultimately achieving liberation.

[86] PP 1849 (217) *Transportation. Convicts. Transportation (Cape of Good Hope):* Smith to Grey, 19 December 1848, enc. The humble Petition of Her Majesty's faithful People of the Cape of Good Hope, 18 November 1848; TNA CO48/297 17 July 1849 no. 116: Grey to Smith, 30 November 1849; TNA CO48/304 14 February 1850 no. 21: Smith to Grey, 14 and 27 February 1850. See also Philip Harling, 'The Trouble with Convicts: From Transportation to Penal Servitude, 1840–67', *Journal of British Studies*, 53, 1 (2014), 91–4 (80–110); McConville, *Irish Political Prisoners*, 50–4; Kirsten McKenzie, 'Discourses of Scandal: Bourgeois Respectability and the End of Slavery and Transportation at the Cape and New South Wales, 1830–1850', *Journal of Colonialism and Colonial History*, 4, 3 (2003), doi:10.1353/cch.2004.0011.

Mitchel's great friend John Martin and Thomas Meagher, Kevin O'Doherty, and William Smith O'Brien. O'Brien was the only member of the British parliament (MP) ever transported as a convict to the Australian colonies.[87]

In 1854, Mitchel published *Jail Journal; or, Five Years in British Prisons*.[88] Now viewed as a classic republican text, the key concerns of the book are somewhat incompatible. This is because Mitchel wanted to describe the horrors that he had suffered as a transported convict, but at the same time he wished to distinguish himself from the mass of ordinary convicts, whom he viewed as brutal, immoral, and corrupt. In *Jail Journal*, he made many exaggerated claims about treatment akin to torture, despite the reality of considerable privileges and little contact with the mass of convicts. In Bermuda, as in Van Diemen's Land, he had his own quarters, did not wear uniform, and never performed hard labour.[89] Because of this, during his sojourn in Bermuda, rumours had even reached London that the ships' officers doffed their hats to him and that he had a servant. These Governor Elliot strictly denied. He had, he reported, opened all letters to and from Mitchel and his family, which confirmed that he was 'in the depths of distress'. Moreover, the only reason he had not put Mitchel out to public works was fear of his 'baneful influence over large bodies of his countrymen'. He allowed him to wear his own clothes; not out of compassion, but because he believed that it made it more difficult for him to escape by blending in with a convict gang.[90]

By the time Mitchel got to Hobart, the Irish Directory in New York had raised funds to support Young Ireland, and it directed that those monies should be used to assist Mitchel and others to escape. Though Mitchel's ticket-of-leave prohibited him from leaving Van Diemen's Land, in 1853 he made it to San Francisco, disguised as a Catholic priest. Mitchel's experience of the British in Ireland might have made him a republican, but it was a republicanism grounded in the privileges of educated white men of his social class. On the one hand, in *Jail Journal* he described Irish

---

[87] McConville, *Irish Political Prisoners*, 54, 79.
[88] John Mitchel, *Jail Journal; or, Five Years in British Prisons* (New York: Office of the 'Citizen', 1854).
[89] Tim Causer, '"On British Felony the Sun Never Sets": Narratives of Political Prisoners in New South Wales and Van Diemen's Land, 1838–53', *Cultural and Social History*, 5, 4 (2008), 423–35. See also G. Kearns, '"Educate that Holy Hatred": Place, Trauma and Identity in the Irish Nationalism of John Mitchel', *Political Geography*, 20 (2001), 885–911; Kenney, '"I felt a kind of pleasure in seeing them treat us brutally"; McConville, *Irish Political Prisoners*, 50–1, 68.
[90] TNA CO37/122/40 21 September 1848 no. 80 folios 250–60: Elliot to Grey, 21 September 1848.

Catholics as slaves and believed that Irish peasants were treated worse than the enslaved Africans he saw when the *Neptune* stopped in Brazil. On the other, in Van Diemen's Land, he found satisfyingly natural parallels between negative views of convicts and enslaved African-Americans: 'Here, a freeman is a king; and the convict-class is regarded just as the negroes must be in South Carolina: which, indeed, is perfectly right.'[91] After his escape to the USA, it is perhaps unsurprising that he sided with the southern states in the civil war, praised enslavement, and went so far as to propose a reinvigoration of the African trade.[92]

It would be easy to interpret the sailing of the *Neptune* to the Cape as a straightforward consequence of Bermuda's desire to get rid of John Mitchel and other Irish republicans. However, this was only part of the story. Rather, and first, the sailing of the *Neptune* was part of a reconfiguration of punishment in Britain that relied on the ability to move prisoners through penal stages by moving them through the colonies. In this regard, sentences of imprisonment and transportation became intertwined to create new forms of punitive mobility, and the penal history of Britain became inextricably linked to the history of empire.[93] This important point cannot be overstated. A key innovation in punishment here was the establishment of the 'exile' system, which blended incarceration and penal transportation. This evolved in the aftermath of the Molesworth Committee of 1837–8 which, as explained in Chapter 5, recommended the abolition of transportation to the Australian colonies and its replacement with imprisonment and hard labour at home, or (for those sentenced to longer terms) in unspecified overseas destinations.[94] The 'exile' system, on the other hand, divided

---

[91] Mitchel, *Jail Journal*, 243.
[92] Mitchel, *Jail Journal*, 29, 170. See also Causer, '"On British Felony the Sun Never Sets"', 430; McConville, *Irish Political Prisoners*, 74.
[93] See also Harling, 'The Trouble with Convicts'.
[94] PP 1837 (518) *Report from the Select Committee on Transportation; together with the minutes of evidence, appendix, and index*, 14 July 1837; PP 1837–38 (669) *Report from the Select Committee on Transportation; together with the minutes of evidence, appendix, and index*, 3 August 1838. See also Raymond Evans, '19 June 1822: Creating "An Object of Real Terror": the Tabling of the First Bigge Report', in Martin Crotty and David Andrew Roberts, eds., *Turning Points in Australian History* (Sydney: University of New South Wales Press, 2009), 48–61; J. B. Hirst, *Convict Society and Its Enemies: A history of early New South Wales* (Sydney, NSW: Allen and Unwin, 1983), 26–7; Kirsten McKenzie, *Scandal in the Colonies: Sydney and Cape Town 1820–50* (Melbourne University Press, 2004); McKenzie, 'Discourses of Scandal'; Isobelle Barrett Meyering, 'Abolitionism, Settler Violence and the Case Against Flogging: A Reassessment of Sir William Molesworth's Contribution to the Transportation Debate', *History Australia*, 7, 1 (2010), 6.1–6.18; John Ritchie, *Punishment and Profit: The reports of Commissioner John Bigge on the Colonies of New South Wales and Van Diemen's Land, 1822–1823; their origins, nature and significance* (Melbourne, VIC: Heinemann, 1970); *The Evidence to the Bigge*

transportation into penal stages through which convicts could move on the basis of time served and conduct. Consequently, convicts sentenced to up to ten years' transportation were placed in separate confinement in Millbank, Pentonville, or Parkhurst prisons prior to their shipment to the Australian colonies, where they were given a conditional pardon. Between 1844 and 1849, 1,723 such 'exiles' (or Pentonvillians) were the first and only convicts transported to the Port Phillip District of New South Wales (which was later separated to become the colony of Victoria).[95]

This new form of imperial penal discipline impacted on other colonies too, to the extent that from the early planning stage Bermuda and Gibraltar were included in what was in effect a triangular convict trade, straddling the northern Atlantic and southern Indian Oceans. Convicts underwent a period of up to a year in separate confinement in Britain, followed by up to five years of public works in Britain or on the hulks of Bermuda or Gibraltar. They were then sent on to one of the Australian colonies, receiving probationary tickets of leave if they behaved well during the voyage. After serving half their term, they would receive a remission of the rest of their sentence, or conditional pardon, though this prohibited them from returning to Britain or Ireland.[96] Several vessels sailed to Van Diemen's Land from Bermuda and Gibraltar during

---

Reports: New South Wales under Governor Macquarie, Volume 2: the written evidence, selected and edited by John Ritchie (Melbourne, VIC: Heinemann, 1971); John Ritchie, 'Towards Ending an Unclean Thing: The Molesworth Committee and the Abolition of Transportation to New South Wales, 1837–40', *Australian Historical Studies*, 17, 67 (1976), 144–64; David Andrew Roberts, 'Beyond "the Stain": Rethinking the Nature and Impact of the Anti-transportation Movement', *Journal of Australian Colonial History*, 14 (2012), 205–79; Norma Townsend, '"The clamour of ... inconsistent Persons": Attitudes to Transportation within New South Wales in the 1830s', *Australian Journal of Politics and History*, 25, 3 (1979), 345–57.

[95] Colleen Wood, Great Britain's exiles sent to Port Phillip, Australia, 1844–1849: Lord Stanley's experiment, PhD thesis, The University of Melbourne, 2014.

[96] TNA CO37/117/49 17 July 1847 folios 402–19 (confidential): Grey to Elliot, 18 June 1847; TNA CO91/187 3 January 1848 nos. 5, 3, and 26: Governor Robert T. Wilson, Gibraltar, to Grey, 3 January 1848, 3 February 1848, 8 February 1848. This overlaid the triangular trade that existed between Britain and Ireland, the Australian colonies, and EIC Asia. The British government chartered convict ships to disembark convicts in New South Wales and Van Diemen's Land. The ships then took on cargoes of oil, sealskins, coals, wool, and sandalwood, and traded them in the South Sea islands and China. They then returned to Bengal with tea. See PP 1812 (341) *Report from the Select Committee on Transportation*, 10 July 1812, 4; Appendix 1: Minutes of evidence, Vice Admiral Governor John Hunter 19 February 1812, 23, Alexander McLeay, secretary to transport board, 28–9. Note that other EIC ships traded with the colony direct from Bengal, though by the terms of the EIC charter, the on-trade in sandalwood with China was illegal. See PP 1812 (341) *Report from the Select Committee on Transportation*, 10 July 1812, Appendix 1: Minutes of evidence, Robert Campbell, 68–9, 76. Lauren Darwin argues that this was a means through which merchants could break into the EIC monopoly on trade. See Lauren Darwin, Convict Transportation in the Age of Abolition, 1787–1807, PhD thesis, University of Hull, 2016, chapter 2.

this period. This included the *Mount Stewart Elphinstone* in 1848, which deposited 140 convicts in Gibraltar, and took 140 convicts from Gibraltar to Van Diemen's Land.[97] Two months later, a second group of 203 men sailed from Bermuda to the same destination on the *Bangalore*, after it had deposited 258 Irish convicts at the dockyard.[98] The *Rodney* in 1851 landed 118 English and Irish convicts in Gibraltar, collected 140 for Van Diemen's Land, picking up convicts in Portsmouth, Portland, Plymouth, and Cork on the way.[99] During that year, 440 convicts left Gibraltar for the colony.[100] In 1852, the *Cornwallis* took 300 convicts to Gibraltar, and embarked 300 embarked for Van Diemen's Land.[101] Having taken 296 English convicts to Bermuda, the ill-fated *Neptune* was the third such vessel to depart for the Antipodes with convicts from the imperial hulks on board.[102] The innovation in its sailing was not so much the idea of the Cape as a transportation colony, but Earl Grey's incorporation of it into an already existing extractive empire-wide carceral circuit of punitive mobility.[103]

The mutual constitution of Britain and its empire in the relocation of convicts was further codified in law with the passing of the Penal Servitude Acts of 1853 and 1857. The 1853 Penal Servitude Act abolished transportation for more than fourteen years. It replaced it with imprisonment and hard labour on public works, and prisoners received terms of years of just under half of what they would have served previously, in transportation. The 1857 Act abolished sentences of transportation altogether but differed from the 1853 Act because prisoners were given the same term of penal servitude as they would have served in

---

[97] TNA CO91/192 25 January 1849 no. 192: Gibraltar annual report, 1848 (*Elphinstone*); TNA CO37/121/30 15 April 1848 no. 26 folios 207–19: Elliot to Grey, 15 April 1848.
[98] TNA CO37/139 18 March 1852 no. 18: Elliot to Grey, 18 March 1852, enc. return of convicts sent to Bermuda, n.d. See also Hollis Hallett, *Forty Years of Convict Labour*, 112–3.
[99] TNA CO91/201 5 October 1851 no. 118: Governor Robert Gardiner, Gibraltar, to Grey, 5 October 1851; CO91/202 (Home Office): H. Waddington, permanent under-secretary of state Home Department, to Herman Merivale, under-secretary of state for the colonies, 5 September 1851.
[100] TNA CO91/204 26 January 1852 no. 12: Annual Report, year ending 31 December 1851.
[101] TNA CO91/200 13 March 1851 no. 36: Gardiner to Grey, 13 March 1851.
[102] TNA CO37/121/3015 April 1848 no. 26 folios 207–19: Elliot to Grey, 15 April 1848; TNA CO37/139 18 March 1852 no. 18: Elliot to Grey, 18 March 1852, enc. return of convicts sent to Bermuda, n.d.; Hollis Hallett, *Forty Years of Convict Labour*, 112–3.
[103] PP 1849 (217) *Transportation. Convicts. Transportation (Cape of Good Hope):* Grey to Smith, 7 August 1848; Grey to Governor Peregrine Maitland, 10 September 1847; Grey to Smith, 23 March 1849. See also Nick Gill, Deirdre Conlon, Dominique Moran, and Andrew Burridge, 'Carceral Circuitry: New Directions in Carceral Geography', *Progress in Human Geography*, 42, 2 (2018), 183–204.

transportation. In both cases, convicts could serve their sentence in Britain, Bermuda, or Gibraltar.[104]

Meantime, the departure of the 1848 ships for the Australian colonies coincided with a period of economic depression, following the low price of wool and recession in Britain, the collapse of markets for grain and livestock, and the lack of British capital investment. Land revenues fell as did settler demand for labour. The colony encouraged free immigration, hoping this would stimulate consumption and investment. However, immigrants flooded the labour market, and they competed with ticket-of-leave convicts. This led to mass unemployment, and it was only with the recovery of wool prices that the economy improved.[105] Just two weeks after the arrival of the *Bangalore* in Van Diemen's Land, a letter from convict Henry Hewitt to overseer of the *Tenedos* hulk in Bermuda, John Kirkham, complained of labour conditions. Only thirty-five of the ticket-of-leave men had been able to find work, and only at very low wages. 'Most of the men now bitterly repent having put down their names', Hewitt wrote. 'This colony is in a very depressed state, most of those who can leave are preparing to do so, and many have done so.' He much lamented the prohibition on leaving the colony, which meant that he could not try his luck in the less economically depressed New South Wales.[106]

The fact that the labour market of Van Diemen's Land was flooded during this period certainly fed into Earl Grey's designation of the Cape as an alternative destination for the *Neptune*. As he suggested in a letter to Governor Harry Smith, he knew that they would have no prospect of finding employment in the Australian colonies.[107] It also influenced another contemporary proposal for the Bermuda exiles from the Caribbean. Frederick Forth, Council President of the Turks and Caicos Islands, wrote: 'The demand here for mechanics and domestic servants is great and urgent ... any men possessed of ... Trades &c &c ... would find immediate and constant employment ... provided they prove themselves honest sober and industrious.' Before his posting to the Bahamas, Forth

---

[104] TNA CO37/154 (Home Office): Waddington to Governor Freeman Murray, Bermuda, 23 May 1856; Penal Servitude Act 1853 (16 & 17 Vict., cap. 99); Penal Servitude Act 1857 (20 & 21 Vict., cap. 3), http://www.legislation.gov.uk/ukpga/Vict/20-21/3/contents. See also Harling, 'The Trouble with Convicts', 100.

[105] David Meredith and Deborah Oxley, 'The Convict Economy', in Simon P. Ville and G. A. Withers, eds., *The Cambridge Economic History of Australia* (Cambridge University Press, 2014), 97–122.

[106] TNA CO37/126/21 1 March 1848 folios 159–66 (private): Elliot to Grey, enc. Henry H. Hewitt to John K. Kirkham, overseer of the *Tenedos*, 30 July 1848; TNA CO48/297: Grey to Smith, 30 November 1849.

[107] TNA CO48/297 17 July 1849 no. 116: Grey to Smith, 30 November 1849.

had been first visiting magistrate in Van Diemen's Land under the administration of George Arthur (see Chapter 4). He later became the police magistrate in Campbell Town, where he supervised convict labour gangs, and eventually rose to the position of director of public works (1841–7). It was this experience, he noted, that led him to believe that the exiles would find employment, as skilled labour, in the salt-ponds or agriculture. They could also be employed on public works, including of water tanks, a lighthouse, a marketplace, wharves, and military barracks.[108] The Colonial Office rejected Forth's proposition, on the grounds that the cost of securing the establishment was not worth the small number of exiles that the islands was willing to receive.[109] Forth countered that the reefs around the islands would make it difficult for convicts to escape. The trees and shrubs had all been cut down so, excepting a few caves, there was nowhere to hide. 'Few Islands, not even Port Arthur in Tasmania or Norfolk Island, are so well adapted to the safe keeping of convicts as Grand Turk and Salt Cay', he added.[110] When, again, the Colonial Office rejected his plan, he proposed the sending of under-sentence convicts, as opposed to exiles, to build a harbour in North Creek. However, there was considerable local opposition to this, and the islands' population started an anti-transportation campaign that much resembled that of the Cape Colony. Forth claimed that a Baptist missionary called William Rycroft had whipped up agitation grounded in exaggerated claims that the convicts were a 'demoralizing population' that would displace emancipated slaves in the labour market.[111] Rycroft had convened a public meeting which passed resolutions that echoed the objections to white convict transportation to the Caribbean and New South Wales in the 1830s as noted in Chapter 5.[112] He even forwarded a petition to anti-transportationist, Sir William

---

[108] TNA CO301/2/21 31 December 1849 no. 21 folios 270–87: Council President Frederick Forth, Turks and Caicos, to Governor Sir Charles Grey, Jamaica, 5 April 1849, enc. Forth to Elliot, 23 March 1849, and Schedule of Trades required at the Turks Islands, n.d. Note that at this time, the islands were governed indirectly through Jamaica.

[109] TNA CO301/3/8 21 January 1850 no. 8 folios 79–108: [Earl] Grey to [Charles] Grey, 7 March 1850.

[110] TNA CO301/3/8 21 January 1850 no. 8 folios 79–108: Forth to [Charles] Grey, 10 December 1849.

[111] TNA CO301/3/20 7 May 1850 no. 19 folios 218–304: Forth to [Charles] Grey, 20 February 1850; enc. Report of the Committee appointed on the 7th instant for the purpose of investigating and reporting upon the contents of a Petition laid before the Board by His Honor the President; [Earl] Grey to [Charles] Grey, 12 June 1850.

[112] TNA CO301/4 (Individuals): George Gibbs: George Gibbs to [Earl] Grey, 8 February 1850, enc. Resolutions of a Meeting held at Grand Key Turks Islands, 31 January 1850.

Molesworth.[113] Again, the Colonial Office rejected the idea, repeating that the value of the convict labour would not offset the cost.[114]

Beyond this important penal context, a second factor in the sailing of the *Neptune* to the Australian colonies was the local view of *Irish* convicts specifically, and their youthful character. Transported in the aftermath of the famine, the Irish were different from ordinary transportation convicts. As Bermudian governor Elliot put it in 1848: '[M]any of them were convicted of stealing food, and agrarian offences; the first, no doubt, chiefly attributable to the dreadful calamity that befell the poorest classes of people during the last two years, and the last in a high degree to the inflammatory practices of others, in the time of their desperate need.'[115] Earl Grey even compared them to the Swing rioters of 1831.[116] But their arrival also coincided with controversy over sexual activity on the hulks. At the end of 1847, the medical officer in charge of the naval hospital reported that some of the convicts had told him that other convicts were committing 'unnatural offences' in their ward. The problem for Governor Elliot was, of course, proving it, for one of the keystones of penal management practice was the encouragement of convict informing against their fellow men, in exchange for mitigation of sentence or the issue of other privileges. Meanwhile, he asked that only convicts aged over 21 be sent, and with the agreement of the colonial secretary put into action the plan to build new barracks on shore at Boaz Island, for healthy and sick men.[117] A sizeable proportion of the Irish convicts were juveniles, and in a private despatch Governor Elliot wrote of his feelings of 'shame and grief' at the thought of the consequences of their mixing with older convict men. 'Poor and scanty food, and the hard things of their infancy', he added, 'have for the most part left these lads with a lower stature and more childish appearance than their age alone would explain.'[118] The colony's Roman Catholic priest James Kennedy wrote that many had

---

[113] TNA CO301/5/3 n.d. May 1850 no. 3 folios 32–41: Forth to [Charles] Grey, n.d. May 1850, enc. A true copy of a letter sent to the people at the Caicos by W. Rycroft received February 21st 1850 (copy at TNA CO301/4/4 7 August 1850 no. 27 folios 125–156); TNA CO301/8 (Individuals), c. 270 inhabitants of Grand Cay: Petition of Inhabitants of Grand Cay, 30 November 1850.
[114] TNA CO301/4 (Individuals): George Gibbs to [Earl] Grey, 8 February 1850, enc. Resolutions of a Meeting held at Grand Key Turks Islands, 31 January 1850.
[115] PP 1849 (217) *Transportation. Convicts. Transportation (Cape of Good Hope)*: Elliot to Grey, 22 June 1848.
[116] TNA CO48/297 17 July 1849 no. 116: Grey to Smith, 30 November 1849.
[117] TNA CO37/118/45 19 November 1847 nos. 313–23 (confidential): Elliot to Grey, 19 November 1847, Grey to Eliot, 16 December 1847.
[118] PP 1849 (217) *Transportation. Convicts. Transportation (Cape of Good Hope)*: Elliot to Grey (private), 3 July 1848. The original document is located at TNA CO37/122/13 3 July 1848 folios 93–5 (confidential): Elliot to Grey, 3 July 1848.

been 'the mere creatures of others'. Elliot requested permission to return to Ireland sixty-eight recently arrived Irish boys, twelve of whom were under 16 years of age and one was aged just 13.[119]

To some extent, the circumstances in which the Irish were transported played in their favour, as far as remission of sentence was concerned. In 1852, for instance, the wife of one man, Martin Rourke, turned up in Bermuda, having travelled all the way from Ireland via New York, Boston, and Halifax. The Wexford court had sentenced her husband to ten years' transportation for sheep stealing in 1848. Reverend Thomas Lyons wrote: 'Her fidelity and devoted affection for her husband prompted her to sacrifice her earning and brave all the difficulties and inconveniences of a long voyage.' The Colonial Office agreed that the 'heroic exertions' of Rourke's wife deserved consideration, and the Home Office issued a warrant for his conditional pardon.[120] It was not always so generous. In 1856, Governor Freeman Murray sent to London a list of Irish convicts who he recommended for pardon on the grounds of good conduct. However, Lord-Lieutenant of Ireland Colonel Thomas Larcom only permitted the release of a few of them, and suggested that the remainder go to Western Australia, if the Colonial Office agreed.[121] Neither was the positive view of Irish convicts mirrored in Gibraltar. In 1852, Superintendent of Convicts Robert Armstrong complained that the unruliest had been selected for transportation.[122] Even in Bermuda, the largely sympathetic view of the Irish came to an abrupt end with a violent riot on the *Medway*, in 1859.[123]

The last transportations of Irish rebels to the Australian colonies were the sixty-two Fenians who reached Swan River in 1867.[124] The Fenian movement combined Irish republicans with American supporters of armed struggle, and these transportations followed a failed plan for an uprising in 1865. In contrast to the Young Irelanders, upon their conviction the Fenians were neither separated from ordinary convicts nor granted special privileges. The government issued amnesties and

---

[119] PP 1849 (217) *Transportation. Convicts. Transportation (Cape of Good Hope):* James Kennedy, Roman Catholic priest, to Elliot, 3 February 1849.
[120] TNA CO37/140 no. 46: Elliot to John Somerset Pakington (1st Baron Hampton), secretary of state for war and the colonies, 28 June 1852, enc. Reverend Thomas Lyons to Elliot, 26 June 1852, and Name, age, conviction &c Sentence of the undermentioned convict, Dromedary Hulk, Ireland Island, 21 June 1852; Pakington to Elliot, 8 September 1852. The records do not specify Mrs Rourke's first name.
[121] TNA CO37/158 (Home Office): Waddington to Merivale, 31 January 1856.
[122] TNA CO91/204 no. 43: Superintendent Robert Armstrong, Bermuda, to George Adderley, colonial secretary Gibraltar, 8 April 1852.
[123] Hollis Hallett, *Forty Years of Convict Labour*, 27–8.
[124] TNA CO91/288 (Home Office): A. Liddell to G. F. Elliot, 18 November 1867; draft letter to Governor Richard Airey, n.d. December 1867.

pardons, and these convicts either settled in the colony, returned to Ireland, or went to the USA. By 1876, there were just six of them remaining. In that year, an American group of supporters purchased a whaling ship, *Catalpa*, recruited a crew, and sent out a rescue party from New York. The convicts absconded from a working party where their rescuers awaited. They rowed out to the *Catalpa*, which managed to evade both its pursuers and Royal Navy ships. And here we complete the circle of relationality between punitive mobility, politics, insurgency, and mutiny, because remarkably the six Fenians with their supporters made it all the way to America's Atlantic shores.[125]

Spain and Latin America

As previous chapters argued, Spanish penal mobility was multi-directional, connected to that of other migrants, and inseparable from the structure and labour needs of the empire.[126] Included in convict flows were political deportees, such as insurgents, intellectuals, and revolutionaries subject to administrative deportation. This is reflected in the history of the *presidio* of Ceuta which, until its closure in 1912, received convicts and political prisoners, including those deported from the colony of Cuba during many insurgencies, notably the Ten Years' War (1868–78) and War of Independence (1895–8).[127] One group, the 'Ñañigos', reconstituted their cultural practices in the *presidio*.[128] In 1901, criminologist Rafael Salillas made observations on the carnivalesque performances of what he claimed was a 'secret society' from Africa, carried to Cuba by slaves, and then on to Ceuta by convicts. Salillas called this 'ethnic re-importation' a 'second and extended localisation'.[129] We now know that he was describing the transfer of male only Abakuá mutual aid societies originating in the Cross River region of southeastern Nigeria. In Cuba, the enslaved established the first Abakuá lodge in 1836, and its adherents

---

[125] Keith Amos, *The Fenians in Australia, 1865–80* (Sydney: New South Wales University Press, 1988); Philip Fennel and Marie King, *John Devoy's* Catalpa *Expedition* (New York University Press, 2006); McConville, *Irish Political Prisoners*, 153, 201, 206–13.

[126] Christian G. De Vito, 'The Spanish Empire, 1500–1898', in Anderson, ed., *A Global History of Convicts and Penal Colonies*, 65–95.

[127] Christian G. De Vito, 'Punitive Entanglements: Connected Histories of Penal Transportation, Deportation, and Incarceration in the Spanish Empire (1830s–1898)', *International Review of Social History*, 63, S26 (2018), 169–70, 171–2, 175, 178–9 (169–89).

[128] Rafael Salillas, 'Los ñañigos en Ceuta', *Revista General de Legislacion y Jurisprudencia*, 49, 98 (1901), 337–60 (quote, 337). I am grateful to Christian G. De Vito for this and subsequent references on the Ñañigos.

[129] Salillas, 'Los ñañigos en Ceuta', 337, 342.

became known as Ñáñigos. Though members of the first Abakuá Society were largely African-descended Creoles (specifically, the Efik people), the lodges later included other Africans, as well as Creoles, Europeans, and Chinese. From the second half of the nineteenth century, the Abakuá enjoyed considerable economic power by controlling labour in the ports and raising labour disputes. Their economic and labour struggles were, as anthropologist Kenneth Routon explains, 'informed by a magical economy and ritual cosmology through which the society lays claim to a privileged source of autonomous power.' For this reason, they became associated with the criminal underworld, and were thus targets of Spanish colonial repression[130]

As a consequence of their economic and spiritual activities, and the relationship between them, the Spanish authorities believed that the Abakuá were engaged in secret but organized forms of criminality and outlawed the society in 1875. However, they continued to constitute a well-known political group whose members were among those who protested against the Spanish monarchy during the War of Independence. Subsequently, the Cuban authorities sentenced several hundred Abakuá insurgents to deportation. They shipped some to the island of Fernando Po (Bioko), in the Bight of Biafra, and others to Cádiz and Figueres in Spain, the Chafarinas islands (near Melilla in North Africa), and the rest to Ceuta.[131] Depending on the precise nature of their sentence, those sent to Ceuta were either confined in the notorious Hacho prison, which Spanish government functionary Juan José Relosillas described as the Siberia of the *presidio*, or alternatively allowed to live in private apartments, with their families, in the town.[132] This had unintended consequences, for as De Vito notes punitive relocation introduced new forms of collective agency, strengthened identities and 'triggered processes that reached beyond the repressive settings'. One element of this was convict politicization, with networks both within and outside the *presidios* facilitating negotiation and escape. Whereas earlier revolts were the joint response of convicts and soldiers to poor conditions, from the third quarter of the nineteenth century, *presidio* convicts rebelled

---

[130] Kenneth Routon, 'Unimaginable Homelands? "Africa" and the Abakuá Historical Imagination', *Journal of Latin American Anthropology*, 10, 2 (2010), 372 (370–400).
[131] Ivor L. Miller, *Voice of the Leopard: African Secret Societies and Cuba* (Jackson: University Press of Mississippi, 2009), 122–3; De Vito, 'Punitive Entanglements'. On Fernando Po, see Isabela de Aranzadi, 'El legado cubano en África: Ñáñigos deportados a Fernando Poo. Memoria viva y archive escrito', *Afro-Hispanic Review*, 31, 1 (2012), 29–60. For a contemporary account, see Miguel Bravo Sentíes, *Revolución Cubana. Deportación a Femando Poo. Relación que hace uno de los deportados* (New York: Hallet de Breen, 1869). On Ceuta, see also Salillas, 'Los ñañigos en Ceuta', 338–9.
[132] Relosillas, *Catorce meses en Ceuta*, 30, 31, 44.

under cries and slogans of 'Spain must die' and 'Long live the National Party'.[133]

Meantime, Salillas described listening to and watching Abakuá music, singing, dancing, and chanting, and took a series of photographs of them dressed up in what he called 'fantastic masquerades'. He noted that in the relatively open penal environment of the *presidio*, Abakuá were able to make their own drums and costumes, as well as to stage and participate in ceremonies. It is interesting to note that these photographs informed Salillas's wider interest in crime and biological determinism. Like all the Spanish *presidios*, Ceuta's population was highly cosmopolitan, and against this background Salillas wrote that photographs of convicts could facilitate the study of racial typologies, and in particular 'the various stages of purity and miscegenation [*mestizaje*]'.[134] As Chapter 8 will show, during this period scientists and others commonly used convicts in studies of the relationship between race, criminality, biology, and culture, and Ceuta in this regard was far from unusual. Indeed, the writings of Relosillas, who was employed in the *presidio* in the 1880s, noted the presence among others of Spanish *navarro* (inhabitants of Navarre), *andaluz* (from Andalusia), *aragonés* (Aragona), *vizcaino* (Vizcaya), and *valenciano*, alongside *chinos* (Chinese) and *gente negra* (black people), among whom numbered the Cuban Abakuá. In common with Salillas, Relosillas attempted to generalize the characteristics of this most cosmopolitan of penal populations, writing of their respective rudeness, frivolity, bravery, passion, superstition, and vengefulness.[135] Moreover, and precisely because convicts in Ceuta had diverse origins from across the Spanish Empire, Salillas himself noted that if they eventually returned to their homes, as some did, they took with them from the demographically diverse environment of the *presidio* further transformed and creolized versions of Abakuá.[136]

Following the decolonization of much of the Spanish Empire in the early nineteenth century, successor regimes used carceral networks to get rid of their political opponents. This was not a twentieth-century or modern phenomenon, but always coexisted with the judicial transportation or administrative deportation of convicts and social 'undesirables'. For example, Ecuador and Chile sent political convicts to the Galapagos

---

[133] De Vito, 'Punitive Entanglements', 184–6 (quote, 184).
[134] Salillas, 'Los ñañigos en Ceuta', 343.
[135] Relosillas, *Catorce meses en Ceuta*, chapter 5, esp. 39–41.
[136] Miller, *Voice of the Leopard*, 124–7. During his field work, anthropologist Miller showed some of Salillas's materials to Cubans and, drawing on their responses to them, was able to demonstrate that the photographs were staged. For instance, as he learned from his respondents, in some cases a single photograph incorporates a juxtaposition of objects that denote both initiation rituals and funerary rites (125).

and Juan Fernández islands, respectively. In the latter case, leader of the first government Bernardo O'Higgins deported followers of the Carrera brothers to Juan Fernández after 1821. They had led the independence wars but then opposed the new government. Similar deportations continued under new governments, when exiles also included liberals (*pipiolos*). Decades later, in the early 1900s, to counter labour radicalism, Argentina deported socialists and anarchists to Ushuaia. It codified the practice through the 1910 Law of Social Defence, with deportees famously including Simón Radowisky who in 1909 had killed the chief of police in Buenos Aires.[137] In the 1930s, in the *Década Infame* (Infamous Decade) that followed the military coup of José Félix Uriburu, government sent further numbers of political dissenters to Ushuaia. At least some of them were kept separately from ordinary labouring convicts, and allocated housing and wages.[138]

Punitive relocation was also a means of the political repression for women during the Mexican revolution of 1910–20. Mexico had been sending convicts since the 1860s, to Yucatan, Oaxaca, and Quintana Roo, and in 1908 government established a penal colony in Ilas Marías. As in the parallel case of the Spanish in the Caribbean, many transportations were 'preventative'. The authorities did not subject individuals to judicial process but selected 'undesirables' for *relegación* to the islands. Building on practices for convicted offenders in numerous other global locations, the regime gradually evolved into one of penal stages, with labour seen as rehabilitative. Transportation and deportation were thus experienced identically.[139] In the 1920s, Irish journalist Francis McCullagh managed to get into Ilas Marías by passing himself off as an American merchant. The islands of María Madre, María Magdalena, María Cleófas, and the islet of San Juanico then held 1,700 convicts (*los deportados*). They were mainly Catholics, and unusually for Latin America included many women and girls. McCullagh published a detailed account of his visit in 1928.[140]

---

[137] Richard D. Salvatore and Carlos Aguirre, 'Colonies of Settlement or Places of Banishment and Torment? Penal Colonies and Convict Labour in Latin America, c. 1800–1940', in De Vito and Lichtenstein, eds., *Global Convict Labour*, 277, 278, 285, 287, 291 (273–309); Edwards, 'Post-Colonial Latin America', 258–9; Ryan Edwards, 'From the Depths of Patagonia: The Ushuaia Penal Colony and the Nature of "The End of the World"', *Hispanic American Historical Review*, 94, 2 (2014), 279 (271–302).

[138] Edwards, 'From the Depths of Patagonia', 290–1.

[139] Salvatore and Aguirre, 'Colonies of Settlement or Places of Banishment and Torment?', 296–306. On preventive deportation in the Spanish Empire, see De Vito, 'Punitive Entanglements', 172.

[140] Francis McCullagh, *Red Mexico: a reign of terror in America* (New York: L. Carrier and Co., 1928).

There were many stages to the Mexican revolution, during which perhaps 10 per cent of the population died. The Cristero war of 1926–9, a rebellion against a secularist anti-Catholic and anti-clerical government, followed the military phase but was nonetheless part of the revolution. The government had seized church property, and closed monasteries, convents, and religious schools. Many women became involved, establishing and joining the feminine brigades of St Joan of Arc. By the end of the war they numbered 25,000. The law prevented the execution of women, and so President Plutarco Elías Calles ordered their removal to the Islas Marías.[141] The Cristeros were subjected to anti-Catholic lectures and put to hard labour, carrying stones. For this reason, by this time, the islands became known as the Mexican Bastille.[142] McCullagh was bitingly critical of President Calles. He described how political convicts, many of whom were persecuted Catholics, were sent in gangs (*cuerda*), with ordinary criminal offenders, first by train, and then by steam launch. He described how they were herded together into goods wagons, in suffocating, 'nightmare' heat. When they arrived at Mazatlán station and the train doors opened, on view were 'masses of human beings piled together like negros in the hold of a slaver'. They then marched to the pier, and from there embarked on the *barco de Guerra*, which journeyed to El Valleto, the capital of Maria Madre, once per month. The convicts were kept there for a few days, and then engaged on public works or in agriculture, and finally were sent out to the district *campamentos* (camps). Their work included logging, brick making, stone collecting, and labouring on the *Salinas* (salt pans). Toil on the salt pans was the hardest work of all, for convicts had to manage the huge pumps that brought the seawater in. McCullagh had little sympathy for ordinary convicts, writing: 'To send into such a hell delicate women and young men ... none of them criminals, all of them accustomed to an atmosphere of moral purity, is to inflict on them a punishment worse than death.'[143]

Another Latin American example is Peru's use of the island of El Frontón for political prisoners. The violence of El Frontón was a key theme in their memoirs. Writers included René Mendoza, deported for spying in 1921, and Julio Garrido Malaver, an activist in the Aprista

---

[141] Barbara Miller, 'The Role of Women in the Mexican Cristero Rebellion: Las Señoras y Las Religiosas', *The Americas*, 40, 3 (1984), 316, 320 (303–23).

[142] Salvatore and Aguirre, 'Colonies of Settlement or Places of Banishment and Torment?', 303.

[143] McCullagh, *Red Mexico*, 151–2, 252–3, 255, 257, 259, 261, 263–4 (quotes, 257, 265). Note that the translation of *cuerda* is rope, and that McCullagh translated the *barco de Guerra* as the floating coffin, though its literal meaning is battleship.

movement, who was detained on the island during 1940–44.[144] Mendoza later claimed that he was treated with such respect that the authorities and soldiers on the island called him Señor.[145] In 1921, Peru opened the island of San Lorenzo for journalists, labour organizers, and political opponents, including communists.[146] However, as in the cases discussed earlier in the chapter, exile provided a means of concentration and convergence, and opportunities to radicalize ordinary prisoners. This was the case in Cuba's Isla de Pinos, which after independence in 1898 housed revolutionary Fidel Castro before the success of the 1959 socialist revolution.[147] For this reason, Ryan Edwards has described the islands as 'incubators of a new politics' which shifted 'the political and intellectual epicentres of the nation'.[148] The extent to which elite political prisoners were concerned with the treatment of ordinary 'criminal' convicts is highly contested. Edwards suggests that the men sent to Ushuaia usually distanced themselves from common men.[149] In some cases, and as has been seen in the case of the Irish in Bermuda, such segregation was encouraged by the authorities. In other examples, Portugal shipped political prisoners (*deportados*) to Angola and Mozambique, but they were not placed in the *depósitos* with ordinary convicts, and were granted a great deal of liberty. The *deportados* included trades union activists and journalists, and eventually all were relocated to Terceira Island in the Azores. After the start of the Spanish Civil War in 1936, the New State (*Estado Novo*) under António de Oliveira Salazar established a prison camp in Tarrafal for the same purpose, and it remained open until 1954. At least one *deportado*, Mário Castelhano, was held in both locations.[150]

*

There were multiple points of intersection between punitive mobility, insurgency, politics, and religion, beginning in the fifteenth century. Further developing the arguments about enslavement and imperial governance in Chapters 4 and 5, the narrative has shown that there was an

---

[144] Carlos Aguirre, *The Criminals of Lima and Their Worlds: The Prison Experience, 1850–1935* (Durham, NC: Duke University Press, 2005), 106–7. The Aprista movement was another name for the American Popular Revolutionary Alliance. It was anti-capitalist and anti-imperialist.
[145] Aguirre, *The Criminals of Lima and Their Worlds*, 104–7, 261n92.
[146] Aguirre, *The Criminals of Lima and Their Worlds*, 132–9.
[147] Ryan C. Edwards, 'Post-Colonial Latin America, since 1800', in Anderson, ed., *A Global History of Convicts and Penal Colonies*, 258 (245–70).
[148] Edwards, 'Post-Colonial Latin America', 258, 259 (quote).
[149] Edwards, 'Post-Colonial Latin America', 258.
[150] Castelhano died in Tarrafal in 1940, for want of basic medical attention. Timothy J. Coates, *Convict Labor in the Portuguese Empire, 1740–1932: Redefining the Empire with Forced Labor and New Imperialism* (Leiden: Brill, 2014), 75–7.

intensely political dimension to punitive relocation across global sites, and no sharp divide between early-modern and modern practices. The discussion of the Dutch East Indies and Cape Colony, the Atlantic empire of Denmark–Norway, EIC penal settlements, and British colonial Mauritius has revealed that convict relocation was a means of getting rid of political enemies and a vector for the transmission and adaptation of insurgency, rebellion, and religious practice. The chapter has also suggested that convict journeys sometimes became spaces for the development and extension of various kinds of solidarities. These formed the basis of convict agency and resistance in continents, islands, and at sea, in locations from Europe and Asia to the Indian Ocean. Such associations and patterns in sites of punitive relocation continued into the twentieth century, notably in the Spanish Empire's successor states in Latin America. This was also the case, as the chapter has suggested, in Bermuda, the Australian colonies, and the Andaman Islands (British Empire), and in Spain's *presidio* of Ceuta. Across these very different places, deportation and transportation created new spaces of political education and resistance, which were quite remarkable in terms of their mobility and transformation.

This chapter brings to a close Part I of the book, which has stressed the importance of convicts as penal labour, explored punitive mobility as a means of governance, discussed its political, social, and cultural impacts, and examined aspects of the relationships between convicts and other workers, including enslaved and indentured labour. Next, we turn to Chapter 7, which opens Part II and shifts our gaze to the relationship between convict transportation and the creation of knowledge systems and classifications, largely through a focus on the modern period. As we will see, the subaltern circulations explored here actually preceded the emergence of elite and global discussions about punishment, which only developed from the late eighteenth century onwards. The book has already touched upon the influence of Crofton's Irish system of convict rehabilitation and France's interest in Britain's Australian penal colonies. The pages that follow develop this theme more fully, examining international meetings, reports, and tours concerned with punitive mobility, and drawing out what they reveal about some of the inherent tensions between punishment and work.

Part II

7 Punishment and Penal Systems

Part 1 of this book discussed the scope and scale of punitive mobility across a wide range of national and imperial contexts, and its multilayered associations with migration, forced labour, enslavement, and governance. The chapters detailed some of the strains experienced in the movement of convicts, and the difficulty administrators faced in reconciling their employment with changing ideas about the nature and purpose of punishment in the face of convict resistance and agency. In regard to the latter, Chapter 6 stressed the way in which deportation, transportation, and exile had unintended effects. They became means of spreading resistance and insurgency, and of creating new or syncretic cosmopolitan cultures. Here, we return to the question of the purpose of punishment, by bringing attention to the circulation and exchange of ideas about punitive mobility during the nineteenth and twentieth centuries. Opening with a discussion of European views on convicts and penal colonies up to the 1850s, it moves on to explore the background to the establishment of the International Penitentiary Congress in 1872, and the tenor of its consideration of convicts and penal colonies over the next fifty years. Of especial concern is an analysis of the tensions between the penal and economic ambitions of punitive relocation, as noted earlier in the book, as they were observed by a range of contemporaries.

The chapter next examines the global influences brought to bear on the development of penal systems developed in sites of punitive relocation, notably the innovations of Alexander Maconochie and Sir Walter Crofton in Norfolk Island (Australia) and Ireland respectively. It then analyses the motivations and observations of global penal tours by German criminologist Robert Heindl and British prison commissioner Alexander Paterson. Taking further Chapter 3's discussion of Japan's investment in European penal codes, and the multiple connections between and across global European empires examined in Chapter 2, it demonstrates the extent of the flow and spread of ideas about punishment around the established French and British empires, and highlights the interest in them from new colonizing nations like Germany. It suggests that global discussions and tours were instigated by the desire to investigate and compare innovations in punishment, and as part of the long history of connecting convicts to political and territorial ambitions. These included Germany's wish to expand its empire in Africa and the Pacific in the early 1900s, Russia's desire to settle the Far East, and Britain's hope that France would move to abolish transportation in the period between the two world wars.

Global Exchanges and the International Penitentiary Congress

The idea for the first International Penitentiary Congress was the outcome of an already vibrant circulation of ideas and practices about punishment and penal reform in the USA, Latin America, and European nation states and their colonies. Indeed, the 1872 Congress itself marked the near-centenary of the death of the British pro-penitentiary and anti-transportation reformer John Howard during a fact-finding tour of Turkey and Russia.[1] Meetings of experts had been held in Frankfurt am Main in 1846, in Brussels in 1847, and again in Frankfurt in 1857.[2] In discussions of penal transportation, they were keen to investigate the successes or failures of various convict colonies. For instance, from the 1810s, following the disastrous effort to establish a penal colony in French Guiana, the French began to explore the possibility of finding an

---

[1] John Howard, *The State of the Prisons in England and Wales with Preliminary Observations and an Account of Some Foreign Prisons* (Warrington: William Eyres, 1777); Rod Morgan, 'Howard, John (1726?–1790)', *Oxford Dictionary of National Biography* (Oxford University Press, 2004); online edition 23 September 2004, https://doi.org/10.1093/ref:odnb/13922 (accessed 23 September 2021). See also Hepworth Dixon, *John Howard, and the Prison-World of Europe* (Webster, MA: Frederick Charlton, 1852); J. Field, *The Life of John Howard; with comments on his character and philanthropic labours* (London: Longman, Brown, Green, and Longmans, 1850). Howard's opposition to transportation anticipated the later arguments of pro-penitentiary Jeremy Bentham, *in Panopticon versus New South Wales, or, The panopticon penitentiary system and the penal colonization system compared* (London: Wilks and Taylor, 1812). I thank Tim Causer for generously sharing his knowledge about this and other sources by Bentham.

[2] [Martino] Beltrani Scalia (inspector of prisons Italy), 'Historical Sketch of National and International Penitentiary Conferences in Europe and America', in *Transactions of the National Congress of Penitentiary and Reformatory Discipline, held at Cincinnati, Ohio, October 12–18 1870*, edited by E. C. Wines, Chairman of the Publishing Committee (Albany, OH: The Argus Company, 1871); *Débats du Congrès Pénitentiaire de Bruxelles. Session de 1847. Séances des 20, 21, 22 et 25 Septembre* (Brussels: Imprimerie de Deltombe, 1847), 267–77; Negley K. Teeters, 'The First International Penitentiary Congresses, 1846-46-57', *The Prison Journal*, 26 (1946), 190–210. The Brussels congress considered a wide range of documents, books, and jail plans, in English, French, Dutch, Italian, and German, from across Europe, including Britain, France, Germany, Italy, Switzerland, and The Netherlands.

alternative site.³ They were particularly active in research on Britain's Australian colonies, including in the translation of numerous parliamentary papers and documents. At the time, New South Wales and Van Diemen's Land (which separated from New South Wales to form a separate colony in 1825) were the largest penal colonies in the world. Two pro-transportation reports by State Councillor of the Committee for the Navy and Colonies M. Forestier, who advocated the founding of a French penal settlement neighbouring Britain's, were especially important to debates.⁴ Forestier's work was followed by the publication of numerous texts on the Australian colonies, many based on the detailed accounts of the French visitors to Sydney in the 1830s, which will be considered in Chapter 8.⁵ During that decade also, the French government dispatched Gustav de Beaumont and Alexis de Tocqueville to the USA in order to consider the alternative merits of its penitentiaries. They incorporated an extraordinary range of documents into their report, sourced from the USA, Britain, France, and Germany. Writing against the growing French enthusiasm for penal colonies, they drew upon contemporary anti-transportation critique of New South Wales, and urged that the desire to colonize overseas territories should not be confused with punishment.⁶ By the early 1820s, the works of Jeremy Bentham, whose panopticon prison design proposed convict rehabilitation through

---

³ Miranda F. Spieler, *Empire and Underworld: captivity in French Guiana* (Cambridge, MA: Harvard University Press, 2012).

⁴ ANOM H1 Traduction de documents sur la déportation à Botany-Bay, régime pénitentiaire dans les colonies australiennes et en général dans les colonies étrangères: mémoires sur le choix d'un lieu de deportation: M. Forestier, *Memoire sur le choix d'un lieu de déportation*, 14 October 1816; Forestier, *Deuxieme rapport du commission de deportation*, March 1819; *Traduction de divers documents relatifs aux condamnés déportés à Botany Bay*, n.d.; ADG IX64 Administration pénitentiaire: rapport de la commission d'enquête sur la déportation de 1838. For an in-depth discussion of Forestier's memoirs, see Jacqueline Dutton, 'Imperial Eyes on the Pacific Prize: French Visions of a Perfect Penal Colony in the South Seas', in John West-Sooby, ed., *Discovery and Empire: The French in the South Seas* (University of Adelaide Press, 2013), 245–82.

⁵ Jules de la Pilorgerie, *Histoire de Botany Bay, état présent des colonies pénales de l'Angleterre dans l'Australie ou examen des effets de la déportation* (Paris: Paulin, 1836); Paul Merruau, *Les Convicts En Australie* (Paris: Librarie de L. Hachette et Cie, 1853); Ernest de Blosseville, *Historie de la Colonisation Pénale et des Établissements de l'Angleterre en Australie* (Évreux: Imprimerie de Auguste Hérissey, 1859); Peter Kropotkin, *In Russian and French Prisons* (London: Ward and Downey, 1887); Ivan Foinitski and Georges Bonet-Maury, *La Transportation Russe et Anglaise avec une Étude Historique sur La Transportation* (Paris: Lecène, Oudin et Cie., 1895). See also Colin Forster, *France and Botany Bay: the lure of a penal colony* (Melbourne University Press, 1996); Dutton, 'Imperial Eyes on the Pacific Prize'; Marc Serge Rivière, 'Distant Echoes of the Enlightenment: Private and Public Observations on Convict Life by Baudin's Disgraced Officer, Hyacinthe de Bougainville (1825)', *Australian Journal of French Studies*, 41, 2 (2004), 171–85.

⁶ *On the Penitentiary System in the United States, and Its Application in France; with an appendix on penal colonies, and also, statistical notes by G. de Beaumont and A. de Tocqueville, translated from the French, with an introduction, notes and additions, by Francis Lieber* (Philadelphia, PA:

observation and work, were widely discussed in Europe and available in French and Portuguese translation.[7] Bentham remained influential later in the nineteenth century, in other global locations, including Mexico.[8] The Indian Prison Discipline Committee of 1838, set up by the governing East India Company (EIC), was similarly expansive in the scope of its global consultations. It included in its discussions of imprisonment and transportation across EIC Asia (notably in Burma and the Straits Settlements) comparative reports from Britain, Australia, and the USA, and in addition Beaumont and Tocqueville's work.[9]

It was not just France and EIC Asia which engaged in the close study of convict transportation practices among other global powers. Following the initiation of the penitentiary congress, Britain's Australian colonies, French Guiana, New Caledonia, and the Russian Far East were of particular interest and concern.[10] By the 1870s, still in possession of sites of

---

Cery, Lea and Blanchard, 1833). Beaumont and Tocqueville considered prison reports, notes, statistics, contemporary publications, and even the 1833 British parliamentary report on the poor law, which ran to over one thousand pages. Tocqueville is best known for his work *Democracy in America* and Beaumont for the novel *Marie*, which were companion volumes and centrally concerned with the importance of enslavement in the founding of America. For a reading of the texts in association, see Victoria Margree and Gurminder K. Bhambra, 'Tocqueville, Beaumont and the Silences in Histories of the United States: An Interdisciplinary Endeavour across Literature and Sociology', *Journal of Historical Sociology*, 24, 1 (2011), 116–31.

[7] Pierre-Louis Etienne Dumont, *Théorie des peines et recompenses par Jérémie Bentham*, 2 volumes (London: L'Imprimerie de Vogle et Schulze, 1811); See also Emmanuelle de Champs, *Enlightenment and Utility: Bentham in French, Bentham in France* (Cambridge University Press, 2015); Timothy J. Coates, *Convict Labor in the Portuguese Empire, 1740–1932: Redefining the Empire with Forced Labor and New Imperialism* (Leiden: Brill, 2014), 26.

[8] Ricardo D. Salvatore and Carlos Aguirre, 'The Birth of the Penitentiary in Latin America: Toward an Interpretive Social History of Prisons', in Ricardo D. Salvatore and Carlos Aguirre, eds., *The Birth of the Penitentiary in Latin America: Essays on Criminology, Prison Reform, and Social Control, 1830–1940* (Austin: University of Texas Press, 1996), 9–17 (1–43); Ryan C. Edwards, 'Post-Colonial Latin America, since 1800', in Clare Anderson, ed., *A Global History of Convicts and Penal Colonies* (London: Bloomsbury, 2018), 348 (245–70).

[9] *Report of the Committee on Prison Discipline* (Calcutta: Baptist Mission Press, 1838), 38–137. On the EIC's penal settlements, see Clare Anderson, 'The British Indian Empire, 1789–1945', in Anderson, ed., *A Global History of Convicts and Penal Colonies*, 211–43.

[10] Pierre-Louis Etienne Dumont, *Théorie des peines et recompenses par Jérémie Bentham*, 2 volumes (London: L'Imprimerie de Vogle et Schulze, 1811); *On the Penitentiary System in the United States, and Its Application in France*; Pilorgerie, *Histoire de Botany Bay*; Merruau, *Les Convicts En Australie*; Blosseville, *Historie de la Colonisation Pénale*; Kropotkin, *In Russian and French Prisons*; Foinitski and Bonet-Maury, *La Transportation Russe et Anglaise*. See also de Champs, *Enlightenment and Utility*; Dutton, 'Imperial Eyes on the Pacific Prize'; Forster, *France and Botany Bay*; Briony Neilson, 'The Paradox of Penal Colonization: Debates on Convict Transportation at the International Prison Congresses 1872–1895', *French History and Civilization*, 6 (2015), 198–211; Marc Serge Rivière, 'Distant Echoes of the Enlightenment: Private and Public Observations on Convict Life by Baudin's Disgraced

punitive location in the Philippines, Puerto Rico, and Cuba, the Spanish government was even debating the extension of penal transportation.[11] It considered French practice in some detail.[12] During this period, like France, Spain was engaged in an assessment of the success or otherwise of convict Australia. Indeed, almost a century earlier in 1793, five years after the arrival of the first fleet of convicts at Botany Bay, the Spanish had dispatched explorer Alejandro Malaspina to New South Wales, supposedly to refresh his ship and carry out scientific research. However, during a period when Britain and Spain were allies, the Spanish government also requested that he report on the purpose and strength of the colony. This was part of a larger tour of 'imperial inspection' of Spanish *presidios* and colonies in the Americas, and of knowledge gathering about the territorial interests of other global powers (Figure 7.1). Malaspina wrote of New South Wales, 'The transportation of the convicts constituted the means and the not the object of the enterprise. The extension of Dominion, mercantile speculations, and the discovery of Mines were the real object.' He criticized the agricultural failure of the colony and argued that in seeking strategic advantage the British had sacrificed law, 'sane policy', and 'the compassionate cries of oppressed Humanity'.[13] At the same time that he condemned the Australian colonies, Malaspina praised

---

Officer, Hyacinthe de Bougainville (1825)', *Australian Journal of French Studies*, 41, 2 (2004), 171–85.

[11] Ruth Pike, *Penal Servitude in Early-Modern Spain* (Madison: University of Wisconsin Press, 1993); Eva Mehl, *Forced Migration in the Spanish Pacific World: From Mexico to the Philippines, 1765–1811* (Cambridge University Press, 2016); Stephanie Mawson, 'Unruly Plebeians and the *Forzado* System: Convict Transportation, between New Spain and the Philippines during the Seventeenth Century', *Revista de Indias*, 73, 259 (2013), 693–730; Stephanie Mawson, 'Convicts or *conquistadores*? Spanish soldiers in the Seventeenth-Century Pacific', *Past and Present*, 232, 1 (2016), 87–125.

[12] AHN Ultramar, 341, Exp. 7: Expediente general sobre colonización en isla Culebra o Pasaje (1881). I thank Christian G. De Vito for this reference.

[13] Donald C. Cutter, 'Introduction', in Andrew David, Felipe Fernandez-Armesto, Carlos Novi, and Glyndwr Williams, eds., *The Malaspina Expedition 1789–1794: Journal of the Voyage by Alejandro Malaspina, Volume 1 Cadiz to Panama* (The Hakluyt Society, London, in association with the Museo Naval, Madrid: 2001), lxxi; Andrew David, Felipe Fernandez-Armesto, Carlos Novi, and Glyndwr Williams, eds., translated by Sylvia Jamieson, *The Malaspina Expedition 1789–1794: Journal of the Voyage by Alejandro Malaspina, Volume III Manila to Cadiz* (The Hakluyt Society, London, in association with the Museo Naval, Madrid: 2004), 71; Robert J. King, *The Secret History of the Convict Colony: Alexandro Malaspina's report on the British settlement of New South Wales* (Sydney, NSW: Allen and Unwin, 1990), 5–6, 96. See also Peter Barber, 'Malaspina and George III, Brambila, and Watling: Three discovered drawings of Sydney and Parramatta by Fernando Brambila', *Australian Journal of Art*, 11 (1993), 31–55; Robert J. King, 'George Vancouver and the Contemplated Settlement at Nootka Sound', *The Great Circle*, 32, 1 (2010), 3–30; John West-Sooby, 'A Case of Peripheral Vision: Early Spanish and French Perceptions of the British Colony at Port Jackson', in West-Sooby, ed., *Discovery and Empire*, 141–69.

Figure 7.1 Convictos en la Nueva Olanda [Convicts in New Holland], by Felipe Bauza, c. 1790
Source: Mitchell Library, State Library of New South Wales SAFE/ DGD 2: Felipe Bauza – drawings made on the Spanish Scientific Expedition to Australia and the Pacific in the ships Descubierta and Atrevida under the command of Alessandro Malaspina, 1789–94.

Britain's earlier transportations to the Americas. He was not entirely correct when he stated that, in the eighteenth century, Britain banished and then freed convicts, for, in fact, it sold them into indenture. However, it is the case that, as he noted, the Americas were much closer to Britain than the Australian colonies, and that many convicts found employment in the production of in-demand goods like tobacco.[14]

[14] Alexandro Malaspina, 'A Political Examination of the English Colonies in the Pacific', 92–119, cited in King, *The Secret History of the Convict Colony*, 101.

Later in the nineteenth century, the Spanish returned once again to Britain's transportation of convicts to the Americas in the eighteenth century, and then also considered the new penal colonies of Russia, France, Portugal, Chile, and Peru.[15] In 1881, they planned a new penal colony for Isla de Culebra, situated between Puerto Rico and Tortola in the Caribbean. Though this came to nothing, the Spanish gathered extensive information on the French experience, including in Cayenne and New Caledonia, as well as on the juvenile establishment of Mettray (Chapter 1).[16]

The first International Penitentiary Congress was held in London in 1872. (Figure 7.2). The National Prison Association of the USA had instigated its foundation, through a new International Prison Commission. Its brief was to organize meetings, collect statistics, and encourage penal reform. Until the middle of the twentieth century, the congress convened every five to eight years, interrupted only by the two world wars. It rotated around the cities of Stockholm (1878), Rome (1885), St Petersburg (1890), Paris (1895), Brussels (1900), Budapest (1905), Washington (1910), London (1925), Prague (1930), Berlin (1935), and The Hague (1950).[17] The congress can be conceptualized as an 'epistemic community',

---

[15] Fernando José Burillo Albacete, *La cuestión penitenciaria. Del Sexenio a la Restauración (1868–1913)* (Prensas Universitarias de Zaragoza, 2011), esp. 62–67. Thanks to Christian G. De Vito for this reference, and those of the following three footnotes. For contemporary debates, see Fernando Cadalso, *Principios de la colonización y colonias penales* (Madrid: J. Góngora y Álvarez, 1896); Francisco Lastres, *Estudios penitenciarios* (Madrid: Establecimiento tipográfico de Pedro Nuñez, 1887); Pere Armengol y Cornet, *¿A las islas Marianas ó al golfo de Guinea?* (Madrid: Eduardo Martínez, 1878); Concepción Arenal, *Las colonias penales de la Australia y la pena de deportación* (Madrid: Librería de Victoriano Suárez, 1895).

[16] Albacete, *La cuestión penitenciaria,* esp. 62–67. The key thinkers on these issues in the 1870s, 1880s, and 1890s were Francisco Lastres, Pere Armengol y Cornet, Concepción Arenal, and Fernando Cadalso, the latter the governor of Madrid's cellular jail.

[17] The National Prison Association of the USA was formed in 1870, and at its first meeting in Cincinnati, it appointed the secretary of the New York Prison Association (est. 1844) E. C. Wines as commissioner to organize the first international congress. See National Prison Association of the United States of America, *Proceedings of the National Prison Congress, Held at Atlanta, GA., 1886* (Chicago, IL: R. R. Donnelley and Sons, The Lakeside Press, 1887), 7–8; *International Congress on the Prevention and Repression of Crime, including penal and reformatory treatment: preliminary report of the commissioner [E. C. Wines] appointed by the president to represent the United States in the Congress, in compliance with a join resolution of March 7, 1871* (Washington DC: Government Printing Office, 1872). The International Prison Commission (IPC) affiliated with the League of Nations in 1910 and became the International Penal and Penitentiary Commission (IPPC) in 1929. For a history of science-focused analysis of the penitentiary congresses during the second half of the nineteenth century, see Nir Shafir, 'The international congress as scientific and diplomatic technology: global intellectual exchange in the International Prison Congress, 1860–90,' *Journal of Global History*, 9, 1 (2014), 72–93. See also the chapter by Martina Henze, 'Transnational Cooperation and Criminal Policy: The prison reform movement, 1820s–1950s', in Davide Rodogno,

Figure 7.2 The International Prison Congress in the Middle Temple Hall [London]
Source: *The Graphic*, 13 July 1872.

a gathering and sharing of the views and knowledge of a range of transnational actors who met together to debate issues of collective interest, and to formulate an agenda for reform.[18] The same people were involved in numerous organizations and congresses, and attended many different meetings, centred on the discussion of poverty, welfare, education, and related topics. Their commitment was to the study of poor and socially marginal people, driven by a combination of political ambition, the desire for change, and religious faith. 'Social reform', as Chris Leonards and Nico Randeraad explain for Western Europe, 'was considered a matter of exchange par excellence'.[19] The penitentiary congress as a transnational network and

---

Bernhard Struck, and Jakob Vogel, eds., *Shaping the Transnational Sphere: Experts, Networks and Issues from the 1840s to the 1930s* (Oxford: Berghahn, 2015), 197–217.

[18] Davide Rodogno, Bernhard Struck, and Jakob Vogel, 'Introduction', in Rodogno, Struck and Vogel, eds., *Shaping the Transnational Sphere*, 6 (1–20).

[19] Chris Leonards and Nico Randeraad, 'Building a Transnational Network of Social Reform in the Nineteenth Century', in Rodogno, Struck, and Vogel, eds., *Shaping the Transnational Sphere*, 114 (111–30).

international organization would become what Martina Henze has called 'the largest and most influential association in the field of criminal policy'.[20]

An organizing committee invited all nations of the world to contribute papers, to comment on pre-circulated questions and to send delegates. The chair of the British committee of the first London meeting was the architect of Fernando de Noronha's modified penal regime (Chapter 1), Sir Walter Crofton. The congress had 400 members, including representatives from 20 countries. In this and later years, delegates hailed from as far afield as the USA and Canada, Chile, Mexico, Haiti, Jamaica, Denmark, Austria, Switzerland, Belgium, France, Germany, Greece, Holland, Italy, Spain, Turkey, India, Russia, Siam (now, Thailand), and Japan. The new independent nations of Latin America were also well represented in these global discussions and meetings. Mexico sent delegates to the inaugural 1872 meeting, and Argentina attended the Stockholm Congress in 1878. The topics of discussion changed over the decades, reflecting developments in penological thinking, but generally included prison labour, the classification of offenders, corporal punishment, the separation and association of prisoners, the treatment of women, probation, officer training, prisoner release, and rehabilitation – as well as internationally pressing questions related to the identification of suspected criminals who had gone overseas and were subjects for legal extradition, and penal transportation.[21] The International Prison Commission was composed of official government delegates, and the prison congresses were lavish affairs. Politicians gave opening addresses;

---

[20] Henze, 'Transnational Cooperation and Criminal Policy', 199–200 (quote, 200).

[21] There are extensive reports on the congresses in IPC president Sir Evelyn Ruggles-Brise's *Prison Reform At Home and Abroad: A short history of the international movement since the London Congress, 1872* (London: Macmillan, 1925) and Negley K. Teeters, *Deliberations of the International Penal and Penitentiary Congresses, Questions and Answers, 1872–1935* (Philadelphia: Temple University Book Store, 1949). There are multiple accounts of individual congresses, written by various delegates in numerous languages. A selection on the first seven meetings includes: E. C. Wines, *Report on the International Penitentiary Congress of London, held July 3–13, 1872* [second annual report of the NY Prison Association of the United States] (Washington DC: Government Printing Office, 1873); E. C. Wines, *The Actual State of Prison Reform Throughout the Civilized World: A discourse pronounced at the opening of the international prison congress of Stockholm, August 10, 1878* (Stockholm: Centra-Tryckeriet, 1878); *Actes du Congrès Pénitentiaire International de Rome, Novembre 1885, Volume 1* (Rome: Mantellate, 1887); C. D. Randall, *The Fourth International Prison Congress St. Petersburg, Russia* (Washington DC: Government Printing Office, 1891); *Congress held at Paris, France, in July, 1895* (Washington DC: Government Printing Office, 1896) (Senate, 54th Congress, 1st session, document no. 181); Samuel J. Barrows, *The Sixth International Prison Congress, held at Brussels, Belgium, August 1900: Report of its proceedings and conclusions* (Washington DC: Government Printing Office, 1903); Samuel J. Barrows, *Report of Proceedings of the Seventh International Prison Congress, Budapest, Hungary, September, 1905* (Washington DC: Government Printing Office, 1907).

and governments hosted state dinners and evening receptions. The congress of Rome included a visit to Italy's 'internal' penal colonies of Trois-Fontaines near Rome and Castiadas in Sardinia, exhibitions of prison manufacture, and the display of models of prisons, complete with mannequins dressed up as convicts and guards.[22] The St Petersburg organizers threw a banquet at the tsar's winter palace, and took delegates on an excursion to the Moscow transfer jail for convicts awaiting transportation to Siberia.[23]

Given the extent of global interest in convicts and penal colonies, it is far from surprising that the international penitentiary congresses debated them at each of their meetings. With their large settlements in French Guiana, New Caledonia, and Siberia, France and Russia dominated discussions.[24] However, over the course of its many gatherings, the Congress never reached a full consensus on their penal value. On the one hand, delegates did not wish to criticize openly the global powers who still engaged in punitive relocation, and on the other they struggled to separate theory and practice. One of the questions put to the first 1872 meeting was 'Ought transportation to be admitted as a punishment? If so, what ought to be its nature?' Only the Russian delegates and one Italian, Adolfo de Foresta, the public prosecutor of Bologna, came out in favour of it.[25] The 1878 congress in Stockholm addressed a similar question, 'What are the conditions under which the punishments of deportation or transportation can perform a useful service in the administration of penal justice?' It is worth dwelling on this debate, which was the most extensive of any congress meeting. The Stockholm delegates discussed the reasons for the abolition of penal transportation to the Australian colonies and debated the merits or otherwise of Italy's Tuscan penitentiary islands.

---

[22] Teeters, *Deliberations of the International Penal and Penitentiary Congresses*, 51. See also Mary Gibson, *Italian Prisons in the Age of Positivism, 1861–1914* (London: Bloomsbury, 2019), 73–5.

[23] Randall, *The Fourth International Prison Congress St. Petersburg*, 202, 221–2, 219.

[24] Interestingly, though not a focus in 1872, penal transportation by Spain and Portugal were discussed in some detail at the US National Prison Reform Congress a couple of years later. See 'State of Penitentiary Reform in Europe and the East', in *Transactions of the Third National Prison Reform Congress, held at Saint Louis, Missouri, May 13–16, 1874: Being the third annual report of the National Prison Association of the United States*, edited by E. C. Wines, secretary of the association (New York: Office of the Association, 1874), 467–53.

[25] The Chairman, Count Frank von Holtzendorff, brought a third consideration into play. He noted that the general opposition of the congress to transportation did not preclude the free emigration of released prisoners or the use of juvenile offenders for what he called 'inland colonization'. See Teeters, *Deliberations of the International Penal and Penitentiary Congresses*, 31–2. On discussions of transportation in 1872, see also Reverend Nehemiah Pierce, *Origin, Organization and Opening Addresses of the International Prison Congress, January 1 1873* (Springfield, IL: publisher unknown, 1873), 20–1; Wines, *Report on the International Penitentiary Congress of London*, 154–5.

They considered the history of Siberia, French Guiana, and New Caledonia, and noted that abolitionist sentiments towards the Andaman Islands penal colony had been expressed at Britain's 1877 Indian Jail Conference.[26] The congress eventually passed a compromise resolution that was the outcome of impassioned debate. If experience to date was not definitely against the continuation of penal transportation, it resolved, neither did it recommend its introduction in other countries, for it did not meet all the conditions necessary for good justice.[27]

Here, Italian public prosecutor de Foresta elaborated on his pro-transportation position. He expressed his admiration of French New Caledonia and drew attention to the value of transportation as a penal stage within a larger system of punishment. He urged Italy to adopt transportation, warning that if government decided against it, if it were to meet the rising demand for jail accommodation it would need to construct 70,000 prison cells at great expense. It would also lose the potential advantage of convict labour. Upon sentence, prisoners should be confined separately in cells, they should next undertake forced gang labour in a colony, and then be issued with a conditional pardon, subject to continuing residence in that colony. E. Michaux, deputy-director of the French Ministry of the Navy and the Colonies, also gave a strong defence of transportation, claiming great success in New Caledonia, and arguing that metropolitan prisons should only be used for term prisoners and incorrigible offenders. F. J. Mouat, former inspector-general of prisons in Bengal presidency, with responsibility for the Indian penal settlements of the Straits Settlements (Penang, Malacca, and Singapore), and a member of the survey party sent to select the best site for a penal colony in the Andaman Islands in 1857, also spoke in favour.[28]

The inspector-general of prisons in South Australia, in contrast, pointed out the long-term difficulties of penal transportation. He stated that once substantial free migration had changed the demography of colonies, continuing transportation had a negative moral effect, 'The bad engendered in these new countries and provoked by the presence of criminals imported are more considerable than the good that is provided to their country of origin.' Other liberal reformers also expressed their

---

[26] *Le Congrès Pénitentiaire International de Stockholm, 15–26 Août 1878, Comptes-Rendus des Séances, publiés sous la direction de a Commission Pénitentiaire Internationale, par le Dr Guillaume* [director of Neuchatel Penitentiary and secretary general of the congress] (Stockholm: Bureau de la Commission Pénitentiaire Internationale, 1879), 595–6; *Report of the Indian Jail Conference Assembled in Calcutta in January–March 1877, under the orders of His Excellency the Governor General in Council, with appendices* (Calcutta: Home Secretariat Press, 1877), 25–31.
[27] *Le Congrès Pénitentiaire International de Stockholm*, 171–202.
[28] *Le Congrès Pénitentiaire International de Stockholm*, 171–200, 590–7.

opposition to transportation, though like de Foresta some had earlier extolled its virtue as a penal stage in Crofton's Irish system. They included Leo Mechelin (Finland), Dona Concepción Arenal (Spain), the Italian president of the congress, Beltrani Scalia, and Franz von Holtzendorff (Germany). The Spanish delegate Francisco Lastres, initially a supporter of penal colonies, changed his views following the meeting.[29] Overall, the delegates of the congress found it hard to reconcile the diversity of views, particularly without appearing to attack their French colleagues, and so ultimately passed the following compromise resolution, 'The penalty of transportation involves difficulties in its execution, which do not admit of its adoption by *all* nations, nor allow the hope that it can *everywhere* be made to realize all the conditions of an effective criminal administration.'[30]

Subsequent meetings in Rome (1885) and St Petersburg (1890) again heard opposing opinions. On the one hand, delegates condemned transportation as contrary to 'good penal justice'. On the other, especially at the Russian congress, delegates mooted its value for the supply of labour to the state and as a means for the rehabilitation of habitual offenders. George Dubois, a member of the board of directors of the French *Société générale des prisons* (General Society of Prisons), drew attention to the relationship between transportation and empire, in Portugal and Russia as well as France. He also noted that Italy's island penal colonies were 'a kind of transportation ... in default of distant colonies'.[31] De Foresta too remained resolute in his support for the punishment, and at the Rome meeting reminded delegates that no penitentiary congress had ever actually condemned transportation, either directly or indirectly, and that in Italy, public opinion was strongly in favour of it. The Lisbon lawyer M. de Silva Matos, who was a representative of Portugal, however, pointed out that though Portugal still sent convicts to penal colonies in Africa, transportation had lost its deterrent appeal, for convicts preferred to undertake their punishment in the open air of the African colonies rather than in

---

[29] *Gaceta de Madrid*, 8 September 1879, cited in Burillo Albacete, *La cuestión penitenciaria*, 67n13. I am grateful to Christian G. De Vito for this reference. See also *Le Congrès Pénitentiaire International de Stockholm*, 171–200, 590–7. On Holtzendorff's earlier support of overseas penal colonies, see Warren Rosenblum, *Beyond the Prison Gates: Punishment and Welfare in Germany, 1850–1933* (Chapel Hill: University of North Carolina Press, 2008), 33.

[30] Wines, *The Actual State of Prison Reform*, 6 (my emphasis). For the resolution in French, see also *Le Congrès Pénitentiaire International de Stockholm*, 202, 597 ('*La peine de la transportation présente des difficulties qui ne permettent pas de l'adopter dans tous les pays, ni d'espérer qu'elle y realise toutes les conditions d'une bonne justice*').

[31] Randall, *The Fourth International Prison Congress St. Petersburg*, 129–30 (quote, 130).

metropolitan central jails. He also believed that French people committed offences deliberately to court transportation.[32]

In St Petersburg, discussions between representative of the largest transporters in Europe at the time, France and Russia, reveal reformers' interest in the relationship between punishment and labour, which was discussed in Chapters 2 and 3. Indeed, following the congress, Demetrius Komorsky, inspector-general of prisons in Siberia, attended a meeting of the *Société générale des prisons* in Paris, where he spoke about convicts in the Russian Far East. Penal transportation in Russia had a long history, he noted, dating from the middle of the seventeenth century. Initially, capitally sentenced convicts were pardoned and sent to the silver and gold mines of the Transbaikal region of Siberia, and they were later joined by ordinary convicts. Komorsky reflected on the two categories of punishments associated with transportation. Criminal punishment deprived felons of their status and all common rights, including to property and family, and thus resulted in civil death. Criminal convicts could be transported with or without hard labour, for a term of years or for life. Local communes inflicted correctional punishments, which sent convicts into transportation for five years, after which they could apply for the right of return. Few did, Komorsky reported, because Siberia was rich in agriculture. Thus, penal transportation and Russia's desire to colonize the region and to exploit its natural resources were intertwined. Indeed, until the second half of the nineteenth century, convicts were subject not to a penal regime but to labour laws, and there was no prison administration until 1869. Further, around 30 per cent of convicts were women, and the authorities encouraged marriage between people Komorsky described as 'transported colonists' as a means of encouraging permanent settlement. Moreover, after serving their sentence, or after ten years, convicts became 'free colonists', but unless they were pardoned, they did not have the right of return to European Russia. Many of those in the Transbaikal found labour in the gold and silver mines at Nerchinsk. Free labourers resented exiles, because they were willing to work for lower wages. This led to 'a certain hostility'. Komorsky noted that this was similar to the labour situation in French Guiana. 'It is an economic question', he argued.[33]

---

[32] *Actes du Congrès Pénitentiaire International de Rome*: closing meeting, 24 November 1885, 654–7. *Actes du Congrès Pénitentiaire International de Rome, Novembre 1885, Volume 2* (Rome: Mantellate, 1888) contains a summary of Italy's pro-transportation arguments in Stockholm, 167–74.

[33] Randall, *The Fourth International Prison Congress St. Petersburg*, 'Mr Komorsky, inspector-general of the prisons of Siberia, interviewed in Paris, November 1890', 246 (241–53). In the intervening period, when the National Prison Congress of the USA met in 1887, Alaska was suggested as an ideal site for a penal colony. This was because it would

From the 1850s, Sakhalin Island became a further destination for convicts sentenced to hard labour, including after 1883, all healthy women. As on mainland Siberia, government permitted male convicts' wives to accompany their husbands into transportation, if they wished. Sakhalin was considered 'a prison surrounded by floating walls', and though convicts were not incarcerated in jails or penal barracks, they were forced to work. Their occupations included road building, land improvement, and construction, and they were also employed in the general administration of the colony. Around 400 capitally convicted convicts and recidivists (out of a total of 3,200 convicts) worked in above-ground coal mines in the mountains. After their release, as in Siberia generally they were not allowed to leave. However, they were maintained by government for a period of two years, and issued with land, tools, livestock, and rations, and were allowed to work as they pleased. Though, as we will see below, the true picture was more complex, Komorksy's French audience was impressed by his representation of Russian affairs and marvelled at his vision of an inexpensive transportation system after which recidivism was rare, and ex-convicts found a social standing. 'Ah, well, if we could do something like it in New Caledonia we should [be very] happy', the society's president said as he closed the meeting.[34]

Only at the Paris Congress (1895) was transportation overwhelmingly viewed with sympathy, and delegates defensive over France's retention of French Guiana and New Caledonia again stressed its merits as a means of enforcing long sentences and punishing habitual offenders and recidivists (Figure 7.3). The pre-circulated question read: 'Can transportation, taken in its broadest sense, be admitted in a rational system of repression; and if so, what particular role would it be called upon to fill?' Congress passed the following resolution: 'Transportation, under different forms, with the improvements already realized and still realizable, has its utility, both for

---

'provide a future and open a career in a new land to such of the convicts as chose to reform and live honest lives'. See Charles Nordhoff, 'Alaska as a Possible Penal Colony', in *Proceedings of the National Prison Congress, Held at Atlanta, GA., 1886* (Chicago, IL: R. R. Donnelley and Sons, The Lakeside Press, 1887), 270–8 (quote, 276). On convicts in Siberia, see Sarah Badcock, *A Prison without Walls? Eastern Siberian Exile in the Last Years of Tsarism* (Oxford University Press, 2016); Daniel Beer, *The House of the Dead: Siberian Exile under the Tsars* (London: Allen Lane, 2016); Daniel Beer, 'Penal Transportation to Siberia and the Limits of State Power, 1801–81', *Kritika: Explorations in Russian and Eurasian History*, 16, 3 (2015), 621–50; Andrew A. Gentes, *Exile to Siberia, 1590–1822* (Basingstoke: Palgrave, 2008); Andrew A. Gentes, *Exile, Murder and Madness in Siberia, 1823–61* (Basingstoke: Palgrave, 2010); Zhanna Popova, 'Exile as Imperial Practice: Western Siberia and the Russian Empire, 1879–1900', *International Review of Social History*, 63, S26 (2018), 131–50.

[34] Randall, *The Fourth International Prison Congress St. Petersburg*, 'Mr Komorsky, inspector-general of the prisons of Siberia, interviewed in Paris, November 1890', 241–53 (quote, 253).

Figure 7.3 *Pénitencier dépôt des condamnés aux travaux forces*.
Photographer: E. Robin, c. 1870
Source: Archives de la Nouvelle-Calédonie: ANC 1 Num 1-19.

the execution of long sentences for great crimes, and for the repression of habitual criminals and determined recidivists.'[35] It continued to attract support at later congresses, largely when discussing situations where labour was in short supply. Thus the 1900 Brussels Congress was approving of the use of convicts on the Trans-Siberian railway; largely because delegates were informed that free labour could not be found.[36]

Penal Marks, Stages, and Tours

Related to debates on penal colonies was discussion of the 'mark system' of progressive classification, through which convicts could earn 'marks' and ultimately tickets-of-leave (probatory certificate), for their conduct and work. The reason for the connection was that Alexander

---

[35] Ruggles-Brise, *Prison Reform At Home and Abroad*, 37, 39, 56, 73–5. The pre-circulated question and resolution are cited in Teeters, *Deliberations of the International Penal and Penitentiary Congresses*, 86–7.
[36] Ruggles-Brise, *Prison Reform at Home and Abroad*, 140.

Maconochie had first implemented the system in the penal colony of Norfolk Island, and Sir Walter Crofton much admired it.[37] Indeed, Penitentiary Congress Chairman E. C. Wines pre-circulated Maconochie's principles of prison discipline to participating nations before the start of the 1872 meeting. These included the key point: 'Unsuitable indulgence in prison management is as pernicious as unsuitable severity. The true principle is, to place the prisoner in a position of stern adversity, from which he must work his way out by his own exertions – by diligent labor and a constant course of voluntary self-command and self-denial.'[38] This approach had greatly influenced Crofton as he devised the Irish system. As E. C. Wines's son Frederick wrote in the USA later in 1899: 'Its germ was sown in Australia, transplanted to Ireland, cultivated by Sir Walter Crofton, brought to this country, modified to suit local conditions, and it has here taken deep root and is rapidly spreading over the surface of the land ... it is bound ultimately to make the circuit of the globe.'[39] This indeed proved to be the case, for the Crofton system was adopted in locally modified form all over the world, including not just Fernando de Noronha (Chapter 1), but elsewhere in Latin America, and the whole of British India, including the Andaman Islands.[40] Other places that used it included landlocked Switzerland and Italy's Tuscan archipelago, where convicts farmed grapes, olives, and cereals.[41] At the Stockholm Congress of 1878, E. C. Wines described the latter as 'the intermediate prison of the Crofton system in its best form'. He

---

[37] John V. Barry, 'Maconochie, Alexander (1787–1860)', http://adb.anu.edu.au/biography/maconochie-alexander-2417/text3207, published first in hardcopy 1967 (accessed online 17 September 2020). Original texts at: Captain Maconochie, *Australiana: Some Thoughts on Convict Management, and Other Subjects Connected with the Australian Penal Colonies* (Hobart Town, Van Diemen's Land: J. C. MacDougall, 1839); Captain Maconochie, *Crime and Punishment: The Mark System, Framed to Mix Persuasion with Punishment, and Make Their Effect Improving, Yet Their Operation Severe* (London: J. Hatchard and Son, 1846). See also J. M. Moore, 'Alexander Maconochie's mark system', *Prison Service Journal*, 198 (2011), 38–46; Norval Morris, *Maconochie's Gentlemen: The Story of Norfolk Island and the Roots of Modern Prison Reform* (Oxford University Press, 2003).

[38] *International Congress on the Prevention and Repression of Crime*, 10, 163–203 (quote, 192). See also *Débats du Congrès Pénitentiaire de Bruxelles*, 29 (Maconochie is listed as a member of the Congress); *Transactions of the National Congress of Penitentiary and Reformatory Discipline, held at Cincinnati*, 170–1.

[39] *Proceedings of the Annual Congress of the National Prison Association of the United States, held at Indianapolis, Ind., October 15–19 1898* (Pittsburgh, PA: Shaw Bros., 1899): Frederick Howard Wines, 'Objections to the Indeterminate System', 164–81.

[40] Wines, *Report on the International Penitentiary Congress of London*, 21, 26, 40, 75; E. C. Wines, *The State of Prisons and of Child-Saving Institutions in the Civilized World* (Cambridge, MA: University Press, John Wilson and Son, 1880), 301, 325–6, 548.

[41] Wines, *Report*, 21, 26, 40, 75. For Crofton's address at the 1872 London Congress, see Pierce, *Origin, Organization and Opening Addresses of the International Prison Congress*, 24–5.

praised the way in which they kept prisoners occupied and helped them to imagine a better future. Because they were allowed to keep any profits, they were invested in their work. Moreover, the open-air work kept them fit and healthy.[42] Noted prison reformer Mary Carpenter had previously described islands as ideal locations for the implementation of Crofton's system. '[B]etter still', she wrote, 'two or three or even four islands, sufficiently near to each other to be within one general surveillance.'[43]

Maconochie's mark system and Crofton's progressive classification together constituted the roots of the ticket-of-leave, or probation, system which was ultimately introduced into jails, and remains a familiar part of modern criminal justice. Here, prisoners undergo imprisonment, gradual release from discipline and eventually conditional liberation. But this key feature of modern incarceration has its historic roots not in jails, but in penal colonies, where the promise of remission of sentence according to good work and conduct was one of the key principles of punishment for transportation convicts. The centrality of this carceral rhythm to the development of jail routines was widely recognized in the first part of the twentieth century, including by the director of the International Prison Commission, Sir Evelyn Ruggles-Brise.[44] What has been lost since the 1920s is an appreciation of the historic origins of probation, which was awarded in the context of a mutually constitutive relationship between penal colonies and prisons. Convicts achieved relative freedom in stages and served out their probation: either by moving through different carceral architectures of punishment and rehabilitation, often across large geographical distances, or within penal sites of relatively open character. This opens up the question of whether a penal discipline designed for empires and expansionist nations, but now used behind the closed walls of prisons, is doomed to fail.[45] The exception here is perhaps post-Soviet Russia where, as Sarah Badcock and Judith Pallot have shown, distance remains a key element of punishment.[46]

As noted earlier, the first International Penitentiary Congress took place almost a century after the death of the famous British penal

---

[42] Wines, *The Actual State of Prison Reform*, 18.
[43] Mary Carpenter, 'Suggestions on reformatory schools and prison discipline founded on observations made during a visit to the United States', in *Transactions of the Third National Prison Reform Congress*, 172.
[44] Ruggles-Brise, *Prison Reform at Home and Abroad*, 20.
[45] A related issue is the comparative success of incarceration and penal transportation for rates of re-offending. See Barry Godfrey, 'Prison versus Western Australia: Which Worked Best, the Australian Penal Colony or the English Convict Prison System?', *The British Journal of Criminology*, 59, 5, (2019), 1139–60.
[46] Sarah Badcock and Judith Pallot, 'Russia and the Soviet Union from the Nineteenth to the Twenty-First Century', in Anderson, ed., *A Global History of Convicts and Penal Colonies*, 284, 294–6 (271–305).

reformer, John Howard, during a tour of prison sites in Turkey and Russia. The 100th anniversary came during the year of the St Petersburg Congress (1890).[47] In the years that followed Howard's death, many individuals went on prison tours. Sometimes, as in the case of Beaumont and Tocqueville's trip from France to the USA, these trips were government sponsored. In other cases, they were self-motivated and organized. In 1855, for example, Superintendent J. P. Walker of the then-largest jail in the world, Agra in the North-West Provinces of British India, spent six months visiting over 50 prisons in Britain, Ireland, and France. At the time, he was on unpaid furlough, but both the EIC's court of directors and the home secretary gave him letters of introduction. Walker's goal was to gather information to implement improved jail discipline and prison education upon his return to India. Less than two years later, during the mass jailbreaks and destructions of the 1857 Revolt, all the Agra prisoners escaped. With Indian prisons in crisis, the British established a new penal colony in the Andaman Islands. Walker became its first superintendent.[48]

The Spanish *presidio* of Ceuta in North Africa was just ten miles from the British colony of Gibraltar, which as Chapter 2 detailed received male convicts from Britain and Ireland between 1842 and 1875. Initially, they were kept on hulks; later they were transferred to a prison located in the dockyard.[49] The British and Spanish governments were certainly aware of the character of their neighbouring regimes, and in 1846 British Governor Sir Robert Wilson and Superintendent of Convicts Dr Julius Williams, made an official visit to Ceuta. Wilson declared himself so

---

[47] Teeters, *Deliberations of the International Penal and Penitentiary Congresses*, 64.

[48] LMA H01/ST/NC/17/1: Letter book including diary of visits to prisons in Britain, Ireland, and France, April–November 1855: J. P. Walker to James Melville, secretary to the East India Company court of directors, 30 April 1855; J. P. Walker's diary of visits to prisons. At this time, Agra central jail held 3,500 prisoners. Walker's career is detailed in Clare Anderson, 'The Making of an Eclectic Archive: Epistemologies of Global Knowledge in the Papers of J. P. Walker (1823–1906)', in Rohan Deb Roy and Guy N. A. Attewell, eds., *Locating the Medical: Explorations in South Asian History* (New Delhi: Oxford University Press, 2017), 151–68. See also Clare Anderson, *The Indian Uprising of 1857–8: Prisons, prisoners and rebellion* (London: Anthem Press, 2007), 34–6, 58–9, 144–56.

[49] Lawrence A. Sawchuk, Lianne Tripp, and Michelle M. Mohan, '"Voluntariness of Exposure": Life in a Convict Station', *Prison Journal*, 90, 2 (2010), 203–19. For a somewhat exuberant account of Gibraltar, written for a popular audience, see Arthur Griffiths, *Secrets of the Prison-House or Gaol Studies and Sketches, Volume I* (London: Chapman and Hall, 1894), 51–142. Griffiths was brigade major (63rd Manchester Regiment) in Gibraltar between 1864 and 1870, when he was appointed in temporary charge of the convict establishment. He later became Britain's inspector of prisons (1878–96), and a prolific writer of works subsequently described as 'sensational and grotesque'. See Bill Forsythe, 'Arthur George Frederick Griffiths (1838–1908)', *Oxford Dictionary of National Biography*, https://doi.org/10.1093/ref:odnb/33581 (accessed 23 September 2021).

impressed by its organization and management that he obtained copies of its regulations from the Spanish governor, General Antonio Ordoñez, and forwarded them to the Colonial Office.[50] The British were not the only visitors to the *presidio*, which attracted great interest in mainland Spain, during a period when, as noted earlier, it was debating the relative merits of 'internal' and 'overseas' penal settlements and colonies. By the 1880s, the famous Spanish criminologist Rafael Salillas, government inspector of prisons, had made several visits there. Initially, Salillas was a follower of Cesare Lombroso, and the idea that criminality was biologically rather than socially determined.[51] Historical interest in Salillas has most usually focused on his work as a criminologist, including a change in his views on crime in the mid-1890s, when he moved away from Lombrosian positivism and began to link crime to poverty.[52] Before then, in his highly influential 1888 work *La vida penal en España* (*Criminal Life in Spain*), Salillas articulated the view that Ceuta was a model penal colony, a place in which convicts could be punished, worked, and reformed, and thus bestow social and economic value on the Spanish nation. Ceuta operated through a graduated system of convict classification, which had arisen not as a consequence of Sir Walter Crofton's globally influential system, but rather so spontaneously that it revealed the 'Irish' system as a 'natural' form of punishment.[53] Noting the close alignment between punishment

---

[50] TNA CO91/177 29 July 1846 no. 108: Governor Robert Wilson, Gibraltar, to Henry Grey (3rd Earl Grey), secretary of state for war and the colonies, 29 July 1846, enc: A moral and corrective system adopted for improving the conduct of the Ceuta convicts, Colonel José de Palacir, commanding at Ceuta, 25 July 1846.

[51] Cesare Lombroso, *Criminal Man*, translated and with a new introduction by Mary Gibson and Nicole Hahn Rafter (Durham, NC: Duke University Press, 2006); Gina Lombroso-Ferrero, *Criminal Man; According to the Classification of Cesare Lombroso. Briefly summarised by his daughter Gina Lombroso Ferrero* (London: Putnam, 1911). See also Neil Davie, *Tracing the Criminal: The rise of scientific criminology in Britain 1860–1920* (Oxford: The Bardwell Press, 2005); Mary Gibson, *Born to Crime: Cesare Lombroso and the origins of biological criminology* (Westport, CT: Praeger, 2002); David G. Horn, *The Criminal Body: Lombroso and the anatomy of deviance* (Abingdon: Routledge, 2003); Daniel Pick, *Faces of Degeneration: a European disorder, c. 1848–1918* (Cambridge University Press, 1989), chapter 5. Mary Gibson notes that the 1885 International Penitentiary Congress in Rome coincided with a Congress of Criminal Anthropology, and members such as Lombroso attended both events. See Gibson, *Italian Prisons in the Age of Positivism*, 73.

[52] Ricardo Campos and Rafael Huertas, 'Criminal anthropology in Spain', in Paul Knepper and P. J. Ystehede, eds., *The Cesare Lombroso Handbook* (London: Routledge, 2013), 314–6 (309–23). See also Rafael Salillas, *El delincuente español: El lenguaje (Estudio filológico, psicológico y sociológico)* (Madrid: Librería de Victoriano Suárez, 1896); Rafael Salillas, *El delincuente español: Hampa (Antropología picaresca)* (Madrid: Librería de Victoriano Suárez, 1896). Again, thanks to Christian G. De Vito here and in the next two footnotes.

[53] Rafael Salillas, *La vida penal en España* (Madrid: Imprenta de la Revista de la Legislación, 1888), 254, 260. This contrasts sharply with the view of one of Salillas's contemporaries,

and the military across empire, he wrote that in Ceuta convicts and soldiers alike were employed in 'organic dependency' on military works. Together they gathered and transported the materials required for fortifications and buildings. Together they built the fort and the barracks. Together they worked as carpenters and blacksmiths; as engineers, draftsmen, painters, photographers, street cleaners, tailors, shoemakers, servants, clerks, and teachers. Besides convicts and soldiers, the only other inhabitants in the *presidio* were clergymen and the families of officers. Salillas concluded, in a rebuke to his critics who wanted the penal colony to shut down: 'Without penal labour, Ceuta would neither be what it is, nor what it will become.'[54]

As discussed in Chapter 3, following the Meiji restoration of 1868, the Japanese government was also actively researching overseas prison regimes. In 1872, Deputy Director of the Prisons Department Shigeya Ohara went on a nine-week-long tour to the British colonies of Hong Kong and Singapore. At this time, Singapore was one of three remaining but soon to be closed Indian penal settlements in Britain's Straits Settlements. Ohara was accompanied by his translator, John C. Hall, the acting British-vice consul in Edo (later, Tokyo), who later noted that they gathered 'several useful hints and suggestions' on convict labour.[55] Ohara afterwards penned the first set of regulations for Japanese institutions, *Kangokusoku narabini zushiki* (*Illustrated Regulations for Prisons*), writing: 'I compared [English practice] with [the] written laws of our country, accommodating our customs and sentiments'. This informed his desire to classify and separate under-trial, male, female, and juvenile prisoners, as well as perhaps his most striking innovation: the adoption and adaptation of Crofton's Irish system of penal stages.

Juan José Relosillas. Relosillas spent fourteen months in Ceuta, where he was employed as first assistant inspector of public works. Among his many criticisms of the *presidio* were poor conditions, the lack of differentiation among prisoners, the use of convicts as guards (*cabos de vara*), and illicit trading between convicts and others. See *Catorce meses en Ceuta* (Ceuta: Caja de Ahorros y Monte de Piedad, 1985) (first published 1886).

[54] Salillas, *La vida penal en España*, 244, 247, 248–9 (quotes, 249).

[55] An English-language report of the tour is located in PP 1875 (1338) *Papers Relating to the Improvement of Prison Discipline in the Colonies*: Governor Sir Harry St George Ord, Straits Settlements, to John Wodehouse (1st Earl Kimberley), secretary of state for the colonies, 4 March 1872, enc. report of John C. Hall, acting British Vice-Consul Yeddo (Tokyo), 20 October 1871. At the time of Ohara's visit, J. F. A. McNair was comptroller general of convicts in the Straits Settlements, and author of *Prisoners Their Own Warders: A Record of the Convict Prison at Singapore in the Straits Settlements Established 1825, Discontinued 1873, Together with a Cursory History of the Convict Establishments at Bencoolen, Penang and Malacca from the Year 1797* (Westminster: Archibald Constable and Co., 1899). See also Lorenz Ködderitzsch, 'The Courts of Law, Appendix: Execution of Penalty', in Wilhelm Röhl, ed., *History of Law in Japan since 1868* (Leiden: Brill, 2005), 756–7 (711–69).

Japanese prisoners could gradually work their way up five classes. They started with work in chains at land clearance or pounding rice, and could rise to the position of an unfettered, first-class overseer, cook, or guard. The length of time prisoners spent in each class depended on their sentence and behaviour.[56]

In 1878, the second International Penitentiary Congress, which was convened in Stockholm, much praised Japan's innovations. Japan did not send delegates to Sweden. However, in what was part of a larger effort to engage in international discussions and thus encourage the revision of the unequal treaties that undergirded diplomatic relations at this time, it submitted a written report.[57] The organizer of the earlier London conference, E. C. Wines, wrote: 'The government of that empire has made the most elaborate, comprehensive and exhaustive report, that has come to the congress from any quarter ... Japan has entered, intelligently and earnestly, on the work of prison reform'. He praised its use of incentives, religious instruction, education, and productive labour (prisoners received 10 per cent of their earnings); and the establishment of houses of refuge for released prisoners with no means of support.[58] In the midst of its international engagements on prison reform, Japan appointed German penologist Kurt von Seebach as an official advisor to government. Home Minister Yamagata had met him during his visit to Europe in 1888. The unfortunate von Seebach died a year later, having fallen ill when inspecting Hokkaido's penal colonies (*shūchikan*). Nonetheless, as Daniel V. Botsman explains, his ideas became foundational for the operation of the Japanese prison system.[59] During this period, penal administrators exchanged and debated materials on the transportation practices of France and Russia.[60] For two decades after 1888, for example, the

---

[56] Yoshirō Hiramatsu, 'History of Penal Institutions: Japan', *Law in Japan: an annual*, 6 (1973), 25–9 (quote, 27) (1–48); Ködderitzsch, 'The Courts of Law, Appendix', 757–9.

[57] Ködderitzsch, 'The Courts of Law, Appendix', 761. On the importance of extraterritoriality, see Daniel V. Botsman, *Punishment and Power in the Making of Modern Japan* (Princeton University Press, 2005), 129–40.

[58] Wines, *The Actual State of Prison Reform*, 24. See also Wines, *The State of Prisons*, 595.

[59] Botsman, *Punishment and Power*, 195. See also Hiramatsu, 'History of Penal Institutions', 38–41.

[60] The following represent a selection, drawn from a three-year period during 1889–91. Paul Bueche (tr. Eiichi Takeda), 'Method of Escorting Prisoners in France', *Dainippon Kangoku Kyōkai Zasshi*, 9 (vol. 2 issue 1, 1889), 34–5 (32–6); Jacques de Boisjoslin (tr. Eiichi Takeda), 'French Penal Colonies and Transportation', *Dainippon Kangoku Kyōkai Zasshi*, 11 (vol. 2, issue 3) (1889), 17–22; Jacques de Boisjoslin (tr. Eiichi Takeda), 'French Penal Colonies and Transportation (continued from no. 11)', *Dainippon Kangoku Kyōkai Zasshi*, 12 (vol. 2, issue 4) (1889), 9–11; 'Number of prisoners sentenced to transportation [Siberia]', *Dainippon Kangoku Kyōkai Zasshi*, 20 (vol. 2, issue 12) (1889), 8–9; 'Russia: Special regulations for using prisoners sentenced to penal transportation with labour [Ussuri railway, Siberia]/Grant of an amnesty for transported

Dainippon Kangoku Kyōkai Zasshi (*Bulletin of the Penitentiary Society of the Empire of Japan*) published an astonishing 338 Japanese translations of English, French, German, and Russian materials.[61]

In regard to Japan's interest in the Russian Empire, it has been well established that from the mid-eighteenth century, exile to settlement and exile to penal labour (*katorga*) in Siberia were part of a state-led effort at colonization. This increased further following the passing of *Ustav o ssyl'nykh* (*Exile and Convoy Regulations*) in 1822.[62] However, as exiles and convicts marched eastwards, they became ill when they sold their clothing for rations, they escaped, and the local authorities would take the healthiest of them for labour purposes. This, the clerical errors on convicts' identity cards, and the switching of identities confounded the labour purpose of the system, for not only were some exiles sent to the wrong place, but often it was only the frail and sick who ended up in their punitive destination. Additionally, over the course of the nineteenth century, tens of thousands of those who reached Siberia escaped, as many as one third of the exile population in some places, including a sizeable proportion of women.[63] By 1900, the state preferred free settlement over penal colonization, and so abolished exile to Siberia. Nonetheless, before the Revolution of 1917 the number of exiles and convicts sent to the region increased, revealing some of the contradictions between punishment and labour exploitation. Exiles were expected to provide for themselves, though often allocated poor quality land and

---

prisoners in Siberia', *Dainippon Kangoku Kyōkai Zasshi*, 38 (vol. 4, issue 6) (1891), 2–7. A later issue of the Bulletin ('Donated foreign books', 40 [vol. 4, issue 8] [1891], 54) noted a gift to the association of four volumes of proceedings of the American National Prison Association, and what seems to have been a copy (or part copy) of Georges Dassonville's 1880 doctoral thesis, which compared the disciplinary and moralizing functions of transportation and penitentiary incarceration in France, Britain, and Russia: Droit Romain: Des peines qui emportaient privation de la liberté naturelle; Droit français Étude comparée de la transportation et de l'emprisonnement cellulaire aux deux points de vue répressif et moralisateurs en droit français: état de la question en France et dans quelques pays. Thèse pour le doctorat (Paris: A. Parent, 1880). Discussing contemporary French and Russian practice, and the history of Britain's Australian penal colonies, Dassonville drew attention to the rejection of transportation as a sound punishment, by the 1878 International Prison Congress in Stockholm, but ultimately he favoured transportation over cellular imprisonment. I am grateful to Takashi Miyamoto for this information.

[61] Of these, eighty-one were from the USA, seventy-five from Britain, eighty-three from France, forty-five from Germany and fifty-four from Russia. Again, I thank Takashi Miyamoto for these insights.

[62] Beer, 'Penal Deportation to Siberia', 622. See also Gentes, *Exile, Murder and Madness in Siberia*, 5–6; Abby M. Schrader, *Languages of the Lash: Corporal Punishment and Identity in Imperial Russia* (DeKalb, IL: Northern Illinois University Press, 2002), 80–3, 185–6.

[63] Badcock, *A Prison Without Walls?*, chapter 2; Beer, 'Penal Deportation to Siberia', 627–8, 639–40; Schrader, *Languages of the Lash*, 85.

unable to compete with cheap convict labour, many fell into poverty, vagrancy, and crime. At the same time, for hard labour convicts, poor food and conditions, insufficient workshops, and the existence of preferred free labour alternatives meant that as Sarah Badcock and Judith Pallot have shown, 'life in hard labour prisons in the early twentieth century was characterized by a lack of work'. The only exception to this was the successful deployment of convicts on railway projects, including the Trans-Siberian route that was much admired by the Japanese.[64]

If Japan was influenced by the exploitation of convict labour in other global contexts, at least some of the Western powers expressed admiration for the Hokkaido settlements. In 1896, Britain's H.M. Inspector of Prisons Arthur Griffiths wrote: 'If we go farthest East, we shall find the penal colony in full use by that most enlightened and progressive nation, Japan.' He praised the use of convicts in road making, mining, and land reclamation, and the openness of a system of 'semi-liberty'. Convicts could work their way up the penal stages, and when they had reached the top, they enjoyed conditions akin to that of free labourers. Griffiths was a brigade-major in the army and had previously served as superintendent of the convict establishment of Gibraltar (1864–70), and in Chatham Hulk and Millbank Prison, where he established public works schemes for prisoners.[65] Meantime, Japanese practices spread to China. The Qing government dispatched officials Japan in 1906, to study its prison system, and used the Japanese model as the basis for reform. Just as the Japanese translated dozens of European and Russian texts, so the Chinese translated Japanese writings on prison reform. In 1908, the

---

[64] Sarah Badcock and Judith Pallot, 'Russia and the Soviet Union from the Nineteenth to the Twenty-First Century', in Anderson, ed., *A Global History of Convicts and Penal Colonies*, 273, 285–7 (quote, 285) (271–305).

[65] Arthur Griffiths (H.M. Inspector of Prisons), 'Penal Colonies – Agricultural and Industrial', *North American Review*, 163, 482 (1896), 685–6 (676–87). A prolific author, in his other work Griffiths discussed European penal transportation more broadly. Most notable perhaps is Arthur Griffiths, *Secrets of the Prison-House or Gaol Studies and Sketches, Volume I* (London: Chapman and Hall, 1894). For a discussion of Griffiths' exaggerated representations of inhumane punishment, see Christine Marlin, 'A Prison and a Gentleman: The prison inspector as imperialist hero in the writings of Major Arthur Griffiths (1838–1908)', in Jason W. Haslam and Julia M. Wright, eds., *Captivating Subjects: Writing Confinement, Citizenship, and Nationhood in the Nineteenth Century* (University of Toronto Press, 2005), 220–40. Marlin argues that Griffiths' representation of Japan as an 'enlightened and progressive country' was connected to its status as Britain's political ally (228–9 [quote, citing Griffiths, *Secrets of the Prison House*, 375]). See also Bill Forsythe, 'Griffiths, Arthur George Frederick (1838-1908)', *Oxford Dictionary of National Biography* (Oxford University Press, 2004), online edition, October 2009, www.oxforddnb.com/view/article/33581 (accessed 7 May 2020).

Chinese even appointed Japanese prison expert Ogawa Shigejiro as an advisor, and he oversaw the construction of Beijing's model prison.[66]

In 1909, German police criminologist named Robert Heindl embarked on a global tour of penal colonies. He began his journey in French New Caledonia, moving on to the Australian states of New South Wales and Queensland, and then to the Andaman Islands and the Spanish *presidio* of Ceuta. In his 470-page account of the voyage, Heindl blended history with ethnographic observations, photographs, statistics, and extracts from official papers. He even offered observations on crime and punishment in China.[67] Heindl undertook his research against the backdrop of a lively debate in Germany about the merits or otherwise of penal colonies. In the early nineteenth century, some German states had deported criminals overseas. Prussia sent offenders to Siberia; and Hamburg, Mecklenburg, and Saxe-Coburg-Gotha to the Americas. Following German unification in 1871, and the acquisition of the colonies of German East Africa, Southwest Africa, New Guinea, and Samoa in the 1880s, there were discussions about the utility of convicts as a means of preparing land for free white settlement. At the time, contemporaries were aware of the history of the Australian colonies, French Guiana, New Caledonia, and Russia's Sakhalin Island, and the potential value of transportation for the expansion of the German Empire. In the early twentieth century, a new organization, the German Deportation League, proposed to government that prisoners could volunteer for transfer from prisons to a penal colony in the Admiralty Islands, part of the Bismarck Archipelago in the western Pacific Ocean. This would not only prevent the spread of 'criminal infection' in jails, but unyielding labour (*ausgiebige Arbeitsbetätigung*) in the open air would enable convicts to break free of the cycle of crime and punishment. Government put off deciding on the proposed penal colony, and so the League put forward an idea for the transfer of ex-prisoner volunteers to the Admiralty Islands. As Warren Rosenblum explains, in this plan, 'ex-offenders would succeed or fail based only upon their readiness to work and their commitment to the community.' Again, government postponed a decision, influenced not just by colonial administrators, but settlers' organizations and missionary societies. They worried about the 'moral infection' of the Indigenous population, and disruptions to a racial hierarchy topped by white settlers. Such opposition

---

[66] Ying Kong, 'A Bibliographic Study of Late Qing Translations of Japanese Prison Books', *Journal of East Asian Cultural Interaction Studies*, 4 (2011), 533–53.
[67] Robert Heindl, *Meine Reise nach der Strafkolonien* (Berlin: Ullstein and Co., 1912). For other penal colony projects, see Richard J. Evans, *Tales from the German Underworld: Crime and Punishment in the Nineteenth Century* (New Haven, CT: Yale University Press, 1998), 78–81.

to penal colonies intensified following the 1904 Herero Rebellion in German Southwest Africa, which shook confidence in colonial rule.[68]

By the time Heindl arrived in his first destination, New Caledonia, the German government had called on its Foreign Office to gather information on convicts and penal colonies in other empires. Heindl himself appears to have travelled quite separately, however, and under the sponsorship of Bavaria.[69] Ultimately, Heindl adopted a strong anti-transportation position. Rosenblum writes that he represented penal colonies as 'archaic systems of power, marked by chaos, brutality, and utter irrationality':

> Alluding repeatedly to Dante's Inferno, he described shadow zones of quiet suffering and unholy copulations, interrupted by public theaters of cruelty and pain and absurd, almost gratuitous displays of domination ... Heindl drew a picture of the colonies as places with endless rules and the unceasing exercise of power, and yet no legitimate or consistent hierarchies and principles of order.[70]

In this regard, Heindl critiqued the fact that penal colonies did not routinely separate prisoners according to their crimes and skills, and claimed that convict labour was inefficient and unproductive. In New Caledonia, which was Heindl's greatest single focus, the French administration hired convicts out to free settlers, which he argued rendered them the de facto masters of the penal colony. Convicts gambled and had sex with each other, and with men far outnumbering women mixed indiscriminately amongst themselves and with both Indigenous peoples and migrants. The undesirable consequence of this, according to Heindl's view, was the birth of mixed-race children.[71]

Heindl did not find comparison with the earlier history of the Australian colonies relevant. Though he believed that the removal of Indigenous peoples would facilitate colonization, he wrote that in a greatly changed era it would not be possible in any future German

---

[68] Warren Rosenblum, *Beyond the Prison Gates: Punishment and Welfare in Germany, 1850–1933* (Chapel Hill: University of North Carolina Press, 2008), 77–87, 91–8, 95 (quote). Rosenthal notes that Germany rejected Italian criminologist Cesare Lombroso's idea that criminals were an 'atavistic' race, instead favouring social and cultural explanations for crime. See also Matthew Fitzpatrick, 'New South Wales in Africa? The Convict Colonialism Debate in Imperial Germany', *Itinerario*, 37, 1 (2013), 59–72.

[69] Fitzpatrick, 'New South Wales in Africa', 68, 71n15; Rosenblum, *Beyond the Prison Gates*, 98–101. Miscellaneous travel papers and letters relating to Heindl's tour are now held in Munich's Staatliches Museum für Völkerkunde (State Museum of Ethnology). I thank Michaela Appel for locating and sharing these records with me.

[70] Rosenblum, *Beyond the Prison Gates*, 99. Rosenblum speculates that *Meine Reise* inspired Franz Kafka's short story *In the Penal Colony*, which was written in 1914 and published in 1919.

[71] Heindl, *Meine Reise nach der Strafkolonien*, 96–120, 125, 162–3, 218, 232–3. See also Rosenblum, *Beyond the Prison Gates*, 100, 263n127.

penal colony. Other reasons were that, first, the Australian colonies had a different climate to the German colonies, making them more conducive to transportation. Second, sentences of transportation had been an alternative to capital punishment for petty crimes that by the early twentieth century attracted short prison sentences, so penal colonies had become defunct. Third, the advent of electricity and steam power in the intervening period had produced profound changes to work practices, rendering convict labour power less valuable. Fourth, the British had maintained convict discipline through the infliction of the no longer acceptable brutal punishments of flogging and execution. And, finally, quicker sea travel between Britain and the Antipodes had removed an important barrier to convict escape.[72] That said, Heindl praised St Helena, an offshore island prison in Queensland's Moreton Bay. Transport costs were minimal for prisoners and prison manufactures and prisoners did not suffer from a change of climate. In part, because medical costs were so low, the island was thus economically productive.[73]

Debates about penal transportation continued in Germany during the First World War and in the Weimar Republic (1919–33), though government never established penal colonies. In 1916, Heindl came back to the issue when he suggested the formation of penal battalions for wartime service. In 1922, he reiterated his opposition to penal colonization, and wrote with satisfaction of the new open-air prisons of Czechoslovakia, Switzerland, and Germany. He then declared himself 'the only criminalist who has studied the English as well as the French and Spanish systems of penal colonization right on the spot'.[74] Repeating the arguments that he had made in 1912, he claimed that the work of ten convicts did not equal that of one man, mortality rates were high, penal colonies were extremely expensive, and they were neither reformative nor rehabilitative. He concluded that after release an ex-convict 'exchanges the spade with the walking stick, and goes forth as a vagabond into the world to look for work with the firm determination not to find it'.[75]

Another important global tour of the twentieth century was that undertaken by Commissioner for Prisons in England and Wales Alexander Paterson, during the 1930s. He visited British imperial prisons, including in East Africa, British India, and the Caribbean, and the penal colony of

---

[72] Heindl, *Meine Reise nach der Strafkolonien*, 301–2.
[73] Heindl, *Meine Reise nach der Strafkolonien*, 315–18. A rich history of the island is Lauren Penny, *St Helena Island, Moreton Bay: An Historical Account* (Brisbane, QLD: Inspire Publishing, 2010).
[74] Robert Heindl and Bertha R. Wolf, 'Penal Settlement and Colonization', *Journal of the American Institute of Criminal Law and Criminology*, 13, 1 (1922), 57 (56–60); Rosenblum, *Beyond the Prison Gates*, 101–2, 138.
[75] Heindl and Wolf, 'Penal Settlement and Colonization', 60.

French Guiana.[76] Like Heindl, Paterson was sympathetic to the idea of open penal settlements, but had a preference for proximate islands or inland regions rather than far-distant sites. John Moore has shown that in this respect Paterson's ideas were 'a faithful reproduction' of Alexander Maconochie's. Indeed, as Commissioner for Prisons Paterson oversaw the establishment of open jails, which were near-identical to Maconochie's 'intermediate' prisons.[77] Like Maconochie, Paterson was also a strong advocate for carceral mobility. For instance, his general view that incarceration 'almost invariably induced a mental and moral deterioration in its inmates' influenced his recommendations on Burma, which was then part of British India. Thus, he advised a maximum two-year sentence in the province, and proposed that government send habitual offenders to island settlements. He identified destinations in the Cocos Islands, northeast of North Andaman Island, and Pyinzalu Island, near Rangoon (now, Yangon). He also recommended, despite the recent abolition of convict transportation, that dacoits and murderers should go to the Andaman Islands penal colony. Paterson made similar points following visits to East Africa and the Caribbean, calling for alternatives to imprisonment. He proposed as possibilities probation, compulsory labour on public works, and the establishment of temporary prison camps. 'Treatment rather than punishment should be the aim of work in prisons', he concluded. Underlying these specific comments was a highly international outlook. Indeed, as Ian Brown demonstrates, Paterson visited Burma after he had attended the 1925 International Penitentiary Congress in London. Brown speculates that it was there that a fellow delegate, former Inspector-General of Prisons of Burma, H. H. G. Knapp, invited him. That Paterson's was a spontaneous rather than an officially sponsored visit perhaps explains why the government of India failed to act on his proposals.[78]

Before he left Britain for a tour of inspection of prisons in the Caribbean colonies, at the end of 1936, Paterson sought permission to visit France's penal colony in French Guiana. He first went to Paris, and secured the

---

[76] Daniel Branch, 'Imprisonment and Colonialism in Kenya, c. 1930–1952: Escaping the Carceral Archipelago', *The International Journal of African Historical Studies*, 38, 2 (2005), 247, 250, 251 (239–65); Ian Brown, 'A Commissioner calls: Alexander Paterson and colonial Burma's prisons', *Journal of Southeast Asian Studies*, 38, 2 (2007), 293, 294, 297, 300–2 (quote, 294) (293–308).

[77] John Moore, 'Alexander Maconochie's "Mark System"', *Prison Service Journal*, 198 (2011), 46, 46n71 (38–46).

[78] Brown, 'A Commissioner calls', 293, 294 (quote), 297, 300–2. Colonial Office discussions of his reports are TNA CO859/19/8: Summary of the contents of Mr Paterson's report on his East African visit, 1939 (quote); TNA CO859/72/13: West Indies, report of Mr Paterson on penal establishments, 1936–7; TNA PCOM9/80: Mr Paterson's visits to American prisons, 1933.

support of the head of the French prison service, and then had a letter sent from the Foreign Office to the French minister of the colonies, via the British ambassador in Paris.[79] Paterson spent four days in the colony, and upon his return to Britain wrote in a private note: 'What I saw in French Guiana disturbed me so profoundly that while I cannot obviously commit myself to any public statement, I feel that I cannot maintain complete silence.'[80] At this time, France had ceased transportation to the colony, but there were still convicts in French Guiana, including those sentenced to life. The continued existence of the penal colony was highly controversial, and public criticism often centred on conditions on Devil's Island, which was a notorious site of confinement for political offenders, including most famously of all, at the end of the nineteenth century, the so-called traitor Captain Alfred Dreyfus (1895-9), transported for life for allegedly betraying military secrets.[81] The French government paid close attention to Paterson's visit, particularly because it coincided with that of Henri Danjou, a famous journalist on *Paris Soir*. After Paterson had left the colony, the governor of French Guiana reported that his visit had come off without incident.[82] Nonetheless, Paterson was highly critical of the penal colony, his perspective rearticulating the concerns of anti-transportationists, including Heindl but dating back at least a century. He wrote:

If you were to ask me at this stage what was my first and last judgement on Guiana, I would say that a convict settlement in a Colony is a fallacy. A country cannot colonise with convicts. It should send the best white men, not the worst white men, to lead and train the coloured men in the Colony. By sending in the first instance the worst of its population to a new country, the Government not only creates there an unfavourable impression, besmirching the name of France, but it blackens also the reputation of the Colony in the ears of France, discouraging the best citizens from going there, to be the pioneers and settlers of a great Empire. The hope of doing two things at once has in practice failed.[83]

---

[79] TNA PCOM 9/81 Visits to Prisons Abroad: proposed visit of Mr Paterson to French Penal Settlement in French Guiana: Alexander Paterson's note, 29 October 1936.

[80] TNA PCOM 9/81 Visits to Prisons Abroad: requesting Foreign Office approval for letter to Head of French Prisons, giving Mr Paterson's observations on his visit to French Guiana, Alexander Paterson's note, 26 May 1937; Paterson to Sir Stephen Gaselee, librarian and keeper of records Foreign Office, 15 July 1937 (quote); Harold Scott, Chairman Prison Commission, to Gaselee, 3 June 1937.

[81] Alfred Dreyfus was Jewish and was transported for life for betraying military secrets to Germany, at a time when anti-Semitism was sweeping France. Five years later, he was exonerated and sent back to France.

[82] ADG IX54 Administration pénitentiaire: Governor René Veber, French Guiana, to Marius Moutet, minister of the colonies, 9 September 1937.

[83] TNA PCOM9/81: Paterson to Mainfroid Andrieu, director French prison service, 19 June 1937. Paterson's reflections on French Guiana are published in *Paterson on*

At the heart of Paterson's condemnation of the penal colony was not just the impossibility of convict colonization, but a second issue: the hopelessness of transportation. Most convicts did not move through penal stages to ultimate liberation but were trapped in the colony forever. This was because under the system of *doublage*, following their release, all convicts sentenced to more than eight years' transportation had to stay for the equivalent number of years. Paterson wrote that the convicts' spiritual despair 'afflicted me more sorely than anything I have ever known', adding that they were like 'ghosts who are not allowed to die'.[84] Though in the aftermath of Paterson's visit, the French condemned transportation at the Fifth Committee of the League of Nations in 1937, the penal colony remained open, and did not close it until after the Second World War. In the meantime, Paterson wrote personally to the inspector-general of the prison administration, Armand Mossé, to cancel a proposed visit of French prison officials to England.[85]

*

This chapter has stressed that circulation and connection underpinned global discussions about punitive mobility in the nineteenth century. It has noted points of convergence and distinction, drawn from nineteenth and twentieth-century debates, the meetings of the International Penitentiary Congress, the development of punitive systems in penal colony sites, and global penal tours. Using examples from the British, French, Spanish, and Russian empires, and Japan, the chapter has highlighted the existence of an intense global interest in Britain's penal colonies in Australia and Singapore, as also the Russian Far East, and French Guiana and New Caledonia. This included through early nineteenth-century French and Spanish visits to New South Wales, and subsequent reports on the merits or otherwise of convict transportation. Detailing and analysing Alexander Maconochie's mark system, Sir Walter Crofton's penal stages, and the international visits of European contemporaries such as Robert Heindl, Gustav Beaumont and Alexis De Tocqueville, J. P. Walker, Shigeya Ohara, and Alexander Paterson, it has suggested that contemporary attitudes to these and other locations provide insights into the tensions between the penal and economic ambitions of convict sites.

In Chapter 8, the theme of circulation continues, through an exploration of other global connections and relationships forged through

Prisons, Being the collected papers of Sir Alexander Paterson, Edited, with an Introduction by S.K. Ruck (London: Frederick Muller Ltd, 1951), 147–52.
[84] TNA PCOM9/81: Paterson to Andrieu, 19 June 1937.
[85] TNA PCOM9/81: Paterson to Armand Mossé, inspector-general of prison administration, 2 February 1939.

convicts and punitive relocation. The chapter opens by examining the impact of punitive mobility on Indigenous populations, underscoring their subjection to devastating violence and marginalization, their encounters with convicts, and the assistance they rendered to the agents of their dispossession. One element of this, dating from the fifteenth and sixteenth centuries, is that convicts and Indigenous peoples alike were key interlocutors in exploration and scientific research. This was in part a consequence of the location of punitive sites in isolated, pristine, or underpopulated places. It was also because convicts and others offered significant levels of assistance and expertise. Currently a shadowy presence in histories of science, as will be suggested, punitive relocation was in fact highly significant for the practice and development of global knowledge gathering.

8 Encounters, Exploration, and Knowledge

If Chapter 7 analysed global discussions, exchanges, and visits around the sites of punitive relocation, this chapter argues that they were also important locations for colonial encounters, exploration, and knowledge formation. Most of the places under consideration in this book were already populated when convicts first arrived. The relatively open character of sites of punitive relocation meant that many convicts lived and settled in dynamic societies in which Indigenous peoples, settlers, labour migrants, and/or enslaved persons lived. Previous chapters have explored aspects of labour and cultural relations between convicts and other populations, free and unfree. This chapter observes that *presidios*, as also penal settlements and colonies, constituted ideal vantage points for the observation of Indigenous peoples, including those represented by expanding polities, as 'backward' or 'primitive'. Relatedly, they were also perfect bases for commodity exchange, including through the creation of relations of dependency by the routine gifting of addictive substances, notably alcohol and narcotics. Central points here are that Indigenous people greatly assisted the process of penal colonization that at the same time dispossessed them, and they encountered the people who came to live in sites of penal relocation in a variety of ways.

The impacts of punitive mobility on Indigenous communities were profound, in terms of the purchase or seizure of land, changes to modes of production, social disruption, the propagation of violence, declarations of war, and the deadly consequences of exposure to new and unfamiliar diseases. As will be shown in examples from the early-modern Americas, the Australian colonies, the Andaman Islands, and French New Caledonia, Indigenous peoples fought back, and with resilience and creativity adopted strategies of resistance. Against this background, from the nineteenth century, various imperial powers attempted to confine Indigenous peoples in ways that mirrored and extended the means used to manage transportation convicts. By this point, the character of penal transportation had changed. No longer was the extraction of convict labour solely a means of punishment, it was also a route to reform and rehabilitation. The same logic, of 'training' Indigenous men, women, and children for useful labour, underpinned efforts to incorporate them into the borders and even governance of penal colonies, and so raise them to 'civilization'.[1] Anthropologist Patrick Wolfe, in a much-cited text on European settler colonialism, has described invasion as a structure, not an event. Settlers desired the dissolution of native societies, and their replacement with settler societies. In places like the Australian colonies, this created a logic of elimination through which settlers looked to both expel and incorporate (and thus erase) Indigenous populations.[2] Wolfe's argument is of great importance in understanding the history of colonization, including through punitive relocation, and the connections between European representations of Indigenous peoples, policies of assimilation and separation, and the rapid decline in Indigenous populations across continents.[3] Narratives of extinction became naturalized through ideas of race, and impacted on the formation of colonial landscapes and cityscapes. These narratives and ideas remain powerful today in settler colonial nations, such as Australia.[4]

From a history of science perspective, it is also significant that the separate penal colonies established in nations and empires from the late

---

[1] Clare Anderson, 'Writing Indigenous Women's Lives in the Bay of Bengal, 1789–1906', *Journal of Social History*, 45, 2 (2011), 480–96; Inga Clendinnen, *Dancing with Strangers: Europeans and Australians at First Contact* (Cambridge University Press, 2005); Jane Carey and Jane Lydon, eds., *Indigenous Networks: Mobility, Connections and Exchange* (Abingdon: Routledge, 2014), 75–94; Martin Daunton and Rick Halpern, eds., *Empire and Others: British Encounters with Indigenous peoples, 1600–1850* (Philadelphia: University of Pennsylvania Press, 1999); Kate Fullagar and Michael McDonnell, eds., *Facing Empire: Indigenous Experiences in a Revolutionary Age*, 1760–1840 (Baltimore, MD: Johns Hopkins University Press, 2018); Tracey Banivanua Mar and Penelope Edmonds, 'Introduction: Making Space in Settler Colonies', in Tracey Banivanua Mar and Penelope Edmonds, eds., *Making Settler Colonial Space: Perspectives on Race, Place and Identity* (Basingstoke: Palgrave, 2010), 1–24; Tracey Banivanua Mar and Penelope Edmonds, 'Indigenous and Settler Relations', in Alison Bashford and Stuart MacIntyre, eds., *The Cambridge History of Australia, Volume 1: Indigenous and Colonial Australia* (Cambridge University Press, 2013), 342–66; Henry Reynolds, *The Other Side of the Frontier: Aboriginal Resistance to the European Invasion of Australia* (Sydney: University of New South Wales Press, 2006 [3rd ed.]); Satadru Sen, *Savagery and Colonialism in the Indian Ocean: Power, Pleasure and the Andaman Islanders* (Abingdon: Routledge, 2010). On how settler colonialism continues to shape the modern world, see Lorenzo Veracini, *The Settler Colonial Present* (Basingstoke: Palgrave, 2015); Lorenzo Veracini, 'The Imagined Geographies of Settler Colonialism', in Banivanua Mar and Edmonds, eds., *Making Settler Colonial Space*, 179–97.

[2] Patrick Wolfe, *Settler Colonialism and the Transformation of Anthropology: The politics and poetics of an ethnographic event* (London: Cassell, 1999), 2. See also Patrick Wolfe, 'Structure and event: Settler colonialism, time and the question of genocide', in A. Dirk Moses, ed., *Empire, Colony, Genocide: Conquest, Occupation, and Subaltern Resistance in World History* (Oxford: Berghahn, 2008), 102–3 (102–32).

[3] Philip D. Morgan, 'Encounters between British and "Indigenous" Peoples, c. 1500–c. 1800', in Daunton and Halpern, eds., *Empire and Others*, 42–78.

[4] Tracey Banivanua Mar and Penelope Edmonds, 'Making Space in Settler Colonies', in Banivanua Mar and Edmonds, eds., *Making Settler Colonial Space*, 3 (1–24).

eighteenth century onwards were often located in relatively pristine natural spaces. They were rich in flora and fauna, as well as shells and rocks. Penal administrators and visiting naturalists, botanists, geologists, and zoologists exploited these natural resources in their scientific research. Moreover, as in the case of Marçal de Corria in Fernando de Noronha, which opened Chapter 1, in locations from Mauritius and New South Wales to the Cape Colony, British India, Mexico, Panama, Sakhalin Island, and the Guianas, scientists and collectors worked with convicts, as well as the Indigenous peoples whose land bordered punitive sites.[5] Convicts and colonized populations played a vital role in Europe's so-called voyages of discovery, clearing paths and carrying equipment, and engaging in the collection, preparation, and identification of specimens and samples. In many instances, scientists drew on their superior local knowledge, and relied upon them to a degree that compels us to rethink the social relations of scientific accumulation during and beyond the nineteenth century. In this regard, the aim of this chapter is to centre convicts and penal colonies in the history of imperial knowledge production.

Indigenous Encounters

In the fifteenth and sixteenth centuries, during shipments in the Portuguese and Spanish empires, convicts undertook punitive voyages with multi-racial groups of settlers including also indentured servants, soldiers, and the enslaved. Evidently, they encountered the peoples already living in their American, African, and Pacific destinations. Because punitive relocation was a component of colonization, and because convicts were colonists, they are part of the history of settler colonialism. During Portuguese voyages of exploration, starting in the 1400s, ships' captains left convicts (*degredados*) convicted of serious crimes on the coasts of Brazil and west and southeast Africa. These men, known as *lançados* (renegades) were supposed to enter local societies, learn languages, and gain cultural knowledge. As Timothy J. Coates explains: 'They could then act as intermediaries when the Portuguese returned on the next voyage.' Simultaneously, and with a view to facilitating trade and commerce, the Portuguese took Africans back to Portugal.[6] The *lançados* played a vital

---

[5] On the history of exploration generally, see Felipe Fernández-Armesto, *Pathfinders: A Global History of Exploration* (London: W. W. Norton and Co., 2007), chapters 7–9; Dane Kennedy, ed., *Reinterpreting Exploration: the West in the World* (Oxford University Press, 2014).

[6] Timothy J. Coates, *Convicts and Orphans: Forced and State-sponsored Colonizers in the Portuguese Empire, 1550–1755* (Stanford University Press, 2001), 86–7. On cultural mediation more broadly, see Morgan, 'Encounters between British and "Indigenous" Peoples', 53.

role as cultural brokers, their influence evident in the widespread adoption of Cape Verde Creole as the language of trade. During the early-modern period, those Portuguese convicts who survived to complete their sentence settled permanently in the colonies, and the consequence was the creation of at least one community of Afro-Portuguese in West Africa. These *lançados* became successful traders (*tangomãos*). Across the Atlantic Ocean in Brazil, such convict intermediaries forged alliances with the survivors of shipwrecks, though little is known about what happened to these groups.[7]

The first Portuguese settlers in Brazil complained about convicts' 'debauched and scandalous relations with the Indians'. And so, the policy of deliberately creating *lançados* gave way to a repeat of Portuguese imperial history in North Africa and Madeira, which Coates describes as 'the controlled, directed use of *degredados*'.[8] This was particularly the case for the Estado da India (Portuguese Asia), which was the most important site of colonization before 1700. Most of the convicts served the Crown as soldiers, and after release or escape, they married or merged into the Luso-Indian communities then developing in Goa, Diu, Bengal, and Madras. Known as *renegados*, these former convicts were said to abandon Christianity, engage in trade and smuggling, and take service in the Mughal or other armies. Though not all soldiers were *degredados*, in the words of Coates: 'many, if not most, *renegados* were those who had little to keep them in the Portuguese world and the most to gain by leaving it'.[9] As political crisis enveloped Portuguese Asia from the 1660s onwards, connections between *degredados* and free populations ran so deep that the Portuguese started to offer pardons to all those convicted of crimes other than the four unpardonable offences (heresy, treason, counterfeiting, and sodomy). This was an attempt to tempt them back into the service of the Crown.[10]

Prior to the arrival of the first Europeans in the Americas, in the middle of the fifteenth century, there were hundreds of separate Indigenous groups spread across the continent, each with distinct cultural practices and speaking different languages. However, as the Iberian empires landed and moved inland, followed by British and French settlers, disease and violence quickly decimated their communities. Eric R. Wolfe terms this

---

[7] Coates, *Convicts and Orphans*, 86–7. Coates notes that *lançado* is rooted in the Portuguese verb *lançar*, to throw, that is, here, a person who has thrown himself to the other side. He defines *tangomãos* as traders who lived as Africans. The state of Brazil was that of the southern two-thirds of what is now the Federative Republic of Brazil.
[8] Coates, *Convicts and Orphans*, 87.
[9] Coates, *Convicts and Orphans*, 79, 86–93 (quote, 89).
[10] Coates, *Convicts and Orphans*, 92.

'the great dying', noting the 'immediate and catastrophic decline' that the earliest Spanish and Portuguese colonists unleashed.[11] The first peoples to be impacted by colonization were those living on Caribbean islands, followed by the inhabitants of Central, South, and North America. Indeed, taking the example of the area that is now the USA, it is likely that by the end of the nineteenth century there were just 240,000 Indigenous inhabitants, compared to a 5,000,000-strong population at first contact.[12]

The Spanish Empire took a variety of approaches to Indigenous relations. On the one hand, it forcefully recruited Indigenous Americans, sending them to work on plantations or impressing them into the army. For instance, the Spanish enslaved Kalinago (Carib) labour from the island of Barbados. Kalinago worked or served alongside convicts (*forzados*) and enslaved Africans. It repeated this pattern in the *presidios* of Mexico as well as in Chile – and further afield in the Philippines. Following judicial trial for crimes such as cattle rustling, or as a punitive measure in the face of refusal to convert to Christianity, the Spanish also sentenced Indigenous peoples to convict labour. They laboured with *forzados* from peninsular Spain, the Americas, and the Pacific in the empire's *obrajes* (textile factories). And yet, on the other hand, and while the Spanish brought convicts and Indigenous peoples together in the context of the army and factory, they used *forzados* to create a *cordon sanitaire* around potentially hostile Indigenous populations, as well as to mark frontiers with Portuguese territory. Paradoxically, this created opportunities for convicts to forge or cement relations with Indigenous Americans. Like the Portuguese in the Estado da India, frequently they escaped, finding refuge with Indigenous peoples, establishing new relationships, and sometimes getting married. Stephanie Mawson writes that though Europeans were essential to the subjugation of Indigenous peoples, they could also destabilize the imperial project. Thus, 'the boundaries between agents and subjects of empire blurred'.[13]

During the seventeenth century, the British also shipped several thousand white convicts to the Caribbean island of Barbados, which was first

---

[11] Eric R. Wolfe, *Europe and the People without History* (Berkeley: University of California Press, 1982), 133–4.

[12] Benjamin Madley, 'Reexamining the American Genocide Debate: Meaning, Historiography, and New Methods', *American Historical Review*, 120, 1 (2015), 98 (98–139).

[13] Stephanie Mawson, 'Convicts or *Conquistadores*? Spanish Soldiers in the Seventeenth-Century Pacific', *Past and Present*, 232, 1 (2016), 94–5, 117 (quote, 95) (87–125). See also Christian G. De Vito, 'The Spanish Empire, 1500–1898', in Clare Anderson, ed., *A Global History of Convicts and Penal Colonies* (London: Bloomsbury, 2018), 75, 80, 86 (65–95).

inhabited by English settlers in 1627. From the 1640s, the British used Indigenous Americans, including enslaved Arawaks from the Guianas, to clear woodland and teach settlers and convicts cultivation skills. Subsequently, the British enslaved other groups of Indigenous workers, from the mainland or other Caribbean islands, and imported them into the colony.[14] The British used Indigenous workers in Barbados for a relatively short period. Because they were inadequate in number, following Thomas Cromwell's invasion of Ireland (1649–53), the British transported more substantial numbers of prisoners of war, vagrants, and convicted felons. Also received in Barbados until the 1660s were thieves and sex workers from Scotland; groups of Monmouth rebels, after the failed rebellion of 1685; and the London poor. Hamish Maxwell-Stewart shows that transportation and indenture in the Caribbean 'helped to shape later attitudes to labour, aiding the subsequent shift to chattel slavery'. Following the enslavement of Indigenous populations, in the mid-1600s British settlers used indentured labour (including convicts sold into indenture) to clear land for sugar production. Planters contracted such labourers to work for short periods, and so they were cheaper than the purchase of enslaved people.[15] They saw convicts as disposable assets, and so subjected them to extremely harsh treatment. Convicts thus enabled the accumulation of the capital necessary for investment in enslaved labour. This began in earnest in the 1660s, when the demand for European labour declined. 'In Barbados', Maxwell-Stewart writes, 'convictism was the ideological precursor of plantation racism.' The British replicated this pattern in Jamaica, which received convicts until 1717.[16] Elsewhere in the Caribbean Sea, Indigenous Caribs formed alliances with maroon (runaway) slaves and went to war with European settlers. There were two full blown wars in eighteenth-century Saint Vincent (1769–73, 1795–6), for instance, leading to the mass deportations described in Chapter 4.[17]

In Britain's eastern colonies in North America, during the same period, colonists perpetrated extreme violence against Indigenous people. This included outright massacres, and bounty programmes for heads and scalps. Indigenous people were dispossessed of land, kidnapped, enslaved, deported, and killed by unfamiliar diseases, such as smallpox and measles.

---

[14] Jerome S. Handler, 'The Amerindian slave population in Barbados in the seventeenth and early eighteenth centuries', *Caribbean Studies*, 8 (1969), 38–64.

[15] Hamish Maxwell-Stewart, 'Transportation from Britain and Ireland, 1615–1875', in Anderson, ed., *A Global History of Convicts and Penal Colonies*, 188–90 (183–210). Barbados became a Crown colony in 1663.

[16] Maxwell-Stewart, 'Transportation from Britain and Ireland', 191–2 (quote, 191).

[17] Michael Craton, *Testing the Chains: Resistance to Slavery in the British West Indies* (Ithaca, NY: Cornell University Press, 1982), 145–53, 190–4, 204–7.

Colonization forced them into competition for resources and many suffered from malnourishment.[18] Those who survived had no choice but to adapt, and they did so in creative ways. They commonly came together to form new communities, groupings which Philip D. Morgan describes as 'an amalgam of survivors, refugees, and war captives'.[19] Fresh groupings and identities in the areas under British control evolved, as Indigenous Americans adapted to form new societies such as the Powhatan in the Chesapeake.[20] During this period, at least 50,000 British and Irish convicts were shipped to the Americas, where they were concentrated in the Chesapeake Bay and in Maryland and Virginia.[21] Maxwell-Stewart has shown that the courts set their penal terms of either seven or fourteen years in order to make them competitive purchases compared to slaves.[22] As in the Caribbean islands, most were indentured into servitude on plantations, and after their term of employment expired many married and settled in the colonies. We know very little about the nature of convict relationships with Indigenous Americans, in regard to trade, intimacy, or other areas of economic, social, and cultural exchange. As colonists, though, convicts were part of the larger history of death, displacement, and expropriation. Indeed, the British even armed a few convicts and sent them into war, including in South Carolina against the Yamasee in 1715–17. Following military defeat, the British then incorporated Indigenous Americans into the new settled colonies. In the areas in which these convicts were most concentrated, Virginia, Maryland, and North Carolina, for instance, they commonly sold Indigenous people into enslavement or indentured servitude. Indeed, this was the fate of the Nanzaticos of Virginia.[23] Indigenous Americans, enslaved Africans, and transported convicts thus co-existed in a complex knot of displacement and exploitation. In the Atlantic world, as Gwenda Morgan and Peter Rushton note: 'The creation of empires brought banishment and forced labour together in the eighteenth century.'[24]

---

[18] Madley, 'Reexamining the American Genocide Debate', 100–1, 109, 114–16, 120–6; Wolfe, *Europe and the People Without History*, 133–4.
[19] Morgan, 'Encounters between British and "Indigenous" Peoples', 48.
[20] Morgan, 'Encounters between British and "Indigenous" Peoples', 48.
[21] A. Roger Ekirch, *Bound for America: The transportation of British Convicts to the Colonies, 1718–1775* (Oxford: Clarendon Press, 1987); Gwenda Morgan and Peter Rushton, *Eighteenth-Century Criminal Transportation: The Formation of the Criminal Atlantic* (Basingstoke: Palgrave, 2004).
[22] Hamish Maxwell-Stewart, 'Transportation from Britain and Ireland 1615–1875'.
[23] John Docker, 'Are Settler-Colonies Inherently Genocidal: Re-reading Lemkin', in Moses, ed., *Empire, Colony, Genocide*, 94–5 (81–101); Gwenda Morgan and Peter Rushton, *Banishment in the Early Atlantic World: Convicts, Rebels and Slaves* (London: Bloomsbury, 2013), 93.
[24] Morgan and Rushton, *Banishment in the Early Atlantic World*, 232–3.

After the Declaration of Independence in 1776, the USA no longer admitted convicts. As Britain searched for a new transportation destination, it turned first to West Africa. In the mid-1770s and again in 1780, the British enlisted convicts into the army and sent them to the garrison of Gorée Island, off the coast of Senegambia, and to other slave forts along the coast. They became implicated in British and Dutch rivalry and worked as guards for the newly enslaved. In these areas, there was extensive contact with African populations, including through sexual relationships between convicts and Africans, and trade with the wealthy Gold Coast Fante. As explained in Chapter 4, by the mid-1780s, the British planned to divert convicts to sites in Africa, but these schemes either failed to get off the ground or ended in disaster.[25] It was against this background that the British despatched the First Fleet of convicts to the Antipodes in 1787. There had been minimal Indigenous–settler contact by the time the British established the first convict settlement in Botany Bay a year later. Penal transportation devastated Indigenous populations, and instigated profound changes in pre-colonial Australian nations, societies, and cultures. Pre-contact, hundreds of Indigenous societies inhabited the continent, speaking at least two hundred distinct languages. There is ample evidence of Indigenous peoples' agency and creativity in their response to the British settlement. Not only did they find advantage for themselves in assisting British expeditions into the interior, they took employment as trackers, returning escaped convicts to their British officers, and worked as servants in colonial households.[26] Their resistance was also widespread, and included foiling settlers through their superior bush craft, raiding settler farms, and spearing livestock.[27] However, from the first years of colonization, Australian Indigenous populations were subject to extreme frontier and domestic violence; made victims of punitive expeditions; decimated by diseases such as smallpox, tuberculosis, and measles; and forced into competition for diminishing natural resources. Perhaps as many as eighty per cent of Indigenous peoples died after the arrival of the First Fleet of convicts. Thus, Indigenous peoples experienced penal colonization as nothing less than invasion.[28]

---

[25] Emma Christopher, *A Merciless Place: The Lost Story of Britain's Convict Disaster in Africa* (Oxford University Press, 2010), 153, 243–4. See also Emma Christopher and Hamish Maxwell-Stewart, 'Convict transportation in global context, c. 1700–88', in Bashford and MacIntyre, eds., *The Cambridge History of Australia, Volume 1*, 75–7 (68–90).

[26] Henry Reynolds, *With the White People: The Crucial Role of Aborigines in the Exploration and Development of Australia* (Ringwood, VIC: Penguin, 1990), 41, 46–50.

[27] Banivanua Mar and Edmonds, 'Indigenous and settler relations', 342–3. See also Reynolds, *With the White People*, 42–6.

[28] Banivanua Mar and Edmonds, 'Indigenous and Settler Relations', 342–3.

As Tracey Banivanua Mar and Penelope Edmonds explain, from the late eighteenth century in New South Wales: 'Contact, conciliation and conflict would always be closely intertwined.'[29] Indeed, in 1814, Governor Lachlan Macquarie established a 'native institution' at Parramatta near Sydney, its purpose to 'effect the civilization of the Aborigines' by training children as farmers and labourers. Macquarie also organized a 'native feast', in a related attempt to bring Indigenous people into contact with the settlement. However, this and the 'native institution' failed. His successor, Sir Thomas Brisbane, later proclaimed martial law, which in effect sanctioned violence on the colonial frontier.[30] Convicts and settlers subjected Indigenous women to sexual violence and physical attacks. These sometimes occurred in camps, which were supposed to be spaces of racial containment but were borderlands, or contact zones, that revealed the asymmetrical power that existed between European men and Indigenous women.[31] The same narrative of 'uneasy coexistence' followed by 'escalated tensions' unfolded in Van Diemen's Land. Famously, in 1828 Lieutenant-Governor George Arthur, one of the architects of the fate of Bussa's rebels (Chapter 4), issued a proclamation dividing the island in two. It prohibited Indigenous peoples from entering settler districts without a pass. Frontier violence escalated, and so Arthur declared martial law. The consequence of this was the decade-long Black War of 1824–34. In 1830, more than one thousand armed convicts joined troops to conduct a military operation known as the 'Black Line', clearing Indigenous peoples from settled land. Indigenous leaders played a key role in negotiating the end of the war. In 1830, Arthur appointed 'Protector of Aborigines', George Augustus Robinson. He worked closely with Truganini, a Nuenonne woman from Bruny Island, travelling around Van Diemen's Land to persuade Indigenous peoples to move to a new settlement on Flinders Island in the Bass Strait. The plan was that they would convert to Christianity and work in settled agriculture. By 1838, just 60 Indigenous Tasmanians, out of an original population of 6,000–8,000, were still alive.[32] A narrative of inevitable 'extinction' evolved during this period, influenced by what was described at the time as the

---

[29] Banivanua Mar and Edmonds, 'Indigenous and settler relations', 342.
[30] Banivanua Mar and Edmonds, 'Indigenous and settler relations', 342, 344–5.
[31] Penelope Edmonds, 'The Intimate, Urbanising Frontier: Native Camps and Settler Colonialism's Violent Array of Spaces around Early Melbourne', in Banivanua Mar and Edmonds, eds., *Making Settler Colonial Space* 140–1 (129–54).
[32] Banivanua Mar and Edmonds, 'Indigenous and Settler Relations', 346–50, 352–4. See also N. J. B. Plomley, ed., *Weep in Silence: A History of the Flinders Island Aboriginal settlement with the Flinders Island journal of George Augustus Robinson, 1835–1839* (Sandy Bay, TAS: Blubber Head Press, 1987).

disappearance of the races of North America.[33] The pattern of Indigenous–settler relations viewed in New South Wales and Van Diemen's Land was later repeated in Moreton Bay, Queensland; the Swan River colony in Western Australia; and, in the Port Phillip District of South Australia. In 1858, the colony of Victoria created reserved land, also known as stations or missions, for Indigenous peoples, which was a means of controlling both residence and mobility.[34] As I have argued elsewhere, there were empire-wide discussions about Indigenous management, in which commentators compared and juxtaposed places like Van Diemen's Land and the Americas. In these, the demise of the so-called dying races was 'tragic but inevitable after first contact with Europeans'.[35]

In the aftermath of the Black War, the innovative penal reformer Alexander Maconochie, discussed in Chapter 7, became private secretary to Arthur's successor as governor, Sir John Franklin. In parallel with his radical ideas on convict rehabilitation, Maconochie outlined ideas for the creation of a 'native police force', which he believed would not only be effective on the frontiers of the settlement, but would inculcate 'European manners and civilization ... order, concert and decorum'.[36] Subsequently, not only were Indigenous peoples employed in colonial police forces, governments established 'native' units in Port Phillip (1842), New South Wales (1848), and Queensland (1849). Indigenous men and women were also targeted for removal to isolated places, including in Western Australia, that resembled the separate stations set up for 'troublesome' convicts. Though the desire to avoid violence motivated Maconochie, these and other measures meant that by the 1860s the government and colonists were in open warfare with Indigenous populations.[37]

There are parallels with the Americas. Indeed, Benjamin Madley argues that in the early seventeenth century, the theory of *vacuum domicilium*, or 'empty domicile', justified conquest and colonization. In Madley's words, this implied that 'American Indians did not inhabit

---

[33] Ann Curthoys, 'Genocide in Tasmania: The History of an Idea', in Moses, ed., *Empire, Colony, Genocide*, 232–7 (229–52). As Curthoys notes, the population of modern Australia includes numerous Tasmanians of Indigenous heritage.

[34] Banivanua Mar and Edmonds, 'Indigenous and Settler Relations', 346–50, 352–4. See also James Boyce, *Van Diemen's Land* (Melbourne, VIC: Black Inc., 2008).

[35] Clare Anderson, 'Convicts, Carcerality and Cape Colony Connections in the 19th Century', *Journal of Southern African Studies*, 42, 3 (2016), 434–5 (429–42).

[36] Cited in Reynolds, *With the White People*, 49.

[37] Ann Curthoys, 'The Beginnings of Transportation in Western Australia: Banishment, Forced Labour, and Punishment at the Aboriginal Prison on Rottnest Island before 1850', *Studies in Western Australian History*, 34 (2020), 59–78; Reynolds, *With the White People*, 40–84. Note that Queensland was part of New South Wales until 1859, when it separated from the colony.

their homelands fully enough, either in population density or in economic development, to justify their having legal ownership, particularly in so-called "empty" areas.'[38] It is useful to think of penal colonization in the Australian colonies as in part motivated by a related idea that the continent was *terra nullius*, or 'nobody's land'. Exceptionally in the British Empire, in the Australian colonies *terra nullius* was enshrined in law, and persisted following Federation in 1901 right up to 1922. The origins of the concept of *terra nullius* might be explained as a consequence of Captain James Cook's 1770 report on the continent's sparse population, the absence of settled agriculture, and crucially Indigenous peoples' disinterest in trade which meant that land could not be purchased from them. However, the first settlers found not only that Indigenous peoples were more numerous than Cook had represented, but that there were established practices of land ownership and property rights. Nonetheless, and connected to colonial ideas of Indigenous peoples as primitive, in a series of legal cases *terra nullius* remained intact. This was because, as Stuart Banner writes, all landowners held land as a consequence of previous government land grants. These were premised on the law of *terra nullius* in which they had a vested interest.[39]

Madhumita Mazumdar and Vishvajit Pandya have shown that the idea of *terra nullius* is relevant to another context, the Andaman Islands of British India, which was a penal colony between 1858 and 1945.[40] The East India Company (EIC) first tried and failed to establish a settlement in the Andamans in the 1790s, during a period when it governed large parts of the India subcontinent. Convicts were not included in the initial colonizing party but were sent later following high death rates among the free Bengali settlers. Having tried to improve conditions by shifting location, without success, the EIC abandoned the Islands, sending the convicts on to its penal settlement in Penang and returning the surviving free settlers to Bengal. But the Andamans lay at the centre of Company trade routes in the Bay of Bengal, and the British did not lose interest in their colonization. The chance came in the aftermath of the 1857 Indian Revolt, during which

---

[38] Madley, 'Reexamining the American Genocide Debate', 100.

[39] Stuart Banner, 'Why *Terra Nullius*? Anthropology and Property Law in Early Australia', *Law and History Review*, 23, 1 (2005), 95–132. See also Merete Borch, 'Rethinking the Origins of *Terra Nullius*', *Australian Historical Studies*, 32, 117 (2001), 222–39; Alan Frost, 'New South Wales as *Terra Nullius*: The British Denial of Aboriginal Land Rights', *Historical Studies*, 19, 77 (1981), 513–23. Shino Konishi and Maria Nugent also note Cook's voyages, in 'Newcomers, c. 1600-1800', in Bashford and MacIntyre, eds., *The Cambridge History of Australia, Volume 1*, 54–60 (43–67).

[40] Madhumita Mazumdar, 'Dwelling in the Fluid Spaces: The Matuas of the Andaman Islands', in Clare Anderson, Madhumita Mazumdar, and Vishvajit Pandya, *New Histories of the Andaman Islands: Landscape, place and identity in the Bay of Bengal, c. 1790–2012* (Cambridge University Press, 2014), 30 (citing Pandya).

mutineers and rebels damaged or destroyed jails across the north of the subcontinent. With over 20,000 prisoners on the loose, and many more tried and convicted for offences connected to the revolt, this produced a penal crisis of unprecedented scale. Thus, with the transfer of the governance of India from the EIC to the British Crown, the government of India transported the first batches of Indian convicts to the Islands in 1858.[41]

Unlike the Australian colonies, the Andamans never enshrined the doctrine of *terra nullius* in law. However, as Mazumdar and Pandya have demonstrated, during the entire period of British rule, the idea was 'subtly and insidiously invoked through survey reports, administrative policies, and schemes for colonization and development'.[42] When the British first invaded the Islands, there were around 7500 people living there, in four major population clusters: the Sentinelese, the Jarawa, the Onge, and the Andamanese (sometimes called the Great Andamanese). There were twelve dialect groups. For the Great Andamanese in particular, colonization led to dramatic population decline, and caused profound disruptions to culture and society. The British subjected them to kidnap and confinement, placing them in 'civilizing' institutions called Andaman Homes. They were the victims of intense violence, warfare, and punitive missions. Newly introduced diseases, including syphilis, had a severe impact on populations, including through producing high rates of stillbirth. As in the Australian colonies, the British switched between attempts to incorporate Islanders into the settlement, to keep them out of the settlement and on 'reserved' land, or to avoid contact altogether. They encouraged them to drink alcohol and smoke tobacco which meant that they became dependent on contact with Europeans.[43] But there existed connections between the penal colonies of the Andamans and Australia that go beyond a comparison of policy. Satadru Sen writes: 'Administrators in the Andamans drew overlapping and not always consistent conclusions from Australian (and especially Tasmanian) history. Very occasionally, they saw it as a model that they might emulate'.[44] In the aftermath of Darwin's *On The Origin of Species*, of particular significance were ideas about where

---

[41] Anderson, *The Indian Uprising of 1857–8: Prisons, prisoners and rebellion* (London: Anthem Press, 2007), 80–4, 118–21, 129–33, 144.
[42] Mazumdar, 'Dwelling in the Fluid Spaces', 30.
[43] Sen, *Savagery and Colonialism in the Indian Ocean*. See also Clare Anderson, 'Colonization, Kidnap And Confinement in the Andamans Penal Colony, 1771–1864', *Journal of Historical Geography*, 37, 1 (2011), 68–81; Clare Anderson, 'Writing Indigenous Women's Lives in the Bay of Bengal, 1789–1906', *Journal of Social History*, 45, 2 (2011), 480–96; Vishvajit Pandya, *In the Forest: Visual and Material Worlds of the Andaman Islanders 1858–2000* (Lanham, MD: University Press of America, 2009).
[44] Satadru Sen, 'Lost between Africa and Tasmania: Racializing the Andamanese', *Journal of Colonialism and Colonial History*, 10, 3 (2009), doi:10.1353/cch.0.0090.

Andaman Islanders were positioned within global hierarchies of race, whether they could provide insights into the origins of humankind, and whether they were a 'dying race', doomed to 'extinction'. Andaman administrators critiqued the Australian colonies for 'a colonialism that had failed to insulate and protect natives from settlers'. The government-appointed Officer in Charge of the Andamanese, M. V. Portman, compared the impacts of white convicts in the Australian colonies with those of Indian and Burmese convicts and white soldiers in the Andamans.[45]

Contact between the penal colony and Andaman Islanders existed at two overlapping scales, involving British administrators and transportation convicts. As Sen shows, Indian and Burmese convicts were at the forefront of settler colonial contact, because they worked in the Andaman Homes, orphanage, nursery, schools, and hospitals. He calls this colonial contact zone, 'the clearing'.[46] Repeatedly, into the 1860s, tales emerged of the existence of secret islands inhabited by Islanders, Malay fishermen, and runaway convicts. But despite this suggestion of the existence of spaces of mutually peaceful domicile, the coexistence of convicts and Islanders was always fraught with contradiction and ambivalence. Islanders sometimes killed escaped convicts or returned them to the settlement. They also attacked guards but left convicts alone. One element of settler-colonial relations was the collection of ethnographic objects, such as baskets and jewellery. Islanders came to produce these specifically for sale to administrators and other collectors.[47] Moreover, as Sen writes: 'The Andamanese maneuvered between licit and illicit relationships with convicts, adopting continent positions of alliance and animosity, intimacy and distance.'[48] Male settlers had sex with female Islanders, who gave birth to children – revealing the idea of 'extinction' to be as erroneous in the Andamans as it was in Van Diemen's Land.[49] One escaped convict, 1857 mutineer Dudhnath Tewari, left a woman pregnant when he returned to the penal colony from a year-long escape. Another escaped mutineer, Sham, reported upon his return to the penal colony: 'I was entreated by the women to have connection with them'.[50] Here, as earlier,

---

[45] Sen, *Savagery and Colonialism in the Indian Ocean*, 35–42 (quote, 41).
[46] Sen, *Savagery and Colonialism in the Indian Ocean*, 176.
[47] Claire Wintle, *Colonial Collecting and Display: Encounters with Material Culture from the Andaman and Nicobar Islands* (Oxford: Berghahn Books, 2013), 25–30.
[48] Sen, *Savagery and Colonialism in the Indian Ocean*, 157–9 (quote, 159).
[49] Sen, *Savagery and Colonialism in the Indian Ocean*, 177–9.
[50] LMA H01/ST/NC/17/9: Statement of convict no. 2467 named Sham son of Sarung, Moosulman … escaped from the settlement … on the 2nd July 1859, and … captured by his voluntary return … on the 2 August 1859; IOR P/206/61: statement of convict no. 276 Doodnath Tewarry, 26 May 1859. On Dudhnath Tewari, see the full discussion in Sen, *Savagery and Colonialism in the Indian Ocean*, 159–70.

we do not have archives that enable insights into the perspectives of women themselves.

Other comparisons can be drawn between the Andamans and two other sites of contemporary penal colonies: French New Caledonia (1863–1931) and Japanese Hokkaido (1881–1908). The existence of both represented substantial encroachments onto Indigenous land, belonging to Kanak and Ainu people, respectively. Alice Bullard explains that the French embarked on a 'civilizing process' in New Caledonia that required the creation of a dehumanized, 'savage' population that was subordinate to colonial rule. This was delivered through the work of administrators, missionaries, anthropologists, and ethnographers.[51] From 1867, the Kanak were placed in *tribus* (reserved land). Bullard states: 'Under the legal fiction of *tribus* the colonial government was able to ignore the Kanak's highly developed system of private property and to pursue the expropriation of Kanak land'.[52] From 1887, with the passing of the *côde indigénat* (Indigenous code), the French established crimes, punishments, and judicial authority specific to the Kanak. The code also compelled the Kanak to live and work in New Caledonia, and so underpinned the production of a supply of forced labour for the colonial state.[53] Conditions on the *tribus* were poor, and the impact of colonial violence and newly imported diseases were devastating. The estimated population in 1887 was 42,000. By 1901, it had fallen to 27,768.[54] Despite this, the French also to some degree assimilated the Kanak into the colony. Not only did Indigenous women have children with French settlers (we do not know if such intimacy was voluntary or coerced), Indigenous men were employed in a native police force charged with returning escaped convicts. The latter played on Kanak 'savagery', for the French administration encouraged them to beat convicts before stringing them to poles by their hands and feet and carrying them back to the nearest camp.[55]

Routinely, during this period, the French sent so-called troublesome Kanak to offshore locations, including the Belep and Loyalty Islands, and the Île des Pins. This accelerated after the war of 1878–9, which broke out after several Indigenous groups, led by Chief Ataï, attacked settlers in La Foa-Fonwhari and Bouloupari. The French greatly feared the spread of insurrection and retaliated with great force. They killed Ataï and almost

---

[51] Alice Bullard, *Exile to Paradise: Savagery and civilization in Paris and the South Pacific, 1790–1800* (Stanford University Press, 2000), chapter 2.
[52] Bullard, *Exile to Paradise*, 222. [53] Bullard, *Exile to Paradise*, 222, 226.
[54] Stephen A. Toth, *Beyond Papillon: The French overseas penal colonies, 1854–1952* (Lincoln: University of Nebraska Press, 2006), 106.
[55] Bullard, *Exile to Paradise*, 210–11, 228–9.

800 of his followers and deported 1000 more. Destinations included mainland institutions such as the 'native depot', and an orphanage, asylum, and 'farm depot'. The French sent at least forty Kanak to Tahiti and to the island of Poulo Condore in Cochinchina. Similar deportations followed later Indigenous 'plots' and conflict, especially from 1887 to 1907, which represented the main period of post-war French conquest in New Caledonia. The French feared that if the Kanak associated with lower-class released convicts (*libérés*), they would lose respect for Europeans. Thus, segregation via the *code indigénat* became a means of keeping convicts and ex-convicts apart from Indigenous peoples and imposing social discipline. But it was insubordination, insolence, threatening behaviour, refusal to pay taxes, and attempts to return to confiscated land that were the most common reasons for internment. Adrian Muckle argues that these were associated with 'widespread resistance to colonization and the extension of the colonial frontier'. At the same time, the Kanak themselves used the *code* as a means of self-governance and expelling disruptive elements from their communities.[56]

In the case of Japan, following land surveys in the 1880s the Meiji regime began to relocate the island peoples of Hokkaido, the Ainu, before the first convicts arrived. Despite nineteenth-century claims that the island was 'barren land' (Chapter 3), penal transportation to Hokkaido had a profound impact on the Ainu. By 1890, the Japanese government had forced many Ainu to move out of their villages and onto reserved land. Their territories then became settlements and co-operative farms for immigrants, as did prison land and farms when convict transportation to each location ceased.[57] Minako Sakata shows that, paradoxically, Ainu relocation not only resulted in segregation but encouraged assimilation, by encouraging settled farming in place of hunter-gathering. The removal of the Ainu accelerated following the introduction of convicts in the early 1880s, because road-building programmes cut through their lands. Moreover, government sold some of it to prospectors and settlers. Also, and as in the Australian colonies, the Andamans, and New Caledonia, the Japanese paid Indigenous peoples to return escaped convicts. According to Sakata, the Ainu suffered greatly at the hands of escaped convicts, and

---

[56] Adrian Muckle, 'Troublesome Chiefs and Disorderly Subjects: The *Indigénat* and the Internment of Kanak in New Caledonia (1887–1928)', *French Colonial History*, 11 (2010), 131–60 (quote, 142). The *indigénat* was introduced in Algeria and most French colonies after 1881. *Libérés* were convicts who had served out their sentence, but under the French law of *doublage*, if transported for eight years or more, were compelled to remain in the colony for a term equivalent to their original sentence.

[57] Minako Sakata, 'Japan in the Eighteenth and Nineteenth Centuries', in Anderson, ed., *A Global History of Convicts and Penal Colonies*, 326–8 (307–35).

it seems clear that they retaliated against Japanese occupation.[58] Indeed, perhaps the island's most famous transportation convict, Rokunosuke Koyama, noted in his memoirs that he had met an Ainu man in Kushiro central prison, imprisoned for arson. Koyama reported that the man had taught him some Ainu words.[59]

The 'Voyages of Discovery' and Scientific Collecting

At the turn of the nineteenth century and into the 1820s, several French naval officers visited New South Wales, under secret political briefs. Notable among them were Jean-François de la Pérouse (1788), Nicolas Baudin (1802), Louis de Freycinet (1819), Hyacinthe de Bougainville (1824), Louis Isidore Duperrey (1824), and Jules Dumont d'Urville (1826). The last two were under government directions to locate a suitable spot for a French penal colony in New South Wales, Swan River (Western Australia), or New Zealand. The different representations of the colony in the published accounts of these French visitors at once both reflected and informed the sharp division of views on the merits of penal transportation that existed in the time.[60] For instance, François Péron, who voyaged with Baudin, published a book that was used by pro-transportation minister, M. Forestier, in his 1819 report to the French

---

[58] Sakata, 'Japan in the Eighteenth and Nineteenth Centuries', 326–8.
[59] Rokunosuke Koyama, *Ikijigoku* (1909), in Kiyoshi Kanzaki, ed., *Meiji bungaku zenshū*, volume 96 (Tokyo: Chikuma Shobō, 1967), 188 (151–201). Thank you to Minako Sakata for supplying this reference. The wholesale removal of Indigenous peoples in some ways anticipated the USSR's 'special settlements', to which whole ethnic groups were sent. See Lynne Viola, 'The Other Archipelago: Kulak Deportations to the North in 1930', *Slavic Review*, 60, 4 (2001), 730–55; Lynne Viola, *The Unknown Gulag: The Lost World of Stalin's Special Settlements* (Oxford University Press, 2007).
[60] Colin Dyer, *The French Explorers and Sydney* (St Lucia: University of Queensland Press, 2009); Robert J. King, 'What brought Lapérouse to Botany Bay?' *Journal of the Royal Australian Historical Society*, 85, 2 (1999), 140–47; Marc Serge Rivière, 'Distant Echoes of the Enlightenment: Private and Public Observations on Convict Life by Baudin's Disgraced Officer, Hyacinthe de Bougainville (1825)', *Australian Journal of French Studies*, 41, 2 (2004), 171–85; John West-Sooby, ed., *Discovery and Empire: The French in the South Seas* (University of Adelaide Press, 2013). See also John Dunmore, ed., *The Journal of Jean-François de Galaup de la Pérouse 1785–1788, Volume 1* (London: The Hakluyt Society, 1994); *Voyages of Discovery to Southern Lands by François Péron, continued by Louis de Freycinet*, second ed. 1824, translated from the French by Christine Cornell, introduction by Anthony J. Brown (Adelaide: Friends of the State Library of South Australia, 2006); *French Designs on Colonial New South Wales: François Péron's Memoir on the English Settlements in New Holland, Van Diemen's Land and the Archipelagos of the Great Pacific Ocean*, translated and edited with an introduction, notes, and Appendices by Jean Fornasiero and John West-Sooby (Adelaide, SA: Friends of the State Library of South Australia, 2014); Louis Freycinet, *Reflections on New South Wales, 1788–1839*, edited by Tom B. Cullity (Potts Point, NSW: Hordern House, 2001).

parliament.[61] In contrast, the critic of transportation Charles Lucas interviewed Louis de Freycinet after his return from Australia in 1820. De Freycinet regaled Lucas with tales of absconders and bushrangers, surmising that convicts 'led an immoral life', and that they had not been reformed by their transportation. Lucas later became French inspector of prisons and was the architect of the country's numerous agricultural colonies for juveniles, which began famously with the opening of Mettray. Later, he was an important figure in the establishment of the 1872 International Penitentiary Congress, analysed in Chapter 7. He viewed these regular meetings as means for what was described at the time as the 'international interchange of ideas for the moral progress of humanity'.[62] De Bougainville's views lay somewhere in between those of these two men. His ambivalence is captured in his claims that convicts were degraded, and yet 'New South Wales is a master-piece of the spirit of colonisation, and all civilised peoples should strive to imitate rather than to destroy such a beautiful establishment.'[63] Péron, who was employed as

---

[61] The original text is: François Péron, *Voyage de decouvertes aux terres australes: exécuté par ordre de sa Majesté, l'Empereur et Roi, sur les corvettes le Géographe, le Naturaliste et la goëlette le Casuarina, pendant les années 1800, 1801, 1802, 1803 et 1804* (Paris: L'Imprimerie Impériale, 1807). In English translation: Francois Péron, *A Voyage of Discovery to the Southern Hemisphere: Performed by Order of the Emperor Napoleon during the Years 1801, 1802, 1803, 1804, One of the Naturalists Appointed for the Expedition ... translated from the French* (London: Richard Phillips, 1809). Note that the leader of the expedition, Baudin, died before the ships returned to France, and Péron died shortly afterwards. De Freycinet completed volume 2 of the manuscript. See *French Designs on Colonial New South Wales: François Péron's Memoir*, 108.

[62] Rivière, 'Distant Echoes of the Enlightenment', 174. Charles Lucas was well known for his work *Du système penal et du système répressif en general, de la peine de mort en particulier* (Paris: Charles Béchet, 1827). He read a paper at the opening of the 1872 congress. See Reverend Nehemiah Pierce, *Origin, Organization and Opening Addresses of the International Prison Congress, January 1 1873* (Springfield, IL: publisher unknown, 1873), 80; Wines, *Report on the International Penitentiary Congress of London*, 1. Numerous anti-transportation contemporaries expressed debts of gratitude to him, including Alm. Lepelletier de la Sarthe, *Système Pénitentiaire: Le Bagne, La Prison Cellulaire, La Déportation* (Le Mans: Mannoyer, 1853); Pilorgerie, *Histoire de Botany Bay*. On Mettray, see Ceri Crossley, 'Using and Transforming the French Countryside: The "Colonies Agricoles" (1820–1850)', *French Studies* 44, 1 (1991), 36–54; Luc Forlivesi, Georges-François Pottier, and Sophie Chassat, *Éduquer et punir. La colonie agricole et pénitentiaire de Mettray (1839–1937)* (Presses Universitaires de Rennes, 2005); Ann Laura Stoler, *Duress: Imperial Durabilities in Our Times* (Durham, NC: Duke University Press, 2016), chapter 3.

[63] Dyer, The French Explorers and Sydney, 138, citing M. le Baron de Bougainville, *Journal de la navigation autour du globe de la frégate La Thétis et de la corvette L'espérance pendant les années 1824, 1825 et 1826* (2 volumes) (Paris: Althus Bertrand, 1837). Bougainville had previously visited New South Wales, with the Baudin expedition of 1802: Rivière, 'Distant Echoes of the Enlightenment', 177.

a naturalist on Baudin's voyage, advocated a complete French takeover of it.[64] If first-hand experience of New South Wales informed French debates about the desirability or otherwise of establishing penal colonies, the French engaged convicts in their voyages of discovery. Indeed, the British government allocated d'Urville five convicts to help prepare his ship for departure from Hobart to the Polar regions. These convicts also guided a French party to the top of Mount Wellington, where it gathered plant specimens. One of the men, M. Dumas, was too sick to go on to the Antarctic, and stayed behind in Hobart where he joined the Tasmanian Natural History Society.[65] French accounts of these voyages also noted numerous encounters with Indigenous Australians.[66]

Charles Darwin's celebrated global voyages of *The Beagle*, 1831–6, which are among the most important scientific expeditions in history, could be represented as not solely the genesis of the account of evolution published as *On The Origin of Species*, but as a worldwide tour of sites of punitive relocation: past, present, and future. This is because the ship stopped not just at Brazil's Fernando de Noronha, as mentioned in Chapter 1, but also in Salvador (site of numerous Portuguese convict *presidios*), Tierra del Fuego (where Argentina's penal colony of Ushuaia was later situated), and the following Spanish convict locations: the Falkland Islands (Malvinas), the Galápagos archipelago, and the Canary Islands. Darwin also called at Britain's Australian penal colonies of New South Wales and Van Diemen's Land, and the British colony of Mauritius, which imported Indian convicts from the EIC presidencies of Bengal and Bombay during the first half of the nineteenth century.[67]

Darwin acknowledged the convict presence in many of the locations that had been or were then sites of transportation. The published account

[64] François Péron, *Mémoire sur les établissements anglais à la Nouvelle Hollande, à la Terre de Diémen et dans les archipels du grand océan Pacifique: le rêve australien de Napoléon: description et projet secret de conquête française*; edited with an introduction, notes, and appendices by Roger Martin; transcribed with the assistance of Jacqueline Bonnemains; preface by Joël Eymeret (Paris: Éditions SPM, 1998). De Freycinet, who completed volume 2 of Péron's manuscript after his death, and had been on Baudin's ship with Péron, was in contrast anti-transportation.
[65] Jules S-C Dumont d'Urville, *An Account in Two Volumes of Two Voyages to the South Seas*, volume 2, translated and edited by Helen Rosenman (Melbourne University Press, 1987), 452–5, 495.
[66] Konishi and Nugent, 'Newcomers, c. 1600–1800', 60–4.
[67] The ship also called at the Cape of Good Hope, though not Robben Island (which received convicts after 1619 under British and Dutch administration), and St Helena, the location for the Emperor Napoleon's six-year exile (1815–21). A history of Indian convicts in Mauritius is Clare Anderson, *Convicts in the Indian Ocean: Transportation from South Asia to Mauritius, 1815–53* (Basingstoke: Macmillan, 2000). On Robben Island, see Harriet Deacon, ed., *The Island: A history of Robben Island 1488–1990* (Cape Town: David Philip, 1997).

of *The Beagle*'s voyages, comprising three volumes edited by Darwin and his commanding officer Captain Robert FitzRoy, included descriptions of the convict site in the Galápagos, which was situated on what the British called Charles Island (Santa Maria de l'Aguada). Otherwise, and seemingly unaware of the prior history of the Spanish Malvinas as a place of punitive relocation, Darwin claimed that the size, climate, isolation, and water supply of the islands then known as the Falklands together constituted 'an admirable place for a penal establishment, a thorough convict colony'.[68] Further, Darwin praised the Indian convicts in Mauritius, as having 'plenty of intellect'.[69] He compared them favourably to the British and Irish convicts then in the Australian colonies, writing: 'These men are generally quiet and well-conducted; from their outward conduct, their cleanliness and faithful observance of their strange religious enactments, it was impossible to look at them with the same eyes as on our wretched convicts in New South Wales.'[70] Indeed, he wrote of Sydney to his friend and fellow botanist Reverend John Henslow in 1836: 'Heaven forfend that I should live where every other man is sure to be somewhere between a petty rogue and a bloodthirsty villain.'[71] He later added: 'Formerly I had entertained Utopian ideas concerning [the penal colony]; but the state of society of the lower classes, from their convict origin, is so disgusting, that this and the sterile monotonous character of the scenery, have driven Utopia and Australia into opposite sides of the World.'[72] Of the Australian colonies, Darwin argued that convicts had what he called a 'demoralizing influence' on free settlers, and noted the existence of frictions between squatters (ticket-of-leave, or probationary, convicts), convict descendants, and the rest of the population. At the same time, and despite these critiques, he recognised the importance of convicts for colonial development, writing: 'The power, which the government

---

[68] Robert FitzRoy, *Narrative of the Surveying Voyages of His Majesty's Ships Adventure and Beagle between the Years 1826 and 1836, Describing Their Examination of the Southern Shores of South America, and the Beagle's Circumnavigation of the Globe. Proceedings of the Second Expedition, 1831–36, under the Command of Captain Robert Fitz-Roy, R.N.*, 3 volumes (London: Henry Colburn, 1839), 263–4, 490, 517, 530–1, 571, 623. The *Narrative* also noted the deleterious presence of an unknown number of escaped convicts in New Zealand and the islands of the Pacific Ocean, 580, 612–4. Despite interest in transportation in the 1840s as a means of populating the colony, the British never sent convicts to the Falklands. See Stephen A. Royle, 'The Falkland Islands, 1833–1876: The Establishment of a Colony', *The Geographical Journal*, 151, 2 (1985), 206 (204–14).
[69] Nora Barlow, ed., *Charles Darwin and the Voyage of the* Beagle (London: Pilot Press, 1945), 252.
[70] FitzRoy, *Narrative of the surveying voyages of His Majesty's Ships Adventure and Beagle*, 571.
[71] CCL UC: OLDLIBRARY-STAN1.27 [6] – Bay of Islands, convict colonies: Charles Darwin to Rev. John Henslow, 28 January 1836.
[72] Barlow, ed., *Charles Darwin and the Voyage of the* Beagle, 132–3.

possesses, by means of forced labour, of at once opening good roads throughout the country, has been, I believe, one main cause of the early prosperity of this colony.'[73] Darwin's observations in this regard cut to the heart of the tension between punishment and colonization that perplexed commentators during this period:

> that any moral reform should take place appears to be quite out of the question ... as a place of punishment the object is scarcely gained; as a real system of reform it has failed ... but as a means of making men outwardly honest, – of converting vagabonds most useless in one hemisphere into active citizens of another, and thus giving birth to a new and splendid country – a grand centre of civilization – it has succeeded to a degree perhaps unparalleled in history.[74]

The voyage of *The Beagle* is, of course, famous for its role in the global history of exploration and collecting, and here too linkages can be made to convicts and penal colonies. Following the second voyage, shipboard artist Conrad Martens settled in Sydney where he painted a series of images showing contact with Tierra del Fuegians.[75] If Martens visually recorded Indigenous peoples in South America, on the third voyage, surgeon Benjamin Bynoe collected indigenous flora and fauna from New South Wales. He sent plants to the Royal Botanic Gardens at Kew, and birds and fish to the British Museum in London. Bynoe's early Australian experience appears to have underpinned his later appointment to the position of surgeon-superintendent of the English convict ships *Blundell* (bound for Norfolk Island), and *Lord Auckland* and *Aboukir* (both destined for Van Diemen's Land).[76]

Joseph Dalton Hooker was a lifelong friend and correspondent of Darwin, and also travelled to the Antipodes. Joseph's father, William Jackson Hooker, was director of London's famous Kew Gardens from 1841 to 1865. Joseph succeeded him, serving between 1865 and 1885. During the period of his father's tenure at Kew, in the early 1840s, Joseph

---

[73] FitzRoy, *Narrative of the Surveying Voyages of His Majesty's Ships Adventure and Beagle*, 517.
[74] FitzRoy, *Narrative of the Surveying Voyages of His Majesty's Ships Adventure and Beagle*, 523.
[75] Richard Darwin Keynes, *Fossils, Finches and Fuegians: Darwin's Adventures and Discoveries on the Beagle* (Oxford University Press, 2003).
[76] CCL CU: OLDLIBRARY-STAN1.34 [7] – document detailing subsequent careers of *Beagle* travellers. See also J. J. Keevil, 'Benjamin Bynoe, Surgeon of HMS Beagle', *Journal of the History of Medicine and Allied Sciences*, 4, 1 (1949), 90–111. A recent biography of Charles Darwin in two parts stresses the importance of networks and patronage for his work: Janet Browne, *Charles Darwin: Voyaging* (London: Pimlico, 2003); Janet Browne, *Charles Darwin: The Power of Place* (London: Pimlico, 2003).

spent a period in Hobart, Van Diemen's Land.[77] With other Tasmanian botanists, notably Ronald Campbell Gunn, former assistant superintendent of convicts in Launceston and director of the Tasmanian Natural History Society, Hooker worked closely with convicts in collecting and identifying plant specimens.[78] Another of Joseph Hooker's correspondents was Andrew Sinclair. Following a period of collecting in Latin America, in 1843 Sinclair went to Van Diemen's Land as surgeon-superintendent of the convict ship *Asiatic*. From there, he travelled on to New Zealand with the new governor, none other than Darwin's commanding officer Robert FitzRoy, and became his colonial secretary. Before he left London, Third Naval Lord of the Admiralty Sir George Seymour had charged Sinclair with reporting on the prospect of procuring naval timber in New Zealand. Sinclair later wrote to Hooker: 'I should like it not for the emolument but for the purpose of collecting and making a step for something better on my return home.'[79]

Collecting in the penal colony of Van Diemen's Land followed early precedent in New South Wales, where convicts gathered specimens on behalf of Charles Fraser, the first superintendent of the Royal Botanic Garden in Sydney. These convicts included a man called John Richardson, transported to New South Wales in 1817. Pardoned in 1821, he returned to England with a cargo of plants destined for Kew Gardens. However, he committed another offence, and in 1822 he was re-transported, this time to Van Diemen's Land. After he arrived, Fraser had Richardson transferred back to Sydney, from where he undertook various collecting missions. These included in the new convict settlement in the tropical north at Moreton Bay (1823–4), and in Melville Island (1826–8) and King George's Sound (1829). Botanists named at least two plants after him: *Hibiscus richardsonii* Lindl and *Alyxia richardsonii* Sweet.[80] The British had settled the northern island of Melville in 1824 and put Richardson in charge of its gardens. Known locally as 'the

---

[77] Jim Endersby, *Imperial Nature: Joseph Hooker and the Practices of Victorian science* (University of Chicago Press, 2008). Joseph Hooker was the first scientist to speak publicly in support of Darwin's *On the Origin of Species*.

[78] Eleanor Cave, Flora Tasmaniae: Tasmanian Naturalists and Imperial Botany, 1829–1860, PhD thesis, University of Tasmania, 2012, chapter 3, 76–80, 275, 350–1.

[79] RBG archives DC 69/305: Andrew Sinclair to W. J. Hooker, from the *Asiatic* convict ship, Sheerness, 18 May 1843; Bryan P.J. Molloy, 'Sinclair, Andrew (1794–1861)', *Dictionary of New Zealand Biography*, volume 1 (1990), available at https://teara.govt.nz/en/biographies/1s12/sinclair-andrew (accessed 21 July 2017).

[80] JSTOR Plants: Richardson, John Matthew (1797–1882), http://plants.jstor.org/stable/10.5555/al.ap.person.bm000391636?searchUri=filter%3Dpeople%26so%3Dps_group_by_genus_species%2Basc%26Query%3D%2528richardson%252C%2Bjohn%2Bmatthew%2529 (accessed 11 July 2017). From Moreton Bay grew the city of Brisbane in Queensland. Melville Island is off the coast of what is now the Northern Territory.

gardener', he planted an extraordinary array of fruits, vegetables, and herbs, as well as sugar cane, coffee, and mustard. This indicates perhaps a desire to render the island productive. Indeed, though still a convict, Richardson even went on a seed collecting expedition to the proximate island of Dutch occupied Timor.[81] Another man, James Lee, Ronald Gunn's convict servant in Van Diemen's Land, assisted in plant collecting and specimen labelling, but also worked as a taxidermist, stuffing and mounting exotic birds for display or sale. Government sent at least some of these to zoological collections in England.[82] Convicts at Macquarie Harbour, a penal station (for convict re-offenders) in the west of the island, also supplied stuffed animal specimens to 'interested gentlemen' in Hobart, including small marsupials known as native cat, or Eastern Quoll (*Dasyurus viverrinus*).[83]

Convicts were also centrally engaged in the production of visual representations of Australian natural history. As early as the 1790s, Surgeon-General of New South Wales John White worked closely with Thomas Watling, transported for forgery, in producing natural history illustrations. In a rare convict-penned record of encounters with Indigenous peoples, Watling described how they would sit with him for hours while he worked. In a letter to his aunt he implored her to find the patronage necessary for his return to England with 'as faithful and finished a set of drawings of the picturesque, botanic, or animate curiosities of N. S. Wales, as has ever yet been received'. However, nothing ever came of this project.[84] The most important botanical artists in the early history of

---

[81] Katherine Ann Roscoe, Island Chains: Carceral Islands and the Colonisation of Australia, 1824–1903, PhD thesis, University of Leicester, 2017, 148–9, 150–1. I am grateful to Katherine Roscoe for sharing details of Richardson's experiences on Melville Island. See also Hazel Marshall, 'Convict pioneers and the failure of the management system on Melville Island, 1824–29', *The Push from the Bush*, 29 (1991), 29–46.

[82] Cave, Flora Tasmaniae, 2–3, 96, 133–8.

[83] I thank Hamish Maxwell-Stewart for this reference. See Hamish Maxwell-Stewart, 'The life and death of James Thomas', *Tasmanian Historical Studies*, 10 (2005), 61, 63 (quote), 64 (55–64). On Macquarie Harbour, see also Hamish Maxwell-Stewart, *Closing Hell's Gates: The Death of a Convict station* (Sydney, NSW: Allen and Unwin, 2008).

[84] Thomas Watling, *Letters from an Exile at Botany Bay, to his Aunt in Dumfries Giving A Particular Account of the Settlement of New South Wales, with the Customs and Manners of the Inhabitants* (Sydney, NSW: University of Sydney Library, 1999 (Prepared from the print edition published by Ann Bell Penrith 1794)). See also Peter Barber, 'Malaspina and George III, Brambila, and Watling: Three discovered drawings of Sydney and Parramatta by Fernando Brambila', *Australian Journal of Art*, 11 (1993), 36 (31–55). Over one hundred of Watling's paintings, including of scenery, Indigenous peoples, birds, and plants are now in London's Natural History Museum. Before working with Watling, John White had published a *Journal of a Voyage to New South Wales: with Sixty-Five Plates of Nondescript Animals, Birds, Lizards, Serpents, Curious Cones of Trees and Other Natural Productions* (London: J. Debrett, 1790). White noted the arrival of Jean-François de la Pérouse's ships *Astrolabe* and *Bousoulle* in 1788, and speculated that the crew had

Van Diemen's Land were also convicts. Thomas Bock painted flora and fauna, as well as Indigenous Tasmanians.[85] William Buelow Gould produced numerous illustrations of plants, birds, and animals, and the celebrated 'Sketchbook of Fishes' (Figure 8.1).[86] In the work of these convict collectors, naturalists, and artists, what are usually considered as imperial and social peripheries can be situated at the heart of empire, science, and knowledge formation.[87]

Administrators routinely employed convicts in the exploration of the hinterlands within or beyond penal colonies and settlements. In this regard, they were part of what Anne Coote and colleagues have called a 'complex commercial supply chain', which developed over time to include a range of exchange, including through auctions, gifts, and barter, and a large number of intermediaries such as retailers and taxidermists.[88] In the mid-1820s, for instance, the governor of the Cape Colony, Charles Somerset, allocated seven convicts to the coastal survey mission of British naval surveyors Captain William Owen and Thomas Boteler. These men included the Dutch-speaker Jakot Msimbiti and a man described as a 'warrior' and called 'Fire'. The British had captured him during the Xhosa Wars and transported him to Robben Island. These two men joined a dozen or so prisoners who had been impressed into Owen's crew from the hulks of Spithead and Woolwich, in the south of England. Owen later recalled that the men acted as intermediaries with the people that they encountered and named for them what he described as the 'countries' that the survey passed. On their return to the Cape Colony, they worked as interpreters for British traders.[89] The Indian

---

taken pity on a French convict called Paris, who disappeared after the ship's departure: 119, 125–6. Both ships were lost at sea on route to the Solomon Islands. See Dunmore, ed., *The Journal of Jean-François de Galaup de la Pérouse 1785–1788, Volume 1*, ccxxviii.

[85] Diane Dunbar, ed., *Thomas Bock: Convict Engraver, Society Portraitist: Exhibition and catalogue* (Launceston, TAS: Queen Victoria Museum and Art Gallery, 1991).

[86] Henry Allport, 'Gould, William Buelow (1801–1853)', Australian Dictionary of Biography, National Centre of Biography, Australian National University, http://adb.anu.edu.au/biography/gould-william-buelow-2114/text2669, published first in hardcopy 1966 (accessed 7 May 2020). Gould's 'Sketchbook of Fishes' is now on UNESCO's Australian memory of the world register. It was the inspiration for Richard Flanagan's novel, *Gould's Book of Fish: A Novel in Twelve Fishes* (London: Atlantic Books, 2002). To view Gould's convict register and illustrations, see https://www.linc.tas.gov.au/allport/Pages/gould.aspx (accessed 10 July 2017).

[87] Cave, Flora Tasmaniae, 7, *10*.

[88] Anne Coote, Alison Haynes, Jude Philp, and Simon Ville, 'When Commerce, Science, and Leisure Collaborated: the Nineteenth-Century Global Trade Boom in Natural History Collections', *Journal of Global History*, 12, 3 (2017), 325–6 (319–39).

[89] Heloise Finch-Boyer, 'Indian Ocean Cosmopolitanisms in the early 19th century: linking Cape Town, Delagoa Bay and Sainte Marie', conference paper presented at 'Durban and Cape Town as Indian Ocean Port Cities: Reconsidering Southern African Studies from the Indian Ocean', University of the Western Cape, South Africa, 12 September 2014.

Figure 8.1 Leafy sea dragon, by William Buelow Gould, c. 1832
Source: Allport Library and Museum of Fine Arts, Hobart, Tasmania HA277: W. B. Gould, Sketchbook of Fishes, c. 1832.

convicts in Mauritius, spoken of so favourably by Darwin, also facilitated British exploration, joining the first successful ascent of the highest mountain on the island, Peter Botte, in 1832. The convicts set up the trail with ropes, crowbars, and ladders, carried the provisions, and dislodged loose rocks for the British party that followed them up the slopes. One British member of the party wrote: 'a more picturesque line of march I have seldom seen'.[90] In 1857, along the same lines,

---

Finch-Boyer draws relevant material from Thomas Boteler, *Narrative of a Voyage of Discovery to Africa and Arabia: Performed in His Majesty's ships, Leven and Barracouta, from 1821 to 1826, under the Command of Capt. F. W. Owen, R.N.* (London: Richard Bentley, 1835), and Boteler's unpublished manuscript, which is in the collections of the National Maritime Museum, Greenwich (MS/77/066). I thank Heloise for sharing this information with me. Note that there were nine Xhosa Wars, during the period 1779–1879.

[90] Lieutenant Taylor, 'Account of the Ascent of the Peter Botte Mountain, Mauritius, on the 7th September, 1832', *Journal of the Royal Geographical Society of London*, 3 (1833), 99–100 (99–104). Taylor wrote that there were between fifteen and twenty convicts in the exploratory party, together with a handful of enslaved people.

Spain allocated some Grenadian convicts (and soldiers) to Britain, France, and the USA, to assist in their joint expedition to the Isthmus of Darien in Panama.[91]

The British in the Australian colonies also relied on convicts – as well as Indigenous peoples – in knowledge acquisition and exploration. In New South Wales, a remarkable young woman named Patygerang assisted First Fleet Lieutenant William Dawes in a study of what is now known to be the Dharug language of the Cadigal people of the Eora nation.[92] When Matthew Flinders circumnavigated the continent between 1801 and 1803, Indigenous guide Bungaree and a child named Nanbaree, said to be an orphan, accompanied him.[93] Such work came in the larger context of settler-colonial violence. This included the acts of dispossession described above, as also Governor Captain Arthur Phillip's policy of capturing Indigenous Australians, with a view to creating go-betweens. Most famous was a man called Bennelong who drifted in and out of the colonial settlement, and who the settlers took to England.[94]

In one of many more such examples, in 1831, Surveyor-General of New South Wales Thomas Mitchell set out to find a river that Indigenous peoples called the Kinder. An Indigenous man who the British called John Piper assisted during the nine-month long journey. Mitchell praised his skills thus: 'In tracing lost cattle, speaking to "the wild natives", hunting, or diving, Piper was the most accomplished man in camp.'[95] When the party returned to Sydney, the British gifted him a brass breastplate inscribed with the title 'Conqueror of the Interior'. As Henry Reynolds notes, Indigenous advisers and expertise played a crucial role in exploration and settlement. Settlers used Indigenous tracks, sought out sites inhabited by Indigenous peoples, which indicated the presence of water and fertile land, and followed their directions to other water sources. They used local guides as cultural intermediaries.[96] Mitchell also took fifteen convicts on the trip, chosen according to their 'character', trade, and qualifications. They included two carpenters, four sailors, a medical assistant, two bullock-drivers, a groom, a blacksmith, a

---

[91] Lionel Gisborne, 'Summary of the Report on the Survey of the Isthmus of Darien', *Journal of the Royal Geographical Society of London*, 27 (1857), 196 (191–206).
[92] Ross Gibson, 'Patyegarang and William Dawes: the space of imagination', in Mar and Edmonds, eds., *Making Settler Colonial Space*, 242–53. Dawes' notebooks can be viewed in the digital collections of SOAS, University of London: https://digital.soas.ac.uk/dawes/about/ (accessed 3 October 2018).
[93] Konishi and Nugent, 'Newcomers', 64–6.
[94] Eleanor Dark, 'Bennelong (c. 1764–1813)', Australian Dictionary of Biography, National Centre of Biography, Australian National University, http://adb.anu.edu.au/biography/bennelong-1769/text1979, published first in hardcopy 1966 (accessed 7 May 2020).
[95] Reynolds, *With the White People*, 5, 19.   [96] Reynolds, *With the White People*, 5–40.

'surveyor's man', and two servants. 'It had been my study, in organising this party', Mitchell wrote, 'to combine proved men of both services with some neat-handed mechanics, as engineers.' He noted that such employment was attractive to convicts, because it could earn them some remission of sentence: 'All were ready to face fire or water, in hopes of regaining by desperate exploits, a portion, at least, of that liberty which had been forfeited to the laws of their country.'[97]

The Andaman Islands were also an important space for convict-assisted exploration, botanical science, and collecting. Situated in the Bay of Bengal, the Islands had remained relatively isolated from outside contact until the end of the eighteenth century. Visitors always admired their natural beauty, and stunning flora and fauna. In 1857, twelve Burmese convicts from the Tenasserim Provinces accompanied Bengal's Inspector-General of Prisons F. J. Mouat, charged by the

---

[97] T. L. Mitchell, *Three Expeditions into the Interior of Eastern Australia; with Descriptions of the Recently Explored Region of Australia Felix, and of the Present Colony of New South Wales*, volume 1 (London: T. and W. Boone, 1839). Mitchell supplied unusually rich details of who the convicts were: 'Alexander Burnett and Robert Whiting, Carpenters. William Woods, John Palmer, Thomas Jones and William Worthington, Sailors. James Souter, Medical Assistant. Robert Muirhead, Daniel Delaney and James Foreham, Bullock-Drivers. Joseph Jones, Groom. Stephen Bombelli, Blacksmith. Timothy Cussack, Surveyor's Man. Anthony Brown, Servant to me. Henry Dawkins, Servant to Mr. White. ... Burnett was the son of a respectable house-carpenter on the banks of the Tweed [in Scotland], where he had been too fond of shooting game, his only cause of trouble. Whiting, a Londoner, had been a soldier in the Guards. Woods had been found useful in the department as a surveyor's man; in which capacity he first came under my notice, after he had been long employed as a boatman in the survey of the coast, and having become, in consequence, ill from scurvy, he made application to me to be employed on shore. The justness of his request, and the services he had performed, prepossessed me in his favour, and I never afterwards had occasion to change my good opinion of him. John Palmer was a sailmaker as well as a sailor, and both he and Jones had been on board a man-of-war, and were very handy fellows. Worthington was a strong youth, recently arrived from Nottingham. He was nicknamed by his comrades Five-o'clock, from his having, on the outset of the journey, disturbed them by insisting that the hour was five o'clock soon after midnight, from his eagerness to be ready in time in the morning. I never saw Souter's diploma, but his experience and skill in surgery were sufficient to satisfy us, and to acquire for him from the men the appellation of The Doctor. Robert Muirhead had been a soldier in India, and banished, for some mutiny, to New South Wales; where his steady conduct had obtained for him an excellent character. Delaney and Foreham were experienced men in driving cattle. Joseph Jones, originally a London groom, I had always found intelligent and trustworthy. Bombelli could shoe horses, and was afterwards transferred to my service by Mr. Sempill in lieu of a very turbulent character, whom I left behind, and who declared it to be his firm determination to be hanged. Cussack had been a bog surveyor in Ireland; he was an honest creature, but had got somehow implicated in a charge of administering unlawful oaths. Brown had been a soldier, and subsequently was assistant coachman to the Marquis of —. Dawkins was an old tar, in whom Mr. White, himself formerly an officer in the Indian navy, placed much confidence.' Mitchell, *Three Expeditions into the Interior of Eastern Australia*, 16–17.

government of India with selecting the best penal colony location. 'Without the aid of these men and of the crew of the *Pluto*', Mouat later recalled, 'we could have made no progress in our explorations, so dense and impenetrable did we find the vegetation everywhere.'[98] A further fifty-seven Burmese convicts volunteered to serve in the colonizing party in 1858, encouraged by the promise of a reduction in their sentences.[99] If convicts had – literally – cleared the path for imperial occupation, later on they greatly assisted scientists in their research. E. H. Man, assistant commissioner in the Andamans (and later deputy chief commissioner), established a fruit, nut, and vegetable plantation and nursery called Royal Dover Garden in Haddo, in 1868. His aim was to supply the Andamans – and Straits Settlements (Malacca, Penang, and Singapore) – with food, and to establish plants and saplings that the convict outstations could then cultivate and grow. The deputy medical officer of the penal colony J. B. King oversaw the gardens, and he relied on convicts in identifying incoming specimens from Burma and Penang. For example, King noted that because some of the plantains were completely unknown to the convicts, they gave them new names. Meantime, probably drawing from his previous experience as medical practitioner in the penal settlement of Penang, he oversaw a system whereby night soil (human waste) from the Haddo convict barracks was repurposed as agricultural manure.[100]

From the earliest years of occupation, officials stationed in the Andamans became keen naturalists and collectors. As noted earlier, at the time of colonization, several hunter-gatherer population groups populated the Islands, but there are few records of their role in colonial knowledge production at this time. However, Mouat's book on the 1857–8 survey mission included an appendix on the zoology of the Islands, written by Edward Blythe, who was curator of the Asiatic Society of Bengal's museum.[101] Captain T. H. Hodge, commander of the guard ship *Sesostris*, sent the museum a large number of fish and

---

[98] F. J. Mouat, 'Narrative of an Expedition to the Andaman Islands in 1857', *Journal of the Royal Geographical Society of London*, 32 (1862), 111 (109–26). On the expedition, and its recommendations, see also Anderson, *The Indian Uprising of 1857–8*, 129–32.

[99] IOR P/206/60 India Judicial Proceedings: Superintendent J. P. Walker to Cecil Beadon, secretary to government of India, 4 September 1858, enc. report on the causes of the severe sickness and great mortality which has prevailed amongst the convicts at Port Blair penal settlement in the Andaman Islands, since the formation of the settlement on the 10th March, up to the 25th August 1858.

[100] RBG archives MR/105 India, Andaman and Nicobar Islands 1870–1928: J. B. King, *Report of the Royal Dover Gardens, Haddo, Port Blair 1870–71*.

[101] Edward Blythe, 'Appendix: The Zoology of the Andaman Islands', in Frederic J. Mouat, *Adventures and Researches among the Andaman Islanders* (London: Hurst and Blackett, 1863), 345–67.

animal specimens, including the skeleton of a small mammal called the palmeivet (part of the Viverridae family).[102] In 1871, Chaplain J. N. Homfray sent sixteen bat specimens to the Indian Museum in Calcutta; in 1876 Chief Superintendent Colonel Tytler added to this collection.[103] They are each listed as museum donors, as are later superintendents John Haughton, Barnett Ford, and Thomas Cadell; the zoologist and photographer George Edward Dobson; and two of the British administrators of the Indian penal settlements in Burma and the Straits Settlements, Lieutenant S. R. Tickell and Alexander C. Maingay, as is noted below.[104]

Another collector was the Reverend Thomas Warneford who in the 1870s enthusiastically gathered shells.[105] Over a period of twelve years, Warneford acquired and catalogued an extensive set of specimens with help from his young daughter, Maud, and their convict servants, including a man they called James. Warneford sent Maud back to England, to school, and shipped boxes of shells on to her for safe keeping. In one letter to her, the limits of his knowledge are clear: 'I am longing to unpack them, and have a look again at my old collection', he wrote. 'You will have to help me name and classify them, and your knowledge of French, which I hope you will then have will be very useful as the only book I have on conchology is in French.'[106] Father also sent daughter a 'pearly nautilus', which he informed her was a gift from James, picked up on Aberdeen beach.[107] Ultimately, Warneford split his collection between the Indian Museum and what is now the Natural History Museum, London, which as noted previously also received Ridley and Bynoe's Brazilian and Australian specimens. Museum personnel later described Warneford's collection as the largest ever amassed in the Islands.[108]

---

[102] Blythe, 'Appendix', 346, 353; Gerrit S. Miller, 'The Mammals of the Andaman and Nicobar Islands', *Proceedings of the National Museum*, 24 (1902), 772 (751–96).

[103] Miller, 'The Mammals of the Andaman and Nicobar Islands', 778–9.

[104] John Anderson, *Catalogue of the Mammalia in the Indian Museum, Calcutta, Part I* (Calcutta: Government of India Central Printing Office, 1881), vii–x, 195, 248; W. L. Sclater, *Catalogue of the Mammalia in the Indian Museum, Calcutta, Part II* (Calcutta: Government of India Central Printing Office, 1891), v–ix, 195, 248.

[105] Warneford became friends with John and Joanna King. In her diary, Joanna mentions visits to his home as well as his shell collecting. See Wellcome Library, London, MSS.7631: Diary kept by Joanna King, 1867–8.

[106] IOR Mss Eur F388/2 Letters to Maud, 1879: Letter from Thomas Warneford to Maud Warneford, 21 September 1879.

[107] IOR Mss Eur F399/1 Letters of Reverend Warneford, 1874–7: Thomas Warneford to Maud Warneford, 31 January [no year given].

[108] H. B. Preston, 'Descriptions of new species of land, marine and freshwater shells from the Andaman Islands', *Records of the India Museum*, 2 (1908), 187–211. See also *Hand List of Mollusca in the Indian Museum, Calcutta* (Calcutta: Office of the Superintendent of Government Printing, 1884). Noted ethnographer E. H. Man later wrote that Warneford had assisted him with identifying shells. See *The Aboriginal Inhabitants of the Andaman Islands* (London: Trübner, 1883), 214.

Superintendent of the Indian Museum John Anderson (who was also professor of comparative anatomy at Calcutta Medical College) also served as surgeon-naturalist on the Indian survey ship *Investigator*, which reached the Andamans in the 1890s. He sent specimens of coral-living crabs back to the mainland.[109] During Violet Talbot's orchid collecting tour of the Andamans in 1907, it was again convicts, led by a Burmese *tindal* (petty officer) named in the records as My Myi, who set out on the overnight sorties necessary for the gathering of the specimens that had eluded her.[110] C. Boden Kloss and W. L. Abbott visited the Islands in 1901, for the purpose of collecting natural history specimens and ethnographic objects for the USA's National Museum in Washington DC. Their collection included 170 birds and mammals, some of which were previously unknown to science. 'Time and place combined', Boden Kloss later wrote, 'to make a naturalist's paradise. ... It is seldom that the work is so easy or the harvest so large.'[111] At the turn of the twentieth century, Russia's Sakhalin Island was visited by several zoologists and botanists. They did not much mention convicts in their initial reports, but when Sakhalin's penal regime came under scrutiny in later years, they republished work which commented on chaos and confusion, and harsh conditions and injustice in the penal settlement.[112]

The remote tropical location of the penal settlement of Mazaruni in British Guiana, discussed in Chapter 5, also rendered it an important site of scientific research. This was closely linked to the strategic desires of the British Empire, as is evident in the instructions given to the first surgeon of the settlement, Dr William McAulay. Governor Henry Light asked him to report on its topography, including soil quality. Afterwards, he was to keep a daily record of 'rainfall, moisture, temperature, wind direction, hour at which sea breeze sets in', and to comment on the impact of the

---

[109] J. R. Henderson, 'On a new species of coral-infesting crab taken by the R.I.M.S. "Investigator" at the Andaman Islands', *The Annals and Magazine of Natural History; Zoology, Botany and Geology*, 18 (1906), 211–19.

[110] My Myi had been transported to the Andamans for life, for murdering a Sikh policeman. See Mrs (Violet) Talbot Clifton, *Pilgrims to the Isles of Penance; Orchid Gathering in the East* (London: John Long, 1911), 88–93, 136–7, 139–42. On Clifton, see Clive Christie, 'British Literary Travellers', *Modern Asian Studies*, 28, 4 (1994), 673–737.

[111] C. Boden Kloss, *In the Andamans and Nicobars: The Narrative of a Cruise in the Schooner "Terrapin," With Notices of the Islands, Their Fauna, Ethnology, Etc.* (London, John Murray: 1903), 35. The National Museum of Natural History is now part of the Smithsonian Institute. See also Miller, 'The Mammals of the Andaman and Nicobar Islands', 751.

[112] Sharyl M. Corrado, The 'End of the Earth': Sakhalin Island in the Russian imperial imagination, 1849–1906, PhD thesis, University of Illinois at Urbana-Champaign, 2010, 79–81.

seasons on plants and trees.[113] By 1860, a German botanist named Carl Ferdinand Appun was working at Mazaruni. He had arrived from neighbouring Venezuela where, for the past ten years and on the recommendation of the famous scientist Alexander von Humboldt, the King of Prussia had employed him to collect specimens for a new museum in Königsberg. His posting to British Guiana followed a request from William Hooker, by then director of the Royal Botanic Garden at Kew, to the governor of the colony, P. E. Wodehouse. He wanted to commission Appun to collect timber and plant specimens on his behalf, but his immediate concern to find out whether Mazaruni timber was suitable for ship-building in Britain's royal dockyards, which at the time were located in Britain as well as overseas in Bermuda and Gibraltar.[114] The governor agreed, and the Court of Policy (the legislative body of the colony) voted for the allocation to Appun of a house in the guards' quarters, a $50 monthly allowance, and a group of convict assistants.[115]

Appun later wrote an account of his experiences at the *strafanstalt* (penal settlement), juxtaposing its natural beauty against its punitive character. Though reserved for the colony's most serious offenders, he described the existence of extensive gardens of orange, guava, papaya, mango, and coconut trees, which meant that it looked more like a beautiful park than a penal settlement.[116] He spent the whole of the autumn of 1860 out in the forests. At the time, many inmates in Mazaruni were of African descent, with a small proportion of Asian indentured labourers imprisoned for breaches of labour laws. Those who did not work in the quarry, forests, or lumberyard were employed in carpentry or boat building. It was perhaps a welcome release to work for Appun, as some of

[113] TNA CO111/191 10 June 1842 no. 100: Governor Henry Light, British Guiana, to Edward Smith-Stanley (14th Earl of Derby), secretary of state for war and the colonies, 10 June 1842, enc. H. E. J. Young, secretary to government, British Guiana, to William McAulay, surgeon Mazaruni, 9 June 1842.

[114] On the relationship between the colonization of Australia and the need for timber for the Royal Navy, see Alan Frost, *Convicts and Empire: A naval question, 1776–1811* (Melbourne, VIC: Oxford University Press, 1980).

[115] RBG archives: Directors' Correspondence (henceforth DC) 65/131: Two newspaper clippings; 'from British Guiana newspaper c. 1860'; DC 65/142 W. H. Campbell to Governor P. E. Wodehouse, British Guiana, 14 and 15 May 1860; DC 65/152: Campbell to Sir William Jackson Hooker, 8 January 1861; Carl Ferdinand Appun, *Unter den Tropen: Wanderungen durch Venezuela, am Orinoco, durch British Guiana und am Amazonenstrome in den jahren 1849–1868* (Jena: Hermann Costenoble, 1871), chapter 2. I am grateful to Svenja Bethke for generously providing translations of the Mazaruni material in Appun's book. See also 'Appun, Karl Ferdinand (1820–1872)', in Anne S. Troelstra, *Bibliography of Natural History Travel Narratives* (Zeist: KNNV publishing, 2016), 41. Appun returned home to Silesia in 1868, but went back to Mazaruni where he died in 1872, apparently after accidentally spilling the sulphuric acid that he kept with him at all times in case of attack.

[116] Appun, *Unter den Tropen*, 51.

them did. Eight prisoners rowed him up and down river. A ninth beat the rhythm of the coxswain. Appun remarked that he got to know the convicts well, acting with unspecified forms of authority to ensure their obedience, and never having reason to complain of their conduct. They dislodged the tree trunks that on occasion blocked their route and built camps and sleeping places on shore at night. They told him the name of a local bird that they called 'the singing Frenchman', and Appun identified as *Cyphorhinus cantans*. In his descriptive narrative, Appun subsequently reported on the properties of dozens of trees, receiving at least some of his information on their sap, oil, seeds, and nuts from his convict assistants, and likely also Indigenous peoples living in the region.[117]

Back in Georgetown, Appun spent several weeks arranging his specimens. He donated some of them to the new colonial museum, and sent several hundred others back to London.[118] Following his initial research, Appun returned to Mazaruni, but the colony's new governor, Francis Hincks, was not enthusiastic about the association between botany and punishment, notably the assistance rendered to Appun by men he described as 'convicts of the worst class'. Hincks wrote to Hooker in 1862: 'To all the arrangements under which the Botanical Collector is connected with a Convict establishment I am strongly opposed and I must be permitted to observe that the duties and responsibilities of yourself and of your correspondents are confined to the procuring of these specimens while I am responsible also of the discipline and economical management of the penal settlement.'[119] Nevertheless, Appun seems to have remained in the field, for in 1864, he collected almost 500 samples comprising plants, bark, and leaves from Mount Roraima, on the border with Brazil and Venezuela. The colonial government sent these to Kew.[120]

Hooker's scientific interest in the extraction of ship-building materials from the forests of British Guiana constituted part of a carceral circuit that looped around the British Empire. Just as convicts were employed to fell and prepare timber for naval ships, convict hulks were moored in many royal dockyards, and routinely hulk prisoners were put to work in

---

[117] Appun, *Unter den Tropen*, 54–55, 71–9, 93, 99, 103.

[118] RBG archives DC 65/142: Campbell to Wodehouse, 14 May 1860; RBG archives 65/152: Campbell to [W. J.] Hooker, 8 January 1861; Lloyd F. Kandasammy, 'A Brief History of the National Museum of Guyana', *Stabroek News*, 27 August 2007. Fossils found at the Mazaruni site also made their way into Georgetown museum. See RBG archives DC 204/248: Campbell to Sir Joseph Dalton Hooker, 5 January 1875.

[119] RBG archives DC 65/239: Governor Francis Hincks to [W. J.] Hooker, 14 November 1862.

[120] RBG archives DC 65/129: Appun to Campbell, 30 April 1864; RBG archives DC 65/158: Campbell to [W. J.] Hooker, 23 May 1864.

dockyard labour.[121] This connects the global history of punitive mobility and unfree labour to the global history of science. Ultimately, Appun found the wood neighbouring the settlement to be unsuitable for naval use. However, following his departure for Europe, botanical work continued under the direction of the superintendent of the penal settlement, Captain Claude Kerr, who was appointed in 1862. Kerr requested that due to his lack of expertise London-based botanists request plants by their 'Anglo-Saxon or vulgar tongue names'. He relied not just on convicts in his knowledge gathering, but on Indigenous peoples too, and the return of specimens included information on their medical use.[122]

The neighbouring penal settlements of Trinidad, also discussed in Chapter 5, were locations of scientific investigation too. Here, note that the first superintendent of the penal settlement in the Irois forest, William Purdie, was simultaneously the superintendent of Trinidad's Royal Botanic Gardens. It was William Hooker who had recommended his appointment.[123] The foundation of the second convict depot in the Chaguanas forest was inspired by the colonial government's desire to exploit its rich resources of timber. Subsequently, Chaguanas also became a centre for both experimental agriculture and local collecting. When Purdie died in 1858, he was replaced in the penal settlement at Irois by one Sylvester Devenish, the inspector of roads, who was said to be familiar with timber works.[124] Meantime, Prestoe, Purdie's successor as superintendent of the Royal Botanic Gardens, became the superintendent of the Chaguanas depot.[125] Purdie and Prestoe both sent duplicate

---

[121] Nick Gill, Deirdre Conlon, Dominique Moran, and Andrew Burridge, 'Carceral Circuitry: New directions in carceral geography', *Progress in Human Geography*, 42, 2 (2018), 183–204. On hulks and dockyards, see Charles Campbell, *The Intolerable Hulks: British Shipboard Confinement, 1776–1857* (Tucson, AZ: Fenestra Books, 2001); C. F. E. Hollis Hallet, *Forty Years of Convict Labour: Bermuda 1823–1863* (Bermuda: Juniperhill Press, 1999); Lawrence A. Sawchuk, Lianne Tripp, and Michelle M. Mohan, '"Voluntariness of Exposure": Life in a Convict Station', *Prison Journal*, 90, 2 (2010), 203–19.

[122] RBG archives DC 204/573: Captain Claude Kerr, superintendent HMPS Mazaruni, to the Royal Botanic Gardens, Kew, 27 November 1867. For Kerr's appointment, see TNA CO111/340 20 May 1863 no. 91: Hincks to Henry Pelham-Clinton (5th Duke of Newcastle), secretary of state for the colonies, 22 May 1863.

[123] TNA CO295/199 2 April 1858 no. 53: Governor Robert William Keate, Trinidad, to Lord Edward Stanley (15th Earl of Derby), secretary of state for the colonies, 2 April 1858; RBG Library, Art and Archives Blog: Kat Harrington, 'Happy 200th birthday to the Royal Botanic Gardens, Trinidad', 29 June 2018 https://www.kew.org/read-and-watch/happy-200th-birthday-to-the-royal-botanic-gardens-trinidad (accessed 5 September 2018).

[124] TNA CO295/199 2 April 1858 no. 53: Keate to Stanley, 2 April 1858, enc. regulations for the government of the Convict Establishment at the Irois Forest.

[125] RBG archives DC 213/410: Henry Prestoe, superintendent Royal Botanic Gardens Trinidad, to the Royal Botanic Gardens Kew, 23 March 1868; RBG archives DC 213/3: W. E. Broadway, assistant superintendent Royal Botanic Gardens Trinidad, to Daniel Morris, assistant director Royal Botanic Gardens Kew, 17 September 1891. For

herbarium specimens to Kew, and renowned botanist August Henrich Rudolf Grisebach used them to write some of the descriptions in his famous *Flora of the British West Indian Islands*. This was the first of a series initiated by William Hooker at Kew, the publication of which was motivated by the desire for better botanical knowledge of the various colonies.[126] In the late 1880s, in the Chaguanas penal settlement there were experiments in the cultivation of groundnuts and ginger, resulting in careful calculations of likely financial returns including through exports to the USA. The superintendent of convicts at this time was Charles Meaden, formerly assistant warder in London's Pentonville prison, and he was charged with harvesting and preparing crops.[127] These included incense gum, samples of which were sent to Kew in 1890.[128]

It is evident that the reach of the Royal Botanic Gardens in Kew into sites of punitive relocation was globally expansive in scope. In the late 1860s and early 1870s, its correspondent in Southeast Asia was Alexander C. Maingay, the resident assistant surgeon of the Straits Settlements. Penang had first received convicts from India in 1789, and Malacca and Singapore in 1826. Maingay relied on these convicts in the collection of plants and seeds and lamented that he was unable to send them on missions beyond the limits of British territory: 'there is a risk of them bolting altogether'. Though transportation to the settlements had ceased in 1866, the penal settlements remained open for under-sentence convicts at this time.[129] Also engaging with Kew, later in the 1920s and 30s, were administrators in the penal colonies of Mexico and the Philippines, and, as late as 1961, Panama.[130] In autumn 1924, for instance, Roxana Ferris gathered samples in María Madre, the penal

---

a nineteenth-century history of the Trinidad gardens, see Rita A. Pemberton, 'The Trinidad botanic gardens and colonial resource development, 1818–1899', *Revista/ Review Interamericana*, 29, 1–4 (1999).

[126] Harrington, 'Happy 200th birthday to the Royal Botanic Gardens, Trinidad'.

[127] TNA CO295/317/49 28 March 1888 no. 77 folios 398–409: Governor Sir William Robinson, Trinidad, to Henry Holland (1st Viscount Knutsford), secretary of state for the colonies, 28 March 1888, enc. O. Harley, superintendent of prisons Royal Gaol, to Knutsford, 23 March 1888 and Charles Meaden, superintendent of convicts HMPS Chaguanas, to Harley, 19 March 1888; Knutsford's Minute, 18 April 1888.

[128] RBG archives DC 213/114: J. H. Hart, superintendent Royal Botanic Gardens Trinidad, to Morris, 27 February 1890.

[129] RBG archives DC 153/111b: Alexander C. Maingay, resident assistant surgeon Straits Settlements, to [J. D.] Hooker, 18 May 1865; RBG archives DC 153/113: Maingay to [J. D.] Hooker, 11 April 1869; RBG archives, Specimens: A. C. Maingay, 1871 – Type of *Neesia synandra* Mast. [family BOMBACACEAE] (stored under name). Penang. Found half way going up the hill, near where some convicts are stationed. Maingay reported the presence of 1300 convicts in the Straits Settlements at this time.

[130] On collecting in the Philippines (Davao), see the RBG archives, Specimens: E. B. Copeland (1873–1964), 30 August 1932 – Lomariopsidaceae: *Lomariopsis papyracea* and *Lomariopsis lineata*. Collected in Davao Penal Colony, Philippines. There is no

colony island of Islas Marías. She stayed for a week, relying on the trails and roads built by convicts, and noting the deforestation associated with the penal colony's development of farmland and production of charcoal.[131] In the 1950s, Secretary of the Smithsonian Institution, Alexander Wetmore, made annual trips to Panama, including to Coiba Island penal colony. An ornithologist and avian palaeontologist, Wetmore was assisted by convicts in collecting bird and iguana specimens.[132]

Finally, in South America, the Guianas were important places for research into and the collection of butterflies. In 1929, the new superintendent of Mazaruni, H. A. Frere, reported to the London entomological society on the direction, duration, and speed of butterfly migration.[133] In the 1930s, the colony's forest officer was stationed at the penal settlement. Like Frere, he used his base as a means of observing butterfly migration.[134] But the most important site in the colonial Americas for butterfly research and collecting was the penal colony of French Guiana, in which both convicts and ex-convicts (*libérés*) engaged. This kind of convict collecting merged scientific interest with a developing commerce for interesting specimens. Under a system known as *doublage*, ex-convicts had to remain in the colony for a term equal to their actual sentence, where they had been transported for less than eight years. If transported for more than eight years, they were obliged to remain for life. In the context of a labour market that was saturated by unpaid convict workers, as a result many of these men fell into hardship and destitution. *Doublage*

academic literature on Davao, but an excellent study of a parallel institution established in 1906 is Michael Salman, '"The prison that makes men free": The Iwahig Penal Colony and the Simulacra of the American State in the Philippines', in Alfred W. McCoy and Francisco A. Scarano, eds., *The Colonial Crucible: Empire in the making of the modern American state* (Madison: University of Wisconsin Press, 2009), 116–28. On Coiba Island, Panama, see RBG archives, Specimens: J.D. Dwyer, 18 August 1961 – Malpighiaceae: *Bunchosia dwyeri* Cuatrec. Collected in Isla de Coiba Penal Colony, Panama. Examples of Dwyer's specimens are included in the JSTOR Global Plants database: https://plants.jstor.org/ (accessed 11 July 2017).

[131] RBG archives: Roxana S. Ferris [1895–1978], Preliminary report on the Flora of the Tres Marías (Stanford University Press, 1927), 63–4; RBG archives, Specimens: Roxana Stinchfield Ferris, 21 October 1927 – Euphoribiaceae (stored under name). Collected in Nayarit, María Madre, Tres Marías Islands; woods just south of penal colony, Mexico. More generally on María Madre, see Salvatore and Aguirre, 'Colonies of Settlement', 296–306. Examples of Ferris' specimens are included in the JSTOR Global Plants database: https://plants.jstor.org/ (accessed 11 July 2017).

[132] Alexander Wetmore, *The Birds of the Republic of Panama, Part 1* (Washington DC: Smithsonian Institution, 1965), 356. Wetmore's photographs of the penal colony are available in the online collections of the Smithsonian Institution: https://siarchives.si.edu/history/alexander-wetmore (accessed 28 July 2021).

[133] L. D. Cleare, 'Butterfly Migrations in British Guiana: II', *Proceedings of the Royal Entomological Society of London*, 77, 2 (1929), 251 (251–64).

[134] T. A. W. Davis, 'Butterfly Migrations in British Guiana', *Proceedings of the Royal Entomological Society of London*, 36, 4–6 (1961), 49 (49–56).

attracted international condemnation, to such a degree that the French government eventually allowed the *Armée du Salut* (Salvation Army) to set up relief efforts in the colony, including the provision of sleeping accommodation and a soup kitchen.[135] Salvationist officers noted that, for many convicts, the catching and sale of butterflies was the sole source of income.[136] Overseas collectors especially desired the species and subspecies of the *Morpho*, many of which shone a beautiful metallic blue-green colour. A key intermediary in butterfly collecting in Cayenne was Eugène Le Moult, who had one time had the third largest collection in the world. Le Moult went to French Guiana with his administrator father, where he remained until 1908, when he moved to Paris. He sold up to 20 million specimens to clients including the Emperor of Japan. His collections can now be found in museums all over Europe. After his posting to the colony in 1935, missionary Father Yves Barbotin became engaged in entomology more broadly; his collections now form an important part of the holdings of the Musée départemental Alexandre-Franconie in Cayenne. Convict René Belbenoit's 1938 account of French Guiana includes one particularly detailed description of the trade in butterflies. He wrote of the exhaustion of convicts worn out by penal labour. Convicts sold butterflies cheaply to guards, often to buy *tafia* (rum); the guards made big profits in selling them abroad. Belbenoit himself used his earnings to fund several escape attempts.[137] Indeed, competition over the trade was so fierce that in 1950 a group of convicts ambushed and

---

[135] ADG IX79 Administration pénitentiaire: Visite du pénitencier par l'Armée du Salut, 23 March 1935.

[136] SAIHC S.61: Charles Péan, *The Conquest of Devil's Island* (London: Max Parrish, n.d.), 123; SAIHC CAR/4 French Guiana: Charles Péan, *Devil's Island* (London: Hodder and Stoughton, 1939), 17. The 'lucrative occupation' of butterfly catching was also noted in *Hell Beyond the Seas: A Convict's Own Story of His Experiences in the French Penal Settlement in Guiana retold by A. Krarup-Nielsen, translated by E. C. Ramsden* (London, John Lane: 1935), 58. The fact of convict butterfly collecting will come as no surprise for readers familiar with Henri Charrière's epic book *Papillon [Butterfly]*, which is loosely based on the author's experiences as a convict, and was later made into a film starring Steve Macqueen and Dustin Hoffman.

[137] René Belbenoit, *Dry Guillotine: Fifteen Years Among the Living Dead* (New York: E. P. Dutton and Co., 1939), 65, 67, 87, 96. Belbenoit noted that a blue *Morpho* was worth 2 francs (67). He used his butterfly catching skills when passing through Colombia during his final escape, when he stayed with convict *évadé* Charlot Gautier, and in just four months made $100 by sending butterflies for sale to tourists in Cartagena. He later offered Indigenous *Kuna* people two *pesos* a piece to collect *Morpho* on his behalf, and spent some months living with them and collecting near their villages. He eventually sold his entire collection to an American dealer in Panama City (317–9, 321, 323, 336, 338). There is an image of Belbenoit with a collection of butterflies in his papers, which are in the Harry Ransom Center, The University of Texas at Austin. See Edgar Walters, 'The storied escapes of René Belbenoit', 14 May 2014, https://sites.utexas.edu/ransomcenter magazine/2013/05/14/rene-belbenoit/ (accessed 28 July 2021).

murdered six collectors who were on their way to sell their butterflies in Cayenne. The colonial administration banned such collecting, and in the larger context of post-war deprivation in the run-up to the abolition of the penal colony in 1953, this caused a convict labour strike.[138]

Belbenoit also made money by selling his manuscripts on French Guiana to the American reporter, Blair Niles. She used them as the basis for a sensational condemnation of the penal colony, subtitled *The Biography of an Unknown Convict*, and published in 1930.[139] Another American visitor, Richard Halliburton, also bought convict writing in Cayenne at this time. He had paid a convict named André to get him the red striped shirt, trousers, and straw hat that constituted the men's uniform, and disguised himself as a *bagnard* (convict) during his stay.[140] There is no evidence that Belbenoit himself sold to Halliburton, but the men were certainly in correspondence.[141] Halliburton did, however, purchase French language materials from three convicts who he named as Leonce Haulard, Du Greny, and Margat Eugène. They included crude sketches in their texts.[142] Aided by his French-speaking assistant Paul Mooney, Halliburton translated the convicts' writing into English. His American literary agent later wrote: 'The stories the men wrote themselves, given absolute freedom. Of course they are frightfully rough, frightfully vulgar in spots. It is Halliburton's idea that they could be reshaped into a very worthwhile series. In any event it is the only material of its particular kind in the world.'[143]

In addition to the collection, writing, and sale of butterflies (and manuscripts), convicts in French Guiana also collected and sold birds. M. Jean Delacour was president of the *Ligue Française pour la Protection des Oiseaux* (French Society for the Protection of Birds), and was widely

---

[138] SAIHC CAR/4 French Guiana: *The People*, 30 April 1950 (account of George Seaton). See also George Seaton, *Isle of the Damned: Twenty Years in the Penal Colony of French Guiana* (New York: Farrar, Straus and Young, 1951).

[139] Blair Niles, *Condemned to Devil's Island: The Biography of an Unknown Convict* (London: Jonathan Cape, 1930). Another convict called Adrien Guillerm also sold materials to Niles. See PUL C0247 RHP Box 22: Devil's Island Correspondence for *New Worlds to Conquer*, 1929–33, folder 9, Adrien Guillerm to Richard Halliburton, 20 August 1929.

[140] Richard Halliburton, *New Worlds to Conquer* (Indianapolis, IN: The Bobbs-Merrill Company Publishers, 1929), chapters 24–9. Given Halliburton and Niles' mutual purchase of convict writing, it is perhaps unsurprising that he acknowledged her work as 'the final word on French Guiana' (300). Not long after his visit to French Guiana, Halliburton was lost at sea, in the Pacific Ocean.

[141] PUL CO247 RHP Box 22, folder 26: René Belbenoit to Halliburton, 10 December 1929.

[142] PUL CO247 RHP Box 9: Devil's Island, New Worlds to Conquer: Devil's Island works by prisoners, folders 15 and 26.

[143] PUL C0247 RHP Box 9, folders 6, 15, 26; Box 22, folder 46: Jean Wick (Mrs Achmed Abdullah) to Tom Davin, 22 October 1933.

regarded as one of the leading aviculturists and ornithologists in the world. Before the First World War, he had a collection of around 2,000 birds belonging to 500 species living in the aviaries at his home in Normandy. After the Germans destroyed them, in 1922 he travelled to Venezuela, Trinidad, and French Guiana to restock his collection. When he arrived in Saint-Laurent-du-Maroni, the headquarters of the penal colony in the far west of the colony, the director loaned him a few convict assistants, to build aviaries and birdcages, and to carry his luggage, food, traps, cages, and live and dead specimens. Two North African convicts pushed Delacour and his party in the wooden wagons that constituted the colony's light railway, and two convicts trapped live birds. Delacour later wrote that whilst in Venezuela he had used birdlime to trap birds, in Saint-Laurent he employed convicts who worked as bird catchers and stuffers. 'They know perfectly well when and where the different birds can be found', he wrote, 'and they knock them down with blow-pipes.' He ensured that these contained soft earth, which stunned rather than killed the birds. And thus, the convicts captured sugarbirds, hummingbirds, tanagers, tinamous, doves, and manakins; and other animal specimens including agutis, acuchis, and armadillos.[144]

*

Isolated locations were attractive to governments as remote places in which to punish and exploit convicts to effect colonization and development. They also drew the attention of European and American explorers, collectors, and ethnographers. The chapter has suggested that convicts were somewhat ambivalent cultural intermediaries, as both subjects and proponents of colonial violence, across a wide range of sites of punitive relocation in the Americas, Africa, Australia, Pacific, and Japan. Penal mobility had a devastating impact on Indigenous peoples, who were also subject to the same kinds of technologies of containment, confinement, and 'rehabilitation' as convicts. However, at the same time, in some cases they were incorporated into punitive regimes, and made to labour for the imperial powers under varying degrees of coercion.

Visitors to penal colonies from the late eighteenth century on were interested in Indigenous peoples, as also flora, fauna, and minerals. Convicts and Indigenous peoples possessed skills and expertise that were vital for the co-creation of knowledge, and so in places like New South Wales, Van Diemen's Land, the Andaman Islands, and the Guianas,

---

[144] M. Jean Delacour, 'Live bird collections in French Guiana', *Animal Kingdom: Bulletin of the New York Zoological Society*, 25, 3 (1922), 62–4. Agutis and acuchis are members of the Dasyproctidae family of rodents, related to guinea pigs.

administrators relied on them in scientific exploration and collection, and sometimes in the commodification of natural resources. Not only did Indigenous peoples and convicts assist in colonial expeditions, but sites of punitive relocation became links in a global chain of collectors, botanic gardens, museums, and literary publishers. Thus, the histories of places as diverse as Robben Island, Moreton Bay, Mazaruni, and French Guiana are inseparable from the acquisition of scientific knowledge. Chapter 10 develops the theme of convicts' incorporation into research further, in a study of the role of penal colonies in the development of ethnography and the human sciences, from the turn of the nineteenth century onwards. Meantime, the following chapter centres convicts in other histories of science, during the same period, turning our attention to the role of punitive relocation in discussions and experiments about bodies, race, and medicine.

9 Medicine, Criminality, and Race

From the nineteenth century, across European empires, convict bodies contributed to the creation of knowledge about, and representations of, criminality, race, and ethnicity, and to research into tropical disease. That is the focus of this chapter. The first section discusses the ways in which scientists used convicts to establish causal links between physique, criminal character, and sometimes race. They were especially interested in anthropometry, or the science of physical measurement. In some sites of punitive relocation, including Britain's Australian colonies, Poulo Condore in French Cochinchina, and the Gibraltar hulks, contemporaries attempted to locate criminal traits through close analysis of the cranium (skull) or other bodily features. By the third quarter of the nineteenth century, Italian positivist Cesare Lombroso, author of *L'Uomo Delinquente* (Criminal Man), had made the highly influential, though controversial, proposition that criminality was biologically determined, connected to hierarchies of race, and thus related to degeneration.[1] Lombroso's theory was particularly influential in Latin America, though the Russians, British, and French received it with more ambivalence. Later, scientists became interested in how both sensitivity to pain and flows of blood (including to the face) might be physical manifestations of criminality.[2]

In Portuguese Africa, medical research began in earnest after the closure of the convict *depósitos* (depots) of Angola and Mozambique in

---

[1] Cesare Lombroso, *Criminal Man*, translated and with a new introduction by Mary Gibson and Nicole Hahn Rafter (Durham, NC: Duke University Press, 2006); Gina Lombroso-Ferrero, *Criminal Man; According to the Classification of Cesare Lombroso. Briefly summarised by his daughter Gina Lombroso Ferrero* (London: Putnam, 1911). See also Neil Davie, *Tracing the Criminal: The Rise of Scientific Criminology in Britain 1860–1920* (Oxford: The Bardwell Press, 2005); Mary Gibson, *Born to Crime: Cesare Lombroso and the Origins of Biological Criminology* (Westport, CT: Praeger, 2002); David G. Horn, *The Criminal Body: Lombroso and the Anatomy of Deviance* (Abingdon: Routledge, 2003); Daniel Pick, *Faces of Degeneration: A European Disorder, c. 1848–1918* (Cambridge University Press, 1989), chapter 5.
[2] Horn, *The Criminal Body*, chapters 4 and 5.

the early 1930s.³ This was almost certainly due to the widespread acceptance of ideologies of lusotropicalism. As explained in Chapter 2, lusotropicalism enabled Portugal to claim that the empire was free of racism. In regard to convicts, for instance, note that in the nineteenth and twentieth centuries, Portugal's African colonies received convicts from both the Iberian Peninsula and its imperial possessions, and they lived and worked together, mixed in the same labour companies.⁴ In other imperial locations during the same period, this was not always the case, and from the nineteenth century onwards, penal colonies were important spaces of medical research on morbidity and mortality. In French Guiana and New Caledonia, and in Britain's penal colony in the Andaman Islands, doctors studied and experimented on convicts of diverse origin, in studies of leprosy, hookworm, yellow fever, and malaria. Such study and experimentation lay open to view some of the tensions between the colonial appropriation of convict bodies, and the role of convict engagement and agency, in the creation of narratives of race and criminality, and in the history of medicine at large. These narratives contain their own nuances and distinctions. In French Guiana, for instance, they bolstered the separation and differentiation of convicts from Europe and North Africa. In New Caledonia, they enabled the drawing of a line between French and non-French convicts and migrants and the Indigenous Kanak. Meanwhile, Andamans research fed into larger global investigations into mosquitos as vectors for sickness and disease. Period was as important as place, and changes to the fields of science and medicine during the era under consideration here also impacted on the purpose and method of convict studies.

Phrenology, Physiognomy, Race, and Character

Phrenology was a technique which developed in the 1820s and 1830s, using the skull as a way of explaining an individual's character. It emerged from the earlier science of craniometry. Scientists used peppercorns or other small objects to measure cranial capacity, the size of which they believed indicated intelligence. Phrenologists divided the brain into thirty-seven 'organs' and claimed that each corresponded to a faculty of the human mind. They could therefore measure the strength or weakness of various character traits. These included wit, cautiousness, combativeness,

---

³ Timothy J. Coates, *Convict Labor in the Portuguese Empire, 1740–1932: Redefining the Empire with Forced Labor and New Imperialism* (Leiden: Brill, 2014), 9.
⁴ Coates, *Convict Labor in the Portuguese Empire*, 9.

and secretiveness.[5] Phrenologists obtained the skulls of prisoners, transportation convicts, and capitally convicted criminals, which were easier to source than those of ordinarily deceased persons and had the advantage of enabling the correlation of cranial observations with evidence of their crimes. For instance, in 1837, the Phrenological Society of Edinburgh received and studied the skulls of two executed Australian convict bushrangers, John Jenkins and Edward Tattersdale. They claimed them to be small, but nonetheless revealing of the men's combativeness, self-esteem, and hope – but lack of cautiousness.[6]

Contemporaries sympathetic to the idea of phrenology even proposed the pre-selection of transportation convicts for the Australian colonies on 'phrenological principles'. Critics, on the other hand, attempted to dismiss its utility by setting up investigations into convict character that they hoped would fail. This was the case when in 1826 a surgeon called James Wardrop hired the well-known phrenologist James De Ville to undertake an examination of 148 convicts, before they set sail for New South Wales. De Ville examined around one third of the convicts, and then gave the ship's surgeon Dr George Thomson a list, detailing what this revealed about the character of each man. This was included as a column in the indents that accompanied all convicts into transportation, and in which were recorded each convict's name, age, education, trade or occupation, crime, place and date of conviction, conduct in jail, and conduct on the hulk on which they were confined in anticipation of their shipment. The idea was that after arrival in the Antipodes Thomson would then inscribe in the convict indents details of their behaviour on board ship, which Wardrop believed would reveal De Ville's phrenological examinations to be flawed.

What Wardrop could not have known was that this would be no ordinary voyage. After the *England* set sail, Thomson, who had no previous knowledge of phrenology, recorded in the ship's log extensive details of the convicts' disorderly and mutinous behaviour, as they hatched a plan to murder him and sail for South America. The 'spirit of insubordination' among the convicts, including disobedience of orders, insolence, abusive language, theft, quarrels, and assaults, led surgeon Thomson to put them in irons and handcuffs, withhold their rations,

---

[5] James Poskett, *Materials of the Mind: Phrenology, Race, and the Global History of Science, 1815–1920* (University of Chicago Press, 2019). See also Roger Cooter, *The Cultural Meaning of Popular Science: Phrenology and the organization of consent in nineteenth-century Britain* (Cambridge University Press, 1984); David de Guistino, *Conquest of Mind: Phrenology and Victorian Social Thought* (London: Croom Helm, 1975); John van Wyhe, *Phrenology and the Origins of Victorian Scientific Naturalism* (Aldershot: Ashgate, 2004).

[6] 'Case of John Jenkins, convict executed at Sydney for murder', *Phrenological Journal and Miscellany*, 10 (June 1836–September 1837), 485–9.

and restrict their access to the upper deck. After the ship arrived in Sydney, Thomson noted that De Ville had singled out as troublesome all but one of the men involved. The leading publication in the field, *The Phrenological Journal and Miscellany*, reported that the leader, convict Robert Hughes, had been 'especially marked by him as a person capable of ruthless murder and deep-laid plots'. Thomson later wrote to sceptic Wardrop thanking him for his introduction to De Ville and phrenology, and noting 'All the authorities here have become phrenologists.'[7] Indeed, De Ville's phrenological examination of the convicts and its ensuing character list was later given the credit for preventing an all-out mutiny on the transportation ship.[8] By this time, Thomson had perhaps forgotten the scathing indictment De Ville made of the convict David Campbell: 'This individual may be made useful, he will be repentant, and have some feelings of religion; but his passions when excited will be somewhat violent and he will manifest some cunning.' Thomson noted after the voyage: 'Steady, orderly and industrious'.[9] Nevertheless, in the year or two following this incident, the Australian press not only routinely commented on recent articles in *The Phrenological Journal*, but informed its readers that phrenological meetings were taking place in both Sydney and Hobart.[10] It reported one case of 1827 in which the body of a transportation convict executed for murder was given over for

---

[7] 'Result of an examination by Mr James De Ville, of the Heads of 148 convicts on board the Convict Ship England, when about to sail for New South Wales in the Spring of 1826 (inc. extract from a letter from G. Thomson to James Wardrop, 9 October 1826')', *The Phrenological Journal and Miscellany*, 4 (October 1826–November 1827), 467–71 (quotes, 470). See also TNA ADM/101/26/1 Journal of the England – Convict Ship, George Thomson MD Surgeon and Superintendent, between the 18th March 1826 and 29th September 1826: Thomson's log, 31 May 1826; Thomson's Remarks, 7 October 1826. This document includes an undated list of just thirty of the convicts, of whom De Ville had examined eleven, hence the claim that he recorded details of one third of the men. On the analytical potential of the records of convict ship surgeons, see Katherine Foxhall, *Health, Medicine, and the Sea: Australian voyages, c. 1815–1860* (Manchester University Press, 2012), 4–5.

[8] *Testimonials on Behalf of George Combe, as a Candidate for the Chair of Logic, in the University of Edinburgh* (Edinburgh: John Anderson Jnr, 1836), *Documents Laid before the Right Honourable Lord Glenelg, Secretary for the Colonies, by Sir George S. Mackenzie, Bart, Relative to the Convicts sent to New South Wales, April 1836:* E. Barlow to Charles Grant (1st Baron Glenelg), secretary of state for war and the colonies, 15 March, 1836, Appendix, 4–6.

[9] TNA ADM/101/26/1 Journal of the England: list of convicts, n.d.

[10] From several examples, see *The Sydney Gazette and New South Wales Advertiser*, 9 September 1826. I located these reports by searching the National Library of Australia's newspaper database Trove, www.trove.nla.gov.au (accessed 1 August 2017).

phrenological analysis. As was often the case during this period, his sentence had specified dissection after hanging.[11]

Later, in 1836, George Combe, founder of the Edinburgh Phrenological Society (est. 1820), visited the English city of Newcastle and examined the heads of several prisoners. His aim was to show that 'there is a marked difference in the development of the brain in men of virtuous disposition, and its development in decidedly vicious characters, such as criminals usually are'.[12] Phrenologists viewed Combe's examinations as a great success, for they accorded with the known characters of the prisoners in question. In 1838, Edinburgh Phrenological Society member George S. Mackenzie, writing in the context of 'atrocities' on his sons' estate in New South Wales, even extolled the value of phrenology as a means of pre-selecting convicts. This, he claimed, would put an end to the transportation of violent offenders, and thus help prevent attacks against Indigenous peoples. He proposed that the Secretary of State for the Colonies, Lord Glenelg, draw up a 'catalogue' of the conviction and characteristics of convicts sentenced to transportation. With a phrenologist, he would then inspect them one by one, and produce his own 'catalogue'. This would predict the convicts' former occupation and crimes and summarise their character. Convict selection would take place following comparison of the two documents.[13] Though Mackenzie was supported by numerous and lengthy testimonials to the power and accuracy of phrenological observation, Glenelg was not a believer in it, and ultimately Mackenzie's scheme was never adopted.[14] However, during this period, phrenology was never

---

[11] *The Monitor*, 10 February 1827.

[12] 'Account of Mr Combe's Phrenological Examination of Heads of Criminals in the Jail of Newcastle-on-Tyne, October 1835', in *Testimonials on Behalf of George Combe*, 44–46 (quote, 44).

[13] *Testimonials on Behalf of George Combe*, Appendix, *Documents Laid before the Right Honourable Lord Glenelg*: Representation sent by Sir George S. Mackenzie, Bart, to the Right Honourable Lord Glenelg, Secretary for the Colonies, in reference to Convicts sent to New South Wales, February 1836, ix–xviii (quote, xi). Mackenzie referred to 'slaughter' on his sons' estate in New England (xiii–xiv), which was in Dugong in the Williams River Valley. In 1835, the British hanged a Gringai man, who settlers called 'Charley', for the murder of six convict shepherds, possibly against the background of an alliance between Indigenous people and convict bushrangers. These acts of violence became known as the 'MacKenzie murders'. See https://williamsvalleyhistory.org/aborigines-gringai/ (accessed 28 July 2017). George Mackenzie's letter suggests that there was some truth to the allegation of an Indigenous–convict alliance, or at the very least significant provocation on the part of the convicts. Note that one of Mackenzie's sons later became premier and colonial treasurer of Queensland. See R. B. Joyce, 'Mackenzie, Sir Robert Ramsay (1811–1873)', Australian Dictionary of Biography, National Centre of Biography, Australian National University, http://adb.anu.edu.au/biography/mackenzie-sir-robert-ramsay-4109/text6569, published first in hardcopy 1974 (accessed 7 May 2020).

[14] The testimonials ('certificates') are printed in the appendix of *Testimonials on Behalf of George Combe*, 1–43, 47–52. This text notes Glenelg's scepticism (13).

entirely dismissed. Alexander Maconochie, pioneer of the 'mark system' discussed in Chapter 7, was also sympathetic to the idea of phrenological pre-selection. He also proposed it as a basis for convict rehabilitation. If convicts learned about their character, he argued, they would be more self-aware and learn to show more self-restraint.[15]

One key element of phrenology was the idea that the traits that it identified could be inherited.[16] For this reason, officials and visitors in the Australian colonies were interested in the physical attributes of the children of convicts, known at the time as 'currency lads' and 'currency lasses'.[17] Some people believed that criminal propensity could 'descend' through the generations, in the same way as physique and character. However, overall, commentators were positive about the convicts' children. Commissioner John Bigge described in his 1822 report to the British parliament a group of boys and girls born to convict women in Parramatta, as 'fine and healthy'. He tried to mitigate against negative views of them and stressed the tenor of the evidence presented to him: 'they neither inherit the vices nor the feelings of their parents'. During this period, observers commonly referred to convict children as 'cornstalks', a metaphor for their fast development, height, and slenderness. By the 1820s, the idea of their superior physical development, compared to their counterparts in Britain, became enveloped in the larger idea of the emergence of a new Australian 'race'. Indeed, even during this early period, convict children called themselves 'Australians', and were sometimes referred to as 'natives'.[18] As historian John Molony writes, sojourners in the colony 'were as unwearied in giving to the world their impressions of the native-born as botanists and students of the wildlife were determined to write about Australia's flora and fauna'.[19]

---

[15] George Combe, 'Penal colonies: the management of prisoners in the Australian Colonies', *Phrenological Journal*, 18 (1845), 101–22.
[16] Bill Jenkins, 'Phrenology, heredity and progress in George Combe's Constitution of Man', *The British Journal for the History of Science*, 48, 3 (2015), 455–73.
[17] These were derogatory terms that emerged in the colony following Governor Macquarie's ban on the circulation of any currency except pounds sterling in 1816. They separated those with convict parents from the 'sterling' children born of free settlers.
[18] PP 1822 (448) *New South Wales: Report of the Commissioner of Inquiry into the State of the Colony of New South Wales*, 19 June 1822, 71–2. See also: John Molony *The Native-Born: the First White Australians* (Melbourne University Press, 2000), 23, 25–6, 79, 122–3. New interdisciplinary histories of convict descent show that penal transportation had positive health outcomes in Van Diemen's Land/Tasmania, particularly where the mothers of children were convicts. 'We can find no evidence that the shackles that encumbered the legs of their parents retarded the growth of colonial children of convict descent', write Hamish Maxwell-Stewart, Kris Inwood, and Jim Stankovich. See 'Prison and the Colonial Family', *The History of the Family*, 20, 2 (2015), 245 (231–48). Note that at this time, settlers often called Indigenous Australians 'black' rather than 'native'.
[19] Molony *The Native-Born*, 61–2, 80.

In places such as Brazil's Fernando de Noronha (Chapter 1), where the convict population had diverse geographical origins, visitors offered insights into what they believed this remarkable carceral melting pot revealed about race, and its relationship to criminality. H. G. Ridley, for instance, wrote of 'pure' black and indigenous convicts, as well as 'dark skinned Portuguese' and 'light [T]eutonic races'. He also noted the presence of a boy with 'brown coffee-milk skin covered with fair but copious lanugo, blue eyes light curly hair and teeth filed to sharp points'.[20] Of course, the ethnic constitution of the penal colony reflected that of the Brazilian population at large, which was composed of people of Indigenous, African, and European descent. However, in writing of a child of mixed heritage Ridley was representing Fernando as more than a microcosm of the mainland. For him, it was a place in which Brazil's cosmopolitanism could produce dangerous degradations of wildness and savagery.[21]

Ridley's comments were entirely in keeping with the language of high imperialism, in which Northern Europeans categorized and situated people within global hierarchies of human development. Important here was the publication of Charles Darwin's *On the Origin of Species* (1859), the foundational text of evolutionary biology. Related to debates about whether humankind was descended from one or multiple ancestors (monogenesis or polygenesis), Ridley's observations also drew on the heavily racialized language of criminal character or propensity which was subject to intense discussion in the last quarter of the nineteenth century.[22] Cesare Lombroso's influential *Criminal Man* (1876) first

---

[20] RBG archives HNR/5/4: The Convicts, n.d.
[21] Here, 'cosmopolitanism' refers to a society, colony, or nation composed of people of diverse origins, and which is not necessarily culturally syncretic. See Peter Van der Veer, 'Colonial Cosmopolitanism', in Robin Cohen and Steven Vertovec, eds., *Conceiving Cosmopolitanism: Theory, Context and Practice* (Oxford University Press, 2002), 165–79. On syncretism, or creolization, see Robin Cohen and Paola Toninato, ed., *The Creolization Reader: Studies in Mixed Identities and Cultures* (London: Routledge, 2009), esp. part 1.
[22] Indeed, during an earlier visit of 1876, Branner was highly critical of the convict regime, arguing that the convicts 'belonged to a low, brutal type of men', and that discipline was inconsistent and arbitrary. However, the island's natural beauty stopped him from 'brooding too long over these dark pictures of human depravity'. See John C. Branner 'The Convict-Island of Brazil – Fernando de Noronha', *The Popular Science Monthly*, 25 (1889), 36, 38 (quote, 38) (33–40). Branner criticized T. S. Lea's Royal Geographical Society article on Fernando, for its view of the 'excellence' of the convict system. He stated that if Lea had been able to speak Portuguese, he would have got 'a clear insight' into the true nature of the penal colony, which included an illegal flogging of such violence that Branner himself had been unable to watch. Branner, 'The Convict-Island of Brazil', 36–7 (unnumbered footnote). Of course, their difference in views might also be explained by the introduction of the new three-stage penal regime in 1879, and Fernando's transfer from the authority of the military to the judicial wing of government, in the years between Branner and Lea's visits (1876 and 1887). Branner himself

proposed the idea of hereditary criminality. Lombroso held that the children of convicts would be born criminal, and thus were in a natural state of 'degeneration'. Research into their physiognomy and cranial form would verify their tendency to commit crime. Lombroso linked criminality to race, for he argued that criminals were atavistic and savage, their development stalled in a 'backward' past.[23] Thus, into the 1890s, links were built between criminology, anthropology, and evolutionary biology in studies of criminal types, and their relationship to 'primitive' peoples. For example, the pioneer of eugenics, Francis Galton (Charles Darwin's cousin) was interested in connecting criminal typology to racial degeneration, and argued that criminals shared the psychology of the 'lower races'.[24] As a unique population of what Francesca Di Pasquale has described as 'the "other" at home', the Libyan deportees sent to Italy in the decades before the Second World War were also the subjects of research connecting race, criminality, and degeneration.[25] However, it is important to acknowledge that Lombroso's views were not accepted everywhere. Indeed, they contrasted with those of his French rival Alexandre Lacassagne, who believed that social factors rather than biologically driven character caused crime.[26] Another critic was French anthropologist and anatomist Léonce Manouvrier, who used statistical findings on anatomy and cranial form to argue against the kind of biological determinism favoured by Lombroso and his supporters.[27] Nonetheless, there is more than a hint of Lombrosian thinking in some of Ridley's observations: 'The most dangerous of the Brazilians are the crosses between the Indian and Mulatto or European. Usually very fine men but quarrelsome and wild savages.' He compared these people of mixed heritage to the 'Southern Brazilian half French or Italian murderers whose crimes are far more atrocious and cruel'. At the top of his scale

---

acknowledged the latter change in 'The Convict-Island of Brazil', 40. See also Peter M. Beattie, *Punishment in Paradise: Race, Slavery, Human rights, and a Nineteenth-century Penal Colony* (Durham, NC: Duke University Press, 2015), 83–4, 89, 116–7, 191–2.

[23] Lombroso, *Criminal Man*; Lombroso-Ferrero, *Criminal Man*; Davie, *Tracing the Criminal*; Gibson, *Born to Crime*; Pick, *Faces of Degeneration*, chapter 5. On 'criminal science', specific to Latin America, see Carlos Aguirre, *The Criminals of Lima and Their Worlds: The Prison Experience, 1850–1935* (Durham, NC: Duke University Press, 2005), chapter 2.

[24] Davie, *Tracing the Criminal*, 97–8.

[25] Francesca Di Pasquale, 'The "Other" at Home: Deportation and Transportation of Libyans to Italy during the Colonial Era (1911–1943)', *International Review of Social History*, 63, S26 (2018), 211–31.

[26] Marc Renneville, 'La criminologie perdue d'Alexandre Lacassagne (1843–1924)', *Criminocorpus* (2005) http://criminocorpus.revues.org/112 (accessed 18 July 2017).

[27] Jennifer Michael Hecht, *The End of the Soul: Scientific Modernity, Atheism, and Anthropology in France* (New York: Columbia University Press, 2003) chapter 3, esp. 227–35.

of crime and race sat the 'forgers and more clever criminals' who, he added, were either French or Italian.[28]

In the latter part of the nineteenth century, scientific research on convicts in penal colonies emerged from and dwelt at the intersections of these concerns and debates about crime, heredity, and race. Research on convicts spanned investigations of the relationship between biology and criminality, and work on race and ethnicity. Penal colonies offered easy access to research subjects and had the further advantage of containing an exceptionally diverse carceral community, including people from a wide range of geographical, social, and cultural origins and backgrounds. As former inspector-general of jails in the Bengal Presidency of British India, F. J. Mouat, wrote shortly before the publication of *Criminal Man*: 'Prisoners are so completely and absolutely under control, and having during the time of their incarceration so forfeited all liberty of action as to render it possible to subject them to a closeness of observation and examination, impracticable with any other class.'[29] Except in Britain where phrenology fell from favour from the middle of the nineteenth century, there is no doubt that the publication of Lombroso's *Criminal Man* reinvigorated cranial analysis as a means of research. Developed by Paul Broca, who invented several craniometric measuring instruments (craniometers), sympathetic researchers believed that statistical, empirical evidence on the form of the skull could provide objective truth about distinctions of race, gender, and character.[30] Famously, Alphonse Bertillon devised a system for the identification of criminal offenders according to the recording of anthropometric measurements and other physical attributes such as the shape of the nose, and the colour of the skin, hair, and eyes.[31] He was a delegate at the Rome International Penitentiary Congress of 1885, which discussed his anthropometric methods in some detail.[32] Bertillon's methods were adopted not just in France, but in the setting up of anthropometry studios in French Guiana

---

[28] RBG archives HNR/5/4: The Convicts, n.d. This file also contains three unattributed news clippings ('The convict island of Brazil', parts 1, 2, and 3), which, given their duplication of the material found in Ridley's notes, he likely authored. It is not known which newspaper published this material.

[29] IOR Mss Eur/F/98/31: F. J. Mouat, *The Prison System of India* (London: National Association for the Promotion of Social Science, 1872), 12.

[30] Stephen J. Gould, *The Mismeasure of Man* (London: Norton, 1981).

[31] Alphonse Bertillon, *The Identification of the Criminal Classes by the Anthropometric Method*, translated by E. R. Spearman (London: Spottiswoode and Co., 1889); Alphonse Bertillon, *Identification Anthropométrique: Instructions Signalétiques* (Paris: Melun, 1893).

[32] *Actes du Congrès Pénitentiaire International de Rome*, annexe, 'Conférence de M. Bertillon sur le fonctionnement du service d'identification part les signalements anthropométriques, 22 novembre 1885', 687–706.

Figure 9.1 Anthropometry Studio, Saint-Laurent-du-Maroni, French Guiana
Photograph by the author, 2014.

(Figure 9.1), New Caledonia, French Indochina, British India, Argentina, Uruguay, Brazil, and the USA.[33]

Colonial administrations subjected convicts to research in other ways too. Across British Asia and the French Empire, the law required colonial doctors to conduct post-mortems on deceased convicts. Issues other than the immediate cause of death often motivated these dissections, which included the removal and study of bodily organs. There are many examples of the use of convict bodies in such scientific investigations. In the 1880s, Paul Neïs, for example, a well-known naval surgeon in the

---

[33] Pierre Piazza, 'Bertillonage: The international circulation of practices and technologies of a system of forensic identification', *Criminocorpus* (2014) http://criminocorpus.revues.org /341 (accessed 25 July 2017). See also: Clare Anderson, *Legible Bodies: Race, Criminality and Colonialism in South Asia* (Oxford: Berg, 2004), 162–8; Martine Kaluszynski, 'Republican Identity: Bertillonage as Government Technique', in Jane Caplan and John Torpey, eds., *Documenting Individual Identity: The development of State practices since the French Revolution* (Princeton University Press, 2001), 123–39; Suren Lalvani, *Photography, Vision and the Production of Modern Bodies* (Albany: State University of New York Press, 1996), 108–17.

French medical service, conducted post-mortem investigations in the French penal colony of Poulo Condore. In a written summary of the dissection of some 23 men, he divided his subjects by race, noting whether they were 'Annamites' (from Annam), Cambodians, or Chinese. He then recorded their age, height, and cause of death, and the size and weight of their brains, presenting averages for each group and in aggregate. He claimed that the brains of the Cambodians were lighter than those of the Chinese, and Chinese brains were lighter than those of the Vietnamese. In their discussion of his study, members of the Anthropological Society of Paris compared his findings, especially his views on the relationship between the size and weight of the brain, with research on European, African, and Oceanic populations. Manouvrier, mentioned above, was among the discussants. The debate sidestepped the issue of biological determinism and criminality and instead focused on race. For his part, Manouvrier was unwilling to draw conclusions based on what he described as a small sample.[34] However, during the same period, another French doctor, L. Lorion, also used convicts in Poulo Condore in a study of crime and medical jurisprudence in Indochina. Like Manouvrier, Lorion was openly sympathetic to Lacassagne's view that crime had social rather than biological causes.[35]

Skulls formed another area for research. In the 1890s, a naval surgeon named Dr Birroleau sent to the Anthropological Society of Paris fifty-one French and ten Algerian skulls of male convicts who had died in the penal colony of New Caledonia. In the accompanying paperwork, he noted that he had taken the French specimens from men originating from all over the country, and he also included some information about each of them. An American scientist visiting Paris found the Algerian skulls in the set too few to investigate but examined the French skulls. He recorded their cephalic index, weighed and measured their capacity, and took the weight

[34] Paul Neïs, 'Note sur le poids des cerveaux pesés au pénitencier de Poulo-Condore (Cochinchine)', *Bulletin de la Société d'Anthropologie de Paris*, 3rd series, Volume 5 (1882), 471–92. Neïs spent almost two years in Indochina, 1882–4, and is most famous for his work amongst the Vietnamese Muong. See James George Scott, *France and Tongking: A narrative of the campaign of 1884 and the occupation of Further India* (London: T. F. Unwin, 1885). On his anatomical collecting, see also Emmanuelle Sibeud, 'A Useless Colonial Science? Practicing Anthropology in the French Colonial Empire, circa 1880–1960', *Current Anthropology*, 53, Supplement 5 (2012), S87n9 (S83–S93). Sibeud notes that Neïs sent the Anthropological Society of Paris a series of 120 measures taken from living subjects in Poulo Condore in 1880; followed by photos in 1881; and then 33 skulls, 2 skeletons, 16 brains, and 300 hair samples in 1882. Twelve years later, in 1894, another naval surgeon, one Dr Calmette, donated to the society the skulls of sixty-five convicts from New Caledonia.
[35] L. Lorion, *Criminalité et Médecine Judiciaire en Cochinchine* (Lyon: A. Storck, 1888). See also Claire E. Edington, *Beyond the Asylum: Mental Illness in French Colonial Vietnam* (Ithaca, NY: Cornell University Press), 20–3.

of each jawbone. He found little difference between these statistics and those relating to sets of skulls previously examined in France. He also found a direct correlation between the cranial index, and weight and capacity. Both were significant because, as he wrote, they supported Manouvrier's position, which as mentioned above critiqued Lombroso's idea that bodily measurements could be used to identify criminals, because they signified intelligence or character more generally.[36] A year later, in 1897, a member of the Anthropological Society, Eugène Pitard, also examined the French skulls and took various measurements of the neurocranium (the top and back of the head) and the facial skeleton. He then compared them to a sample of the same size, taken at random in France. He found also that there was little difference between them, and thus proposed it was impossible to claim the existence of a distinct criminal 'type'.[37] In other cases, convicts proved easily accessible subjects for research on hierarchies of race. In 1916, for instance, seven escaped Vietnamese convicts from French Guiana, imprisoned in Paramaribo in Dutch Surinam awaiting extradition, were among 622 subjects from all over the world who travelling scientist H. F. C. Ten Kate measured for muscular strength. He used a piece of equipment called a Mathieu dynamometer, hoping to find relationality between height and what he called 'muscular potency'.[38]

At the start of the twentieth century, British military officer and prison administrator Arthur Griffiths was clearly writing for the expectations of his metropolitan audience when he described in a popular account the moment that he took charge of the convict establishment of Gibraltar in 1869.[39] Griffiths recorded his efforts to read convict bodies for evidence of their character, 'curiously observing faces and characteristics in the endeavour to read upon the outward mask some indication of the evil propensities within

---

[36] George Grant MacCurdy, 'Le poids et la capacité du crâne, le poids de la mandibule, les indices crânio-mandibulaire, crânio-cérébral, etc. étudiés sur 61 crânes de criminels', *Bulletins de la Société d'anthropologie de Paris*, 4th series, Volume 8 (1897), 408–20. The cephalic index is the ratio of the maximum width of the skull, multiplied by 100, and divided by its maximum length. On Manouvrier, see Hecht, *The End of the Soul*, chapter 3, esp. 227–35. Though MacCurdy did not have access to women's skulls, note that Manouvrier also argued against Paul Broca's claim that skulls indicated women's inferior intelligence.

[37] Eugène Pitard, 'Étude de 51 cranes de criminels français provenant de la Nouvelle-Calédonie', *Bulletins de la Société d'anthropologie de Paris*, 4th series, Volume 9 (1898), 237–43.

[38] H. F. C. Ten Kate, 'Dynamometric Observations among Various Peoples', *American Anthropologist*, 18, 1 (1916), 15–16 (10–18).

[39] Arthur Griffiths, *Secrets of the Prison-House or Gaol Studies and Sketches, Volume I* (London: Chapman and Hall, 1894), 72.

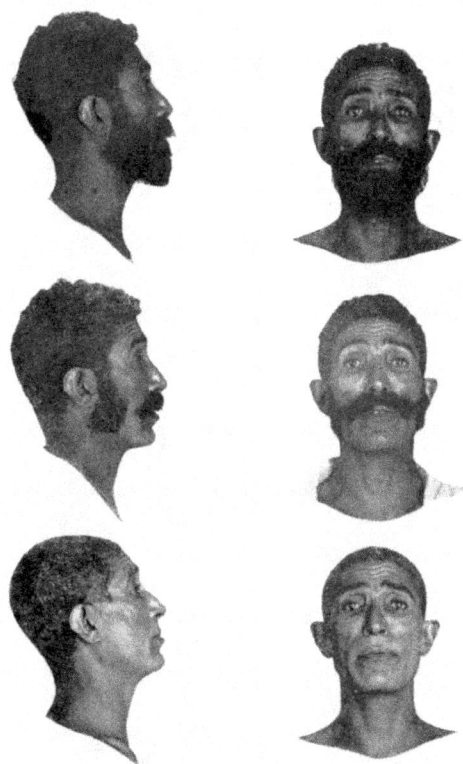

Figure 9.2 An Arab type of convict. A combination of ideality and homicidal mania.

which had culminated in crime'.[40] Journalist and explorer George Griffith too made observations about 'criminal types' in New Caledonia, in a book similarly penned for the popular market during the same period. Griffith presented three series of photographs of convicts, taken during his visit to the colony in 1899 and 1900. They pictured up to four front and profile views of individual convicts: with beards, partial beards, moustaches, and with no facial hair (Figures 9.2 and 9.3). One of the subjects was North African, and another was the famous Polish anarchist who had been transported for the attempted assassination of Napoleon III and Tsar Alexander II in Paris, Antoine Bérézowski. These kinds of photographs may have been of interest to Griffith in regards to what they appeared to reveal about

[40] Griffiths, *Secrets of the Prison-House*, 70–1.

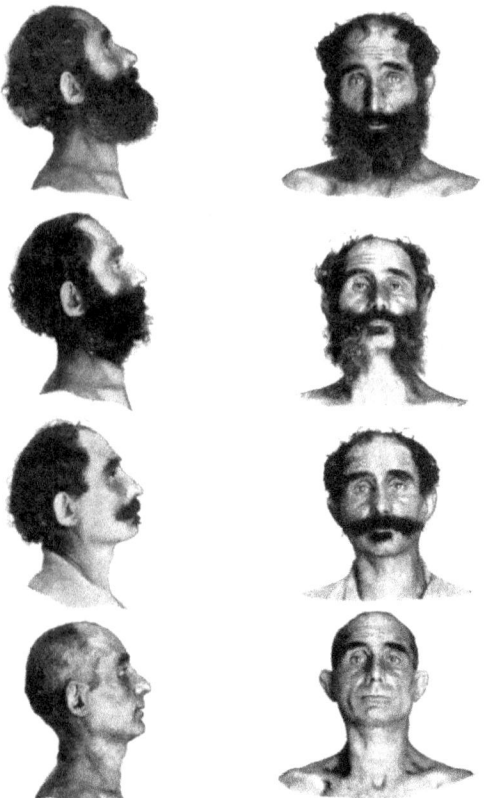

Figure 9.3 Berezowski, the Polish Anarchist who attempted to murder Napoleon III, and Tsar Alexander II, in the Champs Elysées. One of the lowest types of criminal faces. An illustration of the ease with which it is possible to disguise the chin, typical of moral weakness, and the wild-beast mouth, which nearly all criminals have, by means of moustache and beard. *Source*: George Griffith, *In an Unknown Prison Land: an account of convicts and colonists in New Caledonia with jottings out and home* (London, Hutchinson and Co: 1901), 148, 184.

criminal physiognomy, but they were in fact generated out of the desire to recognize convicts in case of escape. Indeed, Griffith noted: 'All Criminals in New Caledonia are photographed in every possible hirsute disguise; and finally cropped and clean shaven.'[41] Across contexts, convict desertion and

[41] George Griffith, *In an Unknown Prison Land: An Account of Convicts and Colonists in New Caledonia with Jottings Out and Home* (London: Hutchinson and Co., 1901), 184.

flight were ongoing and endemic, and their resistance and agency in this respect impacted on the management and operation of all convict sites and penal colonies. Photography and anthropometric measurement were technologies that appeared to offer solutions for the correct identification of suspected escapees. Despite evidence that photographs were difficult to read, and anthropometry inconsistent and unstable, officials used them extensively from the last quarter of the nineteenth century onwards.[42]

Unlike some of his contemporaries in the French medical service, Griffith was sympathetic to Lombrosian ideas about crime and heredity. Writing about a visit to an agricultural school for the sons of convicts in New Caledonia, he found 'distinct reasons for the abolition of convict marriages'. Griffith wrote:

On every face and form were stamped the unmistakable brands of criminality, imbecility, moral crookedness, and general degeneration ... I came away more convinced than ever that crime is a hereditary disease which can finally be cured only by the perpetual celibacy of the criminal.[43]

He later added that criminal physiognomy was such that if a group of French and English convicts stood side by side, it would be impossible to tell the difference between them. 'There is', he wrote, 'no nationality in crime.'[44]

Also during this period came the research of Chief Medical Officer N. S. Lobas in the town of Aleksandrovsk in Russia's far eastern penal colony of Sakhalin Island. He studied eighty ex-convicts sent to the island for murder.[45] After completing their sentence, Sakhalin convicts lived under probationary conditions in local villages for a period. Government then allowed them to leave the island, but not to return to Russia, and so their only option was to stay or to relocate to the Siberian mainland. It was from among these men that Lobas selected the subjects of his study, which took place in 1892–9. Lobas interviewed the men and scrutinized their physiognomy. He concluded that their criminality was the result of the structure of their brains, and that greed or instinct had overridden any empathy that they may have once possessed. He added that none of the men under investigation were 'born criminal' or irreclaimable. In the latter finding, Lobas departed from Lombroso. Sakhalin Island was the base for several other related convict studies, notably investigations

---

[42] For British India, see Anderson, *Legible Bodies*, chapter 5.
[43] Griffith, *In an Unknown Prison Land*, 184.
[44] Griffith, *In an Unknown Prison Land*, 231.
[45] Sharyl Corrado, The 'End of the Earth': Sakhalin Island in the Russian Imperial Imagination, 1849–1906, PhD thesis, University of Illinois at Urbana-Champaign, 2010, 123–4.

into 'criminal types' (*prestupnye tipy*).[46] They included by criminal anthropologist, Dmitrii Dril'. In 1896, under a commission from the Ministry of Justice, Dril' visited Sakhalin – and the French penal colony of New Caledonia. He was under orders to undertake a comparative study of penal colonization, including through a consideration of the earlier history of the Australian colonies. Though Dril' was an advocate of punitive relocation, he was strongly critical of conditions in Sakhalin, and doubtful that the penal regime reformed convicts. Like Lobas, he found explanations for crime in social not biological factors. Furthermore, he criticised the allocation of convicts to labour tasks to which they were unsuited, and complained of the prevalence of alcoholism, gambling, and sex work.[47] Another contemporary study was conducted by psychiatrist Lev Landau, who compiled statistics on mental illness amongst convicts in Sakhalin for the period 1896–1900, added personal observations, and compared them with rates elsewhere in Russia and in other countries.[48]

Generally speaking, Russian doctors and other contemporaries followed Lobas and Dril' in their scepticism about the idea of biological determinism as an explanation for criminality.[49] More generally, scientists attempting to study the issue often found it difficult to reconcile supposedly physiognomic markers of race with those of 'criminality'.[50] For instance, Benjamin Howard, a British trained doctor, visited Russia four times between 1887 and 1897, with the aim of completing a craniological study of convicts in Sakhalin's Korsakov Hospital. However, he did not undertake his planned research, because his initial observations seemed to indicate that all ordinary free Russians were criminals. He wrote: 'high cheek-bones, small, piggish eyes, large mouth, heavy lower jaw, large projecting ears, and receding forehead, are features which are common to the larger proportion of the lower classes in Russia, whether criminal or virtuous'. Nonetheless, he did offer some descriptions of the convicts that he encountered in Sakhalin. Though they were generally of a poor physique, and somewhat pale in

---

[46] Corrado, The 'End of the Earth', 120–6.
[47] Daniel Beer, *Renovating Russia: The Human Sciences and the Fate of liberal modernity, 1880–1930* (Ithaca, NY: Cornell University Press, 2008), chapter 3; Corrado, The 'End of the Earth', 121–3.
[48] Corrado, The 'End of the Earth', 124–6.
[49] On the other hand, note American journalist George Kennan's citation of Lombroso's declaration that revolutionaries 'have a marvelously harmonious physiognomy'. See George Kennan, *Siberia and the Exile System*, 2 volumes (New York: The Century Company, 1891), 454.
[50] This was the case in British India during this period, where supposed physiognomic markers of caste were also important. See Anderson, Legible Bodies, chapter 6.

complexion, a few had fine features. There was also a relative absence of dark-haired convicts, which seemed to contradict ideas about the physiognomy of criminal types. '[A]fter very numerous comparisons I was still unable to discover any single 'mark' which the public perceive in convicted murderers', he concluded.[51]

In contrast to its somewhat mixed reception in Britain, Russia, and France, the independent nations of Latin America were keen adherents of Lombrosian ideas about biological determinism and crime. In the first quarter of the twentieth century, the Institute of Regeneration in Buenos Aires carried out research on prisoners, and this was particularly influential.[52] As late as the 1950s, they processed convicts in central 'prison clinics', questioning them about heredity, measuring them, and ordering them to undertake intelligence tests. With the exception of Brazil, all the nation states ran centralized prison services, meaning that convicts were then despatched to other punitive locations, including agricultural colonies and offshore islands.[53] Ryan C. Edwards has discussed the ways in which Latin American states drew on European debates about the born or socially generated 'criminal' (the Italian positivist and French schools of thought respectively), to produce new ideas about crime, as 'a social pathology that was diagnosed along national lines'. By the early 1900s, as Edwards explains, 'exile and expulsion ... offered forms of political control in changing nation states'. As seen in Chapter 3, anarchists, labour organizers, and student activists were all made subject to internal transportation to distant islands and frontiers. Here, note that contemporaries could explain their activities and actions as the consequence of mental and biological degeneration.[54]

[51] Benjamin Howard, *Prisoners of Russia: A Personal Study of Convict Life in Siberia and Sakhalin* (New York: D. Appleton and Company, 1902), 251, 259, 260, 261 (quotes, 251, 260, 260–1). Note that in Bilibid Prison in the American colonial Philippines, researchers photographed convicts of diverse ethnic backgrounds for display at the Saint Louis Exposition of 1904. See Aaron Abel T. Mallari, 'The Bilibid Prison as an American Colonial Project in the Philippines', *Philippine Sociological Review*, 60 (2012), 185 (165–92).

[52] Carlos Aguirre, 'Prisons and Prisoners in Modernising Latin America (1800–1940)', in Frank Dikötter and Ian Brown, eds., *Cultures of Confinement: A History of the Prison in Africa, Asia and Latin America* (London: Hurst and Company, 2007), 29–35 (14–54).

[53] Ryan C. Edwards, 'Post-Colonial Latin America, since 1800', in Clare Anderson, ed., *A Global History of Convicts and Penal Colonies* (London: Bloomsbury, 2018), 249–56 (245–70); Richard D. Salvatore and Carlos Aguirre, 'Colonies of settlement or places of banishment and torment? Penal colonies and convict labour in Latin America, c. 1800–1940', in Christian G. De Vito and Alex Lichtenstein, eds., *Global Convict Labour* (Leiden: Brill, 2015), 273–309. See also Negley K. Teeters, *Penology from Panama to Cape Horn* (Philadelphia: University of Pennsylvania Press, 1946), 31, 254.

[54] Edwards, 'Post-Colonial Latin America', 257; Ryan Edwards, 'From the Depths of Patagonia: The Ushuaia Penal Colony and the Nature of "The End of the World"', *Hispanic American Historical Review*, 94, 2 (2014), 280 (271–302).

Medical Knowledge and Experimentation

There was a close relationship between the medical and jails services in modern nations and empires, for imperial expansion implied not just the occupation of vast swathes of land, but of the bodies of individuals and communities. In the nineteenth and twentieth centuries, prisons and penal colonies were ideal sites for the process that David Arnold has famously termed 'Colonizing the Body'.[55] Katherine Foxhall has shown that Australian transportation ships were places where doctors could observe, treat, experiment on, and dissect convict bodies. After 1815, following ex-convict doctor William Redfern's critique of medical neglect on board a ship called the *Three Bees*, naval surgeons sailed on board all convict ships. They gave out curatives and rations of wine, and subjected convicts to weekly inspections. Between 1840 and 1844, male convicts on over sixty ships became what Foxhall describes as 'source material' for a massive experiment in the prevention of scurvy. Surgeons issued lime juice, citric acid, and 'nitrate of Potass' to those men showing symptoms of scurvy and reported on their comparative efficacy. The intimacy of life below decks meant that surgeons relied greatly on convicts for information about their shipmates' illness and medical symptoms. Convicts sometimes resisted efforts at treatment, and vaccination against smallpox. However, compared to doctors on land, surgeons also had remarkable access to the bodies of the dead. During one voyage of 1828 (*William Miles*), for example, the surgeon performed six post-mortems on convict men. As Foxhall writes: 'This is a remarkable tally.' In Britain at the time, until the passing of the Anatomy Act in 1832 surgeons could legally dissect only hanged murderers.[56]

British surgeon Frederic J. Mouat took on roles that spanned the departments of the Indian government and is an excellent example of the connected histories of medicine, jails, and penal transportation. Mouat was assistant surgeon, surgeon, surgeon-major, and ultimately deputy inspector-general of hospitals (1840–70), and inspector-general of prisons Bengal (1855–70). He led the British survey expedition to locate the best site for the new Andaman Islands penal colony in 1857–8. The blending of these roles was quite typical of service in British Asia. The first

---

[55] David Arnold, *Colonizing the Body: State Medicine and Epidemic Disease in Nineteenth-Century India* (Berkeley: University of California Press, 1993).

[56] Foxhall, *Health, Medicine, and the Sea*, 13–16, 119–33, 137–41, 155–74 (quote, 38). Redfern was transported for his part in the famous naval mutiny on the Nore in 1797. Following an appointment as assistant surgeon on Norfolk Island, he received a free pardon in 1803. On the Nore mutiny, see Niklas Frykman, 'Connections between Mutinies in European Navies', *International Review of Social History*, 58, S21 (2013), 87–107.

superintendent of the Andamans, J. P. Walker, was also a doctor, and had been previously in charge of Agra jail. At the time, it was said to be the largest prison in the world.[57] Later, W. J. Buchanan was editor of the *Indian Medical Gazette* (1899–1919) and inspector-general of prisons Bengal (1902–1919). Indian jails were places where prisoners' bodies could be readily accessed for vaccination against smallpox, observed during medical trials on the effects of the withdrawal of tobacco and opium, and quantified through the production of statistics on mortality and morbidity.[58] Nonetheless, by the end of the nineteenth century, generally the British in India lacked the resources necessary to become world-leaders in medical research, and lagged behind their European and Asian competitors, including France and Japan, in work on tropical diseases. Despite research on addiction to stimulants, and the development of programmes of smallpox vaccination, only in the 1890s did Britain really start to pioneer research in areas such as leprosy, malaria, cholera, and plague.[59] The penal colony of the Andaman Islands was to play a central role in these medical innovations.

High mortality rates had threatened the permanent colonization of the Islands in 1858, for in the first eighteen months of settlement around one in three of all convicts died. Contemporaries debated the reasons for this. Medical reports included correlations between age and death, and given limitations in supply following transportation, discussions of convicts' pre-conviction use of tobacco, marijuana, and opium, and speculations on the effects of their absence.[60] However, it was not until the convict population had begun to stabilize in the 1870s that convicts first became the subjects of medical experimentation, rather than interrogation or observation. At this time, it was lepers who first came under the purview

---

[57] Clare Anderson, 'The making of an eclectic archive: Epistemologies of global knowledge in the Papers of J.P. Walker (1823–1906)', in Rohan Deb Roy and Guy N. A. Attewell, eds., *Locating the Medical: Explorations in South Asian History* (New Delhi: Oxford University Press, 2017), 151–68.

[58] Clare Anderson, '"The Wisdom of the Barbarian": Rebellion, incarceration, and the santal body politic', *South Asia: Journal of South Asian Studies*, 31, (2008), 223–40; Arnold, *Colonizing the Body*, 129–33.

[59] David Arnold, *The New Cambridge History of India III. 5: Science, Technology and Medicine in Colonial India* (Cambridge University Press, 2000), 71–87; Sanjoy Bhattacharya, Mark Harrison, and Michael Worboys, *Fractured States: Smallpox, Public Health and Vaccination Policy in British India, 1800–1947* (New Delhi: Orient Longman, 2001).

[60] IOR P/206/60 (India judicial proceedings, 12 November 1858): Superintendent J. P. Walker to Cecil Beadon, secretary to government of India, 4 September 1858, enc. report on the causes of the severe sickness and great mortality which has prevailed amongst the convicts at Port Blair penal settlement in the Andaman Islands, since the formation of the settlement on the 10th March, up to the 25th August 1858; IOR P/206/61 (India judicial proceedings, 29 July 1859): Report by Dr G. G. Brown on the sanitary state of the Andamans, March 1859.

of the colonial government. In 1873, the senior medical officer, Surgeon-Major J. Dougall, started to treat twenty-four leprous convicts confined in separate barracks at the convict hospital in Haddo, using resin from a tree that grew locally, *Dipterocarpus turbinatus*. He knew that Indians already used this resin, known as wood oil or gurjun oil, for the treatment of gonorrhoea. Dougall began by giving his patients six drops of the oil per day, gradually increasing the dose to sixty drops. He then issued them with a body rub ointment consisting of a mixture of gurjun and coconut oil. Dougall directed that his patients' bathe twice per day, rub the ointment into their skin for two hours, remove it with dry earth, and wash again. He considered that the lengthy treatment would allow proper absorption of the ointment and promote physical and mental health. Dougall changed the composition of the ointment twice, first replacing the coconut with carbonate of soda, and then with lime water. After settling on the latter, he stopped issuing the drops to his patients, and directed them instead to take a half ounce dose of the ointment twice a day. Dougall claimed noticeable improvements in the convicts' health: healed ulcers, a reduction in the size of tubercles, and the restoration of sensation in various parts of the body. He claimed that the ointment was so popular that the convicts constantly asked for more. Meantime, he removed growths from the foot of one patient, taking them away for microscopic examination. He made other intimate observations, constructing a table detailing his patients' bowel movements, and reporting that his ointment was 'a powerful diuretic and evacuant'.[61]

One of Dougall's supporters, an assistant apothecary in the Madras army, G. W. Phillips, wrote: 'Men who were a spectacle of pity, unable to sit, stand, walk, run, eat, sleep, or answer the calls of nature, and ever troubled with swarm[s] of flies, now possess such healthy constitutions, that one can scarcely believe it without seeing.'[62] The men had restored mobility in their fingers and toes, and the hair on one man's body had even regrown. No fewer than nine surgeons and two deputy surgeons-general visited Haddo to inspect Dougall's leper patients, and one of them declared that he was viewing 'almost a miracle'.[63] However, not everybody was

---

[61] J. Dougall, *Report on the Treatment of Leprosy with Gurjon Oil* (Calcutta: Wyman and Co., 1876), 11. Dougall took two sets of photographs of his patients, taken several months apart, to prove his point. Unfortunately, these photographs were not reproduced in either this pamphlet or *The Indian Medical Gazette*. Dougall died of typhoid a few years later in 1879. This was noted in IOR Mss Eur F388/2: letter from the Reverend Warneford to his daughter Maud Warneford, 31 March 1879.

[62] The Gurjon Oil Treatment of Leprosy, at Port Blair: G. W. Phillips, assistant apothecary Madras army, to G. C. Roy, Bengal medical service, in Dougall, *Report on the Treatment of Leprosy* (59–73).

[63] Phillips to Roy, in Dougall, *Report on the Treatment of Leprosy*, 62–3.

convinced by the power of the treatment. It was pointed out the improvements might have been brought about by better hygiene and regular ablutions, rather than the effects of the ointment *per se*. Indian surgeon G. C. Roy wrote: 'convict warders shake their heads ominously when asked to give their common-sense experience of it'.[64] Nonetheless, the apparently positive palliative effects of Dougall's gurjun ointment led to the adoption of his regime by several hospitals and dispensaries on the Indian mainland, including in Madras. Doctors there reported that it much improved symptoms among patients. In Madura, a native apothecary recently returned from service in Port Blair assisted British doctors 'in getting the treatment carried out properly'.[65] Andamans doctors also adopted Dougall's dry earth rub for the treatment of ulcers in Haddo. G. W. Phillips stated that in sixteen years of service, he had never seen so many and of such large size, the causes including abrasions from falling stones, bamboo and thorns, injuries from working tools, and accidents. During the same period, experiments in the treatment of ulcers in Ross Island hospital claimed the effectiveness of the application of a layer of muslin soaked in carbolic acid between the sore and a poultice of dry earth.[66]

By 1910, around 15 per cent of all prisoners in British India were serving their sentences in the Andamans.[67] Peaking at a standing total of over 14,500 in 1906, the Islands presented a very large number of convicts from diverse regions and communities of the Indian subcontinent, concentrated mainly in a relatively small area of South Andaman, who were readily available for medical research. The British medical officers stationed in the Islands routinely gathered health statistics, employing their data in studies of morbidity and mortality, and including them in the annual reports that the administration sent to the British

---

[64] G. C. Roy, 'Remarks on the Gurjon Oil Treatment of Leprosy at Port Blair', in Dougall, *Report on the Treatment of Leprosy*, 51–9 (quote 56).

[65] *Report on the Treatment of Leprosy with Gurjun Oil and Other Remedies in Hospitals of the Madras Presidency* (Madras: Government Press, 1876), 3–5, 62–63 (quote, 63). Dougall's palliative was widely discussed in India. See, for example, 'Gurjon-Oil in the treatment of skin diseases', *The Indian Medical Gazette*, 1 June 1875, 157. For a discussion of Dougall's Andaman treatments in their larger regional context, see Jane Buckingham, *Leprosy in Colonial South India: Medicine and confinement* (Basingstoke: Palgrave Macmillan, 2001), 88–91.

[66] G. W. Phillips, 'Observations on the Treatment of Ulcers in the Convict Hospital at Haddo, in Medical Charge of Surgeon J. Bird, MD, and Medical Officer, Port Blair', *The Indian Medical Gazette*, 1 February 1875, 37 (37–8).

[67] In 1910, there were 98,032 inmates. 'India', *The British Medical Journal*, 5 October 1912, 902 (901–4).

parliament.[68] Following Dougall's experiments on leprosy, British surgeons used convicts to research other medical concerns and theories, and to test various interventions. They also carried out post-mortems on all deceased convicts, for dissection was compulsory under Andaman regulations. As corpora of statistics, experimentation, and discovery, Andaman convict bodies made a profound contribution to the development of medical knowledge. Indeed, as one of the delegates at London's Sanitary Congress, the physician royal to the queen, put it in 1904: 'the penal settlement of Port Blair affords exceptional opportunities for effective experimental measures'.[69] For example, dysentery rates in the penal colony were high, and Officiating Senior Medical Officer Ernest Waters was convinced that they were caused by the ingestion of mouldy wheat. He undertook experiments in cleaning and grinding wheat in different ways, issuing it to different groups of convicts, and observing whether they became sick or not. Finding the healthiest method, he subsequently made recommendations with a view to reducing the illness.[70]

Another more enduring and systematic focus of medical research in the Andamans was malaria. Following the devastation that afflicted the penal colony during the first two years of settlement during 1858–9, death rates in the Islands remained notoriously high. In the absence of the knowledge that mosquito-borne parasites caused malaria, as Chapter 10 explores, contemporary explanations of them were resonant of the conclusions of Joseph Orgéas in French Guiana at around the same time. In his 1881–2 annual report, for example, Senior Medical Officer James Reid wrote: 'The great and permanent cause of sickness here is the malarial, unhealthy nature of the stations on which convicts are located.' He was referring to swamp reclamation and forest work, and in line with the common belief that effluvia emanating from marshy ground caused malaria, he made the connection between jungle clearance and convict health. '[T]hose very works to which we look *ultimately* for some permanent improvement in convict health are', he wrote, '*during their progress*, themselves powerful causes in the production of sickness.'[71] In the meantime, beginning in 1880, in an effort to control malarial fever, the British issued 1,500 labouring convicts in the northern and southern districts of

---

[68] Analysis of disease and death amongst convicts in the Andaman Islands featured in annual *Reports on the Administration of the Andaman and Nicobar Islands and the Penal Settlement of Port Blair*.

[69] 'Congress of the Sanitary Institute', *The British Medical Journal*, 6 August 1904 (motion of Sir R. Douglas Powell).

[70] PP 1906 (3559) *East India (sanitary measures). Report on sanitary measures in India in 1905–1906*, Volume 39, 77.

[71] PP 1882 (3776) *East India (sanitary measures). Report on Sanitary Measures in India, 1881–82*, 77, 78.

South Andaman three grains of cinchona febrifuge daily. This was a cheaper alternative to quinine.[72]

Perhaps the most famous medical researcher in British India during this period was Ronald Ross. In work carried out in 1895–8, he discovered that it was not contaminated air that spread malaria, but the female *Anopheles* mosquito, which was the vector of the malaria parasite. In 1902, Ross received the Nobel Prize for this discovery.[73] In the years leading up to this award, in 1885 and again in 1886–8, Ross had been stationed in the Andamans, when he was in medical charge of a regiment of the 9th Madras Infantry. Ross's observation that malaria broke out even in the breezy environment of the Islands contributed to his later critique of the conventional medical wisdom that contaminated air emanating from marshy ground or soil transmitted malaria. Ross's insight from the penal colony proved of lasting significance to the development of his work, which was globally important and influential.[74]

Though Ross had long since departed the Islands when he connected malaria to mosquitos, following his discovery, the British administration of the penal colony acted quickly to try and reduce outbreaks of malaria among the convict population. It set out to find the cheapest possible methods of preventing mosquitos from breeding, and established and equipped what it called convict mosquito brigades to undertake any necessary work.[75] The latter were inspired by Ross's handbook *Mosquito Brigades and How to Organise Them*, which included guidance specific to India, and which was circulated around the convict stations.[76] The brigades were part of a larger programme of malaria prevention in the Islands, which had four strands: the maintenance of general good health amongst convicts, the eradication of mosquitos, the prevention of bites,

---

[72] Rohan Deb Roy, *Malarial Subjects: Empire, Medicine and Nonhumans in British India, 1820–1909* (Cambridge University Press, 2017), 184–92.
[73] Arnold, *The New Cambridge History of India III.5*, 145.
[74] Ronald Ross, *Memoirs: With a Full Account of the Great Malaria Problem and Its Solution* (London: John Murray, 1923), 63–72, 130. Ross writes nothing about his medical work in the Islands, noting only that it was 'scanty', 68. On the intertwined histories of quinine, mosquitos, and malaria in South Asia at the turn of the twentieth century, see Rohan Deb Roy, 'Quinine, Mosquitos and Empire: Reassembling Malaria in British India, 1890–1910', *South Asian History and Culture*, 4, 1 (2013), 65–86. As late as 1951, one French scientist used evidence of dozens of dissections from across Indochina, including of seventy-four convicts in Poulo Condore, to confirm the relevance of Ross's findings about the *Anopheles leucosphyrus* mosquito as a vector of malaria throughout Asia. See John McArthur, 'The Importance of *Anopheles leucosphyrus*', *Transactions of the Royal Society of Tropical Medicine and Hygiene*, 44, 6 (1951), 686, 688 (683–94).
[75] 'Congress of the Sanitary Institute', *The British Medical Journal*, 6 August 1904, 289.
[76] Ronald Ross, *Mosquito Brigades and How to Organise Them* (London: George Philip and Son, 1902). On malaria eradication in India more generally, including a discussion of the work of Ross and the 'mosquito brigades', see Deb Roy, *Malarial Subjects*, chapter 5.

and the compulsory issue of doses of quinine. At this time, the settlement's surgeons noted two things. First, that the most established, cleared convict stations like Aberdeen, Haddo, and Phoenix Bay were the least malarial, and second that the greatest number of malaria cases occurred in those who worked outdoors. Drawing on these observations, and following a small trial on Viper Island, the British administration sent out 200-strong convict mosquito brigades to clean drains, fill in puddles, remove rubbish, and cut back undergrowth. They put the blood of all fever cases under the microscope, looking for malarial parasites. This was a huge undertaking: they examined the blood of 10,387 convicts admitted to hospital in 1913–14 alone.[77] Given the scale, it is perhaps not surprising that convicts undertook at least some of this microscopic work. Indeed, Officiating Medical Superintendent Ernest Waters trained them to prepare the samples, identify the different kinds of parasites, and even perform differential blood cell counts.[78] The chapter comes back to the employment of convicts in penal colony hospitals.

The number of mosquitos in the convict stations visibly declined, but disappointingly for the British, the number of malaria cases did not. The strategy to prevent bites was problematic. The burning pastilles smelled so bad that people could not stand to light them. The nets interfered with ventilation and rendered convict barracks unbearably hot. Despite Ross's prize-winning discovery, medical investigations into both the spread and eradication of malaria continued. For instance, Waters conducted an experiment among a 120-strong convict gang, giving quinine to only half the convicts, but found that it made little difference to malaria infection. Neither did another experiment, in which he directed the issue of quinine to 80 per cent of convicts on two successive days each week. Waters concluded that the need to keep convicts fit and in good health, however desirable, was incompatible with punishment, outdoor labour, and ongoing work in land clearance.[79]

Waters also maintained the belief that the inhabitants of the Islands suffered relapses of malaria following exposure to damp and cold

---

[77] Ernest Edwin Waters, 'Malaria in the Andamans Penal Settlement', *The Lancet*, 13 June 1903, 1658–60 (1657–62). This includes material from Waters' article 'Malarias as seen in the Andamans Penal Settlement', *The Indian Medical Gazette*, 38 (December 1903), 419–20, 444–8. See also PP (8087) *East India (Sanitary Measures). Report on sanitary measures in India in 1913–1914*, Volume 47, 68.

[78] Waters, 'Malaria in the Andamans Penal Settlement', 1662.

[79] Waters, 'Malaria in the Andamans Penal Settlement', 1657–62. For an analysis of deaths in the Andamans, directly and indirectly caused by malaria, during the period 1872–1939, see G. Dennis Shanks and David J. Bradley, 'Island Fever: The Historical Determinants of Malaria in the Andaman Islands', *Transactions of the Royal Society of Tropical Medicine and Hygiene*, 104, 3 (2010), 185–90.

weather. He continued an experiment previously initiated by Senior Medical Officer A. R. S. Anderson on the effect of the use of mosquito nets in one of the most malarial parts of the settlement: the female jail, on the outskirts of Port Blair. The men's interest was not solely medical; it also related to their desire to avoid the large number of days lost to public works through convict hospital admissions. In 1902, Waters claimed, the latter was the equivalent of 2,000 people removed from labour for 98 days of the year. Anderson and Waters' experiment divided 37 convict women into three groups. They placed the first group under mosquito nets from dusk to sunrise, issued the second with quinine, and gave the third neither nets nor quinine. The rates of admission to hospital were 1007, 2421, and 4,177 per 1,000 respectively. This proved to the men that the avoidance of mosquito bites was the best way to prevent malaria.[80] They backed up their findings by taking blood samples from all 37 women, examining them for evidence of malaria parasites.[81]

During 1901–6, Anderson oversaw a staggering 73,991 cases of malaria in the convict hospitals, which resulted in 230 deaths. He scrutinized notes on convict post-mortems and carried out his own dissections, looking closely at the spleen, which was known to become swollen in malarial patients, for evidence of ulceration.[82] Assisted by Indian Assistant-Surgeon S. N. Datta, his case records included detailed information on the health histories of individual convicts, both prior to and during transportation, as well as treatment practices.[83] However, rates of infection remained stubbornly high, and so the government of India dispatched S. R. Christophers to investigate rates of malaria in the Andamans. Christophers was director of India's Central Malaria Bureau. He went all over the Islands, choosing the self-supporter villages as the focus of his investigations. Because ticket-of-leave families were less mobile than labouring convicts, he believed that they would best reveal

---

[80] Waters, 'Malaria in the Andamans Penal Settlement', 1658. There are resonances here with the 'quinine parades' introduced in the prisons of the Punjab, where prisoners were made to take a dose of the anti-malarial drug. Malaria rates among prisoners were consequently much lower than in the free population, leading doctors to conclude that jails were models of medical order that they should replicate in wider society. See Deb Roy, 'Quinine, Mosquitos and Empire', 75.

[81] PP (3152) *East India (sanitary measures). Report on sanitary measures in India in 1904–1905*, Volume 38, 80.

[82] 'Splenic Abscess in Malarial Fever', *The Lancet*, 27 October 1906, 1159–60 (discussion of A. R. S. Anderson's article in *The Indian Medical Gazette*). There had also been an additional 3,446 cases in the police hospital (and 5 deaths) and 512 cases in the free hospital. We now know that the spleen becomes swollen because it generates the body's immune response to the malaria parasite, and controls the removal of infected red blood cells.

[83] A. R. S. Anderson, 'Splenic Abscess in Malarial Fever', *The Indian Medical Gazette*, 41 (June 1906), 212–3.

the relative health of locations. He examined these ex-convict families, including their children, for evidence of enlarged spleens and parasite infestation. He then turned to the convict stations, scrutinizing the blood of over 100 convicts, in and out of hospital. He concluded that 61 per cent of convicts in hospital had malaria, and others had a 'high rate of infection'. Christophers also correlated rates of fever with rates of rainfall, concluding that outbreaks of malaria rose during the rainy season. Through comparison with 1911 Census sick rates, and hospital admissions data, he added weight to the turn-of-the-century view that it prevailed amongst convicts employed in outdoor labour. This included excavation work, road building, and cane-cutting. Overall, and for that reason, convicts were more affected by malaria than self-supporters.[84]

The government's immediate concern was health in the penal colony. However, Christophers' research fed into the global interchange of scientific research on the reasons for variable rates of infection. He noted the unknown character of mortality pathways during Indian epidemics and viewed the 'unique' conditions in the Andamans as a means of advancing knowledge in this respect. '[N]ot only is every member of the community under close observation', he wrote, 'but in the case of death an autopsy is performed as a routine practice.' In addition to the drawing of blood from convicts in the labouring stations, to ascertain to what extent convicts brought malarial infection with them in transportation, he examined the spleens of new arrivals in the cellular jail, searching for signs of swelling. He noted that though in some years most deaths occurred amongst those newly arrived in the penal colony, this was not always the case. He weighed the spleens of deceased convicts subject to post-mortems. He concluded that though malaria only directly caused 10 to 14 per cent of deaths amongst convicts, the weight of the spleen in pneumonia cases suggested that it was a contributing factor.[85]

A related research focus was what doctors called 'epidemic jaundice', which broke out in 1892–1901, and again in 1904, 1911, and 1926. Medical officers described its sudden and often-fatal onset, on occasion following attacks of malaria, and set out to investigate its cause.[86] They found that it largely inflicted men who had been working in swamps or paddy fields, and conducted post-mortems on those who died to discover why some but not all malaria patients developed it. A 1928 experiment even included the injection of guinea-pigs with the blood and urine of

---

[84] S. R. Christophers, *Malaria in the Andamans* (Calcutta: Superintendent of Government Printing, 1912), 3–4, 12–19, 23–6, 31.
[85] Christophers, *Malaria in the Andamans*, 29–30, 33, 34, 35, 38 (quote, 30).
[86] A. K. Chowdry, 'Jaundice at Port Blair, Andaman Islands', *The Indian Medical Gazette*, 38 (December 1903), 409–11.

deceased men. The animals did not develop the disease, and so doctors sent serums from the deceased convicts to the mainland and compared them with those from other cases, to see if they could identify a specific Andaman strain. Ultimately, they concluded that the convicts were, in fact, suffering from Weil's disease, a particularly severe type of *leptospirosis*.[87] In 1911, Anderson's successor as senior medical officer, J. M. Woolley, also used medical records and post-mortem dissections to investigate the relationship between malaria and dysentery. Given the continued employment of convicts in timber camps in the Islands' dense forests, he despaired of the possibility of an improvement in general health. Meantime, the death rate in the Andamans remained much higher than in Indian jails, and this was even more marked because, as Woolley noted, government only transported convicts in good health and between the ages of 20 and 40.[88] Into the 1930s, the British engaged in anti-malarial research and prevention programmes, particularly under Chief Commissioner Charles Ferrar. He described malaria as one of the five main challenges in the Islands, and engaging with the medical literature, Ferrar oversaw an acceleration of swamp draining and land reclamation.[89]

It was often individual professional interest that drove medical research in the Andamans, though in the context of larger global debates. Indeed, in 1913, J. M. Woolley, likely influenced by Emile Durkheim's famous book on the social causes of suicide, published work on suicide among convict men. Woolley noted that over the past ten years, five women had attempted suicide, and sixty-five men had committed suicide. For men this equated to a suicide rate of 0.504 per thousand, which was 16.9 times higher than that of Bengal. The rate of suicide attempts among convict women was high, for at the time there were just 720 convict women in the penal colony, but followed Indian patterns because women were more than twice as likely as men to take their own lives. Otherwise, among the men, convicts transported for murder were 3.5 times more likely to commit suicide than who had been convicted of other offences. Hindus were more likely to commit suicide than Burmese or Muslims.[90] Woolley

---

[87] H. C. Brown, 'Epidemic Jaundice in the Andaman Islands', *The Lancet*, 25 February 1928, 388 (388); Chowdry, 'Jaundice at Port Blair', 410.

[88] J. M. Woolley, 'The Andamans: The Prevalence of Malaria and its perverse effect on the health of its convicts', *The Indian Medical Gazette*, 46 (January 1911), 409–15.

[89] Madumita Mazumdar, 'Improving visions, troubled landscapes: The legacies of Colonial Ferrargunj', in Clare Anderson, Madhumita Mazumdar, and Vishvajit Pandya, *New Histories of the Andaman Islands: Landscape, Place and Belonging across the Bay of Bengal, 1790–2012* (Cambridge University Press, 2014), 42–4.

[90] J. M. Woolley, 'Suicide among Indian convicts under transportation', *The British Journal of Psychiatry*, 59, 245 (1913), 339–40, 342 (335–343).

argued that suicide was unrelated to the severity of labour but explained by character and confinement. The 'submissive and docile nature' of Hindus, compared to 'masterful, active and self-reliant' Muslims, meant that they were less able to cope with transportation. Youth, and the absence of what Woolley called 'controlling and steadying influences' were also factors.[91] As for confinement, a cellular jail had been opened in 1906 to receive of all newly arrived convicts for an initial six-month penal stage. Convicts in the jail were more than six times more likely to commit suicide than those outside it. Woolley wrote that this was due to the 'acute mental depression' induced by solitary confinement, particularly for those facing sentences of life.[92] Indeed, convicts who had been in the penal colony for less than two years accounted for almost half of all suicides.[93]

As noted above, the requirement to conduct post-mortems on deceased convicts greatly facilitated medical research in the Andaman Islands, and this was a feature of penal colonies elsewhere. In French Guiana, for example, doctors also used convicts to investigate the causes, effects, and prevention of ulcers, yellow fever, and malaria. They were particularly intrigued by the possibilities that the colony offered for the study of apparent racial variations in prevalence and immunity. This was because convicts of European, Algerian, African, and East Asian descent were all present in the colony, and so it was possible to research patterns of morbidity and mortality specific to each group. In regard to ulcers, for example, in 1885, naval surgeon Le Dantec took skin and tissue from ulcerated Algerian convicts for microscopic analysis. He wanted to see if he could identify a single bacillus common to all, to prove that such ulcers were not location specific.[94] Yellow fever had been a deadly obstacle to colonization since the end of the eighteenth century. In 1881, the Cuban doctor Carlos Finlay first proposed that mosquitos were the vector for the disease, but it was not until 1901 that William Reed, a member of the US Army Medical Corps, then working in Cuba, confirmed the theory. A vaccine followed in 1937.[95] In the meantime, French medical officers

---

[91] Woolley, 'Suicide among Indian Convicts', 340.
[92] Woolley, 'Suicide among Indian Convicts', 338.
[93] Woolley, 'Suicide among Indian Convicts', 338, 341. For Woolley's work on convict marriage, see R. F. Lowis, *Census of India, 1921, Volume II: The Andaman and Nicobar Islands*, (Calcutta: Superintendent of Government Printing, 1923), Appendix B: J. M. Woolley, 'Convict Marriages in the Andamans', reprinted from *The Indian Medical Gazette* 47, 3 (March 1912), 89–94.
[94] Docteur Le Dantec, 'Origine Microbienne de l'Ulcère Phagèdénique des Pays Chauds', *Archives de médicine navale*, 43 (1885), 448–53.
[95] Specifically, yellow fever is a viral disease spread by the female *Aedes aegypti* mosquito. A vaccination was developed in 1937 by South African Max Thelier, for which he was

speculated at length on its origins, impact, and spread, commonly characterizing it as an atmospheric miasma, with disease vectors including infected grain, blankets, and beds. They used convicts, as well as soldiers, guards, and their families, in medical investigation and experimentation. This included detailed discussion of patient histories, and post-mortem dissection, as in the case of E. Maurel's work.[96] In 1880, P. Burot, who in 1877 and 1878 had undertaken medical service in Cayenne and Saint-Laurent-du-Maroni, speculated that yellow fever was related to but distinct from what he called 'la fièvre bilieuse inflammatoire' (inflammatory bilious fever). This was a capacious medical definition that medics used in the nineteenth century to describe many kinds of fevers, and which were thought to arise from disorders of bile. In support of his theory, Burot penned a lengthy history of disease in the colony, drawing from annual reports, hospital case notes, and his own observations. This included detailed reports of the post-mortem dissections of North African and European male convicts, convict women, soldiers, guards and their wives and children, and indentured Indian labourers then working in the interior of the colony.[97]

Post-mortems also fed into research on hookworm in French Guiana, carried out by Chief Medical Officer Riou-Kérangal in the 1860s. He conducted post-mortem research on the presence of the parasite in the intestines of anaemic convicts, finding it to be endemic, especially among Europeans.[98] Forty years later, another French naval surgeon, E. Brimont, carried out research on hookworm on living convicts. He took stool samples from almost 800 men, finding infestation rates averaging as high as 72 per cent. When he looked at the stool samples of 63 patients in the convict hospital in Cayenne, taken at random, he found that rates soared to 89 per cent. Brimont discovered that the longer convicts had spent in the colony, the more likely the presence of the parasite. Indeed, in Saint-Laurent-du-Maroni it affected 88 to 90 per cent of convicts who had been present in the colony for at least three years. Infestations among the local, free population in the same location averaged 35 per cent. Brimont used these findings to argue that though hookworm was not a cause of death, it weakened convicts and

awarded a Nobel Prize in 1951, and became the first African-born recipient of the honour.
[96] Maurel, *Traité des Maladies Pauldéennes à la Guyane.*
[97] P. Burot, *De la Fièvre dite Bilieuse Inflammatoire à la Guyane: application des découvertes de M. Pasteur à la pathologie des pays chauds* (Paris: Octave Doin, 1880), 73, 74–9.
[98] Emile Yves Riou-Kérangal, 'L'Ankylostome duodénal, observé à Cayenne', *Archives de Médicine Navale* (1868), 311. See also J. Orgéas, *La Pathologie Des Races Humaines et le Problème de la Colonisation: Étude anthropologique et économique faite à la Guyane Française* (Paris: Octave Doin, 1886), 173.

rendered them more prone to often-fatal illnesses like malaria, diarrhoea, and pneumonia.[99] To prove this point, he presented a convict case history, in which a man known to us only as 'Samuel' spoke of his debilitated state of health. Brimont took and studied a blood sample and made other medical observations, and after 'Samuel' died he conducted a post-mortem dissection.[100]

In some cases, French doctors used fluids extracted from deceased convicts and penal colony personnel and used them in the experimental inoculation of animals. Burot, for example, injected a dog with forty drops of blood drawn from a man that he believed had died of bilious fever, in the convict hospital at Saint-Laurent-du-Maroni.[101] During an epidemic of yellow fever the Îles du Salut in 1885, Medical Officer C. Rangé similarly used convicts to try to develop a cure. He took samples of fever victims' vomit and blood, and injected it into chickens, dogs, guinea-pigs, and rabbits. He then monitored the animals for disease expressions. A substantial proportion of them died, and despite the ultimate failure of his medical experiments, Rangé concluded that a yellow fever bacillus did exist, and ultimately it would be possible to vaccinate against it.[102] In other cases, convicts volunteered for medical procedures, in exchange for early release or other incentives. Joseph Orgéas detailed 'numerous experiments' to destroy the larvae of *Lucilia hominivorax* (blowflies), which were prevalent in convicts' nostrils and eyes. He described chloroform injections as the most effective treatment, but as they were very painful he preferred to use benzene.[103] In Nouméa, New Caledonia, during the plague epidemic of 1914, a convict named Julien Lespès agreed to be infected, in exchange for the remission of the remainder of his sentence of twenty years forced labour. He survived the experience, but died the following year, possibly by suicide.[104] This was not the first time that an epidemic of plague had hit New Caledonia. As

---

[99] E. Brimont, 'Ankylostomiase en Guyane française', *Bulletin de la Société de Pathologie Exotique*, 2 (1909), 413–17. This represented 15 per cent of the convicts and *relégués* then in the three settlements. The exact rates of infestation were: 72 per cent in Saint-Laurent-du-Maroni, 73 per cent in Saint-Jean-du-Maroni, and 51 per cent in the Îles du Salut.

[100] E. Brimont and M. Ceillier, 'Sur un cas de l'ankylostome maligne avec autopsie', *Bulletin de la Société de Pathologie Exotique*, 2 (1909), 418–23.

[101] Burot, *De la Fièvre dite Bilieuse Inflammatoire à la Guyane*, 480.

[102] Docteur C. Rangé, 'Étude sur l'Épidémie de Fièvre Jaune, ayant sévi aux Îles du Salut (Guyane) du 22 février 1885 au 25 juillet', *Archives de médicine navale*, 45 (1886), 181–206. Prisoners in the Philippines were also used in medical trials, on cholera. See Mallari, 'The Bilibid Prison', 185.

[103] Orgéas, *La Pathologie Des Races Humaines et le Problème de la Colonisation*, 131.

[104] Philippe Collin, 'Poètes au bagne de Nouvelle-Calédonie: Vies et écrits de Julien Lespès et Julien de Sanary ... ou comment survivre par l'écriture', *Criminocorpus* (2015) http://criminocorpus.hypotheses.org/10490 (accessed 5 October 2017).

1899 became a new century, the third global pandemic hit the colony, and consequently it was put into quarantine. Transportation had ceased in 1897, but there remained in the colony convicts under sentence, *libérés* (time-served convicts who were bound to remain in the colony), and convict descendants. Government particularly blamed North African *libérés* for the spread of plague, claiming that like Indigenous Kanak people and Asian and Pacific islander immigrants, they lived in more overcrowded and squalid conditions than free white settlers, which made them more susceptible to infection. There is some evidence to suggest that the French underreported deaths from plague among French settlers, and whether this was the case or not it is abundantly clear that plague enabled the administration to connect race, hygiene, and disease. Indeed, it reported that fifty-nine of the eighty deaths occurred among Asians and Pacific islanders, and just twenty-one among Europeans. Fourteen of the latter were convicts.[105]

If doctors used convicts for medical research, they also employed them in medical service: as compounders, medical assistants, and nurses. Given the respite from hard labour and more generous allowance of rations that they received, despite the risk of infection it is understandable that they regarded hospital work as desirable. Earlier, the chapter detailed the incorporation of convicts into practices of medical research in the Andamans. Note also that the authorities in Korsakov hospital, Sakhalin Island, employed convicts.[106] There exists particularly detailed information on convict nurses in the hospitals of French Guiana and New Caledonia in the writings of Léon Collin, who served six years in the colonial service, from 1907 to 1913. Following previous postings in Indochina, Senegal, and Madagascar, during this period he accompanied at least seven convict convoys into transportation. In 1913, he wrote about the Marais convict hospital of New Caledonia, which was located on Île Nou. The establishment had opened in 1871 following the arrival of the first transportation convoys four years earlier. At first, until at least 1900, the nurses in Marais hospital were nuns from the order of Saint-Joseph de Cluny. Subsequently, convicts replaced them. Collin claimed that convict patients called these convict nurses 'vampires', because they extorted money from them in exchange for the provision of medical care. They would even refuse to administer prescription morphine injections, if they failed to receive payment. When convicts died, Collin wrote, the nurses stole their *plans*, the small cartridges in which convicts concealed

---

[105] William Cavert, 'At the Edge of an Empire: Plague, State and Identity in New Caledonia, 1899–1900', *The Journal of Pacific History*, 51, 1 (2016), 9, 10, 19 (1–20).
[106] Howard, *Prisoners of Russia*, 248.

money and other small items, and which they commonly hid in the anus.[107]

*

This chapter has argued that convicts were subjects of medical observation and research, during a period in which ideas about the relationship between race, criminality, degeneration, and heredity were much debated. Scientists described, measured, and dissected convict bodies, including the skulls and brains of subjects living and dead. Convicts were easily accessible populations, and either they attempted to connect cranial form and other physiognomic features to so-called criminal character, or they appropriated them as subjects of larger studies of racial difference. In the British and French empires, doctors used convicts to study the physical effects of narcotic addiction, to develop treatments for diseases such as scurvy and malaria, and to study outbreaks of plague. Chapter 8 highlighted the ambivalent position of convicts as involuntary settlers, for whilst imperial states incorporated them into expropriative coerced migration and labour, at the same time they possessed agency in regard to some elements of exploration and scientific research. This chapter has revealed similar tensions. Convicts had little choice in complying with intrusive questioning, inspection, and treatment, yet towards the end of the period discussed here they also become involved in medical studies. Whether they were willing subjects or not, the information that convict bodies yielded made key contributions to medical debates and developments in the nineteenth and twentieth centuries. They played a similar role in the history of the human sciences, and it is that which is the subject of the following pages.

---

[107] ANC 61J1: Léon Collin, Fin de bagne en Nouvelle-Calédonie, 1913. This manuscript is reproduced alongside Collin's writings on French Guiana, in Léon Collin, *Des Hommes et des Bagnes: Guyane et Nouvelle-Calédonie un médecin au bagne 1906–1913* (Saint-Laurent-du-Maroni: Éditions Libertalia, 2015). See also Frédéric Angleviel, *Le Paradou: De l'hôpital du Marais au centre hospitalier Albert-Bousequet 1868–2014* (Nouméa: Centre hospitalier Albert-Bousquet, 2013), part 1. George Griffith noted the presence of the nuns of Saint-Joseph, who he called 'Sisters of Mercy', in the hospital, during his visit. See Griffith, *In an Unknown Prison Land*, 155–6.

10 The Human Sciences

Introduction

Penal settlements and colonies were distinct from prisons from a social and cultural point of view, because they received people from an exceptionally wide range of places, often from long distances away. As Chapters 8 and 9 have shown, their often-pristine character or geographical remoteness made them attractive to explorers and naturalists, and the accessibility of their convict populations appealed to medical researchers. This chapter suggests that the cosmopolitanism of convicts, ex-convict settlers, and their descendants also rendered penal colonies ideal places for investigations into the human sciences, and for the development of social science research methods. Administrators and visitors carried out innovative statistical and ethnographic studies in punitive locations, triangulating medical records, and anthropometric measurement with surveys, questionnaires, and interviews. The focus of attention of such research included the pathology of criminal behaviour, the social, cultural, and biological impacts of transportation, and sexuality. In some cases, it emerged out of a concern with the merits or otherwise of penal colonization. In others, it contributed to and shaped contemporary debates on race and, in the Indian context, caste.

The chapter opens with an analysis of the work of French naval surgeon Joseph Orgéas, who was employed in the medical service in French Guiana in the 1880s. Orgéas studied closely the convicts under his charge, collecting a mass of data on the health outcomes of convicts and their children, of European, African, and Asian origin. He compiled statistics, carried out physical examinations, issued questionnaires, and conducted interviews, using his findings to suggest that Europeans could never successfully colonize or settle in the tropics. The second part of the chapter examines two convict censuses. The first is Anton Chekhov's famous study of Sakhalin Island in the Russian Far East during the same period. In common with Orgéas's study of French Guiana, Chekhov was interested in the relationship between human development and the environment, and juxtaposed official statistics with extensive ethnographic work, interviews, and a survey. Many convicts would or could not engage with Chekhov's questioning, and this impacted on the outcome of the study. Nonetheless, like Orgéas, he used his findings to bolster his firm anti-transportation position. The second census took place in 1871 and then every ten years, in the Andaman Islands. The argument here is that the census was not just a means of understanding convict society and culture in the Islands, but of drawing comparative lines of distinction with the populations of British India at large. Indeed, in foregrounding the nature and cultural impacts of convict identity formation, the censuses also reveal a great deal about British understandings of race and caste in South Asia, and how these changed over time. The final section of the chapter returns to French Guiana, and Franck Cazanove's extraordinary 1906 study of sexuality in the *relégué* (repeat offender) settlement of Saint-Jean-du-Maroni. Cazanove's intention was to contribute to contemporary debates about whether sex between men ('depravity') was biologically, socially, or culturally driven, and thus bears relation to the studies discussed in Chapter 9. Indeed, in a context where the focus was increasingly on identities rather than acts, of key concern was the relationship between homosexuality and criminality. However, despite this, Cazanove's ethnographic and medical approach also reveals a great deal about same sex cohabitation, marriage, and love among *relégués*.

Joseph Orgéas: Race, Criminality, and Heredity in the Tropics

In a three-part paper and book published in the 1880s, naval doctor Joseph Orgéas explored the relationship between race, criminality, heredity, and degeneration in French Guiana in rich detail. Orgéas was in medical charge of the hospital for North Africans and black convicts ('*Arabs*' and '*noirs*'), which was separate from that for Europeans, and was in the colony's *commune penitentiare* (penitentiary town) of Saint-Laurent-du-Maroni. From this base, he also made twice-weekly medical visits to Saint-Maurice, which was a *tafia* (sugar cane liquor) distillery, in which only North African and black convicts worked.[1] At this time, the

---

[1] M. le Dt Jh Orgéas, 'Contribution à l'Étude du Non-Cosmopolitisme de l'Homme: La Colonisation de la Guyane par la Transportation, Étude Historique et Démographique', *Archives de médecine navale*, 39 (1883) (in three parts), 161–204, 241–81, 321–58; J. Orgéas, *La Pathologie Des Races Humaines et le Problème de la Colonisation: étude*

North Africans mainly came from the French colony of Algeria, and '*noir*' was a catch-all category that included all non-white, non-Muslim convicts. This incorporated people of African origin and '*gens de couleur*' ('people of colour') from French colonies in Africa and the Caribbean; 'Hindus' (or 'Indians') and 'Chinese', convicted of offences while under contracts of indenture in the French Antilles and Réunion Island; and 'Annamites' from French Indochina.[2] Orgéas's aim was to investigate morbidity and mortality in the penal colony since its foundation in 1852, and what patterns of disease, death, and childbirth could reveal about the larger possibility of European settlement in the tropics. The immediate background to his work was the shipment of substantial numbers of convicts to Guiana from the French colonies after 1867, when France suspended metropolitan transportation because of criticisms about high death rates. It subsequently sent European convicts to the new destination of New Caledonia. A further context was the failed experiment in the introduction of Indian indentured labour into French Guiana, for the same reason, a decade earlier.[3] Orgéas's first paper focused on the penal colony, winning the *prix de médecine navale* (prize for naval medicine) in 1882. His book was broader in scope and included not just convicts but free people of European and African descent: officials, guards, traders, settlers, soldiers, and sailors. It also discussed morbidity and mortality amongst the enslaved, including in the USA; Indian and Chinese indentured migration; and European settlement in India, Africa, Indochina,

---

anthropologique et économique faite à la Guyane Française (Paris: Octave Doin, 1886). Redfield discusses these sources in *Space in the Tropics*, 191–205. The colony used all the *tafia* distilled at St Maurice, because it formed part of the ration for 'black' convicts. (The Europeans received wine, and the North Africans coffee.) See Orgéas, 'Contribution à l'Étude du Non-Cosmopolitisme de l'Homme', 248, 250.

[2] Orgéas, 'Contribution à l'Étude du Non-Cosmopolitisme de l'Homme', 182 (unnumbered footnote). After French occupation in 1881, people from the protectorate of Tunisia also joined the 'Arab' category. At this time, the appellation '*gens de couleur*' implied mixed heritage, for which contemporaries also used the term 'Creole'.

[3] France had abolished slavery across its empire in 1848. To a large extent, penal transportation presented a solution to the desire for an alternative supply of unfree labour, as well as a colony keen to offset the costs of transportation through the value of their work. But notwithstanding the exceptionally high convict death rates during the first years of transportation, the number of convict workers was never likely to be adequate to meet the demand for labour. After 1856, following the example of Mauritius, British Guiana, Trinidad, and Jamaica, French Guiana received indentured labourers from its colony in Pondicherry, via neighbouring regions under British control. The French government sent them inland to pioneer settlements, but they died in large numbers, and in 1876, the British put an end to their recruitment and migration. On 1 January 1885, of the 8,472 immigrants, only 2,483 remained (though 448 children had since been born in the colony). A total of 4,624 others had died; 1,184 had been repatriated to India; and 184 had on-migrated to Guadeloupe. See Orgéas, *La Pathologie Des Races Humaines et le Problème de la Colonisation*, 233–5.

and Indonesia. Further, it compared European settlement in French Guiana to that in the more temperate climes of Canada.[4]

Orgéas explained that he would use a rigorous method, 'to make, in some way ... the physiology of [the convict] collective appear exclusively in numbers, since that language does not need interpretation'. This, he believed, was 'the most precise possible expression of reality'.[5] His desire to represent the success or otherwise of the colony through the presentation of statistics was an approach that resonated with other work in the second half of the nineteenth century, when numerical evidence was commonly generated and then used in support of arguments about the social characteristics of communities and cultures, often undergirded by a social reform agenda, particularly in health and education.[6] The focus of this work included prisoners, paupers, and children, and also Indigenous peoples requiring protection from the devastation of settler colonial contact.[7] Thus, his work can be conceptualized as part of a larger history of the reduction of complex problems to what were then believed to be verifiable and non-interpretable social truths, or what have been described elsewhere as 'epistemological units'.[8] The discipline of statistics appeared to sever the connection between description and interpretation, transforming its findings into what Mary Poovey has famously termed 'modern facts'. Of course, as Poovey has explained, numbers are not free from either theory or interpretation.[9]

Orgéas noted his methodological debt to the statistical approach used by the Parisian researcher Louis-Alphonse Bertillon and used his work to compile what he called his 'terms of comparison'. Bertillon had written about precisely the issues that primarily concerned Orgéas: mortality,

---

[4] First published was Orgéas, 'Contribution a l'Étude du Non-Cosmopolitisme de l'Homme', followed by *La Pathologie Des Races Humaines et le Problème de la Colonisation*.

[5] Orgéas, 'Contribution à l'Étude du Non-Cosmopolitisme de l'Homme', 165–6 (author's translation).

[6] M. J. Cullen, *The Statistical Movement in Early Victorian Britain: The Foundations of Empirical Social Research* (New York: Harvester Press, 1975); Lawrence Goldman, 'The Origins of British "Social Science": Economy, Natural Science and Statistics, 1830–1835', *The Historical Journal*, 26, 3 (1983), 587–616; Lawrence Goldman, 'Statistics and the science of society in early Victorian Britain: An intellectual context for the General Register Office', *Social History of Medicine*, 4, 3 (1991), 415–34; Theodore M. Porter, 'Statistics and Statistical Methods', in Theodore M. Porter and Dorothy Ross, eds., *The Cambridge History of Science: Volume 7* (Cambridge University Press, 2003), 238–50.

[7] Focusing on Australia and New Zealand, see Tim Rowse and Tiffany Shellam, 'The Colonial Emergence of a Statistical Imaginary', *Comparative Studies in Society and History*, 55, 4 (2012), 922–3, (922–54).

[8] Nico Randeraad, 'The International Statistical Congress (1853–1876): Knowledge transfers and their limits', *European History Quarterly*, 41, 1 (2011), 50–65.

[9] Mary Poovey, *A History of the Modern Fact: Problems of Knowledge in the Sciences of Wealth and Society* (University of Chicago Press, 1998), xii.

marriage, childbirth, and childhood.[10] In turn, the Belgian statistician Adolphe Quételet, founder of the International Statistical Congress (1853–76), which sought to establish a framework for the comparison of statistics across nations, had been a great influence on Bertillon.[11] In his famous 1835 book, Quételet had devised the idea of the statistically 'average man', and he had been interested in using small measurements of deviations from the arithmetic mean to explain individual characteristics. These included propensity to crime.[12]

Orgéas's principal provocation, based on his research into convict mortality rates in the colony during the first fifteen years of settlement, was shocking:

[A] European, submissive to the ordinary life of the prison ... becomes, after 5 or 6 years, a man incapable of all work ... he shares his time between light work, hospital and the invalid station, and is finally extinguished by depression or succumbs to a complication ... [T]he probable duration of life of a convict in Guiana (without distinction of race) is 7 years 6 months and 7 days ... the life expectancy for a transported European has been 5 years 5 months and 3 days. That of a transported North African, 7 years, 9 months and 7 days. And of a black convict, 11 years, 8 months and 15 days.[13]

Of the 21,907 men and 399 women transported to the colony between 1852 and 1878, he wrote, 10,837 had died. A further 3,694 had left the colony following their release, and 2,452 had escaped or disappeared. This left just 1,260 ex-convicts living voluntarily in the colony, and 3,663 convicts (including 144 women) still under sentence. Of these, 1,599 were European, 1,285 were from Algeria, and 635 were from other French colonies.[14]

Orgéas presented several examples to show that there were striking differences in survival rates among these convicts. At the settlement of

---

[10] Orgéas, 'Contribution a l'Étude du Non-Cosmopolitisme de l'Homme', 264. Louis-Alphonse Bertillon was Alphonse Bertillon's father.
[11] Following the first meeting in 1853, and despite nine gatherings, the International Statistical Congress failed in its goal to establish transnational uniformity in the presentation and thus international comparability of statistics. It was dissolved in 1876. See Randeraad, 'The International Statistical Congress'.
[12] On Quételet, see also Randeraad, 'The International Statistical Congress', 54; Eileen Janes Yeo, 'Social surveys in the eighteenth and nineteenth centuries', in Porter and Ross, eds., *The Cambridge History of Science: Volume 7*, 88–9 (83–99).
[13] Orgéas, *La Pathologie Des Races Humaines et le Problème de la Colonisation*, 149–50. Orgéas noted that hospital statistics were not broken down by 'race'. However, Riou-Kérangal's 1867 report was. See Orgéas, *La Pathologie Des Races Humaines et le Problème de la Colonisation*, 150–1 (unnumbered footnote).
[14] Orgéas, 'Contribution à l'Étude du Non-Cosmopolitisme de l'Homme', 181–2 ('mouvement de l'effectif des transportés à la Guyane, depuis le début de la transportation en 1852 jusqu'au 1èr janvier 1878').

Saint-Georges, established in 1853 on the Oyapock river, bordering Brazil in the east of the colony, 76 of the 248 European convicts died within eight and a half months of their arrival. This gave an annual mortality rate of 43.2 per cent. Those who survived were so sick and debilitated that the administration removed them to the Îles du Salut, which included the famous Devil's Island (Figure 10.1). Convicts from the French Antilles replaced the Europeans, and by 1855 the annual mortality rate had fallen dramatically, to just 3.75 per cent.[15] The settlement altogether escaped the yellow fever of 1855–6, which claimed the lives of almost one third of the convicts living elsewhere.[16] Taking another of Orgéas's examples, in 1865, 850 convicts were sent to another settlement, Sparouine, on the western side of the colony, just south of Saint-Laurent-du-Maroni. This was part of a forest camp constructed along the railway to Saint-Laurent, which enabled the ready transport of logs to the coast. A year later, just 270 of them were still there. One hundred had died, 119 had disappeared (presumed escaped or dead), and the rest had been admitted to hospital in various states of sickness.[17] The difference in the death rates, Orgéas explained, was the result of the devastating impact of tropical fevers and malaria on Europeans, who unlike black convicts, were unable to acclimatize. The fate of North Africans, he claimed, lay somewhere in between these two groups. They were used to the heat, but they were also habituated to distinct seasons, and so did not fare altogether well.[18] Overall, according to Orgéas, during the first fifteen years of transportation, mortality rates had been 12 per cent for Europeans, 8.54 per cent for North Africans, and 5.75 per cent for black convicts.[19] This distinction was all the more extraordinary because when the extent of white mortality and morbidity became clear, Europeans were kept off road labour, and put to work as servants or in various trades. The administration counted almost exclusively on non-Europeans to work in the harsher work environment in the forests and on public works.[20]

---

[15] Orgéas, 'Contribution à l'Étude du Non-Cosmopolitisme de l'Homme', 194 (citing report of Dr Riou-Kérangal, 1866).
[16] Orgéas, La Pathologie Des Races Humaines et le Problème de la Colonisation, 145–6. Between 18 May 1855 and 31 December 1856, 986 out of 3,188 convicts died.
[17] Orgéas, 'Contribution à l'Étude du Non-Cosmopolitisme de l'Homme', 203–4; Orgéas, La Pathologie Des Races Humaines et le Problème de la Colonisation, 140. The railway was built according to the portable Decauville system.
[18] Orgéas, 'Contribution à l'Étude du Non-Cosmopolitisme de l'Homme', 346; Orgéas, La Pathologie Des Races Humaines et le Problème de la Colonisation, 349.
[19] Orgéas, La Pathologie Des Races Humaines et le Problème de la Colonisation, 151 (unnumbered footnote) (citing report of Dr Riou-Kérangal, March 1867).
[20] Orgéas, La Pathologie Des Races Humaines et le Problème de la Colonisation, 212.

Figure 10.1 Devil's Island, painted by convict
Source: Richard Halliburton Papers, Manuscripts Division, Special Collections, Princeton University Library: C0247 RHP Box 22: Devil's Island Correspondence for *New Worlds to Conquer*, 1929–33, folder 8A. Courtesy of Princeton University Library.

In terms of the prospects of the colony more generally, Orgéas showed that Europeans had little success in having and raising children. Men's semen showed evidence of weakness from age or sickness, he argued, and transmitted these traits to women's ova.[21] Eventually, he predicted, this would lead to European 'extinction' in the colony.[22] There were high rates of sterility and miscarriages amongst convicts, which Orgéas put down to ill health, poor hygiene, and the extreme climate, as well as the effect of impure, malarial air on women and men. This meant that there was no future for French settlers, in Guiana or in places with similar climates. White women were like exotic plants, Orgéas wrote, planted in unsuitable locations, and unable to absorb the nutrients necessary for the production of sap or fruit: 'That is why they dry out and fall before maturity.'[23] 'Pretending that man is cosmopolitan, as seems to have

---

[21] Orgéas, 'Contribution à l'Étude du Non-Cosmopolitisme de l'Homme', 333, 358.
[22] Orgéas, 'Contribution à l'Étude du Non-Cosmopolitisme de l'Homme', 358–9.
[23] Orgéas, 'Contribution à l'Étude du Non-Cosmopolitisme de l'Homme', 334–6 (quote, 336). He used the same metaphor for Europeans more generally in *La Pathologie Des Races Humaines et le Problème de la Colonisation*, 313. Journalist Jean Carol also claimed convict marriages in New Caledonia were 'sterile'. See *Le Bagne (avec photographies)* (Paris: Société d'Éditions Littéraires et Artistiques, 1903), 101.

been the general belief', he added, '... is to pretend that he can live, work, cultivate the soil, and reproduce himself in all corners of the globe.'[24] This was not the case, and the inability of Europeans to settle in hot climates was comparable to the impossibility of cultivating orange, palm, and banana trees in Paris.[25]

Orgéas's calculations of the average life expectancy of convicts in French Guiana, and his predictions about the future of their children, were powerful, not just for their quantification of convict misery, sickness, and mortality during these years, but because exceptionally high death rates since colonization had not gone unremarked, and had always rendered the colony's future existence uncertain. Indeed, Orgéas himself argued that France should have abolished transportation in 1857, because with mortality rates in some parts of the colony as high as 62 per cent it was akin to sentencing men to death. Life expectancy on the Îles du Salut in 1855 was one year, seven months and six days; and at Montagne-d'Argent in 1856, it was just eight months and fifteen days[26] From the earliest days of occupation, convicts had been wracked by malaria and epidemics of yellow fever, afflicted with typhoid and dysentery, and reduced to a state of debility and weakness, often due to the infestations of hookworm noted in Chapter 10. According to Orgéas, it was only following Chief Medical Officer Emile-Yves Riou-Kérangal's reports of 'really appalling' mortality rates in 1867 that the French government had taken the decision to divert all French mainland convicts to the apparently more salubrious penal settlement of New Caledonia. 'Could it have been otherwise?' Riou-Kérangal had asked. 'What becomes of the European, reduced to hard labour, with insufficient rations, often sleeping in damp clothing, and breathing intemperate air?'[27] Subsequently, French Guiana only received the apparently more physically resilient convicts from the colonies: Indochina, Algeria, Senegal, Réunion Island, Pondicherry, Guadeloupe, Martinique, and Madagascar. They included families of rebels from the Martinique insurrection of 1870–1.[28] By the time that Orgéas was writing, non-Europeans

[24] Orgéas, 'Contribution à l'Étude du Non-Cosmopolitisme de l'Homme', 164.
[25] Orgéas, *La Pathologie Des Races Humaines et le Problème de la Colonisation*, 288–9. Another doctor in the French colonial medical service made the same connection, between climate, race, and pathology, shortly after the publication of Orgéas's texts. See E. Maurel, *Traité des Maladies Pauldéennes à la Guyane* (Paris: Octave Doin, 1883).
[26] Orgéas, *La Pathologie Des Races Humaines et le Problème de la Colonisation*, 180. Orgéas used the following figures and devised a mathematical model to support his conclusions on life expectancy: 21.3/31.1 Montagne-d'Argent 1854/1855; 21.5 Georges de l'Oyapock 1855; 35.0 Îles du Salut 1855; 62.3 Comté/Montagne-d'Argent 1856.
[27] Orgéas, *La Pathologie Des Races Humaines et le Problème de la Colonisation*, 140 (quote), 150.
[28] Gilbert Pago, *L'insurrection de Martinique 1870–1871* (Paris: Hachette Livre, 2012).

constituted the convict majority, and were growing in number. At the end of 1880, North African and black convicts constituted 59 per cent of the total, and at the end of 1882 this had risen further to 68 per cent.[29]

Orgéas's research on mortality rates was embedded in a wider global discussion of the relationship between convict transportation and colonization, as had been critiqued for decades and by numerous commentators, including as Chapter 7 demonstrated during the international penitentiary congresses. In his writing, he displayed an impressive knowledge of the history of punitive relocation, including unusually for the era that of The Netherlands, as well as of Spain, Portugal, and Britain.[30] His writings must for this reason be situated within debates about the demography of empires more generally, especially following the publication of Thomas Malthus's bold 1798 *Essay on the Principle of Population*. Malthus had proposed that after the colonization of North America, not taking immigration into consideration, the population had doubled every 25 years. Without an increase in resources to support it, such population growth was unsustainable, and the only limits were disease, famine, war, and sexual abstinence.[31] Orgéas looked not with caution, but with admiration, at the British penal colony of New South Wales, which he believed demonstrated the truth of Malthus's theory. French Guiana had seen no such rise in population, as the French administration had hoped. For this reason, not only had the colonization of this specific locality been a failure, it more generally indicated clearly that white settlement in the tropics was doomed.[32] This contrasted with French settlement in Canada

---

[29] 'Répartition des transportés au 31 décembre 1880', *Notice sur la transportation à la Guyane française et à la Nouvelle-Calédonie pendant les années 1880–1881* (Paris: Imprimerie Nationale, 1884), 31. At the end of 1880, there were 1,238 European men and 82 European women of all penal classes in the colony; compared to 2,205 non-European men and 32 non-European women. The figures for 1882 are: 973 European men and 98 European women, and 2,277 non-European men and 44 non-European women. See 'Répartition des transportés au 31 décembre 1882', *Notice sur la transportation à la Guyane française et à la Nouvelle-Calédonie pendant les années 1882–1883* (Paris: Imprimerie Nationale, 1885), 57. If it included only under-sentence convicts, the proportion was even greater, at 78 per cent. See Orgéas, *La Pathologie Des Races Humaines et le Problème de la Colonisation*, 136 (unnumbered footnote).

[30] Orgéas, *La Pathologie Des Races Humaines et le Problème de la Colonisation*, 170.

[31] For a new postcolonial history of Thomas Malthus that analyses systematically for the first time his global perspective, including his view that the European displacement of Indigenous peoples was unjust, for they had successfully managed their populations within available resources, see Alison Bashford and Joyce E. Chaplin, *The New Worlds of Thomas Robert Malthus: Rereading the Principle of Population* (Princeton University Press, 2016).

[32] Orgéas, 'Contribution à l'Étude du Non-Cosmopolitisme de l'Homme', 162–4. Note that as Bashford and Chaplin stress, in *The New Worlds of Thomas Robert Malthus*, Malthus discussed New South Wales in the second 1803 edition of his *Essay*, though here Orgéas seems to be referring to the first edition of 1798.

which, as for North America more generally, obeyed Malthus's proposition.[33]

In evidencing his argument Orgéas compiled two statistical tables. The first categorized every death that had occurred in the convict hospital at Cayenne between 1854 and 1884. It provided separate columns for free and convict Europeans, and for 'black', 'Arab', 'Hindu', and 'Annamite and Chinese' convicts, and a column for the cause of death, which recorded the devastating impact of malaria and yellow fever on Europeans, in particular.[34] The second was a 'descriptive table of the families of convict colonists', which incorporated all the convict marriages that had been contracted in Saint-Laurent-du-Maroni since 1859.[35] Orgéas's concern was 'the precise, rigorous and I repeat almost mathematical study of the principal physiological and social phenomena presented by this special group of adults and children'.[36] Thus, the second, family table detailed the spouses' age, 'race', literacy, and the dates of the birth and death of any children, for as explained above he was particularly interested in the reproductive outcomes of convict marriage.[37]

Since the foundation of the colony, the government had given land grants in Saint-Laurent-du-Maroni to 431 *concessionaire* households, families which included *libérés* (ex-convicts). Orgéas studied them closely. He noted that European men headed 181 such households, North Africans 170, and other colonially convicted persons the remaining 70.[38] Following the first civil ceremony in October 1859, by the time of Orgéas's research, there had been 418 marriages between convicts or *libérés* in Saint-Laurent, though given death rates in the colony some people had married more than once. Indeed, of the 330 women who contracted marriage, 63 did so twice, and 8 three times.[39] The wives in these relationships were mainly convicts. A dozen or so were free women who had joined their convict husbands from France or the Caribbean colonies (some bringing their children with them, and some remarrying *concessionaires* when their husbands died). Others were daughters of convicts, free black women, and in one case Indigenous. Most convicts married men or women within the racial categories devised by Orgéas:

[33] Orgéas, *La Pathologie Des Races Humaines et le Problème de la Colonisation*, 308.
[34] Orgéas, *La Pathologie Des Races Humaines et le Problème de la Colonisation*, vii ('tableau des décès enregistré à l'hôpital militaire de cayenne du 1èr janvier 1854 à 1èr janvier 1884').
[35] Orgéas, 'Contribution à l'Étude du Non-Cosmopolitisme de l'Homme', 166 ('tableau nominative des familles des *transportés-colons*', 1 January 1882).
[36] Orgéas, *La Pathologie Des Races Humaines et le Problème de la Colonisation*, 257.
[37] Orgéas, *La Pathologie Des Races Humaines et le Problème de la Colonisation*, 166.
[38] Orgéas, 'Contribution à l'Étude du Non-Cosmopolitisme de l'Homme', 257.
[39] Orgéas, 'Contribution à l'Étude du Non-Cosmopolitisme de l'Homme', 276.

European, 'Arab', 'black', 'Indian', and 'Chinese'. A very small number (14 of the 418) married across them, in all cases after 1867.[40] Just one of the male spouses was not a former convict. He had served in the French garrison and married the daughter of a convict. By the time of Orgéas's study, three quarters of all marital unions (301 of the 418) had been dissolved by death, escape, or a free spouse's exit from the colony. In sum, of the 695 men and women who had contracted marriage since 1859, in 1881, just 290 (less than half) were still alive and living in French Guiana.[41]

Excluding from his study, the small number of children born outside French Guiana and brought to the colony with a free spouse, Orgéas remarked that almost half of the married couples in Saint-Laurent-du-Maroni were childless. Black couples were only slightly more fertile than Europeans: one child per couple, compared to 0.90. Orgéas dismissed the idea that this was because convicts and *libérés* practised the 'moral restraint' advocated by Malthus, but rather saw it as a consequence of the extraordinary frequency of miscarriage. Indeed, he had a medical colleague question at random thirty-three European women calling at the Saint-Laurent clinic. Thirty-one of them said that they had had at least one miscarriage. On this basis, Orgéas calculated that miscarriages were at least as common as pregnancies carried to term, and symptomatic of poor hygiene, sickness, and 'non-acclimatisation'.[42] Moreover, though since 1861, 379 children had been born alive to convict parents (notwithstanding 24 stillbirths),[43] 238 of them had since died, which represented a massive 63 per cent of total live births. This did not include the forty children who had left the colony, avoiding in Orgéas's view the very likely prospect of death in French Guiana. Some of these children had left with their parents. They included families returning to Martinique following the 1880 amnesty for 1870-1 insurrectionists. Others went to France with a departing Jesuit order, which placed them in metropolitan schools. At least one child ended up in Mettray, the famous French juvenile reformatory.[44] From a young age, government placed children remaining

---

[40] Orgéas, 'Contribution à l'Étude du Non-Cosmopolitisme de l'Homme', 260 ('Race des époux en function de la race des épouses' ('Race of the husbands according to race of the wives')), 261. The Indigenous woman died two years after marrying a European in 1867.
[41] Orgéas, 'Contribution à l'Étude du Non-Cosmopolitisme de l'Homme', 258–60, 267, 281.
[42] Orgéas, *La Pathologie Des Races Humaines et le Problème de la Colonisation*, 256–7, 273–4 (quote, 274), 301–2, 319; Orgéas, 'Contribution à l'Étude du Non-Cosmopolitisme de l'Homme', 331–4, 340, 357.
[43] There are associations between malaria, sexually transmitted diseases, and stillbirth.
[44] Orgéas, 'Contribution à l'Étude du Non-Cosmopolitisme de l'Homme', 341–3. Orgéas's figures differ slightly from those of Maurel, in part because the latter included the children born to colonial personnel as well as convicts. Maurel's death rates were slightly

in the colony in the care of the sisters (nuns) of the order of Saint Joseph de Cluny. After 1868, it sent older children to primary (elementary) school. The nuns ran the girls' school and the congregation of the Frères de Ploërmel ran the establishment for boys.[45] It is not clear whether these removals took place with or without parental consent, though some of the children were orphans. Note also that although the first convict child was born in April 1861, the administration did not issue rations to children who stayed with their *concessionaire* parents until 1864. This probably forced the decision to separate families for those in straitened circumstances.[46] However, Orgéas concluded that it was not government neglect that was the cause of childhood deaths, but 'congenital weakness', heredity, malaria, and above all the insalubrity of the climate. Indeed, the children of European convicts had much worse prospects than others. Fully one third of European children (117 out of 353) died in the first year of their life. This compared to just 2 out of 19 black children. Acknowledging that the figures were small, Orgéas argued that children of non-European descent had a much better chance of survival before the age of one and declared that this was 'very suggestive' of a larger pattern.[47]

Orgéas compared his findings with Louis-Alphonse Bertillon's French statistics, writing that a child born in France had more chance of reaching the age of 25, and almost the same chance of reaching the age of 30, as a child born in Saint-Laurent-du-Maroni had of reaching the age of 2. And, a child born in France had more chance of reaching the age of 55 as a child from Maroni had of turning 5 years old.[48] They died of the same diseases as their parents and suffered from pica (the craving of non-food substances due to nutritional deficiency). Orgéas wrote of one case of a boy known to us only as 'Ba ... Victor', who gnawed on the iron legs of his hospital bed, and having broken two teeth in the process went on to eat

---

lower, however, totalling 233 of the 392 children born between 1861 and 1876 inclusive. Maurel was in agreement with Orgéas about the relative sterility of convict couples. See Maurel, *Traité des Maladies Pauldéennes à la Guyane,* 46–7.

[45] Orgéas, 'Contribution à l'Étude du Non-Cosmopolitisme de l'Homme', 252. He claimed that the governor and other officials routinely attended the baptism of convicts' children, and numerous members of the penitentiary administration became their godparents. See also Orgéas, *La Pathologie Des Races Humaines et le Problème de la Colonisation,* 66, which notes the attendance of the governor (and a convict musical band) at the wedding of an unnamed European convict woman and Algerian convict Abd-er-Rahman, who had converted to Christianity. According to Orgéas, the governor wanted to show his support for the marriage. The Frères de Ploërmel withdrew from the colony in 1875.

[46] Orgéas, 'Contribution à l'Étude du Non-Cosmopolitisme de l'Homme', 252.

[47] Orgéas, 'Contribution à l'Étude du Non-Cosmopolitisme de l'Homme', 338–41, 357–8.

[48] Orgéas, 'Contribution a l'Étude du Non-Cosmopolitisme de l'Homme', 354–5.

the lime coating on the walls of the ward and pieces of stone from the ground. Pica afflicted lots of children, Orgéas noted, adding that the water contained little salt, and so 'these children looked instinctively for the phosphates and alkaline carbons that their bodies demanded'.[49] Earlier, Chief Medical Officer Riou-Kérangal's report of 1865 had indicated that large numbers of infants died while cutting their teeth. This seems to indicate that at least some of the babies in the colony were suffering from scurvy, which carried symptoms including swollen and ulcerated gums, loose teeth, boils, pain and in adults mental depression, or what observers sometimes called 'nostalgia'.[50] The removal of infants, from the nutritional richness of their mothers' breast to the care of the nuns of Saint Joseph de Cluny, would not have improved their prospects for good health in this regard. But for Orgéas, the problem was not sickness, disease, or nutritional deficiency, but the fact that these children were European in origin, which prevented their proper adaptation to the climate of French Guiana.

Notwithstanding his general claim that statistics were scientifically precise and required minimal explanation, Orgéas provided qualitative evidence in support of his figures and tables. Indeed, he noted that existing statistics on convict families were 'insufficient or doubtful'. And so, he augmented his quantitative work with ethnographic investigations. He went to the places where *libérés* were known to gather, and distributed questionnaires among those who had lived in the colony for a long time. He was particularly interested in finding further information on the individuals and families marked out of interest in the colony's medical records. The *libérés*, he reported, rendered him 'precise information'.[51] Orgéas remarked that it was the peculiarity of local conditions in the *commune penitentiaire* that made his study possible. First, the colony was a small place where everybody knew each other, and as a result it was easy to collect information, even on *libérés*, who were no longer under the direct purview of the French administration. Second, his official position was vital to the success of his investigations; for he was aided not just by

---

[49] Extract from the report of July 1882, addressed to the chief doctor by Dr Rangé, doctor of the 1st class and head of the health service, Îles du Salut, cited in Orgéas, 'Contribution à l'Étude du Non-Cosmopolitisme de l'Homme', 348. See also Orgéas, 'Contribution à l'Étude du Non-Cosmopolitisme de l'Homme', 349 (unnumbered footnote), in which, following Alexander Humboldt, he notes that 'earth-eating' was common in the so-called savage nations.

[50] Orgéas, 'Contribution à l'Étude du Non-Cosmopolitisme de l'Homme', 338. A new study of scurvy stresses its effects in creating 'scorbutic nostalgia' and thus profoundly influencing Europeans' experiences and representations of empire, for example, in the Australian penal colonies. See Jonathan Lamb, *Scurvy: The disease of discovery* (Princeton University Press, 2016), esp. chapter 4.

[51] Orgéas, 'Contribution à l'Étude du Non-Cosmopolitisme de l'Homme', 166–7.

his informants, but by other doctors.[52] Third, given the lengthy sentences of transportation convicts (and importantly the French law of *doublage*), convicts and ex-convicts represented a stable, long-resident population for research – unlike their officers or the troops of the garrison who rotated every two years.[53] Finally, the colony contained convicts from France, Italy, Spain, Belgium, Germany, Britain, and the French colonial world, as also Indigenous and free settler populations. Orgéas wrote:

> French Guiana ... is perhaps in the whole world the country which best lends itself to research on comparative pathology of the human races. There exists a real variety of human types living together on the same soil and under the influence of the same climate. Red Skins, white Europeans, African negroes; later Hindus and Chinese; finally Arab and Annamite transportees.[54]

The appeal of Orgéas's prize-winning work was that it straddled and intervened in contemporary arguments about penal transportation, colonization, and population growth, using what he represented as statistical rigour in making a case about the general fate of European convicts in transportation. However, considering it alongside its more descriptive and narrative elements, it can also be viewed as an innovative medical prosopography, particularly of convict children.[55] Orgéas was engaged in the study of race and colonialism, as distinct from convict morbidity and mortality *tout court*. He supplemented his statistics and mathematical models with personal observations on and details of individual lives, gleaned from his questionnaires and personal meetings with convicts and their families. His research thus lies at the intersection of the history of statistics, empire, and social investigation. Dating from the 1830s, the latter often blended quantitative and qualitative approaches.[56]

---

[52] Orgéas, 'Contribution à l'Étude du Non-Cosmopolitisme de l'Homme', 166, 256, 331–3.
[53] Orgéas, *La Pathologie Des Races Humaines et le Problème de la Colonisation*, 136. This rotation was enforced after 1881.
[54] Orgéas, *La Pathologie Des Races Humaines et le Problème de la Colonisation*, vi.
[55] For a prosopographical approach to convicts and penal settlements in the British Empire including in Asia and the Australian colonies, see Clare Anderson, *Subaltern Lives: Biographies of colonialism in the Indian World, 1790–1920* (Cambridge University Press, 2012).
[56] Samuel William Bloom, *The Word as Scalpel: A History of Medical Sociology* (Oxford University Press, 2002), chapter 1; Martin Bulmer, Kevin Bales, and Kathryn Kish Sklar, eds., *The Social Survey in Historical Perspective, 1880–1940* (Cambridge University Press, 1991); Waltraud Ernst and Bernard Harris, eds., *Race, Science and Medicine, 1700–1960* (London: Routledge, 1999); Yeo, 'Social surveys in the eighteenth and nineteenth centuries'. The classic account of London is Gareth Stedman Jones, *Outcast London: A Study in the Relationship between Classes in Victorian Society* (Oxford: Clarendon Press, 1971).

Orgéas's ethnographic investigations began with examinations of children over the age of 5, on whom he took detailed written notes.[57] He next divided all the children in the colony into four age groups: under 5s, under 10s, under 15s and under 21s. He did not examine the under 5s (30 in number), though noted that he had seen many of them during admissions to hospital with fever, conjunctivitis, and anaemia (the latter of which could of course be symptoms of malaria, scurvy, or hookworm). He stripped naked and inspected closely the rest of the boys, measuring them anthropometrically, subjecting them to physical examinations, asking them intimate questions, and issuing them with basic tests in literacy and arithmetic. He did not physically examine the girls, and noted the limitations of his knowledge on them, though he did ask them a series of questions.[58] Starting with the second group of fifteen children, he reported that three of the nine boys, and three of the five girls, showed signs of 'degeneration'. He wrote that they were underdeveloped for their age, and that they showed signs of cachexia (wasting disease). Orgéas described the girls as '*chétive*' (puny or stunted), and noted that the older the children, the worse this was. As he turned to his third group (16 boys and 20 girls aged 10–14), clearly drawing on the Lombrosian thinking described in the Chapter 9, he recorded the 'vicious deviation of type, and deformation', which was more apparent in the boys than the girls. Their faces were 'irregular', their heads and ears were misshapen, their foreheads were low, and their jaws, noses, and lips were large. He noted also that many of them were extremely small for their age. They had ashen skin, their genitals were small, and a 'constant rule' was microcephaly (a small head associated with cognitive impairment). These bodily characteristics, Orgéas wrote, were not the consequence of heredity or disease, but of the children's failure to acclimatize.[59] Several of them had chronic illnesses or physical disabilities too:

I cite: the young Ba ... Henri, born in 1871 ... The young B ... Dominique, brother of the former, born in 1869, suffering from elephantiasis and limp of the right foot. I name also the young B ... Victor (died 31 July 1882), born 8 January 1868, the older brother of the two brothers I have just cited, suffering from terrible elephantiasis of the two lower limbs. I name also Jon ... (Emile), born 4 January 1867, who died at the age of 15, when he was the size of an 8 year

---

[57] Orgéas, 'Contribution à l'Étude du Non-Cosmopolitisme de l'Homme', 343 (unnumbered footnote).
[58] Orgéas, 'Contribution à l'Étude du Non-Cosmopolitisme de l'Homme', 350.
[59] Orgéas, 'Contribution à l'Étude du Non-Cosmopolitisme de l'Homme', 343–7 (quote, 345). Microcephaly may be inherited or caused by infection during pregnancy (e.g. the mosquito-borne Zika virus, rubella, cytomegalovirus, toxoplasmosis), exposure to harmful chemicals or other causes.

old, with cachexia, rickets, dropsy, elephantiasis, paralysis, suffering from muscular atrophy and idiocy, at the final stage of physiological and muscular feebleness, the most perfect type of human degeneration that one can imagine.[60]

In general, though around half of the girls were thin or anaemic, they were in much better health than the boys. Just two suffered from elephantiasis or oedema, and the rest of the other 50 per cent were in a thriving physical state.[61] Orgéas noted the same pattern in his fourth group, consisting of ten young men and ten young women, aged 15 and over. 'It is among the masculine half of in this group', he wrote, 'that we find the best specimens of human degeneration.'[62] Only one of the five married girls had carried a baby to term, but despite this and the fact that they were rather thin, Orgéas believed that otherwise they showed more signs of physical maturity than the boys. He was especially interested in those girls who had spent periods of time in France (as several had) and returned to the colony. Though concerned with their 'sterility', however, he reported that he had not asked whether they had started to menstruate.[63]

Orgéas gave a particularly detailed account of two of the youths in this group, 'Jacques Lac ... ' and 'Louis Choi ... '. In these, he blended anthropometric measurements with personal observation. Jacques was 20 years old, and the eldest of three siblings, a brother who had died and a sister who had returned to France. Orgéas measured his height and weight, and took down the circumference of his head, neck, chest, arms, and thighs. He described his 'deformed' features, grey pallor, and swollen legs. He was just 1.28 m tall, and weighed 28 kg. The intimacy of the medical exam is evident from his comments on Jacques' penis (said to be as small as that of a two-year-old) and testicles (which had not properly descended), and on the lack of hair on his private parts or underarms. Orgéas questioned him about his sexual desire and noted his response: that he had never experienced it and did not wish to marry or have children. He set him a basic arithmetic test, and despite 11 years of schooling, he could (or did) not do it. Orgéas concluded that he was 'idiotic'. His mother being deceased, Jacques' father was present during the examination, and he told Orgéas that he was surprised by his son's stunted growth, because he had always been well cared for, and had never

---

[60] Orgéas, 'Contribution à l'Étude du Non-Cosmopolitisme de l'Homme', 347–8. The young 'B ... Victor' is the same child discussed above, who was suffering from pica. Elephantiasis is a mosquito-borne disease that causes swelling of the genitals or thighs. Dropsy refers to oedema, or unspecified swelling of the body.
[61] Orgéas, 'Contribution à l'Étude du Non-Cosmopolitisme de l'Homme', 349.
[62] Orgéas, 'Contribution à l'Étude du Non-Cosmopolitisme de l'Homme', 349, 351. This is restated in Orgéas, *La Pathologie Des Races Humaines et le Problème de la Colonisation*, 302 (unnumbered footnote).
[63] Orgéas, 'Contribution à l'Étude du Non-Cosmopolitisme de l'Homme', 350.

been seriously ill. 'Do not think there is a fortune to be made by going to France and putting him on display at fairs', he said, 'unfortunately I am not allowed to leave French Guiana.'[64] Orgéas measured and described 19½ year old 'Louis Cha...', the only survivor of seven siblings, in near-identical terms. He was slight taller and heavier (1.3 m, 29.5 kg), but had, like Jacques, a pallid complexion, undeveloped genitals, and lack of pubic hair. His voice had not broken and seemed 'feminine'. Up to the age of 17, he had spent a great deal of time in hospital, and there he had learned how to read, but not write.[65] Orgéas compared the height of both boys to Quételet's French average (1.67 m), and to the minimum required of army recruits (1.54 m). Finding them lacking, he wrote '[t]here is nothing to add to the language of figures' and added that the children were fit subjects for a museum of human teratology.[66]

Alongside Quételet and Bertillon, scholars often cite the nineteenth and early twentieth-century investigators Henry Mayhew and Charles Booth as the pioneers of modern social research in Europe. In London between 1849 and 1852, in the aftermath of a cholera epidemic and Chartist agitation, Mayhew interviewed the men, women, and children of London for his weekly pamphlets, 'London Labour and the London Poor', which were published in *The Morning Chronicle*.[67] Later, he turned his attention to prisoners in jail, as a means to encourage his reform agenda, in which he praised Alexander Maconochie (Chapter 7).[68] Later, Booth's *Life and Labour of the People in London* (1886–1903) was based on extensive social investigations in the British capital, conducted by Booth and his dozen or so assistants. Their work underpinned the production of poverty maps which conceptualized for the first time the 'poverty line', a mark that divided the city in two, separating rich from

---

[64] Orgéas, 'Contribution à l'Étude du Non-Cosmopolitisme de l'Homme', 351–4 (quote, 354).
[65] Orgéas, 'Contribution à l'Étude du Non-Cosmopolitisme de l'Homme', 355–6.
[66] Orgéas, 'Contribution à l'Étude du Non-Cosmopolitisme de l'Homme', 354. Teratology is the study of abnormalities in physiological development.
[67] Sarah Roddy, Julie-Marie Strange, and Bertrand Taithe, 'Henry Mayhew at 200 – the "Other" Victorian Bicentenary', *Journal of Victorian Culture*, 19, 4 (2014), 481–96; Eileen Yeo and E. P. Thompson. *The Unknown Mayhew* (New York: Pantheon Books, 1971).
[68] In an extraordinary piece of investigation, undertaken without the benefits of the online databases available to researchers today, historian F. B. Smith tracked down the history of one of Mayhew's informants, a man known as 'D', who had returned to England following his transportation to Van Diemen's Land. See F. B. Smith, 'Mayhew's Convict', *Victorian Studies*, 22, 4, (1979), 431–48. See also A. L. Beier, 'Identity, Language, and Resistance in the Making of the Victorian "Criminal Class": Mayhew's Convict Revisited', *Journal of British Studies*, 44, 3 (2005), 499–515.

poor.⁶⁹ The African American scholar W. E. B. Dubois carried out similar work in the USA. Du Bois used the terminology of General William Booth of Britain's Salvation Army – 'the submerged tenth' – in his 1899, *The Philadelphia Negro*, to describe the social, cultural, and economic depravations that he found during a statistical and ethnographic survey of the poorest 10 per cent of people in the city with the largest black population in the north. William Booth had not himself engaged in social research, but *In Darkest England and the Way Out* had offered suggestions to tackle poverty. He offered a scheme of redemption, proposing that the nation's urban poor move from 'city colony', to 'farm colony', and eventually to 'colony over-sea'.⁷⁰ Across the Atlantic, Du Bois interpreted the poverty and exclusion of African Americans as a legacy of enslavement. A decolonized sociology now views him as a pioneer in social research methods, undertaking the first empirical fieldwork in the USA via interviews with Philadelphia residents, and making a profound contribution to the larger field through his innovative research design and data collection.⁷¹

Orgéas's material can be placed in parallel with these studies, for like other researchers he was concerned with what has been described as 'the idea that human disease is always mediated and modified by social activities and the cultural environment'.⁷² However, the point here is that his study was rooted neither in metropolitan Europe nor in post-emancipation

---

⁶⁹ General [William] Booth, *In Darkest England and the Way Out* (London: Funk and Wagnall, 1890); SAIHC S.29: S. Carvosso Gauntlett, *Social Evils The Army Has Challenged*, foreword by General Carpenter (London: Salvationist Publishing and Supplies, 1946), 15; H. Ausubel, 'General Booth's Scheme of Social Salvation', *American Historical Review*, 56, 3 (1951), 519–25. William Booth (who was not related to Charles Booth) was the founder of the Salvation Army. See D. C. Lamb (revised L. E. Lauer), 'Booth, (William) Bramwell (1856–1929)', *Oxford Dictionary of National Biography* (Oxford University Press, 2004); online edition, September 2012, https://doi.org/10.1093/ref:odnb/31969 (accessed 1 May 2020).

⁷⁰ Charles Booth, *Life and Labour of the People of London*, 9 volumes (London: Macmillan, 1892–7). The LSE has digitised the poverty maps alongside Charles Booth's notebooks, at https://booth.lse.ac.uk/ (accessed 20 July 2017). See also John Brown, 'Charles Booth and Labour Colonies, 1889–1905', *The Economic History Review*, 21, 2 (1968), 349–60; Albert Fried and Richard Ellman, eds., *Charles Booth's London* (London: Hutchinson, 1969); Alan Gillie, 'The Origin of the Poverty Line', *The Economic History Review*, 49, 4 (1996), 715–30. I thank Steven Spencer for drawing my attention to Booth's use of the idea of the 'submerged tenth'.

⁷¹ W. E. B. Du Bois, ed., *The Philadelphia Negro: A Social Study* (New York: Cosimo, 1899). See also Martin Bulmer, 'W. E. B. Du Bois as a Social Investigator: The Philadelphia Negro 1899', in Bulmer, Bales, and Kish Sklar, eds., *The Social Survey in Historical Perspective*, 170–88; Hynek Jerabek, 'W. E. B. Du Bois on the history of empirical social research', *Ethnic and Racial Studies Review*, 29, 8 (2016), 1391–7; Aldon D. Morris, *The Scholar Denied: W. E. B. Du Bois and the Birth of Modern Sociology* (Oakland: University of California Press, 2017).

⁷² Bloom, *The Word as Scalpel*, 11.

North America, but in a European colony, assisted by local interlocutors. Moreover, the central focus of this work was on the use of the idea of race as a socio-biological concept that could explain some of the colonizing limits of the French Empire. Unusually, this was not a history of European imperial superiority, but of European failure. Nonetheless, it demonstrates the close link between the science of race, medicine, and colonialism.[73] Indeed, in his work Orgéas followed several other French doctors who were actively researching in the penal colonies of Guiana and New Caledonia. For example, one earlier study on the political exiles transported to the Îles des Pins between 1873 and 1879 drew clear links between climate and health, showing that sickness and hospital admissions peaked during the 'extreme' months of the first quarter of each year.[74] The central role played by Orgéas in the design and delivery of research also adds weight to the argument that governments did not always drive social investigation, but relied on the personal interest of colonial personnel, or non-government actors and their independent initiative.[75] Thus, the history of social surveys and medical investigation is a history of connection and of professionalization, as much as a European, North American or colonial story. Situating Orgéas's work in French Guiana within this larger history of research methods, the history of medicine, and the history of penal transportation enables us to appreciate its wider value. It not only accords convicts and penal colonies a central role in the history of social investigation but centres criminal justice and penal colonization in narratives of race and empire at large.

Convict Censuses in Sakhalin and the Andaman Islands

In its blend of statistical and ethnographic research, in some ways the work of Joseph Orgéas in French Guiana anticipated the better-known investigations of Anton Chekhov in the penal colony of Sakhalin Island in the Russian Far East, a decade later in 1890.[76] Chekhov's visit to Sakhalin

---

[73] Waltraud Ernst, 'Introduction: historical and contemporary perspectives on race, science and medicine', in Ernst and Harris, eds., *Race, Science and Medicine*, 3–5 (1–28).

[74] F. Guyot, 'Contributions à la Géographie Médicale: La Déportation Simple à l'Île des Pins', *Archives de médecine navale*, 36 (1881), 165 (161–75).

[75] Robert Shoemaker and Richard Ward, 'Understanding the Criminal: Record-Keeping, Statistics and the Early History of Criminology in England', *The British Journal of Criminology*, 57, 6 (2017), 1442–61.

[76] Chekhov's work was first translated into English by Luba Terpack and Michael Terpak: *The Island of Sakhalin: A journey to Sakhalin* (New York: Washington Square Press, 1967). In this chapter, I refer to a more recent edition, translated by Brian Reeve: *Sakhalin Island* (London: OneWorld Classics, 2007).

followed the American journalist George Keenan's trip to Siberia in 1885–6. Though he did not go to Sakhalin, Keenan's work on convicts and exiles in Siberia was certainly read by Chekhov, for though it was initially published in the USA, it was almost immediately translated into Russian.[77] Individual convicts and exiles are little present in Keenan's book, which is more concerned with painting a general picture of horrific conditions, than with dwelling on the details of individual lives.[78] Though Kennan inspired Chekhov, Chekhov's labours produced a quite different kind of study.[79]

Most often, historians represent Chekhov's research on Sakhalin as a remarkable piece of investigative journalism, for his goal was to make the convicts and exiles transported there a matter of public knowledge. Indeed, subsequently he published his work: first during 1892–3 in the periodical *Russkaia mysl'* (*Russian Thought*), and then in 1895 as a book.[80] However, Chekhov's interests were also underpinned by his prior medical training, and he intended his writing both as a contribution to medicine and as an intervention in contemporary penological debates.[81] Like Orgéas's study of French Guiana, it might best be described as 'medical geography', a work that explored the relationship between human development and the environment. Like Orgéas, Chekhov proceeded on the basis of an already worked out hypothesis, from his position as an opponent of penal colonization.[82] *Ostrov Sakhalin* (*Sakhalin Island*) was an incredibly ambitious piece of research. It was based on months of study

---

[77] George Kennan, *Siberia and the Exile System*, 2 volumes (New York: The Century Company, 1891). See also Andrew A. Gentes, 'Sakhalin as cause célèbre: The re-signification of Tsarist Russia's penal colony', *Acta Slavica Iaponica*, 32 (2012), 59–60 (55–72); Daniel Beer, 'Penal deportation to Siberia and the limits of State Power', *Kritika: Explorations in Russian and Eurasian History*, 16, 3 (2015) 631 (621–50); Sarah J. Young, 'Knowing Russia's Convicts: The Other in Narratives of Imprisonment and Exile of the Late Imperial Era', *Europe-Asia Studies*, 65, 9 (2013), 1702, 1704 (1700–15). Gentes argues that Kennan's purpose was twofold: to highlight American in contrast to Russian 'freedom', and to give succour to Russian reformers and revolutionaries, and in this he succeeded. Russia as a consequence sponsored Harry De Windt and Benjamin Howard to visit Sakhalin, and they presented the penal colony on the island in a much more sympathetic light. See Gentes, 'Sakhalin as cause célèbre', 60–2.

[78] Young, 'Knowing Russia's convicts', 1702–4.

[79] Gentes, 'Sakhalin as cause célèbre', 61.

[80] Cathy Popkin, 'Chekhov as ethnographer: Epistemological crisis on Sakhalin Island', *Slavic Review*, 51, 1 (1992), 37 (36–51).

[81] Gentes argues that Chekhov's investigations were literary, fact-driven, and artistic. See 'Sakhalin as cause célèbre', 66.

[82] Whether or not Chekhov intended his research to constitute a dissertation for the degree of Doctor of Medical Sciences is disputed. On this, and Chekhov in Sakhalin more broadly, see Sharyl M. Corrado, The 'End of the Earth': Sakhalin Island in the Russian imperial imagination, 1849–1906, PhD thesis, University of Illinois at Urbana-Champaign, 2010, 77–8.

before departure, analysis of official statistics, and extensive ethnographic work on the island, including through personal interviews and a survey. Chekhov called it a *'nauchnyi plan'*, a great scientific project.[83] After an arduous three-month journey to Sakhalin, suffering from tuberculosis, he began with a rough count of the penal population, and then undertook a census. He printed 10,000 cards at the island's police station, inscribed with the following categories: name of settlement, house number, penal status, name, age, religion, birthplace, year of arrival, literacy, marital status (pre-transportation and in Sakhalin), and whether assistance was received by the prison administration. He then went around the colony issuing the cards, interviewing the convicts and exiles, and taking extensive supplementary notes. Sometimes, he was assisted by a convict or settled exile, who 'had taken on the role of guide out of boredom'. Almost 8,000 of these cards still survive.[84]

In his census, Chekhov failed to a greater or lesser degree, for he found convicts and exiles unable or unwilling to give information about their birthplace or age, how long they had been in the penal colony, and even whether they were married before their transportation. Indeed, Chekhov noted that his subjects were suspicious of his motives, and some believed that the census was a precursor to their resettlement on the mainland. Many had no recollection of or refused to reveal their surnames, giving Chekhov new ones such as *'Nepomnyashchii'* ('Don't-remember').[85] Chekhov despaired too about the inaccurate and unreliable nature of the existing statistics, which had been poorly kept and were fraudulent or full of errors. These included shortcomings in the island's medical records. He found it difficult to make sense of the statistical data that he collected, and it has been argued that he presented a large amount of irrelevant data (e.g. how many pencils were in use on the island), and produced 'peculiar correlations'.[86] Nonetheless, Chekhov combined what has been described as a scientific and artistic approach to draw significant conclusions.[87] As in the early colonial New South Wales described in Chapter 9, but in stark contrast to French Guiana, this

---

[83] Popkin, 'Chekhov as ethnographer', 38.
[84] Chekhov describes the taking of the census in chapter 3 of *Sakhalin Island*. He refers to his convict and exile assistants on p. 70, and to suspicions about his motives on p. 73. See also Popkin, 'Chekhov as Ethnographer'; Young, 'Knowing Russia's Convicts'.
[85] Chekhov *Sakhalin Island*, 66–7. Popkin, 'Chekhov as ethnographer', 38–9; Young, 'Knowing Russia's convicts', 1708.
[86] Popkin, 'Chekhov as ethnographer', 39–40, 44–5 (quote, 45). Leonard A. Polakiewicz argues that Popkin is too harsh in her evaluation of Chekhov, and that she is herself prey to overstatement and distortion. See Leonard A. Polakiewicz, 'Western critical response to Chekhov's *The Island of Sakhalin*', *Russian History/Histoire Russe*, 33, 1 (2006), 78–81 (73–82).
[87] Polakiewicz, 'Western critical response to Chekhov's *The Island of Sakhalin*', 82.

included the fact that women on Sakhalin were considerably more fertile than their counterparts in Russia, and that the child mortality rate was very low. In the ten years between 1880 and 1890, 2,275 children were born. In 1891, there were 2,122 children on the island, of whom 644 arrived from European Russia with their parents, and the remainder either had been born during their mother's journey eastwards, or on Sakhalin itself. Though Chekhov thought that these children gave their parents 'moral support', he noted their unproductivity and expense. Indeed, despite their low mortality rates, and though the administration issued them with either money allowances or food subsidies, he claimed that they were 'pale, emaciated ... dressed in rags and always hungry'.[88] Like Orgéas and countless others, Chekhov believed that penal transportation was incompatible with colonization. Not only was the convict and exile population in constant flux and lacking the knowledge of the land necessary for its permanent development, transportation had caused moral and social collapse, producing official brutality and general lawlessness, and encouraging the prostitution of women and girls. Punishment necessitated colonial compromise, and the two were 'in inverse relation to each other'. Moreover, as soon as convicts and exiles had served their sentence and were permitted to leave for the mainland, they did so, taking their children with them. This explained the fact that at the time of Chekhov's writing, there were just 185 people in the colony between the ages of 15 and 20 years, and only 27 of them had been born on their mothers' journey to Sakhalin, or on the island itself.[89]

After publication, Chekhov's book circulated widely, and its historical significance was its representational transformation of Sakhalin from a land ripe for colonization to the most dreaded place in the Russian Empire: 'the end of the world'.[90] This representation of the island was bolstered following the publication of the somewhat sensationalized 'personal testimony' of Vlas Doroshevich, first as columns in the *Odesskii listok* (*Odessa Flier*), *Rossiia* (*Russia*), and *Russkoe slovo* (*The Russian Word*) during 1897–1902, and then as a two-volume book in 1903. Doroshevich was influenced by Chekhov, but wrote about the island exclusively on the basis of interviews, not data.[91] Chekhov's work, meanwhile, like Orgéas's

---

[88] Chekhov *Sakhalin Island*, 238, 242–4, 247 (quote, 247). A terrific new gender history is Carrie Crockett, Excavating Exile: Women of the Sakhalin Penal Colony, 1868–1905, PhD thesis, University of Leicester, 2020.
[89] Chekhov *Sakhalin Island*, 238; Young, 'Knowing Russia's convicts', 1709–10, 1712 (quote, 1712).
[90] This is Corrado's insight in The 'End of the Earth', 78. See also Young, 'Knowing Russia's convicts', 1701.
[91] Corrado, The 'End of the Earth', 82; Gentes, 'Sakhalin as cause célèbre; Popkin, 'Chekhov as ethnographer', 50–1; Young, 'Knowing Russia's convicts', 1701.

French Guiana study, was part of a larger history of research in penal colonies, where convicts were accessible subjects who could be reduced to statistics, and interviewed, and represented both as an anomalous part of humanity, or as representatives of larger populations. Indeed, Chekhov's research in Sakhalin produced a statistical and ethnographic vision of a penal colony that government censuses in other locations had anticipated for at least a century before. For example, the British government took the first muster of convict New South Wales shortly after the First Fleet arrived in 1788, followed by annual musters between 1785 and 1825. It took the first census in 1828, over a decade before that of Britain. There was an important labour history dimension to these musters and censuses, for they enabled the tracking of convict work gangs and more effective assignment.[92] This was also the case in Brazil's Fernando de Noronha, where an 1881 survey detailed age, illness, and disability, and shows evidence of occupational skills matching.[93]

The first Indian census of 1871 included sets of statistical tables on the Andaman Islands. It enumerated and categorized the convict and free populations, the latter at this time including officers and others employed in the colonial establishment, and their families. The level of detail is extraordinary, in large part because the census forms allowed for open ended answers. It divided the 11,490-strong convict population by age and education and recorded the existence of twelve Hindu and five Muslim 'sects'. It noted that there were 170 Europeans in the Islands, all of whom were employed in the penal establishment. The figure for Indigenous Andaman islanders (2,000) is clearly an estimate, but that for the Nicobar Islands (847) appears to represent an actual enumeration.[94] Nonetheless, the published all-India census (known as the 'imperial' census) excluded all the Andaman statistics from its tables, because the government decided that the Islands were not 'strictly within Indian

---

The original text is V. M. Doroshevich, *Sakhalin (Katorga)*, 2 volumes (Moscow: Tipografiia Tovarishchestva I. D. Sytina, 1903). An excellent English language version is now available: Vlas Doroshevich, translated by Andrew A. Gentes, *Russia's Penal Colony in the Far East: A translation of Vlas Doroshevich's 'Sakhalin'* (New York: Anthem Press, 2009). Gentes notes that Doroshevich allowed the convicts and exiles to speak in their own words and, in this sense, he took a more humanistic approach to his subjects than Chekhov (xvii).

[92] Jayne Elizabeth Bisman, 'The census as accounting artefact: A research note with Illustrations from the Early Australian Colonial Period', *Accounting History*, 14 (2009), 297, 299 (293–314).

[93] Peter M. Beattie, *Punishment in Paradise: Race, slavery, human rights, and a nineteenth-century penal colony* (Durham, NC: Duke University Press, 2015), 181–91.

[94] National Archives of India Home (Port Blair, A proceedings), October 1873, nos. 49–59: Census of the Andaman Islands, December 1871.

limits'.[95] The terminology of the Islands' exclusion is hard to decipher. It may have referred to the Islands' geographical position in the Bay of Bengal, or its character as a penal colony. More likely perhaps was the difficulty of fitting the social and cultural diversity and cosmopolitanism of the convicts into a census that was interwoven with the colonial desire to categorize 'traditional' India according to an unchanging cultural and religious essence, which could be located within and across regions of the subcontinent. In this regard, is noteworthy that the imperial census did not include the port of Aden either, though it was part of the Bombay Presidency at the time.

The next census of the Andamans, which took place in 1881, recorded details of the penal settlement only, though it gave another estimate of the Indigenous population. It presented more information than the 1871 report, in a format that was consistent with that of the more prescriptive imperial census tables. This included convicts' birthplace and occupation, whether they could read or write, and how many were of 'unsound mind', blind, or leprous. This time, the general convict population figures for the Andamans (14,628) were included in the published census for all India, but the more detailed information (e.g. age, language spoken, and religious affiliation) was not.[96] The third Andaman census of 1891 again did not collect information on the Indigenous peoples of the Islands, noting only that they were 'said to be dying out'. The statistics on convicts, however, were once more included in the general tables and appendices of the imperial census tables, and in more detail than in 1881. They reveal an enumeration of a total population of 15,609 convicts, 2,234 of whom were men, and 9,433 of whom were Hindus. They lived in 2,997 households in 59 villages. There were 1,909 locally born, free people, with an exceptionally skewed gender ration of 1,523 males to 386 females. This suggests that many women born in the Islands left for the mainland with their time-served or free-born husbands.[97]

Chief Commissioner of the Andamans, Richard C. Temple, directed the 1901 census. He was an enthusiastic anthropological writer and collector, and one of the editors of the journal of 'oriental research', *The Indian Antiquary*. Previously, he had published collaboratively on

---

[95] *Memorandum on the Census of British India, of 1871–72* (London: Eyre and Spottiswoode, 1875), 6.

[96] IOR W7869/6: *Statistics of the Population Enumerated in the Andamans, 17th February 1881* (Calcutta: Office of the Superintendent of Government Printing, 1883); Appendix: Table 1 Area and Population of India, including Native States; *Report on the Census of British India Taken on the 17th February 1881* (London: Eyre and Spottiswoode, 1883).

[97] *General Report on the Census of India, 1891* (London: Eyre and Spottiswoode, 1893), 35, Appendix: Table A. General Statement; Table B. Variation in Population Since 1881; Table C. The Population by Religion; Table E. The Population by Birthplace.

Andamanese languages and grammar, in addition to several scholarly works, including on the Punjab where he had previously served.[98] Temple's census was the first large-scale attempt to enumerate and describe the entire population of the Islands. It excluded only the 'hostile' Jarawas, and Onge peoples, for whom he estimated populations. Overall in the Islands, the census employed 60 government officials and 70 convict clerks (*munshis*), and it enumerated the total population at 16,256 in the penal settlement (of whom 11,947 were convicts), 1,882 Indigenous Andamanese, and 6,511 Nicobarese. Extensive descriptions and reflections accompanied the statistical work. Temple made brief reference to the idea of criminal heredity, as explored in Chapter 9, but was largely unconcerned with using biological determinism as a means of understanding the cultural and social lives of convicts and their children. Unlike Orgéas and Chekhov, whilst presenting a few tables on mortality and morbidity in the Andamans, neither did he construct arguments about the success or failure of penal colonization. To be sure, child mortality rates in the Andamans were so low that in most cases all the children born in a single family survived into adulthood.[99] Temple's motivation in studying the penal colony was partly compelled by the standardized questions required for the census returns, but he was also driven by his own interest in Indian culture and society. The 1901 census is thus an extraordinary piece of research on Indigenous Islanders, and the cultural and religious lives of convicts, ex-convicts, and their descendants. It analysed the nature and pace of social and cultural change since the colonization of the Islands in 1858 and can be read as an extended essay on the distinctiveness of the Islands from mainland society.[100]

The census commissioners responsible for Indigenous enumeration were Temple's sometime collaborator E. H. Man, retired deputy chief commissioner, and renowned photographer and ethnographer,[101] Senior

---

[98] Claire Wintle, *Colonial Collecting and Display: Encounters with Material Culture from the Andaman and Nicobar Islands* (Oxford: Berghahn, 2013). Temple was editor of *The Indian Antiquary*, 1885–1921.

[99] Richard C. Temple, *Census of India, 1901. Volume 3: The Andaman and Nicobar Islands. Report on the Census* (Calcutta: Office of the Superintendent of Government Printing, 1903), Part 3: The Penal Settlement, 400 (285–415).

[100] Some of the descriptions in Temple's census report were used as the basis for the entries on the Andaman and Nicobar Islands in: W. W. Hunter's *Imperial Gazetteer of India. Volume V: Abazai to Arcot* (Oxford: Clarendon Press, 1908), 350–72, and, especially (sometimes verbatim, sometimes in abbreviated form, and sometimes updated beyond 1901), [R. C. Temple], *Imperial Gazetteer of India, Provincial Series: Andaman and Nicobar Islands* (Calcutta: Office of the Superintendent of Government Printing, 1908).

[101] E. H. Man, *The Aboriginal Inhabitants of the Andaman Islands* (London: Trübner, 1883); E. H. Man, 'On the Andamanese and Nicobarese Objects presented to Major-General Pitt Rivers', *Journal of the Anthropological Institute*, 9 (1882), 268–94; E. H. Man, 'On the

Medical Officer A. R. S. Anderson, and H. H. D'Oyly, who was third assistant superintendent. With a convict at the tiller of the census boat, they went on two tours into some of the remotest parts of the Islands, where it seems some of the Andamanese 'took a great deal of trouble in going to places where Europeans could not follow'. The British commissioners took a few islanders with them, encouraging them to shout out 'friendly' words, and trying to bribe their subjects with rice, sugar, biscuits, tea, tobacco, and pipes. One of the Andamanese men, Boya, who the British called Snowball, used coloured beads to count islanders. Every time he encountered a person, he transferred a bead from a full bag into another bag. He used different colours for men, women, boys, and girls. Islanders did not always welcome the enumerators. Indeed, one man met Senior Medical Officer Anderson's greeting with an arrow, which hit him squarely in the thigh.[102]

Deputy Superintendent F. E. Tuson was in charge of the census of the penal settlement. Given the routine daily musters of all convicts, and the annual musters of the entire population, Temple described this element of the census as relatively straightforward. Tuson took as the basis for his convict population figures the daily 'morning report'. This was a count of convicts by district officers, sent each day to the superintendent of the penal settlement, who checked the total numbers against the 'strength register' of the Islands. The administration also counted ex-convicts on probation, who were known as self-supporters or ticket-of-leave holders, every month; the numbers were checked with the superintendent in the same way. In addition, government generated a descriptive roll for each convict, to which clerks added additional information on conduct and other matters including progression through the penal classes and further punishment whilst they were under sentence or on probation. From this, census clerks gleaned further details regarding convicts' place of origin, marital status, religion, and caste. They located information about literacy and health in other locally kept records or by direct interviews. Chief Commissioner Temple added contextual information to accompany the numerous statistical tables that this process generated. These went well beyond what the census itself required. It included not just a detailed account of convict morbidity and mortality, but a detailed ethnographic

---

Aboriginal Inhabitants of the Andaman Islands', *Journal of the Anthropological Institute*, 12 (1883), 69–175, 327–434. On Man's photographic work, see also Elizabeth Edwards, 'Science Visualized: E. H. Man in the Andaman Islands', in Elizabeth Edwards, ed., *Anthropology and Photography, 1860–1920* (London: Royal Anthropological Institute, 1994), 108–21.

[102] CJML 'The Census, 1901': Diary of A. R. S. Anderson, 15–18 February 1901 (uncatalogued typescript).

study as well. In regard to convict health, for example, Temple presented figures to suggest that there existed correlations between morbidity and the length of time a convict had been in the Islands. Those who had spent less than a year in the penal colony had the highest rates of sickness, and self-supporters had the lowest. In between, there was a steady annual decline for the first six years, after which time the rates remained stable.[103] The latter, the ethnographic study, was particularly focused on the transformation of religion and caste among convicts over the previous forty years.[104]

It is well known that the Indian census was preoccupied with caste, for the British viewed it as a signifier of a person or community's occupation that both prescribed and limited the extent of their social, cultural, and religious engagement with others. Investigations of caste were an important constituent of all statistical and ethnographic work in colonial India, which from the turn of the twentieth century included the anthropometric measurement of individuals and caste groups. The British viewed caste as uniquely Indian and saw it as one of the key markers of cultural difference and social distinction in the subcontinent. It is widely accepted that, to at least some extent, from the 1860s and 1870s, the British rendered caste more unchanging and static than heretofore, and used it as category through which society could be understood and ordered, and thus effectively administered and ruled.[105] Though Indians were key informants and centrally engaged in research and knowledge production, censuses created the social categories that they claimed to describe.[106] The Andamans were both especially interesting and especially perplexing for census enumerators, ethnographers, and ultimately anthropometrists,

---

[103] Richard C. Temple, *Census of India, 1901. Volume 3: The Andaman and Nicobar Islands. Report on the Census* (Calcutta: Office of the Superintendent of Government Printing, 1903), Part 3: The Penal Settlement, 384 (285–415).
[104] Temple, *Census of India, 1901. Volume 3*, 285. Appendix A of this report includes all the tables discussed in the report (298–328), and Appendices B and C present tables from the 1881 and 1891 censuses (328–49).
[105] Arjun Appadurai, 'Number in the colonial imagination', in Carol A. Breckenridge and Peter van der Veer, eds., *Orientalism and the Postcolonial Predicament: Perspectives on South Asia* (Philadelphia: University of Pennsylvania Press, 1993), 314–39; Susan Bayly, 'Caste and "race" in the colonial ethnography of India', in Peter Robb, ed., *The Concept of Race in South Asia* (New Delhi: Oxford University Press, 1997), 165–218; Nicholas Dirks, *Castes of Mind: Colonialism and the Making of Modern India* (Princeton University Press, 2001).
[106] Bernard S. Cohn, *An Anthropologist among the Historians and Other Essays* (New Delhi: Oxford University Press, 1987), 224–54; Norbert Peabody, 'Cents, Sense and Census: Human Inventories in Late Precolonial and Early Colonial India', *Comparative Studies in Society and History*, 43, 4 (2001), 819–50; Kevin Walby and Michael Haan, 'Caste Confusion and Census Enumeration in Colonial India, 1871–1921', *Histoire Sociale / Social History*, 45, 90 (2012), 301–18.

not only due to their large Indigenous population, but because convicts were sent to the Islands from all over British India, including continental South Asia and Burma, and from the British Crown colony of Ceylon. They came from hugely diverse regions, climates, and cultures, and from numerous religions and religious sects. They had lived in villages, towns, and cities, they spoke many languages and dialects, and they were habituated to wearing different kinds of clothes and eating a variety of foods. During the first ten years of penal colonization, there is no question that the Andamans was the most cosmopolitan place in British Asia. However, it was not long before new social formations emerged, and gradually the Islands' cosmopolitanism gave way to remarkable forms of cultural hybridity. Contemporary surveys of the Andamans noted both their diversity and their syncretism. In both cases, it was difficult to slot Andaman statistics and descriptions neatly into all-India censuses, for the form of the census was such that they little recognized geographical or social mobility, let alone religious or cultural change, or newly generated social formations.

Indeed, in 1901, Temple described the difficulties that he faced in using the forms supplied by the government of India, writing that they had 'always proved a stumbling block to both enumerators and tabulators'. The forms were, he noted, 'little suited to so highly specialized and small a population as that of the Penal Settlement'. This difficulty meant that he had to get his tabulators to fill them in twice, and though he had checked them and made extensive corrections, he still believed that they were inaccurate. Moreover, the 'small artificial population' of the Islands, comprising convicts, ex-convicts, and their descendants, alongside a free establishment, made it impossible to fill out certain tables, including 'urban population and its variation', and 'education by caste and tribe'.[107] Age was also an issue, as convicts under the age of 16 and over the age of 60 were rarely transported, and this made this element of the Islands' demography unusual.[108] As for occupation, what was to be recorded: a convict's trade or work before conviction, or that to which he or she was allocated in the penal colony? Temple settled on both, but noted the unsatisfactory nature of his pre-conviction categories, which did not appear adequately detailed, and which he could not check.[109]

The biggest problem for Temple, however, was the census of religion and caste. First, the Andamanese and Nicobarese were mainly Animists, and as they constituted an estimated one third of the Islands' population,

---

[107] Temple, *Census of India, 1901. Volume 3*, 288.
[108] Temple, *Census of India, 1901. Volume 3*, 367.
[109] Temple, *Census of India, 1901. Volume 3*, 368.

he decided to exclude them from the table 'population by religion', for fear of skewing the figures. This elision is highly revealing of a social vision of an empire in which Indigenous people could be neither included nor classified as part of the so-called essence of India. Second, following the Third Anglo-Burmese War of 1885, the British started to send Burmese convicts in large numbers to the Andamans. They were largely Buddhists. However, the British had not kept separate statistics on the number of Buddhists in the Islands, but had classified them as 'others' to Christians, Muslims, and Hindus. Given the large rise in the number of Buddhists in the Islands that had taken place by 1901, the Andamans contradicted the mainland census view that Buddhism was in decline.[110] Third, one of the principles of transportation as a punishment was to cause multiple social dislocations. At the same time, penal movement into a new society enabled convicts to transform their caste and thus their status. Temple noted that convicts often tried to 'raise' their caste, adopting the manners of those who claimed higher status for themselves, including in one case when a sweeper (low caste) pretended to be a Brahmin (high caste) cook. This, he noted, would be 'quite inadmissible' in their home villages. On the other hand, other convicts pretended to be lowly sweepers to secure cleaning work, which they found lighter than public works labour.[111]

Whatever cultural formations it revealed, and whatever problems it raised, the inclusion of the Andaman Islands penal colony in the Indian census envelops convicts, ex-convicts, and their descendants into an intellectual history most usually reserved for colonial and Indian elites and their free informants. The difficulties of incorporating the Andaman penal colony into the imperial census is also particularly illuminating of some of the shortcomings of the all-India study. Over time, the census became increasingly predicated on pre-defined categories of caste, and increasingly closed to caste mobility or the redefinition of cultural and religious categories as they changed over time. Because of the enormous diversity among transportation convicts, and because of the pace at which the cosmopolitanism of the Islands gradually dissolved and culturally transformed into a new kind of carceral society, the Andamans census is perhaps best described as a microcosm of the challenges that beset the Indian census at large, particularly with respect to the classification of religion and caste.

Indeed, Temple described convicts as lacking in 'nice distinctions in religious matters', which meant that he found it difficult to classify

---

[110] Temple, *Census of India, 1901. Volume 3*, 368.
[111] Temple, *Census of India, 1901. Volume 3*, 369. Sweepers belong to a *dalit* or 'scheduled' caste.

Hindus according to caste. Important here was the exceptionally imbalanced gender ratio in the penal colony, which in 1901 was comprised of 14,122 men compared to just 2,134 women. Temple noted that men and women could not marry each other from within customary groups, as on the mainland, and in this context a new system of marriage had emerged and given rise to 'local castes'. He explained that these had the same names as those on the mainland but were fundamentally different from them. He included extensive notes on both the marriage process, and the social and cultural outcomes of partnerships that were necessarily between people from diverse social origins. His findings were based on records of marriages in the penal colony, and questions put to married convicts and their families.[112]

From the earliest years of colonization in 1858, the British administration had favoured marriage between convicts as a means of encouraging permanent settlement, and so these potential limitations presented it with a conundrum. The first list of convict marriages dates from as early as 1861. It carefully detailed each spouse's place of origin and the husband's occupation in the Andamans, but without further comment.[113] Though male self-supporters were allowed to call for their families in India, very few free women and children could be persuaded to undertake the journey, and so male self-supporters were allowed to marry convict women.[114] They had to make an application to the superintendent of convicts, and he approved the match as long as the man was able to support his family, and the marriage was acceptable to what were called 'social conditions in India'. For instance, government prohibited marriages between Hindus and Muslims, and marriages between men and divorced women. The couple undertook religious ceremonies appropriate to the spouses' ritual preferences, and then went to the superintendent for the legal registration of their union. Initially, after 1858, government only allowed Hindu and Muslim self-supporters and convicts to marry from within each group, and on occasion this almost certainly breached customary forms of mainland endogamy. In 1881, as the population grew, for the purpose of marriage all Hindus in the Andamans were placed in one of the four mainland caste *varna* (divisions), which in the Islands were called 'castes'. These were Brahman, Kshatriya (known as

---

[112] Temple, *Census of India, 1901. Volume 3*, 289, 297.
[113] *Statement Exhibiting the Moral and Material Progress and Condition of India, during the Year 1861–2, Part I* (Ordered by the House of Commons to be printed, 15 May 1863), Appendix IV: List of convicts who have married at Port Blair.
[114] Satadru Sen, 'Domesticated Convicts: Producing Families in the Andaman Islands', in Indrani Chatterjee, ed., *Unfamiliar Relations: Family and history in South Asia* (Brunswick, NJ: Rutgers University Press, 2004), 261–91.

Khatris in the Andamans), Vaisyas, and Sudras. Only endogamous marriages within these four 'castes' were permitted. Temple was optimistic that if the children of these unions were studied over time, Andamans statistics would gradually reveal 'the birth of caste and the progress of caste construction'.[115] Children, Temple wrote, took the caste of their father, and divided themselves into high and low castes generally, with Brahmans, Khatris, and Vaisyas holding themselves above those of Sudra origin.[116]

One of the remarkable findings of the 1901 census was the rapid growth of the 'local-born' community: the name given to the children of self-supporting convicts and their descendants. Indeed, it revealed that this population had increased between two and three times in two decades: from 754 in 1881 to 1,499 in 1891 and 2,030 in 1901. In addition to the 1,499 local-born people living in the Andamans in 1891, were 410 children who had returned to the mainland with their parents on release: the largest majority (129) to the Punjab. There was, Temple noted, 'a marked difference maintained at present between the "free" introduced from India and the "free" with the taint of convict blood'. Free people from India saw marriage to the locally born as 'degrading'.[117] However, the children of convicts had worked out new marriage customs among themselves. Ideally, locally born men married the daughters of men of the same caste as their fathers. However, the demographics of the penal colony and in particular, the shortage of women meant that this was not always possible, and so more usually men ignored their wives' caste, and passed their own caste onto their children. Moreover, and quite differently to mainland practice, the man's family often paid for the wedding, unless they did not have the means, in which case the woman's family covered the expenses. Women's families never paid dowries. Women could marry a man of higher or lower caste to themselves, and thus move up or down the caste *varna*.[118] Overall, rates of marriage were relatively low for the daughters of convicts, and Temple believed that this was the result of a profound change of cultural practice stemming from the colony's prohibition of child marriage, which self-supporters had themselves extended to girls older than 16.[119]

---

[115] Temple, *Census of India, 1901. Volume 3*, 398–9 (quote, 399).
[116] Temple, *Census of India, 1901. Volume 3*, 399.
[117] Temple, *Census of India, 1901. Volume 3*, 295–6, 353, 398.
[118] Temple, *Census of India, 1901. Volume 3*, 399–400, and Appendix D, Results of enquiry into the Caste History of Local Born Men and Women in the Penal Settlement at Port Blair, 405–9.
[119] Temple, *Census of India, 1901. Volume 3*, 291.

Though Temple despaired of the shortcomings of his Andamans census, in fact its failure to conform to the imperial template means that it is better conceived as an archive of cultural change in the penal colony than as a population count. Beyond religion and caste, for instance, Temple noted that 41 of the languages listed in the Indian census indexes were spoken in the Islands. The main languages were Hindi, Punjabi, Burmese, and Bengali. A handful of convicts, or in some cases one sole man or woman, spoke others, including Gondi, Kharia, and Peshwari.[120] However, the vernacular in most widespread use was Urdu, which Temple noted was 'really hybrid Urdu filled with local terms partly derived from English, partly from Urdu and partly specialised adaptations of all sorts of words to local requirements and circumstances.'[121] All locally born people, whatever their parents' background, spoke this vernacular. The 'specialised adaptations' incorporated the semantics of the penal colony. So, *peti afsar* (petty officer) derived from the Hindustani word for 'belt' (*peti*) and a revised pronunciation of the English word 'officer' (*afsar*). A European overseer of convicts was a *sher* (tiger) *sahib* (white man). Self-supporters on probation were *tikat* (ticket) *wallahs* (people), that is, ticket-of-leave holders. Many locations in the colony, sometimes named after British officers and their families, or ships, were also subject to this accented 'corruption'. Thus, Port Mouat, named after F. J. Mouat, was *Potmot*; Mount Harriet, named after the wife of Superintendent R. C. Tytler in the 1860s, was *Mohan Ret*; and Navy Bay became *Nabbi Beg*.[122]

As mentioned above, Temple did not refer to theories of biological determinism and criminality. However, he reproduced sets of tables dating from 1895, comparing the incidence of violent crime in the penal colony to that in selected areas of the mainland. He surmised that rates in the Andamans were much higher than anywhere in India or Burma: 15.45 per 10,000 of the population, compared to 0.20 in Madras, the highest mainland rate. Given that most convicts were transported for dacoity (gang robbery), violent crimes against the person or property, or murder and attempted murder, Temple drew attention to the fact that this represented a statistical chance of violence of just 0.154 per cent per annum, thus revealing the value of 'continuous severe restraint'. A similar phenomenon has been identified for New South Wales in the nineteenth century, where a relatively low crime society succeeded the penal colony. This has been explained as a result of the success of the social

---

[120] Temple, *Census of India, 1901. Volume 3*, 308.
[121] Temple, *Census of India, 1901. Volume 3*, 293.
[122] Temple, *Census of India, 1901. Volume 3*, 363–4.

reintegration, as opposed to social exclusion, that underpinned the penal transportation model.[123] Also of interest here are Temple's extensive comments on the character of the descendants of convicts. He echoed the observations of visitors to the Australian colonies almost a century earlier. The children of convicts in the Andamans might not have been the 'cornstalks' of the Antipodes, but they were 'bright, intelligent, and unusually healthy'. They certainly did not display any criminal tendencies that could be anchored to characteristics inherited from their parents. 'Heredity', Temple concluded, 'seems to show itself in both sexes rather in a tendency towards the meaner qualities than towards violence of temperament … On the whole, considering their parentage, the local born population is of a much higher type than the inexperienced would expect to find them.'[124]

In his closing comments on caste in the Andamans, Temple wrote: 'That in time caste will rule marriages and social relations in the Penal Settlement in all its accustomed force there appears to be little doubt.' Bound to contemporary mainland representations on the power of caste to define all areas of people's lives, as it turned out, he was quite wrong. In fact, quite the opposite happened. As superintendent of operations for the next census in 1911, R. F. Lowis, noted the combination of penal discipline and a gender ratio of 18 men to every woman rendered caste subject to further disintegration. Except in cooking and the cleaning and removal of waste, government did not allocate convicts to caste-based work. Convicts 'of all castes and creeds' were forced to work alongside each other, and to form friendships with each other in ways that would not have occurred naturally on the mainland. Whilst convicts married within broad caste groups, among the local-born population the 'breaking down of the caste system' produced what Lowis described as 'the most chaotic conditions with regard to marriage'. There were no endogamous or exogamous groups, or prohibited relationships. This was an effect of the transportation regime, but also a consequence of government policy. Neither the building of places of worship, nor the establishment of caste *panchayats* (governing councils) in self-supporters' villages were permitted. Whatever their traditional occupation, most self-supporters became cultivators. Their children went to school together. This constituted 'a deadening and levelling process', where caste had very little influence on the younger generations of the local-born. Otherwise, the 1911 census

---

[123] Temple, *Census of India, 1901. Volume 3*, 370–4; John Braithwaite, 'Crime in a convict Republic', *The Modern Law Review*, 64, 1 (2001), 11–50. Braithwaite compares the fate of post-convict New South Wales to that of the post-emancipation USA. He argues that the latter became a high crime society because of the social exclusions of enslavement.

[124] Temple, *Census of India, 1901, Volume 3*, 400.

enumerated and estimated the Indigenous population at 455, and the rest of the population at 16,324 (of whom just 2,215 were women, and 11,897 were convicts). Lowis explained the small decline in convict numbers since 1901 as the result of the government's subsequent prohibition of the transportation of all but convicts sentenced for life. Subsequently, government offered ex-convicts various inducements to settle in the Islands following their release.[125]

In 1911 and again 1921, Lowis used census operations as an opportunity to research the Islands' Indigenous peoples, as well as its penal colony. He presented most of the statistics and tables required for the imperial census, though like Temple noted that the 'artificiality' and small size of the penal colony made it impossible to address some of the required correlations.[126] For instance, figures on age were of no 'scientific' value. Those on sex were more interesting. The gender ratio of 18:1 was the result of the effects of transportation, but Lowis found that among convicts' children there were 461 boys to 376 girls, which was also an extraordinary figure. Lowis acknowledged that the numbers were small, but wrote: 'so far as anything can be argued from them, they would tend to show that the disproportion of females to males in eastern countries is not altogether due to the condition of subjection in which the women live'.[127] A medical report appended to the 1911 census noted that, compared to the mainland, birth rates in the penal colony were low, and that around 25 per cent of married convict couples did not have children. This was in part because ex-convict women were comparatively older when they got married but given that the large majority were under the age of 35, this was not the whole reason. Senior Medical Officer J. M. Woolley explained the low rates as the consequence of high rates of venereal disease and the prevalence of stillbirth. Inadvertently, Woolley revealed some of the limits to research. He noted that convicts and self-supporters suffering from venereal disease did not routinely present themselves for treatment, in the knowledge that they would receive punishment for it. Thus, he could not quantify its prevalence. Neither did he offer statistics on stillbirths.[128] There are interesting parallels here with Orgéas's findings for French Guiana, where the gender ratio was even more skewed. It is interesting to speculate about whether the men and

---

[125] R. F. Lowis, *Census of India, 1911. Volume 2: The Andaman and Nicobar Islands* (Calcutta: Office of the Superintendent of Government Printing, 1912), 63–4, 66–7, 71–2 (quotes, 67, 71, 72).
[126] Lowis, *Census of India, 1911. Volume 2*, i, 96.
[127] Lowis, *Census of India, 1911. Volume 2*, 66–7 (quote, 67).
[128] J. M. Woolley, 'Convict marriages in the Andamans', *Indian Medical Gazette*, 47, 3 (1912), 89–94 (reprinted as Appendix B of the 1911 census, 111–15).

women of Saint-Laurent-du-Maroni were similarly afflicted with sexually transmitted diseases, which they successfully hid from Orgéas and his medical assistants, or whether the cause was malaria.

In 1919–20, the Indian jails committee recommended the abolition of penal transportation, claiming homosexual relations were so common in the Andamans that the colony was immoral, and that the Islands had no chance of becoming economically self-sufficient and were thus a drain on imperial resource. Abolition, however, was not practical, for a combination of reasons: the number of locally born people then living in the Islands (around 3,000) who had no mainland home, the value of the Islands' timber, their strategic importance, and the desire to see a return on the initial investment in establishing the colony. Against a background of the stationary character of convict numbers revealed in the 1911 census, and the comparatively low number of children born to ex-convicts and their descendants, the government of India offered mainland prisoners the opportunity to go to the Andamans as 'voluntary' settlers, under favourable penal terms. It also paid for convicts' families to join their kin in the Islands, and gave them generous occupancy rights in order to encourage them to settle permanently.[129] The effect of this policy was a dramatic increase in the number of probationary convicts, as well as the number of women and children in the Islands, including families who came to the colony from the mainland, and children who had been born in the Islands and were not returned to India when their parents were repatriated.

Lowis dealt only briefly with the penal settlement in the 1921 census. He had been away during the previous month and left the arrangements to locally appointed district census officer Bunyad Hussain. He again wrote of the penal colony as 'a purely artificial institution', and declared that the statistics on convicts 'are of little or no value'. Overall, the number of convicts had fallen by 342. However, there were 2,725 ex-convicts and their descendants living in the Islands, which was a rise from the 2,030 recorded by Temple in 1901. In total, there were 17,268 non-Indigenous people.[130] The recommendations of the Indian jails commission spurred a period of rapid change, its full extent revealed a decade later, in the census of 1931. This was carried out under the direction of

---

[129] *Report of the Indian Jails Committee, 1919–20* (London: H.M.'s Stationery Office, 1921), chapter 21; M. C. C. Bonington, *Census of India, 1931. Volume 2: The Andaman and Nicobar Islands* (Calcutta: Government of India Central Publication Branch, 1932), 25. See also Taylor C. Sherman, 'From Hell to Paradise? Voluntary Transfer of Convicts to the Andaman Islands, 1921–1940', *Modern Asian Studies*, 43, 2 (2009), 367–88.

[130] R. F. Lowis, *Census of India, 1921. Volume 2: The Andaman and Nicobar Islands* (Calcutta: Office of the Superintendent of Government Printing, 1923), iii, 9.

forestry officer M. C. C. Bonington. The 230 convict wives present in 1921 had increased to 1,004 in 1931; the number of children under the age of 16 rose from 1,427 to 4,075; and the number of girls and women over the age of 15 excluding convicts' wives went up by 756 to 1,842. They largely constituted the near doubling of the free population in just ten years.[131] The consequence of this was that a much larger proportion of male convicts were married than had been the case in 1921: one in seven convicts, compared to one in 47 in 1921.[132] As in previous years, some of the imperial tables in the 1931 census were left blank: on towns, caste and occupation, education and employment, and literacy and caste. This was because there were no towns in the Islands, caste had no bearing on convicts' occupations, no educated convicts were unemployed, and some of the literacy figures would have enumerated just a handful of people, rendering the statistics meaningless. As in previous years, the report included observations on Indigenous peoples, convicts, self-supporters, and their descendants. Like Temple, Bonington took a sympathetic view of marriage practices in the penal colony, writing that though free Indians stationed in the Islands looked down on its population, this was the inevitable and entirely logical result of 'the fact that races and creeds from all parts of India are represented in the Andamans and that there is therefore no homogenous community of any caste'.[133]

The huge increase in convict marriages, which followed the imperial drive to settle the Islands with prisoners and ex-convicts after the Indian jails committee met, enabled Bonington to produce the first detailed data on convict fertility, some two decades after the publication of Temple's detailed statistical and ethnographic account of local-born people. Bonington tabulated the sex of the first-born children of convicts, the size of families by the occupation of the husband, and the size of families by religion, and correlated the age of wives at marriage with average family size.[134] Given that no such statistics were available in previous censuses, and Woolley's 1911 figures were not presented in the same way, it is hard to compare them to the period before 1921, when far fewer convicts were married, and far fewer children were born. That said, in one regard there was one big change. Bonington's tables reveal that though infant marriage

---

[131] Bonington, *Census of India, 1931*, 34. There were also small increases in the amount of Forest Department labour, mainly Ranchis imported from India (increase of 316), and ships' crews (320), as well as 103 people sent to work in the Islands' first free enterprise, the matchstick factory.
[132] Bonington, *Census of India, 1931*, 39.
[133] Bonington, *Census of India, 1931*, 29 (quote), 101.
[134] Bonington, *Census of India, 1931*, 34–5.

among the local-born was rare, more than 400 girls had married at the age of 16 or under, by far the largest number of whom (234) had been 13 years old. This was a stark contrast to the turn of the century, when if Temple's claims are to be believed, penal regulations did not allow such unions.[135] Likely, this was the result of the renewed importation of mainland practices into the Islands during a decade of rapid change.

Sexual Depravation in Saint-Jean-du-Maroni

We return to French Guiana through the publication of a study of sex and sexuality in the *relégué* (recidivist) camp in Saint-Jean-du-Maroni. In general, evidence of sex between men, sexual predation, and violence was a focus of anti-penal colony writing, but this does not reveal much on the larger question of what the homosocial character of many penal sites meant for convict experiences and lives. In 1906, Dr Franck Cazanove, a medical major in the French colonial army, published a study of the *relégués* of French Guiana, in the academic journal *Archives de l'Anthropologie Criminelle*.[136] *Relégués* were repeat offenders, sent to the colony for life for petty crimes such as theft or vagrancy. Following the passing of the law of *relégation* in 1885, in the years before the closure of the penal colony in 1954, government shipped over 17,000 of them to French Guiana. They were in a different legal category to ordinary transportation convicts, and as such they were subject to a different penal regime and allowed to seek their own livelihoods. Those who could not were either kept in prison in Saint-Jean-du-Maroni, or sent to neighbouring sites such as La Forestière, Tolinche, Saint-Louis, and Nouveau Camp, from where they were put to hard labour.[137] At the end of 1905, at the time Cazanove was researching his article, there were 2,354 male and 202 female *relégués* in French Guiana.[138] Writing in the context of debates about the so-called born criminal (Chapter 9), Cazanove declared them vastly inferior to ordinary convicts. They were,

---

[135] Bonington, *Census of India, 1931*, 35, 39. These girls and young women had given birth to more than 1,200 children. See also Temple, *Census of India, 1901, Volume 3*, 291.

[136] Dr Cazanove, 'La Dépravation Sexuelle chez les Relégués à Saint-Jean-du-Maroni', *Archives de l'Anthropologie Criminelle*, 21 (1906), 44–58. First published in 1895, the *Archives* was the first academic journal in France to focus on crime and criminality. See Marc Renneville, 'Les Archives d'anthropologie criminelle: a journal fit for a nascent scientific field', *Criminocorpus*, Histoire de la criminologie, Présentation du dossier, 2015, http://journals.openedition.org/criminocorpus/2959 (accessed 2 January 2019). Cazanove was later chief medical officer of French troops in Senegal.

[137] Jean-Lucien Sanchez, *À perpétuité. Relégués au bagne de Guyane* (Paris: Vendémiaire, 2013).

[138] *Notice sur La Relégation à la Guyane Française et à la Nouvelle-Calédonie: années 1906–1907* (Paris: Melun, 1913), 'Effectif au 31 décembre 1906', 8.

he claimed, defective both physically and intellectually. This was because they were less 'criminal' than 'anti-social' and afflicted by decrepitude and physical and moral corruption. According to Cazanove, this was evident in high mortality rates, which were partly the consequence of one of the causes of ill health amongst general populations: 'sexual perversion'. This finding was entirely in keeping with Cesare Lombroso's writings on the relationship between criminality and sexuality, which was part of a larger move away from a focus on sexual acts and towards the idea of a homosexual identity. Jordan Blair Woods describes how by the end of the nineteenth century homosexual men came to be viewed as 'a distinct class of criminals marked by biological inferiority'.[139] Following a government report of 1904, which had asserted that half of all *relégués* had engaged in sexual activity with other men, it was this which was the focus of Cazanove's study.[140]

Cazanove claimed that the concentration of recidivists in French Guiana created a peculiar environment in which men acquired perverse habits that became contagious.[141] In this he departed from the 1904 report, which argued that convicts brought homosexual desires and practices with them from France.[142] Cazanove's assertion was that the creation of same sex desire in the Saint-Jean camp was the result of two factors. First was a violent culture in which following the arrival of new convict convoys the strong (*les fort-à-bras*) selected sexual partners from the weak (*les faibles*), forming what Cazanove called 'a monstrous, muscular aristocracy'. The chosen men came to secure advantage in this arrangement, finding security and in some cases financial benefits. Second were those who were unable to work. Lacking resources, they succumbed to the sexual advances of other men. Cazanove outlined three 'classes' of sexual activity among both groups of men: '*les faiseurs de soupe*' (soup-makers), in which a couple reciprocated in giving and receiving sexual pleasure; '*les ménages*' (households), where roles during intercourse were more static; and '*les individus sans attache*' (unattached individuals), men who undertook sex work. In each case the so-called passive partners were sometimes known as *mômes*, or wives.[143] At night, they dressed in women's underwear and clothing and applied make-up, wearing hats adorned with ribbons, bracelets, earrings, rings, perfume, and

---

[139] Jordan Blair Woods, 'The Birth of Modern Criminology and Gendered Constructions of Homosexual Criminal Identity', *Journal of Homosexuality*, 62, 2 (2015), 155 (131–66).
[140] Cazanove, 'La Dépravation Sexuelle', 44–5. See also Sanchez, *À perpétuité*, 125.
[141] Cazanove, 'La Dépravation Sexuelle', 46–7.   [142] Sanchez, *À perpétuité*, 125.
[143] Cazanove, 'La Dépravation Sexuelle', 47–8. See also Michael Lucey, *Never Say I: Sexuality and the First Person in Colette, Gide, and Proust* (Durham, NC: Duke University Press, 2006), 37–9.

lipstick. They went by names including *L'Hirondelle* (Swallow); *L'Ange* (Angel); *Rose Pompon* (Pink Pompom); Nana; *Bébé* (Baby); Angèle; and Marguerite. Cazanove referred to physical examinations of these *relégués*, and his observations suggest that with their unbroken voices, smooth skin, atrophied genitals, and undescended or small testicles, at least some of them self-identified as non-binary.[144] He distinguished them from other convicts because they did not conform to gender stereotypes to create a new kind of physically inferior 'criminal'.[145]

Immorality and sexual violence in the penal colony were familiar themes in French convict memoirs, notably those that emerged during campaigns for the abolition of penal colonies in the 1930s. These included René Belbenoit's *Dry Guillotine* and Aage Krarup-Nielsen's *Hell beyond the Seas*.[146] Chapter 11 describes in more detail international condemnation of French Guiana in the twentieth century. Meanwhile, note that Cazanove described elements of sex work in French Guiana, effected through what he described as specially created 'matrimonial agencies', as 'a perfectly organized white slave trade'.[147] However, Cazanove departed from what became familiar patterns in writing about the penal colony to discuss not just sexual violence, but love between men. Though the 1904 government report had noted that convicts tolerated male couples, Cazanove went into more detail in his description of how *relégué* couples (*ménages*) would exchange vows of love and fidelity, combine their possessions, and escape into the forest. They would take a honeymoon in a hut specially constructed for the purpose, and then return to the settlement to face punishment for absconding. Following this, all *relégués* considered their union as a marriage.[148] To support his case, Cazanove presented extracts from a letter from one such man (known as La Marquise) to his lover (Georgette), written when he was in confinement for attempted escape. La Marquise was worried that Georgette was indulging in sex with other men and tortured himself by imagining scenes in which they were kissing her 'beautiful body'. Following their release from punishment, the men were placed in separate camps, but they managed to find each other once again and escaped to Georgetown in British Guiana. However, they were arrested and returned to Cayenne. It was at this point that their relationship turned sour.

---

[144] Cazanove, 'La Dépravation Sexuelle', 51–5. The themes of Cazanove's study are also evident in a 1907 government report on Saint-Jean. See Sanchez, *À perpétuité*, 119–28.
[145] Woods, 'The Birth of Modern Criminology', 136.
[146] Stephen A. Toth, *Beyond Papillon: The French Overseas Penal Colonies, 1854–1952* (Lincoln: University of Nebraska Press, 2006), 53–4.
[147] Cazanove, 'La Dépravation Sexuelle', 57–8.
[148] Cazanove, 'La Dépravation Sexuelle', 48–9. See also Sanchez, *À perpétuité*, 125–6.

Georgette told the authorities that her partner was 'as jealous as a cat' and that she was tired of him. Meantime, Cazanove cited numerous other cases when men who were separated from their partners would do anything to reunite. He also noted the grief that struck them when lovers died. He counted 92 couples which were not, he stressed, relationships constituted solely through sexual pleasure. He wrote that the men formed a real attachment to each other; through deep affection and true love (*'grand amour'*).[149] In making such observations, Cazanove's writings were ethnographic as well as medical, and like Orgéas's more statistical work were a means of addressing social questions by linking them to pathology and the human body.

*

This chapter has suggested that Orgéas's ideas about the 'non-cosmopolitanism' of European convicts in French Guiana, Chekhov's 'great scientific project' in Sakhalin Island, the decennial censuses of the Andaman Islands, and Cazanove's ethnography of sexual 'deviance' constitute part of the history of social science research. Indeed, during this period commentators in Britain, France, and the USA were focusing similarly on issues of criminal pathology, poverty, race, and sexuality. From the second half of the nineteenth century, convicts were the subjects of statistical and ethnographic observation and enquiry, within a larger context in which the stakeholders of punitive mobility were debating the merits or otherwise of penal colonization. Despite some limitations in male researchers' access to convict women, and some convicts' refusal to engage in the research process, research on morbidity and mortality, sex, pregnancy, childbirth, and the health of children, fed into these discussions. Where convicts were from different regions, countries, and colonies, a further interest was what transportation might reveal about health outcomes for convicts sent to live in unfamiliar climates and disease environments, particularly where they married and had children.

In French Guiana and Sakhalin, Orgéas and Chekhov used their findings to add weight to calls for the abolition of penal colonies, and in the case of the former to suggest that Europeans could never establish colonies in challenging and unfamiliar climates. Cazanove studied sex between men to argue for the corrupting nature of the penal colony and to connect homosexuality to criminality. In this regard, debates about convict origins and experience, as well as health and fitness, can be positioned at the heart of understandings of criminality, punishment and empire, as well as the body and intimacy. In the Andamans, the

---

[149] Cazanove, 'La Dépravation Sexuelle', 50–1.

censuses had other purposes. Whilst they fed into all-India 'imperial' studies, local administrators also used them as an opportunity to develop their own research interests on the cultural and social impact of convict transportation, including intergenerationally. Convicts were the objects of such studies, and despite their status in penal sites in some cases became researchers themselves. Though inequalities of power meant that there were always limitations to this, there exists evidence that they sometimes engaged in the research process on their own terms. It is the tension between such agency and restriction that is the focus of Chapter 11. It explores the multiple border crossings that characterized escape, evasion, and extradition between territories and colonies in the nineteenth and twentieth centuries.

11 Escape and Extradition

Focused on a discussion of escape within and across national and imperial borders, this chapter further develops several themes of this book. These include convicts' agency in resisting penal and labour demands; convicts' insurgency, which fostered and globalized forms of religious and political practice; convicts' construction of new societies, communities, and identities; and convicts' importance and participation in the formation of knowledge of various kinds. During the first part of the nineteenth century, there were several cases in which transportation convicts escaped into the jurisdictions of other colonies. As the first part of the chapter will demonstrate, they fled from and to British, Spanish, French, and Danish islands in the Caribbean and from British Gibraltar to the Spanish peninsular. The second part focuses on French Guiana, for the scale of transportation to the colony from the mid-nineteenth to early-twentieth centuries, coupled with a highly organized traffic of convicts over river and sea borders enabled and facilitated large numbers of escapes. The chapter looks especially closely at the punitive experiences of a group of 1848 revolutionaries. Their penal journey took them from France to North Africa and then to the Îles du Salut. They escaped from the capital of the colony at Cayenne to Surinam (now, Suriname), and ultimately reached the American city of Boston. They took their revolutionary politics with them, and in contrast to Irish nationalist convict John Mitchel's pro-slavery writings in the Australian colonies (Chapter 6), they became involved in anti-slavery campaigns in the USA.

Other convicts from French Guiana – *deportés, transportés,* and *relégués* – took flight all over the Atlantic world, travelling to Surinam, Venezuela, and Colombia, the USA, and Britain's West Indian colonies. Here, the chapter stresses that convict absconding not only offers insights into convict agency and experience, but had profound and enduring legal consequences, for it underpinned the development of a series of international agreements and ultimately laws on extradition and deportation. Governments used these against escaped convicts, as well as suspected criminals who they represented as fugitives from justice. The experiences of these runaways varied widely, and whilst they sometimes demonstrated a sophisticated understanding of legal process and ingenuity and ambition in determining their fate, the difficulties of remaining at large often confounded their desire for freedom. Nonetheless, by the 1920s, international condemnation of the penal colony in French Guiana was growing, and in some cases and for reasons that the chapter will explain nations like Britain refused to return escaped convicts to the colony. At the same time, such convicts gave testimony to appalling conditions, which contributed to the anti-transportation arguments of other nations.

Insurgent Border Crossings in the Caribbean and Mediterranean

In January 1836, the Spanish convict ship *Especulacion*, sailing from Havana to Cadiz, was shipwrecked off the coast of Britain's Grand Bahama island. The thirteen Spanish convicts on board were undergoing transportation for a variety of offences. They included robbery, carrying prohibited weapons, murder, and accomplice to murder. Two of the men were soldiers, court-martialled for assault and repeated desertion. Another, José Felix Rodrigues, had been subject to administrative rather than judicial transportation, on the advice of the colonial *fiscal* (attorney general). It was said that he had instigated 'frequent quarrels' in the courts and possessed a 'very immoral' character. He had 'debauched' the wife and 'seduced' the daughter of a rich merchant named Juan Dias, whom he drove to the lunatic asylum. The *fiscal*'s recommendation of transportation was for his disturbance of 'good order, peace and happiness'. His sentence was eight years, and he was forbidden from ever returning to Cuba.[1]

The Spanish convicts were destined for public works at the *presidio* of Ceuta, but when the *Especulacion* ran aground, they took the opportunity to break their irons. English wreckers working on four sloops nearby

---

[1] TNA CO23/96/23 20 February 1836 no. 17 folios 175–90: Lieutenant-Governor Sir William MacBean George Colebrooke, Grand Bahama, to Charles Grant (1st Baron Glenelg), secretary of state for war and the colonies, 20 February 1836, Colebrooke to Glenelg, 13 May 1836, enc. Colebrooke to Captain-General Don Miguel Taçon, Cuba, 2 February 1836, and Colebrooke to Taçon, 11 February 1836. In an enclosed 'Return of Spanish prisoners wrecked in the Spanish Brig "Especulacion" now in the common jail of Nassau' (n.d.), police magistrate C. R. Nesbitt listed the convicts: Francisco del Castello, Tomas Puertolas, Antonio Frias, Sebatn. Marin, José Felix Rodrigues, Desiderio Manresa, Tomas Gonzales, Gabriel Flores, Gregorio Gonzales, Gregorio Hernandez, Francisco Camero, and José Claro Hernandez. Presumably, the thirteenth man (Ignatio Abad) had died or escaped, for he had earlier signed a petition to the lieutenant-governor (see footnote 4).

boarded the vessel and took the convicts to Nassau with the master, crew, and other passengers. The British magistrates on Grand Bahama detained the convicts under the colony's vagrancy laws, intending to deport them.[2] Lieutenant-Governor and Commander-in-Chief Sir William Colebrooke wrote twice to the Captain-General in Cuba, Don Miguel Taçon, first asking him to send a vessel to the Bahamas to collect the convicts and second requesting details of their conviction so that he could decide whether they should be returned to the Spanish authorities at all. Because some of the convicts were under sentences of transportation for offences that would not have invoked the penalty under English law, and because others carried no paperwork, the attorney general had doubts about the legality of their return.[3] Indeed, the convicts themselves petitioned Lieutenant-Governor Colebrooke, writing that they were 'free agents', and thus 'at liberty to exercise their own discretion in proceeding either to the port of their original destination or elsewhere as they might think fit.' They wrote that they had the means of supporting themselves, and could with ease find a passage to an onward destination.[4] In Cuba, both the *fiscal* and the chief justice took the opposite view, and Taçon requested their return.[5] Colebrooke wrote to London for advice, and the secretary of state for war and the colonies referred the matter to King's Advocate. He declared that as the convicts had liberated themselves and gone voluntarily to Nassau they were entitled to be dealt with 'as free agents', as long as they broke no laws.[6]

The case of the *Especulacion* was one of many that arose in the nineteenth century, where the issue of how to deal with the escape of convicted persons from one polity to another vexed officials. A decade earlier in

---

[2] TNA CO23/96/64 13 May 1836 no. 46 folios 432–71: Taçon to Colebrooke, 22 February 1836, enc. opinion of Pedro Alcantara, Havana, 20 February 1836; Colebrooke to Taçon, 12 May 1836.

[3] TNA CO23/96/23 20 February 1836 no. 17 folios 175–90: Colebrooke to Glenelg, 20 February 1836, Colebrooke to Glenelg, 13 May 1836, enc. Colebrooke to Captain-General Don Miguel Taçon, Cuba, 2 February 1836, and Colebrooke to Taçon, 11 February 1836; TNA CO23/96/64 13 May 1836 no. 46 folios 432–71: Taçon to Colebrooke, 22 February 1836, enc. opinion of Pedro Alcantara, Havana, 20 February 1836; Colebrooke to Taçon, 12 May 1836, enc. opinion of the attorney general, 22 March 1836.

[4] TNA CO23/96/64 13 May 1836 no. 46 folios 432–71: The Petition of the Undersigned, 27 January 1836.

[5] TNA CO23/96/64 13 May 1836 no. 46 folios 432–71: Taçon to Colebrooke, 22 February 1836, enc. opinion of Pedro Alcantara, Havana, 20 February 1836.

[6] TNA CO23/96/64 13 May 1836 no. 46 folios 432–71: Glenelg to Colebrooke, 11 October 1836, Return of Spanish prisoners wrecked in the Spanish Brig "Especulacion" now in the common jail of Nassau, n.d.; TNA CO23/97/25 4 August 1836 no. 85 folios 198–216: Colebrooke to Glenelg, 4 August 1836; Glenelg to Colebrooke, 15 October 1836; TNA CO23/98 (Law Officers): Sir John Dodson, King's Advocate, to Glenelg, 30 April 1836.

Saint Vincent, for example, three enslaved persons named Destiny, Castalio, and Liverpool were sentenced to life transportation as 'incorrigible runaways' and, through the process explained in Chapter 4, they were sold into plantation slavery in Gran Colombia. In 1830, they escaped to Trinidad, the same year that eighteen runaway slaves arrived from French Guiana and were immediately claimed by the French administration in Martinique. Seeking advice on the Saint Vincent runaways, Governor Charles Smith informed the Colonial Office that the Spanish law that was still in force in Trinidad authorized him to banish 'suspicious characters'. Therefore, he proposed to banish the French 'fugitive slaves' to Sierra Leone and send the enslaved convicts sent back to their new owner in Gran Colombia as 'a reciprocal act of courtesy'.[7] During the 1830s, both the Danish and the French approached the British government to request its co-operation in the return of other fugitives.[8] In the latter case, four on remand prisoners escaped from Martinique to Saint Lucia. One of them, Florimond Castaing, was accused of murder and found a passage on to Trinidad. The other three, Pier Désir, Louis Lolo, and Lucian Camille, were accused of 'being employed in assisting people in Slavery to escape'. Because by this time the British had abolished slavery, the three men did not break British law. Thus, the attorney general of Saint Lucia refused to extradite them on the basis that their case did not satisfy one of the key principles of extradition.[9] These were detailed in the agreements that at this time existed between other proximate colonies and polities: Trinidad and Venezuela (1847), Labuan and Borneo (1856), and British Honduras and Guatemala (1862).[10]

---

[7] TNA CO295/85 22 September 1830 no. 24: Governor Charles Felix Smith, Trinidad, to Sir George Murray, secretary of state for war and the colonies, 22 September 1830; TNA CO295/87 11 June 1831 no. 78: Smith to Frederick John Goderich (1st Viscount Goderich), secretary of state for war and the colonies, 11 June 1831. It is not clear how the case was resolved. Note that at this time Gran Colombia incorporated parts of northern South America and southern Central America.

[8] TNA CO28/127/28 18 February 1839 no. 23 folios 147–48A: Governor Sir E. J. Murray MacGregor, Barbados, to Glenelg, 18 February 1839.

[9] TNA CO28/129/18 10 December 1839 no no. folios 98–136: Murray MacGregor to Lord John Russell, secretary of state for war and the colonies, 10 December 1839, enc. Governor Alphonse Louis Théodore de Mogès, Martinique, to Murray MacGregor, 22 July 1839; Lieutenant Colonel Everard, administering the government of Saint Lucia, to Murray MacGregor, 28 September 1839.

[10] TNA CO144/14 (Foreign Office): Wodehouse to Herman Merivale, permanent undersecretary Colonial Office, 15 March 1856; TNA CO111/328 8 October 1860 no. 124: Governor Philip Edmond Wodehouse, British Guiana, to Henry Pelham-Clinton (5th Duke of Newcastle), secretary of state for the colonies, 8 October 1860; TNA CO123/110 21 July 1861 no. 64: Proclamation of Lieutenant-Governor Frederick Seymour, British Honduras, 3 July 1862.

In the absence of extradition agreements, convicts found means to remain on the run, entirely legally, and this almost certainly encouraged escape. For instance, there was never a treaty between Britain and Spain relevant to the proximate punitive sites of Gibraltar and Ceuta, apparently because successive governments in Spain were nervous that this might be viewed as ceding of territory.[11] In a series of cases dating from the 1840s, British convicts ran from Gibraltar to Spain, and though officials knew of their whereabouts, they had no legal means of either forcing the Spanish to give them up or of recapturing them. In 1852, for instance, a man named Thomas Hotchin swam to Cádiz, and then went on to Algeciras where he awaited a ship to take him to the USA.[12] In another case of 1859, a British convict warder crossed the border into Spain to bring back convict Patrick Lawler. He and three others had fled the garrison for Algeciras and found work as shoemaker to the governor. The governor described Lawler's recapture as a kidnap and insisted that the British return him to Spanish territory and allow him to choose whether to cross back over to British lines. Following advice from the law officers of the Colonial Office, which considered the warder's actions to have been illegal, they did so, and Lawler decided to remain in Spain.[13]

For most convicts, though, there were significant challenges to remaining at large. These are apparent in a remarkable statement, given by convicts Henry Fawcett and John Kerswell. They had escaped from Gibraltar in 1848 during a violent storm, but returned to the British settlement after a few months at large:

On quitting the Boat, we proceeded direct to the Spanish Lines. [We] were there well treated by a Spaniard who gave us Spirits and a Breakfast. From the Spanish Lines we went to 'Algeciras' and obtained a passport ... from the Governor, who gave us three Dollars. From 'Algeciras' we proceeded to 'Cadiz' where another passport was procured from the Governor of that place, but from whom we received no further assistance, than a promise of protection through Spain. Employ'd at 'Cadiz' at the Gas Company and also under Mr White, Contractor ... at ½ dollar per diem ... we were at work at 'Cadiz' six weeks, but remained altogether ten. From 'Cadiz' we both went to 'Malaga,' were there employed by Mr Young (who had previously engaged us at 'Cadiz') ... remained

---

[11] TNA CO91/185 23 October 1847 nos. 191–4: Governor Sir Robert Wilson, Gibraltar, to Henry Grey (3rd Earl Grey), 23 October 1847; TNA CO91/185 1 November 1847 no. 198: Wilson to Grey, 1 November 1847; TNA CO91/200 10 January 1855 nos. 12–13: Governor Sir Robert Gardiner, Gibraltar, to Newcastle, 10 January 1855.

[12] TNA CO91/204 24 March 1852 no. 36: Gardiner to Sir John Pakington (1st Baron Hampton), secretary of state for war and the colonies, 24 March 1852.

[13] TNA CO91/236 28 November 1859 no. 35: Governor Sir William Codrington, Gibraltar, to Newcastle, 28 November 1859; TNA CO91/246 8 December 1859 no. 40: Statement of Convict Pat. Lawler, 15 November 1859; TNA CO91/246 14 July 1860 no. 80: Codrington to Newcastle, 14 July 1860.

in 'Malaga' a period of six weeks. Subsisted on our earnings, received no commiseration from Spaniards, but every hospitality shown by Englishmen, particularly Mr Young, who took notice of us at 'Cadiz' who clothed us, gave us protection and work and who on our leaving 'Malaga' raised a subscription at the British Hotel of Thirteen Dollars, and presented us with that amount. We were robb'd of eight dollars, about three leagues this side of 'Almeria' by ... 5 men, who attacked us with long knives, and compell'd us to give up the money. Could obtain no employment, were actually starving, with no money and obliged to part with our clothing in order to subsist. Had made up our minds to return when at 'Almeria', stopp'd three days on the journey at 'Malaga', obtained no assistance at that place, with the exception of one loaf and a pound of cheese from an Englishman, from 'Malaga' we came direct to 'Gibraltar', to give ourselves up to the authorities, as the only means to be adopted in our unfortunate situation, trusting to the merciful consideration of the head of the Department, by our voluntary return to exile and imprisonment.[14]

After detailing their mixed fortunes, Fawcett and Kerswell added that three of their fellow absconders were still working at Cádiz, two had gone to the USA, and they presumed the sixth man had been murdered. Though they went back to the convict establishment of their own accord, to deter others from following their example, Governor Robert Wilson ordered that they be placed in double irons for a month and put to severe labour.[15]

Jean Léon Chautard's *Escapes from Cayenne*

In September 1857, three Frenchmen arrived in the coastal city of Salem, in the eastern American state of Massachusetts. Jean Léon Chautard, Louis Antoine Hippolyte Paon, and Charles Bivors made no attempt to hide the fact that they were political prisoners (*deportés*), escaped from French Guiana. Shortly afterwards, Chautard published a short pamphlet about their punishment, deportation, and evasion: *Escapes from Cayenne*. From this and the conduct register kept by the French government we learn that he was a former army corporal and accountant whose removal from France was ordered following his participation in the 'Bloody June Days' insurrection in Paris in 1848. Editor of the journal *La Révolution de 1848* (*The 1848 Revolution*), president of the revolutionary *club de la Montagne* (Mountain Club), and member of the *Societé des droits de l'homme* (Society of the Rights of

---

[14] TNA CO91/188 13 May 1848 no. 77: Wilson to Grey, 13 May 1848, enc. Statement of two convicts who have returned to this Garrison after escaping from the Public Works, 27 November 1847.
[15] TNA CO91/188 13 May 1848 no. 77: Wilson to Grey, 13 May 1848, enc. Statement of two convicts who have returned to this Garrison after escaping from the Public Works, 27 November 1847.

Man), he had joined in the fighting in the city's barricades. Initially sent to Le Havre, and then moved around Brittany's *bagnes* and public works in Brest, Belle Île, Lorient and Vannes, Chautard first escaped and was recaptured, and then received additional punishment for refusing to follow orders. He was returned to Belle Île, where he participated in what he described as a collective act of 'passive resistance', but which government described as a revolt. This followed its decision to grant amnesty to 700 of the 1,200 prisoners on the island, which led to unrest among the remainder. Chautard was one of ten men who appeared in court in Vannes, and though he was acquitted of the charge of mutiny, government decided to send him to its colony of Algeria. He rode the 600 miles overland to Toulon in a wagon and then boarded a ship to Bône (now, Annaba), where he was placed in the Casbah. At the time, this was the holding site for 1848 exiles. A charge of insulting his commander in June 1851 led to a court martial and a five-year sentence of penal labour. For this, Chautard was first confined in the civil prison of Algiers, and then transferred to Fort Saint-Grégoire in Oran. In May 1852, France passed a decree which ordered the transfer of the 1848 prisoners in Algeria to French Guiana, if they had been punished for insubordination or other crimes. Consequently, Chautard was moved to Fort Lamalgue in Toulon, and in September 1852 sailed for French Guiana on board the ship *La Fortune*. Of the men discussed here, only Chautard was married, though there is no record that he had any children. He wrote that he had left his wife of seven years (Clémentine Colat) with an exclamation of deep sorrow: 'Adieu, my beloved, adieu forever, but remember me!'[16]

[16] This account is drawn from Leon Chautard, *Escapes from Cayenne* (Salem, MA: The Observer Office, 1857) and ANOM COL H569/chautardje (Jean Léon Chautard's conduct register). With a few minor exceptions, in regards to Chautard's life in France and French Guiana, the conduct register confirms Chautard's text. See also https://maitron.fr/spip.php?article188256, CHAUTARD Jean, Léon, Ricard, by Michaël Roy, 3 January 2017, revised 26 April 2021 (accessed 1 August 2021); ANOM COL H576/paonlouisa (Louis Antoine Hippolyte Paon's conduct register); https://maitron.fr/spip.php?article35747, 'PAON Hippolyte' (2009), 20 February 2009, revised 5 February 2020 (accessed 1 August 2021); ANOM COL H568/bivorschars (Charles Bivor's conduct register). For broader context on these mid-nineteenth-century deportations, see Louis-José Barbançon, *L'archipel des forçats. Histoire du bagne de Nouvelle-Calédonie (1863–1931)* (Lille: Presses universitaires du Septentrion, 2003), 61–5; Louis-José Barbançon, 'Transporter les Insurgés de juin 1848', *Criminocorpus* (2008), http://journals.openedition.org/criminocorpus/153 (accessed 24 January 2019); Louis-José Barbançon, 'Les transportés de 1848 (statistiques, analyse, commentaires)', *Criminocorpus* (2008) http://journals.openedition.org/criminocorpus/148 (accessed 24 January 2019); Patricia O'Brien, *The Promise of Punishment: Prisons in Nineteenth-century France* (Princeton University Press, 1982), 259–64; Miranda Frances Spieler, *Empire and Underworld: Captivity in French Guiana* (Cambridge, MA: Harvard University Press 2012), 127–9; Sylvie Thénault, *Violence Ordinaire dans l'Algérie Coloniale: camps, internements, assignations à residence* (Paris: Odile Jacob, 2010), chapter 6. Barbançon produces a complete list of the political prisoners of 1848 as an appendix to 'Les transportés de 1848'. On the Bône Casbah, see Charles Ribeyrolles (translated by Louisa

One of Chautard's fellow deserters to the American port of Salem, Louis Paon, was a locksmith who was also deported to Algeria after the 1848 insurgency. Paon wrote a short text about his experiences, and Chautard included his translation of it in *Escapes from Cayenne*. Like Chautard, Paon first went to Bône. Described in his conduct register as brutal, insolent, and violent, Paon got into trouble on several occasions, and ultimately a court martial sentenced him to five years in irons, also for insulting his officers. He too was moved to Algiers, from where he was sent to Fort Lamalgue to await shipment to French Guiana.[17] Chautard and Paon were joined in Algeria by a man called Théodore Louis Tassilier. He was first convicted of encouraging looting and raising workers against the national guard, in June 1848. With Chautard, he was acquitted of mutiny at Belle Île. Government confined Tassilier in Constantine, where he committed multiple offences and was described as a 'very dangerous' man who required careful surveillance. Having picked up a sentence of two years' imprisonment for attempted escape, by a court martial in the city, Tassilier returned to Toulon for transfer to Cayenne.[18] The deportation of the fourth man, day labourer Charles Bivors, followed the same pattern. He was removed from France for his involvement in the 1848 insurgency, and his first destination was Algeria. He committed a series of offences against prison discipline, including fighting with fellow prisoners and insolence towards his officers, for which he was imprisoned in Algiers, and then transferred to Fort Lamalgue. Six months after Chautard's departure, and also under the terms of the 1852 decree, Paon, Tassilier, and Bivors left Toulon on the ship *l'Allier*.[19]

Following a new law of 1850, the men's penal journeys to Algeria had taken place without a trial, for in the crackdown that followed the 'June Days' of 1848 President Napoleon III had sanctioned administrative deportation as a means of removing his political enemies.[20] Subsequently, Chautard, Tassilier, Paon, and Bivors were among some thirty insubordinate political convicts who were transferred from Algeria to Cayenne after the passing of the May 1852 decree noted above. As the men travelled from

Julia Norman), *The Prisons of Africa, Gui[a]na, and Cayenne* (Melton Mowbray: W. Darley, 1857), 82–4.

[17] ANOM COL H576/paonlouisa; ANOM COL H579/tassiliert (Théodore Louis Tassilier's conduct register) (note also the variant spellings 'Tassillier' and 'Tassiliez'); Chautard, *Escapes from Cayenne*, 14, 17 and 'Paon's Narrative', 27–36 (Chautard's English translation of Paon's French writings).

[18] ANOM COL H579/tassiliert; Michel Cordillot, *La Sociale en Amérique: Dictionnaire biographique du mouvement social francophone aux États-Unis, 1848–1922* (Paris: Éditions de l'Atelier, 2002), 405–6.

[19] ANOM COL H576/paonlouisa; ANOM COL HH579/tassiliert; ANOM COL H568/bivorschars; Chautard, *Escapes from Cayenne*, 14, 17.

[20] Barbançon, *L'archipel des forçats*, 61, 64.

France to North Africa, and from North Africa to France and on to South America, the geography of their punitive mobility appears striking but was, in fact, routine. Indeed, during the middle decades of the nineteenth century, France was shipping metropolitan political prisoners and convicts to Algeria and French Guiana, and colonial insurgents from Algeria and the Caribbean colonies of Guadeloupe and Martinique to France, including to Île Sainte-Marguerite off the coast at Cannes, and to the island of Corsica, as well as to mainland prisons.[21] As discussed in Chapters 1 and 5, into the twentieth century France sent convicts from all over its empire to the penal colonies of French Guiana and New Caledonia. They originated in places as far apart as French Indochina, Pondicherry, Réunion Island, Algeria, Tunisia, Guadeloupe, and Martinique.

After they arrived in French Guiana, in common with other political prisoners and criminal convicts (*transportés*), the mobility of Chautard, Tassilier, Paon, and Bivors was restricted. Chautard landed in October 1852, and initially government took advantage of his professional skills and put him to work as a clerk in the Naval Stores in the capital. In April 1853, it transferred him to the *cachot* (dark cells) in an island off the coast: Îlet La Mère. Chautard claimed that this was a punishment for writing a petition, though his dossier records it as a sanction for an escape attempt. Three months later, Tassilier, Paon, and Bivors arrived in the colony, and joined Chautard in Îlet La Mère, with about one hundred other political prisoners from France and Algeria. Shortly afterwards, in July 1853, there was an attempted uprising, in which Tassilier apparently played a leading role. A court martial sentenced him to five years in irons, and his petition for mercy, addressed to Napoleon III, now Emperor of France, failed.[22] Afterwards, government transferred Chautard to one of the Îles du Salut, Île Saint-Joseph, where he was put to hard labour in chains. 'We were ... treated worse than convicts', he later wrote, with a quarter of the political prisoners dying in the harsh conditions. The island was in such a state of insubordination that in January 1855 Governor Louis Adolphe Bonard declared a state of siege and banned *déportés* from sending or receiving letters or

---

[21] For example: ANOM H21B Governor of Martinique to the Minister of the Navy and the Colonies, 28 July and 19 October 1862. See also Allyson Jaye Delnore, 'Empire by Example? Deportees in France and the re-making of a Modern Empire, 1846–1854', *French Politics, Culture and Society*, 33, 1 (2015), 35 (33–54); John Savage, 'Unwanted Slaves: The punishment of transportation and the making of Legal Subjects in early nineteenth-century Martinique', *Citizenship Studies*, 10, 1 (2006), 35–53. Allyson Jaye Delnore mentions Chautard in Political Convictions: French Deportation Projects in the Age of Revolution, 1791–1854, PhD thesis, University of Virginia, 2004, 4, 239.

[22] ANOM COL H579/tassiliert; *Bulletin officiel de la Guyane française, de l'année 1854* (Cayenne: Imprimerie du gouvernement, 1855), 396–7.

other written materials that might incite disorder. A month later, government transferred Chautard and the other survivors to a second island in the group, Île du Diable (Devil's Island), where Chautard oversaw the construction of convict *cazes* (huts or barracks). As Chapter 7 explained, Devil's Island was later famous as the site of Alfred Dreyfus's imprisonment, but even in the middle of the nineteenth century its name was understood as a shorthand reference for the penal colony at large. When the convicts completed their building work, government sent Chautard to the remaining island in Îles du Salut, Île Royale. From there, he petitioned for a free pardon, and government gave him a four-year reduction in his sentence.[23]

After the Îlet La Mère insurrection, in July 1853, government sent Tassilier, Paon, and Bivors to Cayenne, and they spent a month in the city's civil prison before they were sent back to the island. They next joined Chautard in Île Saint-Joseph, where only *deportés* were kept.[24] From here, and before the state of siege was declared, Tassilier managed to smuggle two letters out. It seems that they were carried by four escaped prisoners, who reached England and passed them on to moderate socialist Louis Blanc, who had exiled himself in London in 1848. From there, he published *Le Nouveau Monde: journal historique et politique*, much of which was also translated for *Louis Blanc's Monthly Review*.[25] The first of these letters was published as a French language pamphlet in Manchester, England, in 1855. Tassilier echoed Chautard in complaining that the *deportés* were treated worse than the *transportés*. Their beards were cut, they had to work, and their food rations were poor. Another grievance was that unlike ordinary convicts most of them did not receive a ration of wine. Tassilier also wrote of the inhumanity of the penal colony. He described the 'instruments of torture' in use in the Îles du Salut, which included stakes, gags, ropes, fetters, bread and water rations, and the *cachot*. He added that guards had placed thirteen of the 1848 deportees in

---

[23] Chautard, *Escapes from Cayenne*, 11–13, 20–1; 'ARRÊTE qui déclare l'île Saint-Joseph en état de siege, 29 December 1854, cited in *Bulletin officiel de la Guyane française, de l'année 1853* (Cayenne: Imprimerie du gouvernement, 1855), 491–2.

[24] ANOM COL H579/tassiliert; ANOM COL H568/bivorschars; ANOM COL H576/paonlouisa.

[25] Bensimon, 'The French Exiles and the British', 88–90; Thomas C. Jones and Constance Bantman, 'From Republicanism to Anarchism: 50 Years of French Exilic Newspaper Publishing', in Constance Bantman and Ana Cláudia Suriani da Silva, eds., *The Foreign Political Press in Nineteenth-Century London: Politics from a Distance* (London: Bloomsbury, 2018), 92 (91–112); Ansgar Reiss, 'Home alone? Reflections on political exiles return to their native countries', in Sabine Freitag, ed., *Exiles from European Revolutions: Refugees in Mid-Victorian England* (Oxford: Berghahn, 2003), 307–9 (297–318). Initially, *Le Nouveau Monde* was published in Paris; later it was published in London. Blanc returned to France in 1870.

double irons, with a ball and chain weighing between fourteen and fifteen pounds, and that *deportés* had their fingers broken. Men died from dysentery, deprivation, and injury, and at Île Royale suicide was frequent. Tassilier added that he had never asked for a pardon, nor would he do so in future, because he did not recognize the law that had deported him. He only wished to protest his arbitrary imprisonment and seek justice. In the 1855 pamphlet, Tassilier's signature appears as follows: 'typographer, June 1848 *transporté*, deported to French Guiana without a lawful sentence'.[26]

Both *The Morning Chronicle* and *The Times* reproduced extracts from Tassilier's letters. *The Morning Chronicle* included his complaints of having been treated 'more cruelly than the blacks during their period of slavery', of being forced to labour alongside 'vile criminals', and of the deleterious effects of starvation, sorrow, and the deadly climate.[27] Both these extracts and those published in *The Times* were introduced by Louis Blanc, who noted: 'I was requested to lay before the civilized world the heartrending details, which I did as far as my power went.'[28] In 1856, Blanc received two further letters from the Saint-Joseph political prisoners, one of which was signed by thirty-eight individuals, including Bivors (though not Chautard, Paon or Tassilier). They asked him to make their sufferings known, which according to their account included 'barbarity', violence, forced labour, bad food, and inadequate clothing. Blanc stressed that these men had never been convicted in a court of law and lamented that their situation had not changed since Tassilier's earlier letter, with all the writers calling Île Saint-Joseph the 'Island of Despair'.[29]

At some point during his enforced residence in French Guiana, Bivors was transferred from Île Saint-Joseph to Devil's Island, and in July 1856, he escaped. Paon remained in Île Saint-Joseph for another two months, from where he too absconded. Chautard was the third of the men to run.

---

[26] IISG Bro F926-250: [Signed by Tassilier], *Cayenne* (Manchester: no publisher, 1855) 7–8, 17–18, 19–21. This letter is also reproduced in BL 10408.aa.33(2) Cayenne: letters from republicans sentenced to transportation, 11–22. A second, collective but unsigned, letter from Île Saint-Joseph, dated 1 January 1854, is also reproduced in this volume. In this, the exiles gave 'a cry of despair' and complained of conditions on the island. See pp. 5–10.

[27] 'Sufferings of the French Exiles at Guiana', *The Morning Chronicle*, 15 February 1855. Note that in 1856 *The Morning Chronicle* published a translation of an article from the French newspaper *Le Moniteur* refuting the claims of the political prisoners. See 'The French Political Exiles in Guiana', *The Morning Chronicle*, 4 October 1856.

[28] 'The French political prisoners at Cayenne', *The Times*, 25 August 1856.

[29] 'Sufferings of the French Exiles at Guiana', *The Morning Chronicle*, 15 February 1855; 'The French political prisoners at Cayenne', *The Times*, 25 August 1856. The original French letter was published two days' earlier, in BL LOU.EW S90: *L'Homme: Journal de la Démocratie universelle*, 23 August 1856.

With his reduced sentence, he was among the small group of meritorious convicts who were allowed to live in Cayenne, in what Miranda Frances Spieler has described as a 'neo-Australian experiment' in using convicts as settlers. Under the terms of his residence, Chautard did not have to wear a uniform but was under curfew and constant police surveillance. Afterwards, he asserted that the authorities had repeatedly jailed him on trumped-up charges, and after several attempts in July 1857, he finally succeeded in escaping.[30] A week later, Tassilier, also by then living in Cayenne, likely under the same conditions as Chautard, fled.[31]

The first leg of Bivors and Paon's voyage took them to Surinam. Paon reached the Dutch colony on one of two hand-built rafts, which travelled along the coast and crossed the Maroni River border. Paon's account of the journey articulated the hardships that the men endured, including a hurricane at sea, great thirst, and hunger.[32] In leaving French Guiana, the group had taken advantage of the western current, strapped water barrels to the makeshift vessel, and tied their shirts together to make a sail.[33] Also travelling with Paon was political prisoner François Attibert, who in August 1855 had led the famous Marianne à Trélazé insurrection: a republican and socialist workers' revolt in Angers. Attibert later penned a lengthy account of his transportation in which he repeatedly reminded his readers that transportation separated men from their wives and children. He wrote that when he left French Guiana a convict named Riotto asked him to take a letter to his wife and son in France. Riotto was so sick that he feared he did not have long to live.[34] 'C'est une vie cruelle, que vous endurez, sous les tyrans de France, femmes des transportés!' ('You endure a cruel life under French tyrants, convict wives!') Attibert wrote.[35] He also described numerous previous attempts at escape. As the absconders' raft left the Îles du Salut, he wrote, they sang the revolutionary La Marseillaise:

Allons! enfants de la patrie/ Le jour de gloire est arrivé!
(Arise, children of the homeland/ The day of glory has arrived!)[36]

---

[30] ANOM COL H579/tassiliert; ANOM COL H568/bivorschars; ANOM COL H576/paonlouisa; Spieler, *Empire and Underworld*, 188–9 (quote, 188).

[31] ANOM COL H579/tassiliert.

[32] ANOM COL H568/bivorschars; ANOM COL H576/paonlouisa; 'Paon's Narrative', in *Escapes from Cayenne*, 27–36.

[33] A. Kapler, *Holländisch-Guiana: Erlebnisse und Erfahrungen, während eines 43 jährigen Aufenthalts in der Kolonie Surinam* (Stuttgart: Commissions Verla von W. Kohlhammer, 1881), 296–7.

[34] François Attibert, *Quatre Ans A Cayenne: Notes de Fr. Attibert, Déporté* (Brussels: de la Veuve Verteneuil, 1859), 25–6, 71, 122–3.

[35] Attibert, *Quatre Ans A Cayenne*, 122.

[36] ANOM COL H567/attibertfr; Attibert, *Quatre Ans A Cayenne*, passim (quote, 88). On the Angers revolt, see https://maitron.fr/spip.php?article25341, ATTIBERT François', 20 February 2009, revised 5 February 2020 (accessed 1 August 2021).

Here, Attibert was making a direct appeal to patriotism, and in this way his narrative mirrors those penned by Chautard and Paon, which are similarly inflected with the politics of the age. Beyond descriptions of where, when, and why they were transported, Chautard and Paon's texts include numerous references to revolutionary ideology. In particular, they lamented the politics of the French Second Republic under Napoleon III, explained shifts in the global power balance that meant Britain was entering a period of imperial decline, and expressed anti-slavery ideals. Following the French revolution of 1789, in 1794 the French National Convention had briefly abolished slavery. Napoleon Bonaparte revoked the 1794 decree in 1802, but radicals remained committed to abolition and anti-slavery was a prominent theme in the 1848 revolution.[37]

This is similarly apparent in Paon's description of what happened when the escaped convicts landed on the Dutch coast and (he claimed) encountered a hostile group of Indigenous people. The head of the group tried to force the men to go with him to French territory, telling Paon that he could then claim a reward for their capture. The men refused, telling the man they called Captain Feather (for he wore a feathered cap) that they preferred death to enslavement. A stand-off ensued, at which point Paon claimed the timely arrival of two other men. He wrote that on learning that they were political prisoners, escaped from French Guiana, one of them said: 'I know you; you fought in the year 1848, for the abolition of slavery, and you co-operated to the downfall of that degrading institution. You are in safety here; you are as safe as in your own homes.' This man implored the hostile party to put down their weapons, and the escapees were able to go on their way.[38]

Following this encounter (real, exaggerated, or fabricated), Paon narrated how the group made for Albina, the home of the German botanist and settler August Kapler.[39] In a later work, Kapler confirmed that the men had arrived on his plantation, noting that the Dutch returned escaped convicts to the French, but not political prisoners.[40] Paon wrote that Kapler was of great assistance, and that he and his companions were able to continue their journey to the capital of Surinam at Paramaribo. On arrival, magistrates

---

[37] On this period, see Lawrence C. Jennings, *French Anti-Slavery: The Movement for the Abolition of Slavery in France, 1802–1848* (Cambridge University Press, 2000).

[38] Chautard, *Escape from Cayenne*, 37–8 (quote, 37). On Indigenous peoples, European encounters, and the flow of revolutionary knowledge in the British Empire to the period c. 1840, see Kate Fullagar and Michael A. McDonnell, 'Introduction: Empire, Indigeneity, and Revolution', in Kate Fullagar and Michael A. McDonnell, eds., *Facing Empire: Indigenous Experiences in a Revolutionary Age* (Baltimore, MD: Johns Hopkins University Press, 2018), 1–24.

[39] Chautard, *Escape from Cayenne*, 37–8.   [40] Kapler, *Holländisch-Guiana*, 296–7.

arrested them, and took them to Fort Zeelandia, and it was there that they met the group which had earlier escaped from Devil's Island.[41] Because Paon, Attibert, and Bivors were political prisoners, the Dutch did not return them to French Guiana. Instead, they found passage to British Guiana, arriving in Georgetown in November 1856. They went to see the British governor, William Walker, and he offered them work, which they accepted. Attibert later wrote that after just three weeks he decided to leave for England, embarking on a ship destined for Liverpool. From there, he made his way to London where he met fellow political exiles, including, he claimed, fellow escapees from Îlet La Mère. Perhaps also some of them were time-expired, having arrived in Georgetown with their certificates of freedom in 1855, from where Governor Philip Edmond Wodehouse ordered their return to Europe via England.[42]

Attibert became part of what Fabrice Bensimon has described as a 'significant French community', around 800 strong, which lived in London after 1848. Some stayed for a short period of time, and others for over twenty years.[43] During this period, several French newspapers were published in England, the most important of which was *L'Homme: Journal de la Démocratie Universelle*. Published weekly from 1853 to 1856, it sought to maintain relationships between the geographically dispersed 1848 exiles and, in Constance Bantman's words, played a role 'in fostering a sense of collective identity'. Its editor was Charles Ribeyrolles, who faced deportation to French Guiana, but exiled himself in London before he could be sent.[44] The periodical publicized the plight of the men it called the Cayenne exiles, and in one article Ribeyrolles described them as 'poor martyrs'. 'Love of country is not dead', he added, 'but is held captive'.[45] In

---

[41] Paon claimed in his text that he escaped with Bivors, but this does not appear to have been the case. The conduct registers note that Bivors escaped from Devil's Island, and Paon from 'Îles du Salut', several weeks apart. It seems more likely that Paon and Bivors met again at Zeelandia Fort in Paramaribo. Also with Bivors was Gustav Pauline Dime. See Cordillot, *La Sociale en Amérique*, 163.

[42] Chautard, *Escapes from Cayenne*, 51; Attibert, *Quatre Ans A Cayenne*, 101–3; TNA CO111/304 17 April 1855 no. 45: Governor Philip Edmond Wodehouse, British Guiana, to Lord John Russell, secretary of state for the colonies, 17 April 1855.

[43] Fabrice Bensimon, 'The French Exiles and the British', in Freitag, ed., *Exiles from European Revolutions*, 88 (quote), 99n1 (88–102).

[44] Sylvie Aprile, 'Voices of Exile: French Newspapers in England', in Freitag, ed., *Exiles from European Revolutions*, 152–3 (149–63). See also Constance Bantman, 'Introduction', in Bantman and Suriani da Silva, eds., *The Foreign Political Press in Nineteenth-Century London*, 11 (quote) (1–14). *L'Homme* was published in Jersey until November 1855, when it relocated to London. See Jones and Bantman, 'From Republicanism to Anarchism', 94.

[45] BL LOU.EW S90: *L'Homme: Journal de la Démocratie universelle*, 23 August 1856. See also BL LOU.EW S90: *L'Homme: Journal de la Démocratie universelle*, 'The Martyrs of Cayenne', 26 April 1856.

1853, whilst in London, Ribeyrolles published the highly polemical *Les Bagnes d'Afrique*, and in 1856 the book appeared in English.[46] The work drew on official letters and regulations, and the writings of exiles themselves. They included the famous feminist Pauline Roland, who had been sent to Algeria following her opposition to Napoleon III's coup d'état of December 1851. The purpose of the book was to raise awareness of the punishment of transportation in France. As Ribeyrolles put it, men were shipped to Algeria without trial, and there subjected to hardships, insults, misery, and despair.[47]

No doubt encouraged by the success of his 1848 compatriots, Chautard absconded from Cayenne on board an English coal ship that was on its way British Guiana. He stated that the captain and his crew were sympathetic to his politics and colluded in his escape, and that when he reached the colony's capital at Georgetown, people who opposed Napoleon III welcomed him. The French consul, however, refused to help Chautard get to the USA, because under the terms of his transportation he had undergone civil death, and was no longer a French subject.[48] Chautard had better luck in seeking out men he called 'Republican refugees', escapees like Bivors and Paon who he found working in the city. He noted that one of them was about to get married.[49] Despite the lack of support, the three men decided to try and find a ship to take them to America. They eventually secured a passage, assisted by the American consul and a grant of money from British governor William Walker. There is a short interlude in *Escapes from Cayenne* in which Chautard reproduced a conversation that he said he had with the master of the coal ship that took him to Georgetown, Captain Foskey. They covered the topics of socialism, communism, and the governments of England, France, and the USA. In concluding the book, he wrote that when he got to his destination, he intended to make replicas of convict chains, and tour the country making known his sufferings.[50]

---

[46] Charles Ribeyrolles, *Les Bagnes d'Afrique, Histoire de la Transportation de décembre* (London: Jeffs Bookshop, 1853); Ribeyrolles, *The Prisons of Africa*. During this period, William Jeffs published numerous French works, including political texts by exiles. See Juliette Atkinson, 'William Jeffs, Victorian Bookseller and Publisher of French Literature', *The Library: The Transactions of the Bibliographical Society*, 13, 3 (2012), 269–70 (256–78).

[47] Ribeyrolles, *The Prisons of Africa*, vii.

[48] On the form and importance of the legal incapacitation of convicts in French Guiana, see Spieler, *Empire and Underworld*, 112–15.

[49] Chautard, *Escapes from Cayenne*, 14–17, 59.

[50] Chautard, *Escapes from Cayenne*, 51, 57–8.

Chautard, Paon, and Bivors first arrived at the port of Boston, and then they took the train to Salem.[51] They were far from the first absconders from French Guiana to make it to the city. Four years previous, ordinary convict (*transporté*) Antoine Eugène Quesne and *deporté* Claude Chambonnière had reached Salem, and just three weeks before Chautard and his compatriots arrived, *deporté* Théodore Louis Tassilier had also passed through.[52] By this time, the state of Massachusetts had abolished slavery, and it was not long before abolitionists deployed Chautard and his companions' experiences in their larger campaigns for emancipation. Just a few months after they reached Salem, an account of their escape appeared in the pro-abolition newspaper *The Liberator*, under the title 'Liberty for All Mankind'. This described them as 'political refugees'. Chautard's writings were published in serial form in the *Salem Register*, and the almost immediate production of the full pamphlet (*Escapes from Cayenne*) was a means of raising money for his support.[53] Chautard tried to garner the sympathy of Americans by making an explicit comparison between his experience as a political prisoner in French Guiana and that of the men who he described as exiled Puritans and Quakers who had fled persecution in England and Germany and settled on the east coast. 'These models of freedom will, perhaps, admit us in their Commonwealth; they will give us asylum, protection, and honorable employment', he wrote.[54] Here, Chautard echoed an earlier letter to the American press, from 'schoolmaster' *deporté* Riboulet. He was one of a party of twelve convicts who escaped from Îlet La Mère in 1852, just three months after his arrival, but the only one of them to get to New York. The others had remained in Surinam and British Guiana but wanted to join him. 'Brothers of America', Riboulet wrote, 'I have now an appeal to make to your hearts. . . . all desire to come to America; they want a new, free country! They want to clasp the hand of friends. Is there no means of helping them?'[55]

---

[51] Chautard, *Escapes from Cayenne*, 63.
[52] ANOM COL H579/tassiliert; ANOM COL H577/quesneanto (Antoine Eugène Quesne's conduct register); ANOM COL H569/chambonnie (Claude Chambonnière's conduct register). Entries on Quesne and Tassilier, and another escaped convict Gustave Paulin Dime, can be found in Cordillot, *La Sociale en Amérique*, 98–9, 163–4, 360, 405–6.
[53] William Lloyd Garrison to Theodore Parker (Unitarian minister and anti-slavery leader), 8 November 1857, cited in Louis Ruchames, ed., *The Letters of William Lloyd Garrison, Vol. IV, From disunionism to the brink of war, 1850–1860* (Cambridge, MA: The Belknap Press of Harvard University Press, 1975), 499. Garrison was co-founder of *The Liberator*.
[54] Chautard, *Escapes from Cayenne*, 36.
[55] Riboulet wrote to the editor of the 'Courier' (likely the *Morning Courier and New-York Enquirer*). The letter is reproduced in Ribeyrolles, *The Prisons of Africa*, 122–4. See also ANOM COL H577/ribouletse (Sébastien Riboulet's conduct register).

In other ways, the political stance of *Escapes from Cayenne* appealed to American anti-slavery campaigns. Paon's account of Surinam was noted above, and his other representations of Surinam are particularly interesting in this regard. He wrote: 'Persons believing that black people are unable to work without being slaves, will do well to come here; they will see that black men are not lazier than white when they are well paid, well treated and well ruled.'[56] It is highly unlikely that he argued with the Dutch governor of the colony about enslavement, as he purported, though his account of what he had said to him would have found a receptive audience with American abolitionists:

> Nature or God – as you like, – has made all men equal in rights at their birth; no one is or can be the property of another. If you make man property, you go against the laws of nature, you insult God, you cease to be a man ... Man has a three fold life; he lives physically, morally and intellectually. By slavery you kill both his moral and intellectual life; you, then, kill two thirds of him; you destroy God's work. ... You say that we must not interfere in the question of slavery? – But a negro is a man as well as you and I; he is a member of humanity.[57]

Whether the conversation took place or not, this part of Paon's text connected the French revolution of 1848 to the larger global context. As Merle Curti has argued, the early republican phase of 1848 was 'greeted with sympathy and even enthusiasm' in the USA, with mass meetings taking place in east coast locations. In part, this can be explained by American hatred of monarchical government, viewed as tyrannical, but it was also an expression of support for abstract political rights, a reminder of the way in which early American settlers had severed 'the chains of British rule'.[58] According to Curti, the arrival of French refugees also had a series of specific impacts, including the invigoration of anti-slavery campaigns.[59]

Indeed, Tassilier ended up in New York, where as a professional typographer he was one of the founding shareholder editors (*actionnaires-adhérens*) of the radical weekly periodical *Le Revendicateur (The Claimant)*. The first issue, published in December 1860, established the newspaper's 'humanitarian and socialistic ideas'. Its stated aim was to counter tyranny, power and authority on behalf of men and women, old and young, black and white, whether it came from the church, state, government,

---

[56] Chautard, *Escapes from Cayenne*, 39.
[57] Chautard, *Escapes from Cayenne*, 47–9 (quote, 48).
[58] Merle Curti, 'The Impact of the Revolutions of 1848 on American Thought', *Proceedings of the American Philosophical Society*, 93, 3 (1949), 209–11 (209–15).
[59] Curti, 'The Impact of the Revolutions of 1848', 212, 214. Later in the nineteenth century, liberated convict and socialist Humbert Rullière settled in the USA, under the pseudonym Laurent Casas. See Cordillot, *La Sociale en Amérique*, 98–9.

community, family, or 'skin colour'. Published mainly in French, with some English translations, the newspaper put out an unequivocal call '*aux travaillieurs* [to the workers]!' It proposed that libraries should be set up in the nation's main towns, with books and an accompanying programme of public lectures for the purpose of worker education, and called for practical suggestions on their organization. Further, it set out the social questions with which it would be concerned in future issues:

1. Which are the best means to establish a collective and harmonious society producing the great amount of well-being and happiness?
2. What are the transitions, immediate and practical, necessary to ensure progress, towards absolute equality?
3. Those transitions once known, how can we obtain their adoption by the privileged classes?[60]

These, it proposed, would be addressed in columns concerned with the 'intellectual work of emancipation and social progress, from whatever source it may come'.[61]

The number of *actionnaires-adhérens* grew substantially by the time the second and third issues of *Le Revendicateur* appeared, in January and February 1861, and by this time it had published discourses on the French Revolution, the Opium Wars, and enslavement, including what turned out to be the background to the American Civil War. It supported the abolition of standing armies, the suppression of the clergy, absolute equality, and worker ownership of the means of production.[62] In particular, the newspaper drew connections between the emancipation of enslaved and working people. 'Do they consider you as brothers, those arrogant planters, who pretend a variety of classes of slaves?' it asked, '[T]he American producer of the North is destined to shoe them, to dress them, and to manufacture all the articles of luxury and comfort, for the use of the creole lords of the South. . . . What do they care for your misery? Have they not wealth . . . ?'[63] However, the newspaper disappeared as quickly as it had begun, and it folded after just three issues.[64] This was

---

[60] IISG Microfiche 2494-2: *Le Revendicateur: Journal Social, Politique et Littéraire*, 8 December 1860. Note that the list of questions appeared in English.

[61] IISG Microfiche 2494-2: *Le Revendicateur*, 8 December 1860. The original quote is in English.

[62] IISG Microfiche 2494-2: *Le Revendicateur*, 8 December 1860, 19 January 1861, 9 February 1861. I have not been able to establish that any other French Guiana convicts, escaped or emancipated, were involved in this newspaper, though it is possible that the use of pseudonyms obfuscates this history. See also https://maitron.fr/spip.php?article 159457, 'TASSILIER Théodore, Louis' [*Dictionnaire biographique du mouvement social francophone aux États-Unis*] by Michel Cordillot, 4 June 2014, revised 16 April 2020 (accessed 3 August 2021); Cordillot, *La Sociale en Amérique*, 405–6.

[63] IISG Microfiche 2494–2: *Le Revendicateur*, 19 January 1861.

[64] Michel Cordillot, *La Sociale en Amérique*, 225–6, 297.

perhaps in part a consequence of Tassilier's desire for direction action. During the Civil War he enlisted as Captain in the New York 39th Infantry Regiment, serving for three months in 1861 until he was discharged.[65]

Clearly, the escape of convicts like Chautard, Paon, Bivors, and Tassilier fostered the geographical expansion of networks of political association. Incorporating their experiences, writing, and skills into the history of global radicalism suggests that ideologies of liberty and emancipation in the age of revolution travelled between Europe and North America. Through the deportation of the men known as 'Forty-Eighters', they reached the Guianas, and connected French, Dutch, and British colonial territory to France, England, and the USA. The point here is to stress the convict dynamics of what with Niklas Frykman, Lex Heerma van Voss, Marcus Rediker, and I have referred to as 'the mobility, circulation, and connection of radical ideas and action', across large distances, where seas and oceans were 'cradles and conduits of radical thought'. This adds weight to our suggestion that a more global perspective on the age of revolutions compels us to extend its Eurocentric endpoint beyond 1840, and to encompass insurgency in India and the Caribbean from the 1850s to 1870s.[66] Indeed, Chautard was writing in 1857, the year of the great uprising in British India, of which he was aware. He mentioned reading newspapers that described the massacre of English men and interpreted this as part of the wave of Britain's imperial downfall.[67]

Law and Flight in the Atlantic World

Following the extraordinary journeying of Chautard and his compatriots, it was with the opening of penal colonies to ordinary convicts in French Guiana and New Caledonia during the second half of the nineteenth century that legal issues around the question of extradition became urgent. This was due to the scale of transportation, and the sheer number of convicts who attempted to abscond. As early as 1852, France had approached the British Foreign Office to warn of the possibility of convict escape. Initially, officials such as Governor Sir Henry Barkly in British Guiana dismissed French fears. He noted the prior escape of

---

[65] *U.S., Civil War Soldier Records and Profiles, 1861–1865* (available via paid subscription to ancestry.com) (accessed 31 January 2019).

[66] Clare Anderson, Niklas Frykman, Lex Heerma van Voss, and Marcus Rediker, 'Mutiny and Maritime Radicalism in the Age of Revolution: A Global Survey', *International Review of Social History*, 58, S21, (2013), 4, 11 (quote) (1–14). The pioneering text in this field is David Armitage and Sanjay Subrahmanyam eds., *The Age of Revolutions in Global Context, c. 1760–1840* (Basingstoke: Palgrave, 2009).

[67] Chautard, *Escapes from Cayenne*, 54.

revolutionary *déportés* to Demerara, but thought that the immense difficulty of travelling through swamps and forests or travelling by sea made absconding to the colony a near-impossibility.[68] How wrong Barkly was, for following in the footsteps of the 1848 men, each year hundreds of convicts, *relégués*, and *libérés* attempted to flee the borders of the colony, dozens successfully.[69]

Convicts, *relégués*, and *libérés* from French Guiana crossed the border into Dutch Surinam, which was relatively straightforward given the extent of the colony's uncultivated and unpopulated coastline. At first, the Netherlands did not have an extradition treaty with France, and during the American Civil War (1861–5) got rid of escaped convicts by paying American captains to take them to the USA, where presumably they were able to disappear into newly mobile populations or enlist in military service. When the war ended, the Dutch paid their passage elsewhere, including to British colonies like British Guiana and Barbados. In one case, a ship's captain carried twenty-eight men to Barbados, having been told 'to ask no questions'. At this time, Britain also lacked an extradition treaty, and could do little about the situation, except to express its objection to the arrival of escaped convicts in the strongest possible terms.[70] Eventually, France and the Netherlands signed a treaty, and the governor of Surinam extradited escaped convicts by putting them on one of the boats that travelled between the Dutch and French banks of the Maroni River, which separated the colonies. He simply deported *libérés*, because in law they had served out their sentences. There were incentives on offer, however, with the French awarding the Dutch police ten francs for each

---

[68] TNA CO111/289 22 April 1852 no. 77: Governor Sir Henry Barkly, British Guiana, to Pakington, 22 April 1852.

[69] See the voluminous correspondence in TNA CO111, dating from 1861, and the numerous folios on extradition in ANOM H1854 and H5353. There are no consolidated statistics, but it seems that 459 escapees arrived in British Guiana over a six-year period at the turn of the twentieth century, and 189 in Surinam in 1895 alone. See ANOM H1854: Statement of Expenses incurred in connection with French Alien Criminals by the Government of British Guiana under the Police, Prison and Health Departments during the six years 1898–1903; Governor Titus van Asch van Wijck, Surinam, to Governor Henri de Lamothe, French Guiana, 25 February 1896. Sanchez calculates that on average 580 convicts escaped per year, though the large majority (68 per cent) were recaptured. See Jean-Lucien Sanchez, *À perpétuité. Relégués au bagne de Guyane* (Paris: Vendémiaire, 2013), 227.

[70] TNA CO111/351 31 July 1865 no. 126: Governor Francis Hincks, British Guiana, to Edward Cardwell, secretary of state for the colonies, 31 July 1865 enc. D. C. Munro, Her Britannic Majesty's Consul Surinam, to Hinks, 14 July 1865; TNA CO111/355 30 January 1866 no. 30: Hincks to Cardwell, 30 January 1866; TNA CO111/357 7 May 1866 no. 102: Hincks to Cardwell, 7 May 1866, enc. Governor Reinhart Frans Cornelis van Lansberge, Surinam, to Hincks, 5 May 1866; TNA CO28/202 22 January 1866 no. 437. Governor Sir James Walker, Barbados, to Cardwell, 22 January 1866, enc. Munro to Walker, 10 January 1866.

return.⁷¹ Escapes to Surinam continued well into the twentieth century, by which time deserters routinely carried forged papers. In 1917, the Dutch arrested escaped convict Louis Marius Pellissier in Paramaribo. Pellissier claimed that he was a Venezuelan secret agent of the French government, though he had was under sentence of transportation for twenty years for the theft of military documents and secrets.⁷² Most often, the French alleged, Dutch settlers employed deserters in gold prospecting. According to a *relégué* named Badaire, who returned to Saint-Laurent-du-Maroni of his own accord in 1894, there were around 50 *relégués* then in Surinam. Labour recruiters keen to hire them sent *pirogues* (canoes) over the Maroni River. After they arrived, the Dutch searched them and robbed them of their rations, clothes, and valuables. They then signed labour contracts, generally for periods of four months, for salaries and rations that were less substantial than those they received in French Guiana. Already exhausted from penal labour and their escape, many fell sick in what the French described as the *relégués* trade (*traite du relégués*); an obvious allusion to the slave trade (*la traite*).⁷³

During this period, other destinations for absconders from French Guiana included the Dominican Republic (on the island of Hispaniola), and Santa Marta, Barranquilla, and Colón in Colombia.⁷⁴ In one case, a North African convict named in the records as Ben Romdan Mehamed made it as far as Las Palmas in the Canary Islands. A Franco-Spanish convention had been passed in 1877, and this enabled his extradition to Cayenne.⁷⁵ Over time, the passage of those escaping overland into South America was eased by increased river traffic on the Maroni and Oyapock rivers, and the growing number of roads and paths that cut through previously impenetrable forests. In some instances, escapees were destitute and sought the assistance of French consular agents. They claimed that convicts and ex-convicts told them that their desertion was effected through well-organized *agences d'évasion* (escape agencies), though the

---

⁷¹ ANOM H5352: Governor Émile Joseph Merwart, French Guiana, to the French Vice-Consul in Georgetown, 28 August 1901 – on the subjection of introducing modifications to the convention of 14 August 1876 on the extradition of criminals.
⁷² ANOM H1854: Pierre de Margerie, secretary general of the Ministry of Foreign Affairs, to André Maginot, Minister of the Colonies, 6 July 1917.
⁷³ ANOM H1854: Extracts from the monthly report of Saint-Jean-du-Maroni, August 1894.
⁷⁴ ANOM H1854: Governor Pierre Didelot, French Guiana, to Albert François Lebrun, minister for the colonies, 9 April 1912, enc. Report on the presence of escaped convicts in St-Domingue, 29 June 1912; Stephen Pichon, Minister of Foreign Affairs, to Maginot, 22 May 1913, enc. Minister plenipotentiary of the French Republic in Bogotá, to Pichon, 12 April 1913; Didelot to Pichon, 26 August 1913.
⁷⁵ ANOM H1854: Louis Nail, Minister of Justice, to Henry Simon, minister for the colonies, 10 January 1918.

governor of Guiana denied that this was the case.[76] Both feared the impact of escape on France's international reputation. Indeed, in 1913, the French minister plenipotentiary in Bogotá warned that France would be accused of dumping lawbreakers on South American nations.[77] Meantime, convicts often faced multi-staged return to French Guiana, including through the French colony of Martinique.[78]

During the period of the Contestado War in Brazil (1912–16), desertion from Saint-Georges on French Guiana's eastern border to the military post of Santo-Antõnio in Brazil was a route into service in the Brazilian army.[79] Remarkably, only 184 out of 715 *relégués individuelles* turned up for compulsory annual muster of 1912. It was claimed at the time that most of the remainder had fled into Brazil. Indeed, the North African convict Mohammed Ben M'Ahmed Lazrek took this route when he had served half of a ten-year sentence for murder. He wrote to his mother and brother at the end of 1915, telling them that he had been living in Brazil for the past four years, under the name El Hadj Sliman ben Amar. He hoped that he would see them when he went on *hajj* (pilgrimage) to Mecca.[80] Government tried to stem the flow of escapes, recommending a series of measures including an increase in the number of guards, new limits to *relégations individuelles,* and a ban on their residence in Saint-Georges. It is unclear whether these were fully implemented or successful.[81] Whatever the case, no doubt Brazil was attractive as an escape destination because it failed to formally complain about convict absconders. By 1939, there were at least 500 of them living in Pará, and with plentiful work in the nation's mines and the forests they were a useful source of labour.[82]

French Guiana was also geographically proximate to British Guiana and Trinidad, and they also became escape destinations. Initially, the British lacked the legal means to return deserters to the French

---

[76] ANOM H1854: Governor Pierre Didelot, French Guiana, to Albert François Lebrun, minister for the colonies, 9 April 1912, enc. Report on the presence of escaped convicts in St-Domingue, 29 June 1912; Stéphen Pichon, Minister of Foreign Affairs, to Maginot, 22 May 1913, enc. Enc: Minister plenipotentiary of the French Republic in Bogotá, to Pichon, 12 April 1913; Didelot to Pichon, 26 August 1913.
[77] ANOM H1854: Pichon to Maginot, 22 May 1913, enc. Minister plenipotentiary of the French Republic in Bogotá, to Pichon, 12 April 1913.
[78] ADM 1M7011/B: Emile Gissot, French Consul Barranquilla, to Governor Matteo Alfassa, Martinique, 29 June 1934.
[79] ANOM H1854: Didelot to Lebrun, 27 September 1912.
[80] ANOM H1854: Aristide Briand, Minister of Foreign Affairs, Gaston Doumergue, minister for the colonies, 22 February 1916, 9 March 1916, 16 April 1916.
[81] ANOM H1854: Report on the presence of escaped convicts in St-Domingue, 29 June 1912.
[82] Sanchez, *À perpétuité*, 254.

authorities, and they held the view that in any case they were not obliged to return men who had escaped through the carelessness of the state.[83] Britain and France failed to reach agreement on the mutual extradition of such convicts in 1861, following which the Colonial Office instructed the colonies to treat them as 'destitute foreigners', which meant that they should be taken care of by the consul of their country.[84] Of particular concern to the British was the arrival of convicts who had completed their sentence, and under its terms were permitted to leave French Guiana but not to return to France. The first such individuals had arrived in British Guiana in 1861, petitioning Governor William Walker that they were destitute, and asking either for work or onward passage. At first, the colony provided for their maintenance, and the travel costs for those who wished to leave.[85] However wary that this might eventually prove a hefty burden on colonial finances, it warned that in future they would receive no support.[86] As the consul for French Guiana wrote in 1862: 'What is to be done with them? They arrive in a starving condition and speak not a word of English, which alone makes it very difficult for them to find employment of any description, besides the very fact of their being escaped convicts disinclines persons from giving them work, consequently they must *almost* necessarily again become criminals.'[87] Subsequently British Guiana, and the colonies of Trinidad, Saint Lucia and Grenada, passed laws which enabled them to turn ex-convicts away if they wished to do so. In later years, the USA also refused to receive them. The French authorities thus advised ex-convicts not to try to land in these locations, or they would risk deportation.[88]

The British went on to pass extradition acts in 1870 and 1873, and a treaty with France followed in 1876. The latter detailed that for extradition to take place it must be requested by the consul general and

---

[83] TNA CO111/326 23 January 1860 no. 10: Wodehouse to Newcastle, 23 January 1860; Wodehouse to Governor Louis Tardy de Montravel, French Guiana, 23 January 1860; TNA CO111/330 9 March 1861 no. 30: Wodehouse to Newcastle, 9 March 1861, enc. Wodehouse to G. F. Pairandeau, vice-consul of France, British Guiana, 9 March 1861.

[84] TNA CO111/337 15 December 1862 no. 209: Hincks to Newcastle, 15 December 1862; TNA CO111/351 31 July 1865 no. 126: Newcastle to Hincks, 28 October 1865.

[85] TNA CO111/331 23 May 1861 no. 6: Governor William Walker to Newcastle, 23 May 1861, Walker to Newcastle, 7 June 1861, enc. collective petition signed by B. Salusse, 26 May 1861.

[86] TNA CO111/331 23 May 1861 no. 6: Walker to Newcastle, 8 July 1861, Walker to de Montravel, 7 July 1861.

[87] TNA CO111/335 22 July 1862 no. 135: Hincks to Newcastle, 22 July 1862, enc. G. R. Perry, Consul for French Guiana, to Montraval, 12 July 1862.

[88] TNA CO111/331 23 May 1861 no. 6: Walker to Newcastle, 23 May 1861; TNA CO101/130/32 18 August 1870 no. 32, folios 197–199: Rawson William Rawson, governor of the Windward Islands (inc. Grenada, Saint Lucia, and Trinidad), to John Wodehouse (1st Earl of Kimberley), secretary of state for the colonies, 18 August 1870.

accompanied by: an extract from the convict's descriptive role, including details of their crime and sentence; the notice of the escape; and a request for the convict's return, written by the commissioner of the special tribunal that oversaw escape cases. The Franco-British treaty was extended to the colonies through the passing of ordinances (laws). Later, British Guiana also passed an Aliens Ordinance (1886), which authorized the governor to repatriate anybody who threatened 'the preservation of the peace and good order of the Colony'. In Trinidad, the 1876 treaty was the basis of an 1877 ordinance which was modified twice, in 1889 and 1894. Supplements specific to convicts from French Guiana authorized Trinidad to detain suspected escapees (termed 'fugitive criminals') for up to three months, pending receipt of a request for their return from the governor in Cayenne. Whilst the treaty specified that a French officer identify the detainees in person, the 1894 ordinance allowed the use of authenticated documents instead. These included the convict's description, conviction, crime, sentence, date of sentence, and 'other particulars', sealed with the stamp and signature of the governor. The law on extradition stated that if these documents showed that a convict had not committed a crime under English law, they should be discharged from custody. If any of the necessary documentation was missing, or if it was not properly authenticated, no extradition could take place.[89]

In 1899, the number of arrivals was such that the governor of British Guiana asked his counterpart in French Guiana to send quarterly returns of escapes. This would enable the police in the colony to check the convicts described in these lists against suspects, or men in custody, in Georgetown, and to take the necessary legal steps.[90] By the 1930s, there were around 500 escape attempts in French Guiana each year, though most of the convicts gave themselves up or were recaptured. Only a few

---

[89] The process has been pieced together from a range of sources: TNA CO111/333 (Foreign Office): E. Hammond, Foreign Office, to Frederic Rogers, 23 October 1861; TNA CO295/286/19 17 February 1880 no. 46 folios 106–16: Attorney General Henry Ludlow to Governor Sir Henry Turner Irving, Trinidad, 28 October 1879; TNA CO295/288/61 (Foreign Office): Charles Abbott (3rd Baron Tenterden), permanent under-secretary Foreign Office, to George Cadogan (5th Earl Cadogan), under-secretary Colonial Office, 31 May 1880; ADG IX76 Administration pénitentiaire, 7406, 7415: Translation of a sentence awarded by the Police Magistrate of St Georges West (Trinidad), C. W. W. Greenidge, with respect to the extradition of Joseph Rey and Giovanni Diana, n.d. (1931); ANOM H1854: Georges Biard d'Aunet, Consul General of France, Sydney, to Théophile Delcassé, Minister of Foreign Affairs, 16 October 1902; ANOM H5352: Extract from the "Official Gazette" [Trinidad], 18 March 1905; An ordinance to make special provision with regard to the Extradition of Fugitive criminals from French Guiana, Governor Sir Frederick Napier Broome, Trinidad, 26 April 1894.

[90] ANOM H5352: Governor Sir Walter Joseph Sendall, British Guiana, to Governor Louis Guillaume Mouttet, French Guiana, 1 May 1899.

dozen remained at large.[91] Nonetheless, the *agences d'évasion* that were set up to assist escapes – including to Venezuela and other Latin American states as well as British colonies – seem to have constituted a lucrative business.[92] Some convicts did not use agencies but exploited networks of race and filiation. Indeed, has Lorraine M. Paterson has argued, a few of the convicts transported from French Indochina to French Guiana escaped to Trinidad. There was an established Chinese community on the island, and they owned several small businesses and shops. The escaped Vietnamese headed for locations in which these traders lived, and where they could take employment and 'pass' as free. In at least some cases, they hid their identity as escaped convicts very well, even from the women that they married.[93]

There was a similar pattern of escape by convicts in France's Pacific island colony of New Caledonia. They tried to reach Australia's shores, their flight provoking lengthy discussions on and changes to the law.[94] This was especially the case after 1883, when the number of absconders rose, because the colony introduced a new policy of dispersing convicts, rather than keeping them on large public works projects. This created opportunities for escape.[95] The arrival of almost 600 deserters in Queensland during the period 1866–1913, some of whom were North African, had important effects. At the end of the nineteenth century, the presence of French convicts in Australia fed into the protests which contributed to the desire to restrict non-European immigration, through what was known as the 'White Australia' policy. By focusing on French

---

[91] ADG IX76 Administration pénitentiaire, 7353: Director of the Penitentiary Administration to Governor René Veber, French Guiana, 16 November 1936, enc. Escapes since 1 January 1931.

[92] ADG IX76 Administration pénitentiaire, 7385: François Piétri, minister for the colonies, to Governor Julien Georges Lamy, French Guiana, 3 April 1933.

[93] Lorraine M. Paterson, 'Ethnoscapes of Exile: Political Prisoners from Indochina in a Colonial Asian World', *International Review of Social History*, 63, S26 (2018), 89–108.

[94] A fairly substantial literature on French convict escapes has emerged in recent years, particularly focused on New Caledonia. See Alexis Bergantz, '"The Scum of France": Australian Anxieties towards French convicts in the nineteenth century', *Australian Historical Studies*, 49, 2 (2018), 150–66; Russell Brennan and Jonathan Richards, '"The Scum of French Criminals and Convicts": Australia and New Caledonia Escapees', *History Compass*, 12, 7 (2014), 559–66; Briony Neilson, '"Moral Rubbish in close proximity": Penal colonization and strategies of distance in Australia and New Caledonia, c.1853–1897', *International Review of Social History*, 64, 3 (2019), 445–71; Sanchez, *À perpétuité*, 226–54; Jean-Lucien Sanchez, 'Les évasions de relégués au bagne de Guyane (XIXe–XXe siècle)', *Criminocorpus* (2014) http://journals.openedition.org/criminocorpus/2837 (accessed 9 January 2018); Karin Speedy, '"Arab Castaways"/ "French Escapees": Mobilities, Border Protection and White Australia', *Law, Crime and History*, 6, 2 (2016), 15–30.

[95] Stephen A. Toth, *Beyond Papillon: The French Overseas Penal Colonies, 1854–1952* (Lincoln: University of Nebraska Press, 2006), 77–8.

practice, it also allowed Australians to direct attention away from their convict past. As Alexis Bergantz has argued, ultimately this fed into the development of a shared nationalist mood that underpinned Federation in 1901.[96]

In the early twentieth century, Britain's Howard League for Penal Reform became highly critical of French Guiana and used evidence of convict escape as a means of publicizing and protesting against poor conditions in the penal colony. In 1935, France abolished both transportation to French Guiana and the law of *doublage*, but transportations continued, and a substantial convict population remained. As noted in Chapter 7, a year later in 1936 the Commissioner for Prisons in England and Wales, Alexander Paterson, visited the colony. He had condemned the principle of colonization using convicts, and the hopelessness of the convicts who under the system of *doublage* could not leave. By this time, and in response to an appeal to the Privy Council by the convicts Gregoire Kossokhatko, Robert Rotzinger, and Albert Caullier, the Howard League for Penal Reform was already campaigning on the issue of extradition. The background was this: in 1930, Kossokhatko (a Russian national) had arrived in Trinidad with seven other escaped convicts after eighteen days at sea. A request for extradition was received and succeeded – at exactly the same time as an extradition request for a near-identical group of convicts was turned down. Britain returned five of the men to French Guiana, but the Howard League funded the appeal of Kossokhatko, Rotzinger, and Caullier to the Privy Council in London. It won the case and used the opportunity to press for the abolition of the penal colony. Calling upon the League of Nations to demand improved prison standards, Honorary Secretary Cecily M. Craven critiqued extradition to places that 'civilized nations' deemed 'barbarous'.[97]

Paterson was sympathetic to the Howard League's position. This was evident during meetings of the Colonial Office's Penal Advisory Committee, which included himself and the Howard League's former secretary Margery Fry.[98] Following his visit to French Guiana, in other

---

[96] Bergantz, 'The Scum of France', 159, 165–6. See also Marilyn Lake and Henry Reynolds, *Drawing the Global Colour Line: White Men's Countries and the International Challenge of Racial Equality* (Cambridge University Press, 2008).

[97] Cicely M. Craven, 'Extradition – the case of fugitive criminals from French Guiana', *The Howard Journal*, 3, 2 (1931), 33–5. Emily Whewell's fascinating article on the Kossokhatko case appeared as this book was going to press: 'Seeking Refuge in Hostility: The Caribbean "British Isle of Freedom" and the Right to Remove Fugitive Convicts', *The Journal of Imperial and Commonwealth History*, 48, 1 (2020), 149–67.

[98] TNA CO318/437/12: Extract from the minutes of the 10th meeting of the Colonial Penal Advisory Committee, 13 November 1941. Fry's membership was 'unofficial', but the Colonial Office saw her presence as an important means of protecting it from the Howard League's critique. See TNA CO318/458/1: Note of P. Rogers, 26 October 1944.

discussions with the colonial secretary, Paterson expressed the view that conditions were so appalling that the British ought to do everything possible to avoid sending fugitives back.[99] Nonetheless, the colonies continued to view escaped convicts with suspicion, and this only increased during the Second World War. Because the French sent a few men of 'enemy nationality or associations' to the penal colony, when Germans, Italians, and others turned up as 'fugitives' in British territory, they aroused concern because of fears that they might be spies.[100]

In the aftermath of the Kossokhatko case, Trinidad no longer extradited convicts to French Guiana. Instead, it offered deserters support to continue their journey elsewhere. The law in British Guiana remained unchanged. Consequently, the colony became what the governor described as 'a haven of refuge', and by 1940 dozens of men it termed 'fugitives' were arriving each month. The government placed these people in jail before paying their passage on, and this entailed considerable expense. The colonial secretary sympathized.[101] The increase in fugitive numbers stimulated a change in the Trinidad process. Trinidad asked French Guiana for information about a suspected escapee's nationality and offence, and how they had left the colony. The Colonial Office reported that Trinidad's concern was 'genuinely and merely to rid the Colony of undesirable aliens in the Colony's own interest'. As for any other 'undesirable alien', the governor then made an expulsion order, and the escapee had to make their own arrangements to leave. If they did not, government used the Expulsion of Undesirables Ordinance to prosecute them. If found guilty, after serving their sentence, it deported them to their home nation.[102]

Escaped convicts in Trinidad gave detailed statements to the police, and in mentioning their willingness to work under police supervision, and their desire to see French consul-generals, these suggest that they understood their legal rights. Eventually, the British developed a system through which it compiled lists of names, eventually accompanied by sets of fingerprints, anthropometric measurements, and photographs, often of men in small groups of four of five (Figure 11.1). They sent

---

[99] TNA CO318/437/11: Note of a discussion with Mr Paterson and Mr Keith [and Lloyd] on 11th March [1940].
[100] TNA CO318/437/12: Acting Governor French Guiana, to Oliver Stanley, secretary of state for the colonies, 29 September 1943; Young to Robert Gascoyne-Cecil (5th Marquess of Salisbury), secretary of state for the colonies, 6 August 1942.
[101] TNA CO318/437/11: Young to Lloyd, 7 March 1940; TNA CO318/437/12: Extract from the minutes of the 10th meeting of the Colonial Administration Penal Advisory Committee, 13 November 1941.
[102] TNA CO318/437/12: Colonial Administration Penal Advisory Committee, Colonial Office's note, 10 December 1941.

Figure 11.1 Five escaped French convicts in British Guiana, 1902
Source: Archives nationales d'outre mer: H5352 Guyane anglaise (1902): Gustave Richter, French Consul British Guiana, to Governor E. Merwart, French Guiana, 24 December 1902, enc. Description of five French Fugitives who arrived on 9 November 1902.

these to Cayenne, asking officials if they recognized any of them. In one case dating from 1944, the list included convict no. 51,367, Henri Charrière, who had escaped from Cascades. Charrière later found fame as the author of the bestselling book *Papillon*.[103]

The number of escapes increased dramatically during the Second World War. No doubt this was the result of interruptions to supplies in French Guiana, and thus convict desperation, but with many former soldiers in the penal colony the opportunity to serve their country may also have been a factor. Indeed, at this time several men requested release

---

[103] ANOM H5353: Stéphen Psaila, Consular Agent for France, British Guiana, to Governor Jules Eucher Surlemont, French Guiana, 28 September 1944. See also Henri Charrière, *Papillon* (Paris: Robert Laffont, 1969). *Papillon* is now considered a work of fact-based fiction. Indeed, note that the escape notice detailed here was drawn up during the period when Charrière claimed that he was living in Venezuela.

on condition of enlistment.[104] They included two Polish convicts, arrested in British Guiana, who addressed a letter to this effect to their president, then part of the government-in-exile in London.[105] The Colonial Office proposed the transfer of the eighty or so escaped convicts then in Georgetown to HMPS Mazaruni. By this time, Mazaruni had been closed to ordinary prisoners and had interned German and Italian enemy aliens.[106] With shipping so disrupted in the region during this period, even where it was desirable, deportation and repatriation were difficult. Thus, six escaped convicts, including three Vietnamese, who had arrived in the Bahamas in 1940 were still there five years later in 1945. In the meantime, they worked, and in three cases even got married.[107]

By the end of the war, between forty and fifty suspected 'fugitive criminals' were still living in and around the capital of British Guiana, Georgetown, working in lumber yards, and as shoemakers or hawkers. The penal colony of French Guiana was by then subject to even more attacks by the international community, for appalling conditions and high mortality rates. Escaped convicts in British Guiana aroused considerable sympathy, and they were increasingly described not as 'convicts' or 'fugitives', but as 'refugees'.[108] Of particular importance was the status of these convicts, and to which category they belonged: convicts under sentence; *relégués*, repeat offenders who were either supported by the state (*relégués collectifs*) or made their own living subject to annual musters (*relégués individuelles*); or *libérés*, who had served their sentence (of eight or more years), but were compelled to remain in the colony for an equal term. The British could extradite those under sentence but did not have to deport those who were time served. In discussions between the British and French, it is possible to see how two of the key principles of extradition played out: that those subject to extradition had committed actions that would have been offences under English law, and Britain's belief that

---

[104] TNA CO318/437/6: J. L. Keith, Welfare Section of the Colonial Office, to Mr Beckett [?], 8 January 1940, enc. Cecily Craven, Honorary Secretary, Howard League for Penal Reform, to Keith, 18 January 1940; TNA CO318/437/11: Governor Sir Wilfrid Edward Francis Jackson, British Guiana, to George Lloyd (1st Baron Lloyd), secretary of state for the colonies, 20 July 1940; Governor Sir Hubert Winthrop Young, Trinidad and Tobago, to Robert Gascoyne-Cecil (5th Marquess of Salisbury), secretary of state for the colonies, 6 August 1942.
[105] TNA CO318/437/11: Jackson to Lloyd, 6 February 1941, enc. Grayda Wladyslav and Thomas Paz to the President of Poland in London, 18 December 1940.
[106] TNA CO318/437/11: Telegrams from British Guiana to the Colonial Office, 28 July 1940, 7 January 1941.
[107] TNA CO318/458/1: Governor Sir William Lindsay Murphy, Bahamas, to George Henry Hall, secretary of state for the colonies, 28 November 1945.
[108] ANOM H5353: Psaila to Surlemont, 15 May 1944; chief of the penitentiary administration to Surlemont, 24 May 1944; 'Refugees from Cayenne, Georgetown', *The Daily Argosy*, 25 January 1945.

they had been detained and punished with fairness and humanity. For both reasons, the British did not extradite either *libérés* or political offenders. They did have the right, however, to make them leave British territory, and thus could expel them if they so desired.[109]

*

In focusing on convict escape, this chapter is connected to earlier discussions of labour, resistance, and other forms of agency. As we have seen, straddling European polities in the early nineteenth-century Caribbean, the experience of dealing with escapees became linked to discussions on slavery and abolition, and there and in Gibraltar ultimately led to the development of standard practices and treaties relating to deportation and extradition. Whilst it is embedded in larger histories of revolutionary ideology in important ways, Chautard's *Escapes from Cayenne*, together with the petitions, statements, and writings of other convicts, also offers further insights into punitive mobility as a means for the spread and circulation of radical political thought. In this regard, this convict authored text, alongside official records, enables us to significantly develop the arguments of Chapter 6. The focus on escape and extradition more generally also enables us to foreground agency in an exploration of the relationship between convicts, insurgency, and the global age of revolution. Chautard's narrative is an extraordinary account of dozens of attempted and successful escapes, within the Guianas and to North America and England. It adds texture to evidence gleaned from the bureaucratic processes that accompanied the arrest or return of convict absconders.

As noted above, by the later period considered here, the Dutch and British no longer returned political prisoners to French Guiana, only ordinary convicts. Over time, they and other polities developed a series of complex mechanisms to deport or extradite released and escaped convicts. Indeed, the chapter has suggested that concerns about convict escape to and ex-convict mobility in parts of Australia were even factors in the push towards federation in 1901. Later in the twentieth century, following the closure of New Caledonia to convicts in 1922, the international community also used the presence and testimonies of convicts escaped from French Guiana to support their claims that the penal colony was unfit for purpose and ultimately inhumane. As convicts became 'refugees', even where escapes ultimately failed, evasions had significant repercussions, for they both stimulated political debate and changes to international law.

---

[109] Craven, 'Extradition', 35. See also ANOM H5353: Surlemont to Psaila, 30 May 1944.

12   Conclusion

The endurance of convict mobility globally over a period of five centuries disrupts the dominant narrative of the history of punishment, which has foregrounded the rise of prisons and penitentiaries as the key means of effecting governance and enforcing social discipline in the nineteenth century and later. Indeed, what emerges from the global perspective on penality presented in this book is not just evidence of the survival of early-modern forms of punitive mobility into the modern period, but their ongoing expansion, development, and refinement. Convict movement was connected to other architectures of punishment and confinement and was part of a broader repertoire of governmentality and social control, including the management of labour, and which was sometimes judicial and sometimes extra-legal or administrative. This was true of the widely varying case studies addressed here, ranging from petty criminals, soldiers, vagrants, and sex workers in European capitals to the insurgent slave societies of their colonies, and from political opponents to military mutineers in nations and empires alike. Enveloped in global penal flows, convicts moved between and around ever-evolving penal spaces – *presidios*, hulks, prisons, barracks, and camps – located on islands, littorals, and borderlands. Except in the case of elites, who were sometimes subject to removal without labour, there were often few if any practical distinctions between the different legal categories that put convicts into motion. Convicts experienced banishment, transportation, and exile in remarkably similar ways. In turn, as we have seen, diverse sites of punitive relocation became connected to other forms of punishment, including short rations, additional labour, gagging, chaining, fines, solitary confinement, flogging, execution, and incarceration. In some cases, for instance in inland penal spots and offshore islands in British Guiana and Trinidad, and post-Independence Latin America, punishment blended features of mobility, imprisonment, and additional sanctions, whilst retaining the focus on work and resource extraction.

Convict mobility and penal colonies remained central to penal strategies into the twentieth century (and in post-Soviet Russia and other nations they are still used today). Moreover, even after prisons and penitentiaries emerged, it was often the existence of colonies and borderlands that lay at the heart of the development of new rhythms of punishment. This is because they enabled the movement of convicts through penal stages, for example from architectures of cellular accommodation to relatively open barracks or villages. At the same time, onward mobility to ever more remote hard labour could be inflicted on those who refused to submit to penal regimes. Here, the use of offshore islands and inland sites, such as agricultural and other settlements, was especially important. This was the case, for instance, both inland and on islands in the penal colonies of New South Wales, Van Diemen's Land, and Western Australia.[1] However, by the nineteenth century punitive mobility had become a distinct form of punishment compared to other modes of penal control because it had a much longer association with forced labour, notably the clearance of land, logging, mining, and the development of infrastructures of local, regional, and global communication. Convicts occupied territories and could at once quarry the stone used to construct streets, bridges, bunds, and lighthouses, and hew the timber and mine the coal used to build and, later, power ships. The significance of convicts as unfree workers was such that there existed inverse relationships between the incidence of penal transportation and capital punishment in ways that are only beginning to be properly understood.[2]

The use of punitive mobility to satisfy the aims of getting rid of socially 'undesirable' groups, managing labour, and achieving expansionist ambitions, meant that convict journeys were often multi-staged and multi-directional, including travel overland, upriver, and overseas. Some of the extraordinary, yet routine, voyages described in this book followed the global tracks of the Iberian empires, straddled the Netherlands VOC's Asian and African possessions, moved 'slave-convicts' around the

---

[1] Lisa Ford and David Andrew Roberts, 'New South Wales Penal Settlements and the Transformation of Secondary Punishment in the Nineteenth-Century British Empire', *Journal of Colonialism and Colonial History*, 15, 3 (2014) doi:10.1353/cch.2014.0038. Hamish Maxwell-Stewart, 'Convict Workers, "Penal Labour" and Sarah Island: Life at Macquarie Harbour, 1822–1834', in Ian Duffield and James Bradley, eds., *Representing Convicts: New perspectives of convict forced labour migration* (Leicester University Press, 2000), 142–62; Katherine Roscoe, 'A Natural Hulk: Australia's Carceral Islands in the Colonial Period, 1788–1901', *International Review of Social History*, 63, S 26 (2018), 45–63.

[2] Hamish Maxwell-Stewart, 'Western Australia and Transportation in the British Empire 1615–1939', *Studies in Western Australian History*, 34 (2020), 5–21. See also Timothy J. Coates, 'The Portuguese Empire, 1100–1932', in Clare Anderson, ed., *A Global History of Convicts and Penal Colonies* (London: Bloomsbury, 2018), 38–9 (37–64).

Caribbean and to Sierra Leone, and took French revolutionaries first to offshore islands and then on to colonies in North Africa and South America. Despite the practical difficulties of enforcing sentences in colonies that lacked regular shipping links, such as in Réunion Island, the various ambitions delivered through convict mobility bestow logic on the fact that the same territory could send *and* receive convicts, as was the case not just in Réunion itself but across other carceral circuits of the European empires. In this way, *presidios*, penal settlements, and penal colonies were intimately connected to both strategies of governance and territorial aims. There were, perhaps inevitably, both links and disjuncture between punishment and labour, and work regimes, and these became evident in the other layers that permeated punitive mobility too. In the Caribbean world, for example, despite important distinctions the punitive strategies of European empires were intertwined, and revolution in Haiti and independence across Latin America had significant implications in their disruption of shared geographical and legal networks.

Whilst men and women could be ripped from their homes and families, becoming never-again-seen deterrents to criminal offending or resistance against authority, as Part I of the book has stressed, the imperial and other powers often used them as an occupying force. They sometimes preferred them over less controllable forms of free labour (Indigenous or otherwise) to the extent that convicts could constitute majority immigrant populations in new settlements. An important exception here is turn-of-the-twentieth-century Hokkaido, which received Japanese convicts only after other forms of migration proved unsuccessful. This was also the case in Britain's penal colony of Western Australia.[3] Convicts engaged in all types of work – brickmaking, carpentry, coal and tin mining, road making, dock building – and over time as separate penal colonies emerged, they became incorporated into attempts to render them self-sufficient. Thus, convicts made uniforms and shoes, farmed, cleaned and cooked, and became clerks, teachers, and in some locations, such as Britain's Southeast Asian penal settlements and the Andaman Islands, overseers. Convicts even made crafts, furniture, and fancy goods for sale to local populations, as was the case in Bermuda and New Caledonia. Some of these were displayed alongside their various manufactures at international exhibitions such as those curated by the International Penitentiary Congress from the third quarter of the nineteenth century. Even as over time penal settlements and colonies closed, or convicts were displaced by free labour, during times of crisis such as the Second World

---

[3] Kellie Moss, 'The Swan River Experiment: Coerced Labour in Western Australia 1829-1868', *Studies in Western Australian History*, 34 (2020), 23–40.

War in Asia, global powers like Japan sometimes reverted to using convicts as forced workers. Indeed, the exploitation of people under administrative or judicial sentences of removal had begun many decades before.

Just as previously convict mobility has not been properly integrated into the history of punishment, until recently convicts have been positioned outside global labour history.[4] This is despite the strong association between penal transportation and imperial settlement, and widespread recognition of the local significance of convict workers.[5] Whilst this book calls for the incorporation of convict mobility into standard narratives of penal change, and adds depth to our understanding of patterns of global labour, it also urges the inclusion of convicts in general histories of migration.[6] Noting the continuities of punitive mobility during an era more usually characterized as an age of penal rupture and change, and highlighting the significance of convicts as unfree workers, the book sets out to encourage further appreciation of the importance of convicts for the occupation and development of nations and colonies all over the world. Convicts settled in many destinations, post-sentence. In others, convicts were introduced following previously unsuccessful efforts at encouraging voluntary migration, and whilst they may have departed penal sites at the first opportunity when they became free, they had developed land sufficiently to make it attractive for later settlers. Ironically, perhaps, it was this which led at least to some extent to the development of anti-transportation sentiments, as free settlers displaced convicts, in part by undercutting the cost of their labour, and did not wish to compete against them in the labour market.

Then, as earlier, the modalities of convict labour were undergirded by race. Despite their exploitation, from the fifteenth to nineteenth centuries, as we have seen, convicts were settler colonists and became agents of the dispossession of Indigenous peoples in numerous settings, from the Americas to the Pacific world. Thus, punitive mobility contributed to and in some cases set patterns of Indigenous relocation, disease, disruption, violence, and war. The idea if not the reality of *terra nullius* (empty land) could facilitate occupation, after which parallel forms of confinement developed to include deportation and transportation for resistant or

---

[4] Anderson, ed., *A Global History of Convicts and Penal Colonies*. See also Christian G. De Vito and Alex Lichtenstein, eds., *Global Convict Labour* (Leiden: Brill, 2015).
[5] I borrow here from the pioneering collection of essays focused on Australian labour history, edited by Stephen Nicholas: *Convict Workers: Reinterpreting Australia's past* (Cambridge University Press, 1989).
[6] For instance, convicts feature in only a limited way in seminal texts such as Dirk Hoerder, *Cultures in Contact: World migrations in the second millennium* (Durham, NC: Duke University Press, 2002) and Patrick Manning, *Migration in World History* (London: Routledge, 2005).

insurgent populations such as Indigenous Australians and New Caledonia's Kanak.[7] Though most (not all) punitive sites absorbed convicts of various European, African, Asian, and/or Indigenous origins, only rarely were convicts sent inwards from borderlands, peripheries, and colonies to national and imperial centres. The key exceptions were, for a few short years in the nineteenth century, France, and Italy's African colonies, from the 1880s until the collapse of the Italian Empire in the 1940s. In the latter case, Italy used collective deportation primarily as a means of preventing insurgency, and it was not primarily associated with forced labour.[8] The more usual flow was the mobility of convicts outwards from the mainland and, for European empires, between colonies. Sometimes, as in the case of transportation from the Caribbean to the Australian penal colonies, convicts passed through European places of confinement, notably hulks, during their punitive journeys. On the other hand, the Netherlands Empire was unique in only employing transportation for colonized populations, and this was largely due to plentiful colonial labour in contexts lacking direct sovereignty.[9] Denmark–Norway, meantime, only sent convicts outwards from or within northern Europe and for a relatively short period of time.

There is a mixed picture of the association or separation of convicts of different origins, and this varied over time including according to factors such as the overall demographic profile of convict populations, their skills base, and labour needs. In colonial Van Diemen's Land, for example, African, Asian, and Creole convicts from Mauritius and Hong Kong were both mixed with, and separated from, the wider population at different historical points in time.[10] French Guiana, in contrast, kept colonially convicted convicts separated from Europeans, removing the latter altogether from unhealthy locales, whilst Portugal paid little attention to separation in its urban penal colonies in Mozambique Island and Luanda. Note here also that the racialization of convict regimes was such that it was knotted together with the expropriation of other forms of colonial work, including several failed experiments in other types of labour

---

[7] Kristyn Harman, *Aboriginal Convicts: Australian, Khoisan and Maori Exiles* (Sydney: University of New South Wales Press, 2012); Adrian Muckle, 'Troublesome Chiefs and Disorderly Subjects: The *Indigénat* and the Internment of Kanak in New Caledonia (1887–1928)', *French Colonial History*, 11 (2010), 131–60.

[8] Francesca Di Pasquale, 'The "Other" at Home: Deportation and Transportation of Libyans to Italy During the Colonial Era (1911–1943)', *International Review of Social History*, 63, S26 (2018), 211–31.

[9] Robert Cribb, 'Convict Exile and Penal Settlement in Colonial Indonesia', *Journal of Colonialism and Colonial History*, 18, 3 (2017); doi:10.1353/cch.2017.0043.

[10] Clare Anderson, *Subaltern Lives: Biographies of colonialism in the Indian Ocean world, 1790–1920* (Cambridge University Press, 2012), chapter 5.

importation. As mentioned above, enslaved men and women worked alongside convicts in the early Americas, as did soldiers, and Indigenous people there and in the later Australian colonies were also forcibly recruited and incorporated into colonial labour regimes.[11] Elsewhere, convicts worked with bonded and contract migrants of other kinds, as in the case of the integration of the formerly enslaved 1816 Barbados rebels with the receptives, or 'Liberated Africans', of Sierra Leone.

Especially from the early nineteenth century onwards, the conflation of penal and labour desires produced incompatibilities and tensions within convict systems, as evidenced in the example of mid-Qing China. Fundamentally, punitive mobility could not simultaneously inflict severe punishment, deter against crime, rehabilitate, and meet labour demands. Indeed, the disease environment in some new penal settlements, such as French Guiana and the Andaman Islands, led to critique that penal transportation was little more than a death sentence, in the former case particularly for Europeans. Otherwise, as on Italian penal islands, there was insufficient work in locations chosen for their isolation; alternatively, public works could be so severe that convict labour was overwhelmingly repressive – and deadly – in character. This was the case for convict road-building programmes in Hokkaido. A further difficulty beginning in the nineteenth century arose from the incorporation of education and religious practice into daily routines, though this was not the case everywhere and is perhaps most closely linked to Britain's Australian colonies and convict hulks in Bermuda and Gibraltar. Whilst study and worship worked toward some of the rehabilitative aspects of mobile convict regimes – including in Japan Buddhism and Shinto as well as Christianity – they took convicts away from work, leading to conflicts between administrators, chaplains, and priests. The impossibility of reconciling these elements, alongside fears that the stigma attached to convicts would deter free labour migration, sometimes sounded the death knell not just for extant convict sites but for planned penal relocations. This was true of the proposed penal colony in the nineteenth-century British West Indies, which was never built, whilst the same reservations inflected German debates about the perceived failure of convicts as colonizers into the twentieth century.

After exploiting convicts as workers, on occasion governments viewed their permanent settlement as desirable. However, this was not always the case. In Latin America, for instance, the order, trajectory, and

---

[11] Moss, 'The Swan River Experiment'; Katherine Roscoe, 'Work on Wadjemup: Entanglements between Aboriginal Prison Labour and the Imperial Convict System in Western Australia', *Studies in Western Australian History*, 34 (2020), 79–96.

relationships between punitive mobility, settlement, and free migration were particularly varied. Where settlement was the goal, the shipment of convict women (or in some instances the transfer of male convicts' free female family members) was central, and this was attempted or realized in numerous destinations. With the important exception of Russia, women were always a minority of convicts, often a very small one, and were treated in ways that reflected ideas about ideal family units and appropriately gendered labour. Arguably, their minority status empowered them in establishing family relationships and winning concessions in their working lives.[12] However, even where settlement was desired, the use of convicts as a colonizing force was not always successful, especially after changing ideas about punishment led to the gradual disaggregation of convict groups from other workers during the nineteenth century. This is evidenced in the global shift towards the creation of separate penal colonies, which represented a different form of organization to the earlier integration of convict gangs with other working peoples. Sometimes, this was because convict labour could not be rendered productive, or because ex-convicts could not find work. Otherwise, in Portuguese Angola and Mozambique, it can be put down to their return or repatriation. Again, localities varied widely, though it is the case that in numerous instances the agricultural and infrastructural legacies of convict work encouraged free migration, and thus dramatic population growth. There were also occasions where gangs of convict men were used on specific public works projects, including road building and the construction of dockyards. No women were sent to such locations, including Britain's dockyard hulks in the Atlantic and Mediterranean, or put to work in ports in East India Company (EIC) Burma, from which convicts were removed following completion.[13]

Convicts were linked to other work regimes such as enslavement and indenture (European and Asian), and military labour including through impressment. They could move in and out of categories in ways that elude easy definition but at the same time perhaps capture often-shared experiences of repression and exploitation. Indeed, in locations as different as the expansive Portuguese Empire and the compact site of British Gibraltar, soldiers and convicts worked side-by-side, leading in the latter case to unfavourable representations of the conditions of military service compared to penal labour. Furthermore, and as the

---

[12] For an especially rich examination of convict women's agency, see Kirsty Reid, *Gender, Crime and Empire: Convicts, settlers and the state in early colonial Australia* (Manchester University Press, 2007).

[13] Clare Anderson, 'Convicts, Commodities, and Connections in British Asia and the Indian Ocean, 1789–1866', *International Review of Social History*, 64, S27 (2019), 205–27.

book has suggested, there are particularly close connections between punitive mobility and enslavement. In some instances, convict transportation was instigated due to the shortage of enslaved workers. Also, the ties between repression, governmentality, punitive mobility, and bondage meant that in Europe's Caribbean colonies, enslaved men and women could be resold as convicts; whilst in mid-Qing China convicts could also be enslaved. At the same time, in the nineteenth and twentieth centuries, the idea of 'slave trading' and 'slavery' became rhetorical devices for both insurgent convicts and critics of penal colonies, who compared the slave trade and enslavement to convict shipment and convict work. Indeed, in the years before the American Civil War, escaped convicts from French Guiana even joined anti-slavery campaigns in the USA, bolstering their credibility by presenting parallels with their own experiences. Further, globally, in both the early-modern and later period, convicts were sold into indenture or impressed into the military, leading to the further blending of the labour force, as in the Spanish Empire, and the routine formation of penal battalions which endured in the case of France into the early 1970s.

Though it was rationalized as a means of effecting punishment and deterrence, usually through unfree labour, convict relocation had both unintended consequences and broader impacts. At the time, these were perhaps unanticipated, or at least were not policy motivations. One important feature of punitive mobility is that it became a vector for resistance and insurgency. Convict agency permeated all aspects of punitive relocation, and without exception impacted on the experience and operation of all sites. Acts of resistance varied from everyday and individual efforts to evade control and work, to collective attempts to refuse or renegotiate labour conditions, and riots, uprisings, and escape. As elaborated in previous chapters, during the early nineteenth century, the fate of convicts who fled between polities became bound up with debates about legal rights, slavery and abolition, human trafficking, and comparative punishment. Later on, escape was especially endemic in French Guiana. Right up to the Second World War convicts fled up the coast to Surinam, British Guiana, and Trinidad, or overland to Latin American nations such as Brazil and Venezuela. Ultimately, from Europe to the Caribbean, South American, and Pacific worlds, convict evasions contributed to anti-transportation sentiments and stimulated legal change in the form of new international agreements and formal treaties regarding extradition and deportation. In the case of escapes from New Caledonia to Australia, they even contributed to profound political change, the condemnation of a still-extant French penal colony allowing a new Federation to unite and distance itself from its convict past.

Convict mobility is notable for spreading pre-existing forms of insurgency and rebellion and was also important for the expansion and remaking of global networks of culture and belief. The experience of journeying into punishment, often in cramped conditions and following confinement in groups, nurtured the creation of solidarities. Of the examples discussed in the book, this included among groups of Indian convicts transported following wars of occupation with the EIC. As such, punitive mobility facilitated the movement and connection of radical ideas and actions, on seas and rivers as also on land.[14] Convicts also took political education and consciousness with them on their voyages. This can be seen across various contexts, including in the Empire of Denmark–Norway, among the Irish in the Australian colonies, and through the transnational radical connections forged by escaped French convicts in the USA during the Age of Revolution. From the earliest centuries, convict destinations became spaces of cultural transformation too, through the transference or remaking of social practices and hierarchies, and religious worship. This was the case in the cosmopolitan worlds of the Iberian empires, for the spread of Islam across the Dutch Empire, and later on in the cultural transmissions of both the Garifuna in South America and the 'local-born' society of the Andamans penal colony.

Part II of the book has stressed that aside from their connection to empire and nation building, and punitive and labour functions, sites of convict relocation became locales for the creation of knowledge systems and classifications. In regard to the history of exploration and collecting, this brings a new subaltern history dimension to what is usually viewed as an elite pursuit. Global linkages were forged through the incorporation of convicts (and Indigenous peoples) into Europeans' first trips up rivers and mountains, and inland, and into cultures of specimen gathering. From the early-modern Americas to nineteenth-century southern Africa, Brazil, and the Australian colonies, collectors and scientists drew on local expertise and took advantage of the allocation of convict and Indigenous assistants in securing and preparing specimens, from plants and seeds, and rocks and shells to butterflies and birds. This meant that convicts and penal colonies entered into global circuits of collecting, commerce, and display, including through work in botanical gardens, especially with England's Kew Gardens, and engagement in other forms of experimental agriculture.

---

[14] In regard to EIC Asia, stemming from the penal transportation of soldiers following the Anglo-Sikh Wars, an important theme of Anderson, 'Convicts, Commodities, and Connections'.

Conclusion

Another element of such knowledge formation was that, from at least the start of the nineteenth century, information about new penal thinking circulated around governments and ministries. This was partly spurred on by meetings of experts, including from the third quarter of the nineteenth century through the International Penitentiary Congress. Earlier, and during the same period, administrators with a stake in penal systems undertook global tours, investigating and comparing penal colonies, sometimes through reciprocal visits. Australian New South Wales and Van Diemen's Land, and French Guiana and New Caledonia, were central to such work, and became embroiled in debates on the viability and relative success of colonization through convict settlement. In the case of French Guiana, this contributed to larger controversies about the possibility of equatorial colonization *tout court*. Otherwise, information and administrative norms could follow administrators, like British colonial officer George Arthur, who themselves moved between overseas postings. Government reports were translated, read, and considered, instigating changes to policy and practice. This was not, then, a case of the diffusion of penal practices straightforwardly outwards from Europe and North America. In observing and evaluating global punishments in Britain, continental Europe and the USA, as also Latin America, the Caribbean, and South and East Asia, empires and polities reproduced, adapted, or recreated them anew. Japan was intrigued by penal practices in Europe and Russia, whilst Japanese penological thinking was itself translated and used in China. Britain admired the penal stages in force in Spain's nineteenth-century *presidio* of Ceuta, as well as Japan's *shūchikan* (penitentiaries) in Hokkaido. Sir Walter Crofton's three-stage Irish system of punishment, itself derived from Alexander Maconochie's work in Norfolk Island, was globally influential; the latter's mark system, developed in the Australian colonies, was also adopted all over the world. In these ways, convicts and penal colonies not only played a role in the ordering of the natural world, but themselves formed part of experiments in criminal justice classification systems. Moreover, their association with progressive classification can accurately be described as the origin of the modern probation system, lending a key aspect of colonial punishment a perhaps surprising post-colonial resonance.

Sites of punitive mobility usually incorporated people from diverse backgrounds, in terms of factors such as place of origin, language, ethnicity, and culture. Thus, beyond the value of their labour and expertise in research expeditions, convicts constituted a broad and yet accessible population for medical and ethnographic research. This too rendered them significant in the history of classification systems, and in particular those connected with intertwined understandings of offending patterns and ideologies of race. In the nineteenth century, with the establishment of separate penal colonies, convicts became incorporated into new thinking about criminality, heredity, and degeneration. In the early years of the century this included their appropriation in studies of phrenology and craniology and, in the latter part, techniques such as anthropometric measurement which were used in broader assessments of the validity of Cesare Lombroso's ideas about the 'biological' basis of crime. One element of this was that convicts were commonly subject to post-mortems, which facilitated investigations into the comparative size and weight of skulls and brains. Ultimately, the broader significance of this and other work was its contribution to the idea that 'criminals' were stuck in a backward, 'savage' past, and even where transported convicts were white Europeans this connected discussions about human development to race. There was an uneven picture here, though. Latin American nations followed Lombrosian thinking, but in other places across the British and French empires and in imperial Russia commentators were more sympathetic to the idea that crime was rooted in social factors, as articulated by Lombroso's intellectual rival, Alexandre Lacassagne.

The diversity and ready availability of convicts for the purpose of research also meant that they were used in studies of health and sickness. During the first half of the nineteenth century, Australian convict ships became locations for experimentation on scurvy. Following the settlement of the Andaman Islands in 1858, officers observed convicts for signs of tobacco and opium withdrawal, and later on used them in attempts to ameliorate the symptoms of leprosy and eradicate malaria. Such work also took place in French Guiana during the same period, as doctors investigated yellow fever and hookworm infection among convicts. As noted above, post-mortems were also routinely conducted on deceased convicts, often for research purposes. Such research was driven by the close association between jails and medical services, where doctors also served as penal superintendents, and also by the professional interests of individual administrators and doctors. One feature common to numerous penal colonies were intimate examinations; to a greater or lesser degree convicts were compelled to comply with them. Otherwise, there were at least some limits to the degree to which convicts presented themselves with symptoms of ill health or were willing to engage with medical studies, such as that of Joseph Orgéas in French Guiana. On the other hand, at least in some cases, convicts participated in medical research as 'volunteers'. For example, they became subjects of experimental work in exchange for remission of sentence and worked as nurses and medical attendants.

During this period, from the second half of the nineteenth century into the twentieth, some locations generated quite detailed medical statistics.

As Part II of the book has shown, these were used alongside other research methods in wider investigations of both convict experiences and the outcomes of penal transportation. As in the case of medical research, they were often the product of the interests of individuals, including visitors and officials. Convicts, ex-convicts, their children and descendants sometimes participated in these studies, but on occasion refused. Beyond its local value, this ethnographic work formed part of the larger global development of social science research methods, which grew to incorporate the use of surveys, questionnaires and interviews, all of which were trialled in penal colonies. Here, the pathology of criminal behaviour was a central concern, as were the social, cultural, and biological impacts of punitive mobility. From this work, archives of cultural change were generated in sites such as the Andaman Islands, in regard to marriage practices and caste adaptations. Franck Cazanove's early twentieth-century Saint-Laurent-du-Maroni study is perhaps a unique exploration of intimacy between convict men, revealed through its concern with the relationship between criminality and same sex desire. It provides an important counter to the focus on 'depravity' that inflected anti-transportation sentiments, most famously in Norfolk Island.[15] Otherwise, as with more general debates these labours on occasion emerged out of concerns with the merits of penal colonization, and in particular assessments of its success as a longer-term strategy for colonial occupation and settlement. Here, commentators like Joseph Orgéas in French Guiana and Anton Chekhov in Sakhalin Island used their writing to argue against the use of convicts as colonists or settlers, in the former case bolstering arguments by relating penal colonies to Malthusian theories of population growth. The outcomes of penal transportation for convicts of different ethnicities, and fertility, disability and child health and death rates, were central concerns. As such, research in penal colonies was intertwined with the development of broader ideas about colonization and racial distinction, including additionally in British India caste.

If it is the case that convict relocation was central to labour, migration, governance, classification, and research, what remains of these histories of punitive relocation in the world today? Until the end of the eighteenth century, as the first part of this book has stressed, convicts merged with other labour flows and were not kept in separate penal locations. This means that ultimately, they integrated with wider populations, including Indigenous, indentured, and enslaved peoples. In this regard, convict

---

[15] Tim Causer, 'Anti-transportation, "unnatural crime", and the "horrors" of Norfolk Island', *Journal of Australian Colonial History*, 14 (2012), 230–40.

histories are impossible to untangle from those of other groups, but nonetheless they are important because they stand for complex histories of colonization and occupation, and in particular the ambivalence of forms of settler colonialism underpinned by coercion. Things are rather different for the later period, when modern forms of record-keeping emerged, and the architecture of penal mobility created new forms of built infrastructure. In some places, both survive today, though the picture here is extremely uneven. Remnants – or what scholars of French Guiana have termed the 'ruins' – of convict mobility are present in numerous historic convict sites, even where they are opaque or have been silenced or interpreted in partial or problematic ways.[16] Given the volume of transportations to New South Wales and Van Diemen's Land, and the existence of detailed records of penal flows well into the nineteenth century, it is perhaps unsurprising that there exist self-aware convict descendants in Australia today. Changing social attitudes and awareness that convicts were not some sort of 'criminal class', but representative of wider society, means that earlier stigma has faded. Relatedly, historical and sociological research on genealogy and the 'convict stain' has linked family history and convict identity to nation building and identity formation in important ways.[17] An interesting new development in historical research is the exploration of the intergenerational outcomes of penal transportation in Van Diemen's Land (now, Tasmania), especially focused on height, morbidity, and mortality, as well as reoffending patterns.[18] Otherwise, we know remarkably little about the outcomes of penal transportation, not just in terms of health, but in regard to wider impacts on economy and society. In part, this is because historic records

---

[16] Max Silverman, 'Memory Traces: Patrick Chamoiseau and Rodolphe Hammadi's *Guyane: traces-mémoires du bagne*', Yale French Studies, 118, 19 (2010), 225–38; Michel-Rolph Trouillot, *Silencing the Past: Power and the production of history* (Boston, MA: Beacon Press, 1995).

[17] Ashley Barnwell, 'Convict shame to convict chic: Intergenerational memory and family histories', Memory Studies, 12, 4 (2019), 398–411; Lucy Frost, 'The Politics of Writing Convict Lives: Academic Research, State Archives and Family History', Life Writing, 8, 1 (2011), 19–33; Ronald D. Lambert, 'Reclaiming the ancestral past: narrative, rhetoric and the "convict stain"', Journal of Sociology, 38, 2 (2002), 111–27; Babette Smith, *Australia's Birthstain: The startling legacy of the convict era* (Crows Nest NSW: Allen and Unwin, 2008); Bruce Tranter and Jed Donoghue, 'Convict ancestry: a neglected aspect of Australian identity', Nations and Nationalism, 9, 4 (2003), 555–77.

[18] Barry Godfrey, 'Prison Versus Western Australia: Which Worked Best, the Australian Penal Colony or the English Convict Prison System?', The British Journal of Criminology, 59, 5, (2019), 1139–60; Barry Godfrey, Kris Inwood, and Hamish Maxwell-Stewart, 'Exploring the life course and intergenerational impact of convict transportation', in Veroni I. Eichelsheim and Steve G.A. van de Weijer, eds., *Intergenerational Continuity of Criminal and Antisocial Behaviour: An international overview of current studies* (London: Routledge, 2018), 61–75.

have not survived, and there exists a lack of awareness of penal history, but it is also to do with the assimilation of convicts and their descendants with Indigenous peoples as well as other settlers.

Where the cultural practices of convicts have remained at least partially intact, anthropologists have, however, articulated some of the outcomes of punitive mobility in other contexts. For instance, there exists work on the Garifuna, descendants of slave rebels who the British deported from Saint Vincent to Honduras after the Second Carib War of 1796-7. In 2008, their language, dance, and music were inscribed on UNESCO's intangible heritage list.[19] There is also research on the descendants of Algerians sent to New Caledonia following the 1871 Mokrani Revolt (*Unfaq urrumi*), including notably studies of foodways.[20] This bears relationship to ethnographic work on rituals, dress, music, and dance among the descendants of Cuban exiles (*ñáñigos*) sent to Spain's colony of Fernando Po in the nineteenth century.[21] Finally, research on 'local born' people in the Andamans today, including my own, has drawn on historical and community-generated archives as well as ethnographic work among convict descendants. Penal transportation to the Andamans stimulated interesting adaptations of religion and Hindu caste practices, as well as the creation of a new national history for post-Independence India. This represents convicts as glorious 'freedom fighters', rather than as ordinary criminal offenders.[22] Alongside this work has emerged a very recent literature that foregrounds the extent of segregation and intermixing between convicts and free populations in French Guiana and New Caledonia. It notes the displacement of *bagne* (penal colony) history in French Guiana (if not in France itself), replaced by a focus on enslavement. It also details the shame and stigma that accompanied convict history in New Caledonia for many years, and explains how

---

[19] Christopher Taylor, *The Black Carib Wars: Freedom, survival, and the making of the Garifuna* (Jackson: University Press of Mississippi, 2016).

[20] Louis-José Barbançon and Christophe Sand, *Caledoun: histoire des Arabes et Berbères de Nouvelle-Calédonie* (Bourail: Association des Arabes et Amis de Nouvelle-Calédonie, 2013); Mélica Ouennoughi, *Les déportés maghrébins en Nouvelle-Calédonie* (Paris: Editions L'Harmattan, 2005); Mélica Ouennoughi, 'Les déportés maghrébins en Nouvelle-Calédonie', *Revue Insaniyat*, 32 (2006), 53–68; Rachid Oulahal, Zohra Guerraoui, and Patrick Denoux, 'Entre Mémoire Collective et Émergence Diasporique, Le Cas des Descendants d'Algériens en Nouvelle-Calédonie', *Journal de la Société des Océanistes*, 147, 2 (2018), 373–82.

[21] Isabela de Aranzadi, 'El legado cubano en África. Ñáñigos deportados a Fernando Poo. Memoria viva y archivoescrito', *Afro-Hispanic Review*, 31, 1 (2012), 29–60; Isabela de Aranzadi, 'Cuban heritage in Africa: Deported Ñáñigos to Fernando Po in the 19th century', *African Sociological Review*, 18, 2 (2014), 2–41.

[22] Clare Anderson, Madhumita Mazumdar, and Vishvajit Pandya, *New Histories of the Andaman Islands: Landscape, place and identity in the Bay of Bengal, 1790–2012* (Cambridge University Press, 2016).

convict genealogy has emerged on the island in recent years against the background of political calls for self-determination.[23]

In many convict destinations, historic penal infrastructure still exists, and is well known and celebrated. This includes, for example, the local museums that nineteenth-century political exiles built in the Russian peripheries.[24] In Australia, there is a network of convict heritage sites, mainly centred in New South Wales and Tasmania, and inscribed on UNESCO's world heritage list. Their curation and interpretation have become the subject of intense debate by historians and genealogists.[25] Historic convict sites have become tourist attractions in other places too. These include Abashiri in Hokkaido and The Dockyard in Bermuda. Most famous, perhaps, are Robben Island in South Africa and the Andamans Cellular Jail, both of which have become central to the narration of national histories of resistance against oppression.[26] Perhaps less remembered and memorialized, but no less important, are the ecological and infrastructural impacts of punitive mobility: the land clearance, agricultural development, mining, quarrying, road building, and other kinds of construction that have left their mark in territories and nations all over the world. From Central and South America to Russia, Africa, and Asia, across the Caribbean, Mediterranean, and Indian Ocean and Pacific oceans, whether they are recognized or not, convict histories are thus inscribed upon rural and urban landscapes.

On the other hand, some sites of punitive relocation have been repurposed into new forms of confinement, producing layers of carcerality that can survive into the present day. In 1938, the Brazilian island of Fernando de Noronha, which opened this book, became a prison for political prisoners under the dictatorship of Getúlio Dornelles Vargas. The historic penal colony of Île Nou in New Caledonia today houses both a prison and a secure psychiatric facility (the latter partially occupying former penal colony buildings). Where sites were located in remote interior regions, similar continuities are also in evidence. For instance, HMPS Mazaruni in British Guiana is, today, Mazaruni Prison in the

---

[23] Isabelle Merle and Marine Coquet, 'The Penal World in the French Empire: A Comparative Study of French Transportation and its Legacy in Guyana and New Caledonia', *The Journal of Imperial and Commonwealth History*, 47, 2 (2019), 247–74.

[24] Emily D. Johnson, *How St. Petersburg Learned to Study Itself: The Russian idea of kraevedenie* (University Park: Penn State University Press, 2006).

[25] Clare Anderson, Eureka Henrich, Sarah Longair, and Katherine Roscoe, 'Empire and Its Aftermath in Four (Post-)Colonial Settings', in Jacqueline Z. Wilson, Sarah Hodgkinson, Justin Piche, and Kevin Walby, eds., *The Palgrave Handbook of Prison Tourism* (Basingstoke: Palgrave, 2017), 609–30; Hamish Maxwell-Stewart and Lydia Nicholson, 'Penal Transportation, Family History and Convict Tourism', in Wilson et al., eds., *Palgrave Handbook*, 713–34.

[26] Anderson et al., 'Empire and Its Aftermath'.

independent Republic of Guyana. Much of the original nineteenth-century infrastructure remains intact, whilst the penal settlement's chapel now lies in ruins. China's Xinjiang is today a location in which 're-education' camps exist, and in recent years these have been heavily criticized by human rights activists. Finally, the geography of modern Russia's penal system in many ways echoes its imperial past, which was itself overlaid with the *gulag* archipelago during the Soviet era.[27] There is, it would seem, much work to be done to uncover the outcomes and legacies of punitive relocation, in these and the other contexts explored in this book. Meanwhile, a global approach to convict histories has revealed close and enduring connections between punishment, governance, repression, and nation and empire building. Penal mobility became intertwined with other forms of labour and migration, at the same time as convict agency enabled the spread of insurgency and cultural transformation, and shaped the local practices and global circulations that undergirded knowledge production. In all these ways we see that not only is the history of convicts a global history, global history itself was profoundly shaped by the mobility, labour, and diversity of convict lives.

---

[27] Laura Piacentini and Judith Pallot, '"In Exile Imprisonment" in Russia', *The British Journal of Criminology*, 54, 1 (2014), 20–37.

Appendix: Principal and Selected Imperial and Latin American Sites of Punitive Relocation

Portuguese Empire

Ceuta	1415	1640
Tangier	1471	1662
Sao Tome & Principe	1471	1974
Mozambique	1490	1974
Brazil	1500	1822
Mazagão	1500	1769
Goa	1510	1961
Diu	1535	1961
Malacca (Melaka)	1550	1641
Ceylon (Sri Lanka)	1550	1656
Timor	1550	1974
Santa Catarina	1600	1822
Pará	1600	1822
Angola	1600	1974

Spanish Empire

Santo Domingo (Haiti)	1494	1801
Cuba	1494	1898
Puerto Rico	1500	1898
New Spain (Viceroyalty of)	1520	1810

(cont.)

Chile (Captaincy General of)	1540	1818
Peru (Viceroyalty of)	1542	1820
Canary Islands	1556	1950
Philippines	1571	1898
Mariana Islands	1600	1898
Río de la Plata (Viceroyalty of)	1650	1820
Oran	1668	1792
Melilla	1668	1906
Ceuta	1668	1912
New Granada (Viceroyalty of)	1717	1820
Juan Fernández Islands	1750	1821
Louisiana	1762	1802
Malvinas/ Falkland Islands	1767	1811
Colonia del Sacramento	1776	1816
Patagonia	1779	1816
Caroline Islands	1860	1898
Fernando Po (Bioko)	1865	1950
Rio de Oro	1890s	1976

French Empire

Quebec	1541	1543
Louisiana	1717	1720
French Guiana	1797	1801
	1852	1953
Île Sainte-Marguerite	1830	1884
Algeria	1848	1859
Poulo Condore	1850	1950
Congo	1850	1900
Réunion Island	1850	1900

(cont.)

Martinique	1850	1900
Guadeloupe	1850	1900
Nuka Hiva	1850	1900
New Caledonia	1864	1922
Corsica	1884	1902
Obock (Djibouti)	1886	1895
Gabon	1898	1913

Netherlands East Indies

Cape Colony inc. Robben Island	1619	1806
Batavia (Jakarta)	1619	1942
Ceylon (Sri Lanka)	1619	1815
Allelande Island	1619	1815
Moluccas (Maluku) Islands	1619	1942
Edam & Onrust Islands	1619	1942
Banda Islands	1619	1942

British Empire

British Americas (Chesapeake, Barbados, & Jamaica)	1618	1775
Tangier	1661	1685
Cuba	1750	1825
Puerto Rico	1750	1825
Gorée Island	1775	1804
Whydah (Ouidah)	1783	1785
Honduras	1784	1817
New South Wales	1788	1849
Norfolk Island	1788 1825	1814 1853

(cont.)

Penang	1789	1873
Andaman Islands	1793	1796
	1858	1945
Nova Scotia	1796	?
Bencoolen (Bengkulu)	1797	1823
Amboyna	1797	1823
Van Diemen's Land (Tasmania)	1804	1853
Robben Island	1806	1880s
Mauritius	1815	1853
Sierra Leone	1819	1840s
Bermuda	1824	1863
Malacca (Melaka)	1826	1866
Singapore	1826	1873
Burma (Myanmar)	1830	1862
Bombay Presidency (India)	1836	1864
Madras Presidency (India)	1836	1864
Aden	1841	1850
Gibraltar	1841	1874
Western Australia	1850	1868
Labuan	1851	1858
Nicobar Islands	1869	1888

Sweden and Empire of Denmark–Norway

New Sweden	1640	1655
Danish West Indies	1672	1689
(Saint Thomas, Saint John & Saint Croix)	1750	1755
The Finnmark[a]	1755	1765
Greenland	1728	1729

[a] In law, dating back to the seventeenth century, Finnmark was a place of banishment from Norway, though it is unclear whether the penalty was ever used.

China

Xinjiang	1644	1912

Imperial Russia

Tomsk	1600s	1917
Nerchinsk	1700s	1906
Kutomarskaya	1700s	1917
Maltsevskaya	1700s	1917
Aleksandrovskaya (Irkutsk)	1700s	1917
Tobolsk	1855	1917
Sakhalin	1870s	1906
Kadai	1870s	1906
Zerentui	1870s	1906

Japan (Hokkaido)

Sorachi	1882	1901
Kabato	1881	1908
Abashiri	1891	1908
Kushiro	1885	1901
Tokachi	1895	1908

Argentina

Carmen de Patagones	1810	2000
Chaco	1810	present
Ushuaia	1873	1947
Isla de los Estados	1884	1899

Brazil

Fernando de Noronha	1857	1897
Dourados	1900	1950

Appendix

Chile

Juan Fernández Islands	1821	1930
Santa María Island	1900	1950
Quiriquina Island	1900	1975

Colombia

Gorgona Island	1900	1980s
Oriente (Colombian Amazonia)	1930	present
Araracuara	1938	1971

Costa Rica

San Lucas Island	1900	1990s

Ecuador

Galapagos Islands	1837	1958
Napo (Ecuadorian Amazonia)	1850	1870s
Mera (Ecuadorian Amazonia)	1936	1948

Mexico

Quintana Roo	1821	1900
Marías Islands	1908	present

Panama

Coiba Island	1919	2004

Paraguay

Ybycuí	1811	1900

Peru

Chincha Islands	1821	1900
El Frontón Island	1918	1990s

Sources: These are too numerous to be listed here; information was drawn from the works and archives detailed in the footnotes and Bibliography. See especially the essays collected in Clare Anderson, ed., *A Global History of Convicts and Penal Colonies* (London: Bloomsbury, 2018). Thanks also to Carrie Crockett, Christian G. De Vito, and Tim Coates.

Note: The dates above do not necessarily represent continuous punitive relocations, or the years in which the first and last convicts arrived. They show the date from the first convict arrivals to the date of the penal site's closure, as known to the author.

Bibliography

Published Material, Pre-1945

Actes du Congrès Pénitentiaire International de Rome, Novembre 1885, 2 vols (Rome: Mantellate, 1887–8).
Anderson, A. R. S. 'Splenic Abscess in Malarial Fever'. *The Indian Medical Gazette* 41 (June 1906), 212–3.
Anderson, John. *Catalogue of the Mammalia in the Indian Museum, Calcutta, Part I* (Calcutta: Government of India Central Printing Office, 1881).
Annual Reports on the Convict Establishments at Bermuda and Gibraltar (London: George E. Eyre and William Spottiswoode, 1859–63).
Appun, Carl Ferdinand. *Unter den Tropen: Wanderungen durch Venezuela, am Orinoco, durch British Guiana und am Amazonenstrome in den jahren 1849–1868* (Jena: Hermann Costenoble, 1871).
Arenal, Concepción. *Las colonias penales de la Australia y la pena de deportación* (Madrid: Librería de Victoriano Suárez, 1895).
Attibert, François. *Quatre Ans À Cayenne: Notes de Fr. Attibert, Déporté* (Brussels: de la Veuve Verteneuil, 1859).
Atwood, Thomas. *The History of the Island of Dominica: Containing a description of its situation, extent, climate, mountains, rivers, natural productions, &c. &c. Together with an account of the civil government, trade, laws, customs and manners of the different inhabitants of that island. Its conquest by the French, and restoration to the British dominions* (London: J. Johnson, 1791).
Barlow, Nora (ed.). *Charles Darwin and the Voyage of the Beagle* (London: Pilot Press, 1945).
Barrows, Samuel J. *Report of Proceedings of the Seventh International Prison Congress, Budapest, Hungary, September, 1905* (Washington DC: Government Printing Office, 1907).
Belbenoît, René. *Dry Guillotine: Fifteen years among the living dead* (New York: E. P. Dutton and Co., 1939).
Beltrani Scalia, [Martino]. 'Historical Sketch of National and International Penitentiary Conferences in Europe and America', *Débats du Congrès Pénitentiaire de Bruxelles. Session de 1847. Séances des 20, 21, 22 et 25 Septembre* (Brussels: Imprimerie de Deltombe, 1847).
Bentham, Jeremy. *Panopticon versus New South Wales, or, The panopticon penitentiary system and the penal colonization system compared* (London: Wilks and Taylor, 1812).

Bertillon, Alphonse. *Identification anthropométrique: Instructions signalétiques* (Paris:Melun, 1893).
  The Identification of the Criminal Classes by the Anthropometric Method, translated by E. R. Spearman (London: Spottiswoode and Co., 1889).
Blythe, Edward. 'Appendix: The Zoology of the Andaman Islands'. In Frederic John Mouat (ed.) *Adventures and Researches among the Andaman Islanders* (London: Hurst and Blackett, 1863), pp. 345–67.
Boisjoslin, Jacques de. (translated by Eiichi Takeda), 'French Penal Colonies and Transportation'. *Dainippon Kangoku Kyōkai Zasshi*, 11 (vol. 2, issue 3, 1889), 17–22.
  (translated by Eiichi Takeda), 'French Penal Colonies and Transportation (continued from no. 11)'. *Dainippon Kangoku Kyōkai Zasshi*, 12 (vol. 2, issue 4, 1889), 9–11.
Bonington, M. C. C. *Census of India, 1931. Volume 2: The Andaman and Nicobar Islands* (Calcutta: Government of India Central Publication Branch, 1932).
Booth, Charles. *Life and Labour of the People of London*, 9 vols (London: Macmillan, 1892–7).
Boteler, Thomas. *Narrative of a Voyage of Discovery to Africa and Arabia: performed in His Majesty's ships, Leven and Barracouta, from 1821 to 1826, under the command of Capt. F. W. Owen, R.N.* (London: Richard Bentley, 1835).
Branner, John C. 'The Convict-Island of Brazil – Fernando de Noronha'. *The Popular Science Monthly*, 25 (1889), 33–40.
  'Notes on the Fauna of the Islands of Fernando de Noronha'. *The American Naturalist*, 22, 262 (1888), 861–71.
'A Brazilian Convict Island', *Chambers Journal* (25 February 1893), 116–19.
Brimont, E. 'Ankylostomiase en Guyane française'. *Bulletin de la Société de Pathologie Exotique*, 2 (1909), 413–17.
Brimont, E. and M. Ceillier, 'Sur un cas de l'ankylostome maligne avec autopsie'. *Bulletin de la Société de Pathologie Exotique*, 2 (1909), 418–23.
Brown, H. C. 'Epidemic Jaundice in the Andaman Islands'. *The Lancet*, 211 (25 February 1928), 388.
Browning, Colin Arrott. *The Convict Ship, and England's Exiles* (London: Hamilton, Adams, and Co., 1847).
Bueche, Paul. (translated by Eiichi Takeda), 'Method of Escorting Prisoners in France'. *Dainippon Kangoku Kyōkai Zasshi*, 9 (vol. 2 issue 1, 1889), 32–6.
Bulletin officiel de la Guyane française, de l'année 1854 (Cayenne: Imprimerie du gouvernement, 1855).
Burdon, John. *Archives of British Honduras: Volume I, from the earliest date to A.D. 1800* (London: Sifton Praed and Co., 1931).
  Archives of British Honduras, Volume II, from 1801 to 1840 (London: Sifton Praed and Co., 1934).
Burot, P. *De la fièvre dite bilieuse inflammatoire à la Guyane: application des découvertes de M. Pasteur à la pathologie des pays chauds* (Paris: Octave Doin, 1880).
Butterfield, Agnes. 'Notes on the Records of the Supreme Court, the Chancery, and the Vice-Admiralty Courts of Jamaica'. *Bulletin of the Institute for Historical Research*, 15 (1938), 88–99.

Cadalso, Fernando. *Principios de la colonización y colonias penales* (Madrid, J. Góngora y Álvarez, 1896).
Carol, Jean. *Le Bagne (avec photographies)* (Paris: Société d'Éditions Littéraires et Artistiques, 1903).
Carpenter, Mary. 'Suggestions on Reformatory Schools and Prison Discipline Founded on Observations made during a Visit to the United States', *Transactions of the Third National Prison Reform Congress, held at Saint Louis, Missouri, May 13–16, 1874: Being the third annual report of the National Prison Association of the United States* (New York: Office of the Association, 1874).
'Case of John Jenkins, Convict Executed at Sydney for Murder', *Phrenological Journal and Miscellany*, 10 (June 1836–Sept. 1837), 485–9.
Catorce meses en Ceuta (Ceuta: Caja de Ahorros y Monte de Piedad, 1985) [first published 1886].
Cazanove, [Dr Franck]. 'La dépravation sexuelle chez les relégués à Saint-Jean-du-Maroni'. *Archives de l'Anthropologie Criminelle*, 21 (1906), 44–58.
Chautard, Leon. *Escapes from Cayenne* (Salem, MA: The Observer Office, 1857).
Chowdry, A. K. 'Jaundice at Port Blair, Andaman Islands'. *The Indian Medical Gazette*, 38 (December 1903), 409–11.
Christophers, S. R. *Malaria in the Andamans* (Calcutta: Office of the Superintendent of Government Printing, 1912).
Cleare, L. D. 'Butterfly Migrations in British Guiana: II'. *Proceedings of the Royal Entomological Society of London*, 77, 2 (1929), 251–64.
Clifton, Mrs (Violet) Talbot. *Pilgrims to the Isles of Penance; Orchid Gathering in the East* (London: John Long, 1911).
Collens, J. H. *A Guide to Trinidad: A handbook for the use of tourists and visitors* (London: Elliot Stock, 1888).
Colonial and Indian Exhibition, 1886: Empire of India, Special Catalogue of Exhibits by the Government of India and Private Exhibitors (London: William Clowes and Sons, 1886).
Combe, George. 'Penal Colonies: the management of prisoners in the Australian colonies'. *Phrenological Journal*, 18 (1845), 101–22.
Le Congrès Pénitentiaire International de Stockholm, 15–26 Août 1878, Comptes-Rendus des Séances, publiés sous la direction de a Commission Pénitentiaire Internationale, par le Dr Guillaume (Stockholm: Bureau de la Commission Pénitentiaire Internationale, 1879).
'Congress of the Sanitary Institute'. *British Medical Journal*, (6 August 1904), 289–92.
Cornet, Pere Armengol y. *¿A las islas Marianas ó al golfo de Guinea?* (Madrid: E. Martinez, 1878).
Craven, Cicely M. 'Extradition – the case of fugitive criminals from French Guiana'. *The Howard Journal*, 3, 2 (1931), 33–5.
Curtis, William W. *Applied Christianity in Hokkaido: An attempt at prison reform in Japan* (Boston, MA: American Board of Commissioners for Foreign Missions, n.d. [c. 1894]).
Dantec, [Docteur Le]. 'Origine Microbienne de l'Ulcère Phagédénique des Pays Chauds'. *Archives de médecine navale*, 43 (1885), 448–53.
Dassonville, Georges. *Droit Romain: Des peines qui emportaient privation de la liberté naturelle; Droit français Étude comparée de la transportation et de l'emprisonnement*

cellulaire aux deux points de vue répressif et moralisateurs en droit français: état de la question en France et dans quelques pays. Thèse pour le doctorat (Paris: A. Parent, 1880).
de Blosseville, Ernest. *Historie de la Colonisation Pénale et des Établissements de l'Angleterre en Australie* (Évreux: Imprimerie de Auguste Hérissey, 1859).
Demetz, M. *Report on Agricultural Colonies*. (Glasgow: James Maclehose, 1856).
Dixon, Hepworth. *John Howard, and The Prison-World of Europe* (Webster, MA: Frederick Charlton, 1852).
'Donated foreign books', *Dainippon Kangoku Kyōkai Zasshi* (vol. 4, issue 8, 1891), 54.
Doroshevich, V. M. *Sakhalin (Katorga)*, 2 vols (Moscow: Tipografiia Tovarishchestva I. D. Sytina, 1903).
Dougall, J. *Report on the Treatment of Leprosy with Gurjon Oil* (Calcutta: Wyman and Co., 1876).
Du Bois, W. E. B. (ed.). *The Philadelphia Negro: A social study* (New York: Cosimo, 1899).
Dubois, George. *Report on Incorrigibility*, in E. C. Wines, *The Actual State of Prison Reform Throughout the Civilized World: A discourse pronounced at the opening of the international prison congress of Stockholm, August 10, 1878* (Stockholm: Centra-Tryckeriet, 1878).
Dumont, Pierre-Louis Etienne. *Théorie des peines and recompenses par Jérémie Bentham*, 2 vols (London: L'Imprimerie de Vogle et Schulze, 1811).
Ferris, Roxana S. *Preliminary report on the Flora of the Tres Marías* (Stanford University Press, 1927).
'Exhibitions at the International Prison Congress', *Dainippon Kangoku Kyōkai Zasshi*, 23 (vol. 3, issue 3, 1890).
Field, J. *The Life of John Howard; with comments on his character and philanthropic labours* (London: Longman, Brown, Green, and Longmans, 1850).
FitzRoy, Robert. *Narrative of the surveying voyages of His Majesty's Ships Adventure and Beagle between the years 1826 and 1836, describing their examination of the southern shores of South America, and the Beagle's circumnavigation of the globe. Proceedings of the second expedition, 1831–36, under the command of Captain Robert Fitz-Roy, R.N.*, 3 vols (London: Henry Colburn, 1839).
Foinitski, Ivan and Georges Bonet-Maury. *La Transportation Russe et Anglaise avec une Étude Historique sur La Transportation* (Paris: Lecène, Oudin et Cie., 1895).
Fraser, Lionel M. *Papers Relating to the Improvement of Prison Discipline in the Colonies* (London: H.M.'s Stationery Office, 1875).
General Report on the Census of India, 1891 (London: Eyre and Spottiswoode, 1893).
George, Grant MacCurdy. 'Le poids et la capacité du crâne, le poids de la mandibule, les indices crânio-mandibulaire, crânio-cérébral, etc. étudiés sur 61 crânes de criminels'. *Bulletins de la Société d'anthropologie de Paris*, 4th series, 8 (1897), 408–20.
Ghose, Barendra Kumar. *The Tale of My Exile* (Pondicherry: Arya Office, 1922).
Gisborne, Lionel. 'Summary of the Report on the Survey of the Isthmus of Darien'. *Journal of the Royal Geographical Society of London*, 27 (1857), 191–206.

Griffith, George. *In An Unknown Prison Land: An account of convicts and colonists in New Caledonia with jottings out and home* (London: Hutchinson and Co., 1901).
Griffiths, Arthur. 'Penal Colonies – Agricultural and Industrial'. *North American Review*, 163, 481 (1896), 676–87.
 Secrets of the Prison-House or Gaol Studies and Sketches, Volume I (London: Chapman and Hall, 1894).
'Government Gazette', *Dainippon Kangoku Kyōkai Zasshi*. 23 (vol. 3, issue 3, 1890).
'Gurjon-Oil in the Treatment of Skin Diseases'. *The Indian Medical Gazette* (1 June 1875), 157.
Guyot, F. 'Contributions à la Géographie Médicale: La Déportation Simple à l'Ile des Pins'. *Archives de médecine navale*, 36 (1881), 161–75.
Halliburton, Richard. *New Worlds to Conquer* (Indianapolis, IN: The Bobbs-Merrill Company Publishers, 1929).
Hand List of Mollusca in the Indian Museum, Calcutta (Calcutta: Office of the Superintendent of Government Printing, 1884).
Heindl, Robert. *Meine Reise nach den Strafkolonien, mit vielen originalaufnahmen* (Berlin-Wien: Ullstein und Co., 1913).
 (translated by Bertha R. Wolf), 'Penal Settlement and Colonization'. *Journal of the American Institute of Criminal Law and Criminology*, 13, 1 (1922), 56–60.
Henderson, J. R. 'On a New Species of Coral-Infesting Crab Taken by the R.I.M.S. "Investigator" at the Andaman Islands'. *The Annals and Magazine of Natural History; Zoology, Botany and Geology*, 18 (1906), 211–19.
Henry, J. *Report on the Criminal Law at Demerara, and in the Ceded Dutch Colonies: drawn up by the desire of the Right Hon. The Earl Bathurst* (London: Henry Butterworth, 1821).
Hill, Matthew Davenport. *Mettray: A Letter from the Recorder of Birmingham to Charles Bowyer Adderley, Esq., M.P.* (London: Cash, 1858).
Hokkaidō shūchikan nenpō (Tokyo: Hokkaidō shūchikan, 1896–1900).
Hokkaidō shūchikan tōkeisho (3 vols) (Tokyo: Hokkaidō shūchikan, 1892–94).
Howard, Benjamin. *Prisoners of Russia: A personal study of convict life in Siberia and Sakhalin* (New York: D. Appleton and Company, 1902).
Howard, John. *The State of the Prisons in England and Wales with Preliminary Observations and an Account of Some Foreign Prisons* (Warrington: William Eyres, 1777).
Hunter, W. W. *Imperial Gazetteer of India. Volume V: Abazai to Arcot* (Oxford: Clarendon Press, 1908).
Hutchinson, G. *Reformatory Measures Connected with the Treatment of Criminals in India* (Lahore: Punjab Printing Company's Press, 1866).
Imperial Gazetteer of India, Volume XV: Karachi to Kotayam (Oxford: Clarendon Press, 1908).
'India', *The British Medical Journal*, 5 October 1912, 901–4.
International Congress on the Prevention and Repression of Crime, including penal and reformatory treatment: preliminary report of the commissioner [E. C. Wines] appointed by the president to represent the United States in the Congress, in

compliance with a joint resolution of March 7, 1871 (Washington DC: Government Printing Office, 1872).
Isambert, François-André. *Affaire des déportés de la Martinique, 1823–1824: mémoires, consultations, pieces justificatives, etc.* (Paris: Constantin, 1825).
Josa, F. P. L. *The Apostle of the Indians of Guiana: A memoir of the life and labours of the Rev. W.H. Brett, B.D., for forty years a missionary in British Guiana* (London: Wells, Gardner, Darton and Co., 1887).
Kapler, A. *Holländisch-Guiana: Erlebnisse und Erfahrungen, während eines 43 jährigen Aufenthalts in der Kolonie Surinam* (Stuttgart: Commissions Verla von W. Kohlhammer, 1881).
Kate, H. F. C. Ten. 'Dynamometric Observations among Various Peoples'. *American Anthropologist*, 18, 1 (1916), 10–18.
Kennan, George. *Siberia and the Exile System*, 2 vols (New York: The Century Company, 1891).
Kloss, C. Boden. *In the Andamans and Nicobars: The narrative of a cruise in the schooner "Terrapin," with notices of the islands, their fauna, ethnology, etc.* (London: John Murray: 1903).
Krarup-Nielsen, A. *Hell beyond the Seas: A convict's own story of his experiences in the French Penal Settlement in Guiana*, translated by E. C. Ramsden (London: John Lane, 1935).
Kropotkin, Peter. *In Russian and French Prisons* (London: Ward and Downey, 1887).
Lastres, Francisco. *Estudios penitenciarios* (Madrid: Establecimiento tipográfico de Pedro Nuñez, 1887).
Lea, T. S. 'The Island of Fernando do Noronha in 1887' *Proceedings of the Royal Geographical Society*, 10 (1888), 424–34.
Lieber, Francis. *On The Penitentiary System in The United States, and Its Application in France; with an appendix on penal colonies, and also, statistical notes by G. de Beaumont and A. de Tocqueville: Translated from the French, with an introduction, notes and additions.* (Philadelphia: Cery, Lea and Blanchard, 1833).
Livingstone, David, and Edmund Gabriel, 'Explorations into the Interior of Africa'. *Journal of the Royal Geographical Society of London*, 25 (1855), 218–37.
Lombroso-Ferrero, Gina. *Criminal Man; According to the classification of Cesare Lombroso. Briefly summarised by his daughter Gina Lombroso Ferrero* (London: Putnam, 1911).
Long, Edward. *The History of Jamaica or, General Survey of the Antient and Modern State of that Island: With Reflections on its Situation, Settlements, Inhabitants, Climate, Products, Commerce, Laws, and Government, Volume 2* (London: T. Lowndes, 1774).
Lorion, L. *Criminalité et Médicine Judiciaire en Cochinchine* (Lyon: A. Storck, 1888).
Lowis, R. F. *Census of India, 1911. Volume 2: The Andaman and Nicobar Islands* (Calcutta: Office of the Superintendent of Government Printing, 1912).
Census of India, 1921. Volume 2: The Andaman and Nicobar Islands (Calcutta: Office of the Superintendent of Government Printing, 1923).

Lucas, Charles. *Du système penal et du système répressif en general, de la peine de mort en particulier* (Paris: Charles Béchet, 1827).

Maconochie, Alexander. *Australiana: Some thoughts on convict management, and other subjects connected with the Australian penal colonies* (Hobart Town, Van Diemen's Land: J. C. MacDougall, 1839).

Crime and Punishment: The mark system, framed to mix persuasion with punishment, and make their effect improving, yet their operation severe (London: J. Hatchard and Son, 1846).

Man, E. H. 'On the Andamanese and Nicobarese Objects Presented to Major-General Pitt Rivers', *Journal of the Anthropological Institute*, 9 (1882), 268–94

'On the Aboriginal Inhabitants of the Andaman Islands', *Journal of the Anthropological Institute*, 12 (1883), 69–175, 327–434.

The Aboriginal Inhabitants of the Andaman Islands (London: Trübner, 1883).

Sugimoto, Mankichi. 'Reformatory Projects in Hokkaido', *Dainippon Kangoku Kyōkai Zasshi*, 29 (vol. 3, issue 9, 1890), 46.

Maurel, E. *Traité des Maladies Pauldéennes à la Guyane* (Paris: Octave Doin, 1883).

McClelland, James. *On Reformatories for the Destitute and Fallen (being the substance of a paper read at the statistical section of the British Association), to which is appended, Report on Agricultural Colonies, by M. Demetz, Honorary Counsellor of the Imperial Court of Paris* (Glasgow: James Maclehose, 1856).

McNair, J. F. A. *Prisoners Their Own Warders: A record of the convict prison at Singapore in the Straits Settlements established 1825, discontinued 1873, together with a cursory history of the convict establishments at Bencoolen, Penang and Malacca from the year 1797* (Westminster: Archibald Constable and Co., 1899).

Measor, C. P. *The Convict Service: A Letter to Sir George Cornewall Lewis* [Home Secretary] *on the administration, results and expense of the present convict system; with suggestions* (London: Robert Hardwicke, 1861).

Memorandum on the Census of British India, of 1871–72 (London: Eyre and Spottiswoode, 1875).

Merruau, Paul. *Les Convicts En Australie* (Paris: Librarie de L. Hachette et Cie, 1853).

Miller, Gerrit S. 'The Mammals of the Andaman and Nicobar Islands'. *Proceedings of the National Museum*, 24 (1902), 751–96.

Mitchel, John. *Jail Journal; or, Five Years in British Prisons* (New York: Office of the 'Citizen', 1854).

Mitchell, T. L. *Three Expeditions Into the Interior of Eastern Australia; with descriptions of the recently explored region of Australia Felix, and of the present colony of New South Wales, Volume 1* (London: T. and W. Boone, 1839).

Mouat, Fred. J. *Report on the Jails of the Lower Provinces of the Bengal Presidency for 1858–59* (Calcutta: John Gray General Printing Department, 1859).

Report on the Jails of the Lower Provinces of the Bengal Presidency for 1859–60 (Calcutta: Savielle and Cranenburgh Printers, Bengal Printing Co. Ltd, 1860).

'Narrative of an Expedition to the Andaman Islands in 1857'. *Journal of the Royal Geographical Society of London*, 32 (1862), 109–26.

The Narrative of the Honourable John Byron (Commodore in a Late Expedition round the World) Containing an Account of the Great Distresses Suffered by Himself and His Companions on the Coast of Patagonia, From the Year 1740, till their Arrival in England, 1746. With a Description of St. Jago de Chili, and the manners and customs of the inhabitants. Written by himself (London: S. Baker and G. Leigh, 1768).

Neïs, Paul. 'Note sur le poids des cerveaux pesés au pénitencier de Poulo-Condore (Cochinchine)', *Bulletin de la Société d'Anthropologie de Paris*, 3rd series, 5 (1882), 471–92.

Niles, Blair. *Condemned to Devil's Island: The biography of an unknown convict* (London: Jonathan Cape, 1930).

Nordhoff, Charles. 'Alaska as a Possible Penal Colony', in *Proceedings of the National Prison Congress, held at Atlanta, GA., 1886* (Chicago, IL: R. R. Donnelley and Sons, The Lakeside Press, 1887).

Notice sur La Relégation à la Guyane Française et à la Nouvelle-Calédonie: années 1906-1907 (Paris: Melun, 1913).

Notice sur la transportation à la Guyane française et à la Nouvelle-Calédonie pendant les années 1880–1881 (Paris: Imprimerie Nationale, 1884).

Notice sur la transportation à la Guyane française et à la Nouvelle-Calédonie pendant les années 1882–1883 (Paris: Imprimerie Nationale, 1885).

'Number of prisoners sentenced to transportation [Siberia]'. *Dainippon Kangoku Kyōkai Zasshi*, 20 (vol. 2, issue 12, 1889), 8–9.

Ogawa, Shigejiro and Kosuke Tomeoka. 'Prisons and Prisoners'. In Marcus B. Huish (ed.) *Fifty Years of New Japan, Volume I, compiled by Shigenobu Okuma* (London: Smith, Elder and Co., 1910), 296–319.

Orgéas, J. 'Contribution à l'Étude du Non-Cosmopolitisme de l'Homme: La Colonisation de la Guyane par la Transportation, Étude Historique et Démographique', *Archives de médecine navale*, 39 (1883), 161–204; 241–81; 321–59.

La Pathologie Des Races Humaines et le Problème de la Colonisation: étude anthropologique et économique faite à la Guyane Française (Paris: Octave Doin, 1886).

Péan, Charles. *Devil's Island* (London: Hodder and Stoughton, 1939).

Péron, Francis. *A Voyage of Discovery to the Southern Hemisphere: Performed by order of the Emperor Napoleon during the years 1801, 1802, 1803, 1804, one of the naturalists appointed for the expedition . . . translated from the French* (London: Richard Phillips, 1809).

Péron, François. *Voyage de decouvertes aux terres australes: exécuté par ordre de sa Majesté, l'Empereur et Roi, sur les corvettes le Géographe, le Naturaliste et la goëlette le Casuarina, pendant les années 1800, 1801, 1802, 1803 et 1804* (Paris: L'Imprimerie Impériale, 1807).

Phillips, G. W. 'Observations on the treatment of ulcers in the convict hospital at Haddo, in medical charge of Surgeon J. Bird, M.D., and medical officer, Port Blair', *The Indian Medical Gazette*, (1 February 1875), 37–8.

Pierce, Nehemiah. *Origin, Organization and Opening Addresses of the International Prison Congress, January 1 1873* (Springfield, IL: publisher unknown, 1873).

Pilorgerie, Jules de la. *Histoire de Botany Bay, état présent des colonies pénales de'Angleterre dans l'Australie ou examen des effets de la déportation* (Paris: Paulin, 1836).

Pitard, Eugène. 'Étude de 51 cranes de criminels français provenant de la Nouvelle-Calédonie', *Bulletins de la Société d'anthropologie de Paris,* 4th series, 9 (1898), 237–43.

Portman, M. V. *A History of our Relations with the Andamanese, Volume I* (Calcutta: Office of the Superintendent of Government Printing, 1899).

Preston, H. B. 'Descriptions of New Species of Land, Marine and Freshwater Shells from the Andaman Islands', *Records of the India Museum,* 2 (1908), 187–211.

Proceedings of the Annual Congress of the National Prison Association of the United States, held at Indianapolis, Ind., October 15–19 1898 (Pittsburgh: Shaw Bros., 1899).

Proceedings of the National Prison Congress, held at Atlanta, GA., 1886, National Prison Association of the United States of America, (Chicago, IL: R.R. Donnelley and Sons, The Lakeside Press, 1887).

Raikes, Charles. *Notes on the Revolt in the North-Western Provinces of India* (London: Longman, Brown, Green, Longmans and Roberts, 1858).

Randall, C. D. *The Fourth International Prison Congress St. Petersburg, Russia* (Washington DC: Government Printing Office, 1891).

Rangé, C. 'Étude sur l'Épidémie de Fièvre Jaune, ayant sévi aux Îles du Salut (Guyane) du 22 février 1885 au 25 juillet', *Archives de médecine navale,* 45 (1886), 181–206.

Rattray, Alexander. 'A Visit to Fernando Noronha', *Journal of the Royal Geographical Society of London,* 42 (1872), 431–8.

Report on the Census of British India taken on the 17th February 1881 (London: Eyre and Spottiswoode, 1883).

Report of the Committee on Prison Discipline (Calcutta: Baptist Mission Press, 1838).

Report of the Delegates of the United States to the Fifth International Prison Congress held at Paris, France, in July, 1895 (Washington DC: Government Printing Office, 1896).

Reports of the Directors of Convict Prisons on the Discipline and Management of . . . the Convict Establishments at Gibraltar . . . (London: George E. Eyre and William Spottiswoode, 1864–1875).

Report on the Treatment of Leprosy with Gurjun Oil and Other Remedies in Hospitals of the Madras Presidency (Madras: Government Press, 1876).

Report from A Select Committee of the House of Assembly, appointed to inquire into the origin, causes, and progress, of the late insurrection (Barbados: W. Walker, Mercury and Gazette Office/London: T. Cadell and W. Davies, 1818).

Report of the Indian Jails Committee, 1919–20 (London: H.M.'s Stationery Office, 1921).

Report of the Indian Jail Conference Assembled in Calcutta in January – March 1877, under the orders of His Excellency the Governor General in Council, with appendices (Calcutta: Home Secretariat Press, 1877).

Report of the Delegates of the United States to the Fifth International Prison Congress held at Paris, France, in July, 1895 (Washington DC: Government Printing Office, 1896).

'Result of an Examination by Mr James De Ville, of the Heads of 148 Convicts on Board the Convict Ship England, when about to sail for New South Wales in the Spring of 1826 (inc. extract from a letter from G. Thomson to James Wardrop, 9 October 1826)', *The Phrenological Journal and Miscellany*, 4 (October 1826 - November 1827).

Ribeyrolles, Charles. *Les Bagnes d'Afrique, Histoire de la Transportation de décembre* (London: Jeffs Bookshop, 1853).

The Prisons of Africa, Gui[a]na, and Cayenne, translated by Louisa Julia Norman (Melton Mowbray: W. Darley, 1857).

Riou-Kérangal, Emile Yves. 'L'Ankylostome duodénal, observé à Cayenne', *Archives de médecine navale* (1868), 31.

Ross, Ronald. *Mosquito Brigades and How to Organise Them* (London: George Philip and Son, 1902).

Memoirs: With a full account of the great malaria problem and its solution (London: John Murray, 1923).

Ruggles-Brise, Evelyn. *Prison Reform At Home and Abroad: A short history of the international movement since the London Congress, 1872* (London: Macmillan, 1925).

'Russia: Special regulations for using prisoners sentenced to penal transportation with labour [Ussuri railway, Siberia]/ Grant of an amnesty for transported prisoners in Siberia', *Dainippon Kangoku Kyōkai Zasshi*, 38 (vol. 4, issue 6) (1891), 2–7.

Salillas, Rafael. *La vida penal en España* (Madrid: Imprenta de la Revista de la Legislación, 1888).

'Los ñañigos en Ceuta'. *Revista General de Legislacion y Jurisprudencia* 49, 98 (1901), 337–60.

Sarthe, Alm. Lepelletier de la. *Système Pénitentiaire: Le Bagne, La Prison Cellulaire, La Déportation* (Le Mans: Mannoyer, 1853).

Sclater, W. L. *Catalogue of the Mammalia in the Indian Museum, Calcutta, Part II* (Calcutta: Government of India Central Printing Office, 1891).

Scott, James George. *France and Tongking: A narrative of the campaign of 1884 and the occupation of Further India* (London: T. F. Unwin, 1885).

Schomburgk, Richard. *Reisen in Britisch-Guiana in den Jahren 1840-44* (Leipzig: Verlagsbuchhandlung von J.J. Weber, 1847).

Richard Schomburgk's Travels in British Guiana 1840–1844. Translated and edited, with geographical and general indices, and route maps, by Walter E. Roth, Volume I (Georgetown: 'Daily Chronicle' Office, 1922).

Senties, Miguel Bravo. *Revolución Cubana. Deportación a Femando Poo. Relación que hace uno de los deportados* (New York: Hallet de Breen, 1869).

Société Paternelle, *Fondation d'une colonie agricole de jeunes détenus à Mettray* (Paris: Benjamin Duprat, 1839).

'Splenic Abscess in Malarial Fever'. *The Lancet* (27 October 1906), 1159–60.

Statistics of the Population Enumerated in the Andamans, 17th February 1881 (Calcutta: Office of the Superintendent of Government Printing, 1883).

Substance of the Three Reports of the Commissioner of Inquiry, into the Administration of Civil and Criminal Justice in the West Indies, extracted from the parliamentary paper, with the general conclusions, and the commissioner's scheme of improvement, complete and in full (London: Joseph Butterworth and Son, 1827).

Taylor, [Lieutenant]. 'Account of the Ascent of the Peter Botte Mountain, Mauritius, on the 7th September, 1832', *Journal of the Royal Geographical Society of London*, 3 (1833), 99–104.

Temple, Richard C. *Census of India, 1901. Volume 3: The Andaman and Nicobar Islands. Report on the Census* (Calcutta: Office of the Superintendent of Government Printing, 1903).

Imperial Gazetteer of India, Provincial Series: Andaman and Nicobar Islands (Calcutta: Office of the Superintendent of Government Printing, 1908).

Testimonials on Behalf of George Combe, as a Candidate for the Chair of Logic, in the University of Edinburgh. (Edinburgh: John Anderson Jnr, 1836).

Tsukigata, Kiyoshi. 'Hokkaidō kairanki, 1880'. In Tsukigatamurashi hensan iinkai, (ed.) *Tsukigatamurashi* (Tsukigata: Tsukigatamura Yakuba, 1942), 142–56.

Waters, Ernest Edwin. 'Malaria in the Andamans Penal Settlement'. *The Lancet* (13 June 1903), 1657–62.

'Malaria as seen in the Andamans Penal Settlement'. *The Indian Medical Gazette*, 38 (December 1903), 419–20, 444–8.

Whately, Richard. *Remarks on Transportation, and on a recent defence of the system; in a second letter to Earl Grey* (London: B. Fellowes, 1834).

Thoughts on Secondary Punishments, in a letter to Earl Grey: To which are appended, two articles on transportation to New South Wales, and on secondary punishments; and some observations on colonization (London: B. Fellowes, 1832).

White, John. *Journal of a Voyage to New South Wales: With sixty-five plates of nondescript animals, birds, lizards, serpents, curious cones of trees and other natural productions* (London: J. Debrett, 1790).

Wines, E. C. *Transactions of the National Congress of Penitentiary and Reformatory Discipline, held at Cincinnati, Ohio, October 12–18, 1870, Chairman of the Publishing Committee* (Albany, OH: The Argus Company, 1871).

Report on the International Penitentiary Congress of London, held July 3-13, 1872 (Washington DC: Government Printing Office, 1873).

The Actual State of Prison Reform Throughout the Civilized World: A discourse pronounced at the opening of the international prison congress of Stockholm, August 10, 1878 (Stockholm: Centra-Tryckeriet, 1878).

The State of Prisons and of Child-Saving Institutions in the Civilized World (Cambridge, MA: University Press, John Wilson and Son, 1880).

Wines, E. C. (ed.) *Transactions of the Third National Prison Reform Congress, held at Saint Louis, Missouri, May 13–16, 1874: Being the third annual report of the National Prison Association of the United States* (New York: Office of the Association, 1874).

Woolley, J. M. 'The Andamans: The Prevalence of Malaria and its Perverse Effect on the Health of its Convicts', *The Indian Medical Gazette*, 46, 11 (January 1911), 409–15.

'Convict marriages in the Andamans', *The Indian Medical Gazette* 47, 3 (March 1912), 89–94.

'Suicide among Indian Convicts under Transportation'. *The British Journal of Psychiatry* 59, 245 (1913), 335–43.

Young, John. *Narrative of a Residence on the Mosquito Shore: With an account of Truxillo, and the adjacent islands of Bonacca and Roatan; and a vocabulary of the Mosquitian language* (London: Smith, Elder and Co., 1847).

Published Material, Post-1945

Aguirre, Carlos. *The Criminals of Lima and Their Worlds: The prison experience, 1850–1935* (Durham, NC: Duke University Press, 2005).
'Prisons and Prisoners in Modernising Latin America (1800–1940)'. In Frank Dikötter and Ian Brown (eds.) *Cultures of Confinement: A history of the prison in Africa, Asia and Latin America* (London: Hurst and Company, 2007), 14–54.
Alapatt, George K. 'The Sepoy Mutiny of 1857: Indian Indentured Labour and Plantation Politics in British Guiana'. *Journal of Indian History* 59, 1–3 (1981), 295–314.
Albacete, Fernando José Burillo. *La cuestión penitenciaria. Del Sexenio a la Restauración (1868–1913)* (Prensas Universitarias de Zaragoza, 2011).
Aldrich, Robert. 'Out of Ceylon: The Exile of the Last King of Kandy', in Ronit Ricci *Exile in Colonial Asia: Kings, convicts, commemoration* (Honolulu: University of Hawai'i Press, 2016), pp.48–70.
Banished Potentates: Dethroning and exiling indigenous monarchs under British and French colonial rule, 1815–1955 (Manchester University Press, 2018).
Alexander, Jocelyn. 'Prisoners' Memoirs in Zimbabwe: Narratives of Self and Nation'. *Cultural and Social History* 5, 4 (2008), 395–409.
Allaire, Bernard. *La rumeur dorée: Roberval et l'Amérique* (Montreal: Les Éditions La Presse, 2013).
Allport, Henry. 'Gould, William Buelow (1801–1853)', Australian Dictionary of Biography, National Centre of Biography, Australian National University, http://adb.anu.edu.au/biography/gould-william-buelow-2114/text2669, published first in hardcopy 1966.
Amos, Keith. *The Fenians in Australia, 1865–80* (Kensington: New South Wales University Press, 1988).
Anderson, Clare *Convicts in the Indian Ocean: Transportation from South Asia to Mauritius* (Basingstoke: Macmillan, 2000).
'The Execution of Rughobursing: The Political Economy of Convict Transportation and Penal Labour in Early Colonial Mauritius'. *Studies in History*, 19, 2 (2003), 185–97.
'The Politics of Convict Space: Indian Penal Settlements and the Andamans'. In Alison Bashford and Carolyn Strange (eds.) *Isolation: Places and practices of exclusion* (London: Routledge, 2003), pp. 40–55.
Legible Bodies: Race, criminality and colonialism in South Asia (Oxford: Berg, 2004).
'"The Ferringees are Flying - the ship is ours!": The Convict Middle Passage In Colonial South and Southeast Asia, 1790–1860'. *Indian Economic and Social History Review*, 41, 3 (2005), 143–86.
'The Bel Ombre Rebellion: Indian Convicts in Mauritius, 1815–53'. In Gwyn Campbell (ed.) *Abolition and its Aftermath in Indian Ocean Africa and Asia* (London: Routledge, 2005), pp. 50–65.
'Convict Passages in the Indian Ocean, c. 1790–1860'. In Marcus Rediker, Cassandra Pybus, and Emma Christopher (eds.) *Other Middle Passages* (Berkeley: University of California Press, 2007), pp. 129–49.

The Indian Uprising of 1857–8: Prisons, Prisoners and Rebellion (London: Anthem Press, 2007).

'"The Wisdom of the Barbarian": Rebellion, Incarceration, and the Santal Body Politic'. *South Asia: Journal of South Asian Studies*, 31, 2 (2008), 223–40.

'Convicts and Coolies: Rethinking Indentured Labour in the Nineteenth century'. *Slavery and Abolition*, 30, 1 (2009), 93–109.

'Writing Indigenous Women's Lives in the Bay of Bengal, 1789–1906'. *Journal of Social History*, 45, 2 (2011), 480–96.

'Colonization, Kidnap and Confinement in the Andamans Penal Colony, 1771–1864'. *Journal of Historical Geography*, 37, 1 (2011), 68–81l.

Subaltern Lives: Biographies of colonialism in the Indian Ocean world, 1790–1920 (Cambridge University Press, 2012).

'The Age of Revolution in the Indian Ocean, Bay of Bengal and South China Sea: A Maritime Perspective'. *International Review of Social History*, 58, S21 (2013), 229–51.

'After Emancipation: Empires and Imperial Formations'. In Catherine Hall, Nicholas Draper, and Keith McClelland (eds.) *Emancipation and the Remaking of the British Imperial World* (Manchester University Press, 2014), pp.113–27.

'Transnational Histories of Penal Transportation: Punishment, Labour and Governance in the British Imperial World, 1788–1939'. *Australian Historical Studies*, 47, 3 (2016), 381–97.

'Convicts, Carcerality and Cape Colony Connections in the 19th Century'. *Journal of Southern African Studies*, 42, 3 (2016), 429–42.

'A Global History of Exile in Asia, c. 1700–1900'. In Ronit Ricci (ed.) *Exile in Colonial Asia: Kings, convicts, commemoration* (Honolulu: University of Hawai'i Press, 2016), pp. 37–79.

'The Making of an Eclectic Archive: Epistemologies of Global Knowledge in the Papers of J.P. Walker (1823–1906)'. In Rohan Deb Roy and Guy N. A. Attewell (eds.) *Locating the Medical: Explorations in South Asian history* (New Delhi: Oxford University Press, 2017), pp. 151–68.

'The British Indian Empire, 1789–1939'. In Clare Anderson (ed.) *A Global History of Convicts and Penal Colonies* (London: Bloomsbury, 2018), pp. 211–44.

'Convicts, Commodities, and Connections in British Asia and the Indian Ocean, 1789–1866'. *International Review of Social History*, 64, S27 (2019), 205–27.

Anderson, Clare, Eureka Henrich, Sarah Longair, and Katherine Roscoe. 'Empire and Its Aftermath in Four (Post-)Colonial Settings'. In Jacqueline Z. Wilson, Sarah Hodgkinson, Justin Piche, and Kevin Walby (eds.), *The Palgrave Handbook of Prison Tourism* (Basingstoke: Palgrave, 2017), 609–30.

Anderson, Clare and Hamish Maxwell-Stewart. 'Convict Labour and the Western Empires, 1415–1954'. In Robert Aldrich and Kirsten McKenzie (eds.) *The Routledge History of Western Empires* (London: Routledge, 2014), pp. 102–17.

Anderson, Clare, Carrie M. Crockett, Christian G. De Vito, et al. 'Locating Penal Transportation: Punishment, Space, and Place c. 1750 to 1900'. In Karen

M. Morin and Dominique Moran (eds.) *Historical Geographies of Prisons: Unlocking the usable carceral past* (London: Routledge, 2015), pp. 147–67.

Anderson, Clare, Niklas Frykman, Lex Heerma van Voss, and Marcus Rediker. 'Mutiny and Maritime Radicalism in the Age of Revolution: A Global Survey'. *International Review of Social History*, 58, S21, (2013), 1–14.

Anderson, Clare, Madhumita Mazumdar, and Vishvajit Pandya. *New Histories of the Andaman Islands: Landscape, Place and Identity in the Bay of Bengal, 1790–2012* (Cambridge University Press, 2016).

Anderson, Richard. 'The Diaspora of Sierra Leone's Liberated Africans: Enlistment, Forced Migration, and "Liberation" at Freetown, 1808-1863'. *African Economic History*, 41 (2013), 103–40.

Anderson, Richard Peter. *Abolition in Sierra Leone: Re-Building Lives and Identities in Nineteenth-Century West Africa* (Cambridge University Press, 2020).

Anderson, Richard, and Henry B. Lovejoy, eds., *Liberated Africans and the Abolition of the Slave Trade, 1807–1896* (University of Rochester Press, 2020).

Angleviel, Frédéric. *Le Paradou: De l'hôpital du Marais au centre hospitalier Albert-Bousequet 1868-2014* (Nouméa: Centre hospitalier Albert-Bousquet, 2013).

Appadurai, Arjun. 'Number in the Colonial Imagination'. In Carol A. Breckenridge and Peter van der Veer, (eds.) *Orientalism and the Postcolonial Predicament: Perspectives on South Asia* (Philadelphia: University of Pennsylvania Press, 1993), pp. 314–39.

Applebaum, Anne. *Gulag: A history of the Soviet camps* (London: Penguin, 2003).

de Aranzadi, Isabela. 'El legado cubano en África. Ñáñigos deportados a Fernando Poo. Memoria viva y archivoescrito', *Afro-Hispanic Review*, 31, 1 (2012), 29–60.

'Cuban heritage in Africa: Deported Ñáñigos to Fernando Po in the 19th century', *African Sociological Review*, 18, 2 (2014), 2–41.

Armitage, David, and Sanjay Subrahmanyam (eds.). *The Age of Revolutions in Global Context, c. 1760–1840* (Basingstoke: Palgrave, 2009).

Arnold, David. *Colonizing the Body: State medicine and epidemic disease in nineteenth-century India* (Berkeley: University of California Press: 1993).

The New Cambridge History of India III.5: Science, technology and medicine in colonial India (Cambridge University Press, 2000).

'The Self and the Cell: Indian Prison Narratives as Life Histories'. In David Arnold and Stuart Blackburn (eds.) *Telling Lives in India: Biography, autobiography, and life history* (Bloomington: Indiana University Press, 2004), pp. 29–53.

The Tropics and the Traveling Gaze: India, landscape, and science, 1800–1856 (Seattle: University of Washington Press, 2006).

Atkinson, Juliette, 'William Jeffs, Victorian Bookseller and Publisher of French Literature'. *The Library: The Transactions of the Bibliographical Society*, 13, 3 (2012), 256–78.

Ausubel, H. 'General Booth's Scheme of Social Salvation'. *American Historical Review*, 56, 3 (1951), 519–25.

Badcock, Sarah. *A Prison without Walls? Eastern Siberian exile in the last years of tsarism* (Oxford University Press, 2016).

Badcock, Sarah and Judith Pallot, 'Russia and the Soviet Union from the Nineteenth to the Twenty-First Century'. In Clare Anderson (ed.)

A Global History of Convicts and Penal Colonies (London: Bloomsbury, 2018) pp. 271–305.
Ballantyne, Tony. 'Mobility, Empire, Colonisation', *History Australia*, 11, 2 (2016), 7–37.
Ballantyne Tony and Antoinette Burton, (eds.). *World Histories from Below* (London: Bloomsbury, 2016).
Banner, Stuart. 'Why *Terra Nullius?* Anthropology and Property Law in Early Australia', *Law and History Review*, 23, 1 (2005), 95–132.
Bantman, Constance. 'Introduction'. In Constance Bantman and Suriani da Silva (eds.). *The Foreign Political Press in Nineteenth-Century London: Politics from a distance* (London: Bloomsbury, 2018).
Barbançon, Louis-José. *L'archipel des forçats. Histoire du bagne de Nouvelle-Calédonie (1863–1931)* (Lille: Presses universitaires du Septentrion, 2003).
'Les transportés de 1848 (statistiques, analyse, commentaires)', *Criminocorpus* (2008). http://journals.openedition.org/criminocorpus/148.
'Transporter les Insurgés de juin 1848', *Criminocorpus* (2008). http://journals.openedition.org/criminocorpus/153.
Barbançon, Louis-José and Christophe Sand. *Caledoun: histoire des Arabes et Berbères de Nouvelle-Calédonie* (Bourail: Association des Arabes et Amis de Nouvelle-Calédonie, 2013).
Barber, Peter. 'Malaspina and George III, Brambila, and Watling: Three discovered drawings of Sydney and Parramatta by Fernando Brambila'. *Australian Journal of Art*, 11 (1993), 31–55.
Barker, Anthony. *Slavery and Anti-Slavery in Mauritius, 1810–33: The conflict between economic expansion and humanitarian reform under British rule* (Basingstoke: Palgrave, 1996).
Barnwell, Ashley. 'Convict shame to convict chic: Intergenerational Memory and Family Histories'. *Memory Studies*, 12, 4 (2019), 398–411.
Barry, John V. 'Maconochie, Alexander (1787–1860)', Australian Dictionary of Biography, National Centre of Biography, Australian National University, http://adb.anu.edu.au/biography/maconochie-alexander-2417/text3207, published first in hardcopy 1967.
Bashford, Alison and Joyce E. Chaplin, *The New Worlds of Thomas Robert Malthus: Rereading the principle of population* (Princeton University Press, 2016).
Bates, Crispin et al., eds., *Mutiny at the Margins: New perspectives on the Indian uprising of 1857* [6 vols] (London: Sage, 2013–2014).
Bateson, Charles. 'Browning, Colin Arrott (1791–1856)', Australian Dictionary of Biography, National Centre of Biography, Australian National University, http://adb.anu.edu.au/biography/browning-colin-arrott-1838/text2121, published first in hardcopy 1966.
Bayly, C. A. *The New Cambridge History of India II: Indian society and the making of the British Empire* (Cambridge University Press, 1988).
Bayly, Susan. 'Caste and "race" in the colonial ethnography of India'. In Peter Robb (ed.) *The Concept of Race in South Asia* (New Delhi: Oxford University Press, 1997), pp. 165–218.
Beattie, Peter M. '"Born Under the Cruel Rigor of Captivity, the Supplicant Left It Unexpectedly by Committing a Crime": Categorizing and Punishing Slave Convicts in Brazil, 1830–1897'. *The Americas*, 66, 1 (2009), 11–55.

Punishment in Paradise: Race, slavery, human rights, and a nineteenth-century penal colony (Durham, NC: Duke University Press, 2015).

Beckles, Hilary McD. *Bussa: The 1816 revolution in Barbados* (Cave Hill and St Ann's Garrison, Barbados: University of the West Indies and Barbados Museum and Historical Society: 1998).

'The Slave-Drivers War: Bussa and the 1816 Barbados Slave Rebellion', *Boletín de Estudios Latinoamericanos y del Caribe*, 39 (1985), 85–110.

Bender, Gerald J. *Angola under the Portuguese: The myth and the reality* (London: Heinemann, 1978).

Beer, Daniel. *Renovating Russia: The human sciences and the fate of liberal modernity, 1880–1930* (Ithaca, NY: Cornell University Press, 2008).

'Penal Transportation to Siberia and the Limits of State Power, 1801–81', *Kritika: Explorations in Russian and Eurasian History*, (2015), 621–50.

The House of the Dead: Siberian exile under the Tsars (London: Allen Lane, 2016).

Beier, A. L. 'Identity, Language, and Resistance in the Making of the Victorian "Criminal Class": Mayhew's Convict Revisited', *Journal of British Studies*, 44, 3 (2005), 499–15.

Bender, Jill C. *The 1857 Uprising and the British Empire* (Cambridge University Press, 2016).

Bennett, J. M. 'Bigge, John Thomas (1780–1843)', Australian Dictionary of Biography, National Centre of Biography, Australian National University, http://adb.anu.edu.au/biography/bigge-john-thomas-1779/text1999, published first in hardcopy 1966.

Bensimon, Fabrice. 'The French Exiles and the British'. In Sabine Freitag (ed.) *Exiles From European Revolutions: Refugees in Mid-Victorian England* (Oxford: Berghahn, 2003), pp. 88–102.

Benton, Lauren. *A Search for Sovereignty. Law and geography in European empires, 1400–1900* (Cambridge University Press, 2010).

Bergantz, Alexis. '"The Scum of France": Australian Anxieties towards French Convicts in the Nineteenth Century'. *Australian Historical Studies*, 49, 2 (2018), 150–66.

Bhattacharya, Sanjoy, Mark Harrison, and Michael Worboys. *Fractured States: Smallpox, public health and vaccination policy in British India, 1800–1947* (New Delhi: Orient Longman, 2001).

Bisman, Jayne Elizabeth. 'The Census as Accounting Artefact: A Research Note with Illustrations from the Early Australian Colonial Period'. *Accounting History*, 14 (2009), 293–314.

Bloom, Samuel William. *The Word as Scalpel: A history of medical sociology* (Oxford University Press, 2002).

Boase, G. C. (revised by Elizabeth Baigent), 'Edmonstone, Sir Archibald, third baronet (1795–1871)', *Oxford Dictionary of National Biography* (Oxford University Press, 2004); online edn, 23 September 2004. https://doi.org/10.1093/ref:odnb/8496.

Boehmer, Elleke. 'Robben Island'. *Journal of Postcolonial Writing*, 41, 2 (2005), 223–31.

Bolland, Nigel O. *The Formation of a Colonial Society: Belize, from Conquest to Crown Colony* (Baltimore, MD: Johns Hopkins University Press: 1977).

Borch, Merete. 'Rethinking the origins of *terra nullius*', *Australian Historical Studies*, 32, 117 (2001), 222–39.
Botsman, Daniel V. *Punishment and Power in the Making of Modern Japan* (Princeton University Press, 2005).
Boulind, Richard. 'Shipwreck and Mutiny in Spain's Galleys on the Santo Domingo Station, 1583', *The Mariner's Mirror*, 58, 3 (1972), 297–330.
Boyce, James. *Van Diemen's Land* (Melbourne, VIC: Black Inc., 2008).
Bradley, James and Cassandra Pybus, 'From Slavery to Servitude: The Australian Exile of Elizabeth and Constance'. *Journal of Australian Colonial History*, 9 (2007), 29–50.
Braidwood, Stephen. *Black Poor and White Philanthropists: London's Blacks and the foundation of the Sierra Leone Settlement 1786–1791* (Liverpool University Press, 1994).
Braithwaite, John. 'Crime in a Convict Republic'. *The Modern Law Review*, 64, 1 (2001), 11–50.
Branch, Daniel. 'Imprisonment and Colonialism in Kenya, c. 1930–1952: Escaping the Carceral Archipelago', *The International Journal of African Historical Studies*, 38, 2 (2005), 239–65.
Brennan, Russell and Jonathan Richards, '"The Scum of French Criminals and Convicts": Australia and New Caledonia Escapees". *History Compass*, 12, 7 (2014), 559–66.
Brown, Bruce W. The Machine Breaker Convicts from the *Proteus* and the *Eliza*, MA thesis, University of Tasmania, 2004.
Brown, Ian. 'A Commissioner Calls: Alexander Paterson and Colonial Burma's Prisons'. *Journal of Southeast Asian Studies*, 38, 2 (2007), 293–308.
Brown, John. 'Charles Booth and Labour Colonies, 1889–1905'. *The Economic History Review*, 21, 2 (1968), 349–60.
Browne, Janet *Charles Darwin: The power of place* (London: Pimlico, 2003).
 Charles Darwin: Voyaging (London: Pimlico, 2003).
Buckingham, Jane. *Leprosy in Colonial South India: Medicine and confinement* (Basingstoke: Palgrave Macmillan, 2001).
Buggeln, Marc. 'Forced Labour in Nazi Concentration Camps'. In Christian G. De Vito and Alex Lichtenstein (eds.) *Global Convict Labour* (Leiden: Brill, 2014), pp. 333–60
Bullard, Alice. *Exile to Paradise: Savagery and civilization in Paris and the South Pacific* (Stanford University Press, 2000).
Bulmer, Martin. 'W. E. B. Du Bois as a Social Investigator: The Philadelphia Negro 1899'. In Martin Bulmer, Kevin Bales, and Kathryn Kish Sklar (eds.) *The Social Survey in Historical Perspective*, (Cambridge University Press, 1991), pp. 170–88.
Bulmer, Martin, Kevin Bales, and Kathryn Kish Sklar (eds.). *The Social Survey in Historical Perspective, 1880–1940* (Cambridge University Press, 1991).
Buntman, Fran Lisa. 'How Best to Resist? Robben Island after 1976'. In Harriet Deacon (ed.) *The Island: a history of Robben Island 1488–1990* (Cape Town: David Philip, 1997), pp. 137–67.
 'Resistance on Robben Island 1963–1976'. In Harriet Deacon (ed.) *The Island: A history of Robben Island 1488–1990* (Cape Town: David Philip, 1997), pp. 93–136.

Robben Island and Prisoner Resistance to Apartheid (Cambridge University Press, 2003).

Burnard, Trevor. 'European Migration to Jamaica, 1655–1780'. *William and Mary Quarterly*, 53, 4 (1996), 769–96.

Campbell, Charles. *The Intolerable Hulks: British shipboard confinement, 1776–1857* (Tucson, AZ: Fenestra Books, 2001).

Campbell, Mavis C. *Back to Africa. George Ross and the Maroons: From Nova Scotia to Sierra Leone* (Trenton, NJ: Africa World Press, 1993).

Campos, Ricardo and Rafael Huertas. 'Criminal anthropology in Spain'. In Paul Knepper and P. J. Ystehede (eds.) *The Cesare Lombroso Handbook* (London: Routledge, 2013), pp. 309–23.

Candlin, Kit. *The Last Caribbean Frontier, 1795–1815* (Basingstoke: Palgrave, 2012).

'The role of the enslaved in the "Fedon Rebellion" of 1795'. *Slavery and Abolition*, 39, 4 (2018), 685–707.

Caplan, Jane and Nikolaus Wachsmann (eds.). *Concentration Camps in Nazi Germany: The new histories* (London: Routledge, 2010).

Carey, Hilary. *Empire of Hell: Religion and the campaign to end convict transportation in the British Empire, 1788–1875* (Cambridge University Press, 2019).

Carey, Jane, and Jane Lydon (eds.). *Indigenous Networks: Mobility, connections and exchange* (Abingdon: Routledge, 2014).

Carlyle, E. I. (revised by Lynn Milne). 'Montagu, John (1797–1853)', *Oxford Dictionary of National Biography* (Oxford University Press, 2004); online edn, 23 September 2004. https://doi.org/10.1093/ref:odnb/19028.

Carter, Marina. *Servants, Sirdars and Settlers: Indians in Mauritius, 1834–1874* (New Delhi: Oxford University Press, 1995).

Carter, Marina, V. Govinden, and S. Peerthum, *The Last Slaves: Liberated Africans in 19th-century Mauritius* (Port-Louis, Mauritius: Centre for Research on Indian Ocean Societies, 2003).

Causer, Tim. '"On British Felony the Sun Never Sets": Narratives of Political Prisoners in New South Wales and Van Diemen's Land, 1838–53'. *Cultural and Social History* 5, 4 (2008): 423–35.

'Anti-transportation, "unnatural crime", and the "horrors" of Norfolk Island'. *Journal of Australian Colonial History*, 14 (2012), 230–40.

Cave, Eleanor. Flora Tasmaniae: Tasmanian naturalists and imperial botany, 1829–1860, PhD thesis, University of Tasmania, 2012.

Cavert, William. 'At the Edge of an Empire: Plague, State and Identity in New Caledonia, 1899–1900'. *The Journal of Pacific History*, 51, 1 (2016), 1–20.

Chakraborty, Titas. 'Slave trading and slave resistance in the Indian Ocean world: the case of early eighteenth-century Bengal'. *Slavery and Abolition*, 40, 4 (2019), 706–26.

Champs, Emmanuelle de. *Enlightenment and Utility: Bentham in French, Bentham in France* (Cambridge University Press, 2015).

Charrière, Henri. *Papillon* (Paris: Robert Laffont, 1969).

Chaturvedi, Vinayak. 'A Revolutionary's Biography: The Case of V. D. Savarkar'. *Postcolonial Studies* 16, 2 (2013), 124–39.

Chekov, Anton. *The Island of Sakhalin: A journey to Sakhalin*, translated by Luba Terpack and Michael Terpak (New York: Washington Square Press, 1967).
  Sakhalin Island, translated by Brian Reeve, (London: OneWorld Classics, 2007).
Chopra, Ruma. *Almost Home: Maroons between slavery and freedom in Jamaica, Nova Scotia, and Sierra Leone* (New Haven, CT: Yale University Press, 2018).
Christie, Clive. 'British Literary Travellers'. *Modern Asian Studies*, 28, 4 (1994), 673–737.
Christopher, Emma. *A Merciless Place: The lost story of Britain's convict disaster in Africa* (Oxford University Press), 2011.
Christopher, Emma and Hamish Maxwell-Stewart. 'Convict Transportation in Global Context, c. 1700–88'. In Alison Bashford and Stuart Macintyre (eds.) *The Cambridge History of Australia, Volume 1: Indigenous and colonial Australia* (Cambridge University Press, 2013), pp. 68–90.
Clendinnen, Inga. *Dancing With Strangers: Europeans and Australians at first contact* (Cambridge University Press, 2005).
Clough, Marshall S. *Mau Mau Memoirs: History, memory and politics* (Boulder, CO: Lynne Rienner Publishers, 1998).
Coats, Ann Veronica and Philip MacDougall (eds.). *The Naval Mutinies of 1797: Unity and perseverance* (Woodbridge: Boydell and Brewer, 2011).
Coates, Timothy J. *Convicts and Orphans: Forced and state-sponsored colonizers in the Portuguese Empire, 1550–1755* (Stanford University Press, 2001).
  'Preliminary Considerations on European Forced Labor in Angola, 1880–1930: Individual Redemption and the "Effective Occupation" of the Colony'. *Portuguese Literary & Cultural Studies 15/16: Remembering Angola* (2010), 79–106.
  Convict Labor in the Portuguese Empire, 1740–1932: Redefining the empire with forced labor and new imperialism (Leiden: Brill, 2014).
  'The Long View of Convict Labour in the Portuguese Empire, 1415–1932'. In Christian G. De Vito and Alex Lichtenstein (eds.) *Global Convict Labour* (Leiden: Brill, 2014), pp. 144–67.
  'The Depósito de Degredados in Luanda, Angola: Binding and Building the Portuguese Empire with Convict Labour, 1880s to 1932'. *International Review of Social History*, 63, S26 (2018), 115–67.
  'The Portuguese Empire, 1100–1932'. In Clare Anderson (ed) *A Global History of Convicts and Penal Colonies* (London: Bloomsbury, 2018), pp. 37–64.
Cohen, Robin and Paola Toninato (eds.). *The Creolization Reader: Studies in mixed identities and cultures* (London: Routledge, 2009).
Cohn, Bernard S. *An Anthropologist among the Historians and Other Essays* (New Delhi: Oxford University Press, 1987).
Coleman, Deirdre. 'Bulama and Sierra Leone: Utopian Islands and Visionary Interiors'. In Rod Edmond and Vanessa Smith (eds.) *Islands in History and Representation* (London: Routledge, 2003), pp. 63–80.
Collin, Léon. *Des Hommes et des Bagnes: Guyane et Nouvelle-Calédonie un médecin au bagne 1906–1913* (Saint-Laurent-du-Maroni: Éditions Libertalia, 2015).

Collin, Philippe. 'Poètes au bagne de Nouvelle-Calédonie: Vies et écrits de Julien Lespès et Julien de Sanary ... ou comment survivre par l'écriture', *Criminocorpus* (2015). http://criminocorpus.hypotheses.org/10490.

The Convict Probation System: Van Diemen's Land 1839–1854: A study of the probation system of convict discipline; together with C. J. La Trobe's 1847 report on its operation, and the 1845 report of James Boyd on the probation station at Darlington, Maria Island. Commentary and notes by Ian Brand (Hobart, TAS: Blubber Head Press, 1990).

Coote Anne, Alison Haynes, Jude Philp, and Simon Ville. 'When commerce, science, and leisure collaborated: the nineteenth-century global trade boom in natural history collections', *Journal of Global History*, 12, 3 (2017), 319–39.

Cooter, Roger. *The Cultural Meaning of Popular Science: Phrenology and the Organization of Consent in Nineteenth-Century Britain* (Cambridge University Press, 1984).

Cordillot, Michel. *La Sociale en Amérique: Dictionnaire biographique du mouvement social francophone aux États-Unis, 1848-1922* (Paris: Éditions de l'Atelier, 2002).

'TASSILIER Théodore, Louis', *Dictionnaire biographique du mouvement social francophone aux États-Unis* (2014) https://maitron.fr/spip.php?article159457.

Corrado, Sharyl M. The 'End of the Earth': Sakhalin Island in the Russian imperial imagination, 1849–1906. PhD thesis, University of Illinois at Urbana–Champaign, 2010.

Cox, Edward L. 'Fedon's Rebellion 1795–96: Causes and Consequences'. *The Journal of Negro History*, 67, 1 (1982), 7–19.

Craton, Michael. *Testing the Chains: Resistance to Slavery in the British West Indies* (Ithaca, NY: Cornell University Press, 1982).

Cribb, Robert. 'Convict Exile and Penal Settlement in Colonial Indonesia', *Journal of Colonialism and Colonial History*, 18, 3 (2017). doi:10.1353/cch.2017.0043.

Crockett, Carrie. Excavating Exile: Women of the Sakhalin Penal Colony, 1868–1905, PhD thesis, University of Leicester, 2020.

Crossley, Ceri. 'Using and Transforming the French Countryside: The "Colonies Agricoles" (1820–1850)'. *French Studies* 44, 1 (1991), 36–54.

Cullen, M. J. *The Statistical Movement in Early Victorian Britain: The Foundations of Empirical Social Research* (New York: Harvester Press, 1975).

Curthoys, Ann. 'Genocide in Tasmania: The History of an Idea'. In A. Dirk Moses (ed.) *Empire, Colony, Genocide: Conquest, occupation, and subaltern resistance in world history* (Oxford: Berghahn, 2008), pp. 229–252.

'The Beginnings of Transportation in Western Australia: Banishment, Forced Labour, and Punishment at the Aboriginal Prison on Rottnest Island before 1850', *Studies in Western Australian History Studies in Western Australian History*, 34 (2020), 59–78.

Curti, Merle. 'The Impact of the Revolutions of 1848 on American Thought'. *Proceedings of the American Philosophical Society*, 93, 3 (1949), 209–15.

Cutter, Donald C. 'Introduction'. In Andrew David, Felipe Fernandez-Armesto, Carlos Novi, and Glyndwr Williams (eds.) *The Malaspina*

Expedition 1789–1794: Journal of the Voyage by Alejandro Malaspina, Volume 1 Cadiz to Panama (London: The Hakluyt Society, 2001), lxxi.
da Costa, Emilia Viotti. *Crowns of Glory, Tears of Blood: The Demerara slave rebellion of 1823* (Oxford University Press, 1994).
Dabydeen, David and Brinsley Samaroo (eds.). *India in the Caribbean* (London: Hansib, 1987).
Dalby, Jonathan. *Crime and Punishment in Jamaica, 1756–1856* (Mona, Jamaica: University of the West Indies Press, 2000).
Dalrymple, William. *The Last Mughal: The fall of a dynasty, Delhi, 1857* (London: Bloomsbury, 2006).
Dark, Eleanor. 'Bennelong (c. 1764–1813)', Australian Dictionary of Biography, National Centre of Biography, Australian National University, http://adb.anu.edu.au/biography/bennelong-1769/text1979, published first in hardcopy 1966.
Darwin, Lauren. Convict Transportation in the Age of Abolition, 1787–1807. PhD thesis, University of Hull, 2016.
Daunton, Martin and Rick Halpern (eds.). *Empire and Others: British encounters with indigenous peoples, 1600–1850* (Philadelphia: University of Pennsylvania Press, 1999).
David, Andrew, Felipe Fernandez-Armesto, Carlos Novi, and Glyndwr Williams (eds.), translated by Sylvia Jamieson, *The Malaspina Expedition 1789–1794: Journal of the Voyage by Alejandro Malaspina, Volume III Manila to Cadiz* (London: The Hakluyt Society, 2004).
Davie, Neil. *Tracing the Criminal: The rise of scientific criminology in Britain 1860–1920* (Oxford: The Bardwell Press, 2005).
Davis, T. A. W. 'Butterfly Migrations in British Guiana', *Proceedings of the Royal Entomological Society of London*, 36, 4-6 (1961), 49–56.
Dawdy, Shannon Lee. *Building the Devil's Empire: French colonial New Orleans* (University of Chicago Press, 2009).
  'Connected Singularities: Convict Labour in Late Colonial Spanish America (1760s-1800)'. In Christian G. De Vito and Anne Gerritsen (eds.) *Micro-Spatial Histories of Global Labour* (London: Palgrave, 2018), pp. 171–202.
  'Punitive Entanglements: Connected Histories of Penal Transportation, Deportation, and Incarceration in the Spanish Empire (1830s–1898)'. *International Review of Social History*, 63, S26 (2018), 176 (169–89).
  'The Spanish Empire, 1500-1898', in Clare Anderson (ed.) *A Global History of Convicts and Penal Colonies* (London: Bloomsbury, 2018), pp. 65–95.
De Vito Christian G. and Alex Lichtenstein, (eds.). *Global Convict Labour* (Leiden: Brill, 2015).
De Vito, Christian G., Clare Anderson, and Ulbe Bosma, 'Penal Transportation, Deportation and Exile: Perspectives from the Colonies in the Nineteenth and Twentieth Centuries'. *International Review of Social History*, 63, S26 (2018), 1–24.
Deacon, Shannon Lee. (ed.). *The Island: A history of Robben Island 1488–1990* (Cape Town: David Philip, 1997).

Deacon, Desley, Penny Russell, and Angela Woollacott (eds.). *Transnational Lives: Biographies of global modernity, 1700–present* (Basingstoke: Palgrave Macmillan, 2010).

Dekker, Jeroen J. H. 'Punir, sauver et éduquer: la colonie agricole "Nederlandsch Mettray" et la rééducation résidentielle aux Pays-Bas, en France, en Allemagne et en Angleterre entre 1814 et 1914'. *Le Mouvement Social*, 153 (1990), 63–90.

   The Will to Change the Child: Re-education homes for children at risk in nineteenth century Western Europe (Frankfurt am Main: Peter Lang, 2001).

Delacour, M. Jean. 'Live Bird Collections in French Guiana', *Animal Kingdom: Bulletin of the New York Zoological Society*, 25, 3 (1922), 62–4.

Delnore, Allyson Jaye. Political Convictions: French Deportation Projects in the Age of Revolution, 1791—1854, PhD thesis, University of Virginia, 2004.

   'Empire by Example? Deportees in France and the Re-Making of a Modern Empire, 1846-1854'. *French Politics, Culture and Society*, 33, 1 (2015), 33—54.

Delbourgo, James and Nicholas Dew (eds.). *Science and Empire in the Atlantic World* (London: Routledge, 2008).

Dirks, Nicholas. *Castes of Mind: Colonialism and the making of modern India* (Princeton University Press, 2001).

Docker, John. 'Are Settler-Colonies Inherently Genocidal: Re-reading Lemkin'. In A. Dirk Moses (ed.) *Empire, Colony, Genocide: Conquest, occupation, and subaltern resistance in world history* (Oxford: Berghahn, 2008), pp. 81–101.

Donet-Vincent, Danielle. *De soleil et de silences. Histoire des bagnes de Guyane* (Paris: La boutique de l'histoire, 2003).

Donoghue, John and Evelyn P. Jennings, (eds.). *Building the Atlantic Empires: Unfree labor and imperial states in the political economy of capitalism, ca. 1500–1914* (Leiden: Brill, 2015).

Donohoe, James Hugh. *The Forgotten Australians: The non-Anglo or Celtic convicts and exiles* (Sydney, NSW: published by the author, 1991).

Drescher, Seymour. 'Capitalism and Slavery after Fifty Years'. *Slavery and Abolition*, 18, 3 (1997), 212–27.

Driver, C. J. 'The View From Makana Island: Some Recent Prison Books from South Africa'. *Journal of Southern African Studies*, 2, 1 (1975), 102–19.

Driver, Felix. 'Discipline without Frontiers? Representations of the Mettray Reformatory Colony in Britain, 1840–1880'. *Journal of Historical Sociology*, 3, 3 (1990), 272–93.

Duffield, Ian. 'From Slave Colonies to Penal Colonies; the West Indians Transported to Australia'. *Slavery and Abolition*, 7, 1 (1986), 25–45.

   'The Life and Death of "Black" John Goff: Aspects of the Black Convict Contribution to Resistance Patterns During the Transportation Era in Eastern Australia'. *Australian Journal of Politics and History*, 33, 1 (1987), 30–44.

   '"Stated This Offence": High-Density Convict Micro-Narratives'. In Lucy Frost and Hamish Maxwell-Stewart (eds.) *Chain Letters: Narrating convict lives* (Melbourne University Press, 2001), pp. 119–35.

'A Storm in a Teapot? Five Stories About the Trials of Priscilla's Life and their Household Remedy, Arsenic Trioxide'. *To the Islands: Australia and the Caribbean*, special edition of *Australian Cultural History*, 21 (2002), 19–31.

'Cutting Out and Taking Liberties: Australia's Convict Pirates, 1790–1829', *International Review of Social History*, 58, S21 (2013), 197–227.

Duly, Lesley C. '"Hottentots to Hobart and Sydney": The Cape Supreme Court's Use of Transportation, 1828–38'. *Australian Journal of Politics and History*, 25 (1979), 39–50.

Dunbar, Diane (ed.). *Thomas Bock: Convict engraver, society portraitist: exhibition and catalogue* (Launceston, TAS: Queen Victoria Museum and Art Gallery, 1991).

Dunmore, John (ed.). *The Journal of Jean-François de Galaup de la Pérouse 1785–1788*, (London: The Hakluyt Society, 1994), vol. 2.

Dutton, Jacqueline. 'Imperial Eyes on the Pacific Prize: French Visions of a Perfect Penal Colony in the South Seas'. In John West-Sooby (ed.) *Discovery and Empire: The French in the South Seas* (University of Adelaide Press, 2013), pp. 245–82.

Dyer, Colin. *The French Explorers and Sydney* (St Lucia: University of Queensland Press, 2009).

Edington, Claire E. *Beyond the Asylum: Mental illness in French colonial Vietnam* (Ithaca, NY: Cornell University Press, 2019).

Edmonds, Penelope. 'The Intimate, Urbanising Frontier: Native Camps and Settler Colonialism's Violent Array of Spaces around Early Melbourne'. In Banivanua Mar and Penelope Edmonds (eds.) *Making Settler Colonial Space: Perspectives on race, place and identity* (Basingstoke: Palgrave, 2010), pp. 129–54.

Edwards, Elizabeth. 'Science Visualized: E. H. Man in the Andaman Islands'. In Elizabeth Edwards (ed.) *Anthropology and Photography, 1860–1920* (London: Royal Anthropological Institute, 1994), pp. 108–21.

Edwards, Ryan. 'From the Depths of Patagonia: The Ushuaia Penal Colony and the Nature of "The End of the World"'. *Hispanic American Historical Review*, 94, 2 (2014), 272–302.

Edwards, Ryan C. 'Convicts and Conservation: Inmate labor, fires and forestry in southernmost Argentina'. *Journal of Historical Geography*, 56, 2 (2017), 1–13.

'Post-Colonial Latin America, since 1800'. In Clare Anderson (ed.) *A Global History of Convicts and Penal Colonies* (London: Bloomsbury, 2018), pp. 245–70.

Ekirch, Roger. *Bound for America: The transportation of British convicts to the colonies, 1718–1775* (Oxford: Clarendon Press, 1987).

Elam, J. Daniel. 'Commonplace Anti-Colonialism: Bhagat Singh's Jail Notebook and the Politics of Reading'. *South Asia: Journal of South Asian Studies*, 39, 3 (2016), 592–607.

Elam, J. Daniel and Chris Moffat (eds.). 'Writing Revolution: Practice, History, Politics in Modern South Asia', *South Asia: Journal of South Asian Studies*, 39, 3 (2016).

Endersby, Jim. *Imperial Nature: Joseph Hooker and the practices of Victorian science* (University of Chicago Press, 2008).

Ernst, Waltraud and Bernard Harris (eds.). *Race, Science and Medicine, 1700–1960* (London: Routledge, 1999).

Evans, Raymond, '19 June 1822: Creating "An Object of Real Terror": the tabling of the first Bigge Report'. In Martin Crotty and David Andrew Roberts (eds.) *Turning Points in Australian History* (Sydney: University of New South Wales Press, 2009), pp. 48–61

Evans, Raymond and William Thorpe, 'Power, Punishment and Penal Labour: *Convict Workers* and Moreton Bay'. *Australian Historical Studies*, 25, 98 (1992), 90–111.

Evans, Richard J. *Tales from the German Underworld: Crime and punishment in the nineteenth century* (New Haven, CT: Yale University Press, 1998).

Everill, Bronwyn. *Abolition and Empire in Sierra Leone and Liberia* (Basingstoke: Palgrave, 2012).

Fennel Philip and Marie King, *John Devoy's* Catalpa *Expedition* (New York University Press, 2006).

Fernández-Armesto, Felipe. *Pathfinders: A global history of exploration* (London: W. W. Norton and Co., 2007).

Finch-Boyer, Heloise. 'Indian Ocean Cosmopolitanisms in the early 19th century: linking Cape Town, Delagoa Bay and Sainte Marie', conference paper presented at 'Durban and Cape Town as Indian Ocean Port Cities: Reconsidering Southern African Studies from the Indian Ocean', University of the Western Cape, South Africa, 12 September 2014.

Fitzpatrick, Matthew. 'New South Wales in Africa? The Convict Colonialism Debate in Imperial Germany'. *Itinerario*, 37, 1 (2013), 59–72.

Ford, Lisa and David Andrew Roberts. 'New South Wales Penal Settlements and the Transformation of Secondary Punishment in the Nineteenth-Century British Empire', *Journal of Colonialism and Colonial History*, 15, 3 (2014). doi:10.1353/cch.2014.0038.

Forlivesi, Luc, Georges-François Pottier, and Sophie Chassat, *Éduquer et punir. La colonie agricole et pénitentiaire de Mettray (1839–1937)* (Presses Universitaires de Rennes, 2005).

Forster, Colin. *France and Botany Bay: The lure of a penal colony* (Melbourne University Press, 1996).

Forsythe, Bill. 'Griffiths, Arthur George Frederick (1838–1908)', *Oxford Dictionary of National Biography* (Oxford University Press, 2004); online edn, 23 September 2004. https://doi.org/10.1093/ref:odnb/33581.

Forth, Aidan. *Barbed-Wire Imperialism: Britain's empire of camps, 1876–1903* (Oakland: University of California Press, 2017).

Fortin, Jeffrey A. '"Blackened Beyond Our Native Hue": Removal, Identity and the Trelawney Maroons on the Margins of the Atlantic World, 1796–1800'. *Citizenship Studies*, 10, 1 (2006), 5–34.

Foucault, Michel. *Madness and Civilization: A history of insanity in the age of reason* (London: Tavistock, 1967).

Discipline and Punish: the birth of the prison (New York: Vintage, 1975).

Foxhall, Katherine. *Health, Medicine, and the Sea: Australian Voyages, c. 1815-1860* (Manchester University Press, 2012).

French Designs on Colonial New South Wales: François Péron's Memoir on the English Settlements in New Holland, Van Diemen's Land and the Archipelagos of the Great Pacific Ocean, translated and edited with an introduction, notes and appendices by Jean Fornasiero and John West-Sooby (Adelaide, SA: Friends of the State Library of South Australia, 2014).

Freycinet, Louis. *Reflections on New South Wales, 1788–1839*. Tom B. Cullity (ed.) (Potts Point, NSW: Hordern House, 2001).

Fried, Albert and Richard Ellman (eds.). *Charles Booth's London* (London: Hutchinson, 1969).

Frost, Alan. *Convicts and Empire: A naval question, 1776–1811* (Melbourne, VIC: Oxford University Press, 1980).

'New South Wales as *terra nullius*: The British denial of Aboriginal land rights', *Historical Studies*, 19, 77 (1981), 513–23.

Frost, Lucy. 'The Politics of Writing Convict Lives: Academic Research, State Archives and Family History'. *Life Writing*, 8, 1 (2011), 19–33

Frykman, Niklas. 'Connections Between Mutinies in European Navies', *International Review of Social History*, 58, S21 (2013), 87–107.

Fullagar, Kate and Michael McDonnell (eds.). *Facing Empire: Indigenous experiences in a revolutionary age, 1760–1840* (Baltimore, MD: Johns Hopkins University Press, 2018).

Kate Fullagar, and Michael A. McDonnell, 'Introduction: Empire, Indigeneity, and Revolution'. In Kate Fullagar and Michael A. McDonnell, (eds.) *Facing Empire: Indigenous experiences in a revolutionary age* (Baltimore, MD: Johns Hopkins University Press, 2018), 1–24.

Fyfe, Christopher. *A History of Sierra Leone* (Oxford University Press, 1962).

Gampat, Ramesh. *Guyana: From slavery to the present: Volume 2. Major diseases* (Bloomington: Xlibris, 2015).

Gauntlett, S. Carvosso. *Social Evils The Army Has Challenged*, Foreword by General Carpenter (London: Salvationist Publishing and Supplies, 1946).

Geggus, David Patrick *Haitian Revolutionary Studies* (Bloomington:Indiana University Press, 2001).

Geggus, David Patrick and Norman Fiering (eds.). *The World of the Haitian Revolution* (Bloomington:Indiana University Press, 2009).

Gentes, Andrew A. '*Katorga*: Penal Labor and Tsarist Siberia.' In Eva-Maria Stolberg (ed.) *The Siberian Saga: A history of Russia's Wild East* (Frankfurt: Peter Lang, 2005), pp. 73–85.

Exile to Siberia, 1590–1822 (Basingstoke: Palgrave, 2008).

Russia's Penal Colony in the Far East: A translation of Vlas Doroshevich's 'Sakhalin' (New York: Anthem Press, 2009).

Exile, Murder and Madness in Siberia, 1823–61 (Basingstoke: Palgrave, 2010).

'Sakhalin as Cause Célèbre: The Re-signification of Tsarist Russia's Penal Colony'. *Acta Slavica Iaponica*, 32 (2012). 55–72.

Gheith, Jehanne M. and Katherine Jolluck. *Gulag Voices: Oral histories of Soviet detention and exile* (Basingstoke: Palgrave, 2010).

Ghosh, Durba. *Gentlemanly Terrorists: Political violence and the colonial state in India, 1919–1947* (Cambridge University Press, 2017).

Gibson, Mary. 'A Global History of the Prison'; David Garland, *Punishment and Modern Society: A study in social theory* (Oxford: Clarendon, 1991).
  Born to Crime: Cesare Lombroso and the origins of biological criminology (Westport, CT: Praeger, 2002).
  'Global Perspectives on the Birth of the Prison'. *American Historical Review*, 116, 4 (2011), 1040–63.
  Italian Prisons in the Age of Positivism, 1861–1914 (London: Bloomsbury, 2019).
Gibson. Mary and Ilaria Poerio, 'Modern Europe, 1750–1950'. In Clare Anderson (ed.) *A Global History of Convicts and Penal Colonies* (London: Bloomsbury, 2018), pp. 337–70.
Gibson, Ross. 'Patyegarang and William Dawes: the Space of Imagination'. In Tracey Banivanua Mar and Penelope Edmonds (Eds.) *Making Colonial Settler Space: Perspectives on race, place and identity* (Basingstoke: Palgrave, 2010), pp. 242–53.
Gill, Nick and Deirdre Conlon, Dominique Moran and Andrew Burridge, 'Carceral circuitry: New directions in carceral geography'. *Progress in Human Geography*, 42, 2 (2018), 183–204.
Gillen, Mollie. 'The Botany Bay Decision, 1786: Convicts, Not Empire'. *The English Historical Review*, 97, 385 (1982), 740–66.
Gillie, Alan. 'The Origin of the Poverty Line'. *The Economic History Review*, 49, 4 (1996), 715–730.
Godfrey, Barry. 'Prison Versus Western Australia: Which Worked Best, the Australian Penal Colony or the English Convict Prison System?'. *The British Journal of Criminology*, 59, 5, (2019), 1139–60.
Godfrey, Barry, Kris Inwood, and Hamish Maxwell-Stewart. 'Exploring the life course and intergenerational impact of convict transportation'. In Veroni I. Eichelsheim and Steve G.A. van de Weijer, eds., *Intergenerational Continuity of Criminal and Antisocial Behaviour: an international overview of current studies* (London: Routledge, 2018), 61–75.
Goldman, Lawrence. '"Social Science": Economy, Natural Science and Statistics, 1830–1835'. *The Historical Journal*, 26, 3 (1983), 587–616.
  'Statistics and the Science of Society in Early Victorian Britain: An Intellectual Context for the General Register Office'. *Social History of Medicine*, 4, 3 (1991), 415–34.
  'Crofton, Sir Walter Frederick (1815–1897)', *Oxford, Dictionary of National Biography* (Oxford University Press, 2004); online edn, 23 September 2004. https://doi.org/10.1093/ref:odnb/65325.
Gould, Stephen J. *The Mismeasure of Man* (London: Norton, 1981).
Grant, John N. *The Maroons in Nova Scotia* (Halifax, NS: Formac Publishing Company Ltd, 2002).
Gready, Paul. 'Autobiography and the "Power of Writing": Political Prison Writing in the Apartheid Era'. *Journal of Southern African Studies*, 19, 3 (1993), 489–523.
  Writing as Resistance: Life stories of imprisonment, exile, and homecoming from apartheid South Africa (Lanham, MD: Lexington Books, 2003).
Groen-Vallinga, Miriam J. and Laurens E. Tacoma. 'Contextualizing Condemnation to Hard Labour in the Roman Empire'. In Christian G. De

Vito and Alex Lichtenstein (eds.) *Global Convict Labour* (Leiden: Brill, 2014), pp. 49–78.

Grubb, Farley. 'The Transatlantic Market for British Convict Labor'. *The Journal of Economic History*, 60, 1 (2000), 94–122.

Guha, Ranajit. *Elementary Aspects of Peasant Insurgency in Colonial India* (New Delhi: Oxford University Press, 1983).

Guistino, David de. *Conquest of Mind: Phrenology and Victorian social thought* (London: Croom Helm, 1975).

Hall, Catherine. *Civilising Subjects: Metropole and COLONY in the English imagination, 1830–1867* (Cambridge University Press, 2002).
  Macaulay and Son: Architects of imperial Britain (New Haven, CT:Yale University Press, 2012).

Handler, Jerome S. 'The Amerindian Slave Population in Barbados in the Seventeenth and Early Eighteenth Centuries'. *Caribbean Studies*, 8 (1969), 38–64.

Handler, Jerome S. and Ronald Hughes. 'The 1816 Slave Revolt in Barbados and the Petition of Samuel Hall Lord'. *Journal of the Barbados Museum and Historical Society*, (2001), 267–86.

Harling, Philip. 'The Trouble with Convicts: From Transportation to Penal Servitude, 1840–67'. *Journal of British Studies*, 53, 1 (2014), 80–110.

Harman, Kristyn. *Aboriginal Convicts: Australian, Khoisan and Maori Exiles* (Sydney: University of New South Wales Press, 2012).

Hecht, Jennifer Michael. *The End of the Soul: Scientific modernity, atheism, and anthropology in France* (New York: Columbia University Press, 2003).

Henze, Martina. 'Transnational Cooperation and Criminal Policy: The Prison Reform Movement, 1820s-1950s'. In Davide Rodogno, Bernhard Struck and Jakob Vogel (eds.) *Shaping the Transnational Sphere: Experts, networks and issues from the 1840s to the 1930s* (Oxford: Berghahn, 2015), pp. 197–217.

Hirst, J. B. *Convict Society and Its Enemies: A history of early New South Wales* (Sydney, NSW: Allen and Unwin, 1983).

Hardy, James D. Jr., 'The Transportation of Convicts to Colonial Louisiana'. *Louisiana History: The Journal of the Louisiana Historical Association*, 7, 3 (1966), 207–20.

Harrington, Kat. Royal Botanic Gardens, Kew. Library, Art and Archives Blog: 'Happy 200th Birthday to the Royal Botanic Gardens, Trinidad', 29 June 2018. https://www.kew.org/read-and-watch/happy-200th-birthday-to-the-royal-botanic-gardens-trinidad.

Harris, Cole. *Making Native Space: Colonialism, resistance and reserves in British Columbia* (Vancouver: University of British Columbia Press, 2002).

Hatakeyama, Hideki. 'Convict labor at the Sumitomo Besshi copper mine in Japan.' *International Journal of Social Economics*, 25, 2/3/4 (1998), 365–9.

Hattersley, A. F. *Convict Crisis and the Growth of Unity: Resistance to transportation in South Africa and Australia* (Pietermaritzburg: University of Natal Press, 1965).

Haywood, A. H. Wightwick. 'Sam Lord and his Castle'. *Journal of the Barbados Museum and Historical Society*, 30 (1963), 114–26.

Heinsen, Johan. *Mutiny in the Danish Atlantic World: Convicts, sailors and a dissonant empire* (London: Bloomsbury, 2017).
  'The Scandinavian Empires in the Seventeenth and Eighteenth Centuries'. In Clare Anderson (ed.) *A Global History of Convicts and Penal Colonies* (London: Bloomsbury, 2018), pp. 97–121.
  'Historicizing Extramural Convict Labour: Trajectories and Transitions in Early Modern Europe', *International Review of Social History*, 66, 1, (2021) 111–33.
Helg, Aline. *Liberty and Equality in Caribbean Colombia, 1770–1835* (Chapel Hill: University of North Carolina Press, 2004).
Hiramatsu, Yoshirō. 'History of Penal Institutions: Japan'. *Law in Japan: An Annual*, 6 (1973), 1–48.
Hobsbawm, Eric and George Rudé, *Captain Swing: A social history of the great English agricultural uprising of 1830* (New York: W. W. Norton and Company, 1973).
Hoerder, Dirk. *Cultures in Contact: World migrations in the second millennium* (Durham, NC: Duke University Press, 2002).
Hollis Hallet, C. F. E. 'Bermuda's Convict Hulks'. *Bermuda Journal of Archaeology and Maritime History* 2 (1990), 87–104.
Hollis Hallet, C. F. E. *Forty Years of Convict Labour; Bermuda 1823–1863* (Pembroke, Bermuda: Juniperhill Press, 1999).
Hongda, Harry Wu. *Laogai: the Chinese gulag* (Boulder, CO: Westview Press, 2004).
Horn, David G. *The Criminal Body: Lombroso and the anatomy of deviance* (Abingdon: Routledge, 2003).
Hunt, Nancy Rose. *A Nervous State: Violence, remedies, and reverie in Colonial Congo* (Durham, NC: Duke University Press, 2016).
Jappie, Saarah. '"Many Makassars": Tracing an African-Southeast Asian Narrative of Shaykh Yusuf of Makassar'. In S. Cornelissen and Y. Mine (eds.) *Migration and Agency in a Globalizing World* (Basingstoke: Palgrave, 2018), pp. 47–66.
Jenkins, Bill. 'Phrenology, Heredity and Progress in George Combe's Constitution of Man', *The British Journal for the History of Science*, 48, 3 (2015), 455–73.
Jennings, Evelyn P. 'The Sinews of Spain's American Empire: Forced Labor in Cuba from the Sixteenth to the Nineteenth Centuries'. In John Donoghue and Evelyn P. Jennings (eds.) *Building the Atlantic Empires: Unfree labor and imperial states in the political economy of capitalism, ca. 1500–1914* (Leiden: Brill, 2015), pp. 25–53.
Jennings, Lawrence C. *French Anti-Slavery: The Movement for the Abolition of Slavery in France, 1802–1848* (Cambridge University Press, 2000).
Jerabek, Hynek. 'W. E. B. Du Bois on the history of empirical social research'. *Ethnic and Racial Studies Review*, 29, 8 (2016), 1391–7.
Johnson, Emily D. *How St. Petersburg Learned to Study Itself: The Russian idea of kraevedenie* (University Park: Penn State University Press, 2006).
Jones, Gareth Stedman. *Outcast London: A study in the relationship between classes in Victorian Society* (Oxford: Clarendon Press, 1971).

Jones, Thomas C. and Constance Bantman 'From Republicanism to Anarchism: 50 Years of French Exilic Newspaper Publishing'. In Constance Bantman and Ana Cláudia Suriani da Silva (eds.) *The Foreign Political Press in Nineteenth-Century London: Politics from a distance* (London: Bloomsbury, 2018), pp. 91–112.

Jordan, William Chester. *From England to France: Felony and exile in the High Middle Ages* (Princeton University Press, 2015).

Joyce, R. B. 'Mackenzie, Sir Robert Ramsay (1811–1873)', Australian Dictionary of Biography, National Centre of Biography, Australian National University, http://adb.anu.edu.au/biography/mackenzie-sir-robert-ramsay-4109/text 6569, published first in hardcopy 1974.

Kabato shūchikan, ed., 'Kabato shūchikan enkaku ryakki', in Asahikawashi henshū kaigi, ed., *Shin Asahikawashishi 6* (c. 1892) (Asahikawa: Asahikawashi, 1993).

Kagan-Guthrie, Zachary. 'Repression and Migration: Forced Labour Exile of Mozambicans to São Tomé, 1948–1955'. *Journal of Southern African Studies*, 37, 3 (2011), 449–62.

Kalifa, Dominique. *Biribi: Les Bagnes coloniaux de l'Armée Française* (Paris: Perrin, 2009).

Kaluszynski, Martine. 'Republican identity: Bertillonnage as government technique'. In Jane Caplan and John Torpey (eds.) *Documenting Individual Identity: The development of state practices since the French Revolution* (Princeton University Press, 2001).

Kandasammy, Lloyd F. 'A brief history of the national museum of Guyana'. *Stabroek News*, 27 August 2007.

Kearns, G. '"Educate that holy hatred": place, trauma and identity in the Irish nationalism of John Mitchel'. *Political Geography*, 20 (2001), 885–911.

Keen, Caroline. *An Imperial Crisis in British India: The Manipur uprising of 1891* (London: I.B. Tauris, 2015).

Keevil, J. J. 'Benjamin Bynoe, Surgeon of H.M.S. Beagle.' *Journal of the History of Medicine and Allied Sciences*, 4, 1 (1949), 90–111.

Kennedy, Dane (ed.). *Reinterpreting Exploration: The West in the world* (Oxford University Press, 2014).

Kenney, Padraic. '"I felt a kind of pleasure in seeing them treat us brutally." The Emergence of the Political Prisoner, 1865–1910'. *Comparative Studies in Society and History*, 54, 4 (2012), 863–89.

Kent, David and Norma Townsend, *The Convicts of the Eleanor: Protest in rural England, new lives in Australia* (London: Pluto Press and Merlin, 2002)

Kent, David and Norma Townsend (eds.). *Joseph Mason: Assigned convict 1831–1837* (Melbourne University Press: 2013).

Keynes, Richard Darwin. *Fossils, Finches and Fuegians: Darwin's adventures and discoveries on the Beagle* (Oxford University Press, 2003).

King, Robert J. *The Secret History of the Convict Colony: Alexandro Malaspina's report on the British settlement of New South Wales* (Sydney, NSW: Allen and Unwin, 1990).

'What brought Lapérouse to Botany Bay?' *Journal of the Royal Australian Historical Society*, 85, 2 (1999), 140–47.

'George Vancouver and the contemplated settlement at Nootka Sound'. *The Great Circle*, 32, 1 (2010), 3–30.

Ködderitzsch, Lorenz. 'The Courts of Law, Appendix: Execution of Penalty'. In Wilhelm Röhl (ed.) *History of Law in Japan since 1868* (Leiden: Brill, 2005), pp. 711–69.

Kong, Ying. 'A Bibliographic Study of Late Qing Translations of Japanese Prison Books'. *Journal of East Asian Cultural Interaction Studies*, 4 (2011), 533–53.

Konishi, Shino and Maria Nugent, 'Newcomers, c. 1600–1800'. In Alison Bashford and Stuart Macintyre (eds.). *The Cambridge History of Australia, Volume 1: Indigenous and colonial Australia* (Cambridge University Press, 2013), pp. 43–67.

Kothari, Uma. 'Contesting Colonial Rule: Politics of Exile in the Indian Ocean'. *Geoforum*, 43 (2012), 697–706.

Koyama, Rokunosuke. *Ikijigoku* (1909). In Kiyoshi Kanzaki (ed.) *Meiji bungaku zenshū, Volume 96* (Tokyo: Chikuma Shobō, 1967), pp. 151–201.

Krakovitch, Odile. *Les femmes bagnardes* (Paris: Perrin, 1998).

Laffan, Michael. 'The Sayyid in the Slippers: An Indian Ocean Itinerary and Visions of Arab Sainthood, 1737–1929'. *Archipel*, 86 (2013), 191–227.

'From Javanese Court to African Grave: How Noriman Became Tuan Skapie, 1717–1806'. *Journal of Indian Ocean World Studies*, 1, 1 (2017), 38–59.

'Looking Back on the Bay of Bengal: An African Isolate Reoriented'. In Michael Laffan (ed.) *Belonging across the Bay of Bengal: Religious rites, colonial migrations, national rights* (London: Bloomsbury, 2017), pp. 207–22.

Laidlaw, Zoë. *Colonial Connections, 1815–45: Patronage, the information revolution and colonial Government* (Manchester University Press, 2005).

Lake, Marilyn and Henry Reynolds. *Drawing the Global Colour Line: White men's countries and the international challenge of racial Equality* (Cambridge University Press, 2008).

Lalvani, Suren. *Photography, Vision and the Production of Modern Bodies* (Albany: State University of New York Press, 1996).

Lamb, D. C. (revised by L. E. Lauer). 'Booth, (William) Bramwell (1856–1929)', revised L. E. Lauer, *Oxford Dictionary of National Biography* (Oxford University Press, 2004); online edn, 4 October 2012. https://doi.org/10.1093/ref:odnb/31969.

Lamb, Jonathan. *Scurvy: The disease of discovery* (Princeton University Press, 2016).

Lambert, David. 'Producing/ Contesting whiteness: rebellion, anti-slavery and enslavement in Barbados, 1816'. *Geoforum*, 36 (2005), 29–43.

Lambert, David and Alan Lester, *Colonial Lives across the British Empire: Imperial Careering in the Long Nineteenth Century* (Cambridge University Press, 2006).

Lambert, Ronald D. 'Reclaiming the ancestral past: narrative, rhetoric and the "convict stain"'. *Journal of Sociology*, 38, 2 (2002), 111–27.

The Largest and Oldest Prison Museum in Japan (Abashiri: Abashiri Prison Museum, 2015),

Lenz, Karl-Friedrich. 'Penal Law'. In Wilhelm Röhl (ed.) *History of Law in Japan since 1868* (Leiden: Brill, 2005), pp. 607–626.
Leonards, Chris and Nico Randeraad, 'Building a Transnational Network of Social Reform in the Nineteenth Century'. In Davide Rodogno, Bernhard Struck, and Jakob Vogel (eds.) *Shaping the Transnational Sphere: Experts, networks and issues from the 1840s to the 1930s* (Oxford: Berghahn, 2015), pp. 111–130.
Lester, Alan. 'Personifying Colonial Governance: George Arthur and the Transition from Humanitarian to Development Discourse'. *Annals of the Association of American Geographers*, 102, 6 (2012), 1468–88.
Lester, Alan and Fae Dussart. *Colonization and the Origins of Humanitarian Governance: Protecting Aborigines across the nineteenth-century British Empire* (Cambridge University Press, 2014).
Lombroso, Cesare. *Criminal Man*, translated and with a new introduction by Mary Gibson and Nicole Hahn Rafter (Durham, NC: Duke University Press, 2006).
Lucey, Michael. *Never Say I: Sexuality and the first person in Colette, Gide, and Proust* (Durham, NC: Duke University Press, 2006).
Madley, Benjamin. 'Reexamining the American Genocide Debate: Meaning, Historiography, and New Methods'. *American Historical Review*, 120, 1 (2015), 98–139.
Maclean, Kama. *A Revolutionary History of Interwar India: Violence, image, voice and text* (London: Hurst and Co., 2015).
Maclean Kama and J. Daniel Elam (eds.). *Revolutionary Lives in South Asia: Acts and afterlives of anticolonial political action* (London: Routledge, 2014).
Malherbe, V. C. 'Khoikhoi and the Question of Convict Transportation from the Cape Colony, 1820-1842'. *South African Historical Journal*, 17 (1985), 19–39.
Mallari, Aaron and Abel T. 'The Bilibid Prison as an American Colonial Project in the Philippines'. *Philippine Sociological Review*, 60 (2012), 165–92.
Mandela, Nelson. *Long Walk to Freedom: The autobiography of Nelson Mandela* (London: Little, Brown, 1994).
Manning, Patrick. *Migration in World History* (London: Routledge, 2005).
Mar, Tracey Banivanua and Penelope Edmonds. 'Introduction: Making Space in Settler Colonies'. In Tracey Banivanua Mar and Penelope Edmonds (eds.) *Making Settler Colonial Space: Perspectives on race, place and identity* (Basingstoke: Palgrave, 2010), pp. 1–24.
'Indigenous and settler relations', in Alison Bashford and Stuart MacIntyre, eds., *The Cambridge History of Australia, Volume 1: Indigenous and colonial Australia* (Cambridge University Press, 2013), pp. 342–66.
Margree, Victoria and Gurminder K. Bhambra. 'Tocqueville, Beaumont and the Silences in Histories of the United States: An Interdisciplinary Endeavour Across Literature and Sociology'. *Journal of Historical Sociology*, 24, 1 (2011), 116–31.
Marlin, Christine. 'A Prison and a Gentleman: The Prison Inspector as Imperialist Hero in the Writings of Major Arthur Griffiths (1838-1908)'. In Jason W. Haslam and Julia M. Wright (eds.) *Captivating Subjects: Writing*

confinement, citizenship, and nationhood in the nineteenth century (University of Toronto Press, 2005), pp. 220–40.

Marshall, Hazel. 'Convict pioneers and the failure of the management system on Melville Island, 1824-29'. *The Push from the Bush*, 29 (1991), 29–46.

Mattingly, David, Paul Newson, Oliver Creighton, *et al.* 'A landscape of imperial power: Roman and Byzantine *Phaino*'. In Graham Barker, David Gilbertson and David Mattingly, (eds.) *Archaeology and Desertification: The Wadi Faynan Landscape Survey, South Jordan* (Oxford: Council for British Research in the Levant, 2007), pp. 305–48.

Mawson, Stephanie. 'Unruly Plebeians and the *Forzado* System: Convict Transportation between New Spain and the Philippines during the Seventeenth Century'. *Revista de Indias*, 73, 259 (2013), 693–730.

'Convicts or *Conquistadores*? Spanish Soldiers in the Seventeenth-Century Pacific'. *Past and Present* 232, 1 (2016): 87–125.

Maxwell-Stewart, Hamish. 'The Life and Death of James Thomas'. *Tasmanian Historical Studies*, 10 (2005), 55–64.

Closing Hell's Gates: The death of a convict station (Sydney, NSW: Allen and Unwin, 2008).

'"Those Lads Contrived A Plan": Attempts at Mutiny on Australia-Bound Convict Vessels'. *International Review of Social History*, 58, S21 (2013), 177–96.

'Transportation'. In Paul Knepper and Anja Johansen (eds.). *The Oxford Handbook of The History of Crime and Criminal Justice* (Oxford University Press, 2016), pp. 635–54.

'Transportation from Britain and Ireland, 1615–1875'. In Clare Anderson (ed.) *A Global History of Convicts and Penal Colonies* (London: Bloomsbury, 2018), pp. 183–210.

'Western Australia and Transportation in the British Empire 1615–1939', *Studies in Western Australian History*, 34 (2020), 5–21.

'Convict Workers, "Penal Labour" and Sarah Island: Life at Macquarie Harbour, 1822-1834', in Ian Duffield and James Bradley, eds., *Representing Convicts: New perspectives of convict forced labour migration* (Leicester University Press, 2000), 142–62.

Maxwell-Stewart, Hamish and Cassandra Pybus. *American Citizens, British Slaves: Yankee Political Prisoners in a British Penal Colony 1839–1850* (East Lansing: University of Michigan Press, 2002).

Maxwell-Stewart, Hamish and Michael Quinlan. 'Female Convict Labour and Absconding Rates in Colonial Australia'. *Tasmanian Historical Studies*, 22 (2017), 19–36.

'Voting with Their Feet: Absconding and Labor Exploitation in Convict Australia". In Marcus Rediker, Titas Chakraborty, and Matthias van Rossum (eds.), *A Global History of Runaways: Workers, mobility, and capitalism, 1600–1850* (Oakland: University of California Press, 2019), pp. 156–77.

Maxwell-Stewart, Hamish, Kris Inwood and Jim Stankovich. 'Prison and the Colonial Family', *The History of the Family*, 20, 2 (2015), 231–48.

Maxwell-Stewart, Hamish and Lydia Nicholson. 'Penal Transportation, Family History and Convict Tourism'. In Jacqueline Z. Wilson, Sarah Hodgkinson,

Justin Piche, and Kevin Walby (eds.), *The Palgrave Handbook of Prison Tourism* (Basingstoke: Palgrave, 2017), pp. 713–34.

Mazumdar, Madhumita. 'Dwelling in the Fluid Spaces: The Matuas of the Andaman Islands'. In Clare Anderson, Madhumita Mazumdar, and Vishvajit Pandya, *New Histories of the Andaman Islands: Landscape, place and identity in the Bay of Bengal, c. 1790–2012* (Cambridge University Press, 2014), pp. 170–200.

'Improving visions, troubled landscapes: the legacies of colonial Ferrargunj'. In Clare Anderson, Madhumita Mazumdar and Vishvajit Pandya, *New Histories of the Andaman Islands: Landscape, place and belonging across the Bay of Bengal, 1790-2012* (Cambridge University Press, 2014), pp. 22–61.

McArthur, John, 'The Importance of *Anopheles leucosphyrus*'. *Transactions of the Royal Society of Tropical Medicine and Hygiene*, 44, 6 (1951), 683–94.

McConville, Seán. *Irish Political Prisoners, 1848–1922: Theatres of war* (London: Routledge, 2003).

McCullagh, Francis. *Red Mexico: A reign of terror in America* (New York: L. Carrier and Co., 1928).

McKenzie, Kirsten. 'Discourses of Scandal: Bourgeois Respectability and the End of Slavery and Transportation at the Cape and New South Wales, 1830–1850'. *Journal of Colonialism and Colonial History*, 4, 3 (2003). doi:10.1353/cch.2004.0011

Scandal in the Colonies: Sydney and Cape Town 1820–50 (Melbourne University Press, 2004).

Meadows, Darrell. 'Engineering Exile'. *French Historical Studies*, 21, 1 (2000), 67–102.

Mehl, Eva. *Forced Migration in the Spanish Pacific World: From Mexico to the Philippines, 1765–1811* (Cambridge University Press, 2016).

Meredith, David and Deborah Oxley. 'The Convict Economy'. In Simon P. Ville and G.A. Withers (eds.) *The Cambridge Economic History of Australia* (Cambridge University Press, 2014), pp. 97–122.

Merle, Isabelle. *Expériences Coloniales: La Nouvelle-Calédonie, 1853–1920* (Paris: Belin, 1995).

Merle, Isabelle and Marine Coquet. 'The Penal World in the French Empire: A Comparative Study of French Transportation and its Legacy in Guyana and New Caledonia', *The Journal of Imperial and Commonwealth History*, 47, 2 (2019), 247–74.

Meyering, Isobelle Barrett. 'Abolitionism, Settler Violence and the Case Against Flogging: A Reassessment of Sir William Molesworth's Contribution to the Transportation Debate'. *History Australia*, 7, 1 (2010), 6.1–6.18.

Miller, Barbara. 'The Role of Women in the Mexican Cristero Rebellion: Las Señoras y Las Religiosas'. *The Americas*, 40, 3 (1984), 303–23.

Miller, Ivor L. *Voice of the Leopard: African secret societies and Cuba* (Jackson: University Press of Mississippi, 2009).

Miyamoto, Takashi. 'Towards an Evolutionary History of Penological Information in Modern Japan' (2016). http://staffblogs.le.ac.uk/carchipelago/2014/04/16/towards-an-evolutionary-history-of-penological-information-in-modern-japan/.

'Convict Labor and Its Commemoration: the Mitsui Miike Coal Mine Experience'. *The Asia-Pacific Journal: Japan Focus*, 15, 1 (2017), 1–15.

Mohapatra, Prabhu. 'Eurocentrism, Forced Labour, and Global Migration: A Critical Assessment.' *International Review of Social History*, 52, 1 (2007), 110–15.

Moitt, Bernard. *Women and Slavery in the French Antilles, 1635–1848* (Bloomington: Indiana University Press, 2001).

Moore, J. M. 'Alexander Maconochie's mark system'. *Prison Service Journal*, 198 (2011), 38–46.

Molloy, Bryan P. J. 'Sinclair, Andrew (1794-1861)', *Dictionary of New Zealand Biography*, Volume 1 (1990). https://teara.govt.nz/en/biographies/1s12/sinclair-andrew.

Molony, John. *The Native-Born: The first white Australians* (Melbourne University Press, 2000).

Morgan, Gwenda and Peter Rushton, *Banishment in the Early Atlantic World: Convicts, rebels and slaves* (London: Bloomsbury, 2013).

Morgan, Philip D. 'Encounters between British and "indigenous" peoples, c. 1500 – c. 1800'. In Martin Daunton and Rick Halpern (eds.) *Empire and Others: British encounters with indigenous peoples, 1600–1850* (Philadelphia: University of Pennsylvania Press, 1999) pp. 42–78.

Morgan, Rod. 'Howard, John (1726?–1790)', *Oxford Dictionary of National Biography*, (Oxford University Press, 2004); online edn 23 September 2004. https://doi.org/10.1093/ref:odnb/13922

Morris, Aldon D. *The Scholar Denied: W. E. B. Du Bois and the birth of modern sociology* (Oakland: University of California Press, 2017).

Morris, Norval. *Maconochie's Gentlemen: The story of Norfolk Island and the roots of modern prison reform* (Oxford University Press, 2003).

Morris, Norval, and David Rothman (eds.). *The Oxford History of the Prison: The practice of punishment in western society* (Oxford University Press, 1998).

Mortimer, Brenda Gean. Rethinking Penal Reform and the Royal Prerogative of Mercy During Robert Peel's Stewardship of the Home Office 1822-7, 1828-30, PhD thesis, University of Leicester, 2017.

Moss, Kellie. 'The Swan River Experiment: Coerced Labour in Western Australia 1829-1868'. *Studies in Western Australian History*, 34 (2020), 23–40

Muckle, Adrian. 'Troublesome Chiefs and Disorderly Subjects: The *Indigénat* and the Internment of Kanak in New Caledonia (1887–1928)'. *French Colonial History*, 11 (2010), 131–60.

Mukherjee, Rudrangshu. *Awadh in Revolt 1857–1858: A study of popular resistance* (New Delhi: Oxford University Press, 1984).

'"Satan Let Loose Upon Earth": The Kanpur Massacres in India in the Revolt of 1857'. *Past and Present*, 128, 1 (1990), 92–116.

Neilson, Briony. 'The Paradox of Penal Colonization: Debates on Convict Transportation at the International Prison Congresses 1872–1895'. *French History and Civilization*, (2015), 198–211.

'"Moral Rubbish in Close Proximity": Penal Colonization and Strategies of Distance in Australia and New Caledonia, c.1853–1897'. *International Review of Social History*, 64, 3 (2019), 445–471.

Newton, Melanie J. 'The King v. Robert James, a Slave, for Rape: Inequality, Gender, and British Slave Amelioration, 1823-1834'. *Comparative Studies in Society and History*, 47, 3 (2005), 583–610.

Nicholas, Stephen, ed. *Convict Workers: Reinterpreting Australia's past* (Cambridge University Press, 1989).

Northrup, David. 'Becoming African: Identity Formation among Liberated Slaves in Nineteenth-Century Sierra Leone'. *Slavery and Abolition*, 27, 1 (2006), 1–21.

O'Brien, Patricia. *The Promise of Punishment: Prisons in nineteenth-century France* (Princeton University Press, 1982).

O'Callaghan, Evelyn. *The Earliest Patriots; Being the true adventures of certain survivors of 'Bussa's Rebellion' (1816), in the island of Barbados and abroad* (London: Karia Press, 1986).

Oguchi, Chiaki. *Nihonjin no sōtaiteki kankyōkan: 'konomarenai kūkan' no rekishi-chirigaku* (Tokyo: Kokon shoin, 2002).

Okunomiya, Kenshi. 'Gokuri no Ware'. In *Okunomiya Kenshi Zenshū* (Tokyo: Kōryūsha, 1988), pp. 141–70.

Oldham, Wilfrid. *Britain's Convicts to the Colonies* (Sydney, NSW: Library of Australian History, 1990).

Ouennoughi, Mélica. *Les déportés maghrébins en Nouvelle-Calédonie* (Paris: Editions L'Harmattan, 2005).

'Les déportés maghrébins en Nouvelle-Calédonie', *Revue Insaniyat*, 32 (2006), 53–68.

Oulahal, Rachid, Zohra Guerraoui and Patrick Denoux. 'Entre Mémoire Collective et Émergence Diasporique, Le Cas des Descendants d'Algériens en Nouvelle-Calédonie', *Journal de la Société des Océanistes*, 147, 2 (2018), 373–82.

Padel, Felix. *The Sacrifice of Human Being: British Rule and the Konds of Orissa* (New Delhi: Oxford University Press, 1995).

Pago, Gilbert. *L'insurrection de Martinique 1870–1871* (Paris: Hachette Livre, 2012).

Pallot, Judith. 'Russia's Penal Peripheries: Space, Place and Penality in Soviet and Post-Soviet Russia', *Transactions of the British Institute of Geographers*, New Series, 30, 1 (2005), 98–112.

Pandya, Vishvajit. *In the Forest: Visual and material worlds of the Andaman Islanders 1858–2000* (Lanham, MD: University Press of America, 2009).

Pasquale, Francesca Di. 'The "Other" at Home: Deportation and Transportation of Libyans to Italy During the Colonial Era (1911–1943)', *International Review of Social History*, 63, S26 (2018), 211–31.

'On the Edge of Penal Colonies: Castiadas (Sardinia) and the "Redemption" of the Land'. *International Review of Social History*, 64, 3 (2019), 427–44.

Paterson on Prisons, Being the collected papers of Sir Alexander Paterson, Edited, with an Introduction by S. K. Ruck (London: Frederick Muller Ltd, 1951).

Paterson, Lorraine M. 'Prisoners from Indochina in the Nineteenth-Century French Colonial World'. In Ronit Ricci (ed.) *Exile in Colonial Asia: Kings, convicts, commemoration* (Honolulu: University of Hawai'i Press, 2016), pp. 220–47.

'Ethnoscapes of Exile: Political Prisoners from Indochina in a Colonial Asian World'. *International Review of Social History*, 63, S26 (2018), 89–108.

Paton, Diana. *No Bond but the Law: Punishment, race and gender in Jamaican state formation, 1780–1870* (Durham, NC: Duke University Press, 2004).

'An "Injurious" Population: Caribbean-Australian Penal Transportation and Imperial Racial Politics'. *Cultural and Social History*, 5, 4 (2008), 449–64.

The Cultural Politics of Obeah: Religion, colonialism and modernity in the Caribbean World (Cambridge University Press, 2015).

Payne, Pauline. *The Diplomatic Gardener: Richard Schomburgk: explorer and botanic garden director* (North Adelaide, SA: Jeffcott Press, 2007).

Peabody, Norbert. 'Cents, Sense and Census: Human Inventories in Late Precolonial and Early Colonial India'. *Comparative Studies in Society and History*, 43, 4 (2001), 819–50.

Pedlar, Neil. *The Imported Pioneers: Westerners who helped build modern Japan* (Sandgate, Kent: Japan Library Ltd, 1990).

Pemberton, Rita A. 'The Trinidad Botanic Gardens and Colonial Resource Development, 1818–1899', *Revista/Review Interamericana*, 29, 1–4 (1999).

Penn, Nigel. 'Robben Island 1488–1805'. In Harriet Deacon (ed.) *The Island: A history of Robben Island 1488–1990* (Cape Town: David Philip, 1997), pp. 9–32.

Penny, Lauren. *St Helena Island, Moreton Bay: An historical account* (Brisbane, QLD: Inspire Publishing, 2010).

Péron, François *Mémoire sur les établissements anglais à la Nouvelle Hollande, à la Terre de Diémen et dans les archipels du grand océan Pacifique: le rêve australien de Napoléon: description et projet secret de conquête française*. (Paris: Éditions SPM, 1998).

Piacentini, Laura and Judith Pallot. '"In Exile Imprisonment" in Russia'. *The British Journal of Criminology*, 54, 1 (2014), 20–37.

Piazza, Pierre. 'Bertillonage: The international circulation of practices and technologies of a system of forensic identification'. *Criminocorpus* (2014). http://criminocorpus.revues.org/341.

Pick, Daniel. *Faces of Degeneration: A European disorder, c. 1848–1918* (Cambridge University Press, 1989).

Pieris, Anoma. *Hidden Hands and Divided Landscapes: A penal history of Singapore's plural society* (Honolulu: University of Hawai'i Press, 2009).

Pierre, Michel. *Bagnards: La terre de la grande punition, Cayenne, 1852–1953* (Paris: Éditions Autrement, 2000).

Pike, Ruth. *Penal Servitude in Early-Modern Spain* (Madison: University of Wisconsin Press, 1993).

Plomley, N. J. B. (ed.). *Weep in Silence: A History of the Flinders Island Aboriginal Settlement with the Flinders Island Journal of George Augustus Robinson, 1835–1839* (Sandy Bay, TAS: Blubber Head Press, 1987).

Polakiewicz, Leonard A. 'Western Critical Response to Chekhov's *The Island of Sakhalin*'. *Russian History/ Histoire Russe*, 33, 1 (2006), 73–82.

Poovey, Mary. *A History of the Modern Fact: Problems of knowledge in the sciences of wealth and society* (University of Chicago Press, 1998).

Popkin, Cathy. 'Chekhov as Ethnographer: Epistemological crisis on Sakhalin Island'. *Slavic Review*, 51, 1 (1992), 36–51.

Popova, Zhanna. 'Exile as Imperial Practice: Western Siberia and the Russian Empire, 1879–1900'. *International Review of Social History*, 63, S26 (2018), 131–50.

Porter, Theodore M. 'Statistics and Statistical Methods'. In Theodore M. Porter and Dorothy Ross (eds.). *The Cambridge History of Science: Volume 7* (Cambridge University Press, 2003), pp. 238–50.

Poskett, James. *Materials of the Mind: Phrenology, race, and the global history of science, 1815–1920* (University of Chicago Press, 2019).

Potter, Neville. Francis Nicolas Rossi: The ambivalent position of a French nobleman in 19th-Century New South Wales, PhD Thesis, Australian National University, 2017.

Price, Richard and Sidney W. Mintz, *The Birth of African-American Culture: An anthropological perspective* (Boston, MA: Beacon, 1992).

Priolkar, Anant Kakba. *The Goa Inquisition* (Bombay University Press, 1961).

Pybus, Cassandra. *Black Founders: The unknown story of Australia's first black settlers* (Sydney: University of New South Wales Press, 1996).

'Washington's Revolution (Harry that is, not George)'. *Atlantic Studies: Global Currents*, 3, 2 (2006), 183–99.

Raj, Kapil. *Relocating Modern Science: Circulation and the construction of knowledge in South Asia and Europe* (Basingstoke: Palgrave, 2006).

Randeraad, Nico. 'The International Statistical Congress (1853–1876): Knowledge Transfers and their Limits'. *European History Quarterly*, 41, 1 (2011), 50–65.

Rausch, Jane M. 'Using Convicts to Settle the Frontier: A Comparison of Agricultural Penal Colonies as Tropical Frontier Institutions in Twentieth-Century Colombia'. *SECOLAS Annals*, 34 (2002): 26–48.

Redfield, Peter. *Space in the Tropics: From convicts to rockets in French Guiana* (Berkeley: University of California Press, 2000).

Rediker, Marcus, Cassandra Pybus, and Emma Christopher. 'Introduction'. In Marcus Rediker, Cassandra Pybus, and Emma Christopher (eds.). *Many Middle Passages: Forced migration and the making of the modern world* (University of California Press: 2007), pp. 1–19.

Reid, Kirsty. *Gender, Crime and Empire: Convicts, settlers and the state in early colonial Australia* (Manchester University Press, 2007).

Reiss, Ansgar. 'Home Alone? Reflections on Political Exiles Return to their Native Countries'. In Sabine Freitag, (ed.) *Exiles from European Revolutions: Refugees in Mid-Victorian England* (Oxford: Berghahn, 2003), pp. 297–318.

Renneville, Marc. 'La criminologie perdue d'Alexandre Lacassagne (1843–1924)', *Criminocorpus* (2005). http://criminocorpus.revues.org/112.

'Les Archives d'anthropologie criminelle: a journal fit for a nascent scientific field', *Criminocorpus*, Histoire de la criminologie, Présentation du dossier (2015). http://journals.openedition.org/criminocorpus/2959.

Reynolds, Henry. *The Other Side of the Frontier: Aboriginal resistance to the European invasion of Australia* (Sydney: University of New South Wales Press, 2006 [3rd edition]).

With the White People: The crucial role of Aborigines in the exploration and development of Australia (Ringwood, VIC: Penguin, 1990).
Ricci, Ronit. (ed.) *Exile in Colonial Asia: Kings, convicts, commemoration* (Honolulu: University of Hawai'i Press, 2016).
  'From Java to Jaffna: Exile in Dutch Asia in the eighteenth century'. In Ronit Ricci (ed.) *Exile in Colonial Asia: Kings, convicts, commemoration* (Honolulu: University of Hawai'i Press, 2016), pp. 94–116.
  Banishment and Belonging: Exile and diaspora in Sarandib, Lanka and Ceylon (Cambridge University Press, 2019).
Ritchie, John. *Punishment and Profit: The reports of Commissioner John Bigge on the Colonies of New South Wales and Van Diemen's Land, 1822-1823; their origins, nature and significance* (Melbourne, VIC: Heinemann, 1970).
  'Towards ending an unclean thing: The Molesworth committee and the abolition of transportation to New South Wales, 1837–40'. *Australian Historical Studies*, 17, 67 (1976), 144–164.
  The Evidence to the Bigge Reports: New South Wales under Governor Macquarie, Volume 2: the written evidence, selected and edited by John Ritchie (Melbourne, VIC: Heinemann, 1971).
Rivière, Marc Serge. 'Distant Echoes of the Enlightenment: Private and Public Observations on Convict Life by Baudin's Disgraced Officer, Hyacinthe de Bougainville (1825)'. *Australian Journal of French Studies* 41, 2 (2004), 171–185.
Roberts, David Andrew. 'Beyond "the stain": Rethinking the nature and impact of the anti-transportation movement'. *Journal of Australian Colonial History*, 14 (2012), 205–79.
Roberts, Lissa. 'Situating Science in Global History: Local Exchanges and Networks of Circulation'. *Itinerario*, 33, 1 (2009), 9–30.
Roddy, Sarah, Julie-Marie Strange and Bertrand Taithe, 'Henry Mayhew at 200 – the "Other" Victorian Bicentenary'. *Journal of Victorian Culture*, 19, 4 (2014), 481–96.
Roscoe, Katherine Ann. Island Chains: Carceral Islands and the Colonisation of Australia, 1824–1903. PhD thesis, University of Leicester, 2017.
  'A Natural Hulk: Australia's Carceral Islands in the Colonial Period, 1788–1901'. *International Review of Social History*, 63, S26 (2018), 45–63.
  'Work on Wadjemup: Entanglements between Aboriginal Prison Labour and the Imperial Convict System in Western Australia', *Studies in Western Australian History*, 34 (2020), 79–96.
Roque, Ricardo and Kim A. Wagner, 'Introduction: Engaging Colonial Knowledge'. In Ricardo Roque and Kim A. Wagner (eds.) *Engaging Colonial Knowledge: Reading European archives in world history* (Basingstoke: Palgrave, 2012), pp. 1–32
Roy, Michaël. 'Chautard Jean, Léon, Ricard', *Dictionnaire biographique du mouvement social francophone aux États-Unis* (2018), https://maitron.fr/spip.php?article188256.
Rodogno, Davide, Bernhard Struck, and Jakob Vogel. 'Introduction'. In Davide Rodogno, Bernhard Struck, and Jakob Vogel (eds.) *Shaping the Transnational Sphere: Experts, networks and issues from the 1840s to the 1930s* (Oxford: Berghahn, 2015), pp. 1–20.

Roger, Gwenda and Peter Rushton. *Eighteenth-Century Criminal Transportation: The formation of the criminal Atlantic* (Basingstoke: Palgrave, 2004).
Rosenblum, Warren. *Beyond the Prison Gates: Punishment and welfare in Germany, 1850–1933* (Chapel Hill: University of North Carolina Press, 2008).
Rossum, Matthias van. 'The Dutch East India Company in Asia, 1595–1811'. In Clare Anderson (ed.) *A Global History of Convicts and Penal Colonies* (London: Bloomsbury, 2018), pp. 157–81.
  'The Carceral Colony – Colonial Exploitation, Coercion and Control in the Netherlands East-Indies, 1810s–1940s'. *International Review of Social History*, 63, S26 (2018), 65–88.
Rothman, David J. 'Perfecting the Prison: United States, 1789-1865', in Norval Morris and David Rothman (eds.) *The Oxford History of the Prison: The practice of punishment in western society* (Oxford University Press, 1998), pp. 100–16.
Routon, Kenneth. 'Unimaginable Homelands? "Africa" and the Abakuá Historical Imagination'. *Journal of Latin American Anthropology* 10, 2 (2010), 370–400.
Rowse, Tim and Tiffany Shellam, 'The Colonial Emergence of a Statistical Imaginary', *Comparative Studies in Society and History*, 55, 4 (2012), 922–54.
Roy, Rohan Deb. Quinine, mosquitos and empire: reassembling malaria in British India, 1890–1910'. *South Asian History and Culture*, 4, 1 (2013), 65–86.
  Malarial Subjects: Empire, medicine and nonhumans in British India, 1820–1909 (Cambridge University Press, 2017).
Royle, Stephen A. 'The Falkland Islands, 1833–1876: The Establishment of a Colony'. *The Geographical Journal*, 151, 2 (1985), 204–14.
Ruchames, Louis. (ed.). *The Letters of William Lloyd Garrison, Vol. IV, From disunionism to the brink of war, 1850–1860* (Cambridge, MA: The Belknap Press of Harvard University Press, 1975).
Rudé, George. *Protest and Punishment: The story of the social and political protesters transported to Australia 1788–1868* (Oxford: Clarendon Press, 1978).
Rupprecht, Anita. 'When he gets among his Countrymen, they tell him that he is free': Slave Trade Abolition, Indentured Africans and a Royal Commission'. *Slavery and Abolition*, 33, 3 (2012), 435–55.
  'From slavery to indenture: scripts for slavery's endings'. In Catherine Hall, Nicholas Draper, and Keith McClelland (eds.) *Emancipation and the Remaking of the British Imperial World* (Manchester University Press, 2014), pp. 77–97.
Ryan, Lyndall. 'The Black Line in Van Diemen's Land: Success or failure?'. *Journal of Australian Studies*, 37, 1 (2013), 3–18.
Sakata, Minako. 'Japan in the eighteenth and nineteenth centuries'. In Clare Anderson (ed.), *A Global History of Convicts and Penal Colonies* (London: Bloomsbury, 2018), pp. 307–35.
  'The Transformation of Hokkaido from Penal Colony to Homeland Territory'. *International Review of Social History*, 63, S26 (2018), 109–30.
Salman, Michael. '"The Prison That Makes Men Free": The Iwahig Penal Colony and the Simulacra of the American State in the Philippines'. In

Alfred W. McCoy and Francisco A. Scarano (eds.) *The Colonial Crucible: Empire in the making of the modern American state* (Madison: University of Wisconsin Press, 2009), pp. 116–28.

Salvatore, Ricardo D. and Carlos Aguirre. 'The Birth of the Penitentiary in Latin America: Toward an Interpretive Social History of Prisons'. In Ricardo D. Salvatore and Carlos Aguirre (eds.) *The Birth of the Penitentiary in Latin America: Essays on criminology, prison reform, and social control, 1830–1940* (Austin: University of Texas Press, 1996), pp. 1–43.

'Colonies of Settlement or Places of Banishment and Torment? Penal Colonies and Convict Labour in Latin America, c. 1800–1940'. In Christian G. De Vito and Alex Lichtenstein (eds.) *Global Convict Labour* (Leiden: Brill, 2015), pp. 273–309.

Sanchez, Jean-Lucien. *À perpétuité. Relégués au bagne de Guyane* (Paris: Vendémiaire, 2013).

'Les évasions de relégués au bagne de Guyane (XIXe-XXe siècle)', *Criminocorpus* (2014). http://journals.openedition.org/criminocorpus/2837.

'The French Empire, 1542–1976'. In Clare Anderson (ed.), *A Global History of Convicts and Penal Colonies* (London: Bloomsbury, 2018), pp. 123–55.

Saunders, Kay (ed.). *Indentured Labour in the British Empire 1834–1920* (London: Croom Helm, 1984).

Savage, John. 'Unwanted Slaves: The Punishment of Transportation and the Making of Legal Subjects in Early Nineteenth-Century Martinique'. *Citizenship Studies*, 10, 1 (2006), 35–53.

Savarkar, V. D. *The Story of My Transportation for Life (A Biography of Black Days of Andamans)* (Bombay: Sadbhakti Publications, 1950).

Sawchuk, Lawrence A., Lianne Tripp, and Michelle M. Mohan. '"Voluntariness of Exposure": Life in a Convict Station'. *Prison Journal*, 90, 2 (2010), 203–19.

Schakwyck, David. 'Writing from Prison'. In Sarah Nuttall and Cheryl-Ann Michael (eds.) *Senses of Culture: South African culture studies* (New York: Oxford University Press, 2000), pp. 279–97.

Schrader, Abby M. *Languages of the Lash: Corporal punishment and identity in imperial Russia* (DeKalb, IL: Northern Illinois University Press, 2002).

Seaton, George. *Isle of the Damned: Twenty years in the penal colony of French Guiana* (New York: Farrar, Straus and Young, 1951).

Semley, Lorelle. *To Be Free and French: Citizenship in France's Atlantic Empire* (Cambridge University Press, 2017).

Sen, Satadru. *Disciplining Punishment: Colonialism and convict society in the Andaman Islands* (New Delhi: Oxford University Press, 2000).

'Domesticated Convicts: Producing families in the Andaman Islands'. In Indrani Chatterjee (ed.) *Unfamiliar Relations: Family and history in South Asia* (New Brunswick, NJ: Rutgers University Press, 2004), pp. 261–291.

'Lost Between Africa and Tasmania: Racializing the Andamanese'. *Journal of Colonialism and Colonial History*, 10, 3 (2009). doi:10.1353/cch.0.0090.

Savagery and Colonialism in the Indian Ocean: Power, pleasure and the Andaman islanders (Abingdon: Routledge, 2010).

Scanlan, Padraic X. 'The Colonial Rebirth of British Anti-Slavery: The Liberated African Villages of Sierra Leone, 1815-1824'. *American Historical Review*, 121, 4 (2016), 1084–113.
  Freedom's Debtors: British Antislavery in Sierra Leone in the Age of Revolution (New Haven, CT:Yale University Press, 2017).
Schaffer, Simon, Lissa Roberts, Kapil Raj, and James Delbourgo (eds.). *The Brokered World: Go-betweens and global intelligence, 1770–1820* (Sagamore Beach, MA: Watson Publishing International, 2009).
Schauwers, Albert. 'The "Benevolent" colonies of Johannes van den Bosch: Continuities in the Administration of Poverty in the Netherlands and Indonesia'. *Comparative Studies in Society and History*, 43, 2 (2001), 298–328.
Schwarz, Suzanne. 'Reconstructing the Life Histories of Liberated Africans: Sierra Leone in the Early Nineteenth Century'. *History in Africa*, 39 (2012), 175–207.
Shafir, Nir. 'The International Congress as Scientific and Diplomatic Technology: Global Intellectual Exchange in the International Prison Congress, 1860–90.' *Journal of Global History*, 9, 1 (2014), 72–93.
Shanks, Dennis G. and David J. Bradley, 'Island Fever: The Historical Determinants of Malaria in the Andaman Islands'. *Transactions of the Royal Society of Tropical Medicine and Hygiene*, 104, 3 (2010), 185–90.
Shaw, A. G. L. *Convicts and the Colonies: A study of penal transportation from Great Britain and Ireland to Australia and other parts of the British Empire* (Melbourne University Press, 1966).
Shaw, A. G. L. *Sir George Arthur, Bart, 1784–1854: Superintendent of British Honduras, Lieutenant-Governor of Van Diemen's Land and of Upper Canada, Governor of the Bombay Presidency* (Melbourne University Press, 1980).
Shepherd, Verene A. *Maharani's Misery: Narratives of a passage from India to the Caribbean* (Mona, Jamaica: University of the West Indies Press, 2002).
Sherman, Taylor C. 'From Hell to Paradise? Voluntary Transfer of Convicts to the Andaman Islands, 1921–1940'. *Modern Asian Studies*, 43, 2 (2009), 367–88.
  State Violence and Punishment in India, 1919–1956 (London: Routledge, 2009).
Shoemaker, Robert and Richard Ward. 'Understanding the Criminal: Record-Keeping, Statistics and the Early History of Criminology in England'. *The British Journal of Criminology*, 57, 6 (2017), 1442–61.
Sibeud, Emmanuelle. 'A Useful Colonial Science? Practicing Anthropology in the French Colonial Empire, circa 1880–1960'. *Current Anthropology*, 53, Supplement 5 (2012) S83–S93.
Silverman, Max. 'Memory Traces: Patrick Chamoiseau and Rodolphe Hammadi's *Guyane: traces-mémoires du bagne*'. *Yale French Studies*, 118, 19 (2010), 225–38.
Singh, Ujjwal Kumar. *Political Prisoners in India* (New Delhi: Oxford University Press, 1998).
Sivasundarum, Sujit. 'Sciences and the Global: On Methods, Questions, and Theory'. *Isis*, 101, 1 (2010), 146–58.

Smith, Babette. *Australia's Birthstain: The startling legacy of the convict era* (Crows Nest, NSW: Allen and Unwin, 2008).
Smith, Billy G. *Ship of Death: A Voyage that changed the Atlantic world* (New Haven, CT:Yale University Press, 2013).
Smith, F. B. 'Mayhew's Convict'. *Victorian Studies*, 22, 4, (1979), 431–48.
St John-McAlister, Michael. 'Edward Angelo Goodall (1819-1908): An Artist's Travels in British Guiana and the Crimea', *British Library e-Journal*, article 5 (2007).
Solzhenitsyn, Aleksandr. *The Gulag Archipelago: An experiment in literary investigation* (New York: Harper and Row, 1974).
Soudien, Crain. 'Nelson Mandela, Robben Island and the Imagination of a New South Africa'. *Journal of Southern African Studies* 41, 2 (2015), 353–366.
Speedy, Karin. '"Arab Castaways"/ "French Escapees": Mobilities, Border Protection and White Australia'. *Law, Crime and History*, 6, 2 (2016), 15–30.
Spieler, Miranda Frances. *Empire and Underworld: Captivity in French Guiana* (Cambridge, MA: Harvard University Press 2012).
Spierenburg, Pieter (ed.). *The Emergence of Carceral Institutions, 1550–1900* (Rotterdam: Erasmus Universiteit Press, 1984).
  'Prison and Convict Labour in Early Modern Europe'. In Christian G. De Vito and Alex Lichtenstein (eds.) *Global Convict Labour* (Leiden: Brill, 2014), pp. 108–25.
Steenstrup, Carl. *A History of Law in Japan until 1868* (Leiden: Brill, 1996).
Steiner, Stephan. '"An Austrian Cayenne": Convict Labour and Deportation in the Habsburg Empire of the Early Modern Period'. In Christian G. De Vito and Alex Lichtenstein (eds.) *Global Convict Labour* (Leiden: Brill, 2014), pp. 126–43.
Stokes, E. T. *The Peasant and the Raj: Studies in agrarian society and peasant rebellion in colonial India* (Cambridge University Press, 1978).
Stokes, E.T. (ed. C.A. Bayly), *The Peasant Armed: the Indian Revolt of 1857* (Oxford: Clarendon Press, 1986).
Stoler, Ann Laura. 'Colony', *Political Concepts: A Critical Lexicon*, 1 (2011) http://www.politicalconcepts.org/issue1/colony/.
  Duress: Imperial durabilities in our times (Durham, NC: Duke University Press, 2016).
Stoler, Ann Laura and Carole McGranahan. 'Refiguring Imperial Terrains'. *Ab Imperio*, 2 (2006), 17–56.
Stutje, Klaas. 'From Across the Water: Nusakambangan and the Making of a Notorious Prison Island', *International Review of Social History*, 64, 3 (2019), 493–513.
Sylvie, Aprile. 'Voices of Exile: French Newspapers in England'. In Sabine Freitag (ed.) *Exiles from European Revolutions: Refugees in Mid-Victorian England* (Oxford: Berghahn, 2003), pp. 149–63.
Tanaka, Osamu. "Shihonshugi kakuritsuki Hokkaidō ni okeru rōdō keitai: Shūjin rōdō o chūshin toshite'. *Keizaironshū* (March 1955), 67–112.
Tarlow, Sarah and Emma Battell Lowman. *Harnessing the Power of the Criminal Corpse* (Basingstoke: Palgrave, 2018).

Taylor, Christopher. *The Black Carib Wars: Freedom, survival, and the making of the Garifuna* (Jackson: University Press of Mississippi, 2016).
Teelock, Vijayalakshmi (ed.) *The Vagrant Depot of Grand River, its Surroundings and Vagrancy in British Mauritius* (Port-Louis: University of Mauritius Press, 2004).
Teeters, Negley K. *Penology from Panama to Cape Horn* (Philadelphia: University of Pennsylvania Press, 1946).
  'The First International Penitentiary Congresses, 1846-46-57', *The Prison Journal*, 26 (1946), 190–210.
  Deliberations of the International Penal and Penitentiary Congresses, Questions and Answers, 1872–1935 (Philadelphia: Temple University Book Store, 1949).
Thénault, Sylvie. *Violence Ordinaire dans l'Algérie Coloniale: camps, internements, assignations à residence* (Paris: Odile Jacob, 2010).
Tinker, Hugh. *A New System of Slavery: The export of Indian labour overseas 1830–1920* (Oxford University Press, 1974).
Toth, Stephen A. *Beyond Papillon: The French overseas penal colonies, 1854–1952* (Lincoln: University of Nebraska Press, 2006).
Townsend, Norma. '"The clamour of ... inconsistent Persons": Attitudes to Transportation within New South Wales in the 1830s'. *Australian Journal of Politics and History*, 25, 3 (1979), 345–57.
Tranter, Bruce and Jed Donoghue. 'Convict Ancestry: A Neglected Aspect of Australian Identity', *Nations and Nationalism*, 9, 4 (2003), 555–77.
Troelstra, Anne S. 'Appun, Karl Ferdinand (1820–1872)'. *Bibliography of Natural History Travel Narratives* (Zeist: KNNV publishing, 2016), p. 41.
Trouillot, Michel-Rolph. *Silencing the Past: Power and the production of history* (Boston, MA: Beacon Press, 1995).
Truter, Paul. 'The Robben Island Rebellion of 1751: A Study of Convict Experience at the Cape of Good Hope'. *Kronos* 31 (2005), 34–49.
Tutino, John. *From Insurrection to Revolution in Mexico: Social bases of agrarian violence, 1750–1940* (Princeton University Press, 1986).
d'Urville, Jules S-C Dumont. *An Account in Two Volumes of Two Voyages to the South Seas, Volume 2*, translated and edited by Helen Rosenman (Melbourne University Press, 1987).
Van der Veer, Peter. 'Colonial Cosmopolitanism'. In Robin Cohen and Steven Vertovec (eds.) *Conceiving Cosmopolitanism: Theory, context and practice* (Oxford University Press, 2002).
Veracini, Lorenzo. 'The Imagined Geographies of Settler Colonialism'. In Banivanua Mar and Penelope Edmonds (eds.) *Making Settler Colonial Space: Perspectives on race, place and identity* (Basingstoke: Palgrave, 2010) pp. 179–97.
  The Settler Colonial Present (Basingstoke: Palgrave, 2015).
Verteuil, Anthony de. *Western Isles of Trinidad* (Port of Spain: The Litho Press, 2002).
Viola, Lynne. 'The Other Archipelago: Kulak Deportations to the North in 1930', *Slavic Review*, 60, 4 (2001), 730–55.
  'The Aesthetic of Stalinist Planning and the World of the Special Villages'. *Kritika: Explorations in Russian and Eurasian History*, 4, 1 (2003), 101–28.

The Unknown Gulag: The lost world of Stalin's special settlements (Oxford University Press, 2007).
'Historicising the Gulag'. In Christian G. De Vito and Alex Lichtenstein (eds.) *Global Convict Labour* (Leiden: Brill, 2014), pp. 361–79.
Voyages of Discovery to Southern Lands by François Péron, continued by Louis de Freycinet, second edition 1824, translated from the French by Christine Cornell, introduction by Anthony J. Brown (Adelaide, SA: Friends of the State Library of South Australia, 2006).
Wachsmann, Nikolaus. *Hitler's Prisons: Legal terror in Nazi Germany* (New Haven, CT: Yale University Press, 2004).
Walby, Kevin and Michael Haan. 'Caste Confusion and Census Enumeration in Colonial India, 1871-1921'. *Histoire Sociale / Social History*, 45, 90 (2012), 301–318.
Waley-Cohen, Joanna. 'Banishment to Xinjiang in Mid-Qing China, 1758–1820'. *Late Imperial China*, 10, 2 (1989), 44–71.
Exile in Mid-Qing China: Banishment to Xinjiang, 1758–1820 (New Haven, CT: Yale University Press, 1991).
Walker, James W. St. G. *The Black Loyalists. The search for a promised land in Nova Scotia and Sierra Leone, 1783–1870* (New York: Africana Publishing and Dalhousie University Press, 1976).
Ward, Kerry. *Networks of Empire: Forced migration in the Dutch East India Company* (Cambridge University Press, 2009).
Watling, Thomas. *Letters From An Exile At Botany Bay, To His Aunt In Dumfries Giving A Particular Account Of The Settlement Of New South Wales, With The Customs And Manners Of The Inhabitants* (Sydney, NSW: University of Sydney Library, 1999).
Webster, Anthony. 'British Expansion in South-East Asia and the Role of Robert Farquhar, Lieutenant-Governor of Penang, 1804-5'. *Journal of Imperial and Commonwealth History*, 23, 1 (1995), 1–25.
West-Sooby, John. 'A Case of Peripheral Vision: Early Spanish and French Perceptions of the British Colony at Port Jackson'. In John West-Sooby (ed.) *Discovery and Empire: The French in the South Seas* (University of Adelaide Press, 2013), pp.141–69.
Wetmore, Alexander. *The Birds of the Republic of Panama, Part 1* (Washington DC: Smithsonian Institution, 1965).
Wheat, David. 'Mediterranean Slavery, New World Transformations: Galley Slaves in the Spanish Caribbean, 1578-1635'. *Slavery and Abolition*, 31, 3 (2010), 327–44.
Whewell, Emily. 'Seeking Refuge in Hostility: The Caribbean "British Isle of Freedom" and the Right to Remove Fugitive Convicts'. *The Journal of Imperial and Commonwealth History*, 48, 1 (2020), 149–67.
White, Ashli. 'The Saint-Dominguan Refugees and American Distinctiveness in the Early Years of the Haitian Revolution'. In David Patrick Geggus and Norman Fiering (eds.) *The World of the Haitian Revolution* (Bloomington: Indiana University Press, 2009) pp. 248–60.
White, Luise. 'Separating the Men from the Boys: Constructions of Gender, Sexuality and Terrorism in Central Kenya, 1939-1959'. *International Journal of African Historical Studies* 23, 1 (1990), 1–25.

Whittaker, Anne-Maree. 'Swords to Ploughshares? The 1798 Rebels in New South Wales'. *Saothar* 23 (1998), 13–22.
  Unfinished revolution: United Irishmen in New South Wales, 1800–1810 (Darlinghurst, NSW: Crossing Press, 2010)
Williams, Philip F. and Yenna Wu. *The Great Wall of Confinement: The Chinese prison camp through contemporary fiction and reportage* (Oakland: University of California Press, 2004).
Wintle, Claire. *Colonial Collecting and Display: Encounters with material culture from the Andaman and Nicobar Islands* (Oxford: Berghahn, 2013).
Wolfe, Eric R. *Europe and the People without History* (Berkeley: University of California Press, 1982).
Wolfe, Patrick. *Settler Colonialism and the Transformation of Anthropology: The Politics and poetics of an ethnographic event* (London: Cassell, 1999).
  'Structure and Event: Settler Colonialism, Time and the Question of Genocide'. In A. Dirk Moses (ed.) *Empire, Colony, Genocide: Conquest, occupation, and subaltern resistance in world history* (Oxford: Berghahn, 2008), 102–32.
Wood, Colleen. Great Britain's exiles sent to Port Phillip, Australia 1844-1849: Lord Stanley's experiment. PhD thesis, The University of Melbourne, 2014.
Woods, Jordan Blair. 'The Birth of Modern Criminology and Gendered Constructions of Homosexual Criminal Identity'. *Journal of Homosexuality*, 62, 2 (2015), 131–66.
Wrigley, A. and R. S. Schofield. *The Population History of England 1541–1871: A reconstruction* (Cambridge University Press, 1981).
Wyhe, John van. *Phrenology and the Origins of Victorian Scientific Naturalism* (Aldershot: Ashgate, 2004).
Yeo, Eileen Janes. 'Social Surveys in the Eighteenth and Nineteenth Centuries'. In Theodore M. Porter and Dorothy Ross (eds.) *The Cambridge History of Science: Volume 7* (Cambridge University Press, 2003), pp. 83–99.
Yeo, Eileen and E. P. Thompson. *The Unknown Mayhew* (New York: Pantheon Books, 1971).
Young, Sarah J. 'Knowing Russia's Convicts: The Other in Narratives of Imprisonment and Exile of the Late Imperial Era'. *Europe-Asia Studies*, 65, 9 (2013), 1700–15.

Archives

ARCHIVES DÉPARTMENTALES DE GUYANE (ADG)

Séries IX Administration pénitentiaire: 54: misc. 1936–1938; 64: rapport de la commission d'enquête sur la deportation de 1838; 76: recherches d'évadés, 1931–6; 79: Visite du pénitentiaire par l'Armée Salut, 1935.

ARCHIVES DÉPARTMENTALES DE LA MARTINIQUE (ADM)

Misc. Correspondence, Governor-General of Martinique, 1934.

ARCHIVES DÉPARTMENTALES DE LA RÉUNION (ADLR)

Saint-Denis Court of Assizes (Extracts, Indictments, and Correspondence): 1837, 1840, 1842, 1844, 1845, 1846, 1850.

ARCHIVES DE LA NOUVELLE-CALÉDONIE (ANC)

Unpublished manuscript, Léon Collin, Fin de bagne en Nouvelle-Calédonie, 1913.

ARCHIVES NATIONALES D'OUTRE MER (ANOM)

Administration pénitentiaire coloniale et bagnes de Guyane et Nouvelle Calédonie, Séries H: 1816, 1819, 1844, 1845, 1851, 1854, 1862, 1864, 1894, 1898–1903, 1905, 1912–13, 1916–18, 1944.

Mémoire sur la Déportation des Forçats, présenté en 1828, par M. Martemarie (Havre: Imprimerie de Stanislas Faure, 1840).

ARCHIVES OF THE ROYAL BOTANIC GARDENS, KEW (RBG)

Directors' Correspondence (DC): 1843, 1860–62, 1864–65, 1867–69, 1875, 1890–91.
Papers of Henry Nicholas Ridley, Director of Gardens and Forest, the Straits Settlements, 1887–1912.
India, Andaman and Nicobar Islands 1870–1928: J. B. King, Report of the Royal Dover Gardens, Haddo, Port Blair, 1870–1871.
Specimens: E. B. Copeland, 1932; J. D. Dwyer, 1961; Roxana Stinchfield Ferris, 1927; A. C. Maingay, 1871.

BRITISH LIBRARY, LONDON

British Library (BL)

L'Homme: Journal de la Démocratie universelle, 1856.
Cayenne: letters from republicans sentenced to transportation (Manchester: 1855).

India Office Records (IOR)

Bengal public and judicial despatches (L/PJ) 1858.
Judicial consultations and proceedings (P):
    Bengal, 1824, 1841, 1845, 1859.
    Bombay, 1842, 1845–6.
    India, 1858.
    India, 1858–9.
    Madras, 1803, 1814.
Board of Control (F), 1813, 1836.
Bombay law proceedings (P), 1799.
Correspondence from Thomas Warneford to Maud Warneford, 1874–79.
Mouat, F. J. The Prison System of India (London: National Association for the Promotion of Social Science, 1872).
Reports on the Administration of the Andaman and Nicobar Islands and the Penal Settlement of Port Blair.

CELLULAR JAIL MUSEUM LIBRARY, PORT BLAIR, ANDAMAN ISLANDS (CJML)

'The Census, 1901': Diary of A. R. S. Anderson, 15–18 February 1901 (uncatalogued typescript).

HOKKAIDO UNIVERSITY LIBRARY

Honda, Rimei. *Ezo tochi kaihatsu guzon no taigai*, 1791 (copied in 1854).

INTERNATIONAL INSTITUTE OF SOCIAL HISTORY, AMSTERDAM (IISG)

[Signed by Tassilier]. *Cayenne* (Manchester: no publisher, 1855).
Le Revendicateur: Journal Social, Politique et Littéraire, 1860–1.

LONDON METROPOLITAN ARCHIVES (LMA)

Saint Thomas' Hospital Group: Nightingale Collection, 1855, 1859.

MODERN RECORDS CENTRE, UNIVERSITY OF WARWICK (MRC)

The Howard League for Penal Reform

'Ushuaia, Penal Colony of Argentina in Tierra del Fuego'.

NATIONAL ARCHIVES OF BERMUDA (NAB)

Convict Hulk Establishment, 1847–9.

NATIONAL ARCHIVES OF INDIA, NEW DELHI (NAI)

Census of the Andaman Islands, December 1871.
Port Blair 'A' proceedings, October 1873.
Port Blair 'B' proceedings, May-June 1892.

NATIONAL ARCHIVES OF JAMAICA (NAJ)

Hanover Slave Court, Parish of Hanover, 1819–23, 1825.
Port Royal, summary slave trials, 1819–34.

NATIONAL ARCHIVES OF MAURITIUS (NAM)

Miscellaneous Mauritius secretariat (RA), 1818.
Proceedings of the Court of Assizes (JB), 1817.

NATIONAL ARCHIVES OF TRINIDAD AND TOBAGO (NATT)

Reports of the Inspector of Prisons for the years 1873, 1894, 1897, 1898, 1906–7.

NATIONAL DIET LIBRARY, TOKYO

Tsukigata, Kiyoshi. 'Hokkaidō kaitaku shigi', c. 1885.

THE NATIONAL ARCHIVES, KEW (TNA)

Admiralty and Predecessors

Letters from Commanders-in-Chief, Leeward Islands, 1816.
Office of the Director General of the Medical Department of the Navy and predecessors: Medical journals, 1826, 1833, 1836–7.

Colonial Office, Original Correspondence

Antigua and Montserrat (CO7), 1845, 1849–50, 1856.
Bahamas (CO23), 1834–36.
Barbados (CO28), 1816–19, 1822, 1824–25, 1827–29, 1832–33, 1835–39, 1842–44, 1846, 1849–50, 1853, 1856–58, 1866, 1869.
Bermuda (CO37), 1828–40, 1845–50, 1852–54, 1856–63, 1865.
British Guiana (CO111), 1834–35, 1837, 1839, 1841–44, 1847–48, 1852, 1855, 1857–58, 1860–63, 1865–66.
British Honduras (CO123), 1817–18, 1827, 1849, 1861–62.
Cape of Good Hope Colony (Cape Colony) (CO48), 1825–26, 1842, 1849–50.
Ceylon (CO54), 1819.
Social Services Department and successors (CO859), 1936–7, 1939.
Gibraltar (CO91), 1828, 1831, 1842–65.
Grenada (CO101), 1796–97, 1836–37, 1870, 1879.
Jamaica (CO137), 1807, 1831–32, 1835–36, 1843.
Labuan (CO144), 1856.
Mauritius (CO167), 1817–18.
Sierra Leone (CO267), 1818–19, 1825–9, 1841,1859, 1861.
St Christopher (St Kitts), Nevis and Anguilla. (CO239), 1832.
Trinidad (CO295), 1830–31, 1839, 1857–58, 1864, 1879–80, 1888.
Turks and Caicos Islands (CO301), 1849–50.

West Indies (CO318), 1827, 1837, 1844–45, 1858, 1936–7, 1939, 1940–45.
Windward Islands (CO321), 1877.

Prison Commission

Prison reports and miscellaneous correspondence (PCOM9), 1933, 1936–37.

Public Record Office, Maps and Plans

Sketches of a flag taken from insurgent slaves, Barbados, 1816.

PRINCETON UNIVERSITY LIBRARY (PUL)

Manuscripts Division, Special Collections

Richard Halliburton Papers, 1929–33.

SALVATION ARMY INTERNATIONAL HERITAGE CENTRE, LONDON (SAIHC)

French Guiana: *The People*, 30 April 1950 (account of George Seaton).

Péan, Charles. The Conquest of Devil's Island (London: Max Parrish, n.d.)

Booth, General [William]. In Darkest England and the Way Out (London: Funk and Wagnall, 1890).

TSUKIGATA KABATO MUSEUM ARCHIVES

Tsukigata, Kiyoshi. 'Hokkaidō shūchikan no yakushūjigyō nitsuki jōshin', c. 1885.

UK PUBLIC GENERAL ACTS

Colonial Prisoners Removal Act 1869 (32 & 33 Vict. cap. 10). http://www.legislation.gov.uk/ukpga/Vict/32-33/10/introduction.

Penal Servitude Act 1857(20 & 21 Vict., cap. 3). http://www.legislation.gov.uk/ukpga/Vict/20-21/3/contents.

UK PARLIAMENTARY PAPERS (PP)

Annual Reports and Despatches, Convict Establishments, Bermuda, Gibraltar, 1859–60.

Comptroller's Report, Gibraltar, 1869.

Correspondence, Governors of the Cape of Good Hope, Ceylon, Bermuda, 1849.

Correspondence, Prisons in West Indies, British Colonies in South America, 1830–31.

Papers presented to Parliament for the melioration of the condition of the slave population in in the West Indies, 1831–32.

Papers Relating to the Improvement of Prison Discipline in the Colonies, 1871–72.

Report on Abolition of Slavery, 1837.

Report of Captain J. W. Pringle, on prisons in the West Indies and Jamaica, 17 July 1838.

Reports on the Convict Establishments at Bermuda and Gibraltar, 1859, 1860, 1861.

Report on the Convict Establishments at Gibraltar Western Australia and Tasmania, 1869.

Report of the Commissioners of Enquiry (criminal and civil justice), West Indies and South America, 1828–29.

Report of the Commissioners of Enquiry (criminal and civil justice), Jamaica, 1826–7.

Report of the Commissioners of Enquiry Demerara, Essequebo and Berbice, 1828.

Report of the Commissioners of Inquiry (criminal and civil justice), Honduras and Bahama Islands, 1829.

Reports of the Commissioners of Inquiry (state of colony), New South Wales, 1822–23, 1831.

Report of the Commissioners of Inquiry (state of colony), Sierra Leone, 1826–7.

Report of the Commissioner of Inquiry (judicial establishments), New South Wales and Van Diemen's Land, 1823.

Report of the Commissioner of Inquiry (criminal and civil justice), West Indies, Antigua, Montserrat, Nevis, St Christopher, and the Virgin Islands, 1826–7.

Report of the Directors of Convict Prisons, Pentonville, Millbank, Parkhurst, Portland, Portsmouth, Dartmoor, Chatham, Brixton, Fulham, and Woking, 1870.

Report of the Directors of Convict Establishments, Gibraltar, Western Australia, and Tasmania, 1869.
Report of His Majesty's Commissioners of Legal Enquiry on Trinidad, 1826–7.
Reports on Sanitary Measures in India, 1881–82, 1904–6, 1913–1914.
Report from the Select Committee, Ceylon and British Guiana, 1849.
Report from the Select Committee on Secondary Punishments, 1831.
Reports from the Select Committee on Transportation, 1812, 1837–38.
Report of the Select Committee, West Coast of Africa, 1842.
Reports on Transportation, Cape of Good Hope, 1848–9.
Statement Exhibiting the Moral and Material Progress and Condition of India, during the year 1861–2, Part I.

UNIVERSITY OF CAMBRIDGE (UC)

Christ's College Library (CCL)

Charles Darwin collections.

UNIVERSITY OF PENNSYLVANIA, RARE BOOK AND MANUSCRIPT LIBRARY

John Nicholson diary, 1848–50.

WALTER RODNEY ARCHIVES (NATIONAL ARCHIVES OF GUYANA) (WRNAG)

Court of Policy, 1841, 1842.

WELLCOME LIBRARY, LONDON

Diary kept by Joanna King, 1867–8.

MISCELLANEOUS ONLINE RECORDS

Ancestry. www.ancestry.com.
Board of Guardian Records, 1849.
Church of England Parish Registers, 1849.
Convict prison hulks: registers and letter books, 1838.
England Census, 1841.

US, Civil War Soldier Records and Profiles, 1861–1865.
Bermuda Hulks. http://www.bermudahulks.com/.
Charles Booth's London: Poverty Maps and Police Notebooks. https://booth.lse.ac.uk/.
The Complete Works of Charles Darwin Online. http://darwin-online.org.uk.
William Buelow Gould's 'Sketchbook of Fishes' https://www.linc.tas.gov.au/allport/Pages/gould.aspx.
William Dawes' notebooks, Digital collections of SOAS, University of London: https://digital.soas.ac.uk/dawes/about/.
History in the Williams River Valley. https://williamsvalleyhistory.org/aborigines-gringai/.
International Penal and Penitentiary Commission (IPPC), http://www.unodc.org/congress/en/previous/previous-ippc.html.
JSTOR Global Plants database. https://plants.jstor.org.
Legacies of British Slave-Ownership Database. https://www.ucl.ac.uk/lbs.
Le Maitron: Dictionnaire Biographique: Mouvement Ouvrier Mouvement Social. https://maitron.fr/.
National Library of Australia. "Trove," digitized newspaper catalogue. http://trove.nla.gova.au/newspaper.
Walters, Edgar. 'The storied escapes of René Belbenoit', 14 May 2014. https://sites.utexas.edu/ransomcentermagazine/2013/05/14/rene-belbenoit/.

NEWSPAPERS AND PERIODICALS

The Daily Argosy, 25 January 1945.
Journal of the Royal Geographical Society of London, 1872.
Missionary Herald, June 1896.
The Missionary Review of the World, 1899.
The Monitor, 10 February 1827.
The Morning Chronicle, 15 February 1855, 4 October 1856.
The Sydney Gazette and New South Wales Advertiser, 9 September 1826.
The Times, 25 August 1856, 19 November 1857.

Index

Abakuá mutual aid societies
  Ceuta, 30–2
abolition of slavery
  Britain (1833), 59, 103, 363
  Cuba (1880), 50
  France (1794), 372
  France (1848), 137, 372
  Massachusetts (1783), 375
abolition of the slave trade
  Britain (1807), 100, 104, 132, 135
  Portugal (1836), 42
agricultural penal colonies
  Angola, 10–11, 43, 46
  Belgium, 93
  Italian colonies, 19, 93
  Latin America, 1–2
    Colombia, 97
Ancient World
  changing nature of punitive relocation, 20
Andaman Islands (India), 30–2, 186, 192
  censuses of convict population (generally), 1–2, 320, 358
    marriage between convicts, 5–7, 29–30
    preoccupation with caste/status, 5–7, 28, 29
    shortcomings, 62–63
  exploration of the hinterlands, 29
  first census (1871), 21
  fourth census (1901), 24–6
    census of the penal settlement, 26–8
    children of convicts, 30–2
    incidence of violent crime, 1–5
    indigenous enumeration, 26
    shortcomings, 7–8, 28–9
  French New Caledonia compared, 21–2
  Hokkaido compared, 22–4
  Indigenous peoples, 249
  medical research
    leprosy, 19
    malaria, 20
    withdrawal from addictive substances, 16
  mortality rates, 305
  second census (1881), 21–2
  specimen collection, 29–30
  terra nullius doctrine, 20
  third census (1891), 22–4
Angola
  agricultural penal colonies, 10–11, 43, 46
  colonialization, 42
  political prisoners, 215
  urban penal colonies, 11
anti-transportation sentiment, 265
  impact of, 134
apprenticeship system, 30–2, 129, 134, 161
  Bermuda, 61
  Cuba, 50, 139
  Jamaica, 104, 145
Argentina, 73, 93
  see also Ushuaia (Argentina)
art
  visual representations of natural history, 28
Arthur, Lieutenant Colonel George, 132
Barbados Rebellion (1816), 22–4, 101, 257
Van Diemen's Land, 29, 207
Australian colonies, 221
  economic depression, impact of, 29
  exploration of the hinterlands, 29
  French New Caledonian escapees, 26
  Indigenous peoples, 14–17, 249
  Irish, transportation of, 21, 29–30
    resistance, 26
  political convicts, 26–8
  specimen collection, 266
  terra nullius doctrine, 19
  transportation from Caribbean colonies, 14
    banning of, 1–5, 147
  'White Australia' policy, 384

Index

banishment and penal transportation of slaves
banishment
  Demerara-Essequibo, 13–14
  Dominica, 106
  Trinidad, 107
  British Caribbean, 100
  Bahamas, 9–10
  Garifuna, 110
  Grenada, 8–9
  Jamaica, 3–6
  Montserrat, 105
  Saint Vincent, 105
collective rebellion and treason, 16
  Fédon's Rebellion (British Grenada 1795–6), 14
  Second Maroon War (Jamaica 1795–6), 14–17
compensation for slave owners, 115
French policies, impact on British practice, 135, 171
  French Guiana, 8–9
  Martinique, 7–9
  Saint-Domingue (Haiti), 8–9
Spanish policies, impact on British practice, 135, 171
increase in transportation to Australian penal colonies, 11–13
independence of Spanish colonies, 11
Baptist War (Jamaica) 1831–2, 5–7, 134, 143, 197
Barbados
  Kalingo labour, 253
  see also Barbados Rebellion (1816)
Barbados Rebellion (1816), 7–8, 16–17, 103, 257
  banishment and penal transportation, 1–5
  Honduras, 20
  Sierra Leone, 20
  motivations, 19
  return of maroons to work on plantations, 29
Beaumont, Gustave de, 221, 236, 247
Bentham, Jeremy
  convict rehabilitation theories, 1–5
Bermuda, 37
  military construction, 57–59
    cost-effectiveness of convict labour, 57–61
  indentured and enslaved labour, 59
  see also convict hulks
Bertillon, Louis-Alphonse, 295, 322, 330
Bolivia, 73
  agricultural penal colonies, 97
  free labour migration, 74

Booth, Charles, 62
Boston (USA)
  escaped convicts, 360, 374, 375, 376
Brazil, 93
  escape from French Guiana, 21–2
  farming, 40
  mining, 40
  see also Fernando de Noronha (Brazil)
British Guiana
  Demerara Rebellion (1823), 5–7
  locally convicted felons, 135
  proposal for a new site of transportation Mazaruni, 16–17
  see also Mazaruni (British Guiana)
British Museum, 1, 5, 268
British parliamentary interest in colonial imprisonment, 16, 112, 153, 292, 308
Bussa's Revolt. see Barbados Rebellion (1816)

Cape Colony
  exploration of the hinterlands, 28–9
  Irish, transportation of, 22–4
  Islam, spread of, 8–9
Carrera Island (Trinidad), 152, 153
  convict occupations, 154
  discipline, 155
caste/status, 180, 319
  Andaman Island censuses, 5–7, 28, 29, 320, 344, 346, 348
  caste mobility, 62
  high-caste convicts, 180, 186
  marriage, 64–65
  Mauritius, 172
  social dislocations, 65
Cazanove, Franck, 320
  immorality and sexual depravation in French Guiana, 57–61, 358
Ceuta (Portugal)
  imperial expansion, 9, 40
Ceuta (Spain), 21, 24–6, 37, 212
  African-Cuban secret societies, 30–2
  convict classification, 237
  Gibraltar, information exchange, 236, 364
  political prisoners, 57–59
changing nature of punitive relocation, 14–17
  Ancient World, 20
  European empires
    Denmark-Norway, 26
    France, 22–4
    Germany, 28
    Netherlands, 26–8

Index

changing nature of punitive (cont.)
  Portugal, 21
  17th-century Britain, 24–6
  Spain, 21–2
  imperial China, 20, 29
  imperial Russia, 28–9
  independent Latin American states, 29–30
  Japan
    post-Meiji regime, 29
  Middle Ages, 20
  modern China, 32
  Scandinavian empires, 26
  17th-century Britain, 24–6
  20th-century European dictatorships, 30–2
    Franco's Spain, 30
    Italian Fascist government, 30
    Nazi Germany, 30–2
    USSR, 32
Chautard, Jean Léon
  Boston, 16
  anti-slavery campaigns, involvement in, 16–17
  convictions, 8–9
  escape, 370
  Escapes From Cayenne pamphlet, 8–9
  fellow deserters
    Bivors, 11–13
    Paon, 9–10
  French Guiana, 11
  transfer from Algeria to French Guiana, 10–11
Chekhov, Anton
  census of Sakhalin Island convict population, 19, 319, 320, 358
  shortcomings, 20
  see also Sakhalin Island (Russia)
children
  health of convicts' children, 312, 319, 326
  inherited criminality, 8–9, 343, 351
Chile, 73, 93
  Juan Fernández islands, 30, 94, 213
'civilizing' Indigenous populations, 14–17
  Andaman Islands, 260
  French New Caledonia, 262
Colombia, 73
  agricultural penal colonies, 97
  free labour migration, 74
colonial governance, 1–5
  managing colonial labour
    Mazaruni, 16–17
    Trinidad, 22–4
  see also changing nature of punitive relocation

colonization, relationship with penal colonies, 7–8, 10–13, 57–59, 230, 327
  Hokkaido (Japan), 62–63
  Portuguese empire, 16
    encouragement of free migration, 41, 42, 43
  Ushuaia (Argentina), 96
  Xinjian (China), 29–30
commodity exchange, 147, 151, 162
  addictive substances, 182, 249
  see also trade
communist China
  women, 32
Congo (Belgium)
  agricultural colonies, 57–61
conscripted convicts, 14, 72
  Portuguese empire, 6, 41, 44
    military agrarian penal settlements, 43
  Spanish empire, 46, 51, 139
convict activism, 21–2, 198, 215
convict agency, 10, 33, 34, 56, 171, 195, 211, 216, 219, 301, 360
  Barbados Rebellion, 101
  Carrera Island, 155
  escape, 360, 389
  family and marital relationships, 41
  medical research, 288, 318
  Portuguese degredados, 7–9
  see also resistance
convict flows, 11
convict hulks, 72
  absence of convict women, 37
  Australia compared, 38
  effective punishment and convict reformation, 68
  Irish, transportation of, 21–2
  prohibition on settlement, 37, 71
  Spanish convicts, 67–8
  transportation convicts and penal servitude prisoners, relationship between, 64–5
  see also Bermuda; Gibraltar
convict labour negotiations, 66–7
convict-run and convict-owned businesses, 16–17, 37, 72, 96, 384
criminality
  anthropometry, 3–6, 295
  inherited criminality, 29, 343, 351
    Lobas, 13–14
    Lombroso, 9–10, 29, 237, 287
criticisms of disciplinary regimes
  Australian penal colonies, 26
    Molesworth Committee, 28–9
  Caribbean colonies, 29
  Carrera Island, 24–6
  consideration of new destinations, 26–8

Index

Crofton, Sir Walter, 219
  organisation of convicts, 6
  progressive classification, 13–14, 247
  see also Ireland
Cuba, 50
  labour management, 26
  see also Isla de Pinos (Cuba)

de Beaumont, Gustave. *see* Beaumont, Gustave de
de Tocqueville, Alexis. *see* Tocqueville, Alexis de
degredados (Portuguese empire), 9, 38, 251
  convict agency, 7–9
  women, 40, 42, 45
Demerara Rebellion (1823), 5–7
Demerara-Essequibo
  banishment and penal transportation of slaves, 13–14
Denmark's imperial ambitions, 29
Denmark-Norway, 37, 52, 72
  changing nature of punitive relocation, 26, 216
  solidarities between convicts, 8–9
depósitos (Portuguese empire), 43–4
disease and violence, 249
  Andaman Islands, 20
  Australian Aboriginal populations, 256
  convicts, 29–30
  French New Caledonia, 262
  Indigenous peoples, 11
  North American colonies, 10–11
  see also malaria; yellow fever
dockyard prisons, 28–9, 52, 205, 236
Dominica, 108
  banishment and penal transportation of slaves, 11–13
Dubois, W. E. B., 62
Dutch East India Company, 26, 37
  abolition, 56
  convict labour
    military construction, 55
    plantation work, 55
    public works, 53
  Robben Island, 3–6
  women, 7–8
  see also Netherlands
Dutch pauper colonies, 19

early-modern Americas
  Indigenous peoples, 249
economic development of offshore islands
  Argentina, 30–2
  Chile, 94

Mexico, 96
Peru, 5–7, 94
Ecuador, 73
  agricultural penal colonies, 97
  free labour migration, 74
  education and political consciousness, 70–71
  Andaman Islands, 20
  Robben Island, 20
El Frontón (Peru), 5–7, 74, 98
  political prisoners, 62–63
  see also Peru
English East India Company
  Indian Prison Discipline Committee, 222
  rebellion, 10–11, 186
escape, 11, 29–30, 34, 38
  challenges, 7–9
  export of ideologies, 20
  Indigenous people, relationship with, 253
  multi-directional nature, 360
  Scandinavian empires, 30–2
  Second World War, 29
  Spanish empire, 3–6, 21–2
experimental inoculation
  medical research, 26
exploration of the hinterlands
  Andaman Islands, 29
  Australian colonies, 29
  Cape Colony, 28–9
extradition
  havens of refuge, 386
  legal issues, 378
  see also extradition treaties
extradition treaties
  Britain and France, between, 22–4, 379, 382
  Britain and Spain, between, 6
  Netherlands and France, between, 20
  political prisoners
    Dutch empire, 373
  Spain and France, between, 380

families, 7
  agency, 41
  Andaman Islands census, 341, 353
  health, 312
  medical experimentation, 315
  settlers, 76, 96, 158, 348
  statistical analysis, 328, 329, 331, 332, 354
  ticket-of-leave families, 311
farming, 7, 37
  Brazil, 40
  Japan, post-Meiji restoration, 87
Fédon's Rebellion (British Grenada 1795–6), 14

Fernando de Noronha (Brazil)
  families, 7
  organisation of convicts, 3–6
  phrenology and high imperialism, 10–11
  role in history, 7–9
  specimen collection, 1–5, 266
  types of work
    farmers, 7
    handicrafts, 7
    public works, 7
  Ushuaia (Argentina) compared, 96
fertility rates
  Andaman Islands, 354
forzados (Spanish empire), 20
Franco's Spain
  changing nature of punitive relocation, 30
free migration, 73
  Australian colonies, 229
  Dutch East India Company, 37
  Hokkaido (Japan), 84, 89, 98
  Portuguese empire, 41–2, 43, 74
free settlers, 10, 13, 156
  British Guiana, 151
  Japan, post-Meiji restoration, 24–6
  Portuguese empire, 46
  Siberia, 240
French empire
  changing nature of punitive relocation, 22–4
French Guiana, 220
  criticisms by international community, 388
  escape destinations, 1–5, 360
    Brazil, 21–2
    British Guiana, 24–6, 30–2
    Dutch Surinam, 21
    other destinations, 380
    Trinidad, 381
  immorality and sexual depravation, 57
  sex and sexuality in the *relégué* camp, 57
  sexuality in the *relégué(e)*, 320
  see also Cazanove, Franck
  social survey of convicts, 319
  see also Orgéas, Joseph
  specimen collection, 1–5
French juvenile reformatory at Mettray, 19, 265
French New Caledonia
  criminal physiognomy, 14
  escape destinations
    Australian colonies, 26
    Indigenous peoples, 24–6, 249
frontier penal colonies
  Xinjiang (China), 29–30, 98

Germany
  changing nature of punitive relocation, 28
  penal colonies, 21
Gibraltar, 37
  military construction, 62
  cost-effectiveness of convict labour,
  see also convict hulks
global exchange of penal policies and practice
  Australian colonies, 221
  English East India Company
    Indian Prison Discipline Committee, 222
  French Guiana, failure of, 220
  prison tours, 14–17
    admiration for the Hokkaido settlements, 20
    Ceuta, 16
    Heindl, 20
    Japanese overseas tours (Europe), 16–17
    Japanese overseas tours (Russian empire), 19
    Paterson, 21–2
    US penitentiaries, 221
  Spanish empire, 3–6
  see also International Penitentiary Congress
good behaviour
  reward for, 7, 63, 64, 65, 68, 98, 123, 128, 209
Grenada
  banishment and penal transportation of slaves, 10–11
  Fédon's Rebellion (1795–6), 14
Griffiths, Arthur, 14–17, 64, 241
gulag, 14, 32

Habsburg empire, 28
handicrafts, 7, 37, 61
  Japan, post-Meiji restoration, 87
  Qing-era China, 75
Heindl, Robert, 219, 247
  prison tours, 20
Hokkaido (Japan), 11, 98
  colonization of uncultivated land, 84
  convict profile, 19
  establishment, 16–17
  free migration, 84
  French practice, influence of, 81, 82
  indigenous peoples, relationship with, 22–4
  penal stages, 82
  see also imperial Japan
Honduras
  Barbados Rebellion, 21, 101
  absence of a legal code, 24–6
  historic rejection of convicts, 26

Index

hookworm, 326
  medical research, 24–6, 288
Howard League for Penal Reform, 26–8

immorality and sexual depravation, 57–61, 159, 161, 358
imperial China, 1–5, 73
  changing nature of punitive relocation, 20, 29
  mid-Qing era, 3–6
    colonization aims, 8–9
    punishment, 6
    rehabilitation, 7–9
  see also Xinjiang (China)
imperial Japan, 73
  changing nature of punitive relocation, 14–17, 29
  colonization aims, 11–13
  post-Meiji restoration, 11
    convict rehabilitation, 20
    farming, 85, 87
    forms of outdoor work, 21
    handicrafts, 87
    illness and injury, 89
    mining, 85
    principle of extraterritoriality, 16
    prison reform measures, 14
    public works, 85, 87
    'unequal' treaties, 16
    see also Hokkaido (Japan)
  removal of 'undesirables' to remote islands, 13–14
  Tokugawa Shogunate era, 11–13
imperial Russia
  changing nature of punitive relocation, 28–9
  gulag, 14, 32
  women, 28
indentured and enslaved workers, convicts' relationship with, 10, 13–14
  Dutch East India Company, 1–5
  Scandinavian empires, 5–7
  Spanish empire, 21, 50
  see also slaves and slavery
independent Latin American states
  changing nature of punitive relocation, 29–30
  impact of independence on British practices, 3–6
  political repression, 7–8
  women, 1–5
Indian Rebellion (1857)
  Andaman Islands, 30–2
Indigenous peoples, convicts' relationship with, 10, 57–59
  Andaman Islands, 21
  assisting expeditions, 256
  Barbados
    British empire, 9–10
    Spanish empire, 8–9
  British Guiana, 20
  disease and violence, 8–9, 256
  employment in colonial police forces, 258
  labour, 250
  maroon (runaway) slaves, 254
  North American colonies
    disease and violence, 10–11
    penal transportation, impact of, 1–2, 14
  Portuguese voyages of exploration
    Africa, 6
    Brazil, 252
    lançados, 6
  Portuguese Asia, 7–9
  racial containment, 14–17
  sexual relationships, 256
  Spanish Empire' approach to Indigenous relations, 8–9, 29, 50
  trade, 13–14
internal penal colonies
  dockyard prisons, 28–9
International Penitentiary Congress, 220
  aims and purpose, 8–9
  anti-transportation views, 9–10, 230
  Berlin (1935), 225
  Brussels (1900), 225, 233
  Budapest (1905), 225
  London (1872), 6, 225
  London (1925), 225, 245
  Paris (1895), 225, 232
  Prague (1930), 225
  pro-transportation views, 8–9, 10–13
  punishment and labour, relationship between, 11
  Rome (1885), 225, 228, 230
  St Petersburg (1890), 225, 228, 230, 231, 236
  Stockholm (1878), 7–9, 225, 227, 228, 234
  The Hague (1950), 225
  Washington (1910), 225
  see also global exchange of penal policies and practice
Ireland, 219
  see also Crofton, Sir Walter
Irish, transportation of, 29, 254
  Australian colonies, 21, 29–30
    resistance, 26
  Cape Colony, 22–4
  convict hulks, 21–2
  indentured servants to the Americas, 195

Irish, transportation of (cont.)
  Mitchel, John, 24–6
  plantations, 196
Isla de Pinos (Cuba)
  political prisoners, 215
Islamic practice
  Islamification of the Cape, 7–9, 185
island penal colonies, 98
  British Empire, 29
  Chile, 95
  Dutch East India Company, 176
  Italy, 29
  Japan, post-Meiji restoration, 11
    see also Hokkaido (Japan)
  Mexico, 96
  Ottoman empire, 90
  Peru, 5–7, 94
Islas Marías (Mexico), 1–5
  political prisoners, 1–2
  see also Mexico
Italian fascist government
  changing nature of punitive relocation, 30

Jamaica
  banishment and penal transportation of slaves, 11
  process, 7–9
  Second Maroon War (1795–6), 14–17
  Slave Code (1696), 102
  slave court records, 8–9
  slave courts, 6
  Baptist War (1831–2), 5–7, 134, 143, 197

Kossokhatko affair, 28–9

labour flows, 14
  Spanish empire, 49
lançados (Portuguese empire), 6
leprosy
  medical research, 288, 305
  Andaman Islands, 19
Lobas, N. S., 13–14
Lombroso, Cesare
  hereditary criminality, 9–10
  support in Latin America, 303
  see also criminality
London
  community of French escapees, 14–17
Lowis, R. F. see Andaman Islands (India): censuses of convict population (generally)
lusotropicalism, 41, 288

Maconochie, Alexander, 16, 159, 200
  mark system of progressive classification, 13–14, 219, 247

phrenology, 291
  see also Norfolk Island (Australia)
malaria
  medical research, 288, 305
  Andaman Islands, 20
managing colonial labour
  Mazaruni, 16–17
  Trinidad, 22–4
mark system of progressive classification
  see Maconochie, Alexander
marriage between convicts
  Andaman Islands, 5–7, 29–30, 57–59
  French Guiana, 11–13
  French New Caledonia, 301
Martinique
  banishment and penal transportation of slaves, 7–9
Mayhew, Henry, 62
Mazaruni (British Guiana)
  economic and reformative role, 20, 21
  indigenous men and women, relationship with, 20
  interned enemy aliens, 388
  opposition to white convicts in former slave colonies, 19
  regional penal colony, as, 7–8
  scientific research, 30–2
medical research, 28–9
  convict volunteers
    medical procedures, 26–8
    medical service, 28
  experimental inoculation, 26
  hookworm, 24–6, 288
  leprosy, 288, 305
    Andaman Islands, 19
  malaria, 288, 305
    Andaman Islands, 20
  mortality and morbidity, 288, 305
  racial variations in prevalence of and immunity against diseases, 21
  suicide among convict men, 20
  vaccinations against smallpox, 305
  Weil's disease, 313
  withdrawal from addictive substances, 16–17, 305
    Andaman Islands, 16
  yellow fever, 22–4, 288
  see also scientific research
Mettray. see French juvenile reformatory at Mettray
Mexican revolution (1910–20)
  military phase, 1–5
  political repression, 1–5
  rebellion against secularism, 5–7
Mexican war of independence (1810), 139

Mexico, 73, 93
  see also Islas Marías (Mexico); Mexican revolution (1910–20)
Middle Ages
  changing nature of punitive relocation, 20
military campaigns
  Portugal's overseas possessions, 6
  Spain, 51
military construction, 55
  convict hulks, 37
    Bermuda, 1–2
    Gibraltar, 62–63
    see also Bermuda Gibraltar
  mining, 20, 47, 49, 5555
    Brazil, 40
    Dutch East India Company, 55
    imperial Russia, 22–4, 28
    Japan, post-Meiji restoration, 29, 85, 89, 241
    Mazaruni (British Guiana), 150
    modern Japan, 90
    Spanish colonies, 49, 139
    Xinjiang (China), 76
Mitchel, John, 28, 360
modern China
  changing nature of punitive relocation, 32
modern Japan, 26
Molesworth Committee, 28–9, 134, 147, 161, 162, 171, 203
mortality and morbidity
  French Guiana, 8–9
    racial differences in survival rates, 8–9
  Japan, post-Meiji restoration, 21–2
  medical research, 288, 305
  racial variations, 21–2
  research, 288
  transportation journeys, 13–14
Mozambique
  agricultural penal settlement, 10–11
  colonialization, 42
  political prisoners, 215
  urban penal colonies, 11
mutiny, 10, 21–2
  Danish West India and Guinea Company, 9–10
  differing motivations and ambitions, 19
  English East India Company, 10–11, 186
  political nature, 11–13
    failure to respect cultural practices, 14–17

nation and empire building, relationship with convict relocation, 16–17

Nazi Germany
  changing nature of punitive relocation, 30–2
Netherlands, 37
  changing nature of punitive relocation, 26–8
  see also Dutch East India Company
New Caledonia. see French New Caledonia
New South Wales. see Australian colonies
Norfolk Island (Australia), 219
  see also Maconochie, Alexander
North American colonies
  violence against Indigenous people, 10–11
nutritional deficiency, 66–66

Ohara, Shigeya, 82, 238, 247
Orgéas, Joseph, 16–17, 319, 358
  Bertillon, influence of, 322
  Quételet, influence of, 323
  social survey of French Guiana convicts, 1–5
    background, 3–6
    convict marriage, impact of, 11–13
    ethnographic investigations, 16
    fertility, 9–10, 13–14
    life expectancy, 14
    methodology, 6
    morbidity and mortality, 7–9, 11, 321
    provisos, 14–17
    transportation arguments and policy, impact on, 10–11
Ottoman empire, 26–8

Paterson, Alexander, 219, 247
  prison tours, 21–2
  system of doublage, 385
Penal Servitude Act 1853, 64, 205
Penal Servitude Act 1857, 205
penal settlements defined, 10
penal stages, 5–7
  Andaman Islands (India), 194
  Australian colonies, 128, 161
  'exile' system, 203
  Fernando de Noronha (Brazil), 7, 44
  Hokkaido (Japan), 82
  moving to different colonies, 203
  Ushuaia (Argentina), 95
  see also Maconochie, Alexander
Peru, 73, 74
  Juan Fernández islands, 94
  see also El Frontón (Peru)
Philippines
  labour management, 26–8
phrenology, 6
  criticisms of, 289

phrenology (cont.)
  Edinburgh Phrenological Society, 8–9, 289
  inherited traits, 8–9
  Maconochie, 292
  pre-selection of transportation convicts, 7–9, 291
  supporters of, 289
physiognomy
  hereditary criminality, 294, 300, 301
plantation work, 52, 55
  Irish convicts, 196
  resettlement of Barbadian rebels, 29
political prisoners, 14, 57–61, 69, 360
  Andaman Islands, 65
  Australian colonies, 66
  Cape Colony, 67–8
  Ceuta, 68
  convict hulks, 66–7
  Dutch East India Company, 62
  'exile' system, 203
  extradition/return of
    Dutch empire, 14
    independent Latin American countries, 7–8
    Argentina, 215
    Mexico, 1–2
    Peru, 69
  mutinies, 64–65
  Robben Island, 62
poor health
  Bermuda, 69
  Japan, post-Meiji restoration, 22–4
  see also disease and violence, malaria, nutritional deficiency, scurvy, yellow fever
Portuguese empire, 37
  Africa, sending convicts to, 8–9
  agricultural penal settlements, 10–11
  Angola, 13–14
  Brazil, sending convicts to, 8–9
  categories of convicts, 14–17
  changing nature of punitive relocation, 21
  colonialization policy, 9–10
  conscripted convicts, 6, 41
  convict occupations, 3–6
  depósitos, 11–13
  Mozambique, 14
  multi-directional mobility, 38
  organization of convict work, 16
  settlement post-sentence, 19
  Spanish policy compared, 28–9
  urban penal colonies, 43
Poulo Condore, 263
presidios (Spanish empire), 10, 46

probation system, 14
  see also ticket-of-leave system
prohibition on settlement
  convict hulks, 37, 71
pro-transportation sentiment, 264
  International Penitentiary Congress, 8–9, 10–13
public works, 7, 52
  Ancient World, 20
  Gibraltar, 63
  Japan, 73
  Japan, post-Meiji restoration, 85, 87
  Ushuaia, 96
punishment and deterrence, 66, 73
  poor health, 69
punitive mobility defined, 9–10

Quételet, Adolphe, 323

racial variations in prevalence of and immunity against diseases
  medical research, 21
rehabilitation, 16, 73, 98, 129, 167, 227, 230, 235, 249
  Bentham's theories, 221
  El Frontón (Peru), 74
  Fernando de Noronha (Brazil), 7, 8
  imperial China, 73, 75
  Japan, post-Meiji restoration, 20
  Mazaruni (British Guiana), 20, 21
  religion, 69
  see also Crofton, Sir Walter; Maconochie, Alexander
religion, 7, 14, 69
  Andaman Islands' census, 29
  failure to respect cultural practices
    mutiny, 14–17
    insurgency, 14–17, 360
  see also Islamic practice
relocation of convicts, 28–9
resistance, 172
  community formation, 172
  convict activism, 10
  convict hulks
    escape, 65
    labour resistance, 64, 65
    mutiny, 64
  desertion, 16–17
  differing motivations and ambitions, 19
  Dutch East India Company
    labour resistance, 56
  escape, 11, 13–14, 34, 38
  Indigenous peoples, 249
  labour resistance, 1–5, 360
  mutiny, 10, 38

Index

Danish West India and Guinea
Company, 9–10
English East India Company, 10–11
failure to respect cultural
practices, 186
political reasons, 11–13
punishment and deterrence, 66
Robben Island, 173
Scandinavian empires
escape, 30–2
slave rebellions, 16
Fédon's Rebellion (British Grenada 1795–6), 14
Second Maroon War (Jamaica 1795–6), 110
see also Barbados Rebellion (1816)
Spanish empire
convict activism, 21–2
escape, 21–2
labour resistance, 49
mutiny, 22–4
spread of Islam to the Cape, 8–9
Xinjiang, 10–11
see also solidarities between convicts
Robben Island, 1–5
Dutch United East India Company, 3–6
introduction of Islam to the Cape, 6
Royal Botanic Gardens at Kew, 268, 281

Saint-Domingue (Haiti) revolt (1791–1804), 133, 171
banishment and penal transportation of slaves, 6
Sakhalin Island (Russia)
census of convict population. see Chekhov, Anton
criminal anthropology, 13–14
physiognomy
hereditary criminality, 13–14
specimen collection, 277
Scandinavian empires, 37, 52
changing nature of punitive relocation, 26
science and scientific discovery, relationship with convict relocation, 3–6, 8–9
see also medical research; scientific expeditions;scientific research
scientific expeditions, 5–7
Darwin, 1–2, 26
see also specimen collection
scientific research
anthropometry
physical manifestations of criminality, 1–5
bodies for scientific investigations, 11–13, 304

phrenology, 11
see also medical research
scurvy, 199, 304, 318, 331, 333
17th-century Britain
changing nature of punitive relocation, 24–6
Sierra Leone, 26–8
Barbados Rebellion, 21–2, 101
Barbadian settlers, 29–30
resettlement in Caribbean, 29
slave convicts and liberated Africans, relationship between, 28
slaves and slavery
banishment and penal transportation
Bahamas, 106
Demerara-Essequibo, 13–14
Jamaica, 3–6
Montserrat, 105
Saint Vincent, 105
Caribbean, 100
revolt and rebellion, 16, 100
Fédon's Rebellion (British Grenada 1795–6), 14
Second Maroon War (Jamaica 1795–6), 110
see also Barbados Rebellion (1816)
solidarities between convicts
Bel Ombre sugar estate desertion, 16–17
Danish West India and Guinea Company mutiny, 9–10
English East India Company mutiny, 10–11
escape plans, 11
imperial Denmark-Norway, 8–9
see also resistance
Soviet Union, 14
Spanish empire, 37
Ceuta, 24–6
changing nature of punitive relocation, 21–2
Cuba, 50
employment of convicts, 49
forzados, 10–11, 20
New World, convicts to, 46
North Africa, convicts to, 46
Philippines, 28
Portuguese policy compared, 28–9
presidios, 46
specimen collection, 1–6, 62–63
Andaman Islands (India), 29–30
Australian colonies, 26–8
engagement of convicts, 266
Fernando de Noronha (Brazil), 1–5, 266
French Guiana, 1–5

specimen collection (cont.)
  Mazaruni (British Guiana), 30–2
  medical use, 280
  Sakhalin Island (Russia), 277
  Trinidad, 107
  Ushuaia (Argentina), 266
  visual representations of natural history, 270
  see also scientific expeditions
suicide among convict men, 77
  medical research, 20
Surinam
  escaped convicts, 7–8, 360
Sweden, 37
  New Sweden Company, 52

Tassilier, Théodore Louis
  escape
    radical socialism, 19
Temple, Richard C. see Andaman Islands (India): fourth census (1901)
terra nullius doctrine
  Andaman Islands, 20
  Australian colonies, 19
ticket-of-leave system, 65, 201, 206, 235, 267, 311, 350
  see also probation system
Tocqueville de, Alexis, 329, 350, 368
trade
  collectors, 283
  convict hulks, 72
  Indigenous peoples, with, 255, 256, 259
  learning trade in preparation for freedom, 122, 123, 124, 154
  Portuguese empire, 251, 252
  Xinjiang (China), 76
Trinidad
  banishment and penal transportation of slaves, 107
  depots
    Carrera Island, 21–2
    Chaguanas forest, 153
    Irois Forest, 153
  escaped convicts, 28–9
  locally convicted felons, 135
  scientific research, 7–8
  specimen collection, 7–8
  see also Carrera Island (Trinidad)

Ushuaia (Argentina), 30–2, 73
  Fernando de Noronha (Brazil) compared, 7–8
  political prisoners, 215
  specimen collection, 266
  see also Argentina
USSR
  changing nature of punitive relocation, 32

vaccinations against smallpox
  medical research, 305
vacuum domicilium theory, 16–17
Van Diemen's Land. see Australian colonies
Vereenigde Oost-Indische Compagnie. see Dutch East India Company
violence. see disease and violence
VOC. see Dutch East India Company

Walker, J. P., 247
Weil's disease
  medical research, 313
West Indies
  establishment of a regional penal colony, 29
white convicts to West Indian colonies, 28, 53, 118, 148, 160, 171, 207, 253
withdrawal from addictive substances
  medical research, 16–17, 305
  Andaman Islands, 16
women, 16
  Caribbean women, transportation of, 14–17
  communist China, 32
  Dutch East India Company, 7–8
  imperial China, 77
  imperial Russia, 28
  marriage of convicts, 7
  Andaman Islands, 5–7, 29–30
  Mexican revolution (1910–20)
    political repression, 1–2
  Portuguese degredados, 40, 42, 45

Xinjiang (China), 3–6
  agriculture, 77
  convict labour, 9–10
  women, 77
  yi ju liang de (achieving multiple ends by a single means) principle, 8–9

yellow fever
  medical research, 22–4, 288

For EU product safety concerns, contact us at Calle de José Abascal, 56–1°, 28003 Madrid, Spain or eugpsr@cambridge.org.

www.ingramcontent.com/pod-product-compliance
Lightning Source LLC
LaVergne TN
LVHW011753060526
838200LV00053B/3588